Reference

The Condition of Education 2011

MAY 2011

Susan Aud
William Hussar
Grace Kena
National Center for Education Statistics

Kevin Bianco
Lauren Frohlich
Jana Kemp
Kim Tahan
American Institutes for Research

Katie Mallory
Production Manager
MacroSys, LLC

Thomas Nachazel
Senior Editor
Gretchen Hannes
Editor
American Institutes for Research

NCES 2011-033
U.S. DEPARTMENT OF EDUCATION

ies NATIONAL CENTER FOR EDUCATION STATISTICS
Institute of Education Sciences

U.S. Department of Education
Arne Duncan
Secretary

Institute of Education Sciences
John Q. Easton
Director

National Center for Education Statistics
Jack Buckley
Commissioner

The National Center for Education Statistics (NCES) is the primary federal entity for collecting, analyzing, and reporting data related to education in the United States and other nations. It fulfills a congressional mandate to collect, collate, analyze, and report full and complete statistics on the condition of education in the United States; conduct and publish reports and specialized analyses of the meaning and significance of such statistics; assist state and local education agencies in improving their statistical systems; and review and report on education activities in foreign countries.

NCES activities are designed to address high-priority education data needs; provide consistent, reliable, complete, and accurate indicators of education status and trends; and report timely, useful, and high-quality data to the U.S. Department of Education, the Congress, the states, other education policymakers, practitioners, data users, and the general public. Unless specifically noted all information contained herein is in the public domain.

We strive to make our products available in a variety of formats and in language that is appropriate to a variety of audiences. You, as our customer, are the best judge of our success in communicating information effectively. If you have any comments or suggestions about this or any other NCES product or report, we would like to hear from you. Please direct your comments to

NCES, IES, U.S. Department of Education
1990 K Street NW
Washington, DC 20006-5651

May 2011

The NCES Home Page address is http://nces.ed.gov.
The NCES Publications and Products address is http://nces.ed.gov/pubsearch.

This report was prepared for the National Center for Education Statistics under Contract No. ED-05-CO-0044 with Education Statistics Services Institute—American Institutes for Research. Mention of trade names, commercial products, or organizations does not imply endorsement by the U.S. Government.

Suggested Citation
Aud, S., Hussar, W., Kena, G., Bianco, K., Frohlich, L., Kemp, J., Tahan, K. (2011). *The Condition of Education 2011* (NCES 2011-033). U.S. Department of Education, National Center for Education Statistics. Washington, DC: U.S. Government Printing Office.

For ordering information on this report, write to
ED Pubs, U.S. Department of Education
P.O. Box 22207
Alexandria, VA 22304

or call toll free 1-877-4ED-PUBS or order online at http://www.edpubs.gov.

Content Contact
Susan Aud
(202) 219-7013
susan.aud@ed.gov

Letter from the
Commissioner of the
National Center for Education Statistics

MAY 2011

To ensure reliable, accurate, and timely data, which are necessary to monitor the progress of education in the United States, Congress has mandated that the National Center for Education Statistics (NCES) produce an annual report, *The Condition of Education*. This year's report presents 50 indicators of important developments and trends in U.S. education. These indicators focus on participation and persistence in education, student performance and other measures of achievement, the environment for learning, and resources for education. The report also uses a group of the indicators to take a closer look at changes in postsecondary education in the United States by institution level and control. As more students in the United States pursue education beyond high school, the distribution of students across institutions, such as public, private not-for-profit, and private for-profit, has been shifting. We take a look at these changes to see how they are reshaping postsecondary education.

Enrollment in U.S. schools is expected to grow in the coming years. From 2008 through 2020, public elementary and secondary enrollment is projected to increase to 53 million students. Undergraduate enrollment is expected to increase from 17.6 million students in 2009 to 20.0 million in 2020. Enrollment in postbaccalaureate programs is projected to increase through 2020 to 3.4 million students. These increases in enrollment will be accompanied by a growing diversity of students.

Overall, progress on national assessments in reading and mathematics has been made among 4th- and 8th-graders since the early 1990s. On both mathematics and reading assessments, significant gaps among racial/ethnic groups remain, though the mathematics and reading gaps between White and Black 4th-graders have narrowed since the assessments were first given. In 2007–08, above 75 percent of public high school students graduated on time with a regular diploma, reflecting an increase since 2001 when it was 73 percent. Other measures showing improvements are the status dropout rate, which declined among all racial/ethnic groups and was 8 percent overall in 2009, and rates of postsecondary degree attainment, which increased for Black, Hispanic, Asian/Pacific Islander, and American Indian/Alaska Native students.

NCES produces an array of reports each year that present findings about the U.S. education system. *The Condition of Education 2011* is the culmination of a year-long project. It includes data that were available by April 2011. In the coming months, other reports and surveys informing the nation about education will be released. Along with the indicators in this volume, NCES intends these surveys and reports to help inform policymakers and the American public about trends and conditions in U.S. education.

Jack Buckley
Commissioner
National Center for Education Statistics

This page intentionally left blank.

Reader's Guide

The Condition of Education is available in two forms: this print volume for 2011 and an electronic version on the National Center for Education Statistics (NCES) website (http://nces.ed.gov/programs/coe). *The Condition of Education* website includes the entire content of the 2011 print volume, plus special analyses from the 2000 through 2010 editions, and selected indicators from earlier editions of *The Condition of Education*. (See page xxii for a list of all the indicators that appear on *The Condition of Education* website.)

The print volume of *The Condition of Education 2011* is divided into five sections of indicators. Each section begins with a summary of the general topic areas covered by the indicators in the section both in this volume and on the website. Each indicator consists of a page with key findings and technical notes, one or two figures and/or tables on the adjacent page, and one or more supplemental tables, found in *appendix A*. The supplemental tables feature the estimates used in the indicator discussion as well as additional estimates related to the indicator. Where applicable, tables of standard errors for estimate tables are available on the NCES website (http://nces.ed.gov/programs/coe). Additional information on data sources, analyses conducted, and definitions of variables and measures can be found in the supplemental notes in *appendix B*. Finally, a glossary of key terms, a bibliography, and an index are featured in *appendixes C–E*.

ⓘ This icon on the main indicator page lists references for related indicators, supplemental tables, glossary terms, and other sources that provide more information relating to the indicator. Indicators use the most recent national and international data available from either NCES or other sources that are relevant to the indicator. When the source is an NCES publication, such as the *Digest of Education Statistics 2010* (NCES 2011-015), the publication can be viewed on the NCES website (http://nces.ed.gov/pubsearch).

Data Sources and Estimates

The data in this report were obtained from many different sources—including students and teachers, state education agencies, local elementary and secondary schools, and colleges and universities—using surveys and compilations of administrative records. Users of *The Condition of Education* should be cautious when comparing data from different sources. Differences in aspects such as procedures, timing, question phrasing, and interviewer training can affect the comparability of results across data sources.

Most indicators in *The Condition of Education* summarize data from surveys conducted by NCES or by the Census Bureau with support from NCES. Brief explanations of the major NCES surveys used in this edition of *The Condition of Education* can be found in *supplemental notes 3 and 4* of this volume. More detailed explanations can be obtained on the NCES website (http://nces.ed.gov) under "Surveys and Programs." Information about the Current Population Survey (CPS), another frequent source of survey data used in *The Condition of Education*, can be found in *supplemental note 2* and at http://www.census.gov/cps/.

Data for indicators reported in this volume are obtained primarily from two types of surveys: universe surveys and sample surveys. Some indicators report data taken from entire populations (universe surveys), such as *indicator 37* (Variations in Instruction Expenditures). With this type of survey, information is collected from every member of the population. For example, data for *indicator 37* were obtained from each school district in the United States. When data from an entire population are available, estimates of the total population or a subpopulation are made by simply summing the units in the population or subpopulation. A universe survey is usually expensive and time consuming, so many surveys collect data from a sample of the population of interest (sample survey). For example, *indicator 10* (Reading Performance) reports information from the National Assessment of Educational Progress (NAEP), which assesses a representative sample of students rather than the entire population of students. When a sample survey is used, statistical uncertainty is introduced because data come from only a portion of the entire population. This statistical uncertainty must be considered when reporting estimates and making comparisons.

Various types of statistics derived from universe and sample surveys are reported in *The Condition of Education*. Many indicators report the size of a population or a subpopulation, and often the size of a subpopulation is expressed as a percentage of the total population. In addition, the average (or *mean*) values of some characteristic of the population or subpopulation may be reported. The average is obtained by summing the values for all members of the population and dividing the sum by the size of the population. An example is the annual average salaries of full-time instructional faculty at degree-granting postsecondary institutions (*indicator 44*). Another measure that is sometimes used is the *median*. The median is the midpoint value of a characteristic at or above which 50 percent of the population is estimated to fall, and at or below which 50 percent of the population is estimated to fall. An example is the median annual earnings of young adults who are full-time, full-year wage and salary workers (*indicator 17*).

Estimates based on universe and sample survey data may be affected by a wide range of potential data collection errors, such as coverage errors, response errors, data coding errors, and data entry errors. Estimates of the size of these types of errors are typically not available.

Reader's Guide

Standard Errors

Using estimates calculated from data based on a sample of the population requires consideration of several factors before the estimates become meaningful. When using data from a sample, some margin of error will always be present in estimations of characteristics of the total population or subpopulation because the data are available from only a portion of the total population. Consequently, data from samples can provide only an approximation of the true or actual value. The margin of error of an estimate, or the range of potential true or actual values, depends on several factors such as the amount of variation in the responses, the size and representativeness of the sample, and the size of the subgroup for which the estimate is computed. The magnitude of this margin of error is measured by what statisticians call the "standard error" of an estimate.

When data from sample surveys are reported, as is the case with most of the indicators in *The Condition of Education,* the standard error is calculated for each estimate. The standard errors for all estimated totals, means, medians, or percentages reported in the supplemental tables of *The Condition of Education* can be viewed on the NCES website (http://nces.ed.gov/programs/coe).

The standard errors of the estimates for different subpopulations in an indicator can vary. As an illustration, *indicator 10* reports the average reading scale scores of 12th-grade students between 1992 and 2009. In both 2005 and 2009, the average reading scale score for 12th-grade students in high-poverty schools was 266 (see table A-10-2). In contrast to the similarity of these scores, the standard errors for these estimates were 2.0 and 1.0, respectively (see table S-10-2). The average score with the smaller standard error provides a more reliable approximation of the true value than the average score with a higher standard error. In addition, standard errors tend to diminish in size as the size of the sample (or subsample) increases.

In order to caution the reader when interpreting findings in *The Condition of Education,* estimates from sample surveys are flagged with a "!" when the standard error exceeds 30 percent of the estimate, and suppressed with a "‡" when exceeding 50 percent of the estimate.

Data Analysis and Interpretation

When estimates are from a sample, caution is warranted when drawing conclusions about one estimate in comparison to another, or about whether a time series of estimates is increasing, decreasing, or staying the same. Although one estimate may appear to be larger than another, a statistical test may find that the apparent difference between them is not reliably measurable due to the uncertainty around the estimates. In this case, the estimates will be described as having no measurable difference, meaning that the difference between them is not statistically significant.

Whether differences in means or percentages are statistically significant can be determined using the standard errors of the estimates. In this publication and others produced by NCES, when differences are statistically significant, the probability that the difference occurred by chance is less than 5 percent, according to NCES standards.

For all indicators in *The Condition of Education* that report estimates based on samples, differences between estimates (including increases and decreases) are stated only when they are statistically significant. To determine whether differences reported are statistically significant, two-tailed t tests at the .05 level are typically used. The t test formula for determining statistical significance is adjusted when the samples being compared are dependent. The t test formula is not adjusted for multiple comparisons. When the difference between estimates is not statistically significant, tests of equivalence can be used. An equivalence test determines the probability (generally at the .15 level) that the estimates are statistically equivalent, that is, within the margin of error that the two estimates are not substantively different. When the difference is found to be equivalent, language such as "x" and "y" "were similar" or "about the same" has been used. When the variables to be tested are postulated to form a trend, the relationship may be tested using linear regression, logistic regression, or ANOVA trend analysis instead of a series of t tests. These alternate methods of analysis test for specific relationships (e.g., linear, quadratic, or cubic) among variables. For more information on data analysis, please see the NCES Statistical Standards, Standard 5-1, available at http://nces.ed.gov/statprog/2002/std5_1.asp.

A number of considerations influence the ultimate selection of the data years that are featured in *The Condition of Education.* To make analyses as timely as possible, the latest year of data is shown if it is available during report production. The choice of comparison years is often also based on the need to show the earliest available survey year, as in the case of the NAEP and the international assessment surveys. In the case of surveys with long time frames, such as surveys measuring enrollment, the decade's beginning year (e.g., 1980 or 1990) often starts the trend line. In the figures and tables of the indicators, intervening years are selected in increments in order to show the general trend. The narrative for the indicators typically compares the most current year's data with those from the initial year and then with those from a more recent period. Where applicable, the narrative may also note years in which the data begin to diverge from previous trends.

Rounding and Other Considerations

All calculations within *The Condition of Education* are based on unrounded estimates. Therefore, the reader may find that a calculation, such as a difference or a percentage change, cited in the text or figure may not be identical to the calculation obtained by using the rounded values shown in the accompanying tables. Although values reported in the supplemental tables are generally rounded to one decimal place (e.g., 76.5 percent), values reported in each indicator are generally rounded to whole numbers (with any value of 0.50 or above rounded to the next highest whole number). Due to rounding, cumulative percentages may sometimes equal 99 or 101 percent rather than 100 percent.

Indicators in this volume that use the Current Price Index (CPI) use a base academic year of 2009–10 and a base calendar year of 2009 for constant dollar calculations. For more information on the CPI, see *supplemental note 10.*

Race and ethnicity

The categories denoting race and ethnicity in *The Condition of Education* are in accordance with the 1997 Office of Management and Budget (OMB) standard classification scheme. These classifications are based primarily on the respondent's self-identification, as is the case with data collected by the U.S. Census Bureau, or, in rare instances, on observer identification. Under the OMB standards, race and ethnicity are considered separate concepts. "Hispanic or Latino" is an ethnicity category, not a racial category. Race categories presented in *The Condition of Education 2011* exclude persons of Hispanic ethnicity; thus, the race/ethnicity categories are mutually exclusive.

Ethnicity is categorized as follows:

■ *Hispanic or Latino:* A person of Cuban, Mexican, Puerto Rican, South or Central American, or other Spanish culture or origin, regardless of race.

Racial groupings are as follows:

■ *American Indian or Alaska Native:* A person having origins in any of the original peoples of North and South America (including Central America) who maintains tribal affiliation or community attachment.

■ *Asian:* A person having origins in any of the original peoples of the Far East, Southeast Asia, and the Indian subcontinent: for example, Cambodia, China, India, Japan, Korea, Malaysia, Pakistan, the Philippines, Thailand, and Vietnam.

■ *Black:* A person having origins in any of the Black racial groups of Africa.

■ *Native Hawaiian or Other Pacific Islander:* A person having origins in any of the original peoples of Hawaii, Guam, Samoa, or other Pacific Islands.

■ *White:* A person having origins in any of the original peoples of Europe, North Africa, or the Middle East.

■ *Two or more races:* A person who selected two or more of the following racial categories when offered the option of selecting one or more racial designations: White, Black, Asian, Native Hawaiian or Other Pacific Islander, or American Indian or Alaska Native.

In *The Condition of Education,* the following terms are typically used to represent the above categories: White, Black, Hispanic, Asian, Pacific Islander, American Indian/Alaska Native, and Two or more races. Not all categories are shown in all indicators. For more information on race/ethnicity, see *supplemental note 1.*

Symbols

In accordance with the NCES Statistical Standards, many tables in this volume use a series of symbols to alert the reader to special statistical notes. These symbols, and their meanings, are as follows:

—	Not available.
†	Not applicable.
#	Rounds to zero.
!	Interpret data with caution. The standard error of the estimate is equal to 30 percent or more of the estimate's value.
‡	Reporting standards not met.
*	$p < .05$ Significance level.

This page intentionally left blank.

Contents

Contents

Page

List of Tables

List of Tables

Table		Page

List of Tables

List of Figures

List of Figures

Section 2—Learner Outcomes

Section 3—Student Effort and Educational Progress

Section 4—Contexts of Elementary and Secondary Education

List of Figures

Section 5—Contexts of Postsecondary Education

The List of Indicators on *The Condition of Education* Website (2003–2011)

This List of Indicators includes all the indicators that appear on *The Condition of Education* website (http://nces.ed.gov/programs/coe), drawn from the 2003–2011 print volumes. The list is organized first by section and then by subject area. Thus, the indicator numbers and the years in which the indicators were published are not sequential.

Section 3—Student Effort and Educational Progress

The List of Indicators on *The Condition of Education* Website (2003–2011)

Section 4—Contexts of Elementary and Secondary Education

This page intentionally left blank.

Introduction

To ensure reliable, accurate, and timely data, which are necessary to monitor the progress of education in the United States, Congress has mandated that the National Center for Education Statistics (NCES) produce an annual report, *The Condition of Education*. This year's report presents 50 indicators of important developments and trends in U.S. education. These indicators focus on participation and persistence in education, student performance and other measures of achievement, the environment for learning, and resources for education.

This introduction features an Overview and a Closer Look. The Overview summarizes each section of the volume by highlighting each indicator, which is referenced by its number (e.g., *indicator 19*). Each figure in the Overview can also be found in an indicator in the volume. For indicators with figures highlighted in the Overview, the indicator figure number will follow the Overview figure number in its reference (i.e., figure 3 is figure 19-1). The Closer Look examines a subset of indicators on postsecondary education, using figures and tables from the full indicators. The relevant figures are included and referenced tables can be found in Appendix A: Supplemental Tables.

Overview

Section 1: Participation in Education

■ Between 2000 and 2009, enrollment rates increased for young adults ages 18–19 and adults ages 20–24, 25–29, and 30–34; students in these age groups are typically enrolled in college or graduate school (*indicator 1*). See figure 1 below (figure 1-1, page 21).

■ From 2008–09 through 2020–21, public elementary and secondary school enrollment is projected to increase from 49.3 to 52.7 million students, but with differences across states (*indicator 2*).

■ From 1999–2000 to 2008–09, the number of students enrolled in public charter schools more than tripled from 340,000 to 1.4 million students. In 2008–09, some 5 percent of all public schools were charter schools (*indicator 3*).

■ Private school enrollment in prekindergarten through grade 12 increased from 5.9 million in 1995–96 to 6.3 million in 2001–02, and then decreased to 5.5 million in 2009–10. Some 10 percent of all elementary and secondary school students were in private schools in 2009–10 (*indicator 4*).

Figure 1.   (Figure 1-1) Percentage of the population ages 3–34 enrolled in school, by age group: October 1970–2009

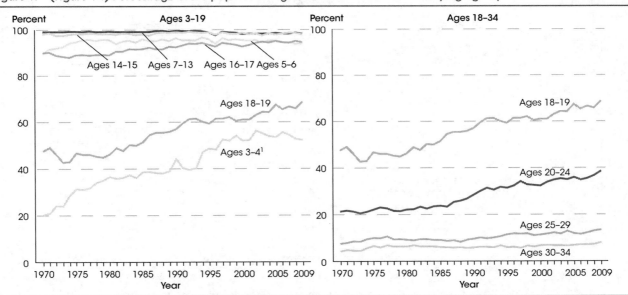

[1] Beginning in 1994, new procedures were used to collect enrollment data on children ages 3–4. As a result, pre-1994 data may not be comparable to data from 1994 or later.
NOTE: Includes enrollment in any type of graded public, parochial, or other private schools. Includes nursery schools, kindergartens, elementary schools, high schools, colleges, universities, and professional schools. Attendance may be on either a full-time or part-time basis and during the day or night. Excluded are enrollments in schools or classes that do not advance students to regular school degrees, such as trade schools, business colleges, or vocational schools. For more information on the Current Population Survey (CPS), see *supplemental note 2*.
SOURCE: U.S. Department of Commerce, Census Bureau, Current Population Survey (CPS), October Supplement, 1970–2009.

Introduction

- Between 1989 and 2009, the percentage of public school students who were White decreased from 68 to 55 percent, and the percentage of those who were Hispanic doubled from 11 to 22 percent *(indicator 5)*.

- In 2009, some 21 percent of children ages 5–17 (or 11.2 million) spoke a language other than English at home, and 5 percent (or 2.7 million) spoke English with difficulty. Seventy-three percent of those who spoke English with difficulty spoke Spanish *(indicator 6)*.

- The number of children and youth ages 3–21 receiving special education services was 6.5 million in 2008–09, corresponding to about 13 percent of all public school enrollment *(indicator 7)*.

- Between 2000 and 2009, undergraduate enrollment in degree-granting postsecondary institutions increased by 34 percent, from 13.2 to 17.6 million students. Projections indicate that it will continue to increase, reaching 19.6 million students in 2020 *(indicator 8)*.

- Postbaccalaureate enrollment has increased every year since 1983, reaching 2.9 million students in 2009. In each year since 1988, women have made up more than half of postbaccalaureate enrollment.

In 2009, postbaccalaureate enrollment was 59 percent female *(indicator 9)*.

Section 2: Learner Outcomes

- Between 2007 and 2009, there was no measurable change in the average grade 4 reading score on the National Assessment of Educational Progress (NAEP); the average grade 8 reading score, however, increased 1 point. At grade 12, the average reading score increased by 2 points between 2005 and 2009 *(indicator 10)*. See figure 2 below (figure 10-1, page 43, for reading scale scores).

- In 2009, White students at grade 12 scored 27 points higher in NAEP reading than Black students and 22 points higher than Hispanic students. Neither score gap was significantly different from the respective score gaps in previous assessment years *(indicator 11)*.

- From 1990 to 2009, average grade 4 NAEP mathematics scores increased by 27 points and average grade 8 scores increased by 20 points. At grade 12, average scores increased by 3 points between 2005 and 2009 *(indicator 12)*. See figure 2 below (figure 12-1, page 47, for mathematics scale scores).

Figure 2. (Figures 10-1 and 12-1) Average reading and mathematics scale scores of 4th-, 8th-, and 12th-grade students: Selected years, 1990–2009

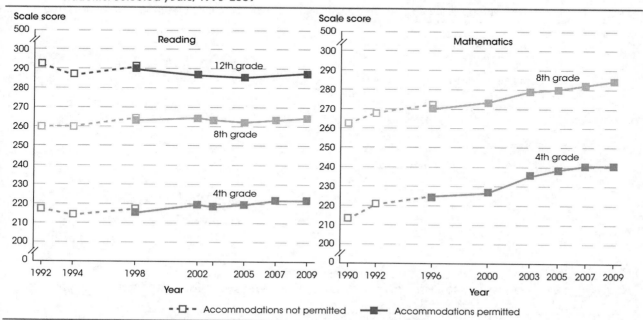

NOTE: The National Assessment of Educational Progress (NAEP) reading and mathematics scales range from 0 to 500. Student assessments are not designed to permit comparisons across subjects or grades. Testing accommodations (e.g., extended time, small group testing) for children with disabilities and limited-English-proficient students were not permitted in 1990, 1992, and 1994; students were tested with and without accommodations in 1996 for mathematics and in 1998 for reading. The 12th-grade NAEP reading assessment was not administered in 2003 or 2007. For more information on NAEP, see *supplemental note 4.*
SOURCE: U.S. Department of Education, National Center for Education Statistics, National Assessment of Educational Progress (NAEP), selected years, 1992–2009 Reading Assessments and 1990–2009 Mathematics Assessments, NAEP Data Explorer.

■ In 2009, White students at grade 12 scored 30 points higher in NAEP mathematics than Black students and 23 points higher than Hispanic students. Neither score gap was measurably different from the corresponding score gaps in 2005 *(indicator 13)*.

■ Thirty-four percent of students at grade 4, some 30 percent of students at grade 8, and 21 percent of students at grade 12 performed at or above the *Proficient* level in the NAEP science assessment in 2009 *(indicator 14)*.

■ In 2009, the average U.S. combined reading literacy score for 15-year-old students was not measurably different from the average score of the 34 Organization for Economic Co-operation and Development (OECD)-member countries. The average U.S. score was lower than that of 6 OECD countries and higher than that of 13 OECD countries *(indicator 15)*.

■ In 2009, the average U.S. mathematics literacy score for 15-year-old students was below the average of the 34 OECD member countries. On the science literacy scale, the average U.S. score was not measurably different from the OECD average *(indicator 16)*.

■ In 2009, young adults ages 25–34 with a bachelor's degree earned more than twice as much as young adults without a high school diploma or its equivalent, 50 percent more than young adult high school completers, and 25 percent more than young adults with an associate's degree *(indicator 17)*.

■ In 2010, young adults ages 25–34 with at least a bachelor's degree had a full-time employment rate that was over 30 percentage points higher than that of their peers who had not completed high school (74 vs. 41 percent) *(indicator 18)*.

Section 3: Student Effort and Educational Progress

■ In 2007–08, about three-quarters of public high school students graduated on time with a regular diploma *(indicator 19)*. See figure 3 below (figure 19-1, page 65).

■ In general, the status dropout rates for Whites, Blacks, and Hispanics each declined between 1980 and 2009. However, in each year during that period, the status dropout rate was lower for Whites and Blacks than for Hispanics *(indicator 20)*.

Figure 3.   (Figure 19-1) Averaged freshman graduation rate for public high school students, by state: School year 2007–08

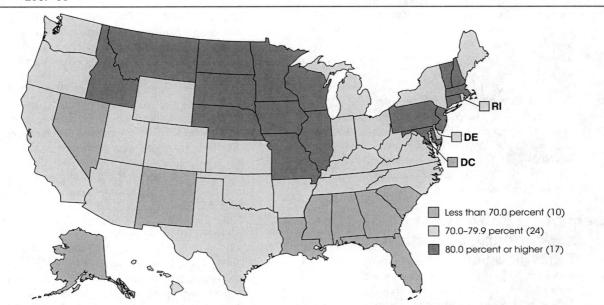

Less than 70.0 percent (10)
70.0–79.9 percent (24)
80.0 percent or higher (17)

NOTE: The rate is the number of graduates divided by the estimated freshman enrollment count 4 years earlier. This count is the sum of the number of 8th-graders 5 years earlier, the number of 9th-graders 4 years earlier, and the number of 10th-graders 3 years earlier, divided by 3. Ungraded students were allocated to individual grades proportional to each state's enrollment in those grades. The estimate for Maine includes graduates of semi-private schools. For more information on the Common Core of Data (CCD), see *supplemental note 3*. For more information on measures of student progress and persistence, see *supplemental note 6*.
SOURCE: U.S. Department of Education, National Center for Education Statistics, Common Core of Data (CCD), "NCES Common Core of Data State Dropout and Completion Data File," school year 2007–08, version 1a.

Introduction

- The immediate college enrollment rate after high school increased from 1975 to 1997 (51 to 67 percent), declined from 1997 to 2001 (to 62 percent), then increased from 2001 to 2009 (70 percent). Gaps in immediate enrollment rates by family income, race/ethnicity, and sex have persisted over time (*indicator 21*).

- In 2007–08, about 36 percent of undergraduate students considered to be in their first year reported having ever taken a remedial course, while 20 percent had actually taken one in that same year. At public 2-year institutions, about 42 percent of students had ever taken a remedial course (*indicator 22*).

- About 54 percent of male and 60 percent of female first-time students who sought a bachelor's degree and enrolled at a 4-year institution full time in fall 2002 completed a bachelor's degree at that institution within 6 years (*indicator 23*).

- In 2010, some 32 percent of 25- to 29-year-olds had completed at least a bachelor's degree. Between 1975 and 2010, the gap in bachelor's degree attainment between Whites and Hispanics widened from 15 to 25 percentage points, and the gap between Whites and Blacks widened from 13 to 19 percentage points (*indicator 24*).

- Greater percentages of the population ages 25 to 64 had earned a bachelor's degree or higher in all reporting OECD countries in 2008 than in 2001 (21 vs. 15 percent). The percentage of the U.S. population with a bachelor's degree or higher was 32 percent in 2008, compared with 28 percent in 2001 (*indicator 25*).

- Between 1998–99 and 2008–09, the number of degrees earned increased by 41 percent for associate's degrees, by 33 percent for bachelor's degrees, and by 49 percent for master's degrees. In 2008–09, females earned the majority of all associate's, bachelor's, master's, and doctoral degrees awarded (*indicator 26*).

Section 4: Contexts of Elementary and Secondary Education

- In 2008–09, charter schools and schools with a magnet program each composed a higher percentage of all public schools than they did in 1998–99 (5 vs. 1 percent for charter schools and 3 vs. 1 percent for schools with a magnet program) (*indicator 27*).

- In 2008–09, greater percentages of Black, Hispanic, and American Indian/Alaska Native students attended high-poverty elementary and secondary public schools than did White or Asian/Pacific Islander students (*indicator 28*). See figure 4 on the following page (figure 28-1, page 87).

- In 2009, some 19 percent of 5- to 17-year-olds were in families living in poverty, compared with 15 percent in 2000 and 17 percent in 1990 (*indicator 29*).

- From 1992 to 2008, the rate of nonfatal incidents of crime against students ages 12–18 at school declined from 144 to 47 crimes per 1,000 students, and for students away from school the rate declined from 138 to 38 crimes per 1,000 students (*indicator 30*).

- A larger percentage of full-time teachers held a postbaccalaureate degree in 2007–08 than in 1999–2000. Forty-nine percent of elementary school teachers and 54 percent of secondary school teachers held a postbaccalaureate degree in 2007–08, compared with 43 percent and 50 percent, respectively, in 1999–2000 (*indicator 31*).

- In 2008–09, some 8 percent of public school teachers left the teaching profession compared with 16 percent of private school teachers. Another 7 percent of all teachers moved from their 2007–08 school to a different school (*indicator 32*).

- From 1999–2000 to 2007–08, the percentage of principals who were female increased from 52 to 59 percent at public elementary schools and from 22 to 29 percent at public secondary schools (*indicator 33*).

- In 2008–09, some 12 percent of all principals left the profession. In addition to principals who left the profession, another 6 percent of all principals moved from their 2007–08 school to a different school for the 2008–09 school year (*indicator 34*).

- From 1989–90 through 2007–08, total elementary and secondary public school revenues increased from $356 billion to $599 billion (in constant 2009–10 dollars), a 68 percent increase after adjusting for inflation (*indicator 35*).

- Total expenditures per student in public elementary and secondary schools rose 39 percent in constant dollars from 1989–90 through 2007–08, with interest on school debt increasing faster than current expenditures or capital outlay (*indicator 36*).

Figure 4. (Figure 28-1) Percentage of public school students in high-poverty schools, by race/ethnicity and school level: School year 2008–09

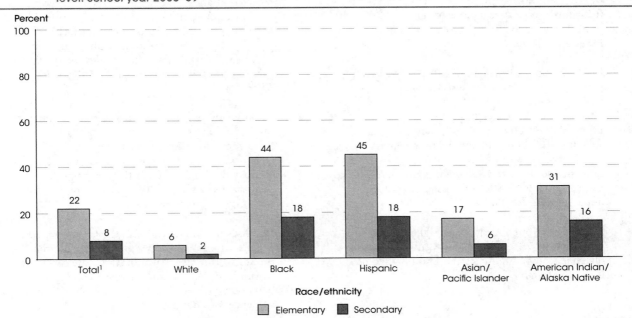

¹ Includes students whose racial/ethnic group was not reported.
NOTE: The National School Lunch Program is a federally assisted meal program. To be eligible, a student must be from a household with an income at or below 130 percent of the poverty threshold for free lunch, or between 130 percent and 185 percent of the poverty threshold for reduced-price lunch. High-poverty schools are public schools where more than 75 percent of the students are eligible for the free or reduced-price lunch program. Race categories exclude persons of Hispanic ethnicity. Persons with unknown race/ethnicity are not shown. For more information on race/ethnicity and poverty, see *supplemental note 1*. For more information on the Common Core of Data (CCD), see *supplemental note 3*.
SOURCE: U.S. Department of Education, National Center for Education Statistics, Common Core of Data (CCD), "Public Elementary/Secondary School Universe Survey," 2008–09.

- Total variation in instruction expenditures per student has increased among public school districts since 1997–98, primarily due to an increase in the variation between states *(indicator 37)*.

- In 2007, the United States spent $10,768 per student on elementary and secondary education, which was 45 percent higher than the OECD average of $7,401. At the postsecondary level, U.S. expenditures per student were $27,010, more than twice as high as the OECD average of $12,471 *(indicator 38)*.

Section 5: Contexts of Postsecondary Education

- In fall 2009, some 11 percent of all full-time undergraduate students attended private for-profit institutions. About 38 percent of full-time students age 35 and over attended private for-profit institutions, compared with 5 percent of full-time students under the age of 25 *(indicator 39)*.

- In 2008–09, more than half of the 1.6 million bachelor's degrees awarded were in five fields: business (22 percent), social sciences and history

(11 percent), health professions and related clinical sciences (8 percent), education (6 percent), and psychology (6 percent) *(indicator 40)*.

- Overall, 656,800 master's degrees and 67,700 doctoral degrees were awarded in 2008–09; these numbers represent increases of 49 and 54 percent, respectively, over the numbers awarded in 1998–99. In 2008–09, females earned 60 percent of master's degrees and 52 percent of doctoral degrees awarded *(indicator 41)*.

- Between 1998–99 and 2008–09, the number of degrees conferred by private for-profit institutions increased by a larger percentage than the number conferred by public institutions and private not-for-profit institutions; this was true for all levels of degrees *(indicator 42)*. See figure 5 on the following page (figure 42-1, page 119).

- In 2007–08, about 4.3 million undergraduate students, or 20 percent of all undergraduates, took at least one distance education course. About 0.8 million, or 4 percent of all undergraduates, took their entire program though distance education *(indicator 43)*.

Introduction

- After increasing by 14 percent during the 1980s and by 5 percent during the 1990s, average salaries for full-time faculty were 4 percent higher in 2009–10 than they were in 1999–2000, after adjusting for inflation *(indicator 44)*.

- In 2009, about 41 percent of full-time and 76 percent of part-time college students ages 16–24 were employed *(indicator 45)*.

- From 1999–2000 to 2007–08, the percentage of full-time, full-year undergraduates receiving federal loans increased from 43 to 49 percent. Over the same period, the average federal grant increased from $3,300 to $3,800 (in constant 2009–10 dollars) *(indicator 46)*.

- The net price of education was higher in 2007-08 than in 1999-2000 for full-time, full-year, dependent undergraduates at all family income levels *(indicator 47)*.

- About 9 out of 10 full-time graduate students received financial aid in 2007–08. The average total price of attending was greater in 2007–08 than in 2003–04 for students in master's or first-professional degree programs at public universities, as well as for students in first-professional degree programs at private not-for-profit universities *(indicator 48)*.

- In 2008–09, average tuition and fees, in constant 2009–10 dollars, at 4-year postsecondary institutions were $12,100. At public 4-year institutions, average tuition and fees were $6,400, compared with $15,300 at private for-profit institutions and $24,900 at private not-for-profit institutions *(indicator 49)*.

- In 2008–09, instruction was the largest per-student expense at public ($7,534) and private not-for-profit institutions ($15,215). At private for-profit institutions, instruction was the second largest per-student expense category, with $3,069 spent per student *(indicator 50)*.

Figure 5. **(Figure 42-1) Number of degrees conferred by degree-granting institutions, by level of degree and control of institution: Academic years 1998–99 and 2008–09**

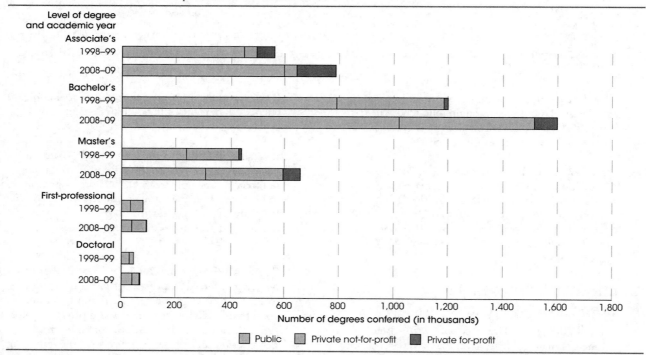

NOTE: Includes only institutions that participated in Title IV federal financial aid programs. For more information on the Integrated Postsecondary Education Data System (IPEDS) and IPEDS classification of institutions, see *supplemental notes 3* and *8*. See the glossary for definitions of first-professional degree and doctoral degree.
SOURCE: U.S. Department of Education, National Center for Education Statistics, 1998–99 and 2008–09 Integrated Postsecondary Education Data System (IPEDS), "Completions Survey" (IPEDS-C:99) and Fall 2009.

A Closer Look at Postsecondary Education by Institution Level and Control

Increasing participation in postsecondary education in the United States has become an issue of vital importance to policymakers. Several indicators in this volume describe the current state of postsecondary education and others describe how it has been changing in recent decades. In this section, we take a closer look at postsecondary education in the United States by examining these indicators by institution level and control, primarily for undergraduate students. These institutional characteristics were selected because postsecondary education in the U.S. has been undergoing changes along these dimensions. Specifically, postsecondary education has traditionally been divided into public and private not-for-profit institutions, but in recent years private for-profit institutions have entered the marketplace in growing numbers. This has created additional opportunities for students seeking a postsecondary education, but it has also brought to light differences in how students pursue and pay for that education.

Enrollment and Degrees Conferred

The past three decades have experienced growth in postsecondary enrollments, primarily in the public sector, and most recently, in the private for-profit sector as well. Between 1980 and 1990, undergraduate enrollment in degree-granting institutions grew from 10.5 to 12.0 million students, an increase of 1.5 million students (see table A-8-2). Eighty-five percent of this increase (representing 1.3 million students) occurred at public institutions; 8 percent, at private not-for-profit institutions; and 7 percent, at private for-profit institutions. Between 1990 and 2000, undergraduate enrollment increased by 1.2 million students; 69 percent of this increase occurred at public institutions; 14 percent, at private not-for-profit institutions; and 16 percent, at private for-profit institutions. The greatest increase was seen in the most recent decade: from 2000 to 2009, undergraduate enrollment at degree-granting institutions increased by 4.4 million students. Of this increase, 65 percent occurred at public institutions, 9 percent at private not-for-profit institutions, and 27 percent (representing 1.2 million students) at private for-profit institutions. Undergraduate enrollment at

private for-profit 4-year institutions increased from 23,000 students in 1980 to 1.2 million students in 2009. During the same period, undergraduate enrollment at private for-profit 2-year institutions increased from 0.1 million to 0.4 million students.

The changes in enrollment numbers are similar to the changes in the number of degrees conferred: the number of undergraduate degrees has increased in the last decade, and changes in the percentage distribution of degrees conferred have differed depending on institution control. Between 1998–99 and 2008–09, there was a 41 percent increase in the number of associate's degrees conferred and a 33 percent increase in the number of bachelor's degrees conferred (see tables CL-1 and A-42-1).

Although most associate's degrees (76 percent in 2008–09) are conferred by public institutions, this percentage has decreased since 1998–99, when 80 percent of associate's degrees were conferred by public institutions; the percentage conferred by private for-profit institutions has increased from 11 to 18 percent over the same period. In 2008–09, degree-granting institutions conferred 787,300 associate's degrees, an increase of 227,400 from the number conferred in 1998–99. Of the additional 227,400 degrees, approximately two-thirds were conferred by public institutions and about one-third were conferred by private for-profit institutions. (Private not-for-profit institutions conferred slightly fewer associate's degrees in 2008–09 than they did in 1998–99.)

At the bachelor's level, the number of degrees conferred by private for-profit institutions more than quadrupled from 1998–99 to 2008–09, from about 16,000 to 85,000. In 1998–99, some 66 percent of bachelor's degrees were conferred by public institutions, compared with 33 percent conferred by private not-for-profit institutions and about 1 percent conferred by private for-profit institutions. By 2008–09, the distribution had changed somewhat: 64 percent of bachelor's degrees were conferred by public institutions; 31 percent by private not-for-profit institutions; and 5 percent by private for-profit institutions.

Introduction

Table CL-1. Number of degrees conferred by degree-granting institutions and percent change, by control of institution and level of degree: Academic years 1998–99 and 2008–09

Level of degree and academic year	Total	Public	Private Total	Private Not-for-profit	Private For-profit
Associate's					
1998–99	559,954	448,334	111,620	47,611	64,009
2008–09	787,325	596,098	191,227	46,929	144,298
Percent change	40.6	33.0	71.3	-1.4	125.4
Bachelor's					
1998–99	1,200,303	790,287	410,016	393,680	16,336
2008–09	1,601,368	1,020,435	580,933	496,260	84,673
Percent change	33.4	29.1	41.7	26.1	418.3
Master's					
1998–99	439,986	238,501	201,485	192,152	9,333
2008–09	656,784	308,206	348,578	285,098	63,480
Percent change	49.3	29.2	73.0	48.4	580.2
First-professional					
1998–99	78,439	31,693	46,746	46,315	431
2008–09	92,004	37,357	54,647	53,572	1,075
Percent change	17.3	17.9	16.9	15.7	149.4
Doctoral					
1998–99	44,077	28,134	15,943	15,501	442
2008–09	67,716	39,911	27,805	25,169	2,636
Percent change	53.6	41.9	74.4	62.4	496.4

NOTE: Includes only institutions that participated in Title IV federal financial aid programs. For more information on the Integrated Postsecondary Education Data System (IPEDS) and IPEDS classification of institutions, see *supplemental notes 3* and *8*. See the glossary for definitions of first-professional degree and doctoral degree.
SOURCE: U.S. Department of Education, National Center for Education Statistics, 1998–99 and 2008–09 Integrated Postsecondary Education Data System (IPEDS), "Completions Survey" (IPEDS-C:99) and Fall 2009.

Of the 17.6 million undergraduate students enrolled in degree-granting institutions in fall 2009, some 36 percent attended public 4-year institutions, 40 percent attended public 2-year institutions, 15 percent attended private not-for-profit 4-year institutions, less than 1 percent attended private not-for-profit 2-year institutions, 7 percent attended private for-profit 4-year institutions, and 2 percent attended private for-profit 2-year institutions, (see table A-39-1). This pattern varied by race/ethnicity. For example, 38 percent of White students attended public 2-year institutions, compared with 40 percent of Black students, 42 percent of Asian/Pacific Islander students, 45 percent of American Indian/Alaska Native students, and 52 percent of Hispanic students. In addition, 17 percent of Black undergraduate students attended private for-profit institutions in 2009, compared with 10 percent of Hispanic students, 9 percent of nonresident alien students, 7 percent of White students, and 5 percent (each) of Asian/Pacific Islander and American Indian/Alaska Native students.

Forty-four percent of full-time undergraduate students who enrolled in degree-granting institutions in fall 2009 attended public 4-year institutions, while 26 percent attended public 2-year institutions, 19 percent attended private not-for-profit 4-year institutions, less than one percent attended private not-for-profit 2-year institutions, 8 percent attended private for-profit 4-year institutions, and 3 percent attended private for-profit 2-year institutions (see figure CL-1). However, 30 percent of full-time students ages 35 and over attended private for-profit 4-year institutions, compared with 3 percent of full-time students under the age of 25. In 2009, some 66 percent of part-time undergraduate students enrolled in public 2-year institutions, 22 percent enrolled in public 4-year institutions, 7 percent enrolled in private not-for-profit 4-year institutions, and 5 percent enrolled in private for-profit 4-year institutions (less than one percent each enrolled in private not-for-profit and private for-profit 2-year institutions). Some 70 percent of part-time students under the age of 25 enrolled in public 2-year institutions, compared with 24 percent of full-time students under the age of 25.

Figure CL-1. Percentage distribution of fall undergraduate enrollment in degree-granting institutions, by student attendance status, age, and control and level of institution: Fall 2009

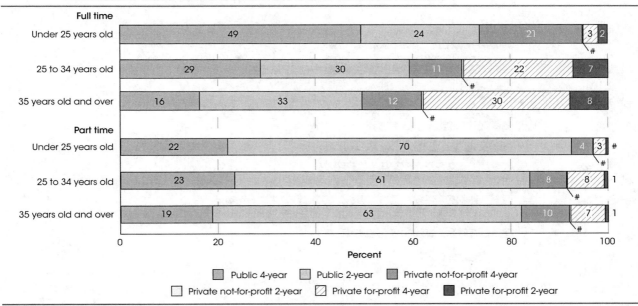

Rounds to zero.
NOTE: Degree-granting institutions grant associate's or higher degrees and participate in Title IV federal financial aid programs. For more information on IPEDS, see *supplemental note 3*. Institutions in this indicator are classified based on the highest degree offered. For more information on the classification of postsecondary institutions, see *supplemental note 8*.
SOURCE: U.S. Department of Education, National Center for Education Statistics, 2009 Integrated Postsecondary Education Data System (IPEDS), Spring 2010.

Use of Resources

The changes in postsecondary undergraduate enrollment by institution level and control have been accompanied by changes in how coursework is delivered. Distance education courses, including those delivered by live, interactive audio or videoconferencing; pre-recorded instructional videos; webcasts; CD-ROM or DVD; and computer-based systems delivered over the Internet, can provide flexible learning opportunities for students. In 2007–08, about one in five undergraduate students, or 4.3 million, took at least one distance education course (see table A-43-1). However, in that year there were differences between institution controls in the percentages of students taking distance education courses and in the percentages who were completing their entire program through distance education. A lower percentage of students at private not-for-profit institutions (14 percent) took distance education courses than did students at public institutions (22 percent) and private for-profit institutions (21 percent) (see figure CL-2). In addition, at private for-profit institutions, 12 percent of students took their entire program through distance education, which was higher than the percentage who did

so at both public and private not-for-profit institutions (3 percent each). Students at private for-profit 4-year institutions had the highest rate of distance course taking (30 percent) of all the institution levels and controls, as well as the highest rate taking their entire program through distance education (19 percent).

Differences in the delivery of education can be associated with how institutions distribute their resources. In 2008–09, total expenses for degree-granting institutions were $273 billion at public institutions, $141 billion at private not-for-profit institutions, and $16 billion at private for-profit institutions (see table A-50-3). Expenses for instruction were 28, 33, and 24 percent of total expenses, respectively, for public, private not-for-profit, and private for-profit institutions (with per FTE student spending in constant 2009–10 dollars of $9,418, $15,289, and $2,659, respectively) (see figure CL-3).Student services, academic support and institutional support expenses were 20, 30, and 67 percent of total expenses for public, private not-for-profit and private for-profit institutions (with per FTE student spending of $6,647, $14,118, and $9,101, respectively).

Introduction

Figure CL-2. Percentage of undergraduate students in postsecondary institutions taking distance education courses, by control and level of institution: 2003–04 and 2007–08

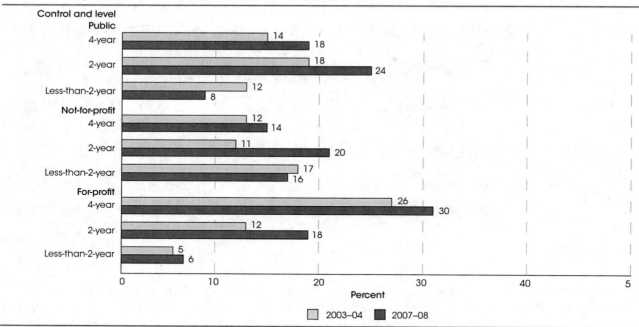

NOTE: Estimates pertain to all postsecondary students who enrolled at any time during the school year at an institution participating in Title IV programs. Distance education participation includes participation at any institution for students attending more than on institution during the school year. Data include Puerto Rico. For more information on the National Postsecondary Student Financial Aid Study (NPSAS), see *supplemental note 3*. For more information on the classification of postsecondary education institutions, see *supplemental note 8*.
SOURCE: U.S. Department of Education, National Center for Education Statistics, 2003–04 and 2007–08 National Postsecondary Student Aid Study (NPSAS:04 and NPSAS:08).

Figure CL-3. Expenses per student at 4-year degree-granting postsecondary institutions, by institutional control and purpose: Academic year 2008–09

[In constant 2009–10 dollars]

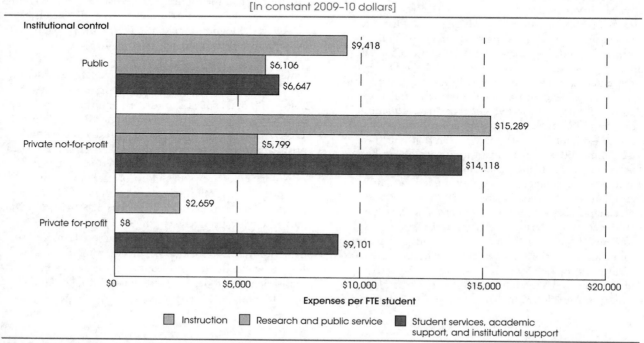

NOTE: Full-time-equivalent (FTE) enrollment includes full-time students plus the full-time equivalent of part-time students. Data are adjusted by the Consumer Price Index (CPI) to constant 2009–10 dollars. For more information on the CPI, see *supplemental note 10*. For more information on the Integrated Postsecondary Education Data System (IPEDS), see *supplemental note 3*.
SOURCE: U.S. Department of Education, National Center for Education Statistics, 2008–09 Integrated Postsecondary Education Data System, Spring 2010.

Student Financing

One major concern for students pursuing postsecondary education is how to pay for it. The total price of attending a postsecondary institution includes tuition and fees, books and materials, and living expenses. In 2007–08, the average total price of attendance (in constant 2009–10 dollars) for students—that is, full-time, full-year, dependent undergraduates who attended only one

institution during the year—was $19,300 at public 4-year institutions and $12,100 at public 2-year institutions (see table A-47-1). At private institutions, the total price was $37,400 at not-for-profit 4-year institutions $23,800 at not-for-profit 2-year institutions, $33,500 at for-profit 4-year institutions and, $27,900 at for-profit 2-year institutions.

Figure CL-4. Average total price, grants, and net price for full-time, full-year, dependent undergraduates at 4-year institutions, by institution control: Academic years 1999–2000, 2003–04, and 2007–08

[In constant 2009–10 dollars]

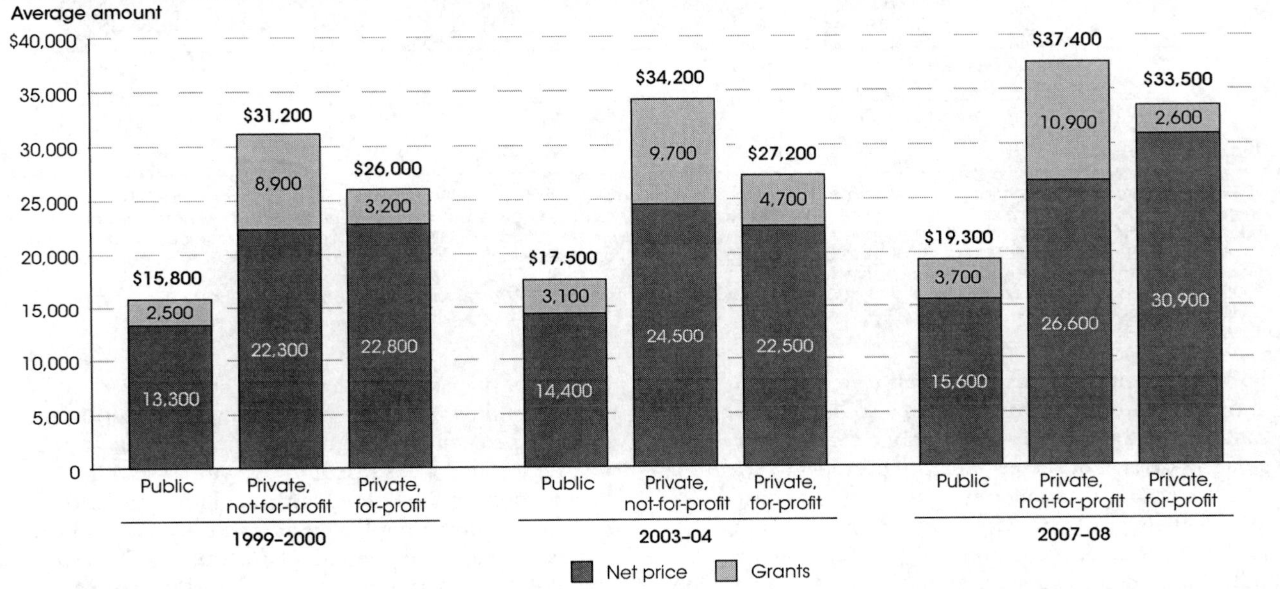

NOTE: *Full time* refers to students who attended full time (as defined by the institution) for the full year (at least 9 months). *Net price* is an estimate of the cash outlay that students and their families need to make in a given year to cover educational expenses. Averages were computed for all students, including those who did not receive financial aid. Data were adjusted by the Consumer Price Index for All Urban Consumers (CPI-U) to constant 2009–10 dollars. For more information on the CPI-U, see *supplemental note 10.* Estimates exclude students who were not U.S. citizens or permanent residents and therefore ineligible for federal student aid and students who attended more than one institution in a year, due to the difficulty of matching information on price and aid. Detail may not sum to totals due to rounding.
SOURCE: U.S. Department of Education, National Center for Education Statistics, 1999–2000, 2003–04, and 2007–08 National Postsecondary Student Aid Studies (NPSAS:2000, NPSAS:04, and NPSAS:08).

Grants and loans are the major forms of federal financial support for postsecondary students. Federal grants (e.g., Pell grants), do not need to be repaid, and are available only to undergraduates who qualify by economic need, whereas loans are available to all students. In addition to federal financial aid, there are also grants from state and local governments, institutions, and private sources. In 2007–08, about two-thirds (65 percent) of full-time, full-year undergraduates received a grant from any source and one-third (33 percent) received a federal grant (see figure

CL-4 and table A-46-1). At public 4-year institutions, some 29 percent of full-time, full-year undergraduates received federal grants in 2007–08, compared with 28 percent of undergraduates at private not-for-profit institutions and 56 percent of undergraduates at private for-profit 4-year institutions. At 2-year institutions, some 37 percent of students at public institutions, 52 percent of students at private not-for-profit institutions, and nearly three-quarters (74 percent) of student at private for-profit institutions received federal grants in 2007–08.

Introduction

Figure CL-5. Average tuition and fees and average loan amounts at postsecondary institutions, by level and control of institution: 2008–09

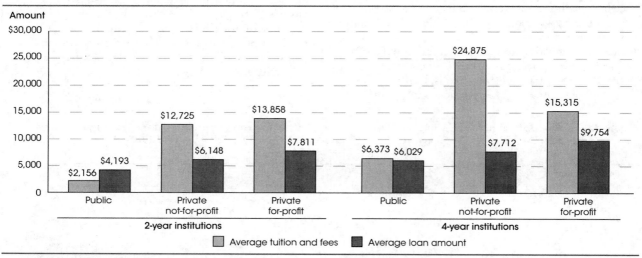

NOTE: Degree-granting institutions grant associate's or higher degrees and participate in Title IV federal financial aid programs. Tuition and fees amounts for public institutions are the averages for in-state students. Tuition and fee data are collected in the fall and loan data are collected in the spring. For more information on the Integrated Postsecondary Data System (IPEDS) and IPEDS classification of institutions, see *supplemental notes 3 and 8.* Data were adjusted to constant 2009–10 dollars using the Consumer Price Index for All Urban Consumers (CPI-U). For more information on the CPI-U, see *supplemental note 10.*
SOURCE: U.S. Department of Education, National Center for Education Statistics, 2009–10 Integrated Postsecondary Education Data System (IPEDS), Spring 2009.

Forty-nine percent of first-time, full-time students at degree-granting institutions had a student loan in 2008–09 (see table A-49-1). At public 4-year institutions, some 47 percent of these students had student loans and the average loan amount was $6,000 (in constant 2009–10 dollars) (see figure CL-5). At private not-for-profit 4-year institutions, some 61 percent of first-time, full-time students had loans and the average loan amount was $7,700. At private for-profit 4-year institutions, 81 percent of these students had loans, and the average loan amount was $9,800. Looking at 2-year institutions, some 21 percent of first-time, full-time students at public institutions had loans in 2008–09, with an average loan amount of $4,200; in contrast, 58 percent of these students at private not-for-profit institutions had a loan, with an average loan amount of $6,100, and 78 percent of these students at private for-profit institutions had a loan, with an average loan amount of $7,800.

Figure CL-6. Two-year student loan cohort default rates at degree-granting institutions, by level and control of institution: Fiscal years 2006–2008

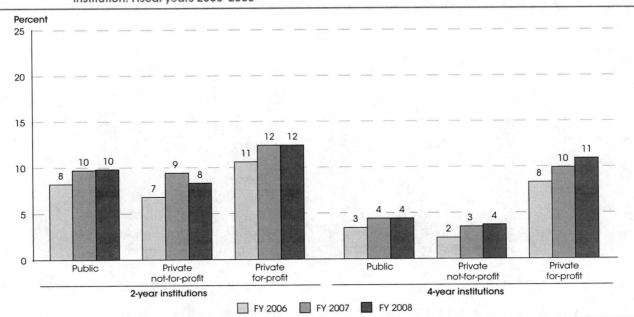

NOTE: Includes undergraduate and postbaccalaureate students. Degree-granting institutions grant associate's or higher degrees and participate in Title IV federal financial aid programs. The 2-year cohort default rate is the percentage of borrowers who enter repayment on certain Federal Family Education Loan (FFEL) Program or William D. Ford Federal Direct Loan (Direct Loan) Program loans during a particular federal fiscal year (a fiscal year runs from October 1 to September 30) and default or meet other specified conditions within the cohort default period. The cohort default period is the two-year period that begins on October 1 of the fiscal year when the borrower enters repayment and ends on September 30 of the following fiscal year. For more information on the Integrated Postsecondary Data System (IPEDS) and IPEDS classification of institutions, see supplemental notes 3 and 8.
SOURCE: U.S. Department of Education, Federal Student Aid, Direct Loan and Federal Family Education Loan Programs, Cohort Default Rate Database, retrieved November 5, 2010, from http://www2.ed.gov/offices/OSFAP/defaultmanagement/cdr.html.

Approximately 3.2 million students entered the repayment phase of their student loans in fiscal year (FY) 2008, meaning their students loans became due between September 30, 2007 and October 1, 2008 (see table A-49-2). Of those students, 7 percent defaulted within 2 years, or by October 1, 2010 (see figure CL-6). The default rates for the FY 2008 cohort were highest at private for-profit 4-year institutions (11 percent) and private for-profit 2-year institutions (12 percent). The lowest default rates for that same cohort were at public and private not-for-profit 4-year institutions (4 percent each).

Persistence and Outcomes

Finally, we turn to persistence and outcomes in postsecondary education. One measure of persistence is the retention rate, defined as the percentage of students who enrolled in an institution in the fall and returned to that same institution the following year to continue their studies (see figure CL-7). Some 77 percent of full-time students and 46 percent of part-time students who entered 4-year institutions in 2008 returned the following year to continue their studies (see table A-39-2). Seventy-eight percent of full-time and 48 percent

of part-time students who enrolled in public 4-year institutions in 2008 returned the following year; 79 percent of full-time and 44 percent of part-time students did so at private not-for-profit 4-year institutions; and 50 percent of full-time and 43 percent of part-time students did so at private for-profit 4-year institutions. At 2-year institutions, the retention rates for those who entered school in 2008 were the following: 59 percent of full-time and 40 percent of part-time students at public institutions, 59 percent of full-time and 60 percent of part-time students at private not-for-profit institutions, and 69 percent of full-time and 47 percent of students at private for-profit institutions.

Turning to outcomes, the bachelor's degree completion rates of students who began seeking a bachelor's degree at 4-year institutions in fall 2002 and did not transfer to another institution varied by the control of institution. Graduation rates were highest at private not-for-profit institutions, followed by public institutions and private for-profit institutions. For example, the 6-year graduation rate at private not-for-profit institutions was 65 percent, compared with 55 percent at public institutions and 22 percent at private for-profit institutions (see table A-23-1).

Introduction

Figure CL-7. Overall annual retention rates and graduation rates within 150 percent of normal time at degree-granting institutions, by level and control of institution and student attendance status: Fall 2009

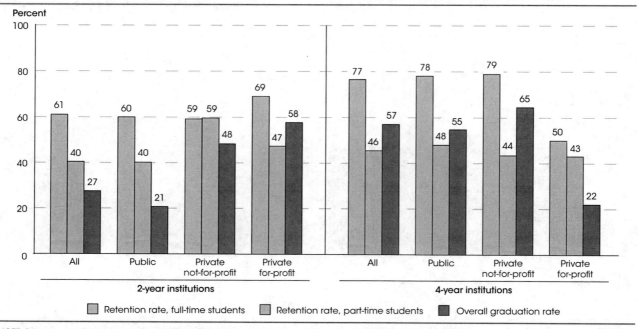

NOTE: Degree-granting institutions grant associate's or higher degrees and participate in Title IV federal financial aid programs. The retention rate is the percentage of first-time, bachelor's degree-seeking students who return to the institution to continue their studies the following year, in this case Fall 2009. The overall graduation rate is the percentage of full-time, first-time students who graduated within 150 percent of normal program completion time, in this case by Fall 2008 for the cohort that enrolled in 4-year institutions in Fall 2002 and for the students that enrolled in 2-year institutions in Fall 2005. For more information on IPEDS, see *supplemental note 3*. Institutions in this indicator are based on the highest degree offered. For more information on the classification of postsecondary institutions, see *supplemental note 8*.
SOURCE: U.S. Department of Education, National Center for Education Statistics, 2009 Integrated Postsecondary Education Data System (IPEDS), Spring 2010.

At both public and private not-for-profit 4-year institutions, the 6-year graduation rates for both males and females who began seeking a bachelor's degree in fall 2002 varied by the acceptance rate of the institution. For example, at public 4-year institutions with open admissions policies, 27 percent of males and 34 percent of females completed a bachelor's degree or its equivalent within 6 years (see table A-23-2). At public 4-year institutions where the acceptance rate was less than 25 percent of applicants, however, the 6-year graduation rate for males was 73 percent and for females, 72 percent.

At 2-year institutions, about 27 percent of first-time, full-time students who enrolled in fall 2005 completed a certificate or associate's degree within 150 percent of the normal time required to complete such a degree (see table A-23-3). For the cohort who enrolled in 1999, the completion rate was 29 percent. The certificate

or associate's degree completion rate of students who enrolled in fall 2005 at 2-year institutions varied by institution control. Twenty-one percent of students graduated within 150 percent of the normal time at public 2-year institutions, 48 percent did so at private not-for-profit institutions, and 58 percent did so at private for-profit public institutions

This Closer Look provides a snapshot on what postsecondary education looks like today, particularly the differences in enrollment, resource use, student financing and outcomes by institution level and control. It is projected that by 2020, there will be nearly 20 million students enrolled in undergraduate institutions (see table A-8-1). The dynamic nature of this sector suggests that these factors may look quite different for those 20 million students.

Technical Notes

When looking at these data it is important to understand who, specifically, they apply to. Undergraduate students are the focus of this Closer Look. However, the indicators on expenses per student and on two-year cohort default rates apply to all postsecondary students. In addition, some indicators, such as the percentage distribution in degree-granting institutions, separate students into full-time and part-time subgroups. Other indicators, such as postsecondary graduation rates and the average total price of attendance, pertain only to full-time (as defined by the institution), full-year (attending at least 9 months out of the year) students who attended only one institution during the year. (The indicator that discusses average total price, grants, and net price is further limited to dependent students.)

Postsecondary education is a term that encompasses a wide range of academic options for students beyond high school, ranging from certificates to advanced degrees. The term postsecondary institution is the category used to refer to institutions with formal instructional programs and a curriculum designed primarily for students who have completed the requirements for a high school diploma or its equivalent. Institutions are characterized by type of financial control—public, private not-for-profit, and private for-profit, as well as by

level—4-year-and-above (4-year), 2-year but less-than-4-year (2-year), and less-than-2-year. For more information on the classification of postsecondary institutions, see *supplemental note 8.*

The postsecondary data used in this Closer Look are from the Integrated Postsecondary Education Data System (IPEDS), the National Postsecondary Student Aid Study (NPSAS), and the Federal Student Aid Direct Loan and Federal Family Education Loan Programs Cohort Default Rate database. IPEDS data are collected at the institution level and participation in the data collection is a requirement for institutions that participate in Title IV federal student financial aid programs, such as Pell grants or Stafford loans. NPSAS data are based on a representative sample of all students in postsecondary education institutions that are eligible to participate in the federal financial aid programs under Title IV. The Federal Student Aid Cohort Default Rate database encompasses all borrowers with Federal Family Education Loans (FFELs) or William D. Ford Federal Direct loans. FFELs include subsidized or unsubsidized Federal Stafford loans and Federal Supplemental Loans for Students (Federal SLS loans). For more information on IPEDS, NPSAS, or Federal Student Aid, see *supplemental note 3.*

Section 1
Participation in Education

Section 1
Participation in Education

Contents

Introduction

The indicators in this section of *The Condition of Education* report trends in enrollments across all levels of education. Enrollment is a key indicator of the scope of and access to educational opportunities, and functions as a basic descriptor of American education. Changes in enrollment have implications for the demand for educational resources such as qualified teachers, physical facilities, and funding levels, all of which are required to provide high-quality education for our nation's students.

The indicators in this section include information on enrollment rates reported by age group, as well as enrollment by level of the education system. These levels are preprimary education, elementary and secondary education, undergraduate education, graduate and professional education, and adult education. Indicators prepared for this year's volume appear on the following pages, and all indicators in this section, including indicators from previous years, appear on the NCES website (see the "List of Indicators on *The Condition of Education* Website" on page xxii for a full listing of indicators).

The first indicator in this section compares rates of enrollment in formal education programs across specific age groups in the population. Trends in enrollment rates provide a perspective on the education of the U.S. population at different ages and over time.

Preprimary education helps prepare children for elementary school and can also serve as child care for parents. An indicator on the website describes participation in center-based early childhood care and education programs such as Head Start, nursery school, and prekindergarten.

Elementary and secondary education provides knowledge and skills that prepare students for further learning and productive membership in society. Because enrollment at the elementary and secondary levels is mandatory in most states until at least age 16 and in a number of states until age 17 or 18, changes in enrollment are driven primarily by shifts in the size and composition of the school-age population, as well as by shifts in the types of schools (e.g., traditional public, public charter, and private schools) that students attend. These factors are examined in this section's indicators. An additional indicator on the website examines the educational option of homeschooling.

Some of the indicators in this section provide information about the characteristics of the students who are enrolled in formal education and, in some cases, how enrollment rates of different types of students vary across schools. For example, indicators that appear in this volume describe the racial/ethnic distributions of public school students, the number and characteristics of children who speak a language other than English at home, and the number and percentage of children with disabilities.

Postsecondary education offers students opportunities to gain advanced knowledge and skills either immediately after high school or later in life. Because postsecondary education is voluntary, changes in total undergraduate enrollment typically reflect fluctuations in enrollment rates and the perceived availability and value of postsecondary education, as well as the size of college-age populations. Postbaccalaureate (which includes graduate and first-professional) enrollment constitutes an important segment of postsecondary education, allowing students to pursue advanced coursework in a variety of areas. Indicators on postsecondary enrollment are found in this volume. An indicator on the website describes adult education, which consists of formal education activities intended to allow adults to upgrade their work skills, change careers, or expand personal interests.

Indicators of participation in education from previous editions of *The Condition of Education* not included in this volume are available at http://nces.ed.gov/programs/coe.

Enrollment Trends by Age

Between 2000 and 2009, enrollment rates increased for young adults ages 18–19 and adults ages 20–24, 25–29, and 30–34; students in these age groups are typically enrolled in college or graduate school.

School enrollment rates for individuals ages 3–4, 5–6, 16–17, 18–19, 20–24, 25–29, and 30–34 were higher in 2009 than in 1970. In contrast, the rates of youth ages 7–13 and 14–15 remained close to 100 percent throughout this period (see table A-1-1). Enrollment patterns may reflect changes in attendance requirements, the perceived value or cost of education, and the time taken to complete degrees.

Between 1970 and 2009, the enrollment rate for children ages 3–4 (the ages at which children are typically enrolled in nursery or preschool) increased from 20 to 52 percent. More recently, from 2000 through 2009, it has remained stable (between 52 and 56 percent). The enrollment rate for children ages 5–6, who are typically enrolled in kindergarten or first grade, rose from 90 percent in 1970 to 96 percent in 1976 and has since remained stable.

For youth ages 7–13 and 14–15, enrollment rates have remained at nearly 100 percent over the past 39 years, reflecting states' compulsory age requirements for school attendance (see tables A-1-1 and A-1-2). The enrollment rates for 7- to 13-year-olds and 14- to 15-year-olds were generally higher than the rate for 16- to 17-year-olds, but the rate for 16- to 17-year-olds did increase from 90 percent in 1970 to 95 percent in 2009. As of August 2010, the maximum compulsory age of attendance was 18 years in 20 states and the District of Columbia (D.C.), 17 years in 11 states, and 16 years in 19 states.

Young adults ages 18–19 are typically transitioning into college education or the workforce. Between 1970 and 2009, the overall enrollment rate for young adults ages 18–19 increased from 48 to 69 percent (see table A-1-1). During this period, the enrollment rate for 18- to 19-year-olds at the secondary level increased from 10 to 19 percent, while at the college level the rate rose from

37 to 50 percent. Between 2000 and 2009, the college enrollment rate increased from 45 to 50 percent.

Adults ages 20–34 who are in school are usually enrolled in college or graduate school. Between 1970 and 2009, the enrollment rate for adults ages 20–24 increased from 22 to 39 percent, and the rate for adults ages 25–29 increased from 8 to 13 percent. The enrollment rate for adults ages 30–34 increased from 4 percent in 1970 to 7 percent in 1975 and has since remained relatively stable (between 6 and 8 percent). Between 2000 and 2009, the enrollment rate for adults ages 20–24 increased from 32 to 39 percent; for adults ages 25–29, from 11 to 13 percent; and for adults ages 30–34, from 7 to 8 percent.

Enrollment rates for all age groups varied by state in 2009 (see table A-1-2). Rates for ages 3–4 ranged from 30 percent in Idaho to 66 percent in New Jersey. For ages 5–17, rates ranged from 95 (North Dakota and West Virginia) to 98 percent (Vermont). Among 18- to 19-year-olds, total rates ranged from 57 percent in Nevada to 84 percent in D.C. Secondary enrollment rates ranged from 14 percent in D.C. to 40 percent in Alaska, while the range for college enrollment rates was the reverse: 21 percent in Alaska to 70 percent in D.C. (There are several major universities in D.C. and the American Community Survey, from which the data come, considers college students to live in the state or district where they are enrolled in college.) Rates for 20- to 24-year-olds ranged from 30 percent (Nevada) to 52 percent (Rhode Island), and for 25- to 34-year-olds, from 9 percent (West Virginia) to 16 percent (Utah, Maryland, and D.C.).

For more information: *Tables A-1-1 and A-1-2*
Glossary: *College, Elementary/secondary school, Nursery school, Private school, Public school*

Technical Notes

Current Population Survey (CPS) estimates include enrollment in any type of graded public, parochial, or other private school. This includes nursery schools, kindergartens, elementary schools, high schools, colleges, universities, and professional schools. American Community Survey (ACS) estimates include enrollment in public, private, and home school. This includes nursery school, kindergarten, elementary and high school, college, and graduate or professional school. Both the ACS and the CPS include only enrollments in regular schooling; that is, schools or classes that advance a person toward an elementary school certificate, a high school diploma, or a college, university, or professional school degree.

Home school is not specifically mentioned in the CPS questionnaire and is included in enrollment estimates only if it meets the definition of regular schooling. Home school is specifically mentioned in the ACS questionnaire and homeschoolers are explicitly included with private school/college students. Due to this and other methodological differences between the CPS and ACS, enrollment estimates from the two surveys are not directly comparable. The age groupings used in this indicator reflect the schooling stages that are typical for students given their age. For more information on the CPS, see *supplemental note 2*. For more information on the ACS, see *supplemental note 3*.

Figure 1-1. Percentage of the population ages 3–34 enrolled in school, by age group: October 1970–2009

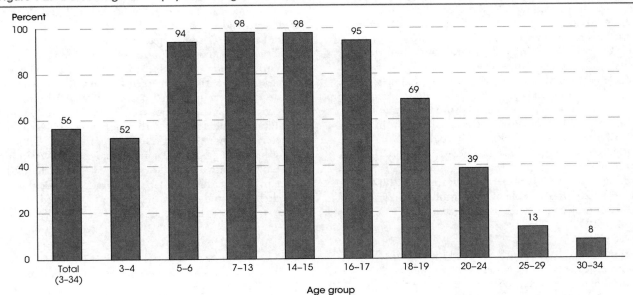

Percent — Ages 3–19

Ages 14–15 Ages 7–13 Ages 16–17 Ages 5–6

Ages 18–19

Ages 3–4[1]

Percent — Ages 18–34

Ages 18–19

Ages 20–24

Ages 25–29

Ages 30–34

Year

[1] Beginning in 1994, new procedures were used to collect enrollment data on children ages 3–4. As a result, pre-1994 data may not be comparable to data from 1994 or later.
NOTE: Includes enrollment in any type of graded public, parochial, or other private schools. Includes nursery schools, kindergartens, elementary schools, high schools, colleges, universities, and professional schools. Attendance may be on either a full-time or part-time basis and during the day or night. Excluded are enrollments in schools or classes that do not advance students to regular school degrees, such as trade schools, business colleges, or vocational schools. For more information on the Current Population Survey (CPS), see *supplemental note 2*.
SOURCE: U.S. Department of Commerce, Census Bureau, Current Population Survey (CPS), October Supplement, 1970–2009.

Figure 1-2. Percentage of the population ages 3–34 enrolled in school, by age group: October 2009

Percent

Age group	Percent
Total (3–34)	56
3–4	52
5–6	94
7–13	98
14–15	98
16–17	95
18–19	69
20–24	39
25–29	13
30–34	8

Age group

NOTE: Includes enrollment in any type of graded public, parochial, or other private schools. Includes nursery or preschools, kindergartens, elementary schools, high schools, colleges, universities, and professional schools. Attendance may be on a full- or part-time basis and during the day or night. Excludes enrollments in schools that do not advance students to regular school degrees, such as trade schools, business colleges, or vocational schools. For more information on the Current Population Survey (CPS), see *supplemental note 2*.
SOURCE: U.S. Department of Commerce, Census Bureau, Current Population Survey (CPS), October Supplement, 2009.

From 2008–09 through 2020–21, public elementary and secondary school enrollment is projected to increase from 49.3 to 52.7 million students, but with differences across states.

In 2008–09, about 49.3 million students were enrolled in public elementary and secondary schools. Of these students, 34.3 million were enrolled in prekindergarten (preK) through grade 8, and 15.0 million were enrolled in grades 9 through 12 (see table A-2-1).

Public school enrollment declined during the 1970s and early 1980s and increased in the latter part of the 1980s. Enrollment continued to increase throughout the 1990s and early 2000s. By 1997–98, public school enrollment had reached 46.1 million students and had surpassed its early 1970s peak. Between 2000–01 and 2006–07, public school enrollment increased by 2.1 million students, reaching 49.3 million students in 2006–07. Total public school enrollment remained at 49.3 million in 2008–09 and is projected to remain at 49.3 million through 2010–11. From 2008–09 to 2020–21, total public school enrollment is projected to increase by 7 percent to 52.7 million (2020–21 is the last year for which projected data are available).

Enrollment trends in grades preK–8 and 9–12 have differed over time as successive cohorts of students have moved through the public school system. For example, enrollment in grades preK–8 decreased throughout the 1970s and early 1980s, while enrollment in grades 9–12 decreased in the late 1970s and throughout the 1980s. Enrollment in grades preK–8 increased from 1985–86 through 2003–04 and remained relatively stable between 2003–04 and 2008–09. Public school enrollment in grades preK–8 is projected to increase from 34.3 million in 2008–09 to an estimated high of 37.4 million in 2020–21. Public school enrollment in grades 9–12 increased from 1990–91 through 2007–08, but is projected to decline through 2012–13. From 2013–14 through 2020–21, enrollment in grades 9–12 is projected to increase, and it is projected to surpass its 2007–08 level by 2020–21. Public school enrollment in grades 9–12 is projected to increase 2 percent from 2007–08 to 2020–21.

Since 1970–71, the South has been the region of the United States with the largest share of public school enrollment. However, the regional distribution of students

in public schools has not remained static. The share of total public school enrollment in the Northeast and the Midwest decreased between 1970–71 and 2008–09 (from 21 to 16 percent and from 28 to 22 percent, respectively), while the share of enrollment in the South and the West increased during the same time period (from 32 to 38 percent and from 18 to 24 percent, respectively). According to projections, by 2020–21 some 15 percent of public school students will be in the Northeast, 21 percent will be in the Midwest, 26 percent will be in the West, and 39 percent will be in the South.

Changes in public school enrollment in grades preK–12 are also projected to differ by state. Nevada, Arizona, and Alaska are projected to see the greatest percent increases in total enrollment from 2008–09 to 2020–21 (25 to 28 percent), and enrollment is projected to increase by 18 percent or more in three other states (see table A-2-2). Michigan and West Virginia are projected to see the largest percent decreases in total enrollment over the same time period (by 6 percent each), and four other states are projected to see decreases of 4 percent or more.

From 2008–09 to 2020–21, the rate of increase in overall public school enrollment is projected to differ by grade level and among states. For example, enrollment in grades preK–8 is projected to increase more than enrollment in grades 9–12 during this period (9 vs. 2 percent). In grades preK–8, enrollment is projected to increase by more than 30 percent in Nevada and Alaska but decrease by more than 7 percent in West Virginia. Projections indicate that between 2008–09 and 2020–21, enrollment in grades 9–12 will experience a wider range of percent change than enrollment in grades preK–8. Enrollments in grades 9–12 in Texas, Nevada, Wyoming, and Colorado are expected to increase by more than 20 percent, while enrollments in these grades in Michigan, Rhode Island, and New Hampshire are projected to decrease by more than 15 percent.

For more information: *Tables A-2-1 and A-2-2*
Glossary: *Elementary/secondary school, Prekindergarten, Public school*

Technical Notes

The most recent year of actual data is 2008–09, and 2020–21 is the last year for which projected data are available. For more information on projections, see NCES 2011-026. Some data have been revised from previously

published figures. Detail may not sum to totals due to rounding. For a list of the states in each region, see *supplemental note 1.*

Figure 2-1. Actual and projected public school enrollment in grades prekindergarten (preK) through 12, by grade level: School years 1970–71 through 2020–21

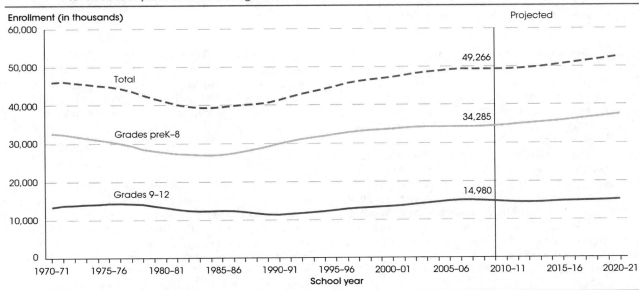

NOTE: The most recent year of actual data is 2008–09, and 2020–21 is the last year for which projected data are available. For more information on projections, see NCES 2011-026. Detail may not sum to totals because of rounding. Some data have been revised from previously published figures.
SOURCE: U.S. Department of Education, National Center for Education Statistics, Statistics of Public Elementary and Secondary Day Schools, 1970-71 through 1984-85; Common Core of Data (CCD), "State Nonfiscal Survey of Public Elementary/Secondary Education," 1985-86 through 2008-09, and National Elementary and Secondary Enrollment Model, 1972–2008.

Figure 2-2. Projected percent change in public school enrollment in grades prekindergarten (preK) through 12, by state or jurisdiction: Between school years 2008–09 and 2020–21

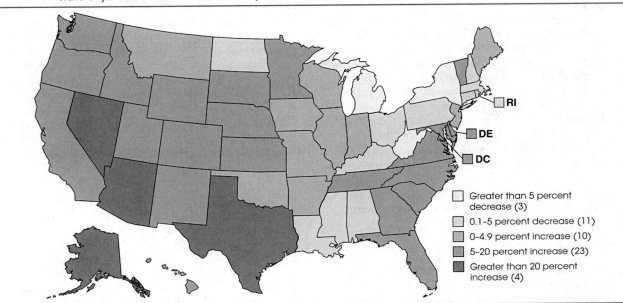

NOTE: The most recent year of actual data is 2008–09, and 2020–21 is the last year for which projected data are available. For more information on projections, see NCES 2011-026.
SOURCE: U.S. Department of Education, National Center for Education Statistics, Common Core of Data (CCD), "State Nonfiscal Survey of Public Elementary/Secondary Education," 2008–09; and Public State Elementary and Secondary Enrollment Model, 1980–2008.

Charter School Enrollment

From 1999–2000 to 2008–09, the number of students enrolled in public charter schools more than tripled from 340,000 to 1.4 million students. In 2008–09, some 5 percent of all public schools were charter schools.

A *public charter school* is a publicly funded school that is typically governed by a group or organization under a legislative contract or charter with the state; the charter exempts the school from selected state or local rules and regulations. In return for funding and autonomy, the charter school must meet the accountability standards articulated in its charter. A school's charter is reviewed periodically (typically every 3 to 5 years) and can be revoked if guidelines on curriculum and management are not followed or if the standards are not met (U.S. Department of Education 2000). As of November 2010, charter schools operated in 40 states and the District of Columbia. In the following states, a charter school law has not been passed: Alabama, Kentucky, Maine, Montana, Nebraska, North Dakota, South Dakota, Vermont, Washington, and West Virginia.

From 1999–2000 to 2008–09, the number of students enrolled in public charter schools more than tripled from 340,000 to 1.4 million students (see table A-3-3). During this period, the percentage of all public schools that were charter schools increased from 2 to 5 percent, comprising 4,700 schools in 2008–09 (see table A-3-1). In addition to the increase in the number of charter schools, the enrollment size of charter schools has grown over time. The percentage of charter schools with enrollments under 300 students decreased from 77 percent in 1999–2000 to 64 percent in 2008–09. Accordingly, the percentage of charter schools with enrollments of 300–499 students increased from 12 to 20 percent during this period; the percentage with 500–999 students, from 9 to 13 percent; and the percentage with 1,000 students or more, from 2 to 3 percent. Though public charter schools have grown in size of enrollment since 1999–2000, they tend to be smaller than traditional public schools, of which 30 percent had fewer than 300 students in 2008–09.

The percentage of charter schools that were high-poverty schools—where 75 percent or more of students were

eligible for free or reduced-price lunch (FRPL)—increased from 13 percent in 1999–2000 to 30 percent in 2008–09. In comparison, 19 percent of traditional public schools were considered high poverty in 2008–09 (see table A-3-2). During this time period, the percentage of charter schools that were low poverty (25 percent of students or less were eligible for FRPL) decreased from 37 to 24 percent.

In 2008–09, over half (54 percent) of charter schools were elementary schools, while secondary and combined schools accounted for 27 and 19 percent of charter schools, respectively. The distribution was different at traditional public schools: 71 percent were elementary schools, 24 percent were secondary schools, and 5 percent were combined schools (see table A-3-2). In 2008–09, about 55 percent of charter schools were located in cities, 21 percent were in suburban areas, 8 percent were in towns, and 16 percent were in rural areas. In contrast, 25 percent of traditional public schools were in cities, 28 percent were in suburban areas, 14 percent were in towns, and 33 percent were in rural areas.

The proportion of public school students enrolled in charter schools varied by region and state. For example, in 2008–09, seven states and the District of Columbia enrolled five or more percent of public school students in charter schools. Four of these states were in the West (Arizona, Colorado, California and Utah), two were in the South (Delaware and the District of Columbia) and two were in the Midwest (Michigan and Ohio). California enrolled the most students in charter schools with about 285,000 enrolled and the District of Columbia enrolled the highest percentage of public school students in charter schools—35 percent, representing some 24,000 students.

For more information: *Tables A-3-1 through A-3-3*
Glossary: *High-poverty schools, Public charter schools, Student membership*

Technical Notes

A *public charter school* is a school that provides free public elementary and/or secondary education to eligible students under a specific charter granted by the state legislature or other appropriate authority. Charter schools can be administered by regular school districts, state education agencies (SEAs), or chartering organizations. Data are based on schools reporting student membership. *Student membership* is defined as an annual headcount of students enrolled in school on October 1 or the school day closest to that date. The Common Core of Data (CCD) allows a student to be reported for only a single school

or agency. For example, a vocational school (identified as a "shared time" school) may provide classes to students from other schools and report no membership of its own. *High-poverty schools* are defined as public schools where more than 75 percent of the students are approved for free or reduced-price lunch (FPRL). *Low-poverty schools* are defined as public schools where 25 percent or fewer students are approved for FRPL. For more information on poverty status, locale, and geographic region, see *supplemental note 1*. For more information on the CCD, see *supplemental note 3*.

Figure 3-1. Number of students enrolled in public charter schools: Selected school years, 1999–2000 through 2008–09

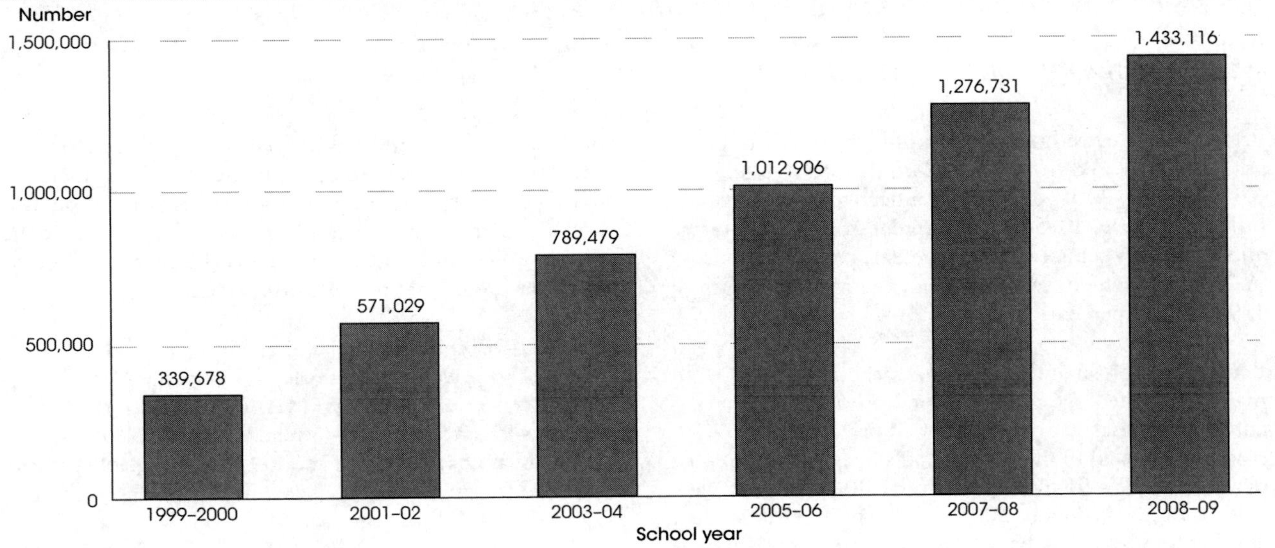

Number

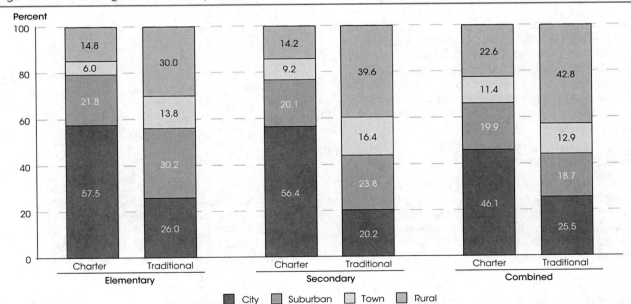

¹ Data for New Jersey were not available and therefore not included in the estimates.
NOTE: A *public charter school* is a school that provides free public elementary and/or secondary education to eligible students under a specific charter granted by the state legislature or other appropriate authority. Charter schools can be administered by regular school districts, state education agencies (SEAs), or chartering organizations. Data are based on schools reporting student membership. *Student membership* is defined as an annual headcount of students enrolled in school on October 1 or the school day closest to that date. The Common Core of Data (CCD) allows a student to be reported for only a single school or agency. For example, a vocational school (identified as a "shared time" school) may provide classes to students from other schools and report no membership of its own. For more information on CCD, see *supplemental note 3*.
SOURCE: U.S. Department of Education, National Center for Education Statistics, Common Core of Data (CCD), "Public Elementary/Secondary School Universe Survey," 1999–2000 (version 1b), 2001–02 (version 1a), 2003–04 (version 1a), 2005–06 (version 1a), 2007–08 (version 1b), and 2008–09 (version 1b).

Figure 3-2. Percentage distribution of public schools, by locale, school type, and level: School year 2008–09

NOTE: A *public charter school* is a school that provides free public elementary and/or secondary education to eligible students under a specific charter granted by the state legislature or other appropriate authority. Charter schools can be administered by regular school districts, state education agencies (SEAs), or chartering organizations. Data are based on schools reporting student membership. *Student membership* is defined as an annual headcount of students enrolled in school on October 1 or the school day closest to that date. The Common Core of Data (CCD) allows a student to be reported for only a single school or agency. For example, a vocational school (identified as a "shared time" school) may provide classes to students from other schools and report no membership of its own. For more information on locale, see *supplemental note 1*. For more information on CCD, see *supplemental note 3*.
SOURCE: U.S. Department of Education, National Center for Education Statistics, Common Core of Data (CCD), "Public Elementary/Secondary School Universe Survey," 2008–09 (version 1b).

Private school enrollment in prekindergarten through grade 12 increased from 5.9 million in 1995–96 to 6.3 million in 2001–02, and then decreased to 5.5 million in 2009–10. Some 10 percent of all elementary and secondary school students were in private schools in 2009–10.

Private school enrollment in prekindergarten through grade 12 increased from 5.9 million in 1995–96 to 6.3 million in 2001–02, and then decreased to 5.5 million in 2009–10. Some 10 percent of all elementary and secondary school students were in private schools in 2009–10, which was lower than the percentage in 1995–96 (12 percent) (see tables A-4-1 and A-4-2).

Between 1995–96 and 2005–06, Catholic schools maintained the largest share of total private school enrollment, but the percentage of all private school students enrolled in Catholic schools decreased from 45 percent in 1995–96 to 39 percent in 2009–10 (see table A-4-1). In 2007–08 and 2009–10, the number of students enrolled in Catholic schools was not measurably different from the number enrolled in other religious schools. The decrease in Catholic school enrollment stemmed from the decline of students enrolled in parochial schools (those run by a parish, not by a diocese or independently). The number of students enrolled in Conservative Christian and Affiliated schools also declined. In contrast, the number and percentage of students enrolled in unaffiliated and nonsectarian schools increased from 1995–96 to 2009–10.

In 2009–10, most private school students were enrolled in schools with a regular program emphasis (85 percent; see table A-4-3). Of the remaining students, 5 percent were enrolled in early childhood schools, 4 percent were enrolled in Montessori schools, and 2 percent each were enrolled in schools with a special program emphasis, special education schools, and alternative schools. The racial/ethnic composition of private schools varied by type of program emphasis. For example, the percentage

of Black students enrolled in special education schools (22 percent) exceeded the percentage of Black students enrolled in the remaining program types (7 to 17 percent), and a higher percentage of Asian/Pacific Islander students were enrolled in Montessori schools (13 percent) than in all other program types (3 to 10 percent).

In 2009–10, the percentage of all students who were enrolled in private schools was higher in the Northeast (14 percent) than in the Midwest (11 percent), the South (9 percent), and the West (8 percent) (see table A-4-2). Looking at changes over time, the percentage of students enrolled in private schools was lower in 2009–10 than in 1995–96 in all four regions.

There were differences in the racial/ethnic composition of private school enrollments (data from 2009–10) compared with public school enrollments (data from 2008–09). White students' share of enrollment was greater in private schools than public schools (73 vs. 55 percent), while the opposite was true for Blacks (9 vs. 17 percent) and Hispanics (9 vs. 21 percent) (see table A-4-3 and NCES 2011-015, table 43). Asians/Pacific Islanders made up 5 and 6 percent of public and private school enrollments respectively. American Indian/Alaska Native students comprised 1 percent of public school enrollment and 0.4 percent of private school enrollment.

For more information: *Tables A-3-1 through A-3-3*
Glossary: *Prekindergarten, Private school, Public school*

Technical Notes

Prekindergarten students who are enrolled in private schools that do not offer at least one grade of kindergarten or higher are not part of this universe. Other religious schools are those with a religious orientation or purpose but are not Catholic. Conservative Christian schools are those with membership in at least 1 of 4 associations, and affiliated schools are those with membership in 1 of 11 associations. Unaffiliated schools are those that have a more general religious orientation or purpose but are not classified as Conservative Christian or affiliated with a specific religion. Nonsectarian schools do not have

a religious orientation or purpose. Vocational schools are included with special program emphasis schools. For more information on private schools, private school program emphases, private school typology, and the Private School Universe Survey (PSS), see *supplemental note 3*. The distribution of private school students by race/ethnicity excludes prekindergarten students. Race categories exclude persons of Hispanic ethnicity. For more information on geographic region and race/ethnicity, see *supplemental note 1*. Detail may not sum to totals because of rounding.

Figure 4-1. Number of private school students in prekindergarten through grade 12, by school type: Various school years, 1995–96 through 2009–10

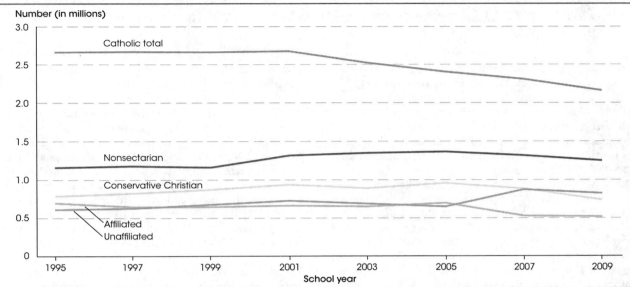

NOTE: Prekindergarten students who are enrolled in private schools that do not offer at least one grade of kindergarten or higher are not part of this universe. Catholic schools include parochial, diocesan, and private Catholic schools. Affiliated religious schools have a specific religious orientation or purpose but are not Catholic. Unaffiliated schools have a more general religious orientation or purpose but are not classified as Conservative Christian or affiliated with a specific religion. Nonsectarian schools do not have a religious orientation or purpose. For more information on the Private School Universe Survey (PSS), see *supplemental note 3*.
SOURCE: U.S. Department of Education, National Center for Education Statistics, Private School Universe Survey (PSS), various years, 1995–96 through 2009–10.

Figure 4-2. Percentage distribution of public and private school enrollments, by race/ethnicity: School year 2009–10

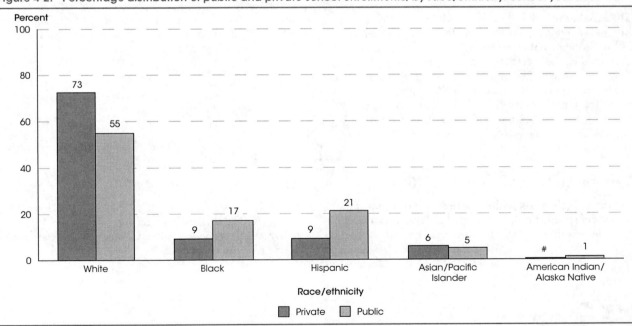

Rounds to zero.
NOTE: Prekindergarten students who are enrolled in private schools that do not offer at least one grade of kindergarten or higher are not part of this universe. The distribution of prekindergarten private school students are excluded due to racial/ethnic information not being available for an estimated 837,719 students. Race categories exclude persons of Hispanic ethnicity. Estimates for persons from other racial/ethnic groups are not shown. Data on public schools are from 2008–09. For more information on race/ethnicity, see *supplemental note 1*. For more information on the Private School Universe Survey (PSS) and the Common Core of Data (CCD), see *supplemental note 3*.
SOURCE: U.S. Department of Education, National Center for Education Statistics, Private School Universe Survey (PSS), 2009–10; and Common Core of Data (CCD), "State Nonfiscal Survey of Public Elementary/Secondary Education," 2008–09.

Racial/Ethnic Enrollment in Public Schools

Between 1989 and 2009, the percentage of public school students who were White decreased from 68 to 55 percent, and the percentage of those who were Hispanic doubled from 11 to 22 percent. By 2009, Hispanic enrollment had exceeded 11 million students.

The shifting racial and ethnic distribution of public school students enrolled in prekindergarten through 12th grade is one aspect of the changing composition of school enrollment. From 1989 through 2009, the number of White students in U.S. public schools fluctuated between 27.9 and 30.9 million, but their share of enrollment decreased from 68 to 55 percent (see table A-5-1). In contrast, during this same period, Hispanic enrollment increased from 4.8 to 11.4 million students and the percentage of Hispanics enrolled doubled from 11 to 22 percent. While the total number of Black students increased (from 7.1 to 7.8 million), their share of enrollment decreased slightly during this time. Hispanic enrollment surpassed Black enrollment for the first time between 2001 and 2003 and has remained higher than Black enrollment in each year through 2009.

Overall, enrollment increased in each region of the country between 1989 and 2009 (see table A-5-2). Enrollment increased from 15.1 to 19.1 million in the South, from 9.1 to 12.3 million in the West, from 10.5 to 11.1 million in the Midwest, and from 7.4 to 8.5 million in the Northeast.

The racial/ethnic distribution of public school enrollment differed by region from 1989 to 2009. The number of White students remained stable in the West and South, decreased in the Northeast, and increased in the Midwest. The percentage of enrollment of White students declined in all four regions. The number of Black students increased slightly in the West and South and remained stable in the Northeast and Midwest during this time period. The percentage of enrollment of Black students

remained stable in all four regions. The number of Hispanic students increased in all four regions as did their share of enrollment. The number of Asian students was stable in the West and increased in the South, Northeast, and Midwest. Their percentage of enrollment remained stable in the West and Northeast and increased in the South and Midwest. Pacific Islander students in all four regions represented less than one percent of enrollment in 2009–10. American Indian/Alaska Native students made up 1 percent or less of student enrollment in all regions of the United States. Students of two or more races made up 4 percent of enrollment in the West, 3 percent in the Midwest, and 2 percent in the Northeast and South.

In 2009, 12 states and the District of Columbia had student racial/ethnic distributions of less than 50 percent White students (see table A-5-4). Black students had the largest share of public school enrollment in Mississippi and the District of Columbia. Hispanic students had the largest share of public school enrollment in four states (Arizona, California, New Mexico, and Texas). Of all the jurisdictions, the District of Columbia enrolled the highest percentage of Black students (76 percent), New Mexico enrolled the highest percentage of Hispanic students (56 percent), and Hawaii enrolled the highest percentage of Asian students (23 percent) and students of two or more races (32 percent).

 For more information: *Tables A-5-1 through A-5-4*
Glossary: *Public school*

Technical Notes

Estimates include all public school students enrolled in prekindergarten through 12th grade. Race categories exclude persons of Hispanic ethnicity. For more information on race/ethnicity and region, see *supplemental*

note 1. For more information on the Current Population Survey (CPS), see *supplemental note 2.* For more information on the American Community Survey (ACS), see *supplemental note 3.*

Figure 5-1. Percentage distribution of the race/ethnicity of public school students enrolled in prekindergarten through 12th grade: Selected years, October 1989–October 2009

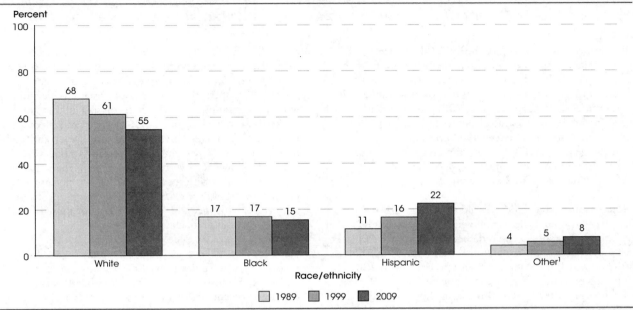

¹ "Other" includes all students who identified themselves as being Asian, Hawaiian, Alaska Native, Pacific Islander, American Indian, or two or more races.
NOTE: Estimates include all public school students enrolled in prekindergarten through 12th grade. Detail may not sum to totals because of rounding. For more information on the Current Population Survey (CPS), see *supplemental note 2*. Race categories exclude persons of Hispanic ethnicity. For more information on race/ethnicity, see *supplemental note 1*.
SOURCE: U.S. Department of Commerce, Census Bureau, Current Population Survey (CPS), October Supplement, 1989, 1999, and 2009.

Figure 5-2. Number of public school students enrolled in prekindergarten through 12th grade, by region and race/ethnicity: October 1989–October 2009

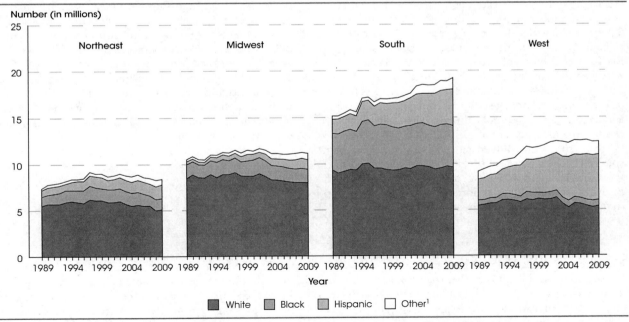

¹ "Other" includes all students who identified themselves as being Asian, Hawaiian, Alaska Native, Pacific Islander, American Indian, or two or more races.
NOTE: Estimates include all public school students enrolled in prekindergarten through 12th grade. Over time, the Current Population Survey (CPS) has had different response options for race/ethnicity. For more information on the Current Population Survey (CPS), see *supplemental note 2*. Race categories exclude persons of Hispanic ethnicity. For more information on race/ethnicity and region, see *supplemental note 1*.
SOURCE: U.S. Department of Commerce, Census Bureau, Current Population Survey (CPS), October Supplement, 1989–2009.

In 2009, some 21 percent of children ages 5–17 (or 11.2 million) spoke a language other than English at home, and 5 percent (or 2.7 million) spoke English with difficulty. Seventy-three percent of those who spoke English with difficulty spoke Spanish.

The number of school-age children (children ages 5–17) who spoke a language other than English at home rose from 4.7 to 11.2 million between 1980 and 2009, or from 10 to 21 percent of the population in this age range (see table A-6-1). From 2006 to 2009, this percentage remained between 20 and 21 percent. After increasing from 4 to 7 percent between 1980 and 2000, the percentage of school-age children who spoke a language other than English at home and spoke English with difficulty decreased to 5 percent in 2009.

Among school-age children who spoke a non-English language at home, the percentage who spoke English with difficulty generally decreased between 1980 and 2009. For example, 41 percent of these children spoke English with difficulty in 1980, compared with 36 percent in 2000, some 25 percent in 2006, and 24 percent in 2009. School enrollment patterns have also changed over time for these children: the enrollment rate increased from 90 to 93 percent between 1980 and 2009.

In 2009, the percentage of school-age children who spoke a language other than English at home and spoke English with difficulty varied by demographic characteristics, including race/ethnicity, citizenship status, poverty status, and age (see table A-6-2). Sixteen percent each of Hispanics and Asians spoke a non-English language at home and spoke English with difficulty, compared with 6 percent of Pacific Islanders, 3 percent of American Indians/Alaska Natives, and 1 percent each of Whites, Blacks, and children of two or more races. Differences were also seen among racial/ethnic subgroups of Hispanic and Asian school-age children. For example, 25 percent of Vietnamese school-age children spoke a non-English language at home and spoke English with difficulty, compared with 8 percent of their Filipino peers. For Hispanic subgroups, 19 percent of Dominican school-age children spoke a non-English language at home and spoke English with difficulty, compared with 7 percent of Puerto Rican school-age children. In terms of citizenship status, 4 percent of U.S.-born citizens spoke a language

other than English at home and spoke English with difficulty, compared with 11 percent of naturalized U.S. citizens and 35 percent of non-U.S. citizens. Regarding poverty status, the percentage of poor school-age children who spoke a language other than English at home and spoke English with difficulty (10 percent) was greater than the percentages for their near-poor (7 percent) and non-poor peers (3 percent). Children in families with incomes below the poverty threshold are classified as *poor,* those in families with incomes at 100–199 percent of the poverty threshold are classified as *near-poor,* and those in families with incomes at 200 percent or more of the poverty threshold are classified as *nonpoor.*

Concerning differences by age, the percentage of 5- to 9-year-olds who spoke a non-English language at home and spoke English with difficulty (7 percent) was greater than the percentages of 10- to 13-year-olds and 14- to 17-year-olds who did so (4 percent each). These patterns by age held across most demographic and socioeconomic characteristics.

Of the 2.7 million school-age children who spoke a language other than English at home and spoke English with difficulty in 2009, about 73 percent spoke Spanish, 13 percent spoke an Asian/Pacific Islander language, 10 percent spoke an Indo-European language other than Spanish, and 4 percent spoke another language (see table A-6-3). English-speaking ability also varied by state in 2009. In five states—Alabama, Louisiana, Mississippi, West Virginia, and Montana—the percentage of 5- to 17-year-olds who spoke a non-English language and spoke English with difficulty was about 1 percent. The states with the highest percentages were Arizona and New York (6 percent each); Nevada and Texas (9 percent each); and California (11 percent).

 For more information: *Tables A-6-1 through A-6-3*

Technical Notes

Respondents were asked whether each child in the household spoke a language other than English at home. Those who answered "yes" were asked how well each child could speak English using the following categories: "very well," "well," "not well," and "not at all." All children who were reported to speak English less than "very well" were considered to have difficulty speaking English. Spanish-language versions of the questionnaires were

available to respondents. Estimates have been revised from previous publications. For more information on the Long Form Decennial Census and the American Community Survey, see *supplemental note 3.* Race categories exclude persons of Hispanic ethnicity. For more information on race/ethnicity, poverty status, and geographic region, see *supplemental note 1.*

Figure 6-1. Percentage of children ages 5–17 who spoke a language other than English at home and percentage who spoke a language other than English at home and spoke English with difficulty: Selected years, 1980–2009

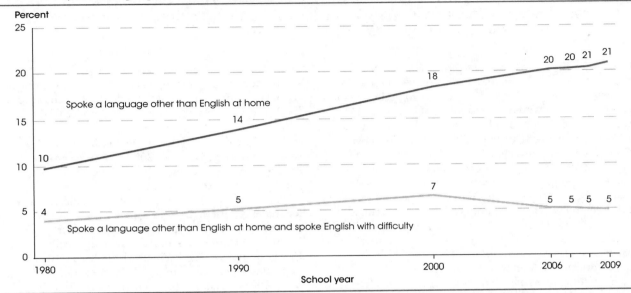

NOTE: Respondents were asked whether each child in the household spoke a language other than English at home. Those who answered "yes" were asked how well each child could speak English using the following categories: "very well," "well," "not well," and "not at all." All children who were reported to speak English less than "very well" were considered to have difficulty speaking English. Spanish-language versions of the questionnaires were available to respondents. For more information on the Long Form Decennial Census and the American Community Survey, see *supplemental note 3*.
SOURCE: U.S. Department of Commerce, Census Bureau, Long Form Decennial Census, 1980, 1990, and 2000, and American Community Survey (ACS), 2006–2009.

Figure 6-2. Percentage of children ages 5–17 who spoke a language other than English at home and spoke English with difficulty, by state or jurisdiction: 2009

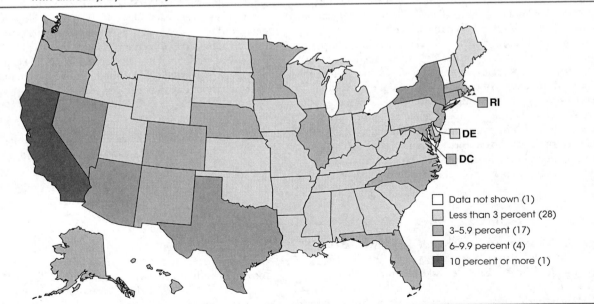

NOTE: Respondents were asked whether each child in the household spoke a language other than English at home. Those who answered "yes" were asked how well each child could speak English using the following categories: "very well," "well," "not well," and "not at all." All children who were reported to speak English less than "very well" were considered to have difficulty speaking English. A Spanish-language version of the questionnaire was available to respondents. For more information on the American Community Survey, see *supplemental note 3*. For more information on geographic region, see *supplemental note 1*.
SOURCE: U.S. Department of Commerce, Census Bureau, American Community Survey (ACS), 2009.

The number of children and youth ages 3–21 receiving special education services was 6.5 million in 2008–09, corresponding to about 13 percent of all public school enrollment. Some 38 percent of these students receiving special education services had specific learning disabilities.

Enacted in 1975, the Individuals with Disabilities Education Act (IDEA) mandates the provision of a free and appropriate public school education for children and youth ages 3–21 who have disabilities. Data collection activities to monitor compliance with IDEA began in 1976. From 1980–81 through 2004–05, the number of children and youth ages 3–21 in IDEA programs increased, as did the number expressed as a percent in relation to public school enrollment (see table A-7-1). Beginning in 2005–06, the number and percentage of children and youth served under IDEA have declined each year through 2008–09. In 1980–81 some 4.1 million children and youth ages 3–21 received special education services. The number of children and youth served under IDEA grew to 6.7 million in 2005–06, or about 14 percent of public school enrollment. By 2008–09, the number of children and youth receiving services declined to 6.5 million, corresponding to about 13 percent of all public school enrollment.

Generally, a greater percentage of children and youth ages 3–21 received special education services under IDEA for specific learning disabilities than for any other type of disability in every school year between 1980–81 and 2008–09 (see table A-7-1). A specific learning disability is a disorder in one or more of the basic psychological processes involved in understanding or in using language, spoken or written, that may manifest itself in an imperfect ability to listen, think, speak, read, write, spell, or do mathematical calculations. In 2008–09, some 38 percent of all children and youth receiving special education services had specific learning disabilities, 22 percent had speech or language impairments, and 10 percent had other health impairments. Students with disabilities such as intellectual disabilities, emotional disturbances, developmental delay, and autism each accounted for between 5 and 7 percent of children and youth served

under IDEA. Children and youth with multiple disabilities; hearing, orthopedic, and visual impairments; traumatic brain injury; and deaf-blindness each accounted for 2 percent or less of children served under IDEA.

About 95 percent of children and youth ages 6–21 who were served under IDEA in 2008–09 were enrolled in regular schools (see table A-7-2). Some 3 percent of children and youth ages 6–21 who were served under IDEA were enrolled in separate schools (public or private) for students with disabilities; 1 percent were placed by their parents in regular private schools; and less than 1 percent each were in separate residential facilities (public and private), homebound or in hospitals, or in correctional facilities. Among all children and youth ages 6–21 who were enrolled in regular schools, the percentage of children and youth who spent most of their school day (more than 80 percent) in general classes was higher in 2008–09 than in any other school year since 1990. For example, in 2008–09, some 58 percent of children and youth spent most of their school day in regular class, compared to 33 percent in 1990–91. In 2008–09, about 86 percent of students with speech or language impairments—the highest percentage of all disability types—spent most of their school day in general classes. Sixty-two percent each of students with developmental delay and of students with visual impairments spent most of their school day in general classes. In contrast, 16 percent of students with intellectual disabilities and 13 percent of students with multiple disabilities spent most of their school day in general classes.

For more information: *Tables A-7-1 and A-7-2*
Glossary: *Disabilities, children with; Individuals with Disabilities Act (IDEA)*

Technical Notes

Special education services through the Individuals with Disabilities Education Act (IDEA) are available only for eligible children. Eligible children and youth are those identified by a team of professionals as having a disability that adversely affects academic performance and being in need of special education and related services. Intellectual disability includes the condition formerly

known as mental retardation. Data include children and youth in the 50 states, the District of Columbia, and the Bureau of Indian Education schools. Data for 2007–08 and 2008–09 do not include Vermont. In 2006–07, the total number of 3- to 21-year-olds served under IDEA in Vermont was 14,010. For more information on the student disabilities presented, see *supplemental note 7.*

Figure 7-1. Percentage distribution of 3- to 21-year-olds served under the Individuals with Disabilities Education Act (IDEA), by type of disability: School year 2008–09

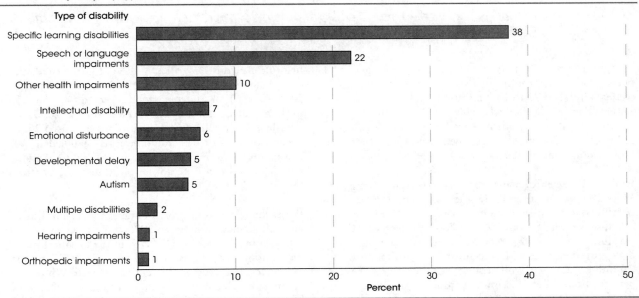

NOTE: Deaf-blindness, traumatic brain injury, and visual impairments are not shown because they each account for less than 1 percent of children served under IDEA. Due to categories not shown, detail does not sum to total. Includes children and youth in the 49 states, the District of Columbia, and the Bureau of Indian Education schools. Data do not include Vermont. For more information on student disabilities, see *supplemental note 7.*
SOURCE: U.S. Department of Education, Office of Special Education Programs, Individuals with Disabilities Education Act (IDEA) database, retrieved October 18, 2010, from http://www.ideadata.org/PartBdata.asp.

Figure 7-2. Percentage distribution of students ages 6–21 served under the Individuals with Disabilities Education Act (IDEA), Part B, placed in a regular school environment, by time spent in general classes: Selected school years, 1995–96 through 2008–09

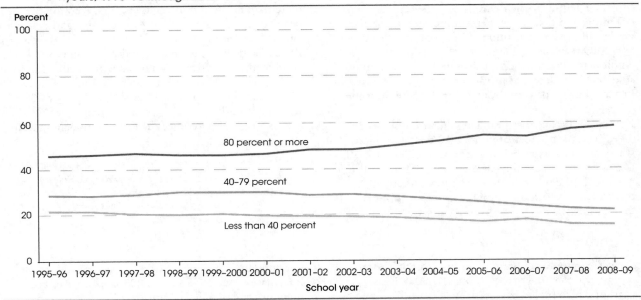

NOTE: Includes children and youth in the 50 states, the District of Columbia, and the Bureau of Indian Education schools. Data for 2007–08 and 2008–09 do not include Vermont. Detail may not sum to totals because of rounding. For more information about student disabilities, see *supplemental note 7.*
SOURCE: U.S. Department of Education, Office of Special Education Programs, Individuals with Disabilities Education Act (IDEA) database, retrieved October 18, 2010, from https://www.ideadata.org/arc_toc9.asp#partbLRE.

Between 2000 and 2009, undergraduate enrollment in degree-granting postsecondary institutions increased by 34 percent, from 13.2 to 17.6 million students. Projections indicate that it will continue to increase, reaching 19.6 million students in 2020.

Total undergraduate enrollment in degree-granting postsecondary institutions increased from 7.4 million students in fall 1970 to 13.2 million in fall 2000 and 17.6 million in fall 2009 (see table A-8-1). According to projections, undergraduate enrollment is expected to reach 19.6 million in fall 2020 (the last year for which projected data are available).

Undergraduate enrollment grew at a faster rate during the 1970s (42 percent) than it did in more recent decades; it continued to increase throughout the 1980s and 1990s, but at slower rates. From 2000 to 2009, undergraduate enrollment rose by 34 percent. During this time period, male enrollment grew 31 percent, from 5.8 million to 7.6 million students, while female enrollment grew 35 percent, from 7.4 to 10.0 million students. In 2009, females accounted for 57 percent of enrollment, and males, 43 percent. Enrollments for both males and females are expected to increase through 2020, reaching 8.1 and 11.5 million students, respectively.

Undergraduate enrollment in public institutions increased from 10.5 million students in 2000 to 13.4 million in 2009, a 27 percent increase. Private institutions experienced a higher rate of growth over this time period, as their enrollment grew from 2.6 to 4.2 million students, a 60 percent increase. Most of the growth in private institution enrollment between 2000 and 2009 occurred among for-profit institutions—their enrollment almost quadrupled from 0.4 to 1.6 million students. Enrollment at private not-for-profit institutions increased by 17 percent, from 2.2 to 2.6 million students.

Between 2000 and 2009, undergraduate enrollment at 4-year institutions increased from 7.2 to 10.0 million students, and is expected to reach 11.1 million in 2020 (see table A-8-2). Enrollment increased 30 percent (from 4.8 to 6.3 million) at public 4-year institutions, 19 percent at private not-for-profit institutions (from 2.2 to 2.6 million), and nearly five-fold at private for-profit

institutions (from 0.2 to 1.2 million). During the same period, enrollment at 2-year institutions increased from 5.9 to 7.5 million students and is expected to reach 8.5 million students by 2020. Between 2000 and 2009, enrollment at public 2-year institutions increased 25 percent (from 5.7 to 7.1 million), nearly doubled at private for-profit institutions (from 192,000 to 385,000), and decreased at private not-for-profit institutions (from 59,000 to 35,000).

For each racial/ethnic group, undergraduate enrollment generally increased between 1976 and 2009, but at different rates, resulting in a shift in the racial/ethnic distribution (see table A-8-3). In 1976, some 7.7 million (82 percent) of undergraduate students were White, compared with 9.0 million (68 percent) in 2000. By 2009, the number of White students had grown to 10.9 million, but White students as a percentage of the total enrollment had decreased to 62 percent. The number of Black students almost tripled between 1976 and 2009, from 0.9 to 2.6 million students. Black students' share of undergraduate enrollment fluctuated between 10 and 12 percent from 1976 to 2000, and in 2009 about 15 percent of undergraduate students were Black. Hispanic and Asian/Pacific Islander enrollment each increased more than five-fold from 1976 to 2009; accordingly, the percentages of students who were Hispanic and Asian/Pacific Islander increased. In 1976, Hispanics and Asians/Pacific Islanders represented 4 and 2 percent of total enrollment, respectively, compared with 13 and 7 percent, respectively, in 2009. While American Indian/Alaska Native enrollment increased from 70,000 to 189,000 students from 1976 to 2009, these students accounted for approximately 1 percent of the total enrollment in 2009.

For more information: *Tables A-8-1 through A-8-3*
Glossary: *Four-year postsecondary institution, Full-time enrollment, Part-time enrollment, Private institution, Public institution, Two-year postsecondary institution, Undergraduate*

Technical Notes

Projections are based on data through 2009. The most recent year of actual data is 2009, and 2020 is the last year for which projected data are available. For more information on projections, see NCES 2011-026. Because of underreporting and nonreporting of racial/ethnic data, some estimates are slightly lower than corresponding data in other published tables. Race categories exclude persons of Hispanic ethnicity. For more information on race/ethnicity, see *supplemental note 1*. Data for 1999

were imputed using alternative procedures. For more information, see NCES 2001-083, appendix E. For more information on the Integrated Postsecondary Education Data System (IPEDS), see *supplemental note 3*. All actual data presented in this indicator are IPEDS fall enrollment data, and thus measure the enrollment in the fall of the academic year. For more information on the classification of postsecondary education institutions, see *supplemental note 8*.

Figure 8-1. Actual and projected undergraduate enrollment in degree-granting postsecondary institutions, by sex and attendance status: Fall 1970–2020

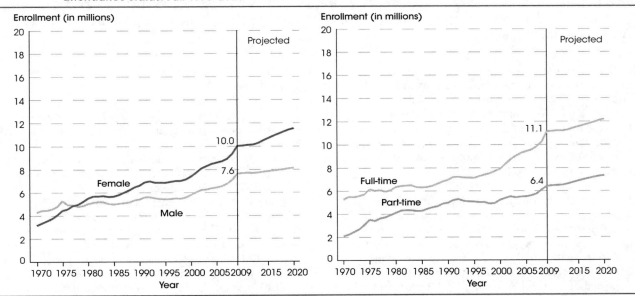

NOTE: Projections are based on reported data through 2009. For more information on projections, see NCES 2011-026. Data through 1995 are for institutions of higher education, while later data are for degree-granting institutions. Data for 1999 were imputed using alternative procedures. For more information, see NCES 2001-083, appendix E. Some data have been revised from previously published figures. For more information on the Integrated Postsecondary Education Data System (IPEDS), see *supplemental note 3*. For more information on the Classification of Postsecondary Education Institutions, see *supplemental note 8*. See the glossary for definitions of full-time and part-time enrollment.
SOURCE: U.S. Department of Education, National Center for Education Statistics, Higher Education General Information Survey (HEGIS), "Fall Enrollment in Colleges and Universities" surveys, 1970 through 1985; 1990 through 2009 Integrated Postsecondary Education Data System, "Fall Enrollment Survey" (IPEDS-EF:90–99) and Spring 2001 through Spring 2010; and Enrollment in Degree-Granting Institutions Model, 1980–2009.

Figure 8-2. Percentage distribution of undergraduate enrollment in degree-granting institutions, by race/ethnicity: Fall 1976, 2000, and 2009

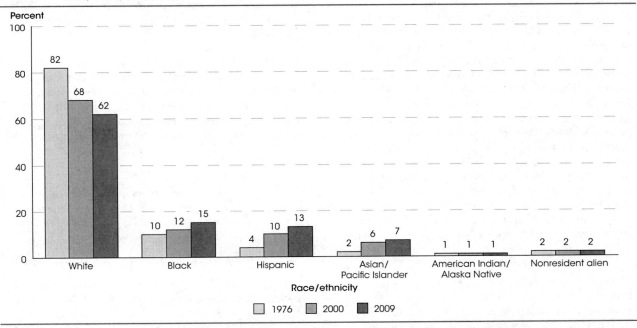

NOTE: Data for 1976 are for institutions of higher education, and data for 2000 and 2009 are for degree-granting institutions. Detail may not sum to totals because of rounding. Race categories exclude persons of Hispanic ethnicity. Because of underreporting and nonreporting of racial/ethnic data, some estimates are slightly lower than corresponding data in other published tables. Nonresident aliens are shown separately because information about their race/ethnicity is not available. See the glossary for the definition of nonresident alien. For more information on race/ethnicity, see *supplemental note 1*. For more information on the Integrated Postsecondary Education Data System (IPEDS), see *supplemental note 3*. For more information on the Classification of Postsecondary Education Institutions, see *supplemental note 8*.
SOURCE: U.S. Department of Education, National Center for Education Statistics, Higher Education General Information Survey (HEGIS), "Fall Enrollment in Colleges and Universities" surveys, 1976; and 2000 and 2009 Integrated Postsecondary Education Data System (IPEDS), Spring 2001 and 2010.

Postbaccalaureate Enrollment

Postbaccalaureate enrollment has increased every year since 1983, reaching 2.9 million students in 2009. In each year since 1988, women have made up more than half of postbaccalaureate enrollment. In 2009, postbaccalaureate enrollment was 59 percent female.

In fall 1976, some 1.6 million students were enrolled in postbaccalaureate programs, which include graduate and first-professional programs (see table A-9-1). Postbaccalaureate enrollment fluctuated during the period from the mid-1970s to the early 1980s, but between 1983 and 2009 it increased from 1.6 to 2.9 million students. Fall enrollment in postbaccalaureate programs is projected to increase through 2020 to 3.4 million students.

More females than males have been enrolled in postbaccalaureate programs every year since 1988. In 1976, some 673,000 females were enrolled in a postbaccalaureate program, compared with 905,000 males. In 1988, female enrollment exceeded male enrollment, and by 2009 postbaccalaureate enrollment consisted of 1.7 million females (59 percent) and 1.2 million males (41 percent). Projections indicate that females will continue to enroll in postbaccalaureate programs at a higher rate than will males, and in 2020 postbaccalaureate enrollment is expected to increase to 2.1 million females (61 percent) and 1.3 million males (39 percent).

As postbaccalaureate enrollment has grown, the distribution of students—in terms of attendance status and control of institutions they attended—has changed. In 1976, more students attended part time than full time, but in each year since 2000 full-time enrollment has been higher than part-time enrollment. Additionally, the percentage of postbaccalaureate students who attended private institutions increased between 1976 and 2009. In 1976, about 35 percent of postbaccalaureate students were enrolled in private institutions, compared with 50 percent in 2009. The growth in total private enrollment is attributable to the growth in enrollment at both private for-profit and private not-for-profit institutions. The number of students attending private for-profit institutions increased from 3,000 students in 1976 (less than 1 percent of total enrollment) to 267,000 students in 2009 (9 percent), while the number of students attending private not-for-profit institutions increased from 541,000

students in 1976 (34 percent) to 1.2 million students in 2009 (41 percent).

For each racial/ethnic group, the number of students enrolled in postbaccalaureate programs generally increased between 1976 and 2009 but at different rates, resulting in a shift in the racial/ethnic distribution. In 1976, some 1.3 million (85 percent) postbaccalaureate students were White. By 2009, the number of White students had grown to 1.8 million, but White enrollment as a percentage of total enrollment had decreased to 63 percent (see table A-9-2). The number of Black postbaccalaureate students more than tripled between 1976 and 2009, from 90,000 to 342,000 students. The percentage of postbaccalaureate students who were Black increased from 6 to 12 percent from 1976 to 2009. Hispanic and Asian/Pacific Islander enrollment increased six- and seven-fold, respectively, from 1976 to 2009; accordingly, the percentages of students who were Hispanic and Asian/Pacific Islander increased. In 1976, Hispanics and Asians/Pacific Islanders each represented 2 percent of total enrollment, and in 2009 they represented 6 and 7 percent, respectively. While American Indian/Alaska Native enrollment increased from 6,000 to 18,000 students during this period, they accounted for less than 1 percent of enrollment in 2009. The percentage of students who were nonresident aliens increased from 5 percent in 1976 to 11 percent in 2009.

In 1976, males outnumbered females in postbaccalaureate programs for each racial/ethnic group shown except for Blacks; however, in 2009, females outnumbered males in all groups except for nonresident aliens. The largest relative gap between female and male enrollment in 2009 was between Black females and males: 71 percent of the total Black enrollment was female in fall 2009.

For more information: *Tables A-9-1 and A-9-2*
Glossary: *Nonresident alien, Postbaccalaureate enrollment, Private institution, Public institution*

Technical Notes

The most recent year of actual data is 2009, and 2020 is the last year for which projected data are available. For more information on projections, see NCES 2011-026. Because of underreporting and nonreporting of racial/ethnic data, some estimates are slightly lower than corresponding data in other published tables. Race categories exclude persons of Hispanic ethnicity. Nonresident aliens are shown separately because information about their race/ethnicity is not available.

For more information on race/ethnicity, see *supplemental note 1*. For information on the Integrated Postsecondary Education Data System (IPEDS), see *supplemental note 3*. All actual data presented in this indicator are IPEDS fall enrollment data and thus measure the enrollment in the fall of the academic year. For more information on the Classification of Postsecondary Education Institutions, see *supplemental note 8*.

Figure 9-1. Actual and projected postbaccalaureate enrollment in degree-granting institutions, by sex: Fall 1976–2020

Enrollment (in thousands)

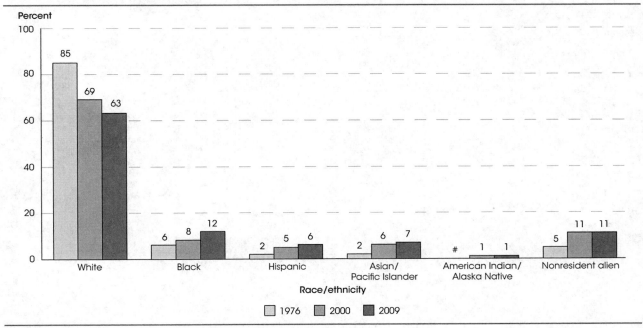

[1] Projections are based on reported data through 2009. The most recent year of actual data is 2009, and 2020 is the last year for which projected data are available. For more information on projections, see NCES 2011-026. Data for 1999 were imputed using alternative procedures. For more information, see NCES 2001-083, appendix E.
NOTE: Postbaccalaureate enrollment is the number of students with a bachelor's degree who are enrolled in graduate-level or first-professional programs. For more information on the Integrated Postsecondary Education Data System (IPEDS), see *supplemental note 3*.
SOURCE: U.S. Department of Education, National Center for Education Statistics, Higher Education General Information Survey (HEGIS), "Fall Enrollment in Colleges and Universities" surveys, 1967 through 1985; 1986 through 2009 Integrated Postsecondary Education Data System, "Fall Enrollment Survey" (IPEDS-EF:86–99), and Spring 2001 through Spring 2010; and Enrollment in Degree-Granting Institutions Model, 1980–2009.

Figure 9-2. Percentage distribution of postbaccalaureate enrollment in degree-granting institutions, by race/ethnicity: Fall 1976, 2000, and 2009

Rounds to zero.
NOTE: Postbaccalaureate enrollment is the number of students with a bachelor's degree who are enrolled in graduate-level or first-professional programs. Detail may not sum to totals because of rounding. Race categories exclude persons of Hispanic ethnicity. Nonresident aliens are shown separately because information about their race/ethnicity is not available. See the glossary for the definition of nonresident alien. For more information on race/ethnicity, see *supplemental note 1*. For more information on the Integrated Postsecondary Education Data System (IPEDS), see *supplemental note 3*. For more information on the Classification of Postsecondary Education Institutions, see *supplemental note 8*.
SOURCE: U.S. Department of Education, National Center for Education Statistics, Higher Education General Information Survey (HEGIS), "Fall Enrollment in Colleges and Universities" surveys, 1976, and 2000 and 2009 Integrated Postsecondary Education Data System (IPEDS), Spring 2001 and 2010.

Section 2
Learner Outcomes

Section 2
Learner Outcomes

Contents

Introduction ————————————————————————————

The indicators in this section of *The Condition of Education* examine student achievement and other outcomes of education among students in elementary and secondary education and among adults in the broader society. The indicators on student achievement illustrate how students are performing on assessments in reading, mathematics, science, and other academic subject areas. They highlight trends over time in student achievement as well as gaps in achievement between groups. Indicators prepared for this year's volume appear on the following pages, and all indicators in this section, including indicators from previous years, appear on the NCES website (see the "List of Indicators on *The Condition of Education* Website" on page xxii for a full listing of indicators).

Children enter school with varying levels of knowledge and skill. Measures of these early childhood competencies represent important indicators of students' future prospects both inside and outside of the classroom. The first indicator in this section (found on the website) traces the gains in achievement and the specific reading and mathematics skills of children through the early years of elementary education. This indicator highlights changes in student achievement for a cohort of kindergarten children as they progressed through the early years of schooling.

As students progress through school, it is important to know the extent to which they are acquiring necessary skills and gaining proficiency in challenging subject matter. Several indicators in this section report trends in assessment performance, either by age or by grade,

among elementary and secondary students. Performance is measured in three ways: (1) as the change in students' average scores over time, (2) as the change in the percentage of students achieving specified levels of achievement, and (3) through international comparisons of national average scores. Indicators in this volume show the reading, mathematics, and science achievement of students in grades 4, 8, and 12. In addition, there are indicators that examine the gaps in achievement by various groups of students. Other indicators that appear on the website highlight achievement in the arts, writing, economics, U.S. history, and geography. Also, two indicators found in this volume examine the reading, mathematics, and science performance of students at the international level.

In addition to academic achievement at the elementary and secondary levels, adult literacy contributes to an educated, capable, and engaged citizenry. Indicators on the website highlight adult literacy, measured here by levels of adult literacy and adult reading habits.

Economic outcomes include the earnings of individuals with varying levels of educational attainment, as well as the likelihood of being employed (both included in this volume). The last indicators in this section look specifically at the economic outcomes of education. An indicator showing the health status of individuals by their educational attainment is featured on the website.

Indicators of learner outcomes from previous editions of *The Condition of Education* not included in this volume are available at http://nces.ed.gov/programs/coe.

Reading Performance

Between 2007 and 2009, there was no measurable change in the average grade 4 reading score; the average grade 8 reading score, however, increased 1 point. At grade 12, the average reading score increased by 2 points between 2005 and 2009.

In 2009, the average National Assessment for Educational Progress (NAEP) reading scale score for 4th-grade students (221) was not measurably different from the 2007 score (221), but higher than the scores on all earlier assessments between 1992 (217) and 2005 (219) (see table A-10-1). From 1992 to 2009, 4th-grade students' average NAEP reading scale scores increased 4 points. For 8th-grade students, the average score in 2009 was 1 point higher than in 2007 (263) and 4 points higher than in 1992 and 1994, but not always measurably different from the scores on the assessments given between 1998 and 2005. The average reading score for 12th-grade students was 2 points higher in 2009 than in 2005 (286), the year of the immediately preceding assessment, but was 4 points lower than the score in 1992 (292). The 2009 score was not measurably different than the scores in 1994 or 2002.

Percentages of 4th-grade students performing at or above the *Basic,* at or above the *Proficient,* and at the *Advanced* achievement levels in reading showed no measurable change from 2007 to 2009. In 2009, about 67 percent of 4th-grade students performed at or above *Basic,* 33 percent performed at or above *Proficient,* and 8 percent performed at *Advanced.* Percentages of 8th-grade students performing at or above *Basic* and at or above *Proficient* each increased 1 percentage point between 2007 and 2009. Additionally, the 2009 percentages of 8th-grade students who reached both these performance levels were higher than in 1992. In 2009, the percentage of 8th-grade students performing at the *Advanced* level (3 percent) was not measurably different from the percentage performing at this level in 2007 (3) or 1992 (3). The percentage of students at grade 12 performing at or above *Basic* (74 percent) in 2009 was not significantly different from the percentage doing so in 2005 (73), but was lower than the percentage doing so in 1992 (80). Thirty-eight percent of 12th-grade students performed at or above *Proficient* in 2009; this was 3 percentage points higher than the 2005 percentage, but not significantly different than percentages in the earlier assessment years. There was no measurable change at the *Advanced* level from 2005 at

grade 12, although it was 1 percentage point higher than in 1992.

At grade 4, the average reading scores in 2009 for White, Black, Hispanic, Asian/Pacific Islander, and American Indian/Alaska Native students were not measurably different from their scores in 2007 (see table A-10-2). The 2009 reading scores for White, Black, and Hispanic students were, however, higher than the scores from assessment years prior to 2007. At grade 8, average reading scores were higher in 2009 than in 2007 for all racial/ethnic groups. At grade 12, the average score for White students was 3 points higher in 2009 than in 2005, and the score for Asian/Pacific Islander students was 11 points higher. Scores for Black, Hispanic, and American Indian/Alaska Native students did not change significantly from 2005 to 2009.

NAEP results also permit state-level comparisons of the reading abilities of 4th- and 8th-grade students in public schools. State measures of the reading abilities of 12th-grade students are available from a 2009 state pilot reading assessment in which 11 states participated. While there was no measurable change from 2007 to 2009 in the overall average score for 4th-grade public school students in the nation, scores increased in two states (Kentucky and Rhode Island) and the District of Columbia and decreased in four states (Alaska, Iowa, New Mexico, and Wyoming) (see table A-10-3). At grade 8, although the average score for public school students in the nation was 1 point higher in 2009 than in 2007, score increases were seen in less than one-quarter of the states. Scores were higher in 2009 than in 2007 for nine states (Alabama, Connecticut, Florida, Hawaii, Kentucky, Missouri, New Mexico, Pennsylvania, and Utah), and in the remaining states and the District of Columbia, scores showed no measurable change.

For more information: *Tables A-10-1 through A-10-3*
Glossary: *Achievement levels, English language learners, Traditional public school*

Technical Notes

NAEP reading scores range from 0 to 500. The 12th-grade NAEP reading assessment was not administered in 2003 or 2007. The achievement levels define what students should know and be able to do: *Basic* indicates partial mastery of fundamental skills, *Proficient* indicates demonstrated competency over challenging subject matter, and *Advanced* indicates superior performance. Testing accommodations (e.g., extended

time, small group testing) for children with disabilities and English language learners were not permitted in 1992 and 1994; students were tested with and without accommodations in 1998. For more information on NAEP, see *supplemental note 4.* Race categories exclude persons of Hispanic ethnicity. For more information on race/ethnicity, see *supplemental note 1.*

Figure 10-1. Average reading scale scores of 4th-, 8th-, and 12th-grade students: Selected years, 1992–2009

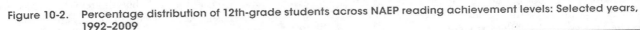

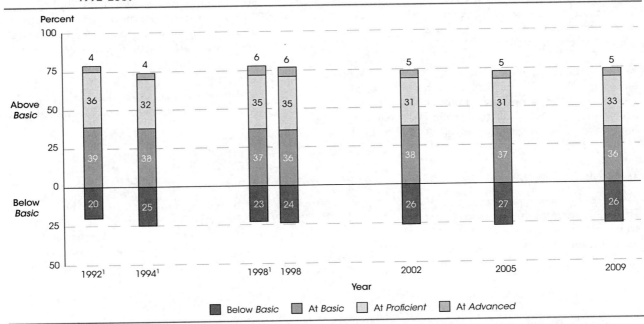

NOTE: The National Assessment of Educational Progress (NAEP) reading scale ranges from 0 to 500. Student assessments are not designed to permit comparisons across subjects or grades. Testing accommodations (e.g., extended time, small group testing) for children with disabilities and English language learners were not permitted in 1992 and 1994; students were tested with and without accommodations in 1998. The 12th-grade NAEP reading assessment was not administered in 2003 or 2007. For more information on NAEP, see *supplemental note 4*.
SOURCE: U.S. Department of Education, National Center for Education Statistics, National Assessment of Educational Progress (NAEP), selected years, 1992–2009 Reading Assessments, NAEP Data Explorer.

Figure 10-2. Percentage distribution of 12th-grade students across NAEP reading achievement levels: Selected years, 1992–2009

[1] Testing accommodations (e.g., extended time, small group testing) for children with disabilities and English language learners were not permitted in 1992 and 1994; students were tested with and without accommodations in 1998. The footnoted column represents the sample without accommodations.
NOTE: Achievement levels define what students should know and be able to do: *Basic* indicates partial mastery of fundamental skills, *Proficient* indicates demonstrated competency over challenging subject matter, and *Advanced* indicates superior performance. Detail may not sum to totals because of rounding. For more information on the National Assessment of Educational Progress (NAEP), see *supplemental note 4*.
SOURCE: U.S. Department of Education, National Center for Education Statistics, National Assessment of Educational Progress (NAEP), selected years, 1992–2009 Reading Assessments, NAEP Data Explorer.

Reading Achievement Gaps

In 2009, White students at grade 12 scored 27 points higher in reading than Black students and 22 points higher than Hispanic students. Neither score gap was significantly different from the respective score gaps in previous assessment years.

In 2009 and in all previous assessment years since 1992, the average National Assessment for Educational Progress (NAEP) reading scale scores of White 4th-, 8th-, and 12th-grade students were higher than their Black and Hispanic peers' scores. This disparity is known as an achievement gap—in NAEP reading scores, the achievement gap is seen by the differences between the average scores of two student subgroups on the standardized assessment. In 2009, the average reading score of Black 4th-grade students was less than that of White 4th-grade students by 26 points; this gap was not measurably different from the gap in 2007, but it was smaller than the gaps in all other assessment years prior to 2007 (see table A-11-1). The reading achievement gap between Hispanic and White 4th-grade students in 2009 (-25 points) was not measurably different from the gaps in 2007 or 1992.

Scores of White, Black, and Hispanic 8th-grade students have all increased from 1992, yet neither the 2009 reading achievement gap between Black and White 8th-grade students (-26 points) nor the gap between Hispanic and White 8th-grade students (-24 points) was measurably different from the corresponding gaps in 2007 and 1992. In 2009, White students at grade 12 scored 27 points higher in reading than Black students and 22 points higher than Hispanic students. Neither score gap was measurably different from the respective score gaps in previous assessment years.

In 2009, female 4th-grade students scored 7 points higher, on average, than male students. This difference was not measurably different from the gaps in 2007 or 1992. Scores for female 8th-grade students in 2009 were not measurably different than their scores in 2007 or 1992,

while male 8th-grade students' average reading score in 2009 was higher than their scores in either of the other two years. The reading score difference between male and female 8th-grade students in 2009 (-9 points) was not measurably different from the difference seen in 2007, but it was smaller than the difference seen in 1992 (-13 points). Average reading scores for both male and female 12th-grade students were lower in 2009 than in 1992. Female students scored 12 points higher on average than male students in 2009, not measurably different from the differences in 2005 or 1992.

In 2009, achievement gaps between students in schools with high percentages of low-income students and students in schools with low percentages of such students existed at all three grade levels (see table A-11-2). For this indicator, students are identified as attending schools with high percentages of low-income students if more than 75 percent of the students in the school are eligible for free or reduced-price lunch. Students are identified as attending schools with low percentages of low-income students if 25 percent or fewer of the students in the school are eligible for free or reduced-price lunch. In 2009, the low-income gap for grade 4 was not measurably different from the gap in 2007 but was smaller than gaps in all years prior to 2007. In grade 8, there were no measurable differences in the 2009 low-income gap and gaps in previous assessment years. In 2009, the low-income gap at grade 12 was larger than gaps reported in all previous assessments.

For more information: *Tables A-11-1 and A-11-2*
Glossary: *Achievement levels, English language learner*

Technical Notes

NAEP reading scores range from 0 to 500. Score gaps are calculated based on differences between unrounded scores. Testing accommodations for children with disabilities and English language learners were not permitted in 1992 and 1994; students were tested

with and without accommodations in 1998 and 2000. The 12th-grade NAEP reading assessment was not administered in 2000, 2003, or 2007. For more information on race/ethnicity, see *supplemental note 1*. For more information on NAEP, see *supplemental note 4*.

Figure 11-1.   Average reading scale scores of 12th-grade students, by race/ethnicity: Selected years, 1992–2009

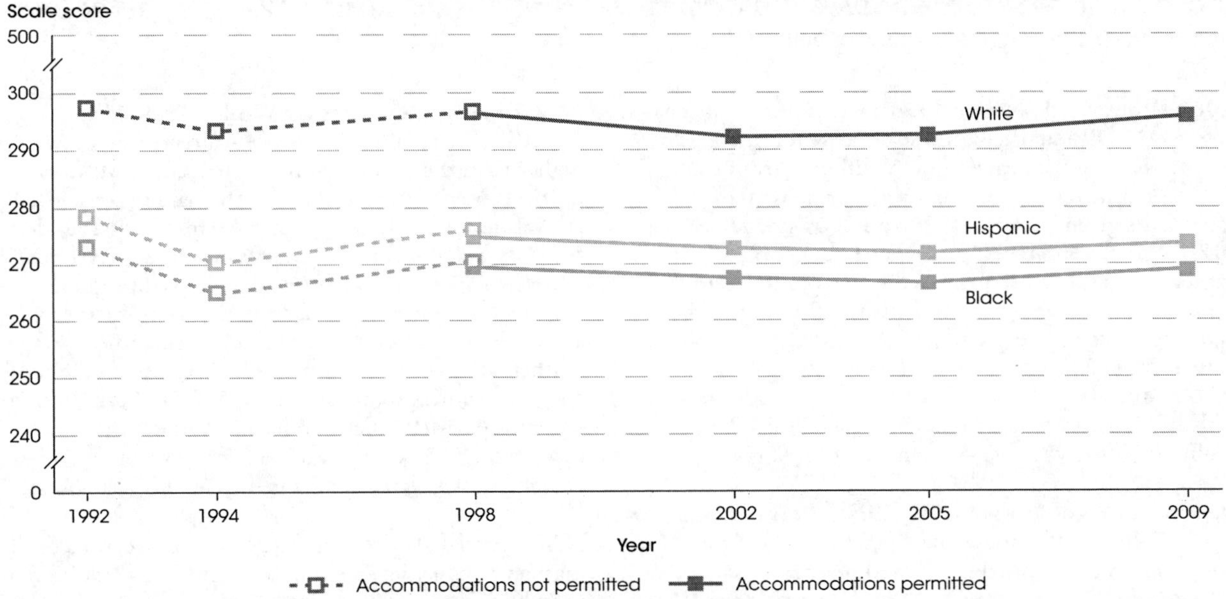

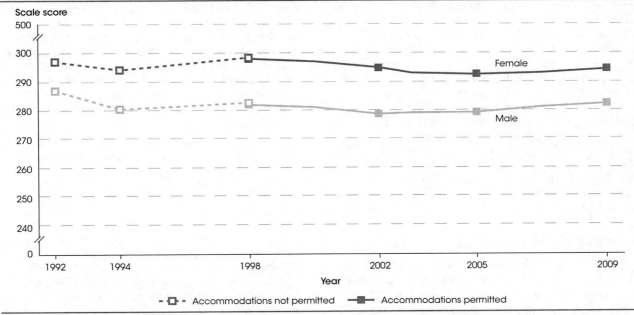

Scale score

- ◻ - Accommodations not permitted   ■ Accommodations permitted

NOTE: The National Assessment of Educational Progress (NAEP) reading scale ranges from 0 to 500. Testing accommodations (e.g., extended time, small group testing) for children with disabilities and English language learners were not permitted in 1992 and 1994; students were tested with and without accommodations in 1998. For more information on NAEP, see *supplemental note 4*. Race categories exclude persons of Hispanic ethnicity. For more information on race/ethnicity, see *supplemental note 1*.
SOURCE: U.S. Department of Education, National Center for Education Statistics, National Assessment of Educational Progress (NAEP), selected years, 1992–2009 Reading Assessments, NAEP Data Explorer.

Figure 11-2.   Average reading scale scores of 12th-grade students, by sex: Selected years 1992–2009

Scale score

- ◻ - Accommodations not permitted   ■ Accommodations permitted

NOTE: The National Assessment of Educational Progress (NAEP) reading scale ranges from 0 to 500. Testing accommodations (e.g., extended time, small group testing) for children with disabilities and English language learners were not permitted in 1992 and 1994; students were tested with and without accommodations in 1998. For more information on NAEP, see *supplemental note 4*.
SOURCE: U.S. Department of Education, National Center for Education Statistics, National Assessment of Educational Progress (NAEP), selected years, 1992–2009 Reading Assessments, NAEP Data Explorer.

From 1990 to 2009, average grade 4 mathematics scores increased by 27 points and average grade 8 scores increased by 20 points. At grade 12, average scores increased by 3 points between 2005 and 2009.

In 2009, the average National Assessment of Educational Progress (NAEP) mathematics scale score for 4th-grade students (240) was not measurably different from the 2007 score but was higher than the scores on all of the assessments given between 1990 and 2005 (see table A-12-1). From 1990 to 2009, average grade 4 NAEP mathematics scale score increased by 27 points. The average score for 8th-grade students in 2009 was higher than the average scores in all previous assessment years. From 1990 to 2009, average grade 8 scores increased by 20 points, from 263 to 283. The average 12th-grade mathematics score was 3 points higher in 2009 than it was in 2005, the year the assessment was first given.

The percentages of 4th-grade students performing at or above the *Basic,* at or above the *Proficient,* and at the *Advanced* achievement levels showed no measurable change from 2007 to 2009. In 2009, some 82 percent of 4th-grade students performed at or above *Basic,* 39 percent performed at or above *Proficient,* and 6 percent performed at *Advanced.* The percentages of 8th-grade students performing at or above *Basic,* at or above *Proficient,* and at the *Advanced* achievement levels each showed increases of 1 to 2 percentage points from 2007 to 2009. In 2009, some 73 percent of 8th-grade students performed at or above *Basic,* 34 percent performed at or above *Proficient,* and 8 percent performed at *Advanced.* The percentage of 12th-grade students performing at or above *Basic* was 3 percentage points higher in 2009 (64 percent) than in 2005. Twenty-six percent of 12th-grade students performed at or above the *Proficient* level in 2009, which was also a 3-point increase from the percentage who did so in 2005. The percentages performing at the *Advanced* level in 2005 and 2009 were not measurably different (2 and 3 percent, respectively).

At grade 4, the average mathematics scores in 2009 for White, Black, Hispanic, Asian/Pacific Islander, and American Indian/Alaska Native students were not measurably different from their scores in 2007 (see table A-12-2). The 2009 scores for White, Black, Hispanic, and Asian/Pacific Islander 4th-grade students were, however, higher than their scores from the assessment years prior to 2007. At grade 8, the average mathematics scores in 2009 for White, Black, Hispanic, and Asian/Pacific Islander students were higher than their scores in 2007. The 2009 score for American Indian/Alaska Native 8th-grade students was not measurably different from their scores in any of the earlier assessment years. At grade 12, average mathematics scores were higher in 2009 than in 2005 for all racial/ethnic groups. From 2005 to 2009, the average score for Asian/Pacific Islander 12th-grade students increased by 13 points, and the average score for American Indian/Alaska Native students increased by 10 points.

NAEP results also permit state-level comparisons of the mathematics achievement of 4th- and 8th-grade students in public schools. While there was no measurable change from 2007 to 2009 in the overall average mathematics score for 4th-grade public school students, scores increased in seven states (Colorado, Kentucky, Maryland, Nevada, New Hampshire, Rhode Island, and Vermont) and the District of Columbia and decreased in four states (Delaware, Indiana, West Virginia, and Wyoming) (see table A-12-3). At grade 8, scores were higher in 2009 than in 2007 in 14 states (Connecticut, Georgia, Hawaii, Idaho, Missouri, Montana, Nevada, New Hampshire, New Jersey, Rhode Island, South Dakota, Utah, Vermont, and Washington) and the District of Columbia. At grade 8, no state had mathematics scores decline from 2007 to 2009. State mathematics results for 12th-grade students are available only for 2009, the pilot year of a NAEP state mathematics assessment in which 11 states participated.

For more information: *Tables A-12-1 through A-12-3*
Glossary: *Achievement levels, English language learner, Traditional public school*

Technical Notes

NAEP mathematics scores range from 0 to 500 for grades 4 and 8. The framework for the 12th-grade mathematics assessment was revised in 2005; as a result, the 2005 and 2009 results cannot be compared with those from previous years. At grade 12, mathematics scores on the revised assessment range from 0 to 300. The achievement levels define what students should know and be able to do: *Basic* indicates partial mastery of fundamental skills, *Proficient* indicates demonstrated competency over challenging subject matter, and *Advanced* indicates superior performance. Testing accommodations (e.g., extended time, small group testing) for children with disabilities and English language learners were not permitted in 1990 and 1992. Students in grades 4 and 8 were tested with and without accommodations in 1996. For more information on NAEP, see *supplemental note 4.* Race categories exclude persons of Hispanic ethnicity. For more information on race/ethnicity, see *supplemental note 1.*

Figure 12-1. Average mathematics scale scores of 4th- and 8th-grade students: Selected years, 1990–2009

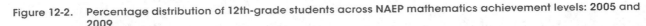

Average scale scores

NOTE: At grades 4 and 8, the National Assessment of Educational Progress (NAEP) mathematics scale ranges from 0 to 500. Testing accommodations (e.g., extended time, small group testing) for children with disabilities and limited-English proficient students were not permitted in 1990 and 1992; students were tested with and without accommodations in 1996. For more information on NAEP, see *supplemental note 4.*
SOURCE: U.S. Department of Education, National Center for Education Statistics, National Assessment of Educational Progress (NAEP), selected years, 1990–2009 Mathematics Assessments, NAEP Data Explorer.

Figure 12-2. Percentage distribution of 12th-grade students across NAEP mathematics achievement levels: 2005 and 2009

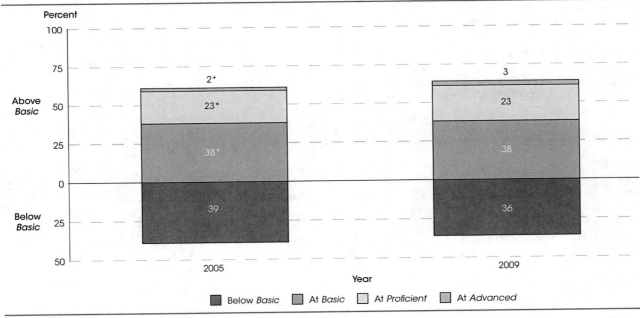

* Percentage is significantly different (*p* < .05) from 2009.
NOTE: Achievement levels define what students should know and be able to do: *Basic* indicates partial mastery of fundamental skills, *Proficient* indicates demonstrated competency over challenging subject matter, and *Advanced* indicates superior performance. Detail may not sum to totals because of rounding. For more information on the National Assessment of Educational Progress (NAEP), see *supplemental note 4.* The framework for the 12th-grade mathematics assessment was revised in 2005; as a result, the 2005 and 2009 results cannot be compared with those from previous years. At grade 12, mathematics scores on the revised assessment range from 0 to 300.
SOURCE: U.S. Department of Education, National Center for Education Statistics, National Assessment of Educational Progress (NAEP), selected years, 2005 and 2009 Mathematics Assessments, NAEP Data Explorer.

Mathematics Achievement Gaps

In 2009, White students at grade 12 scored 30 points higher in mathematics than Black students and 23 points higher than Hispanic students. Neither score gap was measurably different from the corresponding score gaps in 2005.

In 2009 and in all previous assessment years since 1992, the average National Assessment for Educational Progress (NAEP) mathematics scale scores of White 4th-, 8th-, and 12th-grade students were higher than the scores of their Black and Hispanic peers. This disparity is known as an achievement gap—in the NAEP mathematics assessment, it is the difference between the average scores of two student subgroups on the standardized assessment. The achievement gap between Black and White 4th-grade students in 2009 (-26 points) was not measurably different from the gap in 2007, but it was smaller than the gap in 1990 (-32 points). The 21-point achievement gap between White and Hispanic 4th-grade students in 2009 was not measurably different from the gap in 2007 or the gap in 1990 (see table A-13-1).

White, Black, and Hispanic 8th-grade students' scores increased between 2007 and 2009, yet neither the 2009 achievement gap between Black and White 8th-grade students (-32 points) nor the 2009 achievement gap between Hispanic and White 8th-grade students (-26 points) was measurably different from the corresponding gaps in 2007 or 1990. In 2009, White 12th-grade students scored 30 points higher in mathematics than Black students and 23 points higher than Hispanic students. Neither achievement gap was measurably different from the corresponding gaps in 2005.

In 2009, male 4th-grade students scored 2 points higher on average than female 4th-grade students. This difference was not measurably different from the gap in 2007. At grade 8, male students scored 2 points higher than female

students in 2009; since the increases in scale scores were comparable for both males and females since 2007, the 2-point score difference was not measurably different from the difference in 2007. Average mathematics scores for both male and female 12th-grade students were higher in 2009 than in 2005. Male students scored 3 points higher on average than female students in 2009, not measurably different from the score difference in 2005.

In 2009, achievement gaps between students in schools with high percentages of low-income students and students in schools with low percentages of such students exist at all three grade levels (see table A-13-2). For this indicator, students are identified as attending schools with high percentages of low-income students if more than 75 percent of the students in the school are eligible for free or reduced-price lunch. Students are identified as attending schools with low percentages of low-income students if 25 percent or fewer of the students in the school are eligible for free or reduced-price lunch. In 2009, the low-income gap at grade 4 was -31 points, at grade 8 the gap was -38 points, and at grade 12 the gap was -36 points (see table A-13-2). None of the low-income gaps in 2009 were measurably different from previous gaps reported by NAEP.

For more information: *Tables A-13-1 and A-13-2*
Glossary: *Achievement levels, English language leaner*

Technical Notes

NAEP mathematics scores range from 0 to 500 for grades 4 and 8. The framework for the 12th-grade mathematics assessment was revised in 2005; as a result, the 2005 and 2009 results cannot be compared with those from previous years. At grade 12, mathematics scores on the revised assessment range from 0 to 300. Score gaps are calculated based on differences between

unrounded scores. Testing accommodations for children with disabilities and English language learners were not permitted in 1990 and 1992. Students were tested in grades 4 and 8 with and without accommodations in 1996. For more information on race/ethnicity or free or reduced-price lunch, see *supplemental note 1*. For more information on NAEP, see *supplemental note 4*.

Figure 13-1. Average mathematics scale scores of 4th- and 8th-grade students, by school poverty level: Selected years, 2000–09

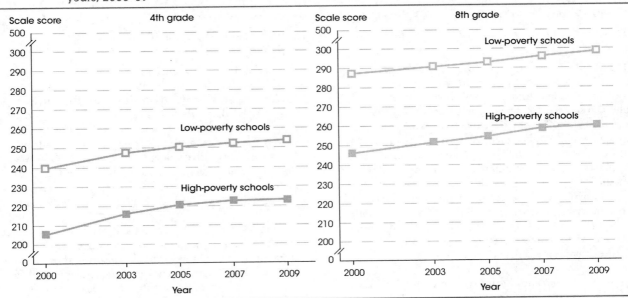

NOTE: The National Assessment of Educational Progress (NAEP) mathematics scores range from 0 to 500 for grades 4 and 8. The percentage of students eligible for free or reduced-price lunch ranges between 0–25 percent in low-poverty schools and between 76–100 percent in high-poverty schools. For more information on NAEP, see *supplemental note 4* and for more information on free or reduced-price lunch, see *supplemental note 1.*
SOURCE: U.S. Department of Education, National Center for Education Statistics, National Assessment of Educational Progress (NAEP), selected years, 2000-2009 Mathematics Assessments, NAEP Data Explorer.

Figure 13-2. Average mathematics scale scores of 12th-grade students, by race/ethnicity: 2005 and 2009

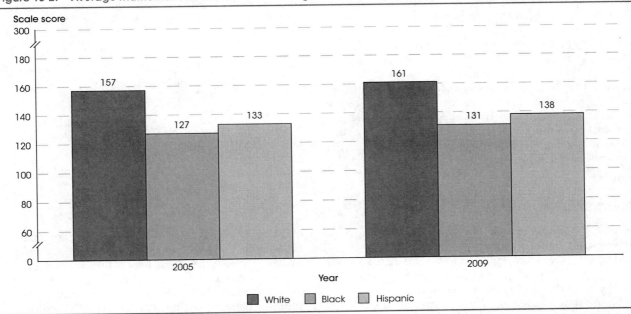

NOTE: The framework for the 12th-grade mathematics assessment was revised in 2005; as a result, the 2005 and 2009 results cannot be compared with those from previous years. At grade 12, mathematics scores on the revised assessment range from 0 to 300. For more information on the National Assessment of Educational Progress (NAEP), see *supplemental note 4.* Race categories exclude persons of Hispanic ethnicity. For more information on race/ethnicity, see *supplemental note 1.*
SOURCE: U.S. Department of Education, National Center for Education Statistics, National Assessment of Educational Progress (NAEP), selected years, 2005 and 2009 Mathematics Assessments, NAEP Data Explorer.

Thirty-four percent of students at grade 4, some 30 percent of students at grade 8, and 21 percent of students at grade 12 performed at or above the Proficient level in the 2009 science assessment. One percent of 4th-grade students, 2 percent of 8th-grade students, and 1 percent of 12th-grade students performed at the Advanced level.

The National Assessment of Educational Progress (NAEP) 2009 science assessment was designed to measure students' knowledge of three content areas: physical science, life science, and Earth and space sciences. In 2009, a new science framework was developed by the National Assessment Governing Board to keep assessment content current with key developments in science, curriculum standards, assessments, and research. As such, the results of the 2009 science assessment are not comparable to results from earlier years. Nevertheless, this indicator presents a snapshot of what the nation's 4th-, 8th-, and 12th-grade students know and can do in science, and it will serve as the basis for comparisons on future science assessments.

Seventy-two percent of 4th-grade students, 63 percent of 8th-grade students, and 60 percent of 12th-grade students performed at or above the *Basic* achievement level in science in 2009 (see table A-14-1). Thirty-four percent of students at grade 4, some 30 percent of students at grade 8, and 21 percent of students at grade 12 performed at or above the *Proficient* level in 2009. Some 1 percent of 4th-grade students, 2 percent of 8th-grade students, and 1 percent of 12th-grade students performed at the *Advanced* level.

On average, male students scored higher than female students at all three grades in 2009 (see table A-14-2). Differences were also reflected in achievement-level results: at grade 4, 35 percent of male students performed at or above *Proficient*, compared with 32 percent of female students. At grades 8 and 12, the percentages of male students performing at or above the *Basic*, at or above the *Proficient*, and at the *Advanced* levels were higher than the percentages of female students.

Results of the 2009 science assessment varied for students of different racial/ethnic groups. At grades 4 and 8, White students had higher average scale scores (163 and 162, respectively) than other racial/ethnic groups. In addition, Asian/Pacific Islander students scored higher (160 at grades 4 and 8) than Black, Hispanic, and American Indian/Alaska Native students. At grade 12, there was no significant difference in scores for White and Asian/Pacific Islander students (159 vs. 164, respectively), and both groups scored higher than other racial/ethnic groups.

At grades 4 and 8, the percentage of students who scored at or above *Basic* and at or above *Proficient* were lowest for students in high-poverty schools, meaning those schools in which more than 75 percent of the students qualify for free or reduced-price lunch. At grade 4, some 46 percent of students in high-poverty schools scored at or above *Basic* and 11 percent scored at or above *Proficient*, compared with 89 and 54 percent, respectively, for students in low-poverty schools, meaning those schools in which 25 percent or fewer of the students qualify for free or reduced-price lunch. At grade 8, some 33 percent of students in high-poverty schools scored at or above *Basic* and 8 percent scored at or above *Proficient*, compared with 81 percent and 46 percent in low-poverty schools.

For more information: *Tables A-14-1 through A-14-3*
Glossary: *Achievement levels, English language learner*

Technical Notes

NAEP science scores range from 0 to 300. The achievement levels define what students should know and be able to do: *Basic* indicates partial mastery of fundamental skills, *Proficient* indicates demonstrated competency over challenging subject matter, and *Advanced* indicates superior performance. In 2009, a new framework was developed for the 4th-, 8th-, and 12th-grade NAEP science assessment. For more information on NAEP, see *supplemental note 4*. Eligibility or approval for the National School Lunch Program also serves as a measure of poverty status. Race categories exclude persons of Hispanic ethnicity. For more information on race/ethnicity or free or reduced-price lunch, see *supplemental note 1*.

Figure 14-1. Percentage of students who performed at or above the *Proficient* achievement level in science, by grade and school poverty level: 2009

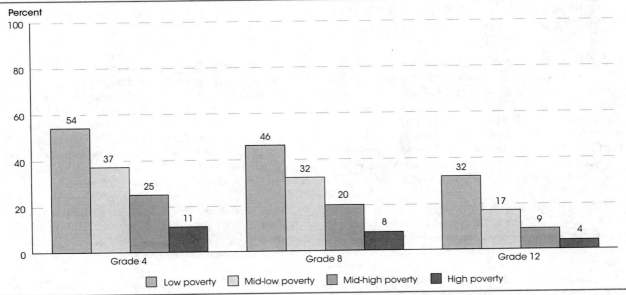

NOTE: The National Assessment of Educational Progress (NAEP) science achievement levels define what students should know and be able to do. *Proficient* indicates demonstrated competency over challenging subject matter, and *Advanced* indicates superior performance. The percentage of students at or above Proficient includes students at the *Proficient* and the *Advanced* achievement levels. *High-poverty schools* are defined as public schools where more than 75 percent of the students are eligible for the free or reduced-price lunch (FRPL) program, and *mid-high poverty schools* are those schools where 51 to 75 percent of students are eligible. *Low-poverty schools* are defined as public schools where 25 percent or fewer students are eligible for FRPL, and *mid-low poverty schools* are those schools where 26 to 50 percent of students are eligible for FRPL. For more information on free or reduced-price lunch, see *supplemental note 1*. For more information on NAEP, see *supplemental note 4*.
SOURCE: U.S. Department of Education, National Center for Education Statistics, National Assessment of Educational Progress (NAEP), 2009 Science Assessment, NAEP Data Explorer.

Figure 14-2. Average science scale scores, by grade and race/ethnicity: 2009

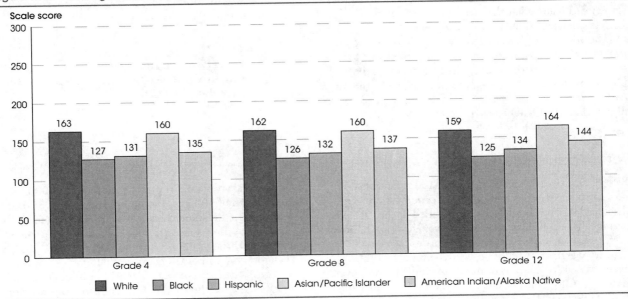

NOTE: Race categories exclude persons of Hispanic ethnicity. For more information on race/ethnicity, see *supplemental note 1*. The National Assessment of Educational Progress (NAEP) science scale ranges from 0 to 300. For more information on NAEP, see *supplemental note 4*.
SOURCE: U.S. Department of Education, National Center for Education Statistics, National Assessment of Educational Progress (NAEP), 2009 Science Assessment, NAEP Data Explorer.

International Reading Literacy

In 2009, the average U.S. combined reading literacy score for 15-year-old students was not measurably different from the average score of the 34 OECD-member countries. The U.S. average score was lower than that of 6 OECD countries and higher than that of 13 OECD countries.

The 2009 Program for International Student Assessment (PISA) reports the performance of 15-year-old students in reading literacy in 65 countries and other education systems, including the 34 Organization for Economic Co-operation and Development (OECD) countries, 26 non-OECD countries, and 5 other education systems. The OECD countries are a group of the world's most advanced economies. Other education systems refer to non-national entities, such as Shanghai-China.

The U.S. students' average score on the combined reading literacy scale (500) was not measurably different from the average score of OECD countries (493) (see table A-15-1). Compared with the other 64 countries and other education systems, the U.S. average was lower than the average in 9 countries and other education systems (6 OECD countries, 1 non-OECD country, and 2 education systems) and higher than the average in 39 countries and other education systems (13 OECD countries, 24 non-OECD countries, and 2 other education systems).

PISA 2009 presents results for three reading literacy subscales that represent reading processes: *access and retrieve, integrate and interpret,* and *reflect and evaluate.* These subscales refer to skills students must apply to draw meaning from reading, (e.g., reflect and evaluate requires students to relate what they read to their own knowledge and experience and judge what they read objectively). On the *access and retrieve* subscale and *integrate and interpret subscale,* U.S. students' averages (492 and 495, respectively) were not measurably different from the OECD averages (495 and 493, respectively). On the *reflect and evaluate* subscale, the U.S. students' average (512) was higher than the OECD average (494).

In all 65 participating countries and other education systems, female students scored higher, on average, than male students on the combined reading literacy scale (see table A-15-2). The average difference between U.S. males and females (25 scale score points) was smaller than the average difference of the 34 OECD countries (39 scale score points) and the difference in 45 countries and other education systems (24 OECD countries, 18 non-OECD countries, and 3 other education systems).

The average scores of U.S. Black and Hispanic students on the combined reading literacy scale (441 and 466, respectively) were lower than the U.S. and OECD averages. In contrast, average scores of U.S. White and Asian students (525 and 541, respectively) were higher than the U.S. and OECD averages (see table A-15-3). The average score of U.S. students who reported being of two or more races (502) was not measurably different from the U.S. and OECD averages.

The U.S. average in reading literacy in 2000 (504), the last PISA cycle in which reading literacy was assessed in depth, was not measurably different from the average in 2009 (500) (see table A-15-4). There were no measurable differences between the U.S. average and the OECD trend average in 2000 (504 and 496, respectively) or in 2009 (500 and 495, respectively).

 For more information: *Tables A-15-1 through A-15-4*
Glossary: *Organization of Economic Co-operation and Development (OECD)*

Technical Notes

PISA is principally an OECD study, and the results for non-OECD countries and other education systems are displayed separately and are not included in the OECD average. The OECD average is the average of the national averages of the OECD member countries, with each country weighted equally, and differs from the OECD average used for analysis of trends in student scores over time. The OECD average used in the analysis of trends in reading literacy is based on the averages of the 27 OECD countries with comparable data for 2000 and 2009. The

reading literacy scale was established in PISA 2000 to have a mean of 500 and a standard deviation of 100. The combined reading literacy scale is made up of all the items in the three subscales, and each scale is computed separately through Item Response Theory (IRT) models. Therefore, the combined reading scale score is not the average of the three subscale scores. For more information on PISA, see *supplemental note 5.* For more information on race/ethnicity, please see *supplemental note 1.*

Figure 15-1. Average scores of 15-year-old students on combined reading literacy scale, by country: 2009

OECD country and average score					
Korea, Republic of	539	Canada	524	Japan	520
Finland	536	New Zealand	521	Australia	515
Netherlands	508	Iceland	500	France	496
Belgium	506	**United States**	**500**	Denmark	495
Norway	503	Sweden	497	United Kingdom	494
Estonia	501	Germany	497	Hungary	494
Switzerland	501	Ireland	496	**OECD average**	**493**
Poland	500				
Portugal	489	Czech Republic	478	Austria	470
Italy	486	Slovak Republic	477	Turkey	464
Slovenia	483	Israel	474	Chile	449
Greece	483	Luxembourg	472	Mexico	425
Spain	481				
Non-OECD country or other education system and average score					
Shanghai-China	556	*Hong Kong-China*	533	Singapore	526
Liechtenstein	499	*Chinese Taipei*	495		
Macao-China	487	Romania	424	Argentina	398
Latvia	484	Thailand	421	Kazakhstan	390
Croatia	476	Trinidad and Tobago	416	Albania	385
Lithuania	468	Colombia	413	Qatar	372
Dubai-UAE	459	Brazil	412	Panama	371
Russian Federation	459	Montenegro, Republic of	408	Peru	370
Serbia, Republic of	442	Jordan	405	Azerbaijan	362
Bulgaria	429	Tunisia	404	Kyrgyz Republic	314
Uruguay	426	Indonesia	402		

■ Average is higher than the U.S. average ☐ Average is not measurably different from the U.S. average ▒ Average is lower than the U.S. average

NOTE: The Organization for Economic Co-operation and Development (OECD) average is the average of the national averages of the OECD member countries, with each country weighted equally. Because the Program for International Student Assessment (PISA) is principally an OECD study, the results for non-OECD countries are displayed separately from those of the OECD countries and are not included in the OECD average. Scores are reported on a scale of 0 to 1,000. Scores are significantly different at the .05 level of statistical significance. Italics indicate education systems in non-national entities. UAE is the United Arab Emirates. For more information on PISA, see *supplemental note 5*.
SOURCE: Fleischman, H.L., Hopstock, P.J., Pelczar, M.P., and Shelley, B.E. (2010). *Highlights From PISA 2009: Performance of U.S. 15-Year-Old Students in Reading, Mathematics, and Science Literacy in an International Context* (NCES 2011-004), table 3; data from the Organization for Economic Co-operation and Development (OECD), Program for International Student Assessment (PISA), 2009.

Figure 15-2. Average scores of 15-year-old students in the United States and OECD countries on combined reading literacy scale: 2000 and 2009

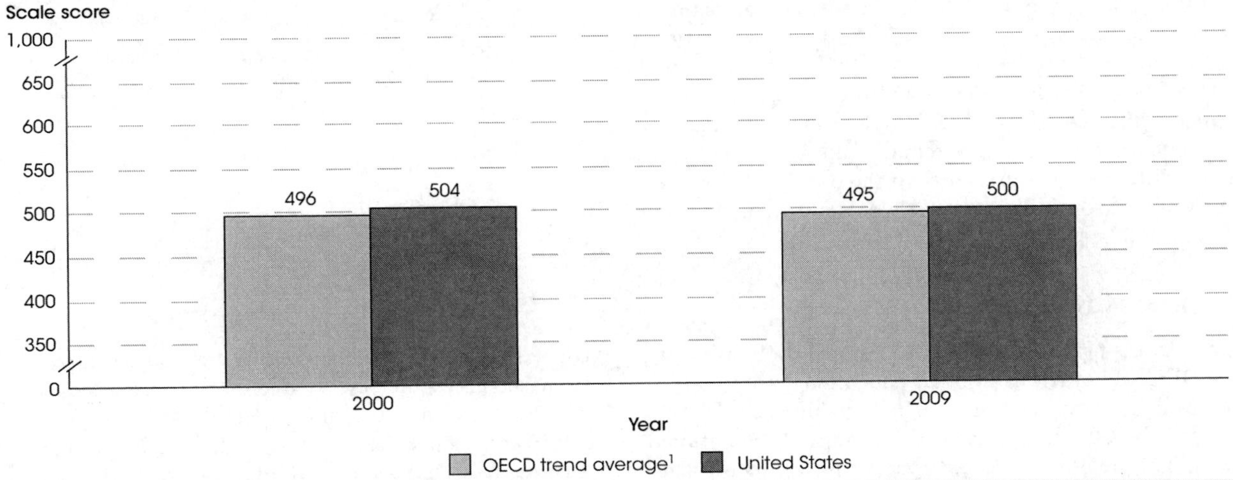

[1] The Organization for Economic Co-operation and Development (OECD) trend average used to report on trends in reading literacy is based on 27 OECD member countries with comparable data for 2000 and 2009. Data for Austria is excluded from OECD trend analyses because of a concern over a data collection issue in 2009; however, after consultation with Austrian officials, the National Center for Education Statistics kept the Austrian data in the U.S. trend reporting. For more information on the OECD average used to report on trends in reading literacy, see *supplemental note 5*.
NOTE: The OECD average is the average of the national averages of the OECD member countries, with each country weighted equally. Scores are reported on a scale of 0 to 1,000. There were no statistically significant differences between the U.S. average score and the OECD average score in 2000 or in 2009 or in the U.S. average between 2000 and 2009. For more information on PISA, see *supplemental note 5*.
SOURCE: Fleischman, H.L., Hopstock, P.J., Pelczar, M.P., and Shelley, B.E. (2010). *Highlights From PISA 2009: Performance of U.S. 15-Year-Old Students in Reading, Mathematics, and Science Literacy in an International Context* (NCES 2011-004), figure 4; data from the Organization for Economic Co-operation and Development (OECD), Program for International Student Assessment (PISA), 2000 and 2009.

International Mathematics and Science Literacy

In 2009, the average U.S. mathematics literacy score for 15-year-old students was below the average score of the 34 OECD member countries. On the science literacy scale, the average U.S. score was not measurably different from the OECD average.

The 2009 Program for International Student Assessment (PISA) reports on the performance of 15-year-olds in mathematics and science literacy in 65 countries and other education systems, including the 34 Organization for Economic Co-operation and Development (OECD) countries, 26 non-OECD countries, and 5 other education systems. The OECD countries are a group of the world's most advanced economies. Other education systems refer to non-national entities, such as Shanghai-China.

The average U.S. mathematics literacy score (487) in 2009 was lower than the average score of the 34 OECD countries (496). In comparison with students in all 64 other countries and education systems, students in the United States on average scored lower than students in 23 (17 OECD countries, 2 non-OECD countries, and 4 other education systems) and higher than students in 29 (5 OECD countries, 23 non-OECD countries, and 1 other education system).

No measurable difference was found between the average U.S. mathematics literacy scores in 2009 (487) and 2003 (483), the earliest time point to which PISA 2009 mathematics literacy scores can be compared (see table A-16-1). In both years, the U.S. average score was lower than the OECD average score.

In 2009, male students outscored their female peers in mathematics literacy in 35 countries and other education systems, and on average among the OECD countries (see table A-16-2). Female students outscored their male peers in 5 countries. On average, U.S. male students scored 20 scale score points above U.S. female students in 2009; this gender difference was greater than the 6-point difference observed in favor of U.S. male students over their female peers in 2003.

The average U.S. science literacy score (502) in 2009 was not measurably different from the average score of the 34 OECD countries (501). In comparison with students in all 64 other countries and education systems, students in the United States on average scored lower than students in 18 (12 OECD countries, 2 non-OECD countries, and 4 other education systems) and higher than students in 33 (9 OECD countries, 23 non-OECD countries, and 1 other education system).

The average U.S. science literacy score was higher in 2009 (502) than in 2006 (489), the only year of data to which PISA 2009 science literacy scores can be compared (see table A-16-3). The U.S. average was lower than the OECD average in 2006, but was not measurably different from the OECD average in 2009.

In 2009, female students outscored their male peers in science literacy in 21 countries and other education systems, while male students outscored their female peers in 11 countries (see table A-16-4). No measurable gender gap in science literacy scores was found among the OECD countries, on average, in 2009. U.S. male students scored 14 scale score points above U.S. female students on average in 2009, whereas no measurable gender difference was observed in 2006.

For more information: *Tables A-16-1 through A-16-4*
Glossary: *Organization for Economic Co-operation and Development (OECD)*

Technical Notes

Since PISA is principally an OECD study, the results for non-OECD countries and other education systems are displayed separately and are not included in the OECD average. The OECD average is the average of the national averages of the 34 OECD member countries, with each country weighted equally, and differs from the OECD average used for analysis of trends in student scores over time. The OECD average used in the analysis of trends in mathematics literacy is based on the averages of the 29 OECD countries with comparable data for 2003 and 2009. For science literacy trends, all 34 OECD countries are used. Scores are reported on a scale from 0 to 1,000. For more information on PISA, see *supplemental note 5.*

Figure 16-1. Average scores of 15-year-old students on mathematics and science literacy scales, by country: 2009

Mathematics literacy scale

OECD country and average score

Country	Score	Country	Score	Country	Score
Korea, Republic of	546	New Zealand	519	Denmark	503
Finland	541	Belgium	515	Slovenia	501
Switzerland	534	Australia	514	Norway	498
Japan	529	Germany	513	France	497
Canada	527	Estonia	512	Slovak Republic	497
Netherlands	526	Iceland	507	**OECD average**	**496**
Austria	496	United Kingdom	492	Ireland	487
Poland	495	Hungary	490	Portugal	487
Sweden	494	Luxembourg	489	Spain	483
Czech Republic	493	**United States**	**487**	Italy	483
Greece	466	Turkey	445	Mexico	419
Israel	447	Chile	421		

Non-OECD country or other education system and average score

Country	Score	Country	Score	Country	Score
Shanghai-China	600	Hong Kong-China	555	Liechtenstein	536
Singapore	562	Chinese Taipei	543	Macao-China	525
Latvia	482				
Lithuania	477	Uruguay	427	Colombia	381
Russian Federation	468	Thailand	419	Albania	377
Croatia	460	Trinidad and Tobago	414	Tunisia	371
Dubai-UAE	453	Kazakhstan	405	Indonesia	371
Serbia, Republic of	442	Montenegro, Republic of	403	Qatar	368
Azerbaijan	431	Argentina	388	Peru	365
Bulgaria	428	Jordan	387	Panama	360
Romania	427	Brazil	386	Kyrgyz Republic	331

Science literary scale

OECD country and average score

Country	Score	Country	Score	Country	Score
Finland	554	Canada	529	Germany	520
Japan	539	Estonia	528	Switzerland	517
Korea, Republic of	538	Australia	527	United Kingdom	514
New Zealand	532	Netherlands	522	Slovenia	512
Poland	508	**OECD average**	**501**	Iceland	496
Ireland	508	Czech Republic	500	Sweden	495
Belgium	507	Norway	500	Austria	494
Hungary	503	Denmark	499	Portugal	493
United States	**502**	France	498		
Slovak Republic	490	Luxembourg	484	Turkey	454
Italy	489	Greece	470	Chile	447
Spain	488	Israel	455	Mexico	416

Non-OECD country or other education system and average score

Country	Score	Country	Score	Country	Score
Shanghai-China	575	Singapore	542	Liechtenstein	520
Hong Kong-China	549	Chinese Taipei	520	Macao-China	511
Latvia	494				
Lithuania	491	Thailand	425	Kazakhstan	400
Croatia	486	Jordan	415	Albania	391
Russian Federation	478	Trinidad and Tobago	410	Indonesia	383
Dubai-UAE	466	Brazil	405	Qatar	379
Serbia, Republic of	443	Colombia	402	Panama	376
Bulgaria	439	Montenegro, Republic of	401	Azerbaijan	373
Romania	428	Argentina	401	Peru	369
Uruguay	427	Tunisia	401	Kyrgyz Republic	330

■ Average is higher than the U.S. average   ☐ Average is not measurably different from the U.S. average   ☐ Average is lower than the U.S. average

NOTE: The Organization for Economic Co-operation and Development (OECD) average is the average of the national averages of the OECD member countries, with each country weighted equally. Because the Program for International Student Assessment (PISA) is principally an OECD study, the results for non-OECD countries are displayed separately from those of the OECD countries and are not included in the OECD average. Countries are ordered on the basis of average scores, from highest to lowest within the OECD countries and non-OECD countries. Scores are significantly different at the .05 level of statistical significance. Italics indicate education systems in non-national entities. UAE is the United Arab Emirates. Scores are reported on a scale from 0 to 1,000. For more information on PISA, see supplemental note 5.
SOURCE: Fleischman, H. L., Hopstock, P. J., Pelczar, M. P., and Shelley, B. E. (2010). Highlights From PISA 2009: Performance of U.S. 15-Year-Old Students in Reading, Mathematics, and Science Literacy in an International Context (NCES 2011-004), table 8; data from the Organization for Economic Co-operation and Development (OECD), Program for International Student Assessment (PISA), 2009.

Annual Earnings of Young Adults

In 2009, young adults ages 25–34 with a bachelor's degree earned more than twice as much as young adults without a high school diploma or its equivalent, 50 percent more than young adult high school completers, and 25 percent more than young adults with an associate's degree.

In 2009, some 61 percent of young adults ages 25–34 who were in the labor force were employed full time throughout a full year. The percentage of young adults working full time throughout a full year was generally higher for those with higher levels of educational attainment. For example, 69 percent of young adults with a bachelor's degree or higher were full-time, full-year workers in 2009, compared with 55 percent of young adults with a high school diploma or its equivalent.

For young adults ages 25–34 who worked full time throughout a full year, higher educational attainment was associated with higher median earnings. This pattern of higher median earnings corresponding with higher levels of educational attainment was consistent for each year examined between 1995 and 2009 (see table A-17-1). For example, young adults with a bachelor's degree consistently had higher median earnings than those with less education. This relationship of higher median earnings corresponding with higher educational attainment also held across sex and race/ethnicity subgroups.

In 2009, the median of the earnings for young adults with a bachelor's degree was $45,000, while the median was $21,000 for those without a high school diploma or its equivalent, $30,000 for those with a high school diploma or its equivalent, and $36,000 for those with an associate's degree. In other words, young adults with a bachelor's degree earned more than twice as much as those without a high school diploma or its equivalent in 2009 (i.e., 114 percent more), 50 percent more than young adult high school completers, and 25 percent more than young adults with an associate's degree. In 2009, the median of the earnings of young adults with a master's degree or higher was $60,000, some 33 percent more than the median for young adults with a bachelor's degree.

Between 1980 and 2009, the difference (in constant 2009 dollars) in median earnings increased between those with a bachelor's degree or higher and those who had completed high school, as did the difference between those with a bachelor's degree or higher and those without a high school diploma or its equivalent. For example, in 1980, young adults with a bachelor's degree or higher earned $18,200 more than those without a high school diploma or its equivalent. This difference increased to $25,500 in 2005 and to $29,000 in 2009. This increase in the differential in median earnings over this period was primarily due to the decrease in earnings for high school completers and young adults without a high school diploma or its equivalent. Between 1995 and 2009, there was no overall linear pattern in the difference in median earnings between those with a bachelor's degree and those with a master's degree or higher. For example, in 1995, young adults with a master's degree or higher earned $12,700 more than their peers with a bachelor's degree; this difference in median earnings was $10,100 in 2005 and $15,000 in 2009.

Earnings differences were also observed by sex and race/ethnicity. In 2009, the median of the earnings for young adult males was higher than the median for young adult females at every education level (see figure 18-2). For example, in 2009, young adult males with a bachelor's degree earned $51,000, while their female counterparts earned $40,100. In the same year, the median of White young adults' earnings was higher than that of Black and Hispanic young adults' earnings at most education levels. Asian young adults with a bachelor's degree or with a master's degree or higher had higher median earnings than did their White, Black, and Hispanic counterparts in 2009. For example, in 2009, the median of earnings for young adults with at least a master's degree was $70,000 for Asians, $58,000 for Whites, $55,000 for Blacks, and $53,000 for Hispanics.

For more information: *Table A-17-1*

Glossary: *Bachelor's degree, Constant dollars, Consumer Price Index (CPI), Educational attainment, High school completer, Master's degree*

Technical Notes

High school completers are those who earned a high school diploma or equivalent (e.g., a General Educational Development [GED] certificate). Median earnings are presented in 2009 constant dollars by means of the Consumer Price Index (CPI) to eliminate inflationary factors and to allow for direct comparison across years. For more information on the CPI, see *supplemental note 10. Full-year worker* refers to those who were employed 50 or more weeks during the previous year; *full-time worker* refers to those who were usually employed 35 or more hours per week. The Current Population Survey (CPS) questions used to obtain educational attainment were changed in 1992. In 1994, the survey instrument for the CPS was changed and weights were adjusted. For more information on changes to the CPS, see *supplemental note 2.* For more information on race/ethnicity, see *supplemental note 1.*

Figure 17-1. Median annual earnings of full-time, full-year wage and salary workers ages 25–34, by educational attainment: 1995–2009

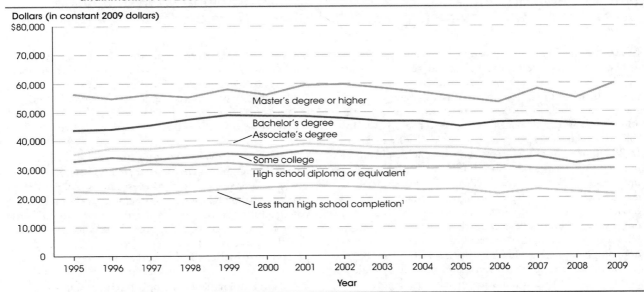

Dollars (in constant 2009 dollars)

[1] Young adults in this category did not earn a high school diploma or receive alternative credentials, such as a General Educational Development (GED) certificate.
NOTE: Earnings are presented in 2009 constant dollars by means of the Consumer Price Index (CPI) to eliminate inflationary factors and to allow for direct comparison across years. For more information on the CPI, see *supplemental note 10*. *Full-year worker* refers to those who were employed 50 or more weeks during the previous year; *full-time worker* refers to those who were usually employed 35 or more hours per week. For more information on the Current Population Survey (CPS), see *supplemental note 2*.
SOURCE: U.S. Department of Commerce, Census Bureau, Current Population Survey (CPS), March and Annual Social and Economic Supplement, 1996–2010.

Figure 17-2. Median annual earnings of full-time, full-year wage and salary workers ages 25–34, by educational attainment and sex: 2009

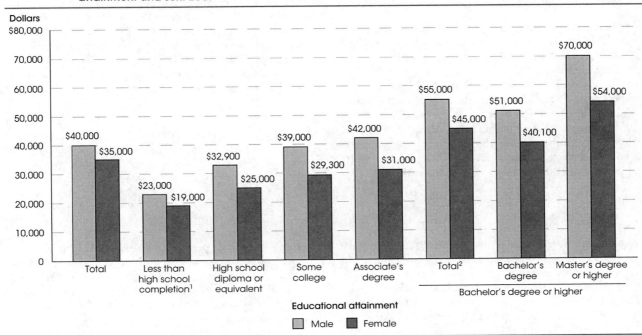

Dollars

[1] Young adults in this category did not earn a high school diploma or receive alternative credentials, such as a General Educational Development (GED) certificate.
[2] Total represents median annual earnings of young adults with a bachelor's degree or higher.
NOTE: *Full-year worker* refers to those who were employed 50 or more weeks during the previous year; *full-time worker* refers to those who were usually employed 35 or more hours per week. For more information on the Current Population Survey (CPS), see *supplemental note 2*.
SOURCE: U.S. Department of Commerce, Census Bureau, Current Population Survey (CPS), March and Annual Social and Economic Supplement, 2010.

Employment Outcomes of Young Adults

In 2010, young adults ages 25–34 with at least a bachelor's degree had a full-time employment rate that was over 30 percentage points higher than that of their peers who had not completed high school (74 vs. 41 percent).

In 2010, some 73 percent of young adults ages 25–34 were employed (61 percent full time and 12 percent part time), 9 percent were unemployed, and 18 percent were not in the labor force (see table A-18-1). In each year shown from 1990 to 2010, a greater percentage of young adults with at least a bachelor's degree were employed full time than were their peers with lower levels of education. In 2010, for example, 74 percent of those with a bachelor's degree or higher were employed full time (including 73 percent of bachelor's degree holders and 77 percent of those with a master's degree or higher), compared with 65 percent of those with an associate's degree, 56 percent of those with some college education, 55 percent of high school completers, and 41 percent of those who had not completed high school (i.e., those without a high school diploma or its equivalent). Additionally, a smaller percentage of young adults with a bachelor's degree or higher were unemployed than were their peers with lower levels of education. In 2010, for example, 4 percent of those with a bachelor's degree or higher were unemployed (including 4 percent of bachelor's degree holders and 3 percent of those with a master's degree or higher), compared with 7 percent of those with an associate's degree, 10 percent of those with some college education, 13 percent of high school completers, and 14 percent of those who had not completed high school.

The percentage of young adults who were unemployed in 2010 (9 percent) was higher than the percentages in 2000 (3 percent) and 2005 (5 percent). The full-time employment rate in 2010 (61 percent) was lower than the rates in these years as well (72 and 67 percent, respectively). In addition, the percentage of young adults who were employed full time was lower in 2010 than in 2000 at each level of educational attainment. For example, 55 percent of young adults who had not completed high school were employed full time in 2000, compared with 41 percent in 2010. Among young adults with at least a

bachelor's degree, the corresponding percentages were 81 percent and 74 percent. Comparing full-time employment rates in 2010 with those in 2005, rates were lower for young adults with less than a bachelor's degree but no measurable changes were found between these two years for young adults with at least a bachelor's degree.

Overall, in 2010, White young adults had the highest rate of full-time employment and American Indian/Alaska Native young adults had the lowest rate (see table A-18-2). Blacks had the highest overall unemployment rate among young adults and Asians had the lowest rate. In 2010, the range in the percentage of young adults who were not in the labor force went from 16 percent for Whites to 27 percent for American Indians/Alaska Natives.

Trends in employment, unemployment, and labor force participation for young adults varied by race/ethnicity and educational attainment in 2010. With the exception of master's degree or higher, at each level of educational attainment, a greater percentage of Black young adults was unemployed than were their peers of other races/ethnicities. Patterns for full-time employment among young adults varied more widely across racial/ethnic groups. For example, among those with at least a bachelor's degree, the rate of full-time employment was lower for Asians (63 percent) than for their peers in the other racial/ethnic groups (71 to 77 percent). In addition, the percentage of young adults with at least a bachelor's degree who were not in the labor force was higher for Asians (24 percent) than for their peers in the other racial/ethnic groups (10 to 14 percent).

For more information: *Tables A-18-1 and A-18-2*
Glossary: *Associate's degree, Bachelor's degree, Educational attainment, High school diploma, Master's degree*

Technical Notes

Persons who were employed 35 or more hours during the previous week were classified as working full time; those who worked fewer hours were classified as working part time. *High school completers* refers to those who earned a high school diploma or equivalent (e.g., a General Educational Development [GED] certificate). Race

categories exclude persons of Hispanic ethnicity. For more information on race/ethnicity, see *supplemental note 1.* The Current Population Survey (CPS) questions used to obtain data on educational attainment were changed in 1992. For more information on the CPS, see *supplemental note 2.*

Figure 18-1. Percentage of adults ages 25–34 who were employed full time, by educational attainment: 2010

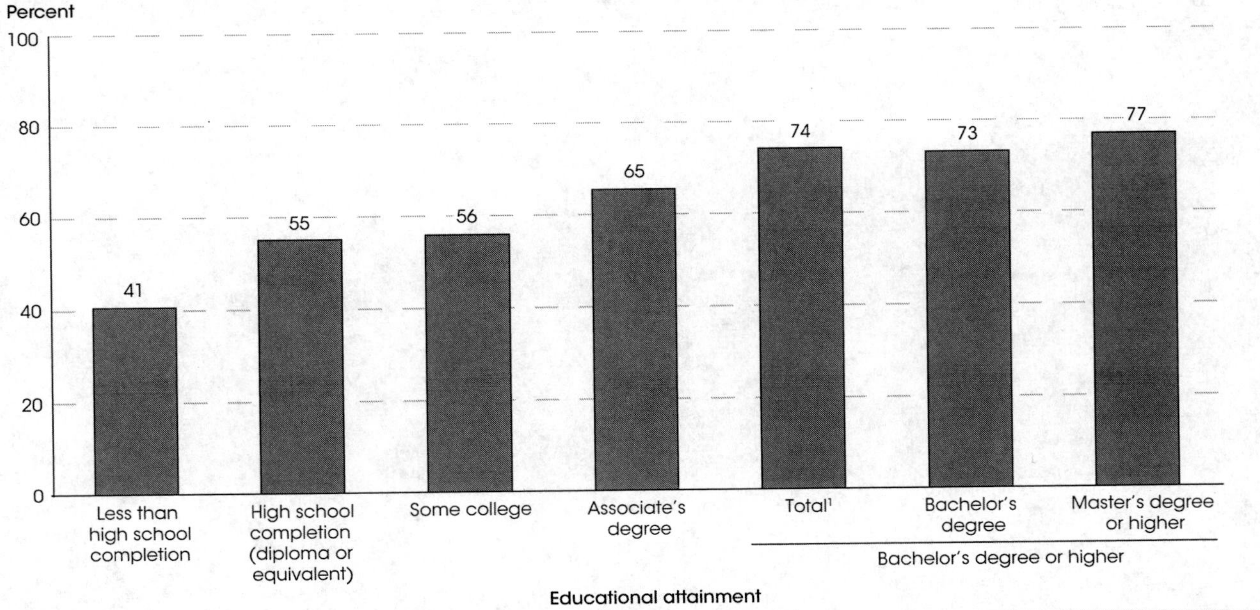

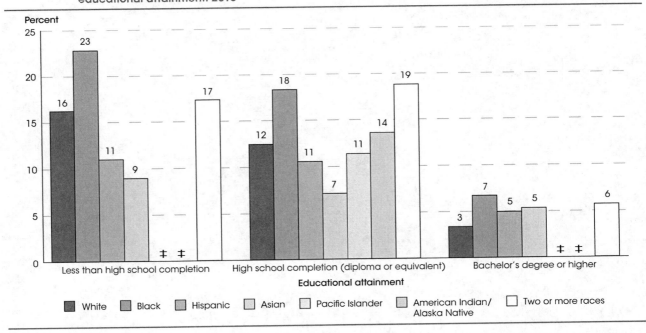

¹ Total represents the percentage of young adults with a bachelor's degree or higher who were employed full time.
NOTE: Persons who were employed 35 or more hours during the previous week were classified as working full time. For more information on the Current Population Survey, see *supplemental note 2.*
SOURCE: U.S. Department of Commerce, Census Bureau, Current Population Survey (CPS), Annual Social and Economic Supplement (ASEC), 2011.

Figure 18-2. Percentage of adults ages 25–34 who were unemployed, by race/ethnicity and selected levels of educational attainment: 2010

‡ Reporting standards not met.
NOTE: For more information on race/ethnicity, see *supplemental note 1.* For more information on the Current Population Survey, see *supplemental note 2.*
SOURCE: U.S. Department of Commerce, Census Bureau, Current Population Survey (CPS), Annual Social and Economic Supplement (ASEC), 2011.

Section 3
Student Effort and Educational Progress

Section 3
Student Effort and Educational Progress

Contents _____

Introduction

The indicators in this section of *The Condition of Education* report on the progress students make as they move through the education system. In this section, particular attention is paid to how various subgroups in the population proceed through school and attain different levels of education, as well as the factors that are associated with their progress along the way. Indicators prepared for this year's volume appear on the following pages, and all indicators in this section, including various indicators from previous years, appear on the NCES website (see the "List of Indicators on *The Condition of Education* Website" on page xxii for a full listing of indicators).

Focusing on the educational aspirations and efforts of students, the first indicators in this section (found on the website) include student measures of time spent on homework, preparedness for academic activities, postsecondary education expectations, and patterns of school attendance.

Included in this section of the volume is an indicator on the averaged freshman graduation rate, which estimates the on-time graduation rate for students in each state. On the website, there are indicators on the percentage of students who have ever been retained in a grade; the percentage of students with disabilities who leave high school with a regular diploma; and the dropout rates by family income. Dropping out of high school is measured here in two ways: (1) by status rates (the percentage of students in a given age range who are not enrolled in school and who have not completed high school) and

(2) by event rates (the percentage of students in an age range who leave school in a given year). Status rates are discussed in an indicator in this volume, while event rates are discussed in an indicator on the website.

Students' transition to college is also examined in this section. One important measure featured in this volume is the percentage of students who enroll in college within one year of completing high school. In addition, this section includes indicators that describe the relationship between the qualifications and characteristics of students who enter postsecondary education, in particular their need for remedial coursework, and their success in earning a credential.

Lastly, this section contains indicators that focus on completion. An overall measure of the progress of the population through the education system is attainment, which is the highest level of education completed by a certain age. *The Condition of Education* annually examines levels of attainment for 25- through 29-year-olds. In addition, this section has an indicator that compares U.S. educational attainment to that of other countries. Another indicator in this volume showcases the number of postsecondary degrees earned over time by gender and race/ethnicity.

Indicators of student effort and educational progress from previous editions of *The Condition of Education* which are not included in this volume are available at http://nces.ed.gov/programs/coe.

Public High School Graduation Rates

In 2007–08, about three-quarters of public high school students graduated on time with a regular diploma.

This indicator examines the percentage of public high school students who graduate on time with a regular diploma. To do so, it uses the *averaged freshman graduation rate*—an estimate of the number of regular diplomas issued in a given year divided by an estimate of the averaged enrollment base for the freshman class four years earlier. For each year, the averaged freshman enrollment count is the sum of the number of 8th-graders 5 years earlier, the number of 9th-graders 4 years earlier (when current-year seniors were freshmen), and the number of 10th-graders 3 years earlier, divided by 3. The intent of this averaging is to account for the high rate of grade retention in the freshman year, which adds 9th-grade repeaters from the previous year to the number of students in the incoming freshman class each year.

Among public high school students in the class of 2007–08, the averaged freshman graduation rate was 74.7 percent; that is, 3 million students graduated on time (see table A-19-1). Wisconsin had the highest graduation rate, at 89.6 percent. Sixteen other states had rates of 80 percent or more (ordered from high to low): Vermont, Minnesota, Iowa, New Jersey, South Dakota, North Dakota, Nebraska, New Hampshire, Pennsylvania, Missouri, Connecticut, Montana, Massachusetts, Maryland, Illinois, and Idaho. The District of Columbia had the lowest rate, at 56.0 percent. Nine other states had graduation rates below 70 percent (ordered from high to low): Alaska, Alabama, Florida, New Mexico, Georgia, Mississippi, Louisiana, South Carolina, and Nevada.

The overall averaged freshman graduation rate was higher for the graduating class of 2007–08 (74.7 percent) than it was for the graduating class of 2001–02 (72.6 percent). However, from 2004–05 to 2005–06, the overall averaged freshman graduation rate decreased from 74.7 percent to 73.4 percent. Looking at changes by state, there was an increase in the graduation rate in 40 states from school year 2001–02 to 2007–08; in 8 of these states (Alabama, Missouri, New Hampshire, New York, Oregon, South Dakota, Tennessee, and Vermont) rates increased by more than 5 percentage points. The graduation rate decreased in 11 states (Arizona, California, Louisiana, Nebraska, Nevada, New Jersey, New Mexico, North Dakota, Texas, Utah, and Washington) and the District of Columbia, with decreases of greater than 5 percentage points observed in Utah (6 percent), the District of Columbia (12 percent), and Nevada (16 percent).

For more information: *Table A-19-1*
Glossary: *High school, High school diploma, Public school*

Technical Notes

Ungraded students were allocated to individual grades proportional to each state's enrollment in those grades. Graduates include only those who earned regular diplomas or diplomas for advanced academic achievement (e.g., honors diploma) as defined by the state or jurisdiction. The 2003–04 national estimates include imputed data for New York and Wisconsin.

The 2005–06 national estimates include imputed data for the District of Columbia, Pennsylvania, and South Carolina. The 2007–08 estimate includes graduates of semi-private schools in Maine. For more information on the Common Core of Data (CCD), see *supplemental note 3*. For more information on measures of student progress and persistence, see *supplemental note 6*.

Figure 19-1. Averaged freshman graduation rate for public high school students, by state or jurisdiction: School year 2007–08

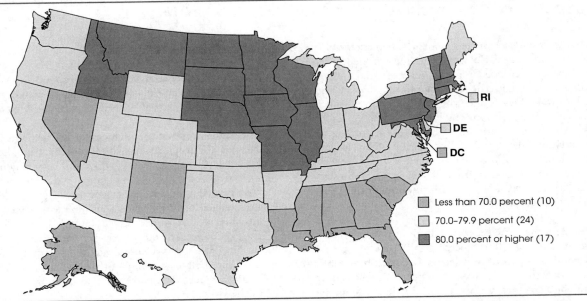

Less than 70.0 percent (10)

70.0–79.9 percent (24)

80.0 percent or higher (17)

NOTE: The rate is the number of graduates divided by the estimated freshman enrollment count 4 years earlier. This count is the sum of the number of 8th-graders 5 years earlier, the number of 9th-graders 4 years earlier, and the number of 10th-graders 3 years earlier, divided by 3. Ungraded students were allocated to individual grades proportional to each state's enrollment in those grades. The estimate for Maine includes graduates of semi-private schools. For more information on the Common Core of Data (CCD), see *supplemental note 3*. For more information on measures of student progress and persistence, see *supplemental note 6*.
SOURCE: U.S. Department of Education, National Center for Education Statistics, Common Core of Data (CCD), "NCES Common Core of Data State Dropout and Completion Data File," school year 2007–08, version 1a.

Figure 19-2. Averaged freshman graduation rate for public high school students: School years 2001–02 through 2007–08

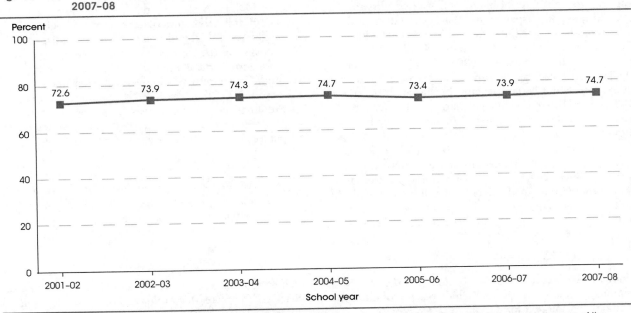

NOTE: The rate is the number of graduates divided by the estimated freshman enrollment count 4 years earlier. This count is the sum of the number of 8th-graders 5 years earlier, the number of 9th-graders 4 years earlier, and the number of 10th-graders 3 years earlier, divided by 3. Ungraded students were allocated to individual grades proportional to each state's enrollment in those grades. The 2003–04 national estimates include imputed data for New York and Wisconsin. The 2005–06 national estimates include imputed data for the District of Columbia, Pennsylvania, and South Carolina. The 2007–08 estimate includes graduates of semi-private schools in Maine. For more information on the Common Core of Data (CCD), see *supplemental note 3*. For more information on measures of student progress and persistence, see *supplemental note 6*.
SOURCE: U.S. Department of Education, National Center for Education Statistics, Common Core of Data (CCD), "NCES Common Core of Data State Dropout and Completion Data File," school year 2007–08, version 1a; and "State Nonfiscal Survey of Public Elementary/Secondary Education," 2002–03, Version 1b; 2003–04, Version 1b; 2004–05, Version 1b; 2005–06, Version 1b; and 2006–07, Version 1b.

In general, the status dropout rates for Whites, Blacks, and Hispanics each declined between 1980 and 2009. However, in each year during that period, the status dropout rate was lower for Whites and Blacks than for Hispanics.

The *status dropout rate* represents the percentage of 16- through 24-year-olds who are not enrolled in school and have not earned a high school credential (either a diploma or an equivalency credential such as a General Educational Development [GED] certificate). In this indicator, status dropout rates are estimated using both the American Community Survey (ACS) and the Current Population Survey (CPS). The 2009 ACS has larger sample sizes than the CPS, which allows for more detailed comparisons of status dropout rates by race/ethnicity, nativity, and sex. For more information on these surveys, see *supplemental notes 2* and *3*.

Based on the CPS, the status dropout rate declined from 14 percent in 1980 to 8 percent in 2009 (see table A-20-1). A significant part of this decline occurred between 2000 and 2009 (from 11 percent to 8 percent). Status dropout rates and changes in these rates over time differed by race/ethnicity. In general, the status dropout rates for Whites, Blacks, and Hispanics each declined between 1980 and 2009. However, in each year during that period, the status dropout rate was lower for Whites and Blacks than for Hispanics. In addition, the rate for Asians/Pacific Islanders was lower than that for Hispanics and Blacks every year between 1989 and 2009. Although the gaps between the rates of Blacks and Whites, Hispanics and Whites, and Hispanics and Blacks have decreased, the decreases occurred in different time periods. The Black-White gap narrowed during the 1980s, with no measurable change between 1990 and 2009. In contrast, the Hispanic-Black gap narrowed between 1990 and 2009, with no measurable change in the gap during the 1980s. The Hispanic-White gap narrowed between 2000 and 2009, with no measurable change in the gap between 1980 and 1999.

The ACS allows for comparisons of status dropout rates for 16- through 24-year-olds residing in households, as well as those in noninstitutionalized and institutionalized group quarters. Among those living in households and noninstitutionalized group quarters, such as college

housing and military quarters, the status dropout rate was 8 percent (see table A-20-2) in 2009. A higher percentage of males than females were status dropouts (9 vs. 7 percent). This pattern was evident across certain racial/ethnic groups, namely Whites, Blacks, and Hispanics.

The status dropout rate includes all 16- through 24-year-old dropouts, regardless of when they last attended school, as well as individuals who may never have attended school in the United States and may never have earned a high school credential. It is possible to isolate data for immigrants and those who were born and attended school in the United States, helping to highlight the experiences of young people in our education system. In 2009, the status dropout rate for Hispanics born in the United States was higher than the rates for Asians, Whites, Blacks, and persons of two or more races born in the United States. No measurable differences were found, however, between U.S.-born Hispanics and Native Hawaiians/Pacific Islanders. Overall, the status dropout rate for U.S.-born 16- through 24-year-olds was lower than the rate for their peers born outside of the United States (7 vs. 20 percent). Hispanics and Asians born in the United States had lower status dropout rates than did their counterparts born outside of the United States, whereas U.S.-born Blacks had higher status dropout rates than did their counterparts born outside of the United States. A higher dropout rate among Hispanics born outside of the United States (32 percent) compared to those born in the United States (10 percent) partially accounts for the relatively high overall Hispanic rate (17 percent). In 2009, the status dropout rate for the institutionalized population was 40 percent (see table A-20-3). This rate varied by race/ethnicity, ranging from 31 percent for Whites to 47 percent for Hispanics.

For more information: *Tables A-20-1 through A-20-3*
Glossary: *GED certificate, High school equivalency certificate, Status dropout rate*

Technical Notes

The United States refers to the 50 states and the District of Columbia. Race categories exclude persons of Hispanic ethnicity. For more information on race/ethnicity, see *supplemental note 1*. Estimates of the status dropout rate using the CPS include civilian, noninstitutionalized 16- through 24-year-olds. Young adults in the military or those who are incarcerated, for instance, are not included in this measure. However, the 2009 ACS

includes noninstitutionalized and institutionalized group quarters. Therefore, due to this and other methodological differences between the CPS and ACS, status dropout estimates from the two surveys are not directly comparable. For more information on these surveys, see *supplemental notes 2* and *3*. For more information on measures of student persistence and progress, see *supplemental note 6*.

Figure 20-1. Status dropout rates of 16- through 24-year-olds in the civilian, noninstitutionalized population, by race/ethnicity: October Current Population Survey (CPS) 1995–2009

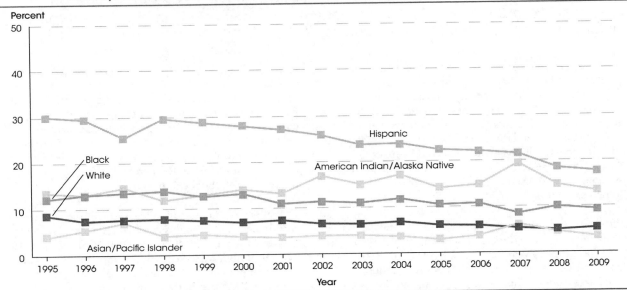

NOTE: The *status dropout rate* is the percentage of 16- through 24-year-olds who are not enrolled in high school and have not earned a high school credential (either a diploma or an equivalency credential such as a General Educational Development [GED] certificate). The status dropout rate includes all dropouts regardless of when they last attended school. Data for American Indians/Alaska Natives in 1999 have been suppressed due to unstable estimates. This figure uses a different data source than figure 20-2; therefore, estimates for 2009 are not directly comparable to the estimates in figure 20-2. Race categories exclude persons of Hispanic ethnicity. One should use caution when making comparisons between data for 1995 and later years because of differing response options for race/ethnicity. For more information on race/ethnicity and the CPS, see *supplemental notes 1* and *2*. For more information on measures of student persistence and progress, see *supplemental note 6*.
SOURCE: U.S. Department of Commerce, Census Bureau, Current Population Survey (CPS), October Supplement, 1995–2009.

Figure 20-2. Status dropout rates of 16- through 24-year-olds in the household and noninstitutionalized group quarters population, by race/ethnicity and nativity: American Community Survey (ACS) 2009

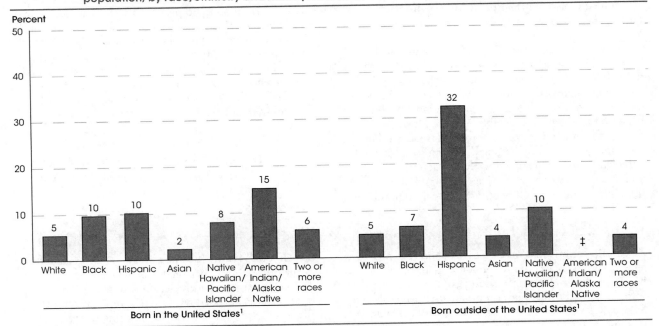

‡ Reporting standards not met.
[1] United States refers to the 50 states and the District of Columbia.
NOTE: This figure uses a different data source than figure 20-1; therefore, estimates are not directly comparable to the 2009 estimates in figure 20-1. Noninstitutionalized group quarters include college and university housing, military quarters, facilities for workers and religious groups, and temporary shelters for the homeless. Among those counted in noninstitutionalized group quarters in the American Community Survey, only the residents of military barracks are not included in the civilian noninstitutionalized population in the Current Population Survey. Race categories exclude persons of Hispanic ethnicity. For more information on race/ethnicity and the ACS, see *supplemental notes 1* and *3*. For more information on measures of student persistence and progress, see *supplemental note 6*.
SOURCE: U.S. Department of Commerce, Census Bureau, American Community Survey (ACS), 2009.

Immediate Transition to College

The immediate college enrollment rate after high school increased from 1975 to 1997 (51 to 67 percent), declined from 1997 to 2001 (to 62 percent), then increased from 2001 to 2009 (70 percent). Gaps in immediate enrollment rates by family income, race/ethnicity, and sex have persisted over time.

The *immediate college enrollment rate* is defined as the percentage of high school completers of a given year who enroll in 2- or 4-year colleges in the fall immediately after completing high school. Between 1975 and 2009, the immediate college enrollment rate ranged from 49 to 70 percent (see table A-21-1). The rate of enrollment immediately after high school increased from 1975 to 1997 (51 to 67 percent), declined from 1997 to 2001 (to 62 percent), then increased from 2001 to 2009 (70 percent).

Differences in immediate college enrollment rates by family income, race/ethnicity, and sex were observed over time. In every year between 1975 and 2009, the immediate college enrollment rates of high school completers from low- and middle-income families were lower than those of high school completers from high-income families (see table A-21-1). Most recently, in 2009, the immediate college enrollment rate of high school completers from low-income families was 55 percent, 29 percentage points lower than the rate of high school completers from high-income families (84 percent). The immediate college enrollment rate of high school completers from middle-income families (67 percent) also trailed the rate of their peers from high-income families by 17 percentage points.

Since 2003, data on Asian high school completers have been collected separately. Between 2003 and 2009, the immediate college enrollment rate of Asian high school completers increased from 80 to 90 percent, while the enrollment rate of White high school completers increased from 66 to 71 percent (see table A-21-2). During this period, the immediate college enrollment rates did not measurably change for Black and Hispanic high school completers (approximately 60 percent each in 2003 and 2009). In every year between 2003 and 2009, the immediate college enrollment rate of Asian high school

completers was higher than the rates of White, Black, and Hispanic high school completers. The immediate college enrollment rate of Asian high school completers was 19 percentage points higher than the immediate college enrollment rate of White high school completers (71 percent). In 2009, the immediate college enrollment rates of White and Asian high school completers were higher than the rates of Black (63 percent) and Hispanic (62 percent) high school completers.

Overall, at 2- and 4-year colleges, the immediate college enrollment rates of high school completers increased between 1975 and 2009 (see table A-21-3). In 1975, 18 percent of high school completers enrolled at a 2-year college immediately after high school, while 28 percent did so in 2009. Similarly, in 1975, some 33 percent of high school completers enrolled at a 4-year college immediately after high school, compared with 42 percent in 2009. In every year between 1975 and 2009, immediate college enrollment rates at 2-year colleges were lower than those at 4-year colleges.

During this period, immediate college enrollment rates increased for both males and females: the rate for males increased from 53 to 66 percent, and for females, from 49 to 74 percent. Thus, the enrollment pattern shifted during this period from higher college enrollment rates for males to higher enrollment rates for females. At 2-year colleges in 2009, the immediate college enrollment rate for males (25 percent) was lower than the rate for females (30 percent), while at 4-year colleges the rates for males and females were not measurably different.

For more information: *Tables A-21-1 through A-21-3*
Glossary: *Educational attainment, High school completer*

Technical Notes

This indicator provides data on high school completers ages 16–24, who account for about 98 percent of all high school completers in a given year. Enrollment rates were calculated using data from the Current Population Survey (CPS). Before 1992, *high school completer* referred to those who had completed 12 years of schooling. As of 1992, *high school completer* refers to those who have received a high school diploma or equivalency certificate. *Low income* refers to the bottom 20 percent of all family incomes, *high income* refers to the top 20

percent of all family incomes, and *middle income* refers to the 60 percent in between. Race categories exclude persons of Hispanic ethnicity. Due to short-term data fluctuations associated with small sample sizes for the Black, Hispanic, Asian, and low-income categories in some years, moving average rates are also presented and discussed in the indicator text. For more information on the CPS, educational attainment, family income, and race/ethnicity, see *supplemental note 2*.

Figure 21-1. Percentage of high school completers who were enrolled in 2- or 4-year colleges the October immediately following high school completion, by family income: 1975–2009

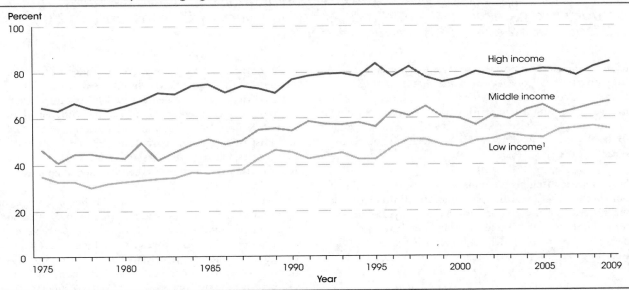

[1] Due to the small sample size for the low-income category, data are subject to relatively large sampling errors. Therefore, moving averages are used to produce more stable estimates. The 3-year moving average is an arithmetic average of the year indicated, the year immediately preceding, and the year immediately following. For 1975 and 2009, a 2-year moving average is used: data for 1975 reflect an average of 1975 and 1976, and data for 2009 reflect an average of 2008 and 2009.

NOTE: Includes high school completers ages 16–24, who account for about 98 percent of all high school completers in a given year. *Low income* refers to the bottom 20 percent of all family incomes, *high income* refers to the top 20 percent of all family incomes, and *middle income* refers to the 60 percent in between. For more information on the Current Population Survey (CPS), educational attainment, and family income, see *supplemental note 2.*

SOURCE: U.S. Department of Commerce, Census Bureau, Current Population Survey (CPS), October Supplement, 1975–2009.

Figure 21-2. Percentage of high school completers who were enrolled in 2- or 4-year colleges the October immediately following high school completion, by race/ethnicity: 2003–09

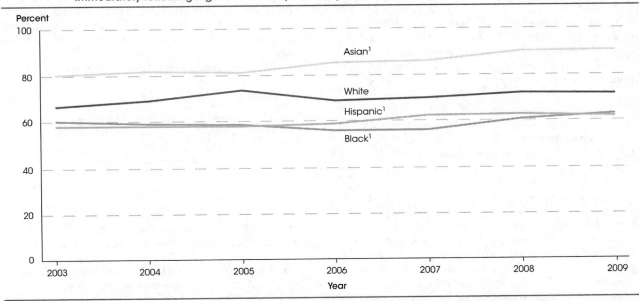

[1] Due to the small sample sizes for the Black, Hispanic, and Asian categories, data are subject to relatively large sampling errors. Therefore, moving averages are used to produce more stable estimates. The 3-year moving average is an arithmetic average of the year indicated, the year immediately preceding, and the year immediately following. For 2009, a 2-year moving average is used: data for 2009 reflect an average of 2008 and 2009.

NOTE: Includes high school completers ages 16–24, who account for about 98 percent of all high school completers in a given year. Race categories exclude persons of Hispanic ethnicity. From 2003 onward, data for Asians and Pacific Islanders are collected separately. Data for the Asian category are not available prior to 2003. For more information on the Current Population Survey (CPS), educational attainment, and race/ethnicity, see *supplemental note 2.*

SOURCE: U.S. Department of Commerce, Census Bureau, Current Population Survey (CPS), October Supplement, 2003–09.

Remedial Coursetaking

In 2007–08, about 36 percent of undergraduate students considered to be in their first year reported having ever taken a remedial course, while 20 percent had actually taken one in that same year. At public 2-year institutions, about 42 percent of students had ever taken a remedial course.

Many students enter postsecondary education not fully prepared for college-level work, requiring them to take remedial courses. Remedial courses, usually in mathematics, English, or writing, provide instruction to improve basic knowledge and skills within a subject and to develop studying and social habits related to academic success at the college level.

Students attending postsecondary education part time or not completing the credit accumulation requirements for second-year status could be considered first-year students for more than 1 year. Therefore, there is a distinction between "first-year" students who reported in 2007–08 that they had "ever" taken a remedial course and those who reported that they had taken one in 2007–08.

In 2007–08, approximately 36 percent of first-year undergraduate students reported that they had ever taken a remedial course, and 20 percent of first-year undergraduates reported that they had taken at least one remedial course in the 2007–08 academic year (see table A-22-1). Some 9 percent of first-year undergraduate students reported that they took one remedial course in 2007–08, while 7 percent took two, and 4 percent took three or more remedial courses in that year.

A higher percentage of female than male undergraduate students reported in 2007–08 that they had ever taken a remedial course (39 percent vs. 33 percent) or that they had taken at least one in 2007–08 (21 percent vs. 19 percent).

In 2007–08, the percentage of White first-year undergraduates (31 percent) who reported that they had ever taken a remedial course in college was smaller than the percentages of undergraduate students who had in

all other racial/ethnic groups, except students of two or more races and students who listed their race as "other." The reported rates of remedial coursetaking for students in these two groups were not measurably different than that of Whites. In addition, higher percentages of Black and Hispanic undergraduate students (45 percent and 43 percent, respectively) than Asian students (38 percent) reported that they had ever taken a remedial course.

There were differences by age group in the percentages of first-year undergraduates who reported in 2007–08 that they had ever taken a remedial course. The percentage of the youngest students (ages 15 to 23 years old) who reported ever taking a remedial course (35 percent) was smaller than the percentages of students ages 24 to 29 (40 percent) or students 30 years or older (38 percent) who reported doing so.

In 2007–08, some 42 percent of first-year undergraduate students at public 2-year institutions (typically community colleges) reported having ever taken a remedial college course—a percentage that was higher than students at institutions of any other level or control. For instance, 4-year institutions in the following categories had smaller percentages of first-year students who reported having ever taken a remedial college course: public non-doctorate institutions (39 percent of students), public doctorate institutions (24 percent), private not-for-profit non-doctorate institutions (26 percent), and private not-for-profit doctorate institutions (22 percent).

For more information: *Table A-22-1*
Glossary: *Four-year postsecondary institution, Postsecondary education, Two-year postsecondary institution, Undergraduate student*

Technical Notes

Data are based on a sample survey of students who enrolled at any time during the school year including those that were not in degree- or certificate-awarding programs. Data include the 50 states, the District of Columbia, and Puerto Rico. *Full time* refers to students who attended full time (as defined by the institution) for the full year (at least 9 months). Race categories exclude persons of Hispanic ethnicity. For more information on race/ethnicity, see *supplemental note 1*. For more

information on the National Postsecondary Student Aid Study (NPSAS), see *supplemental note 3*. Institutions in this indicator are classified based on the number of highest degrees awarded. For example, institutions that award 20 or more doctoral degrees per year are classified as doctoral universities. For more information on the classification of postsecondary institutions, see *supplemental note 8*.

Figure 22-1.   Percentage of first-year undergraduate students who ever took a remedial education course, by institution control and level: 2007–08

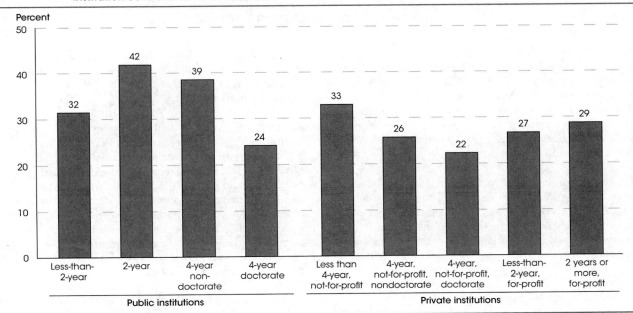

NOTE: Although these data are for first-year undergraduates, student status was determined by accumulation of credits. Students attending postsecondary education part time, or not completing the credit accumulation requirements for second-year status, could be considered first-year students for more than 1 year. Therefore, there is a distinction between having "ever" taken a remedial course and having taken one in 2007–08. Data are based on a sample survey of students who enrolled at any time during the school year. Data include the 50 states, the District of Columbia, and Puerto Rico.
SOURCE: U.S. Department of Education, National Center for Education Statistics, 2007–08 National Postsecondary Student Aid Study (NPSAS:08).

Figure 22-2.   Percentage of first-year undergraduate students who took remedial education courses, by institution control, level, and number of courses: 2007–08

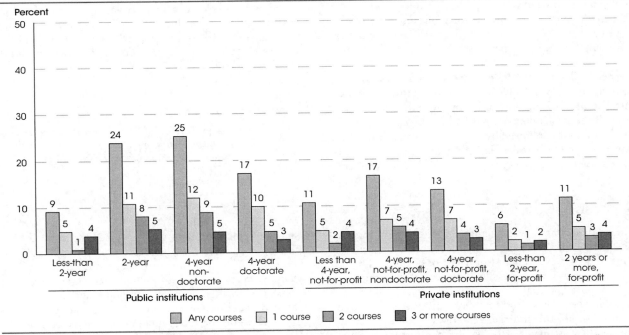

NOTE: Although these data are for first-year undergraduates, student status was determined by accumulation of credits. Students attending postsecondary education part time, or not completing the credit accumulation requirements for second-year status, could be considered first-year students for more than 1 year. Therefore, there is a distinction between having "ever" taken a remedial course and having taken one in 2007–08. Data are based on a sample survey of students who enrolled at any time during the school year. Data include the 50 states, the District of Columbia, and Puerto Rico.
SOURCE: U.S. Department of Education, National Center for Education Statistics, 2007–08 National Postsecondary Student Aid Study (NPSAS:08).

About 54 percent of male and 60 percent of female first-time students who sought a bachelor's degree and enrolled at a 4-year institution full time in fall 2002 completed a bachelor's degree at that institution within 6 years.

Approximately 57 percent of first-time students who sought a bachelor's degree or its equivalent and enrolled at a 4-year institution full time in fall 2002 completed a bachelor's degree or its equivalent at that institution within 6 years (see table A-23-1). By comparison, 55 percent of students in an analogous cohort who began seeking a bachelor's degree or its equivalent in fall 1996 graduated within 6 years.

The bachelor's degree completion rates for students who began seeking a bachelor's degree at 4-year institutions in fall 2002 varied by the control of institution. Graduation rates were highest at private not-for-profit institutions, followed by public institutions and private for-profit institutions. For example, the 6-year graduation rate at private not-for-profit institutions was 65 percent, compared with 55 percent at public institutions and 22 percent at private for-profit institutions.

At both public and private not-for-profit 4-year institutions, the 6-year graduation rates for females who enrolled in fall 2002 were higher than the rates for males. At public institutions, approximately 58 percent of females seeking a bachelor's degree or its equivalent graduated within 6 years, compared with 52 percent of males; at private not-for-profit institutions, 67 percent of females graduated within 6 years, compared with 62 percent of males. At private for-profit institutions, however, the 6-year graduation rate was higher for males than females (24 vs. 21 percent).

Bachelor's degree completion rates for students who sought a bachelor's degree at 4-year institutions and enrolled in fall 2002 also varied by race/ethnicity. Asian/Pacific Islander students had the highest 6-year graduation rate, followed by White, Hispanic, Black, and American Indian/Alaska Native students (see table A-23-2). Approximately 67 percent of Asians/Pacific Islanders graduated with a bachelor's degree or its equivalent within 6 years, compared with 60 percent of Whites, 49 percent of Hispanics, 40 percent of Blacks, and 38 percent of American Indians/Alaska Natives.

At both public and private not-for-profit 4-year institutions, the 6-year graduation rates for both males and females who began seeking a bachelor's degree in fall 2002 varied by the acceptance rate of the institution. For example, at public 4-year institutions with open admissions policies, 27 percent of males and 34 percent of females completed a bachelor's degree or its equivalent within 6 years. At public 4-year institutions where the acceptance rate was less than 25 percent of applicants, however, the 6-year graduation rate for males was 73 percent and for females, 72 percent.

At 2-year institutions, about 27 percent of first-time, full-time students who enrolled in fall 2005 completed a certificate or associate's degree within 150 percent of the normal time required to complete such a degree (see table A-23-3). For the cohort who enrolled in 1999, the completion rate was 29 percent.

The certificate or associate's degree completion rate of students who enrolled in 2-year institutions in fall 2005 varied by institution control. Fifty-eight percent of students graduated within 150 percent of the normal time at private for-profit 2-year institutions, 48 percent did so at private not-for-profit institutions, and 21 percent did so at public institutions.

For more information: *Tables A-23-1 through A-23-3*
Glossary: *Associate's degree, Bachelor's degree, Four-year postsecondary institution, Private institution, Public institution, Two-year postsecondary institution*

Technical Notes

The graduation rate was calculated as the total number of students who completed a degree within the specified time to degree attainment (for bachelor's degrees, 6 years; for less than 4-year degrees, 150 percent of the normal time required to attain such a degree) divided by the revised cohort, meaning the cohort minus any allowable exclusions. For this indicator, the revised cohorts are the spring 2009 estimates of 1) the number of students who entered a 4-year institution in fall 1996, fall 1999, and fall 2002 as first-time, full-time undergraduates seeking a bachelor's or equivalent degree, and 2) the number of students who entered a 2-year institution in fall 1999 and fall 2005 as first-time, full-time undergraduates seeking a certificate or associate's degree. Students who transferred to another institution and graduated are not counted as completers at their initial institution. For more information on the Integrated Postsecondary Education Data System (IPEDS), see *supplemental note 3.* Race categories exclude person of Hispanic ethnicity. For more information on race/ethnicity, see *supplemental note 1.*

Figure 23-1. Percentage of students seeking a bachelor's degree at 4-year institutions who completed a bachelor's degree within 6 years, by control of institution and race/ethnicity: Cohort year 2002

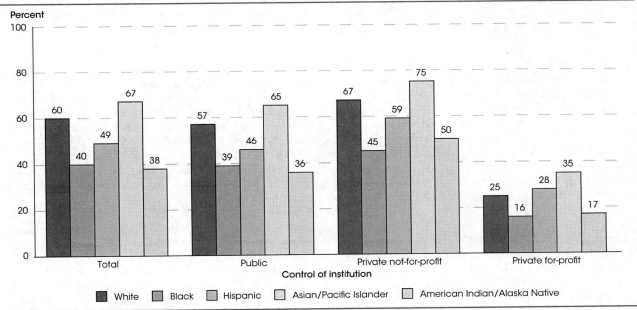

NOTE: The rate was calculated as the total number of students who completed a degree within the specified time to degree attainment (6 years) divided by the revised cohort minus any allowable exclusions. Students who transferred to another institution and graduated from the other institution are not counted as completers at their initial institution. For more information on the Integrated Postsecondary Education Data System (IPEDS), see *supplemental note 3*. Race categories exclude persons of Hispanic ethnicity. For more information on race/ethnicity, see *supplemental note 1*.
SOURCE: U.S. Department of Education, National Center for Education Statistics, Integrated Postsecondary Education Data System (IPEDS), Spring 2009, Graduation Rates component.

Figure 23-2. Percentage of students seeking a certificate or associate's degree at 2-year institutions who completed a certificate or degree within 150 percent of the normal time required to do so, by control of institution and race/ethnicity: Cohort year 2005

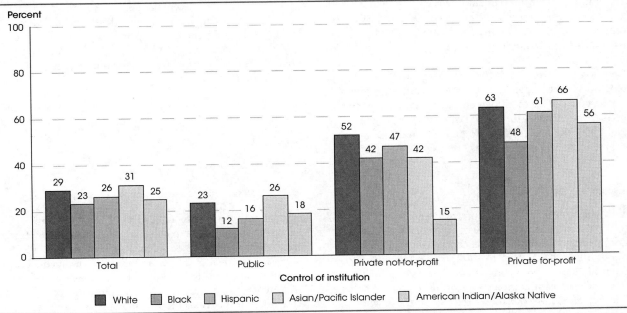

NOTE: The rate was calculated as the total number of students who completed a degree within the specified time to degree attainment (6 years) divided by the revised cohort minus any allowable exclusions. Students who transferred to another institution and graduated from the other institution are not counted as completers at their initial institution. For more information on the Integrated Postsecondary Education Data System (IPEDS), see *supplemental note 3*. Race categories exclude persons of Hispanic ethnicity. For more information on race/ethnicity, see *supplemental note 1*.
SOURCE: U.S. Department of Education, National Center for Education Statistics, Integrated Postsecondary Education Data System (IPEDS), Spring 2009, Graduation Rates component.

Educational Attainment

In 2010, some 32 percent of 25- to 29-year-olds had completed at least a bachelor's degree. Between 1975 and 2010, the gap in bachelor's degree attainment between Whites and Hispanics widened from 15 to 25 percentage points, and the gap between Whites and Blacks widened from 13 to 19 percentage points.

Between 1975 and 2010, the educational attainment of 25- to 29-year-olds increased. For the purpose of this indicator, educational attainment represents the percentage who achieved at least the cited credential, such as a high school diploma or equivalency credential or a bachelor's degree. In 2010, for example, 89 percent of 25- to 29-year-olds had received at least a high school diploma or equivalency certificate, a 6 percentage point increase from 1975 (see table A-24-1). The high school completion rate has remained between 85 and 89 percent since 1980.

In both 1975 and 2010, the percentage of Whites who had completed high school was higher than that of Blacks and Hispanics, although the gaps between Whites and Blacks and Whites and Hispanics have narrowed over the years. Between 1975 and 2010, the high school completion rate for Blacks increased from 71 to 90 percent, and the gap between Blacks and Whites decreased from 15 to 5 percentage points. During this period, the high school completion rate for Hispanics increased from 53 to 69 percent, and the gap between Hispanics and Whites decreased from 34 to 25 percentage points. In 2010, the high school completion rate for Whites was 95 percent. Educational attainment data for Asians/Pacific Islanders were not available until 1990; in that year, 90 percent of Asians/Pacific Islanders had completed high school. Between 1990 and 2010, the high school completion rate for Asians/Pacific Islanders increased from 90 to 94 percent.

Between 1975 and 2010, the percentage of 25- to 29-year-olds who had completed a bachelor's degree or higher increased from 22 to 32 percent; however, most of the increase occurred prior to the last decade. Between 1975 and 2010, the percentage who had attained a bachelor's degree increased from 24 to 39 percent for Whites, from

10 to 19 percent for Blacks, and from 9 to 13 percent for Hispanics. During this period, the gap in bachelor's degree attainment between Blacks and Whites increased from 13 to 19 percentage points, and the gap between Whites and Hispanics increased from 15 to 25 percentage points. Between 1990 and 2005, the percentage of Asians/Pacific Islanders who had attained a bachelor's degree increased from 42 to 60 percent; however, between 2005 and 2010 this percentage decreased from 60 to 53 percent.

In 2010, some 7 percent of 25- to 29-year-olds had completed a master's degree or higher. The percentage of Asians/Pacific Islanders who had attained a master's degree in 2010 (18 percent) was higher than that of their peers from all other races/ethnicities: 8 percent of Whites, 5 percent of Blacks, and 2 percent of Hispanics had attained a master's degree in 2010. Between 1995 and 2010, the rate of master's degree attainment increased for Whites (from 5 to 8 percent), Blacks (from 2 to 5 percent), and Asians/Pacific Islanders (from 11 to 18 percent).

Differences in educational attainment by gender shifted between 1975 and 2010. For example, in 1975, a higher percentage of males than females had completed high school, by a difference of 3 percentage points, but by 2010 females' rate of high school attainment was higher than males', by 3 percentage points. A higher percentage of males than females had attained a bachelor's degree in 1975 (by a difference of 6 percentage points), while by 2010 the percentage of females who had attained a bachelor's degree was 8 percentage points higher than that of males.

 For more information: *Table A-24-1*

Technical Notes

This indicator uses March Current Population Survey (CPS) data to estimate the percentage of civilian, noninstitutionalized people ages 25 through 29 who are out of high school. Prior to 1992, *high school completers* referred to those who completed 12 years of schooling, *some college* meant completing 1 or more years of college, and *bachelor's degree or higher* referred to those who completed 4 years of college; from 1992 to 2010, *high school completers* refers to those who have received a high school diploma or equivalency certificate, *some college*

means completing any college at all, and *bachelor's degree or higher* refers to those who have earned at least a bachelor's degree. For more information on the CPS, see *supplemental note 2*. For more information on educational attainment of 25- to 29-year-olds, see *supplemental note 6*. Some estimates are revised from previous publications. Included in the totals but not shown separately are estimates for persons from other racial/ethnic groups. Race categories exclude persons of Hispanic ethnicity. For more information on race/ethnicity, see *supplemental note 1*.

Figure 24-1. Percentage of 25- to 29-year-olds who completed at least high school, by race/ethnicity: March 1975–2010

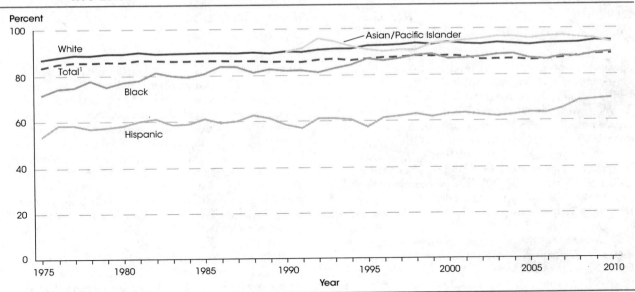

¹ Included in the total but not shown separately are estimates for persons from other racial/ethnic groups.
NOTE: Data for Asians/Pacific Islanders were available beginning in 1990. Prior to 1992, *high school completers* referred to those who completed 12 years of schooling; from 1992 to 2010, the term refers to those who have received a high school diploma or equivalency certificate. For more information on educational attainment of 25- to 29-year-olds, see *supplemental note 6*. For more information on the Current Population Survey (CPS), see *supplemental note 2*. Race categories exclude persons of Hispanic ethnicity. For more information on race/ethnicity, see *supplemental note 1*.
SOURCE: U.S. Department of Commerce, Census Bureau, Current Population Survey (CPS), Annual Social and Economic Supplement, 1975–2010.

Figure 24-2. Percentage of 25- to 29-year-olds with a bachelor's degree or higher, by race/ethnicity: March 1975–2010

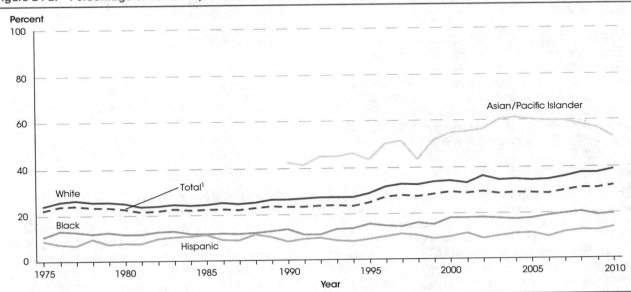

¹ Included in the total but not shown separately are estimates for persons from other racial/ethnic groups.
NOTE: Data for Asians/Pacific Islanders were available beginning in 1990. Data prior to 1992 were for completing 4 years of college; from 1992 to 2010, data are for earning a bachelor's degree. For more information on educational attainment of 25- to 29-year-olds, see *supplemental note 6*. For more information on the Current Population Survey (CPS), see *supplemental note 2*. Race categories exclude persons of Hispanic ethnicity. For more information on race/ethnicity, see *supplemental note 1*.
SOURCE: U.S. Department of Commerce, Census Bureau, Current Population Survey (CPS), Annual Social and Economic Supplement, 1975–2010.

International Comparison of Educational Attainment

Greater percentages of the population ages 25 to 64 had earned a bachelor's degree or higher in all reporting OECD countries in 2008 than in 2001 (21 vs. 15 percent). The percentage of the U.S. population with a bachelor's degree or higher was 32 percent in 2008, compared with 28 percent in 2001.

Member countries of the Organization for Economic Co-operation and Development (OECD) generally reported that the percentages of the adult population (ages 25 to 64) with a high school education or a bachelor's degree or higher were greater in 2008 than in 2001. On average across member countries of the OECD reporting data, the percentage of the population ages 25 to 64 possessing a high school education was 65 percent in 2001 and 72 percent in 2008. The percentage of the adult population possessing a bachelor's degree or higher was 15 percent in 2001 and 21 percent in 2008 (see table A-25-1).

The percentage of the population who had completed high school was higher in 2008 than in 2001 in 24 OECD countries and lower in 2008 than in 2001 in three OECD countries (one OECD country showed no measurable difference from 2001 to 2008). In the United States, 88 percent of the population had completed high school in 2001, compared with 89 percent in 2008. Greater percentages of the population ages 25 to 64 had earned a bachelor's degree or higher in all reporting OECD countries in 2008 than in 2001. The percentage of the U.S. adult population with a bachelor's degree or higher was 32 percent in 2008, compared with 28 percent in 2001.

In 2008 in 27 reporting OECD countries, 60 percent or more of the population ages 25 to 64 had completed at least high school, but differences in educational attainment were seen when the population was broken out by age group. On average across OECD countries, the percentage of 25- to 34-year-olds with at least a high school education was 21 percentage points higher than that of 55- to 64-year-olds with at least a high school

education (81 vs. 60 percent, respectively) (see table A-25-2). The United States was the only country in 2008 where the percentage of 25- to 34-year-olds who had completed high school did not exceed the percentage of 55- to 64-year-olds who had completed high school. The percentage of the population who had completed high school in 2008 was about the same at every age group in the United States (between 88 and 89 percent). Canada, the Czech Republic, Estonia, Germany, the Slovak Republic, and Switzerland were the only other countries where 80 percent or more of 55- to 64-year-olds were high school completers.

In 2008, over 20 percent of the 25- to 64-year-old population in 18 OECD countries had earned a bachelor's degree or higher. In 31 OECD countries and the partner country Brazil, 25- to 34-year-olds had higher levels of attaining a bachelor's degree or higher than did 55- to 64-year-olds. On average across OECD countries, 27 percent of the population ages 25 to 34 had completed a bachelor's degree or higher, compared with 15 percent of the population 55 to 64 years old. In the United States, some 32 percent of 25- to 34-year-olds and 31 percent for 55- to 64-year-olds had attained a bachelor's degree or higher. The United States was the only country where at least 30 percent of 55- to 64-year-olds had attained a bachelor's degree or higher in 2008.

For more information: *Tables A-25-1 and A-25-2*
Glossary: *Educational attainment, Organization for Economic Co-operation and Development (OECD)*

Technical Notes

The OECD is an organization of 34 countries whose purpose is to promote trade and economic growth in both member and nonmember countries. Of the 34 OECD member countries, 29 countries reported high school attainment data in 2001 and 32 countries reported these data in both 2005 and 2008. Twenty-nine OECD member countries reported bachelor's degree or higher attainment data in 2001, and 33 countries reported these data in both 2005 and 2008. The OECD average refers to the mean of the data values for all reporting OECD countries, to which each country reporting data contributes equally. Attainment data for two non-OECD partner countries are displayed separately and are not included in the OECD average. High school attainment data in this indicator refer to degrees classified by the

OECD as International Standard Classification of Education (ISCED) level 3. ISCED level 3 corresponds to high school completion in the United States. ISCED level 3C short programs do not correspond to high school completion; these short programs are excluded from this indicator. Data regarding the attainment of a bachelor's degree or higher in this indicator refer to degrees classified by the OECD as ISCED level 5A or 6. ISCED level 5A, first award, corresponds to the bachelor's degree in the United States; ISCED level 5A, second award, corresponds to master's and first-professional degrees in the United States; and ISCED level 6 corresponds to doctoral degrees. For more information on ISCED levels, see *supplemental note 11.*

Figure 25-1. Percentage of the population 25 to 64 years old who have attained selected levels of education: 2001, 2005, and 2008

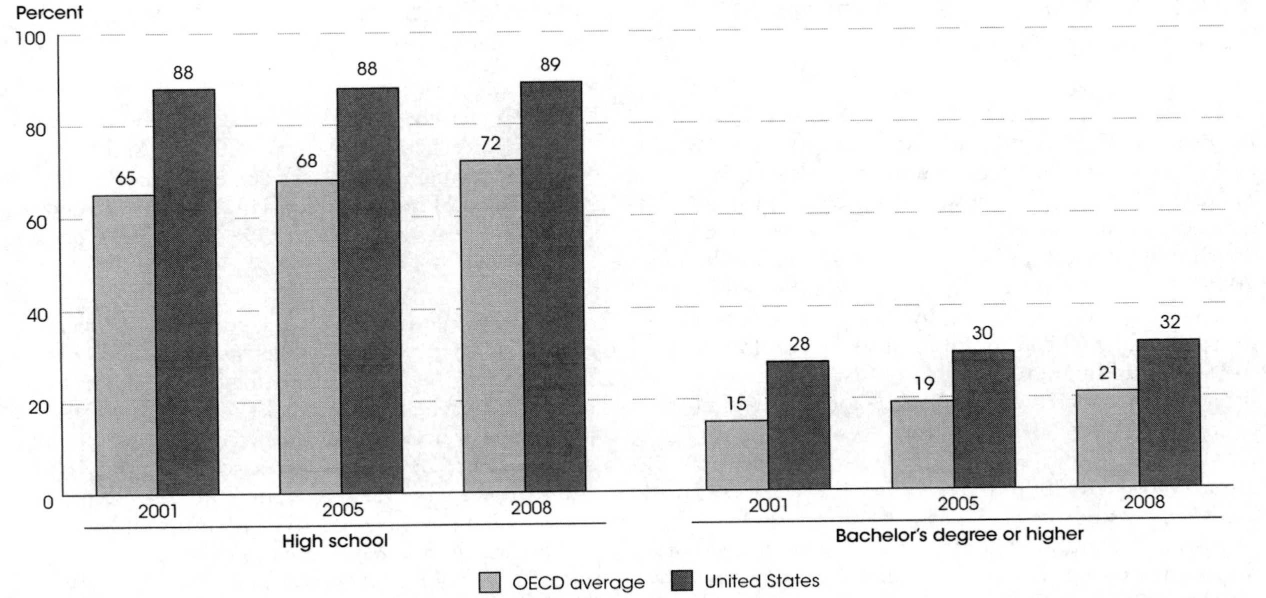

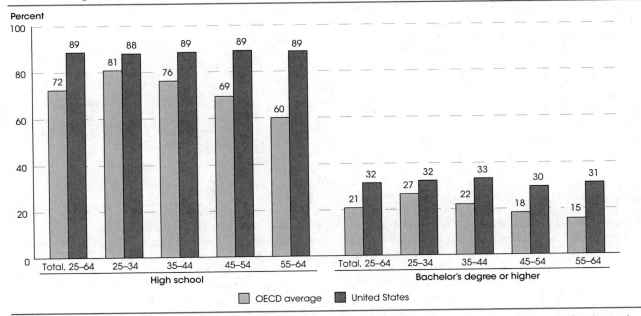

NOTE: Educational attainment data in this figure refer to degrees classified by the Organization for Economic Co-operation and Development (OECD) as International Standard Classification of Education (ISCED) level 3 for high school and level 5A or 6 for bachelor's degree or higher. For more information on ISCED levels, please see *supplemental note 11*. The OECD average refers to the mean of the data values for all reporting OECD countries, to which each country reporting data contributes equally.
SOURCE: Organization for Economic Co-operation and Development (OECD), *Education at a Glance,* 2002, 2007, and 2010, Tables A1.2a and A1.3a.

Figure 25-2. Percentage of the population 25 to 64 years old who have attained selected levels of education, by age group: 2008

NOTE: Educational attainment data in this figure refer to degrees classified by the Organization for Economic Co-operation and Development (OECD) as International Standard Classification of Education (ISCED) level 3 for high school and level 5A or 6 for bachelor's degree or higher. For more information on ISCED levels, please see *supplemental note 11*. The OECD average refers to the mean of the data values for all reporting OECD countries, to which each country reporting data contributes equally.
SOURCE: Organization for Economic Co-operation and Development (OECD), *Education at a Glance,* 2002, 2007, and 2010, Tables A1.2a and A1.3a.

Between 1998–99 and 2008–09, the number of degrees earned increased by 41 percent for associate's degrees, by 33 percent for bachelor's degrees, and by 49 percent for master's degrees. In 2008–09, females earned the majority of all associate's, bachelor's, master's, and doctoral degrees awarded.

Postsecondary enrollment in degree-granting institutions increased by 32 percent from academic years 1998–99 to 2008–09, from 14.5 to 19.1 million students (see *indicators 8* and *9*). This growth was accompanied by a 38 percent increase in the number of degrees earned, which rose from 2.3 million in 1998–99 to 3.2 million in 2008–09. The number of degrees earned increased by 41 percent for associate's degrees, by 33 percent for bachelor's degrees, and by 49 percent for master's degrees (see table A-26-1). In addition, the number of first-professional degrees earned increased by 17 percent, and the number of doctoral degrees, by 54 percent.

From 1998–99 to 2008–09, the number of degrees earned increased for students of all racial/ethnic groups for each level of degree, but at varying rates. For all levels of degrees, the change in percentage distribution of degree recipients was characterized by increased numbers of Black and Hispanic graduates. For more information on changing enrollment patterns in postsecondary education by race/ethnicity, see tables A-8-3 and A-9-2. From 1998–99 to 2008–09, the number of associate's degrees earned by Hispanics more than doubled (increasing by 101 percent), and the number earned by Black students increased by 77 percent, while the number earned by White students increased by 28 percent (see table A-26-2). As a result, in 2008–09, Blacks students earned 13 percent and Hispanic students earned 12 percent of all associate's degrees awarded, up from 10 and 9 percent, respectively, in 1998–99. During the same time period, the number of bachelor's degrees awarded to Black students increased by 53 percent, and the number awarded to Hispanic students increased by 85 percent. The number of bachelor's degrees awarded to White students increased by 26 percent. In 2008–09, Black students earned 10 percent and Hispanics earned

8 percent of all bachelor's degrees conferred, up from 9 and 6 percent, respectively, in 1998–99. Similarly, higher percentages of master's degrees were conferred to Black and Hispanic students in 2008–09 (11 and 6 percent, respectively) than in 1998–99 (7 and 4 percent, respectively).

From 1998–99 to 2008–09, the percentage of degrees earned by females fluctuated between 61 and 62 percent for associate's degrees and remained steady around 57 percent for bachelor's degrees. In contrast, both the percentage of master's and the percentage of doctoral degrees earned by females increased during this period (from 58 to 60 percent and from 43 to 52 percent, respectively) (see table A-26-1). For nearly all levels of degrees within different race/ethnic groups, women earned the majority of degrees in 2008–09. For example, Black females earned 68 percent of associate's degrees, 66 percent of bachelor's degrees, 72 percent of master's degrees, 62 percent of first-professional degrees, and 67 percent of doctoral degrees awarded to Black students (see table A-26-2). Hispanic females earned 62 percent of associate's degrees, 61 percent of bachelor's degrees, 64 percent of master's degrees, 53 percent of first-professional degrees, and 57 percent of doctoral degrees awarded to Hispanic students. White females earned more degrees than White males for each level of degree except first-professional, for which they earned 46 percent of the degrees awarded.

For more information: *Tables A-26-1 and A-26-2*
Glossary: *Associate's degree, Bachelor's degree, Doctoral degree, First-professional degree, Non-resident alien, Private institution, Public institution*

Technical Notes

Reported racial/ethnic distributions of students by level of degree, field of degree, and sex were used to estimate race/ethnicity for students whose race/ethnicity was not reported. Race categories exclude persons of Hispanic ethnicity. Nonresident aliens are featured separately because information about their race/ethnicity is not

available. For more information on race/ethnicity, see *supplemental note 1*. For more information on the Integrated Postsecondary Education Data System (IPEDS), see *supplemental note 3*. For more information on the Classification of Postsecondary Education Institutions, see *supplemental note 8*.

Figure 26-1. Number of degrees conferred by degree-granting institutions, by level of degree: Academic years 1998–99, 2003–04, and 2008–09

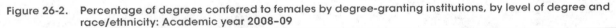

Level of degree

Associate's
1998–99 — 559,954
2003–04 — 665,301
2008–09 — 787,325

Bachelor's
1998–99 — 1,200,303
2003–04 — 1,399,542
2008–09 — 1,601,368

Master's
1998–99 — 439,986
2003–04 — 558,940
2008–09 — 656,784

Number of degrees conferred (in thousands)

NOTE: For more information on the Integrated Postsecondary Education Data System (IPEDS), see *supplemental note 3*. For more information on the Classification of Postsecondary Education Institutions, see *supplemental note 8*.
SOURCE: U.S. Department of Education, National Center for Education Statistics, 1998–99, 2003–04, and 2008–09 Integrated Postsecondary Education Data System (IPEDS), "Completions Survey" (IPEDS-C:99) and Fall 2004 and 2009.

Figure 26-2. Percentage of degrees conferred to females by degree-granting institutions, by level of degree and race/ethnicity: Academic year 2008–09

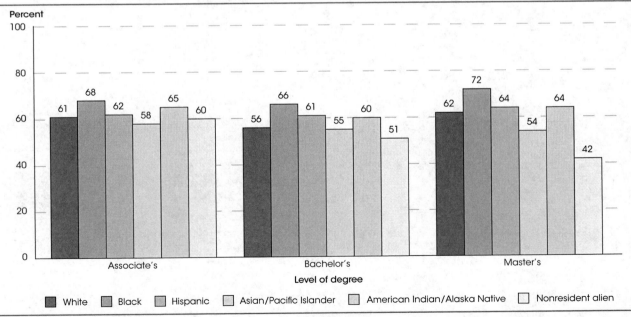

Percent

Associate's: White 61, Black 68, Hispanic 62, Asian/Pacific Islander 58, American Indian/Alaska Native 65, Nonresident alien 60

Bachelor's: White 56, Black 66, Hispanic 61, Asian/Pacific Islander 55, American Indian/Alaska Native 60, Nonresident alien 51

Master's: White 62, Black 72, Hispanic 64, Asian/Pacific Islander 54, American Indian/Alaska Native 64, Nonresident alien 42

Level of degree

■ White   ■ Black   ■ Hispanic   ■ Asian/Pacific Islander   ■ American Indian/Alaska Native   □ Nonresident alien

NOTE: Reported racial/ethnic distributions of students by level of degree, field of degree, and sex were used to estimate race/ethnicity for students whose race/ethnicity was not reported. Race categories exclude persons of Hispanic ethnicity. Nonresident aliens are shown separately because information about their race/ethnicity is not available. Detail may not sum to totals because of rounding. For more information on race/ethnicity, see *supplemental note 1*. For more information on the Integrated Postsecondary Education Data System (IPEDS), see *supplemental note 3*. For more information on the classification of postsecondary education institutions, see *supplemental note 8*.
SOURCE: U.S. Department of Education, National Center for Education Statistics, 2008–09 Integrated Postsecondary Data System (IPEDS), "Completion Survey," Fall 2009.

Section 4
Contexts of Elementary and Secondary Education

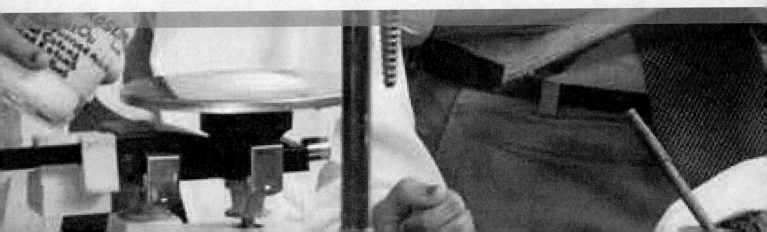

Section 4
Contexts of Elementary and Secondary Education

Contents

Introduction

The indicators in this section of *The Condition of Education* measure aspects of the context for learning in elementary and secondary schools. Such aspects include the content of learning; expectations for student performance; the climate for learning and other organizational aspects of schools; characteristics of teachers, principals, and staff; processes of instruction; mechanisms of choice in education; and financial resources. Indicators prepared for this year's volume appear on the following pages, and all indicators in this section, including indicators from previous years, appear on the NCES website (see the "List of Indicators on *The Condition of Education* Website" on page xxii for a full listing of indicators).

The first indicators in this section consider school characteristics and the climate for learning, which is shaped by different factors in the school environment. First, an indicator provides information on the characteristics of public schools. In addition, indicators found in this volume consider measures of the concentration of poverty in public schools and the pervasiveness of violence in public schools. Indicators on the website feature the concentration of racial and ethnic groups in public schools and the suspension and expulsion of students.

Other indicators in this section look at principals and teachers. Two indicators in this volume examine the characteristics of principals and teachers, while another indicator found on the website compares the extent and nature of teacher training that U.S. teachers receive in certain subject areas with the training received by teachers in foreign countries. In addition, there are indicators in this volume on principal and teacher turnover. Indicators on school staff and international teaching comparisons can be found on the Web.

In this section, there are indicators on the website that focus on the learning opportunities that are afforded to children, including student/teacher ratios in public schools. Other indicators on the website highlight parent and family involvement in education, participation in early literacy activities, and afterschool activities.

School choice provides parents with the opportunity to choose a school for their children other than their assigned public school. Indicators regarding school choice (found on the website) report on the parental choice of charter schools or private schools as an alternative to their child's assigned public school.

The final indicators in this section detail financial support for education. In this section of *The Condition of Education,* the primary focus is on describing the forms and amounts of financial support made available to education from public and private sources and the items on which funds are spent. In this volume of *The Condition of Education,* there are also indicators on variations in expenditures per student, trends in expenditures per student in elementary and secondary education by school poverty level, and international comparisons of education expenditures.

Indicators of contexts of elementary and secondary schooling from previous editions of *The Condition of Education* not included in this volume are available at http://nces.ed.gov/programs/coe.

Characteristics of Public Schools

In 2008–09, charter schools and schools with a magnet program each composed a higher percentage of all public schools than they did in 1998–99 (5 vs. 1 percent for charter schools and 3 vs. 1 percent for schools with a magnet program).

Regular public schools constituted 90 percent of all public schools in 2008–09, with alternative schools for students at risk of school failure (6 percent), special education schools (2 percent), and vocational schools (1 percent) making up the remainder (see table A-27-1). The distributions of public schools by school type differed by school level in 2008–09. Ninety-eight percent of elementary schools were regular schools, with other school types making up less than 2 percent of elementary schools. At the secondary level, 80 percent of schools were regular schools, 14 percent were alternative schools, 5 percent were vocational schools, and 1 percent were special education schools.

Charter schools are publicly funded schools that are typically governed by a group or organization under a legislative contract or charter with the state. They can be regular schools, alternative schools, special education schools, and vocational schools as well as Title I schools and schools with magnet programs (see indicator 3 for more information on charter schools). Some 5 percent of all public schools were charter schools in 2008–09, up from 1 percent in 1998–99.

The percentage of public schools with a magnet program was higher in 2008–09 than it was in 1998–99 (3 vs. 1 percent). A Title I school is designated under appropriate state and federal regulations as a high-poverty school that is eligible for participation in programs authorized by Title I of P.L. 107-110. In 2008–09, some 63 percent of public schools were Title I schools.

The distribution of public schools by school size differed by school level in 2008–09. Some 38 percent of secondary schools were small (enrollment of less than 300 students), as compared to 27 percent of elementary schools. In that same year, 26 percent of secondary schools were large (1,000 or more students), as compared to 4 percent of elementary schools.

The percentage of public schools where White students accounted for more than 50 percent of enrollment was lower in 2008–09 than in 1998–99 (63 vs. 72 percent). In contrast, the percentage of schools where Hispanic students accounted for more than 50 percent of enrollment was higher in 2008–09 than in 1998–99 (13 vs. 8 percent). In both years, the percentage of schools where Black students accounted for more than 50 percent of enrollment was approximately the same (11 percent).

In 2008–09, nineteen percent of public schools were high-poverty schools (i.e., schools where more than 75 percent of the students were eligible for the free or reduced-price lunch program). The distributions of public schools by poverty level differed by school level. In 2008–09, about 22 percent of elementary schools and 11 percent of secondary schools were high-poverty schools.

In 2008–09, the largest percentage of public schools were in rural areas (32 percent), followed by suburbs (28 percent), cities (26 percent), and towns (14 percent).

For more information: *Table A-27-1*

Glossary: *Combined school, Elementary school, Magnet school or program, Public school, Regular school, Secondary school, Title I school*

Technical Notes

Estimates are for public schools in the 50 states and the District of Columbia. The percentage distributions for school size and race/ethnicity exclude schools that did not report enrollment. High-poverty schools are defined as public schools where more than 75 percent of the students are eligible for the free or reduced-price lunch (FRPL) program, and low-poverty schools are defined as public schools where 25 percent or fewer students are eligible for

FRPL. Small schools are defined as public schools with enrollments of less than 300 students, and large schools are defined as public schools with enrollments of 1,000 or more students. For more information on locale, poverty, race/ethnicity, and region, see *supplemental note 1*. For more information on the Common Core of Data (CCD), see *supplemental note 3*.

Figure 27-1. Percentage distribution of public schools, by school level and enrollment size: School year 2008–09

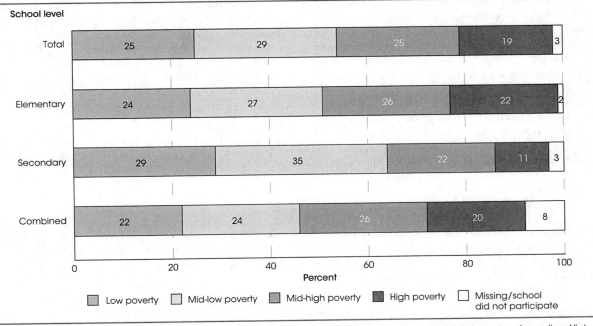

School level

	Less than 300 students	300–499 students	500–999 students	1,000 or more students
Total	31	28	32	9
Elementary	27	33	36	4
Secondary	38	15	22	26
Combined	66	14	15	5

NOTE: Estimates are for public schools reporting enrollment data in the 50 states and the District of Columbia. Detail may not sum to totals because of rounding. For more information on the Common Core of Data (CCD), see *supplemental note 3.*
SOURCE: U.S. Department of Education, National Center for Education Statistics, Common Core of Data (CCD), "Public Elementary/Secondary School Universe Survey," 2008–09 (version 1b).

Figure 27-2. Percentage distribution of public schools, by school level and school poverty level: School year 2008–09

School level

	Low poverty	Mid-low poverty	Mid-high poverty	High poverty	Missing/school did not participate
Total	25	29	25	19	3
Elementary	24	27	26	22	2
Secondary	29	35	22	11	3
Combined	22	24	26	20	8

NOTE: Estimates are for public schools in the 50 states and the District of Columbia. Detail may not sum to totals because of rounding. *High-poverty schools* are defined as public schools where more than 75 percent of the students are eligible for the free or reduced-price lunch (FRPL) program, and *mid-high poverty schools* are those schools where 51 to 75 percent of students are eligible. *Low-poverty schools* are defined as public schools where 25 percent or fewer students are eligible for FRPL, and *mid-low poverty schools* are those schools where 26 to 50 percent of students are eligible for FRPL. For more information on the free or reduced-price lunch program, see *supplemental note 1.* For more information on the Common Core of Data (CCD), see *supplemental note 3.*
SOURCE: U.S. Department of Education, National Center for Education Statistics, Common Core of Data (CCD), "Public Elementary/Secondary School Universe Survey," 2008–09 (version 1b).

In 2008–09, greater percentages of Black, Hispanic, and American Indian/Alaska Native students attended high-poverty elementary and secondary public schools than did White or Asian/Pacific Islander students.

The percentage of students eligible for the free or reduced-price lunch (FRPL) program provides a proxy measure for the concentration of low-income students within a school. In this indicator, schools are divided into categories by FRPL eligibility; high-poverty schools are defined as public schools where more than 75 percent of the students are eligible. In 2008–09, approximately 22 percent of elementary and 8 percent of secondary school students attended high-poverty public schools, up from the 20 percent of elementary and 6 percent of secondary school students who did so in 2007–08 (see table A-28-1 and U.S. Department of Education 2010, indicator 25).

In terms of the racial/ethnic distribution of students across schools of all poverty levels, in 2008–09, greater percentages of Hispanic, Black, and American Indian/Alaska Native students attended high-poverty public elementary and secondary schools than did White or Asian/Pacific Islander students. In addition, greater percentages of Asian/Pacific Islander students attended these schools than did White students. For example, at the elementary level, 45 percent of Hispanic, 44 percent of Black, and 31 percent of American Indian/Alaska Native students were enrolled in high-poverty schools, compared with 17 percent of Asian/Pacific Islander and 6 percent of White students. Smaller percentages of students of all racial/ethnic groups attended high-poverty schools at the secondary level than at the elementary level, but the relative patterns among the racial/ethnic groups were similar at both levels.

Examining the racial/ethnic distributions within schools of a given poverty type provides a more detailed snapshot of the extent to which students of various races/ethnicities are concentrated in certain schools.

While over half (54 percent) of public school students in 2008–09 were White, 14 percent of students attending high-poverty schools were White (see table A-28-2). Black and Hispanic students, in contrast, were overrepresented in high-poverty schools. Blacks made up 17 percent of students overall and 34 percent of students in high-poverty schools, and Hispanics made up 21 percent of students overall and 45 percent of students in high-poverty schools. Asians/Pacific Islanders made up 5 percent of the student population overall and 4 percent of the student population in high-poverty schools, and American Indians/Alaska Natives made up 1 percent of students in all schools and 2 percent of students in high-poverty schools.

The distribution of students in high-poverty schools also differed by the locale (city, suburban, town, and rural) of the schools. In 2008–09, the percentage of students in high-poverty schools who attended city schools was nearly twice as large as the percentage of all students who attended city schools (58 vs. 29 percent). On the other hand, 35 percent of all public school students attended schools in suburban areas, but only 23 percent of students in high-poverty schools attended schools in suburban areas. Students attending schools in towns and rural areas were also underrepresented among students attending high-poverty schools, comprising 12 and 24 percent, respectively, of students in all schools, compared with 9 and 11 percent, respectively, of students in high-poverty schools.

For more information: *Tables A-28-1 and A-28-2*
Glossary: *National School Lunch Program, Public school*

Technical Notes

Private school students are excluded from the analysis because large proportions of private schools do not participate in the FRPL program. Race categories exclude persons of Hispanic ethnicity. For more information on race/ethnicity, locale, and poverty, see *supplemental note 1*. For more information on the Common Core of Data (CCD), see *supplemental note 3*.

Figure 28-1. Percentage of public school students in high-poverty schools, by race/ethnicity and school level: School year 2008–09

Percent

Race/ethnicity

	Elementary	Secondary
Total[1]	22	8
White	6	2
Black	44	18
Hispanic	45	18
Asian/Pacific Islander	17	6
American Indian/Alaska Native	31	16

■ Elementary ■ Secondary

[1] Includes students whose racial/ethnic group was not reported.
NOTE: *High-poverty schools* are defined as public schools where more than 75 percent of the students are eligible for the free or reduced-price lunch (FRPL) program. Race categories exclude persons of Hispanic ethnicity. Persons with unknown race/ethnicity are not shown. For more information on race/ethnicity and poverty, see *supplemental note 1.* For more information on the Common Core of Data (CCD), see *supplemental note 3.*
SOURCE: U.S. Department of Education, National Center for Education Statistics, Common Core of Data (CCD), "Public Elementary/Secondary School Universe Survey," 2008–09.

Figure 28-2. Percentage distribution of the race/ethnicity of public school students, by locale and school poverty level: School year 2008–09

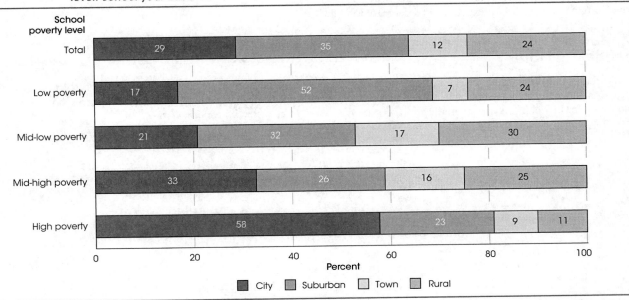

School poverty level	City	Suburban	Town	Rural
Total	29	35	12	24
Low poverty	17	52	7	24
Mid-low poverty	21	32	17	30
Mid-high poverty	33	26	16	25
High poverty	58	23	9	11

■ City ■ Suburban □ Town ■ Rural

NOTE: *High-poverty schools* are defined as public schools where more than 75 percent of the students are eligible for the free or reduced-price lunch (FRPL) program, and *mid-high poverty schools* are those schools where 51 to 75 percent of students are eligible. *Low-poverty schools* are defined as public schools where 25 percent or fewer students are eligible for FRPL, and *mid-low poverty schools* are those schools where 26 to 50 percent of students are eligible for FRPL. For more information on locale and poverty, see *supplemental note 1.* For more information on the Common Core of Data (CCD), see *supplemental note 3.* Detail may not sum to totals because of rounding.
SOURCE: U.S. Department of Education, National Center for Education Statistics, Common Core of Data (CCD), "Public Elementary/Secondary School Universe Survey," 2008–09.

In 2009, some 19 percent of 5- to 17-year-olds were in families living in poverty, compared with 15 percent in 2000 and 17 percent in 1990.

In 2009, approximately 19 percent of 5- to 17-year-old children in the United States were in families living in poverty (see table A-29-1). The region with the highest rate of poverty among school-age children in 2009 was the South (21 percent), followed by the West (18 percent), Midwest (18 percent), and the Northeast (16 percent).

At the state level, child poverty rates across the United States ranged from 10 to 32 percent in 2009. In the District of Columbia and Mississippi, 32 and 29 percent, respectively, of children were living in poverty in 2009. In contrast, New Hampshire and Maryland each had 10 percent of school-age children living in poverty. When compared to the U.S. national rate of child poverty in 2009, some 21 states had rates that were lower than the national average, 16 states and the District of Columbia had rates that were higher than the national average, and 13 states had rates that were not measurably different from the national average. Of the 17 jurisdictions (16 states and the District of Columbia) that had poverty rates above the national average, 14 were located in the South.

In general, child poverty rates across the United States decreased from 1990 to 2000. For the United States as a whole, 17 percent of school-age children in 1990 were in poverty, compared with 15 percent of children in 2000. From 1990 to 2000, the child poverty rate decreased in 38 states. Six states and the District of Columbia had increases in child poverty rates from 1990 to 2000. Both the Midwest and the South experienced a decrease in child

poverty rates over this time period (from 15 to 12 percent and 20 to 18 percent, respectively), while the Northeast and the West did not show a measurable change.

From 2000 to 2009, the percentage of school-age children living in poverty in the United States increased from 15 to 19 percent. The child poverty rate was higher in 2009 than in 2000 for 36 states and all regions. In spite of the general decrease in child poverty rates from 1990 to 2000, some 30 states and the District of Columbia had higher child poverty rates in 2009 than in 1990, while 17 states had child poverty rates that were not measurably different than they were in 1990. Three states, Louisiana, Mississippi, and West Virginia, had significant decreases in the percentages of children living in poverty from 1990 to 2009. The percentages of school-age children living in poverty were higher in 2009 than in 1990 for the West, Midwest, and Northeast, while the child poverty rates in 1990 and 2009 in the South were not measurably different.

From 2008 to 2009 the child poverty rate increased from 17 to 19 percent. All regions experienced increases in child poverty rates between 2008 and 2009, as did 18 states.

For more information: *Table A-29-1*

Technical Notes

Children in families include own children and all other children in the household who are related to the householder by birth, marriage, or adoption. For more

information on poverty and region, see *supplemental note 1*. For more information on the American Community Survey, see *supplemental note 3*.

Figure 29-1. Percentage of 5- to 17-year-olds in families living in poverty, by state: 2009

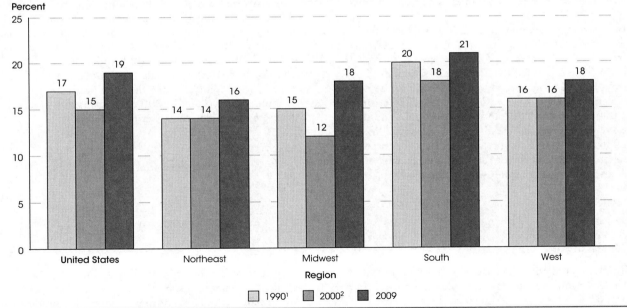

U.S. average = 18.6 percent

- [ ] Less than the U.S. average (21)
- [ ] Not significantly different from the U.S. average (13)
- [ ] More than the U.S. average (17)

NOTE: Children in families include own children and all other children in the household who are related to the householder by birth, marriage, or adoption. For more information on poverty and region, see *supplemental note 1*. For more information on the American Community Survey (ACS), see *supplemental note 3*.
SOURCE: U.S. Department of Commerce, Census Bureau, American Community Survey (ACS), 2009.

Figure 29-2. Percentage of 5- to 17-year-olds in families living in poverty, by region: 1990, 2000, and 2009

Percent

Region	1990[1]	2000[2]	2009
United States	17	15	19
Northeast	14	14	16
Midwest	15	12	18
South	20	18	21
West	16	16	18

[1] Based on 1989 incomes collected in the 1990 decennial census.
[2] Based on 1999 incomes collected in the 2000 decennial census.
NOTE: Children in families include own children and all other children in the household who are related to the householder by birth, marriage, or adoption. For more information on poverty and region, see *supplemental note 1*. For more information on the American Community Survey (ACS), see *supplemental note 3*.
SOURCE: U.S. Department of Commerce, Census Bureau, 1990 Summary Tape File 3 (STF 3), "Median Household Income in 1989" and "Poverty Status in 1989 by Family Type and Age," retrieved May 12, 2005, from http://factfinder.census.gov/servlet/DTGeoSearchByListServlet?ds_name=DEC_1990_STF3_&_lang=en&_ts=134048804959; Decennial Census, 1990, Minority Economic Profiles, unpublished data; Decennial Census, 2000, Summary Social, Economic, and Housing Characteristics; Census 2000 Summary File 4 (SF 4), "Poverty Status in 1999 of Related Children Under 18 Years by Family Type and Age," retrieved March 28, 2005, from http://factfinder.census.gov/servlet/DTGeoSearchByListServlet?ds_name=DEC_2000_SF4_U&_lang=en&_ts=134049420077; and American Community Survey, 2009.

Rates of School Crime

From 1992 to 2008, the rate of nonfatal incidents of crime against students ages 12–18 at school declined from 144 to 47 crimes per 1,000 students, and for students away from school the rate declined from 138 to 38 crimes per 1,000 students.

This indicator examines the rate of nonfatal incidents of crime against students ages 12–18, both at school and away from school. Nonfatal crime includes theft and all violent crime; violent crime includes serious violent crime (rape, sexual assault, robbery, and aggravated assault) and simple assault. The rate of nonfatal crime against students ages 12–18 declined between 1992 and 2008. This pattern held for the crime rate at school and away from school as well as in the following three subcategories: theft, violent crime, and serious violent crime. Specifically, from 1992 to 2008, the rate of nonfatal crime against students at school declined from 144 to 47 crimes per 1,000 students; the theft victimization rate, from 95 to 24 thefts per 1,000 students; the violent crime rate, from 48 to 24 crimes per 1,000 students; and the serious violent crime rate, from 10 to 4 crimes per 1,000 students (see table A-30-1). During the same time period, the total nonfatal crime rate against students away from school declined from 138 to 38 crimes per 1,000 students, the theft victimization rate declined from 68 to 19 thefts per 1,000 students, the rate of violent crime declined from 71 to 19 crimes per 1,000 students, and the serious violent crime rate declined from 32 to 8 crimes per 1,000 students.

In the more recent period from 2007 to 2008, the rate of total nonfatal crime against students at school decreased from 57 to 47 crimes per 1,000 students. During this period, the theft victimization rate at school declined from 31 to 24 thefts per 1,000 students, but the rate of violent crime did not measurably change (26 crimes per 1,000 students in 2007 and 24 in 2008). In addition, there was no measurable difference between 2007 and 2008 in the rate of total crime against students away from school; this was also true for rates of theft, violent crime, and serious violent crime away from school.

Nonfatal crime rates at school and away from school differed depending on the type of crime. From 1992 through 2008, the rate of serious violent crime against students was generally lower at school than away from school. For example, in 2008, the student victimization rate for serious violent crime was four crimes per 1,000 students at school, compared with eight per 1,000 students away from school. In contrast, the rate of theft against students at school was generally higher than the rate of theft away from school.

In 2008, the rate of nonfatal crime against students varied according to student characteristics. The rates of total nonfatal crime and violent crime were lower for female students than for male students both at school and away from school (see table A-30-2). For example, the violent victimization rate at school was 19 crimes per 1,000 female students, compared with 29 per 1,000 male students; away from school, the rate of violent crime was 12 crimes per 1,000 females, compared with 25 per 1,000 males. However, there was no difference between male and female students in the rates of theft against them; this was true for theft at school and away from school. At school, the rate of total nonfatal crime against Black students (68 crimes per 1,000 students) was higher than the rate for White students (44 per 1,000 students) and Hispanic students (47 per 1,000 students). In general, the violent victimization rate (at school and away from school) was higher for students from households with incomes of less than $15,000 than it was for students from households with higher income levels.

For more information: *Tables A-30-1 and A-30-2*

Technical Notes

Total nonfatal crime includes violent crime and theft. Violent crime includes serious violent crime and simple assault. Serious violent crime includes rape, sexual assault, robbery, and aggravated assault. Theft includes purse snatching, pickpocketing, all burglaries, attempted forcible entry, and all attempted and completed thefts except motor vehicle thefts. Theft does not include robbery in which threat or use of force is involved. "At school" includes inside the school building, on school property, or on the way to or from school. Detail may not sum to totals because of rounding and missing data on student characteristics. Race categories exclude persons of Hispanic ethnicity. For more information on race/ethnicity, see *supplemental note 1*. There were changes in the sample design and survey methodology in the 2006 National Crime Victimization Survey (NCVS) that affected survey estimates. Due to this redesign, 2006 data are not presented in this indicator. Data from 2007 onward are comparable to earlier years. For more information on NCVS, see *supplemental note 3*.

Figure 30-1. Rate of nonfatal incidents of crime against students ages 12–18 at school, by type of crime: Selected years, 1992–2008

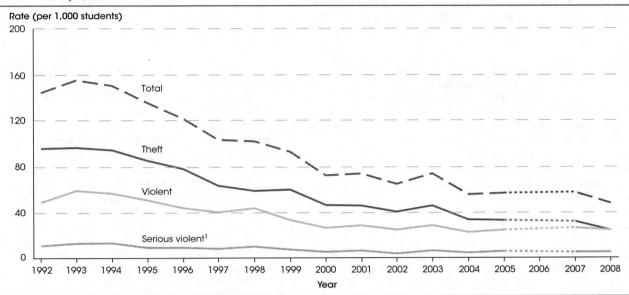

Rate (per 1,000 students)

[1] Serious violent crime is also included in violent crime.
NOTE: Total nonfatal crime includes violent crime and theft. Violent crime includes serious violent crime and simple assault. Serious violent crime includes rape, sexual assault, robbery, and aggravated assault. Theft includes purse snatching, pickpocketing, all burglaries, attempted forcible entry, and all attempted and completed thefts except motor vehicle thefts. Theft does not include robbery in which threat or use of force is involved. "At school" includes inside the school building, on school property, or on the way to or from school. Detail may not sum to totals because of rounding. There were changes in the sample design and survey methodology in the 2006 National Crime Victimization Survey (NCVS) that affected survey estimates. Due to this redesign, 2006 data are not presented. Data from 2007 onward are comparable to earlier years. For more information on NCVS, see *supplemental note 3*.
SOURCE: U.S. Department of Justice, Bureau of Justice Statistics, National Crime Victimization Survey (NCVS), 1992–2005 and 2007–2008.

Figure 30-2. Rate of nonfatal incidents of crime against students ages 12–18 at school and away from school, by type of crime and sex: 2008

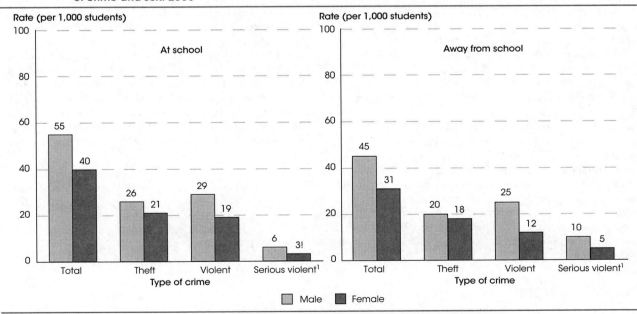

! Interpret data with caution. The standard error of the estimate is equal to 30 percent or more of the estimate's value.
[1] Serious violent crime is also included in violent crime.
NOTE: Total nonfatal crime includes violent crime and theft. Violent crime includes serious violent crime and simple assault. Serious violent crime includes rape, sexual assault, robbery, and aggravated assault. Theft includes purse snatching, pickpocketing, all burglaries, attempted forcible entry, and all attempted and completed thefts except motor vehicle thefts. Theft does not include robbery in which threat or use of force is involved. "At school" includes inside the school building, on school property, or on the way to or from school. Detail may not sum to totals because of rounding. For more information on the National Crime Victimization Survey, see *supplemental note 3*.
SOURCE: U.S. Department of Justice, Bureau of Justice Statistics, National Crime Victimization Survey (NCVS), 2008.

Characteristics of Full-Time Teachers

A larger percentage of full-time teachers held a postbaccalaureate degree in 2007–08 than in 1999–2000. Forty-nine percent of elementary school teachers and 54 percent of secondary school teachers held a postbaccalaureate degree in 2007–08, compared with 43 percent and 50 percent, respectively, in 1999–2000.

In the 2007–08 school year, there were 3.5 million full-time teachers, up from 3.1 million in 1999–2000. There were 2.1 million full-time elementary school teachers in 2007–08, including 1.9 million public school and 167,000 private school teachers (see table A-31-1). At the secondary level, there were 1.1 million full-time teachers, including 1.0 million public school and 61,000 private school teachers. The number of elementary and secondary full-time teachers in public schools increased from 1999–2000 to 2007–08; however, the number of private teachers in 1999–2000 was not measurably different from the number in 2007–08 at either level.

The majority of full-time teachers were women in 2007–08. At the elementary level, 84 percent of public school and 87 percent of private school teachers were female; these estimates were about the same as those in 1999–2000. At the secondary level, 59 percent of public school teachers were female, up from 55 percent in 1999–2000. Females represented 53 percent of private school secondary teachers in 2007–08, an estimate not measurably different from that in 1999–2000.

The racial/ethnic distribution of full-time teachers shifted slightly from 1999–2000 to 2007–08. The percentage of teachers who were Hispanic was higher in 2007–08 than in 1999–2000 (8 vs. 6 percent for elementary, and 7 vs. 5 percent for secondary). At the elementary level, there were no measurable differences from 1999–2000 to 2007–08 in the percentage of teachers who were White or in the percentage who were Black. At the secondary level, the percentage of teachers who were White was lower in 2007–08 (83 percent) than in 1999–2000 (86 percent).

A larger percentage of full-time teachers held a postbaccalaureate degree (master's degree, education specialist or professional diploma, first-professional degree, or doctoral degree) in 2007–08 than in 1999–2000. Forty-nine percent of elementary school teachers and 54 percent of secondary school teachers held a postbaccalaureate degree in 2007–08, compared with 43 percent and 50 percent, respectively, in 1999–2000. In 2007–08, a higher percentage of public elementary school teachers held such degrees than did private elementary school teachers (50 vs. 30 percent).

In general, full-time teachers in public elementary and secondary schools had fewer years of teaching experience in 2007–08 than in 1999–2000, while private elementary school teachers had more teaching experience in 2007–08 than in 1999–2000 (see table A-31-2). Public elementary school teachers averaged 13 years of teaching experience in 2007–08 and 15 years in 1999–2000. In addition, 27 percent of public elementary school teachers had 20 or more years of teaching experience in 2007–08, compared with 34 percent in 1999–2000. Public secondary school teachers had 14 years of teaching experience, on average, in 2007–08, and 15 years in 1999–2000; about 28 percent of these teachers had 20 or more years of teaching experience in 2007–08, compared with 37 percent in 1999–2000. In 2007–08, private elementary school teachers had 14 years of teaching experience, on average, while in 1999–2000 they had 13 years of experience. In addition, 28 percent of them had 20 or more years of experience in 2007–08, compared with 24 percent in 1999–2000. From 1999–2000 to 2007–08, there were no measurable changes in either of these experience measures for secondary private school teachers.

In 2007–08, about 89 percent of elementary and 87 percent of secondary public school teachers held a regular teaching certificate; an additional 4 percent of public school teachers at each level had satisfied all requirements except a probationary period. In comparison, in private schools, 57 percent of elementary and 55 percent of secondary teachers held a regular teaching certificate, with 3 percent of elementary and 2 percent of secondary teachers holding a probationary certification. In 2007–08, approximately 1 percent each of elementary and secondary public school teachers held no teaching certification in the state where they taught, compared with 35 percent of elementary and 41 percent of secondary private school teachers.

For more information: *Tables A-31-1 and A-31-2*
Glossary: *Combined school, Doctoral degree, Education specialist/professional diploma, Elementary school, First-professional degree, Master's degree, Private school, Public school, Secondary school*

Technical Notes

Race categories exclude persons of Hispanic ethnicity. For more information on race/ethnicity, see *supplemental note 1*. Regular certification includes regular or standard state certificates and advanced professional certificates (for both public and private school teachers) and full certificates granted by an accrediting or certifying body other than the state (for private school teachers only). Probationary certificates are for those who have satisfied all requirements except the completion of a probationary period. For more information on the Schools and Staffing Survey (SASS), see *supplemental note 3*.

Figure 31-1. Percentage distribution of full-time school teachers, by school level and highest degree earned: School years 1999–2000 and 2007–08

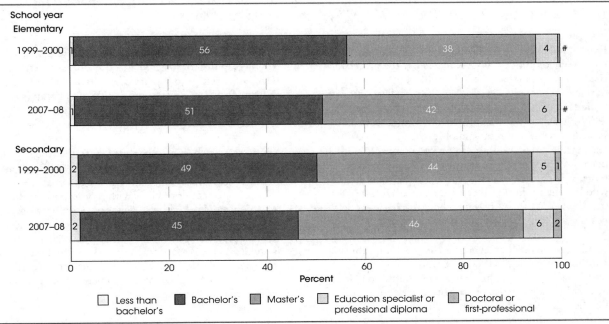

Rounds to zero.
NOTE: "Less than bachelor's" includes teachers with an associate's degree and those without a postsecondary degree; in 2007–08, it also includes those with vocational certificates. "Education specialist/professional diploma" includes teachers with a certificate of advanced graduate studies in. See glossary for the definition and a list of first-professional degrees. Detail may not sum to totals because of rounding.
SOURCE: U.S. Department of Education, National Center for Education Statistics, Schools and Staffing Survey (SASS), "Public School Teacher and Private School Teacher Data Files," 1999–2000 and 2007–08 and "Charter School Teacher Data File," 1999–2000.

Figure 31-2. Percentage distribution of full-time teachers, by sector and certification type: School year 2007–08

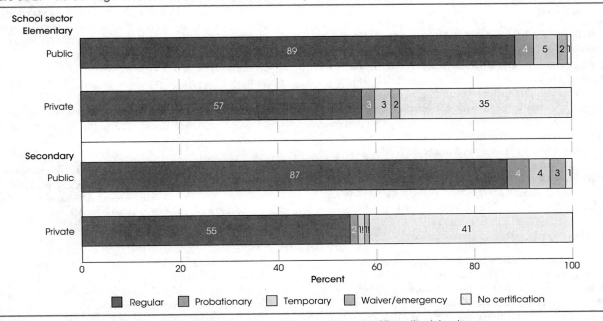

! Interpret with caution. The standard error of the estimate is equal to 30 percent or more of the estimate's value.
NOTE: The regular certification category includes regular or standard state certificates and advanced professional certificates (for both public and private school teachers) and full certificates granted by an accrediting or certifying body other than the state (for private school teachers only). Probationary certificates are for those who have satisfied all requirements except the completion of a probationary period. Temporary certificates are for those who require additional college coursework and/or student teaching. Waivers or emergency certificates are for those with insufficient teacher preparation who must complete a regular certification program in order to continue teaching. No certification indicates that the teacher did not hold any certification in the state where the teacher had taught. Detail may not sum to totals because of rounding.
SOURCE: U.S. Department of Education, National Center for Education Statistics, Schools and Staffing Survey (SASS), "Public School Teacher and Private School Teacher Data Files," 2007–08.

In 2008–09, some 8 percent of public school teachers left the teaching profession compared with 16 percent of private school teachers. Another 7 percent of all teachers moved from their 2007–08 school to a different school.

From school years 1988–89 to 2008–09, a lower percentage of public school teachers left the profession than private school teachers. In 1988–89, 6 percent of public school teachers, or 132,000 teachers, left the profession, while 13 percent of private school teachers, or 40,000 teachers, left the profession. Similarly, in 2008–09, some 8 percent of public school teachers, or 270,000 teachers, left the teaching profession, compared with 16 percent of private school teachers, or 77,000 teachers (see table A-32-1). The percentage of teachers in public schools who left the profession increased from 1988–89 to 2008–09. The percentage of private school teachers who left did not measurably change over the same time period.

In addition to teachers who left the teaching profession, another 7 percent of all teachers moved from their 2007–08 school to a different school (either outside or within their district or within or between sectors) for the following school year (see table A-32-2). Eight percent of public school teachers and 5 percent of private school teachers moved in 2008–09. The percentage of public school teachers who moved in 2008–09 was not measurably different from the percentage who moved in 1988–89 (8 percent in both years), but the percentage of private school teachers who moved was lower in 2008–09 (5 percent) than in 1988–89 (10 percent).

Overall, the percentage of teachers leaving the profession in 2008–09 was higher among teachers with the most teaching experience (20 years or more) and teachers with the least teaching experience (3 years or fewer), compared with teachers with 10 to 19 years of experience. There were no measurable differences in the percentages leaving teaching between teachers with the most or least amount of experience and teachers with 4 to 9 years of experience. Twelve percent of all teachers with 3 or fewer years of experience and 11 percent of teachers with 20 or more years of experience left the teaching profession in 2008–09, compared with 5 percent of teachers with 10 to 19 years of experience. The same pattern held true across experience levels for teachers in public schools who left teaching.

Among private school teachers, a higher percentage of teachers with 3 or fewer years of teaching experience (23 percent) or 4 to 9 years of experience (17 percent) left the teaching profession in 2008–09, compared with private school teachers with 20 or more years of experience (11 percent).

Similar to teachers who left the profession, the percentage of teachers moving schools in 2008–09 was higher among teachers with the least amount of teaching experience. Thirteen percent of teachers with 3 or fewer years of experience moved schools, compared with between 5 and 9 percent of teachers with higher levels of experience. However, in contrast to the pattern observed among leavers, a smaller percentage of teachers with the highest amount of experience moved schools (5 percent), compared with teachers with 3 or fewer years (13 percent) or 4 to 9 years of experiences (9 percent).

Higher percentages of the youngest teachers than of teachers of other ages moved between schools in 2008–09. Overall, 14 percent of teachers under age 30 moved schools, compared with 7 percent of teachers ages 30 to 39, some 6 percent of those ages 40 to 49, some 5 percent of those ages 50 to 59, and 2 percent of those age 60 or over. The same pattern held for the youngest teachers at both public and private schools. The percentage of teachers age 60 or over who moved schools was lowest compared to teachers of all other age groups who moved.

When looking at teacher movers by region, a higher percentage of teachers in the South and West moved schools in 2008–09 than did teachers in the Northeast. The percentage of teachers moving schools in the South was also higher than that of teachers in the Midwest.

For more information: *Tables A-32-1 through A-32-3*
Glossary: *Doctoral degree, Education specialist/professional diploma, First-professional degree, Master's degree, Private school, Public school*

Technical Notes

Stayers are those teachers who remained at the same school. *Movers* are those teachers who moved to a different school. *Leavers* are those teachers who left the profession. Teachers left the profession for a variety of reasons, including taking a job in a field other than elementary or secondary teaching, pursuing further education, leaving for family reasons, retiring, or other miscellaneous reasons. The denominator used to calculate the percentages in this indicator is the weighted number of School and Staffing Survey (SASS) teachers surveyed during the Teacher Follow-up Survey (TFS) year. SASS teachers who died or left the country are excluded. For more information on SASS and TFS, see *supplemental note 3*. Race categories exclude persons of Hispanic ethnicity. For more information on race/ethnicity and poverty, see *supplemental note 1*. Average base salary was calculated in 2009–10 school year constant dollars and adjusted using the Consumer Price Index (CPI). For more information on the CPI, see *supplemental note 10*.

Figure 32-1. Percentage of public and private school teacher leavers: Various school years 1988–89 through 2008–09

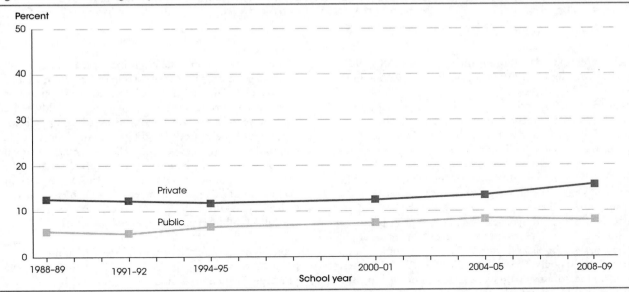

NOTE: *Leavers* are those teachers who left the profession. Denominator used to calculate the percent is the weighted number of SASS teachers surveyed during the Teacher Follow-up Survey (TFS) year; Schools and Staffing Survey (SASS) teachers who died or left the country are excluded. For more information on SASS, see *supplemental note 3*.
SOURCE: Keigher, A. (2010). *Teacher Attrition and Mobility: Results From the 2008–09 Teacher Follow-up Survey* (NCES 2010-353), data from U.S. Department of Education, National Center for Education Statistics, Teacher Follow-up Survey (TFS), "Current Teacher Data File" and "Former Teacher Data File," 1988–89, 1991–92, 1994–95, 2000–2001, 2004–05, and 2008–09.

Figure 32-2. Percentage of teacher leavers, by years as a teacher and school sector: School year 2008–09

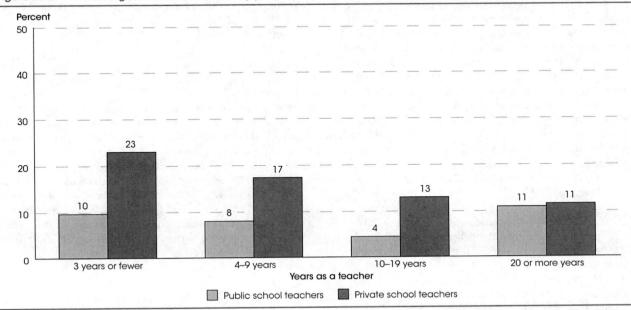

NOTE: *Leavers* are those teachers who left the profession. For more information on the Schools and Staffing Survey (SASS), see *supplemental note 3*.
SOURCE: U.S. Department of Education, National Center for Education Statistics, Teacher Follow-up Survey (TFS), "Current Teacher Data File" and "Former Teacher Data File," 2008–09.

Characteristics of School Principals

From 1999–2000 to 2007–08, the percentage of principals who were female increased from 52 to 59 percent at public elementary schools and from 22 to 29 percent at public secondary schools.

Schools employed 118,400 principals in the 2007–08 school year, up from 110,000 principals in 1999–2000 (see table A-33-1). In 2007–08 there were 78,500 elementary school principals, with 79 percent at public schools and 21 percent at private schools. At the secondary level there were 24,500 principals, with 88 percent at public schools and 12 percent at private schools.

From 1999–2000 to 2007–08, the percentage of public school principals who were female increased at both the elementary and secondary levels, although the gender distribution varied by level. The percentage of principals who were female increased from 52 to 59 percent at public elementary schools and from 22 to 29 percent at public secondary schools. From 1999–2000 to 2007–08, there was no measurable change at either school level in the percentage of private school principals who were female.

There were changes in the distribution of principals by age from 1999–2000 to 2007–08. At public elementary and secondary schools, the percentage of principals under age 40 increased, as did the percentage of principals age 55 and over, while the percentage of principals ages 45 to 49 and 50 to 54 decreased. For example, 10 percent of public elementary school principals were under age 40 in 1999–2000, compared with 19 percent in 2007–08. The percentage of public elementary school principals who were age 55 and over increased from 22 to 33 percent during this time. From 1999–2000 to 2007–08, the percentage of private school principals ages 55 and over also increased at the elementary and secondary levels, while the percentage of principals ages 45 to 49 and 50 to 54 decreased at both levels. However, unlike public school principals, the percentages of elementary and secondary principals at private schools who were under age 40 in 1999–2000 were not measurably different from the percentages in 2007–08.

The percentage of public school principals with 20 or more years of experience as a principal was lower in 2007–08 than in 1999–2000 at both elementary and secondary schools. During this period, the percentage of public secondary school principals with 20 or more years of experience as a principal decreased from 10 to 5 percent. About 36 percent of public secondary school principals had 3 or fewer years' experience as a principal in 2007–08, compared with 30 percent in 1999–2000.

Compared with public school principals, a higher percentage of private school principals had 20 or more years of experience as principals in 2007–08. For example, 19 percent of private elementary school principals had 20 or more years of experience as a principal, compared with 8 percent of their public school peers. However, when comparing teaching experience, the percentage of private school principals with few years of experience was higher than that of public school principals. In 2007–08, about 26 percent of private elementary school principals had 3 or fewer years of teaching experience, compared with 3 percent of public elementary school principals.

Educational attainment differed between public and private school principals. In 2007–08, about 32 percent of private elementary school principals and 18 percent of private secondary school principals had a bachelor's degree or less, while 1 percent each of public elementary and public secondary school teachers had a bachelor's degree or less. A higher percentage of public elementary school principals held a doctoral or first-professional degree (8 percent) than did private elementary school principals (5 percent); there was no measurable difference between public and private school secondary principals in the percentage of principals who held a doctoral or first-professional degree.

Principals' median annual salary, calculated in constant 2009–10 dollars, was generally higher in 2007–08 than in 1999–2000. From 1999–2000 to 2007–08, the median salary of public secondary school principals increased from $86,900 to $90,100. The salary of secondary school principals was higher than the salary of elementary school principals, and the salary of public school principals was higher than the salary of private school principals. In 2007–08, principals at public elementary schools had lower median salaries than those at public secondary schools ($86,000 vs. $90,100). Public school principals outearned their private school peers, whose salaries were $46,100 in private elementary schools and $67,600 in private secondary schools.

For more information: *Table A-33-1*
Glossary: *Elementary school, Private school, Public school, Secondary school*

Technical Notes

Median annual salary estimates were adjusted using the Consumer Price Index (CPI). For more information on the CPI, see *supplemental note 10.* For more information on the Schools and Staffing Survey (SASS), see *supplemental note 3.*

Figure 33-1. Percentage of male principals, by school type and level: School years 1999–2000 and 2007–08

NOTE: Principals from Bureau of Indian Education schools were excluded from the analysis. Detail may not sum to totals because of rounding. For more information on the Schools and Staffing Survey (SASS), see *supplemental note 3*.
SOURCE: U.S. Department of Education, National Center for Education Statistics, Schools and Staffing Survey (SASS), "Public School Principal and Private School Principal Data Files," 1999–2000 and 2007–08, and "Charter School Principal Data File," 1999–2000.

Figure 33-2. Percentage distribution of public school principals, by school level and years of experience as a principal: School years 1999–2000 and 2007–08

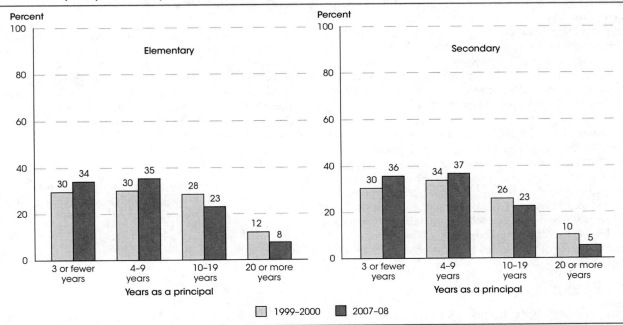

NOTE: Principals from Bureau of Indian Education schools were excluded from the analysis. Detail may not sum to totals because of rounding. For more information on the Schools and Staffing Survey (SASS), see *supplemental note 3*.
SOURCE: U.S. Department of Education, National Center for Education Statistics, Schools and Staffing Survey (SASS), "Public School Principal and Private School Principal Data Files," 1999–2000 and 2007–08, and "Charter School Principal Data File," 1999–2000.

Principal Turnover: Stayers, Leavers, and Movers

In 2008–09, some 12 percent of all principals left the profession. In addition to principals who left the profession, another 6 percent of all principals moved from their 2007–08 school to a different school for the 2008–09 school year.

In 2008–09, some 12 percent of all principals left the profession (see table A-34-1). The percentage of principals in public schools who left the profession ("leavers") was not significantly different from the percentage of those in private schools who left the profession (12 and 11 percent, respectively). Forty-five percent of public school principals who left after the 2007–08 school year were retired in 2008–09, and 22 percent of private school principal leavers were retired (see table A-34-3). In addition to principals who left the profession, another 6 percent of all principals moved from their 2007–08 school to a different school for the 2008–09 school year ("movers") (either outside or within their district or between or within sectors) (see table A-34-1). The percentage of principals who were movers was higher at public schools than at private schools (7 percent vs. 3 percent, respectively).

Generally, a higher percentage of principals over the age of 60 than principals in younger age groups left the profession (see table A-34-2). In 2008–09, some 20 percent of all principals age 60 or over left the profession, compared with 13 percent of principals ages 50 to 59, some 8 percent of principals ages 40 to 49, and 9 percent of principals ages 30 to 39. These differences in percentages of leavers by age group were seen among principals overall as well as among public school principals, while the only significant difference among the percentages of private school principals leaving the profession was that a higher percentage of principals under 30 (24 percent) left the profession than principals ages 40 to 49 (8 percent). Among principals over the age of 60, a higher percentage of public school than private school principals left the profession (27 vs. 10 percent, respectively).

Compared to principals who left the profession in 2008–09, principals who moved to other schools in 2008–09 followed an opposite pattern in terms of age. A lower percentage of all principals over the age of 60 than of principals in most of the younger age groups moved to other schools. Three percent of all principals age 60 or over moved to other schools in 2008–09, compared with 6 percent each of principals ages 50 to 59 or 40 to 49 and 9 percent of principals ages 30 to 39.

Overall, a higher percentage of principals with the highest level of experience at any school (10 or more years) left the profession in 2008–09, compared with principals with the lowest level of experience at any school (less than three years). Among public school principals, 18 percent who had been a principal at any school for 10 or more years left the profession, while 8 percent of those who had been a principal at any school for less than three years left the profession. The patterns by which public and private school principals left the profession differed in terms of levels of experience. A higher percentage of private school principals who had been a principal at any school for less than three years (16 percent) left the profession, compared with those who had been a principal at any school for 10 or more years (8 percent).

Of those public school leavers with the most experience as principals (10 or more years), a higher percentage were retired in 2008–09 (68 percent), compared with those who were working in a K–12 school, but not as a principal (8 percent) or were working in K–12 education, but not in a K–12 school (20 percent) (see table A-34-3). Among the most experienced private school principal leavers, a higher percentage were retired in 2008–09 (40 percent), compared with those were working in a job outside of K–12 education (22 percent).

While a higher percentage of more experienced principals left the profession than less experienced principals, a higher percentage of less experienced principals moved to other schools (see table A-34-2). A lower percentage of all principals with 10 or more years experience as a principal anywhere (5 percent) moved to other schools in 2008–09, compared with principals with less than three years of experience (8 percent).

For more information: *Tables A-34-1 through A-34-3*
Glossary: *Education specialist/professional diploma, Elementary school, Private school, Public school, Secondary school*

Technical Notes

Stayers are 2007–08 principals who were principals in the same schools in 2008–09. *Movers* are 2007–08 principals who were principals in different schools in 2008–09. *Leavers* are 2007–08 principals who were no longer principals in 2008–09. "Other" includes principals who had left their 2007–08 school, but for whom it was not possible to determine a mover or leaver status in 2008–09. For more information on the Schools and Staffing Survey (SASS) and the Principal Follow-up Survey (PFS), see *supplemental note 3*.

Figure 34-1.   Percentage distribution of principal stayers, movers, and leavers, by school sector: School year 2008–09

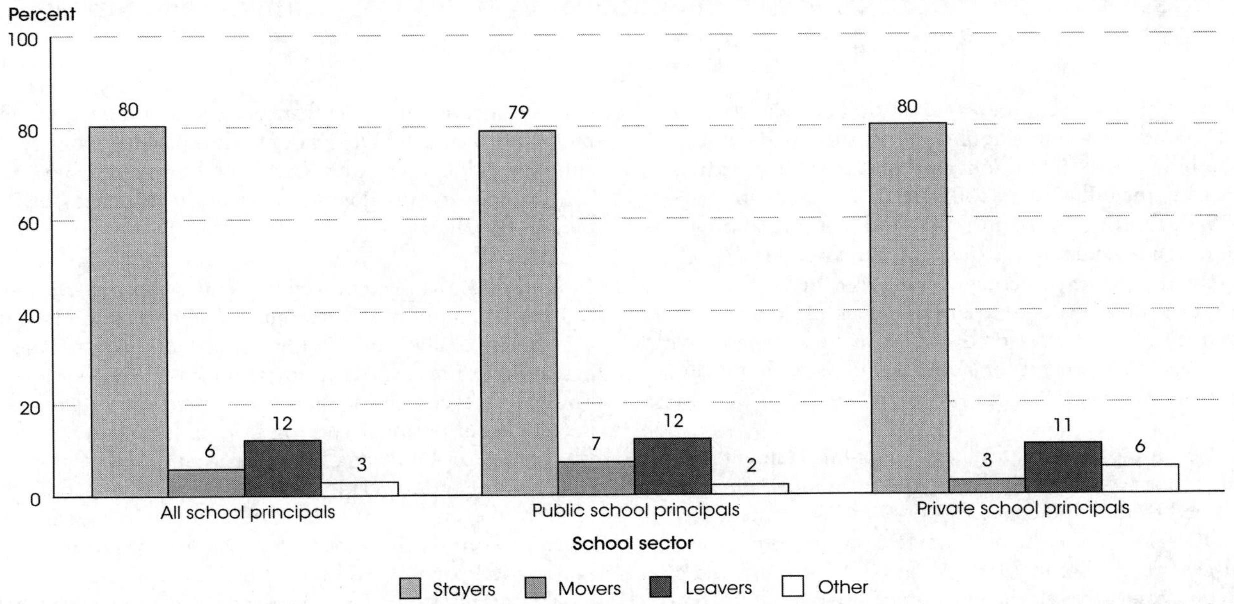

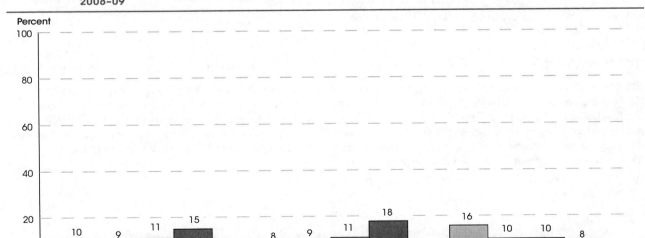

NOTE: *Stayers* are 2007–08 principals who were principals in the same schools in 2008–09. *Movers* are 2007–08 principals who were principals in different schools in 2008–09. *Leavers* are 2007–08 principals who were no longer principals in 2008–09. "Other" includes principals who had left their 2007–08 school, but for whom it was not possible to determine a mover or leaver status in 2008–09. For more information on the Schools and Staffing Survey (SASS), see *supplemental note 3*. Detail may not sum to totals due to rounding.
SOURCE: U.S. Department of Education, National Center for Education Statistics, Schools and Staffing Survey (SASS), "Public School Principal and Private School Principal Data Files," 2007–08; "Public School Principal Status and Private School Principal Status Data Files," 2008–09.

Figure 34-2.   Percentage of principal leavers, by school sector and years as a principal at any school: School year 2008–09

NOTE: *Stayers* are 2007–08 principals who were principals in the same schools in 2008–09. *Movers* are 2007–08 principals who were principals in different schools in 2008–09. *Leavers* are 2007–08 principals who were no longer principals in 2008–09. "Other" includes principals who had left their 2007–08 school, but for whom it was not possible to determine a mover or leaver status in 2008–09. For more information on the Schools and Staffing Survey (SASS), see *supplemental note 3*.
SOURCE: U.S. Department of Education, National Center for Education Statistics, Schools and Staffing Survey (SASS), "Public School Principal and Private School Principal Data Files," 2007–08; "Public School Principal Status and Private School Principal Status Data Files," 2008–09.

Public School Revenue Sources

From 1989-90 through 2007-08, total elementary and secondary public school revenues increased from $356 billion to $599 billion, a 68 percent increase after adjusting for inflation.

From 1989–90 through 2007–08, total elementary and secondary public school revenues increased from $356 billion to $599 billion, a 68 percent increase after adjusting for inflation to 2009–10 dollars (see table A-35-1). During this period, the total amount coming from each revenue source (federal, state, and local) increased, but the percentage increases differed by revenue source. Federal revenues, the smallest of the three revenue sources, increased by 125 percent, compared with increases of 73 percent for state revenues and 56 percent for local revenues.

The percentage of total revenues for public elementary and secondary education that came from local sources declined from 47 percent in 1989–90 to 44 percent in 2007–08. While the percentage coming from state sources was similar in 1989–90 and 2007–08 (47 and 48 percent, respectively), the percentage fluctuated during this period: it was lowest (45 percent) in 1993–94 and highest (50 percent) in 2000–01. The percentage of total revenues from federal sources increased from 6 to 9 percent from 1989–90 through 2004–05, and in 2007–08 it was 8 percent.

In 2007–08, there were significant variations across the states in the percentage of public school revenues coming from each revenue source. In 25 states, the majority of

education revenues came from state governments, while in 15 states and the District of Columbia the majority came from local revenues. In 10 states, no single revenue source made up a majority of education revenues (see table A-35-2).

In 2007–08, the percentage of revenues coming from state sources was highest in Vermont (86 percent) and Hawaii (85 percent). (Hawaii has only one school district.) The percentage of revenues coming from state sources was lowest in Nevada and Illinois (31 percent each). The percentage of revenues coming from federal sources was highest in Louisiana (17 percent) and Mississippi (16 percent) and lowest in New Jersey and Connecticut (4 percent each). Among the states, the percentage of revenues coming from local sources was highest in Nevada (63 percent) and lowest in Hawaii (3 percent) and Vermont (8 percent). The percentage of revenues from property taxes also differed by state, ranging from a high of 54 percent in Connecticut to lows of 0 or nearly 0 percent in Hawaii and Vermont.

For more information: *Tables A-35-1 and A-35-2*
Glossary: *Consumer Price Index (CPI), Elementary school, Secondary school, Property tax, Public school, Revenues*

Technical Notes

Revenues have been adjusted for the effects of inflation using the Consumer Price Index (CPI) and are in constant 2009–10 dollars. For more information about the CPI, see *supplemental note 10*. Other local government revenues includes revenues from sources such as local nonproperty taxes and investments, as well as revenues from student

activities, textbook sales, transportation and tuition fees, and food services. For more information about revenues for public elementary and secondary schools, see *supplemental note 10*. For more information about the Common Core of Data, see *supplemental note 3*.

Figure 35-1. Total revenues for public elementary and secondary schools, by revenue source: School years 1989–90 through 2007–08

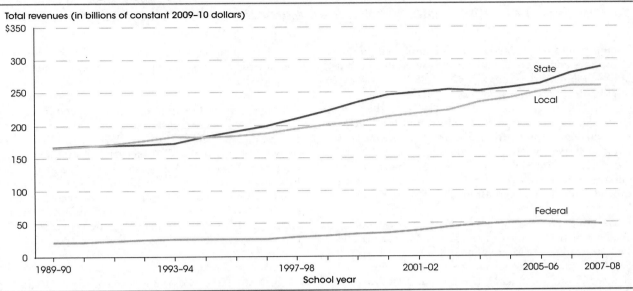

Total revenues (in billions of constant 2009–10 dollars)

NOTE: Revenues are in constant 2009–10 dollars, adjusted using the Consumer Price Index (CPI). For more information about the CPI and revenues for public elementary and secondary schools, see *supplemental note 10.* For more information about the Common Core of Data, see *supplemental note 3.*
SOURCE: U.S. Department of Education, National Center for Education Statistics, Common Core of Data (CCD), "National Public Education Financial Survey," 1989–90 through 2007–08.

Figure 35-2. State revenues for public elementary and secondary schools as a percentage of total school revenues, by state: School year 2007–08

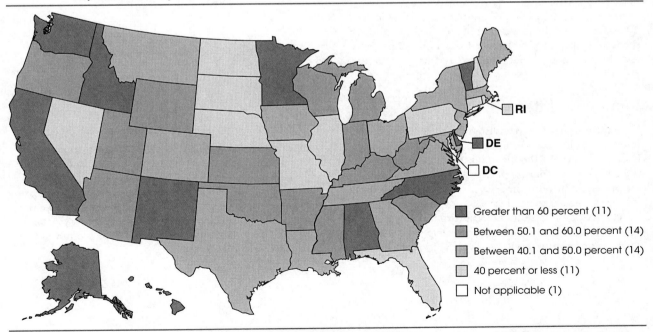

Greater than 60 percent (11)

Between 50.1 and 60.0 percent (14)

Between 40.1 and 50.0 percent (14)

40 percent or less (11)

Not applicable (1)

NOTE: Both the District of Columbia and Hawaii have only one school district each; therefore, neither is comparable to the other states. For more information about revenues for public elementary and secondary schools, see *supplemental note 10.* For more information about the Common Core of Data, see *supplemental note 3.*
SOURCE: U.S. Department of Education, National Center for Education Statistics, Common Core of Data (CCD), "National Public Education Financial Survey," 2007–08.

Public School Expenditures

Total expenditures per student in public elementary and secondary schools rose 39 percent in constant dollars from 1989–90 through 2007–08, with interest on school debt increasing faster than current expenditures or capital outlay.

Total expenditures per student in fall enrollment in public elementary and secondary schools measured in constant 2009–10 dollars rose from $8,832 in 1989–90 to $12,236 in 2007–08, a 39 percent increase (see table A-36-1). Most of this increase occurred after 1998–99. The various components of total expenditures increased at different rates during this time period. Spending on interest on school debt per student increased at the highest rate at 105 percent (from $159 to $326), followed by capital outlay at 83 percent (from $749 to $1,368) and current expenditures at 33 percent (from $7,925 to $10,542).

In the 2007–08 school year, payments of salaries and employee benefits for instructional and noninstructional staff, after adjusting for inflation, together composed $8,464 of current expenditures per student in public elementary and secondary schools. From 1989–90 through 2007–08, the amount of current expenditures per student spent on salaries and employee benefits together increased by 30 percent, with salaries alone increasing 22 percent and employee benefits alone increasing 62 percent. During this period, the amount of current expenditures spent on purchased services increased 57 percent. As a result of these different rates of increases, salaries as a share of current expenditures decreased from 66 to 60 percent between 1989–90 and 2007–08, while the percentage of current expenditures spent on employee benefits rose from 17 to 20 percent, and the percentage spent on purchased services increased

from 8 to 10 percent. The percentage spent on tuition and other items remained around 2 percent throughout the period.

Among the major functions of current expenditures, spending on student and staff support increased at the highest rate (62 percent) between 1989–90 and 2007–08, followed by instruction (34 percent) and transportation (32 percent) (see table A-36-2). Spending also increased by a smaller percentage on three other major functions of current expenditures: operation and maintenance (20 percent), food services (17 percent), and administration (16 percent). Of the seven major functions of current expenditures, only spending on enterprise operations declined (32 percent).

In the 2007–08 school year, 61 percent of the $10,542 spent on current expenditures in public elementary and secondary schools went toward instruction expenditures such as salaries and benefits of teachers (see table A-36-2). About 14 percent went toward student and staff support; 10 percent, operation and maintenance; 8 percent, administration; 4 percent each, transportation and food services; and less than 1 percent, enterprise operations.

For more information: *Tables A-36-1 and A-36-2*
Glossary: *Expenditures, Public school*

Technical Notes

Expenditures have been adjusted for the effects of inflation using the Consumer Price Index (CPI) and are in constant 2009–10 dollars. For more information about the CPI, see *supplemental note 10*. Current expenditures are presented by both the service or commodity bought (object) as well as the activity that is supported by the service or commodity bought (function). Total expenditures exclude "Other current expenditures" such as community services, private school programs,

adult education, and other programs not allocable to expenditures per student at public schools. Enterprise operations include expenditures for operations funded by sales of products or services, along with amounts for direct program support made available by state education agencies for local school districts. For more information about the classifications of expenditures, see *supplemental note 10*. For more information about the Common Core of Data, see *supplemental note 3*.

Figure 36-1. Percentage change in inflation-adjusted total expenditures per student in fall enrollment in public elementary and secondary schools, by expenditure type and objects of current expenditures: School years 1989–90 to 2007–08

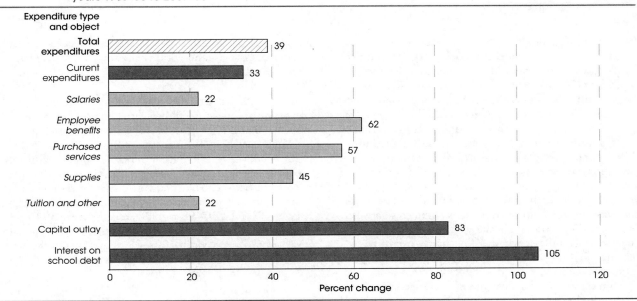

NOTE: "Current expenditures," "Capital outlay," and "Interest on school debt" are subcategories of "Total expenditures"; "Salaries," "Employee benefits," "Purchased services," "Supplies," and "Tuition and other" are subcategories of "Current expenditures." Expenditures have been adjusted for the effects of inflation using the Consumer Price Index (CPI) and are in 2009–10 constant dollars. For more information about the CPI and classifications of expenditures, see *supplemental note 10.* For more information about the Common Core of Data (CCD), see *supplemental note 3.*
SOURCE: U.S. Department of Education, National Center for Education Statistics, Common Core of Data (CCD), "National Public Education Financial Survey," 1989–90 and 2007–08.

Figure 36-2. Current expenditures per student in fall enrollment in public elementary and secondary schools, by expenditure object: School years 1989–90 through 2007–08
[In constant 2009–10 dollars]

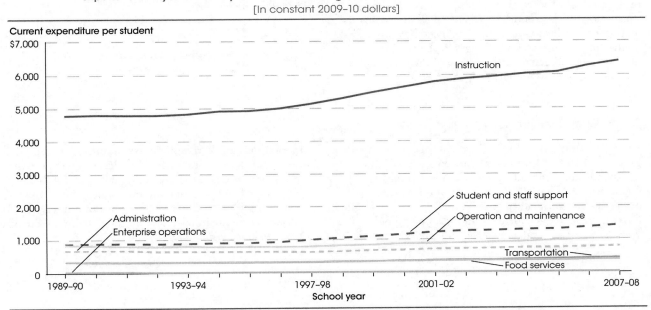

NOTE: Expenditures have been adjusted for the effects of inflation using the Consumer Price Index (CPI) and are in constant 2009–10 dollars. For more information about the CPI, see *supplemental note 10.* For more information about classifications of expenditures, see *supplemental note 10.* For more information about the Common Core of Data (CCD), see *supplemental note 3.*
SOURCE: U.S. Department of Education, National Center for Education Statistics, Common Core of Data (CCD), "National Public Education Financial Survey," 1989–90 through 2007–08.

Variations in Instruction Expenditures

Total variation in instruction expenditures per student has increased among public school districts since 1997–98, primarily due to an increase in the variation between states.

A number of methods can be used to measure the variation in the amount that school districts spend per student on instruction. This indicator uses the *Theil coefficient* to measure the variation in the instruction expenditures per student in unified public school districts for prekindergarten through grade 12. The *Theil coefficient* provides a national measure of differences in instruction expenditures per student that can be decomposed into separate components to measure school district-level variations between and within states. The between-state and within-state components indicate whether the national variation in instruction expenditures per student is primarily due to differences in expenditures between states or within states. Similarly, the trends in the two components indicate whether the change over time in the national variation of instruction expenditures per student is primarily due to changes between states or within states. The *Theil coefficient* can range from zero, indicating no variation, to a maximum possible value of 1.0. The value of the *Theil coefficient* remains unchanged if expenditures in all districts are increased by the same percentage; therefore it was not necessary to adjust instruction expenditures for inflation at the national level.

The variation in instruction expenditures per student over time may reflect differences across school districts in the amount of services or goods purchased, such as the number of classroom teachers hired. These changes may, in part, reflect various state finance litigation, school finance reform efforts, and changes in the composition of student enrollment. Further, some of the variation in expenditures per pupil may be due to cost differences across states and districts within states. Changes in cost differences across and within states may also affect the changes in the variation over time.

Across U.S. districts, the total variation in instruction expenditures per student decreased between school years 1989–90 and 1997–98 and then increased between school years 1997–98 and 2007–08 (see table A-37-1). In 2007–08, the total variation in instruction expenditures per student was greater than it was in the early 1990s. Both the between-state and within-state variations in instruction expenditures per student decreased between 1989–90 and 1997–98 and increased between 1997–98 and 2007–08. Like the total variation, the between-state variation was greater in 2007–08 than it was in the early 1990s. The within-state variation was smaller in 2007–08 than it was in the early 1990s.

Between 1989–90 and 2007–08, differences between states accounted for a greater proportion of the variation in instruction expenditures per student among public school districts than did differences within states. The percentage of the total variation due to between-state differences increased from 72 percent in 1989–90 to 78 percent in 2007–08, while the percentage of the total variation due to within-state differences decreased from 28 to 22 percent.

For more information: *Table A-37-1*
Glossary: *Expenditures, Public school*

Technical Notes

For more information on classifications of expenditures for elementary and secondary education, the variation in expenditures per student, and the *Theil coefficient,* see *supplemental note 10.* This indicator only includes unified public elementary and secondary districts. Unified districts serve both elementary and secondary grades. The *Theil coefficient* was calculated for unified districts only in order to limit any variations in expenditures per pupil due to the grade levels of the school districts or due to districts serving only students in special programs. In 2007–08, approximately 92 percent of all public elementary and secondary school students were enrolled in unified school districts. For more information on the Common Core of Data, see *supplemental note 3.*

Figure 37-1. Variation in instruction expenditures per student in unified public elementary and secondary school districts, by source of variation: School years 1989–90 through 2007–08

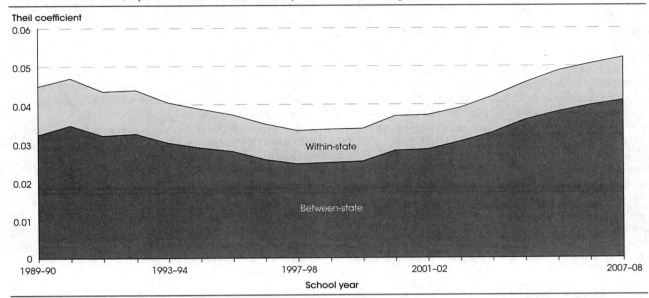

Theil coefficient

NOTE: The *Theil coefficient* measures variation for groups within a set (i.e., states within the country) and indicates relative variation and any differences that may exist among them. It can be decomposed into components measuring between-state and within-state variation in expenditures per student. It has a minimum value of zero, and increasing values indicate increases in the variation, with a maximum possible value of 1.0. The value of the *Theil coefficient* remains unchanged if expenditures in all districts are increased by the same percentage; therefore it was not necessary to adjust instruction expenditures for inflation at the national level. For more information on the variation in expenditures per student and the *Theil coefficient*, see *supplemental note 10.* For more information on the Common Core of Data (CCD), see *supplemental note 3.*
SOURCE: U.S. Department of Education, National Center for Education Statistics (NCES), Common Core of Data (CCD), "NCES Longitudinal School District Fiscal-Nonfiscal (FNF) File, Fiscal Years 1990 through 2002" and "School District Finance Survey (Form F-33)," 2002–03 through 2007–08.

Figure 37-2. Percentage distribution of source of variation in instruction expenditures per student in unified public elementary and secondary school districts: Various school years, 1989–90 through 2007–08

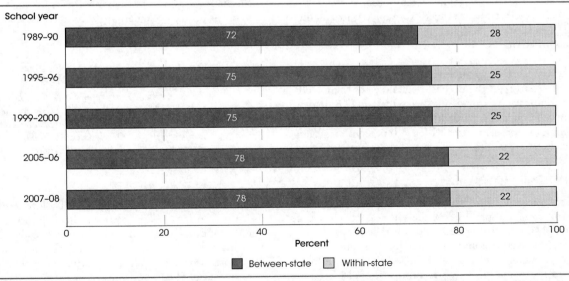

NOTE: Detail may not sum to totals because of rounding. The *Theil coefficient* measures variation for groups within a set (i.e., states within the country) and indicates relative variation and any differences that may exist among them. It can be decomposed into components measuring between-state and within-state variation in expenditures per student. It has a minimum value of zero, and increasing values indicate increases in the variation, with a maximum possible value of 1.0. The value of the *Theil coefficient* remains unchanged if expenditures in all districts are increased by the same percentage; therefore it was not necessary to adjust instruction expenditures for inflation at the national level. For more information on the variation in expenditures per student and the *Theil coefficient*, see *supplemental note 10.* For more information on the Common Core of Data (CCD), see *supplemental note 3.*
SOURCE: U.S. Department of Education, National Center for Education Statistics (NCES), Common Core of Data (CCD), "NCES Longitudinal School District Fiscal-Nonfiscal (FNF) File, Fiscal Years 1990 through 2002" and "School District Finance Survey (Form F-33)," 2003–04, 2005–06 and 2007–08.

In 2007, the United States spent $10,768 per student on elementary and secondary education, which was 45 percent higher than the OECD average of $7,401. At the postsecondary level, U.S. expenditures per student were $27,010, more than twice as high as the OECD average of $12,471.

This indicator uses material from the Organization for Economic Co-operation and Development (OECD) report *Education at a Glance* to compare countries' expenditures on education using *expenditures per student from both public and private sources* and *total education expenditures as a percentage of gross domestic product (GDP)*. The latter measure allows a comparison of countries' expenditures relative to their ability to finance education. Private sources of expenditures include payments from households for school-based expenses such as tuition, transportation fees, book rentals, or food services, as well as private funds raised by institutions.

In 2007, expenditures per student for the United States were $10,768 at the combined elementary and secondary level, which was 45 percent higher than the average of $7,401 for the OECD member countries reporting data (see table A-38-1). The expenditure per student measure is based on full-time-equivalent (FTE) student enrollment rather than headcounts. At the postsecondary level, U.S. expenditures per student were $27,010, which was more than twice as high as the OECD average of $12,471. Expenditures per student varied widely across the OECD countries: at the combined elementary and secondary level, expenditures ranged from $2,165 in Mexico and $2,245 in Chile to $15,579 in Luxembourg; at the postsecondary level, they ranged from $5,576 in Poland to $20,278 in Canada, $20,883 in Switzerland, and $27,010 in the United States.

Among the OECD countries reporting data in 2007, the countries that spent the highest percentage of their GDP on total education expenditures were Iceland (7.8 percent), the United States (7.6 percent), Israel (7.4 percent), Denmark (7.1 percent), and Korea (7.0 percent). Looking at education expenditures by level, the percentage of

its GDP (4.0 percent) that the United States spent on elementary and secondary education was higher than the average percentage by all OECD countries reporting data (3.6 percent). Compared with the percentage of its GDP that the United States spent on elementary and secondary education, 6 countries spent a higher percentage, 20 countries spent a lower percentage, and 3 countries spent the same percentage. Among OECD countries, Iceland spent the highest percentage (5.1 percent) of its GDP on elementary and secondary education. At the postsecondary level, the United States spent 3.1 percent of its GDP on education, which was higher than the average percentage spent by OECD countries (1.5 percent) and higher than the percentage spent by any other OECD country reporting data.

A country's wealth (defined as GDP per capita) is positively associated with expenditures per student on education at the combined elementary/secondary level and at the postsecondary level. For example, the education expenditures per student (both elementary/secondary and postsecondary) for each of the 10 OECD countries with the highest GDP per capita in 2007 were higher than the OECD average expenditures per student. The expenditures per student for the 10 OECD countries with the lowest GDP per capita were below the OECD average at both the elementary/secondary level and at the postsecondary level.

For more information: *Table A-38-1*

Glossary: *Elementary/secondary school, Expenditures per student, Full-time equivalent (FTE) enrollment, Gross Domestic Product (GDP), Organization for Economic Co-operation and Development (OECD), Postsecondary education, Purchasing Power Parity (PPP) indices*

Technical Notes

Education expenditures are from public revenue sources (governments) and private revenue sources. Private sources include payments from households for school-based expenses such as tuition, transportation fees, book rentals, or food services, as well as funds raised by institutions through endowments or returns on investments. Data for private school expenditures at the elementary and secondary levels are estimated for some countries, including the United States. Per student expenditures are based on public and private FTE enrollment figures and on current expenditures and capital outlays from both public and private sources, where data are available. Purchasing power parity (PPP) indices are used to convert

other currencies to U.S. dollars (i.e., absolute terms). Within-country consumer price indices are used to adjust the PPP indices to account for inflation because the fiscal year has a different starting date in different countries. For more information on classification of expenditures for international comparisons, see *supplemental note 10.* Luxembourg data are excluded from the graphs because of anomalies with respect to their GDP per capita data (large revenues from international finance institutions distort the wealth of the population). The OECD average for GDP per capita for each graph is based on the number of countries with data available (31 for figure 38-1 and 30 for figure 38-2).

Figure 38-1. **Annual expenditures per student for elementary and secondary education in selected OECD countries, by GDP per capita: 2007**

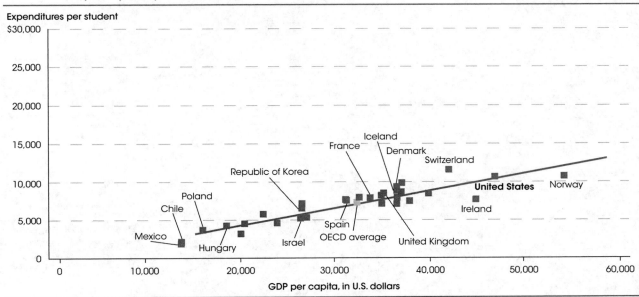

Expenditures per student

— Linear relationship between spending and country wealth for 31 OECD countries reporting data (elementary/secondary): $r^2 = .84$; slope = .23; intercept = -207.
NOTE: Luxembourg data are excluded because of anomalies with respect to their Gross Domestic Product (GDP) per capita data. (Large revenues from international finance institutions distort the wealth of the population.) For more information on the International Standard Classification of Education (ISCED), see *supplemental note 11.*
SOURCE: Organization for Economic Co-operation and Development (OECD), Center for Educational Research and Innovation. (2010). *Education at a Glance, 2010: OECD Indicators,* tables B1.2 and X2.1.

Figure 38-2. **Annual expenditures per student for postsecondary education in selected OECD countries, by GDP per capita: 2007**

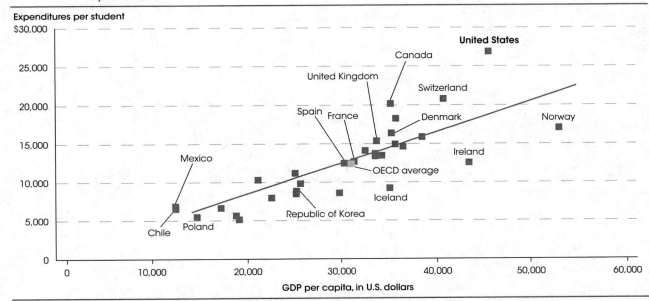

Expenditures per student

— Linear relationship between spending and country wealth for 31 OECD countries reporting data (postsecondary): $r^2 = .67$; slope = .44; intercept = -1,263.
NOTE: Luxembourg data are excluded because they do not report data for postsecondary institutions. For more information on the International Standard Classification of Education (ISCED), see *supplemental note 11.*
SOURCE: Organization for Economic Co-operation and Development (OECD), Center for Educational Research and Innovation. (2010). *Education at a Glance, 2010: OECD Indicators,* tables B1.2 and X2.1.

Section 5
Contexts of Postsecondary Education

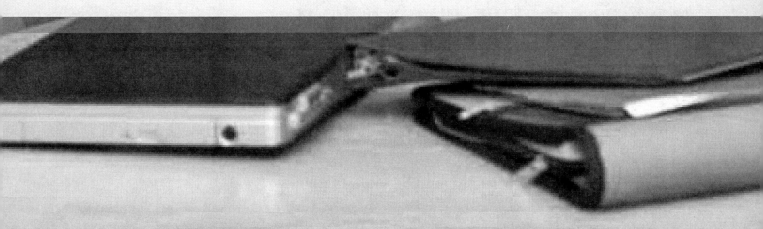

Section 5
Contexts of Postsecondary Education

Contents

Introduction

The indicators in this section of *The Condition of Education* examine features of postsecondary education, many of which parallel those presented in the previous section on elementary and secondary education. Indicators prepared for this year's volume appear on the following pages, and all indicators in this section, including those from previous years, appear on the NCES website (see the "List of Indicators on *The Condition of Education* Website" on page xxii for a full listing of indicators).

Postsecondary education is characterized by diversity both in institutional level and control and in the characteristics of students. Postsecondary institutions vary by the level of degrees awarded, control (public or private), and whether they are operated on a not-for-profit or for-profit basis. Beyond these basic differences, postsecondary institutions have distinctly different missions and provide students with a wide range of learning environments. For example, some institutions are research universities with graduate programs, while others focus on undergraduate education; some have a religious affiliation, while others do not; and some have selective entrance policies, while others have more open admissions.

The first indicator in this section examines postsecondary enrollment by institution level and control. Indicators on the website focus on the racial and ethnic concentration in postsecondary institutions, the number and characteristics of U.S. students who study in foreign countries, and international students who study in U.S. postsecondary institutions.

Indicators in this volume highlight data on degree completion, showing trends in the fields of study that undergraduate and graduate students receive their degrees in; compare the distribution of degrees awarded by institutional control; and examine the percentage of postsecondary student participating in distance education courses.

Faculty members are another defining feature of postsecondary institutions: they teach students, conduct research, and serve their institutions and communities. An indicator in this volume highlights trends in faculty salaries and benefits at different postsecondary levels and across institutional control.

Finally, *The Condition of Education* examines financial support for postsecondary education. Indicators in this volume include the number and characteristics of college students who are employed and an examination of federal grants and loans to undergraduate students. Other indicators provide measures of the price of attending a postsecondary institution, as well as student loan amounts and default rates by institution level and control. The last indicator in this volume examines the levels and sources of postsecondary revenues and expenses. Indicators on the website look at the institutional aid available to students and public funding for postsecondary institutions.

Indicators of the contexts of postsecondary education from previous editions of *The Condition of Education* not included in this volume are available at http://nces.ed.gov/programs/coe.

Characteristics of Undergraduate Institutions

In fall 2009, some 11 percent of all full-time undergraduate students attended private for-profit institutions. About 38 percent of full-time students age 35 and over attended private for-profit institutions, compared with 5 percent of full-time students under the age of 25.

Of the 18 million undergraduate students at degree-granting institutions in the United States in fall 2009, some 76 percent attended public institutions, 15 percent attended private not-for-profit institutions, and 9 percent attended private for-profit institutions (see table A-39-1). Enrollment patterns by institution control varied by race/ethnicity. For example, 17 percent of Black undergraduate students attended private for-profit institutions in fall 2009, compared with 5 percent of Asian/Pacific Islander students. Fifty-two percent of Hispanic undergraduate students and 45 percent of American Indian/Alaska Native undergraduate students attended public 2-year institutions, compared with 38 percent of White students, 40 percent each of Black students, and 42 percent of Asian/Pacific Islander students.

Among undergraduate students who were enrolled full time in fall 2009, some 11 percent attended private for-profit institutions in fall 2009. About 38 percent of full-time students age 35 and over attended private for-profit institutions, compared with 5 percent of full-time students under the age of 25. For part-time undergraduate students under the age of 25, more than two-thirds (70 percent) attended public 2-year institutions in fall 2009.

Some 77 percent of full-time students and 46 percent of part-time students who entered 4-year institutions in 2008 returned the following year to continue their studies; this percentage is the retention rate (see table A-39-2). At 2-year institutions, the retention rates for

those who entered school in 2008 were 61 percent for full-time students and 40 percent for part-time students. Among 4-year institutions, retention rates varied based on the percentage of applicants who were accepted for admission. For 4-year institutions with open admissions policies, 57 percent of full-time students and 46 percent of part-time students who enrolled in fall 2008 returned the following year. Four-year institutions that accepted less than a fourth of applicants had retention rates of 95 percent for full-time students and 60 percent for part-time students.

At 4-year public institutions with open admissions policies, 31 percent of the students who began as first-year, full-time undergraduates in 2002 completed a bachelor's degree within 6 years (by fall 2009) (see table A-39-2). In contrast, at public 4-year institutions that accepted less than a fourth of applicants, 73 percent of students who began attending in 2002 completed a bachelor's degree within 6 years. At private not-for-profit and private for-profit institutions with open admissions, the 6-year graduation rates for the 2002 cohort for bachelor's degree recipients were 35 and 13 percent, respectively.

For more information: *Tables A-39-1 and A-39-2*
Glossary: *College, Four-year postsecondary institution, Full-time enrollment, Part-time enrollment, Private institution, Public institution, Tuition, Two-year postsecondary institution*

Technical Notes

Degree-granting institutions grant associate's or higher degrees and participate in Title IV federal financial aid programs. For 4-year institutions, the retention rate is the percentage of first-time, bachelor's degree-seeking students who return to the institution to continue their studies the following fall. For 2-year institutions, the retention rate is the percentage of first-time degree/certificate-seeking students enrolled in the fall who either returned to the institution or successfully completed their program by the following fall. The overall graduation rate is the percentage of full-time, first-time students who graduated or transferred out of the institution within 150 percent

of normal program completion time. For a bachelor's degree, this represents 6 years. Race categories exclude persons of Hispanic ethnicity. For more information on race/ethnicity, see *supplemental note 1*. Full time refers to students who enrolled full time (as defined by the institution) in the fall. For more information on the Integrated Postsecondary Education Data System (IPEDS), see *supplemental note 3*. Institutions in this indicator are classified based on the highest degree offered. For more information on the classification of postsecondary institutions, see *supplemental note 8*.

Figure 39-1. Percentage distribution of fall undergraduate enrollment in degree-granting institutions, by student attendance status, age, and control and level of institution: Fall 2009

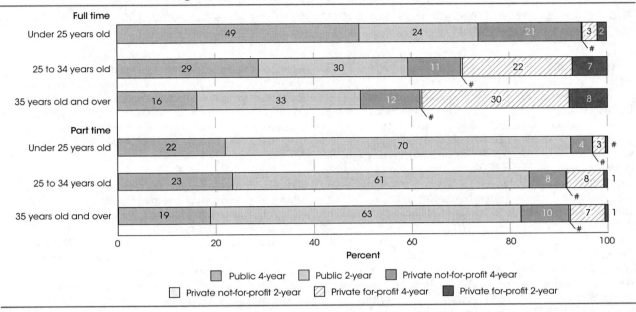

Rounds to zero.
NOTE: Degree-granting institutions grant associate's or higher degrees and participate in Title IV federal financial aid programs. For more information on IPEDS, see *supplemental note 3*. Institutions in this indicator are classified based on the highest degree offered. For more information on the classification of postsecondary institutions, see *supplemental note 8*.
SOURCE: U.S. Department of Education, National Center for Education Statistics, 2009 Integrated Postsecondary Education Data System (IPEDS), Spring 2010.

Figure 39-2. Overall annual retention rates and graduation rates within 150 percent of normal time at degree-granting institutions, by level and control of institution and student attendance status: Fall 2009

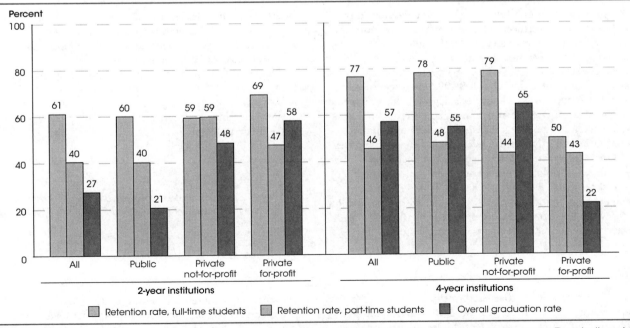

NOTE: Degree-granting institutions grant associate's or higher degrees and participate in Title IV federal financial aid programs. The retention rate is the percentage of first-time, bachelor's degree-seeking students who return to the institution to continue their studies the following year, in this case fall 2009. The overall graduation rate is the percentage of full-time, first-time students who graduated within 150 percent of normal program completion time, in this case by fall 2008 for the cohort that enrolled in 4-year institutions in fall 2002 and for the students that enrolled in 2-year institutions in fall 2005. For more information on IPEDS, see *supplemental note 3*. Institutions in this indicator are based on the highest degree offered. For more information on the classification of postsecondary institutions, see *supplemental note 8*.
SOURCE: U.S. Department of Education, National Center for Education Statistics, 2009 Integrated Postsecondary Education Data System (IPEDS), Spring 2010.

Undergraduate Fields of Study

In 2008–09, more than half of the 1.6 million bachelor's degrees awarded were in five fields: business (22 percent), social sciences and history (11 percent), health professions and related clinical sciences (8 percent), education (6 percent), and psychology (6 percent).

Of the 1.6 million bachelor's degrees awarded in 2008–09, over 50 percent were concentrated in five fields: business (22 percent), social sciences and history (11 percent), health professions and related clinical sciences (8 percent), education (6 percent), and psychology (6 percent) (see table A-40-1). The fields of visual and performing arts (6 percent), engineering and engineering technologies (5 percent), communication and communications technologies (5 percent), and biological and biomedical sciences (5 percent) represented an additional 21 percent of all bachelor's degrees awarded in 2008–09.

Overall, there were 33 percent more bachelor's degrees awarded in 2008–09 than in 1998–99 (an increase of 401,100 bachelor's degrees awarded). Bachelor's degrees awarded in the field of parks, recreation, leisure, and fitness studies had the largest percent change of all fields (from 16,500 to 31,700 degrees, a 92 percent change). The next largest percent change was in the field of security and protective services (from 24,600 to 41,800 degrees, a 70 percent change). Education was the only field in which fewer bachelor's degrees were awarded in 2008–09 than in 1998–99 (a negative percent change of 5 percent).

About 57 percent of all bachelor's degrees conferred in 2008–09 were awarded to females, which was about the same as the percentage awarded to females in 1998–99. Looking at the five most prevalent bachelor's degree fields, females earned between 49 and 85 percent of the degrees awarded in those fields. In 2008–09, females earned the smallest percentages of bachelor's degrees relative to males in the fields of engineering and engineering technologies (16 percent of these degrees were awarded to females) and computer and information sciences and support services (18 percent female), both of which are considered STEM (science, technology, engineering, and mathematics) fields. From 1998–99 to 2008–09, there were changes in the percentages of bachelor's degrees conferred to females in several fields of study. For example, of all the bachelor's degrees conferred in the field of security and protective

services, the percentage that were conferred to females was 50 percent in 2008–09, compared with 43 percent in 1998–99. In contrast, of all the bachelor's degrees conferred in the field of computer and information sciences and support services, the percentage conferred to females was 18 percent in 2008–09, compared with 27 percent in 1998–99.

Of the 787,300 associate's degrees earned in 2008–09, about 54 percent were awarded in two broad areas of study: liberal arts and sciences, general studies, and humanities (34 percent) and health professions and related clinical sciences (21 percent). Overall, there was a 41 percent change in the number of associate's degrees awarded from 1998–99 to 2008–09 (an increase of 227,400 associate's degrees awarded). The field experiencing the largest percent change in the number of associate's degrees awarded over this time period was psychology (143 percent, from 1,600 to 3,900 degrees). Several fields experienced a decline in the number of associate's degrees awarded; for example, 4,400 fewer associate's degrees were awarded in engineering and engineering technologies in 2008–09 than in 1998–99 (a negative percent change of 8 percent).

In 2008–09, females earned 62 percent of all associate's degrees awarded. Females earned the majority of associate's degrees awarded in the fields of family and consumer sciences (96 percent were awarded to females) and legal professions and studies (90 percent female). Females earned fewer associate's degrees than males in fields such as precision production (6 percent female) and engineering and engineering technologies (11 percent female).

For more information: *Table A-40-1*

Glossary: *Associate's degree, Bachelor's degree, Classification of Instructional Programs (CIP), STEM fields*

Technical Notes

The percent increases discussed in this indicator refer to aggregate fields of study. For more information on fields of study for postsecondary degrees, see *supplemental note 9*. The 2000 *Classification of Instructional Programs* was initiated in 2002–03. Estimates for 1998–99 have been reclassified when necessary to conform to the new

taxonomy. For more information on the classification of postsecondary education institutions, see *supplemental note 8*. For more information on the Integrated Postsecondary Education Data System (IPEDS), see *supplemental note 3*.

Figure 40-1. Number of bachelor's degrees awarded by degree-granting institutions in selected fields of study: Academic years 1998–99 and 2008–09

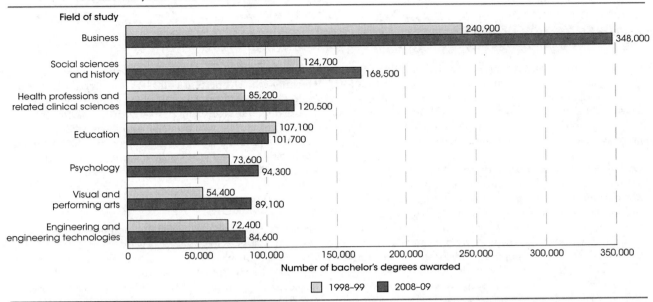

NOTE: For more information on fields of study for postsecondary degrees, see *supplemental note 9*. The 2000 *Classification of Instructional Programs* was initiated in 2002–03. Estimates for 1998–99 have been reclassified when necessary to conform to the new taxonomy. For more information on the classification of postsecondary education institutions, see *supplemental note 8*. For more information on the Integrated Postsecondary Education Data System (IPEDS), see *supplemental note 3*.
SOURCE: U.S. Department of Education, National Center for Education Statistics, 1998–99 and 2008–09 Integrated Postsecondary Education Data System, "Completions Survey" (IPEDS-C:99) and Fall 2009.

Figure 40-2. Percentage of bachelor's degrees awarded to females by degree-granting institutions in selected fields of study: Academic year 2008–09

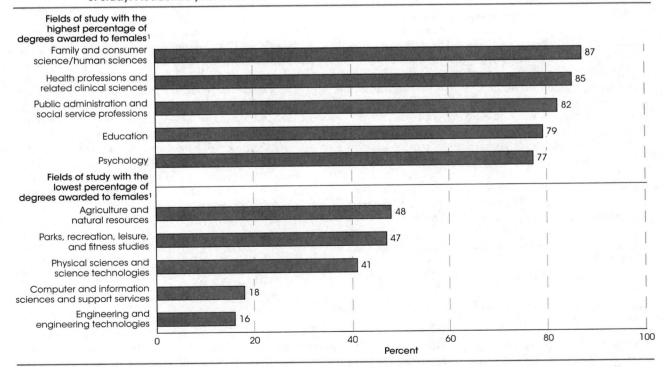

[1] Of the 20 fields of study in which the most bachelor's degrees were awarded in 2008–09.
NOTE: For more information on fields of study for postsecondary degrees, see *supplemental note 9*. For more information on the classification of postsecondary education institutions, see *supplemental note 8*. For more information on the Integrated Postsecondary Education Data System (IPEDS), see *supplemental note 3*.
SOURCE: U.S. Department of Education, National Center for Education Statistics, 2008–09 Integrated Postsecondary Education Data System, "Completions Survey," Fall 2009.

Overall, 656,800 master's degrees and 67,700 doctoral degrees were awarded in 2008–09; these numbers represent increases of 49 and 54 percent, respectively, over the numbers awarded in 1998–99. In 2008–09, females earned 60 percent of master's degrees and 52 percent of doctoral degrees awarded.

Of the 656,800 master's degrees awarded in 2008–09, over 50 percent were concentrated in two fields: education (27 percent) and business (26 percent) (see table A-41-1). During that same academic year, an additional 10 percent of all master's degrees were awarded in the field of health professions and related clinical sciences.

Overall, there were 49 percent more master's degrees awarded in 2008–09 than in 1998–99 (an increase of 216,800 master's degrees awarded). During this period, the two fields awarding the most master's degrees, education and business, saw percent changes of 51 and 57 percent, respectively, in the number of degrees awarded. In each of the 20 most popular fields of study, the number of master's degrees awarded was higher in 2008–09 than in 1998–99. The field of security and protective services had the largest percent change in the number of master's degrees awarded (from 2,200 to 6,100 degrees, a 172 percent increase). The field of physical sciences and science technologies saw the smallest percent change in the number of master's degrees awarded over this period (from 5,100 to 5,700 degrees, a 10 percent increase).

Females earned 60 percent of all master's degrees awarded in 2008–09. In the two fields awarding the most master's degrees, education and business, females earned 77 and 45 percent, respectively, of all master's degrees awarded. In addition, females earned 81 percent of all master's degrees awarded in the field of health professions and related clinical sciences. In fields such as engineering and engineering technologies and computer and information sciences and support services, however, females earned fewer master's degrees than males in 2008–09: females earned 23 percent of the master's degrees awarded in engineering and engineering technologies and 27 percent of master's degrees awarded in computer and information sciences and support services. These fields are part of a larger grouping known as science, technology, engineering, and mathematics (STEM) fields.

Over 50 percent of the 67,700 doctoral degrees awarded in 2008–09 were awarded in four fields: health professions and related clinical sciences (18 percent),

education (13 percent), engineering and engineering technologies (12 percent), and biological and biomedical sciences (10 percent). Overall, there were 54 percent more doctoral degrees in 2008–09 than in 1998–99 (an increase of 23,600 doctoral degrees awarded). In 2008–09, more doctoral degrees were awarded in the field of health professions and related clinical sciences than in any other field, and from 1998–99 to 2008–09 the number of degrees awarded in this field increased by more than 500 percent.

Females earned about 35,400 doctoral degrees (or 52 percent of all doctoral degrees awarded) in 2008–09, an 87 percent increase over the number awarded in 1998–99. Among the top 20 fields of study, females earned the smallest percentages of doctoral degrees relative to males in 2008–09 in the fields engineering and engineering technologies and computer and information sciences and support services (22 percent female each). In contrast, females earned the greatest percentages of doctoral degrees relative to males in family and consumer sciences/human sciences (80 percent female) and health professions and related clinical sciences (74 percent female).

In 2008–09, of the 92,000 first-professional degrees awarded, 48 percent were awarded in the field of law. An additional 17 percent of first-professional degrees were conferred in medicine, and 12 percent were conferred in pharmacy. In 2008–09, 17 percent more first-professional degrees were awarded than were in 1998–99. During this period, the field of pharmacy saw the greatest percentage increase in the number of degrees awarded (183 percent), and the field of chiropractic medicine saw the greatest decrease (31 percent). Females earned 45,100 first-professional degrees in 2008–09 (49 percent of all first-professional degrees awarded in that year), representing a 32 percent increase over the number of degrees awarded to females in 1998–99.

For more information: *Table A-41-1*

Glossary: *Classification of Instructional Programs (CIP), Doctoral degree, First-professional degree, Master's degree, STEM fields*

Technical Notes

The percent increases discussed in this indicator refer to aggregate fields of study. For more information on fields of study for postsecondary degrees, see *supplemental note 9*. The 2000 edition of *Classification of Instructional Programs* was initiated in 2002–03. Estimates for 1998–99 have been reclassified when necessary to conform to the new

taxonomy. For more information on the classification of postsecondary education institutions, see *supplemental note 8*. For more information on the Integrated Postsecondary Education Data System (IPEDS), see *supplemental note 3*.

Figure 41-1. Number of master's degrees awarded by degree-granting institutions in selected fields of study: Academic years 1998–99 and 2008–09

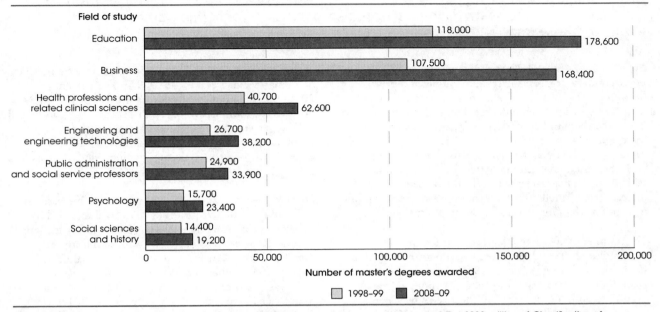

Field of study

NOTE: For more information on fields of study for postsecondary degrees, see *supplemental note 9*. The 2000 edition of *Classification of Instructional Programs* was initiated in 2002–03. Estimates for 1998–99 have been reclassified when necessary to conform to the new taxonomy. For more information on the classification of postsecondary education institutions, see *supplemental note 8*. For more information on the Integrated Postsecondary Education Data System (IPEDS), see *supplemental note 3*.
SOURCE: U.S. Department of Education, National Center for Education Statistics, 1998–99 and 2008–09 Integrated Postsecondary Education Data System, "Completions Survey" (IPEDS-C:99) and Fall 2009.

Figure 41-2. Percentage of master's degrees awarded to females by degree-granting institutions in selected fields of study: Academic year 2008–09

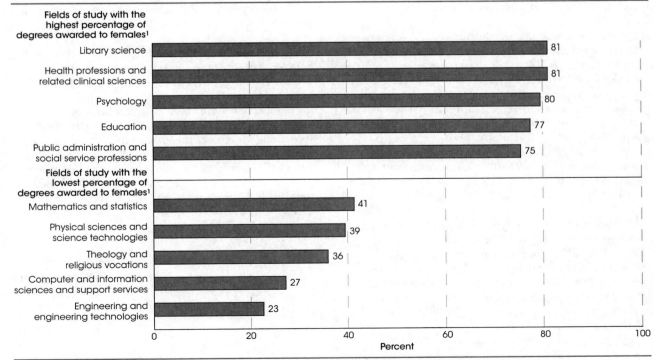

[1] Of the 20 fields of study in which the most master's degrees were awarded in 2008–09.
NOTE: For more information on fields of study for postsecondary degrees, see *supplemental note 9*. For more information on the classification of postsecondary education institutions, see *supplemental note 8*. For more information on the Integrated Postsecondary Education Data System (IPEDS), see *supplemental note 3*.
SOURCE: U.S. Department of Education, National Center for Education Statistics, 2008–09 Integrated Postsecondary Education Data System, Fall 2009.

Between 1998–99 and 2008–09, the number of degrees conferred by private for-profit institutions increased by a larger percentage than the number conferred by public institutions and private not-for-profit institutions; this was true for all levels of degrees.

Between 1998–99 and 2008–09, the number of postsecondary degrees conferred by public and private for-profit and private not-for-profit institutions generally increased for each level of degree. From 1998–99 to 2008–09, the number of associate's degrees awarded increased by 41 percent, bachelor's degrees by 33 percent, master's degrees by 49 percent, first-professional degrees by 17 percent, and doctoral degrees by 54 percent (see table A-42-1). For all degree levels, the percentage increases were smaller for public and private not-for-profit institutions than for private for-profit institutions.

The number of associate's degrees awarded from 1998–99 to 2008–09 increased by 33 percent for public institutions (from 448,300 to 596,100 degrees) and more than doubled for private for-profit institutions (from 64,000 to 144,300 degrees), but decreased by 1 percent for private not-for-profit institutions (from 47,600 to 46,900 degrees). Due to these changes, the percentage of all associate's degrees that were conferred by private for-profit institutions increased from 11 percent in 1998–99 to 18 percent in 2008–09, while the percentage that were conferred by public and private not-for-profit institutions decreased during this period (from 80 to 76 percent and from 9 to 6 percent, respectively).

From 1998–99 to 2008–09, the number of bachelor's degrees awarded by public institutions increased by 29 percent (from 790,300 to 1,020,400 degrees), the number awarded by private not-for-profit institutions increased by 26 percent (from 393,700 to 496,300 degrees), and the number awarded by private for-profit institutions more than quadrupled (from 16,300 to 84,700 degrees). Despite the large gains made by private for-profit institutions, they awarded 5 percent of all bachelor's degrees conferred in 2008–09, while public institutions awarded 64 percent and private not-for-profit institutions awarded 31 percent of all bachelor's degrees.

The number of master's degrees awarded by private not-for-profit institutions increased 48 percent from 1998–99 to 2008–09, yet the percentage of master's degrees conferred by these institutions remained about the same. For public institutions, however, the number of master's degrees conferred increased at a lower rate (29 percent), resulting in a decrease in their share of all

master's degrees: public institutions conferred 54 percent of all master's degrees in 1998–99 and 47 percent in 2008–09. The number of master's degrees conferred by private for-profit institutions, on the other hand, increased by 580 percent, resulting in an increase in their share of total master's degrees conferred. Private for-profit institutions conferred 2 percent of all master's degrees in 1998–99 and 10 percent in 2008–09.

From 1998–99 to 2008–09, the percentage increases in the number of first-professional degrees awarded by public institutions and private not-for-profit institutions (18 and 16 percent, respectively) were similar to the overall 17 percent increase in first-professional degree awards. The number of first-professional degrees awarded by private for-profit institutions in 2008–09 was more than twice the number of degrees awarded in 1998–99. In 2008–09, public institutions conferred 41 percent of all first-professional degrees; private not-for-profit institutions, 58 percent; and private for-profit institutions, 1 percent. From 1998–99 to 2008–09, the number of doctoral degrees conferred increased by 42 percent for public institutions (from 28,100 to 39,900 degrees), by 62 percent for private not-for-profit institutions (from 15,500 to 25,200 degrees), and by almost 500 percent for private for-profit institutions (from 440 to 2,600 degrees).

Although enrollment size is not reported here, the growing number of private for-profit institutions provides context for the percentage increases in the number of degrees conferred by level and control of institution. For example, the number of private for-profit 4-year institutions increased from 190 to 530 from 1998–99 to 2008–09, accounting for most of the increase in the total number of 4-year institutions (from 2,340 to 2,720 institutions) (see table A-42-2). In addition, the number of private for-profit 2-year institutions increased from 480 to 570 during this time, while the total number of all 2-year institutions decreased from 1,710 to 1,690.

For more information: *Tables A-42-1 and A-42-2*
Glossary: *Associate's degree, Bachelor's degree, Doctoral degree, First-professional degree, Private institution, Public institution*

Technical Notes

This indicator includes only degree-granting institutions that participated in Title IV federal financial aid programs. For more information on the Integrated

Postsecondary Education Data System (IPEDS) and IPEDS classification of institutions, see *supplemental notes 3 and 8.*

Table 42-1. Number of degrees conferred by degree-granting institutions and percent change, by control of institution and level of degree: Academic years 1998–99 and 2008–09

Level of degree and academic year	Total	Public	Private		
			Total	Not-for-profit	For-profit
Number of degrees					
Associate's					
1998–99	559,954	448,334	111,620	47,611	64,009
2008–09	787,325	596,098	191,227	46,929	144,298
Percent change	40.6	33.0	71.3	-1.4	125.4
Bachelor's					
1998–99	1,200,303	790,287	410,016	393,680	16,336
2008–09	1,601,368	1,020,435	580,933	496,260	84,673
Percent change	33.4	29.1	41.7	26.1	418.3
Master's					
1998–99	439,986	238,501	201,485	192,152	9,333
2008–09	656,784	308,206	348,578	285,098	63,480
Percent change	49.3	29.2	73.0	48.4	580.2
First-professional					
1998–99	78,439	31,693	46,746	46,315	431
2008–09	92,004	37,357	54,647	53,572	1,075
Percent change	17.3	17.9	16.9	15.7	149.4
Doctoral					
1998–99	44,077	28,134	15,943	15,501	442
2008–09	67,716	39,911	27,805	25,169	2,636
Percent change	53.6	41.9	74.4	62.4	496.4

NOTE: Includes only institutions that participated in Title IV federal financial aid programs. For more information on the Integrated Postsecondary Education Data System (IPEDS) and IPEDS classification of institutions, see *supplemental notes 3* and *8*. See the glossary for definitions of first-professional degree and doctoral degree.
SOURCE: U.S. Department of Education, National Center for Education Statistics, 1998–99 and 2008–09 Integrated Postsecondary Education Data System (IPEDS), "Completions Survey" (IPEDS-C:99) and Fall 2009.

Figure 42-1. Number of degrees conferred by degree-granting institutions, by level of degree and control of institution: Academic years 1998–99 and 2008–09

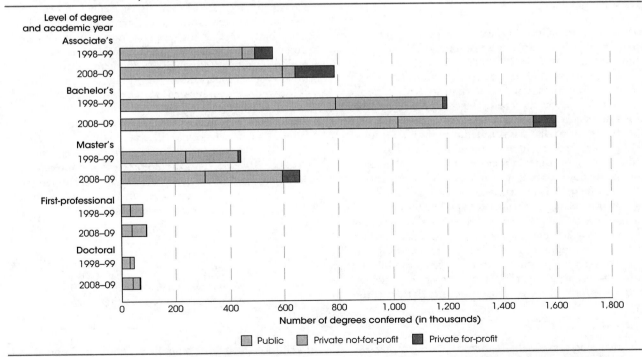

NOTE: Includes only institutions that participated in Title IV federal financial aid programs. For more information on the Integrated Postsecondary Education Data System (IPEDS) and IPEDS classification of institutions, see *supplemental notes 3* and *8*. See the glossary for definitions of first-professional degree and doctoral degree.
SOURCE: U.S. Department of Education, National Center for Education Statistics, 1998–99 and 2008–09 Integrated Postsecondary Education Data System (IPEDS), "Completions Survey" (IPEDS-C:99) and Fall 2009.

Distance Education in Higher Education

In 2007–08, about 4.3 million undergraduate students, or 20 percent of all undergraduates, took at least one distance education course. About 0.8 million, or 4 percent of all undergraduates, took their entire program through distance education.

Distance education courses and programs provide flexible learning opportunities to both undergraduate and postbaccalaureate students. In this indicator, distance education courses include live, interactive audio- or videoconferencing; prerecorded instructional videos; webcasts; CD-ROMs or DVDs; or computer-based systems accessed over the Internet. Distance education does not include correspondence courses. In 2007–08, about 4.3 million undergraduate students, or 20 percent of all undergraduates, took at least one distance education course (see table A-43-1). About 0.8 million, or 4 percent of all undergraduates, took their entire program through distance education. The percentage of undergraduates who took any distance education courses rose from 16 percent in 2003–04 to 20 percent in 2007–08; over the same period, however, the percentage who took their entire program through distance education decreased from 5 to 4 percent. In addition to these undergraduate students, about 0.8 million, or 22 percent, of all postbaccalaureate students took distance education courses in 2007–08 (see table A-43-2). The percentage of postbaccalaureate students who took their entire program through distance education (9 percent) was higher than the percentage at the undergraduate level.

There were differences in the percentage of students participating in distance education programs by institutional control in 2007–08. A lower percentage of students at private not-for-profit institutions (14 percent) took distance education courses than students at public institutions (22 percent) or students at private for-profit institutions (21 percent) (see table A-43-1). Also, a higher percentage of students at private for-profit institutions (12 percent) took their entire program through distance education than students at either public institutions or private not-for-profit institutions (both 3 percent). Within the specific institutional controls and levels, a higher percentage of students at private for-profit 4-year institutions (30 percent) took distance education courses than students at any other control and level of institution, ranging from 6 percent at private for-profit less-than-2-year institutions to 24 percent at public 2-year institutions. Similarly, a higher percentage of students at private for-profit 4-year institutions took their entire

program through distance education (19 percent) than students at any other control and level of institution, ranging from 2 percent at public less-than-2-year, public 4-year, and private for-profit less-than-2-year institutions to 8 percent at private for-profit 2-year institutions.

Participation in distance education programs also varied by student characteristics. A higher percentage of older than younger undergraduate students took distance education courses. In 2007–08, for example, 30 percent of students 30 years old and over took distance education courses, compared to 26 percent of students 24 to 29 years of age and 15 percent of students 15 to 23 years of age (see table A-43-1). A higher percentage of undergraduates who had a job took distance education courses (22 percent) than those who had no job (16 percent) and a higher percentage of students attending classes exclusively part time took distance education courses (25 percent) than those attending classes exclusively full time (17 percent).

There also were differences in distance education participation by student dependency status. In 2007–08, a lower percentage of undergraduates who were financially dependent (14 percent) took distance education courses than undergraduates who were financially independent (see table A-43-1). A higher percentage of independent undergraduates who were married and had dependents took distance education courses (33 percent) than did other types of independent undergraduates, including those who were unmarried, with or without dependents, as well as those who were married and without dependents (percentages for these three groups ranged from 24 to 29 percent). Similarly, a higher percentage of married postbaccalaureate students with dependents took distance education courses (33 percent) and took their entire program through distance education (16 percent) than did unmarried postbaccalaureate students with no dependents (5 percent) (see table A-43-2).

 For more information: *Tables A-43-1 and A-43-2*
Glossary: *College, Four-year postsecondary institution, Public institution, Private institution, Two-year postsecondary institution, Undergraduate student*

Technical Notes

Estimates pertain to all postsecondary students who enrolled at any time during the school year at an institution participating in Title IV programs. Distance education participation includes participation at any institution for students attending more than one

institution during the school year. For more information on the National Postsecondary Student Financial Aid Study (NPSAS), see *supplemental note 3.* For more information on the classification of postsecondary education institutions, see *supplemental note 8.*

Figure 43-1. Percentage of undergraduate students in postsecondary institutions taking distance education courses, by control and level of institution: 2003–04 and 2007–08

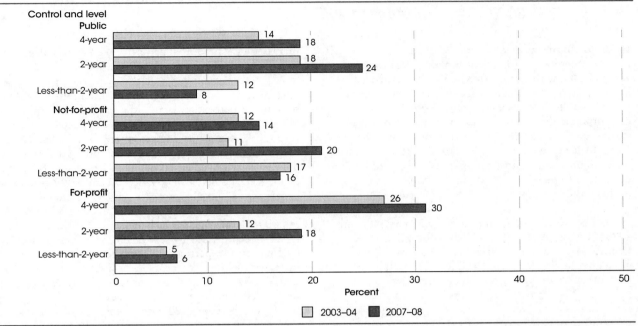

NOTE: Estimates pertain to all postsecondary students who enrolled at any time during the school year at an institution participating in Title IV programs. Distance education participation includes participation at any institution for students attending more than one institution during the school year. Data include Puerto Rico. For more information on the National Postsecondary Student Financial Aid Study (NPSAS), see *supplemental note 3*. For more information on the classification of postsecondary education institutions, see *supplemental note 8*.
SOURCE: U.S. Department of Education, National Center for Education Statistics, 2003–04 and 2007–08 National Postsecondary Student Aid Study (NPSAS:04 and NPSAS:08).

Figure 43-2. Percentage of undergraduate and postbaccalaureate students in postsecondary institutions taking distance education courses, by dependency status: 2007–08

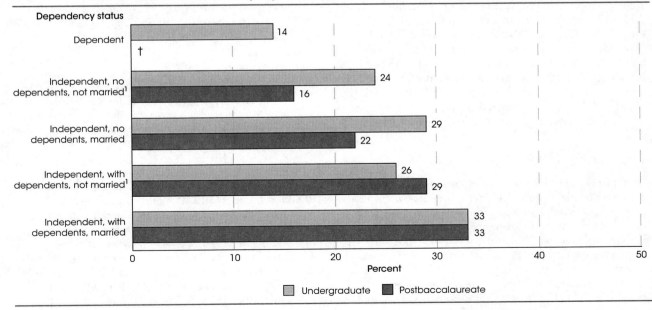

† Not applicable.
[1] Includes separated.
NOTE: Estimates pertain to all postsecondary students who enrolled at any time during the school year at an institution participating in Title IV programs. Distance education participation includes participation at any institution for students attending more than one institution during the school year. Data include Puerto Rico. For more information on the National Postsecondary Student Financial Aid Study (NPSAS), see *supplemental note 3*. For more information on the classification of postsecondary education institutions, see *supplemental note 8*.
SOURCE: U.S. Department of Education, National Center for Education Statistics, 2007–08 National Postsecondary Student Aid Study (NPSAS:08).

Faculty Salaries, Benefits, and Total Compensation

After increasing by 14 percent during the 1980s and by 5 percent during the 1990s, average salaries for full-time faculty were 4 percent higher in 2009–10 than they were in 1999–2000, after adjusting for inflation.

In 2009–10, the average salary for full-time instructional faculty at degree-granting postsecondary institutions was $74,600, with a range of $55,600 for instructors, lecturers, and other faculty with no academic rank to $103,700 for professors (see table A-44-1). Faculty categories are defined by the institution. Salaries at the various levels and controls of institutions ranged from $44,700 at private 2-year colleges to $97,700 at private doctoral universities. Institutions are categorized by the number of highest degrees awarded: doctoral, master's, bachelor's, or associate's.

The average faculty salary increased by 25 percent from 1979–80 to 2009–10, after adjusting for inflation (see table A-44-2). Average salaries increased for each type of faculty during this period as follows: professors (30 percent), assistant professors (28 percent), associate professors (24 percent), and faculty with no academic rank (17 percent). Average salaries were also higher in 2009–10 than they were in 1979–80 at each institution level and control, with increases ranging from 9 percent at public 2-year colleges to 40 percent at private doctoral universities.

Compared with earlier years, growth in average faculty salaries slowed in the recent decade. After increasing by 14 percent during the 1980s and by 5 percent during the 1990s, average faculty salaries were 4 percent higher in 2009–10 than they were in 1999–2000, after adjusting for inflation (data not shown). This pattern differed by institution level and control. Average salaries at public and private master's degree institutions and public and private doctoral universities were between 1 and 4 percent higher in 2009–10 than they were in 1999–2000. Salaries at public other 4-year colleges did not measurably change during this period. In contrast, average faculty salaries

increased by 9 percent at private other 4-year colleges and were 3 percent lower at private 2-year colleges.

Average fringe benefits (adjusted for inflation) increased by a higher percentage than did average faculty salaries (82 vs. 25 percent) between 1979–80 and 2009–10. As a result, fringe benefits accounted for a higher share of total compensation for faculty in 2009–10 than it did in 1979–80 (22 vs. 16 percent). Compared with faculty salaries between 1999–2000 and 2009–10, fringe benefits for faculty increased by larger percentages at most levels and controls of institutions. From 1999–2000 to 2009–10, average fringe benefits for faculty increased by 24 percent, while average faculty salaries increased by 4 percent. In particular, fringe benefits for faculty increased by higher percentages at public institutions than at private institutions. For example, average benefits for faculty at public master's degree institutions increased by 28 percent, compared with an increase of 19 percent for faculty at private master's degree institutions. From 1999–2000 to 2009–10, benefits for faculty at public 2-year colleges increased by 29 percent, while benefits at private 2-year colleges decreased by 2 percent.

Combining salary with benefits, faculty received an average total compensation package in 2009–10 that was about 8 percent higher than the package they received in 1999–2000. In 2009–10, the average compensation package for faculty was about $95,600, including $74,600 in salaries and $21,000 in benefits.

For more information: *Tables A-44-1 and A-44-2*
Glossary: *Consumer Price Index (CPI), Faculty, Four-year postsecondary institution, Private institution, Public institution, Salary, Two-year postsecondary institution*

Technical Notes

Average total compensation is the sum of salary (which excludes outside income) and fringe benefits (which may include benefits such as retirement plans, medical/dental plans, group life insurance, or other benefits). Private institutions include private not-for-profit and private for-profit institutions. Institutions are classified by the number of highest degrees awarded. For example, institutions that award 20 or more doctoral degrees per year are classified as doctoral universities. For more information on the classification of postsecondary institutions, see *supplemental note 8*. Data do not include institutions at which all faculty were part time, contributed their services, were in the military, or taught

preclinical or clinical medicine. Salaries reflect an average of all faculty on 9- and 10-month contracts rather than a weighted average based on contract length that appears in some other National Center for Education Statistics reports. Data exclude faculty on 11- and 12-month contracts (17 percent of faculty in 2009–10) and are reported for the 50 states and D.C. and exclude Puerto Rico and the territories. Data are adjusted by the Consumer Price Index (CPI) to constant 2009–10 dollars. For more information on the CPI, see *supplemental note 10*. Detail may not sum to totals because of rounding. For more information on the Integrated Postsecondary Education Data System (IPEDS), see *supplemental note 3*.

Figure 44-1. Average salary for full-time instructional faculty on 9- and 10-month contracts at degree-granting postsecondary institutions, by level and control of institution: Academic year 2009–10

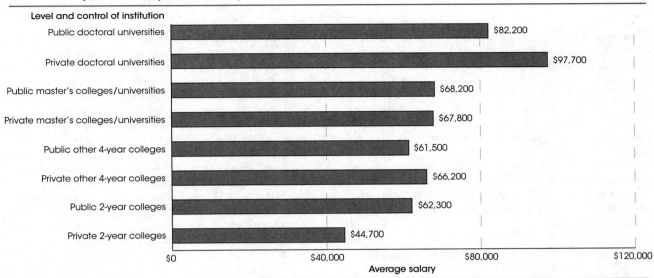

Level and control of institution

Institution	Average salary
Public doctoral universities	$82,200
Private doctoral universities	$97,700
Public master's colleges/universities	$68,200
Private master's colleges/universities	$67,800
Public other 4-year colleges	$61,500
Private other 4-year colleges	$66,200
Public 2-year colleges	$62,300
Private 2-year colleges	$44,700

Average salary

NOTE: Institutions are classified based on the number of highest degrees awarded. For more information on the classification of postsecondary institutions, see *supplemental note 8*. Data are reported for the 50 states and D.C. and exclude Puerto Rico and the territories. Salaries exclude outside income and reflect an average of all faculty on 9- and 10-month contracts rather than a weighted average based on contract length that appears in some other reports of the National Center for Education Statistics. For more information on the Integrated Postsecondary Education Data System (IPEDS), see *supplemental note 3*.
SOURCE: U.S. Department of Education, National Center for Education Statistics, 2009–10 Integrated Postsecondary Education Data System (IPEDS), Fall 2009 and Winter 2009–10.

Figure 44-2. Average total compensation (salary and benefits) for full-time instructional faculty on 9- and 10-month contracts at degree-granting postsecondary institutions: Selected academic years, 1979–80 through 2009–10

[In constant 2009–10 dollars]

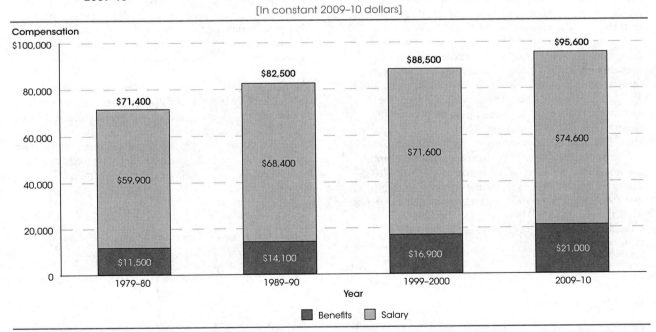

Compensation

Year	Benefits	Salary	Total
1979–80	$11,500	$59,900	$71,400
1989–90	$14,100	$68,400	$82,500
1999–2000	$16,900	$71,600	$88,500
2009–10	$21,000	$74,600	$95,600

Year

■ Benefits   ■ Salary

NOTE: Average total compensation is the sum of salary (which excludes outside income) and fringe benefits (which may include benefits such as retirement plans, medical/dental plans, group life insurance, or other benefits). Data are reported for the 50 states and D.C. and exclude Puerto Rico and the territories. Salaries reflect an average of all faculty on 9- and 10-month contracts rather than a weighted average based on contract length that appears in some other reports of the National Center for Education Statistics. Salaries, benefits, and compensation adjusted by the Consumer Price Index (CPI) to constant 2009–10 dollars. For more information on the CPI, see *supplemental note 10*. For more information on the Integrated Postsecondary Education Data System (IPEDS), see *supplemental note 3*.
SOURCE: U.S. Department of Education, National Center for Education Statistics, 1979–80 Higher Education General Information Survey (HEGIS), "Faculty Salaries, Tenure, and Fringe Benefits Survey"; and 1989–90, 1999–2000, and 2009–10 Integrated Postsecondary Education Data System (IPEDS), "Salaries, Tenure, and Fringe Benefits of Full-Time Instructional Faculty Survey" (IPEDS-SA:89–99), "Completions Survey" (IPEDS-C:89–99), Fall 2009 and Winter 2009–10.

College Student Employment

In 2009, about 41 percent of full-time and 76 percent of part-time college students ages 16–24 were employed.

The percentage of full-time college students ages 16–24 who were employed increased from 34 to 52 percent between 1970 and 2000 and then decreased to 47 percent in 2001, where it remained relatively stable until 2008 before declining to 41 percent in 2009 (see table A-45-1). The percentage of full-time students who worked 20–34 hours per week increased from 10 to 22 percent from 1970 to 2000 and then remained relatively stable (between 20 and 22 percent) through 2008 before declining to 18 percent in 2009. The percentage of these students who worked 35 or more hours per week increased from 4 percent in 1970 to 9 percent in 2000, fluctuated between 8 and 9 percent through 2008, and declined to 6 percent in 2009.

In 2009, about 76 percent of part-time college students ages 16–24 were employed. In contrast to the increase among full-time college students, there was no overall trend between 1970 and 2009 in the percentage of part-time college students who were employed. The percentage of part-time college students working 35 or more hours per week, however, decreased from 60 to 37 percent between 1970 and 2009.

The employment rate of full-time college students at public 4-year institutions fluctuated between 1990 and 2009; it increased between 1990 and 2000, decreased in 2001, and then remained relatively stable until it decreased again in 2009. The employment rate for full-time students at private 4-year institutions also increased between 1990 and 2000 and decreased in 2001, but showed no measurable change between 2001 and 2009. The percentage of full-time students at public 2-year institutions who were employed did not measurably change between 1990 and 2000 but decreased between 2000 and 2009. The percentage of part-time students in public and private 4-year institutions who were employed did not show an overall trend between 1990 and 2009. The employment rate of part-time students in public 2-year institutions in 1990 was not measurably different from the rate in 2007, but from 2007 to 2009, it decreased from 83 to 72 percent.

The percentages of students who were employed differed by level and control of institution. In general, the employment rates of full-time students were higher at public 2-year institutions than at 4-year institutions for nearly all years of data shown between 1990 and 2009. In addition, the employment rate of full-time students at public 4-year institutions was higher than the rate at private 4-year institutions for all years of data shown. In 2009, for example, about 45 percent of full-time students at public 2-year institutions were employed, compared with 41 percent of full-time students at public 4-year institutions and 35 percent at private 4-year institutions. The employment rates for part-time students generally did not differ by level and control of institution between 1990 and 2007, though in 2008 and 2009, a higher percentage of part-time students at public 4-year institutions worked than did those at public 2-year institutions. In 2009, a higher percentage of part-time students at 4-year private institutions were employed than were students at 2- and 4-year public institutions.

In 2009, the percentage of full-time college students ages 16–24 who were employed differed by sex and race/ethnicity. A higher percentage of female full-time students were employed than were male full-time students (45 vs. 36 percent) (see table A-45-2). Also, the employment rates of full-time students were higher among White and Hispanic students and students of two or more races (45, 39, and 44 percent, respectively) than among Black and Asian students (29 and 26 percent, respectively).

The percentage of students who were employed in 2009 also differed by student enrollment level. The percentage of part-time graduate students who were employed was higher than the percentage of part-time undergraduate students who were employed (88 vs. 74 percent). At both the part-time and full-time level, higher percentages of graduate than undergraduate students worked 35 or more hours per week.

For more information: *Tables A-45-1 and A-45-2*
Glossary: *Four-year postsecondary institution, Full-time enrollment, Part-time enrollment, Private institution, Public institution, Two-year postsecondary institution*

Technical Notes

College includes both 2- and 4-year institutions. College students were classified as *full time* if they were taking at least 12 hours of classes (or at least 9 hours of graduate classes) during an average school week and as part time if they were taking fewer hours. *Hours worked per week* refers to the number of hours that the respondent worked

at all jobs during the survey week. For more information on the Current Population Survey (CPS), see *supplemental note 2*. Race categories exclude persons of Hispanic ethnicity. For more information on race/ethnicity, see *supplemental note 1*.

Figure 45-1. Percentage of 16- to 24-year-old college students who were employed, by attendance status and hours worked per week: October 1970 through October 2009

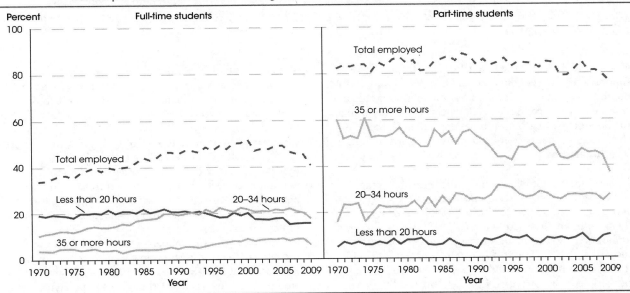

NOTE: College includes both 2- and 4-year institutions. College students were classified as *full time* if they were taking at least 12 hours of classes (or at least 9 hours of graduate classes) during an average school week and as part time if they were taking fewer hours. Percent employed estimates include those who were employed but not at work during the survey week. *Hours worked per week* refers to the number of hours the respondent worked at all jobs during the survey week—these estimates exclude those who were employed but not at work during the survey week; therefore, detail may not sum to total percentage employed. For more information on the Current Population Survey (CPS), see *supplemental note 2.*
SOURCE: U.S. Department of Commerce, Census Bureau, Current Population Survey (CPS), October Supplement, 1970–2009.

Figure 45-2. Percentage of 16- to 24-year-old full-time college students who were employed, by sex and institution level and control: October 2009

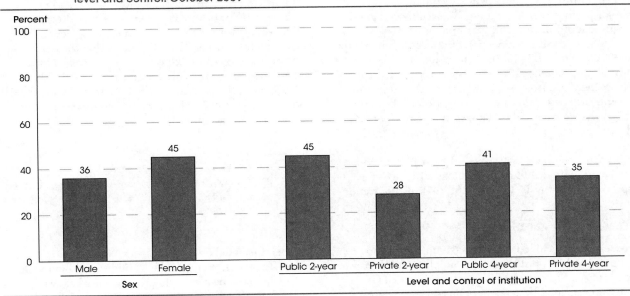

NOTE: College includes both 2- and 4-year institutions. College students were classified as *full time* if they were taking at least 12 hours of classes (or at least 9 hours of graduate classes) during an average school week. Percent employed estimates include those who were employed but not at work during the survey week. For more information on the Current Population Survey (CPS), see *supplemental note 2.*
SOURCE: U.S. Department of Commerce, Census Bureau, Current Population Survey (CPS), October Supplement, 2009.

From 1999–2000 to 2007–08, the percentage of full-time, full-year undergraduates receiving federal loans increased from 43 to 49 percent. Over the same time period, the average federal grant increased from $3,300 to $3,800 (in constant 2009–10 dollars).

Grants and loans are the major forms of federal financial support for postsecondary students. Federal grants, which do not need to be repaid, are available to undergraduates who qualify by economic need, whereas loans are available to all students. In addition to federal financial aid, there are also grants from state and local governments, institutions, and private sources, as well as private loans.

In 2007–08, about 65 percent of full-time, full-year undergraduates received a grant from any source, compared with 59 percent in 1999–2000 (see table A-46-1). From 1999–2000 to 2007–08, the average grant amount received from all sources by these recipients increased from $6,500 to $7,400 (in constant 2009–10 dollars). During this period, the average federal grant per recipient also increased from $3,300 to $3,800. The percentage of low-income dependent undergraduate students who received federal grants increased from 73 percent in 1999–2000 to 80 percent in 2007–08. In 2007–08, about 15 percent of middle-income and less than 1 percent of high-income students received federal grants.

In 2007–08, while some 29 percent of full-time, full-year undergraduates at public 4-year institutions and 28 percent of full-time full-year undergraduates at private not-for-profit 4-year institutions received federal grants, 56 percent of full-time full-year undergraduates at private for-profit 4-year institutions received federal grants. From 1999–2000 to 2007–08, the percentage of students at private for-profit 4-year institutions receiving federal grants increased from 36 to 56 percent. At public 4-year and private not-for-profit 4-year institutions, however, there were no measurable changes during this period in the percentages of students receiving federal grants.

Fifty-three percent of full-time, full-year undergraduates received a loan, including federal loans, in 2007–08, up from 45 percent in 1999–2000. In 2007–08, some

49 percent of all full-time, full-year undergraduates received federal loans, compared with the 43 percent who received federal loans in 1999–2000. Of those undergraduates receiving a loan, the average loan amount from all sources was $8,200 in 2007–08, higher than the average amount in 1999–2000 ($6,500, in constant 2009–10 dollars). From 1999–2000 to 2007–08, the percentage of low-income dependent undergraduates who received federal loans increased from 47 to 51 percent. In 2007–08, there was no measurable difference between low-income and middle-income dependent undergraduates in the percentage who received federal loans (51 and 49 percent, respectively), but the percentages for both groups were higher than the percentage of high-income dependent undergraduates who received federal loans that year (35 percent). Sixty-one percent of independent undergraduates received a federal loan in 2007–08.

In 2007–08, approximately 49 percent of full-time, full-year undergraduates at public 4-year institutions received federal loans, compared with 61 percent of students at private not-for-profit 4-year institutions and 92 percent of students at private-for-profit 4-year institutions. Comparing the percentage of students receiving federal loans at private for-profit 4-year institutions in 1999–2000 with the percentage receiving federal loans at those institutions in 2007–08 shows that the percentage increased from 73 to 92 percent, respectively. However, there were no measurable changes from 1999–2000 to 2007–08 in the percentages of students receiving federal loans at 4-year public institutions and private not-for-profit 4-year institutions.

For more information: *Table A-46-1*

Glossary: *Four-year postsecondary institution, Private institution, Public institution, Two-year postsecondary institution*

Technical Notes

Federal loans include Perkins loans, subsidized and unsubsidized Stafford loans, and Supplemental Loans to Students (SLS); federal grants are primarily Pell Grants and Supplemental Educational Opportunity Grants (SEOG), but also include Byrd scholarships. Parent Loans for Undergraduate Students (PLUS), veterans' benefits, and tax credits are not included in any of the totals. The weights used for the National Postsecondary Student Aid Study (NPSAS) 2000 calculations were revised and produce estimates that differ from those reported in *The Condition of Education 2010*. Income for dependent

students is based on parents' annual income in the prior year. The cutoff points for low, middle, and high income were obtained by identifying the incomes below the 25th percentile (low-income), between the 25th and 75th percentiles (middle-income), and at the 75th percentile and above (high-income). Data were adjusted to 2009–10 dollars using the Consumer Price Index for All Urban Consumers (CPI-U). For more information on the CPI-U, see *supplemental note 10*. For more information on NPSAS, see *supplemental note 3*.

Figure 46-1. Percentage of full-time, full-year dependent undergraduates who had federal loans and grants, by income level: Academic year 2007–08

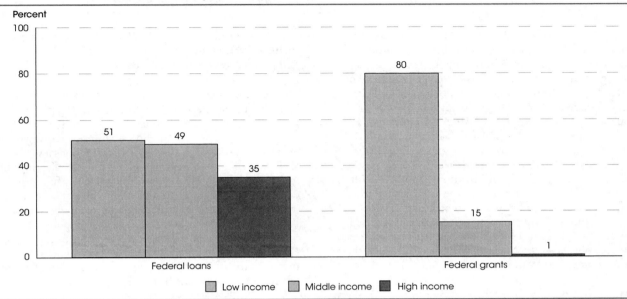

NOTE: Federal loans include Perkins loans, subsidized and unsubsidized Stafford loans, and Supplemental Loans to Students (SLS). Federal grants are primarily Pell Grants and Supplemental Educational Opportunity Grants (SEOG), but also include Byrd scholarships. Income for dependent students is based on parents' annual income in the prior year. The cutoff points for low, middle, and high income were obtained by identifying the incomes below the 25th percentile (low-income), between the 25th and 75th percentiles (middle-income), and at the 75th percentile and above (high-income).
SOURCE: U.S. Department of Education, National Center for Education Statistics, 2007–08 National Postsecondary Student Aid Study (NPSAS:08).

Figure 46-2. Average grants and loans to full-time, full-year dependent undergraduates who had federal loans and grants, by income level: Academic year 2007–08

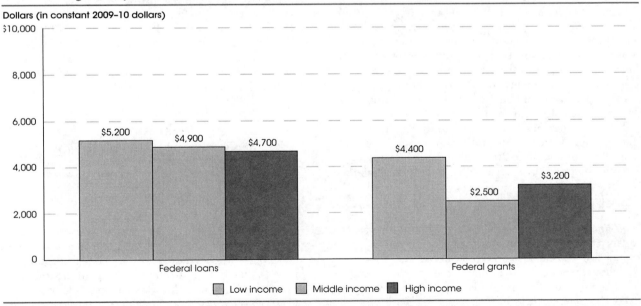

NOTE: Federal loans include Perkins loans, subsidized and unsubsidized Stafford loans, and Supplemental Loans to Students (SLS). Federal grants are primarily Pell Grants and Supplemental Educational Opportunity Grants (SEOG), but also include Byrd scholarships. Income for dependent students is based on parents' annual income in the prior year. The cutoff points for low, middle, and high income were obtained by identifying the incomes below the 25th percentile (low-income), between the 25th and 75th percentiles (middle-income), and at the 75th percentile and above (high-income). Data adjusted to 2009–10 dollars using the Consumer Price Index for All Urban Consumers (CPI-U). For more information about the CPI-U, see *supplemental note 10.*
SOURCE: U.S. Department of Education, National Center for Education Statistics, 2007–08 National Postsecondary Student Aid Study (NPSAS:08).

Price of Attending an Undergraduate Institution

The net price of education was higher in 2007–08 than in 1999–2000 for full-time, full-year, dependent undergraduates at all family income levels.

The total price of attending a postsecondary institution (also called "the student budget") includes tuition and fees, books and materials, and an allowance for living expenses. In 2007–08, the average total price of attendance, in constant 2009–10 dollars, for full-time, full-year, dependent undergraduates was $12,100 at public 2-year institutions and $19,300 at public 4-year institutions (see table A-47-1). At private institutions, the total price was $23,800 at not-for-profit 2-year institutions, $37,400 at not-for-profit 4-year institutions, $27,900 at for-profit 2-year institutions, and $33,500 at for-profit 4-year institutions. The average total price of attendance for students at each of the six major combinations of institution level and control was higher in 2007–08 than in 1999–2000, with the exception of private not-for-profit 2-year institutions, for which there was no measurable difference.

Many students and their families do not pay the full price of attendance because they receive financial aid to help cover their expenses. The primary types of financial aid are grants, which do not have to be repaid, and loans, which must be repaid. Grants, including scholarships, may be awarded on the basis of financial need, merit, or both, and may include tuition aid from employers. The average grant amounts for students at public 2- and 4-year institutions and private not-for-profit 4-year institutions were higher in 2007–08 than in 1999–2000 (see table A-47-1). However, there was no measurable change in the average grant amount for students at private not-for-profit 2-year institutions, private for-profit 2-year institutions, or private for-profit 4-year institutions. The loan amounts reported in this indicator include student borrowing through federal, state, institutional, and alternative (private) loan programs, as well as loans taken out by parents through the federal Parent Loans for Undergraduate Students (PLUS) program. When adjusted for inflation to 2009–10 dollars, the average amount borrowed by students at each of the six major

combinations of institution level and control was higher in 2007–08 than in 1999–2000. Financial aid amounts and percentages exclude tax credits and deductions.

The net price is an estimate of the cash outlay, including loans, that students and their families need to pay in a given year to cover educational expenses. It is calculated here as the total price of attendance minus grants (which decrease the price). Tax credits and deductions are excluded from the calculation of net price. Reflecting the higher total costs, the net price for full-time, full-year, dependent undergraduates was higher in 2007–08 than in 1999–2000 at four of the six major combinations of institution level and control (public 2-year, public 4-year, private not-for-profit 4-year, and private for-profit 4-year). From 2003–04 to 2007–08, the net price of attendance increased for all institutions, with the exception of private not-for-profit 2-year institutions.

Overall, the net price of sending a student to a postsecondary institution was higher in 2007–08 than in 1999–2000 for families at all income levels. For low-income, middle-income and high-income families, the net price increased, respectively by $1,400, $2,200, and $3,600. During this period, net price also increased for students from all racial/ethnic groups, with the exception of American Indian/Alaska Natives (see table A-47-2). For example, the net price for White students increased from $16,000 in 1999–2000 to $18,700 in 2007–08. For Black, Hispanic, Asian, Pacific Islander/Native Hawaiian students, and students of two or more races, the net price increased, respectively, by $2,600, $2,600, $3,100, $5,000, and $3,100.

For more information: *Tables A-47-1 and A-47-2*
Glossary: *Consumer Price Index (CPI), Four-year postsecondary institution, Private institution, Public institution, Two-year postsecondary institution*

Technical Notes

Full time refers to students who attended full time (as defined by the institution) for the full year (at least 9 months). Information on the use of tax credits by individual families is not available and therefore could not be taken into account in calculating net price. Averages were computed for all students, including those who did not receive financial aid. Detail may not sum to totals because of rounding. Data were adjusted by the Consumer Price Index for All Urban Consumers (CPI-U) to constant 2009–10 dollars. For more information on the CPI-U, see *supplemental note 10*. Estimates exclude

students who were not U.S. citizens or permanent residents and therefore ineligible for federal student aid and students who attended more than one institution in a year, due to the difficulty matching information on price and aid. For more information on race/ethnicity, see *supplemental note 1*. The weights used for the National Postsecondary Student Aid Study (NPSAS) 2000 calculations were revised and produce estimates that differ from those reported in *The Condition of Education 2010*. For more information on NPSAS, see *supplemental note 3*.

Figure 47-1. Average total price, grants, and net price for full-time, full-year, dependent undergraduates at 2-year institutions, by institution control: Academic years 1999–2000, 2003–04, and 2007–08

[In constant 2009–10 dollars]

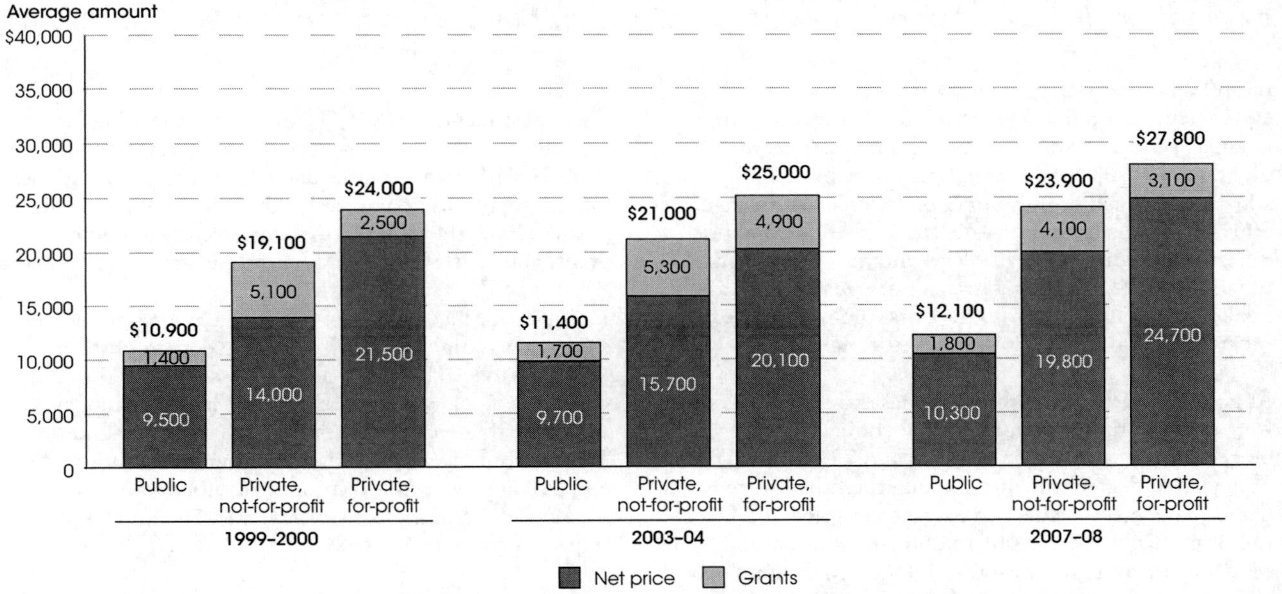

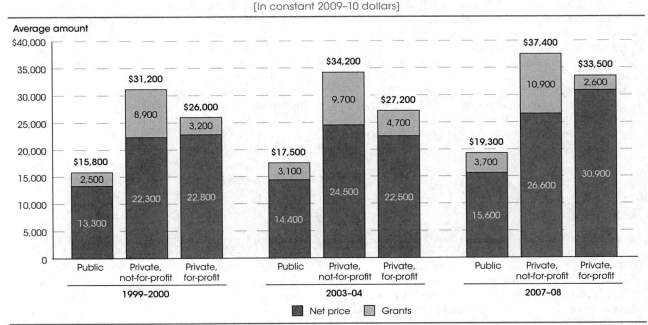

NOTE: *Full time* refers to students who attended full time (as defined by the institution) for the full year (at least 9 months). *Net price* is an estimate of the cash outlay that students and their families need to make in a given year to cover educational expenses. Averages were computed for all students, including those who did not receive financial aid. Data were adjusted by the Consumer Price Index for All Urban Consumers (CPI-U) to constant 2009–10 dollars. For more information on the CPI-U, see *supplemental note 10*. Detail may not sum to totals because of rounding.
SOURCE: U.S. Department of Education, National Center for Education Statistics, 1999–2000, 2003–04, and 2007–08 National Postsecondary Student Aid Studies (NPSAS:2000, NPSAS:04, and NPSAS:08).

Figure 47-2. Average total price, grants, and net price for full-time, full-year, dependent undergraduates at 4-year institutions, by institution control: Academic years 1999–2000, 2003–04, and 2007–08

[In constant 2009–10 dollars]

NOTE: *Full time* refers to students who attended full time (as defined by the institution) for the full year (at least 9 months). *Net price* is an estimate of the cash outlay that students and their families need to make in a given year to cover educational expenses. Averages were computed for all students, including those who did not receive financial aid. Data were adjusted by the Consumer Price Index for All Urban Consumers (CPI-U) to constant 2009–10 dollars. For more information on the CPI-U, see *supplemental note 10*. Detail may not sum to totals due to rounding.
SOURCE: U.S. Department of Education, National Center for Education Statistics, 1999–2000, 2003–04, and 2007–08 National Postsecondary Student Aid Studies (NPSAS:2000, NPSAS:04, and NPSAS:08).

About 9 out of 10 full-time graduate students received financial aid in 2007–08. The average total price of attending was greater in 2007–08 than in 2003–04 for students in master's or first-professional degree programs at public universities, as well as for students in first-professional degree programs at private not-for-profit universities.

In 2007–08, the average total price (tuition and fees, books and materials, and living expenses) for 1 year of full-time graduate education was $34,600 for a master's degree program; $39,700 for a doctoral program; and $46,500 for a first-professional degree program. Prices are in constant 2009–10 dollars (see table A-48-1). The average total price differed depending on degree level and institution control, ranging from $29,000 for a master's degree program at a public institution to $53,700 for a first-professional degree program at a private not-for-profit institution.

About one-fourth (26 percent) of master's degree students were enrolled full time in 2007–08, compared to 53 percent of doctoral degree students and 78 percent of first-professional degree students. Among the full-time master's degree students, the adjusted average net price (total price minus grants) was $23,900 at public institutions and $35,000 at private not-for-profit institutions. Compared with their peers at private not-for profit institutions, on average, full-time master's students at public institutions received more in assistantships and borrowed less in student loans.

In 2007–08, some 85 percent of full-time students at the master's level, 88 percent at the first-professional level, and 93 percent at the doctoral level received some type of financial aid (see table A-48-2). Grants and assistantships are usually awarded on a discretionary basis and are not related to financial need. Financial need must be demonstrated by students in order to obtain Perkins or subsidized Stafford loans, but not to take out unsubsidized Stafford loans, or private loans. Graduate students may receive tuition assistance from their employers (also considered grant aid). For example, in 2007–08, some 48 percent of part-time students in master of business administration programs received this type of financial aid (see table A-48-3).

The average annual net price in 2007–08 for full-time doctoral students was $24,700 at public institutions and $36,300 at private not-for-profit institutions (see table A-49-1). Although full-time doctoral students faced higher average total prices compared with their counterparts at the master's level, they did receive larger average amounts in grants and assistantships and borrowed less in student loans.

In 2007–08, the annual net price paid by first-professional students was higher than that paid by doctoral students in both public and private not-for-profit institutions. Also, first-professional students relied more heavily on loans to pay for their education: in 2007–08 their per annum loan amounts averaged $23,400 at public institutions and $30,500 at private not-for-profit institutions, while doctoral students' per annum loans averaged $4,700 and $9,800, respectively.

The average total price of attending a graduate program was greater in 2007–08 than in 2003–04 (after adjusting for inflation) for master's degree students at public institutions and for first-professional students at both public and private not-for-profit institutions. Tuition and fees were greater in 2007–08 than in 2003–04 for master's degree students at public institutions and for first-professional students at public and private not-for profit institutions. The 2007–08 tuition and fees associated with obtaining a doctoral degree at both public and private not-for-profit institutions were not measurably different from the 2003–04 tuition and fees; the same was true for net price. For students enrolled in first-professional degree programs at private not-for-profit institutions, the total annual price of attendance (in constant 2009–10 dollars) rose from approximately $47,600 in 2003–04 to $53,700 in 2007–08.

For more information: *Tables A-48-1 through A-48-3*
Glossary: *Classification of Instructional Program (CIP), Consumer Price Index (CPI), Doctoral degree, First-professional degree, Master's degree*

Technical Notes

First-professional programs include chiropractic, osteopathic medicine, dentistry, pharmacy, law, podiatry, medicine, theology, optometry, and veterinary medicine. The category labeled "Assistantships and other aid" consists primarily of assistantships but also includes a small amount of other types of aid such as work study, state vocational, rehabilitation and job training grants, federal veterans benefits, and military tuition aid. Analysis is limited to students who attended for the full year at only one institution in 2003–04 and 2007–08 to keep financial aid and prices comparable. Totals include data for private

for-profit institutions, which are not shown separately. *Full time* means enrolled full time (according to the institution's definition) for at least 9 months during the academic year; full-time enrollment does not preclude working. For more information on the National Postsecondary Student Aid Study (NPSAS), see *supplemental note 3*. Data were adjusted to constant 2009–10 dollars using the Consumer Price Index for All Urban Consumers (CPI-U). For more information on the CPI-U, see *supplemental note 10*. Detail may not sum to totals because of rounding.

Figure 48-1. Average annual total price, financial aid, and net price for full-time graduate and first-professional students attending public institutions: Academic years 2003–04 and 2007–08

[In constant 2009–10 dollars]

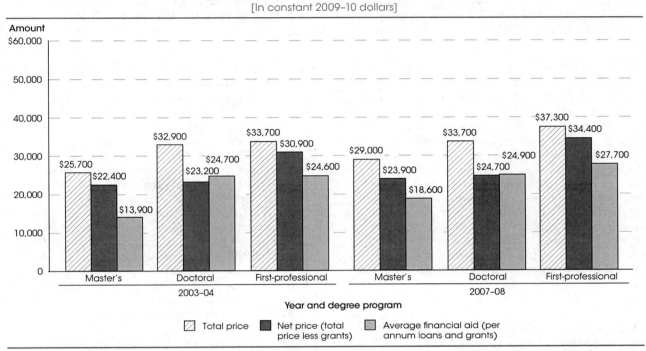

NOTE: Data presented are limited to students who attended for the full year at only one institution to keep financial aid and price data comparable. Detail may not sum to totals because of rounding. For more information on the National Postsecondary Student Aid Study (NPSAS), see *supplemental note 3.*
SOURCE: U.S. Department of Education, National Center for Education Statistics, 2003–04 and 2007–08 National Postsecondary Student Aid Study (NPSAS:04 and NPSAS:08).

Figure 48-2. Average annual total price, financial aid, and net price for full-time graduate and first-professional students attending private not-for-profit institutions: Academic years 2003–04 and 2007–08

[In constant 2009–10 dollars]

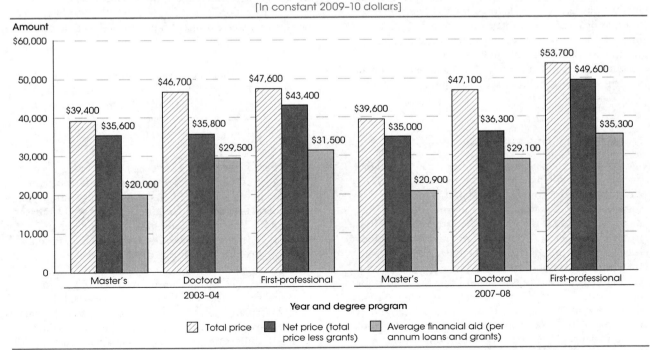

NOTE: Data presented are limited to students who attended for the full year at only one institution to keep financial aid and price data comparable. Detail may not sum to totals because of rounding. For more information on National Postsecondary Student Aid Study (NPSAS), see *supplemental note 3.*
SOURCE: U.S. Department of Education, National Center for Education Statistics, 2003–04 and 2007–08 National Postsecondary Student Aid Study (NPSAS:04 and NPSAS:08).

Tuition and Fees, Student Loans, and Default Rates

In 2008–09, average tuition and fees, in constant 2009–10 dollars, at 4-year postsecondary institutions were $12,100. At public 4-year institutions, average tuition and fees were $6,400, compared with $15,300 at private for-profit institutions and $24,900 at private not-for-profit institutions.

In 2008–09, average tuition and fees, in constant 2009–10 dollars, at 4-year postsecondary degree-granting institutions were $12,100. At public 4-year institutions, average tuition and fees were $6,400, compared with $15,300 at private for-profit institutions and $24,900 at private not-for-profit institutions (see table A-49-1). Among first-time, full-time students attending 4-year institutions in 2008–09, the percentage who had student loans differed by institution control: 56 percent of all students had student loans, compared with 47 percent of students at public institutions, 61 percent of students at private not-for-profit institutions, and 81 percent of students at private for-profit institutions. In 2008–09, average per annum loan amounts, in constant dollars, were highest at private for-profit institutions ($9,800), followed by private not-for-profit institutions ($7,700) and public institutions ($6,000).

At 2-year postsecondary degree-granting institutions, average tuition and fees (in constant 2009–10 dollars) were $2,600 in 2008–09. At public 2-year institutions, average tuition and fees were $2,200; at private not-for-profit 2-year institutions, average tuition and fees were $12,700; and at private for-profit 2-year institutions, average tuition and fees were $13,900. Some 21 percent of first-time, full-time students attending public 2-year institutions had student loans, with an average loan amount of $4,200. At private not-for-profit 2-year institutions, 58 percent of students had student loans, with an average loan amount of $6,100. At private for-profit 2- year institutions, 78 percent of students had student loans, with an average loan amount of $7,800.

Approximately 3.2 million students entered the repayment phase of their student loans in fiscal year (FY) 2008, meaning their student loans became due between October 1, 2007, and September 30, 2008 (see table A-49-2). Of those students, 7 percent had defaulted on the payments on their student loans within 2 years (before FY 2009 ended on September 30, 2009). The percentage of students who enter repayment on their loans in a particular fiscal year and default prior to the end of the next fiscal year is the 2-year cohort default rate. The default rate for students in the FY 2008 cohort was 5 percent at 4-year degree-granting institutions and 11 percent at 2-year degree-granting institutions. Default rates for the FY 2008 cohort were highest at private for-profit 2-year institutions (12 percent) and private for-profit 4-year institutions (11 percent). The lowest default rates were for students at private not-for-profit and public 4-year institutions (4 percent each).

The 7 percent rate of default across all institutions for the FY 2008 cohort was higher than the rates for the FY 2007 (6 percent) and FY 2006 (5 percent) cohorts. The percentage increase in default rates from FY 2006 to FY 2008 was greatest at private for-profit 4-year institutions (from 8 percent to 11 percent). The smallest increases in default rates from FY 2006 to FY 2008 were at public 4-year institutions (from 3 to 4 percent) and private not-for-profit 2-year institutions (from 7 to 8 percent).

For more information: *Tables A-49-1 and A-49-2*

Glossary: *College, Four-year postsecondary institution, Private institution, Public institution, Tuition, Two-year postsecondary institution*

Technical Notes

Degree-granting institutions grant associate's or higher degrees and participate in Title IV federal financial aid programs. Tuition and fees amounts for public institutions are the averages for in-state students. The repayment phase is the period when student loans must be repaid and generally begins 6 months after a student leaves an institution. The 2-year cohort default rate is the percentage of borrowers who enter repayment on certain Federal Family Education Loan (FFEL) Program or William D. Ford Federal Direct Loan (Direct Loan) Program loans during a particular federal fiscal year (a fiscal year runs from October 1 to September 30) and default or meet other specified conditions within the cohort default period. The cohort default period is the two-year period that begins on October 1 of the fiscal

year when the borrower enters repayment and ends on September 30 of the following fiscal year. Default rates were calculated using student counts by institution from the Federal Student Aid Cohort Default Rate Database and the IPEDS classification of institution level and control. For more information on the Federal Student Aid (FSA) cohort default rate database or the Integrated Postsecondary Education Data System (IPEDS), see *supplemental note 3*. Institutions in this indicator are classified based on the highest degrees awarded. For more information on the classification of postsecondary institutions, see *supplemental note 8*. Data were adjusted to 2009–10 dollars using the Consumer Price Index for All Urban Consumers (CPI-U). For more information on the CPI-U, see *supplemental note 10*.

Figure 49-1. Average tuition and fees and average loan amounts at degree-granting institutions, by level and control of institution: 2008–09

[In constant 2009–10 dollars]

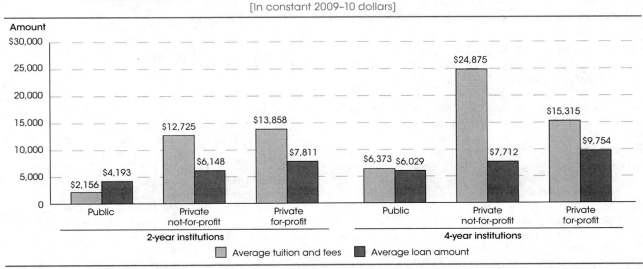

NOTE: Degree-granting institutions grant associate's or higher degrees and participate in Title IV federal financial aid programs. Tuition and fees amounts for public institutions are the averages for in-state students. Tuition and fee data are collected in the fall and loan data are collected in the spring. For more information on the Integrated Postsecondary Data System (IPEDS) and IPEDS classification of institutions, see *supplemental notes 3* and *8*. Data were adjusted to constant 2009–10 dollars using the Consumer Price Index for All Urban Consumers (CPI-U). For more information on the CPI-U, see *supplemental note 10.*
SOURCE: U.S. Department of Education, National Center for Education Statistics, 2009–10 Integrated Postsecondary Education Data System (IPEDS), Spring 2009.

Figure 49-2. Two-year student loan cohort default rates at degree-granting institutions, by level and control of institution: Fiscal years 2006–08

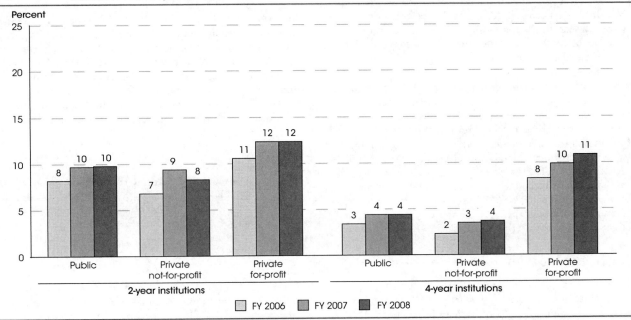

NOTE: Includes undergraduate and postbaccalaureate students. Degree-granting institutions grant associate's or higher degrees and participate in Title IV federal financial aid programs. The 2-year cohort default rate is the percentage of borrowers who enter repayment on certain Federal Family Education Loan (FFEL) Program or William D. Ford Federal Direct Loan (Direct Loan) Program loans during a particular federal fiscal year and default or meet other specified conditions within the cohort default period, which is the two-year period that begins on October 1 of the fiscal year when the borrower enters repayment and ends on September 30 of the following fiscal year. Default rates were calculated using student counts by institution from the Federal Student Aid Cohort Default Rate Database and the Integrated Postsecondary Data System (IPEDS) classification of institution level and control. For more information on IPEDS and IPEDS classification of institutions, see *supplemental notes 3* and *8*.
SOURCE: U.S. Department of Education, Federal Student Aid, Direct Loan and Federal Family Education Loan Programs, Cohort Default Rate Database, retrieved November 5, 2010, from http://www2.ed.gov/offices/OSFAP/defaultmanagement/cdr.html.

Postsecondary Revenues and Expenses

In 2008–09, instruction was the largest per-student expense at public ($7,534) and private not-for-profit institutions ($15,215). At private for-profit institutions, instruction was the second largest expense category, with $3,069 spent per student.

About 19 million undergraduate and graduate students were enrolled in postsecondary degree-granting institutions in 2008–09 (see *indicators 8 and 9*). This indicator examines general patterns in the revenues and expenses of postsecondary degree-granting institutions. Only some financial data may be comparable across institutional control (public, private not-for-profit, and private for-profit) because of differences in accounting procedures for certain categories. In addition, comparisons between institutional levels (2-year vs. 4-year) may also be limited because of different institutional missions.

In 2008–09, total revenue was $267 billion at public institutions, $69 billion at private not-for-profit institutions, and $19 billion at private for-profit institutions (see table A-50-1). The category of student tuition and fees typically accounts for a large percentage of total revenue and was the largest revenue source at both private not-for-profit and for-profit institutions in 2008–09 (78 and 86 percent, respectively). At public institutions, the share of revenue from tuition and fees (19 percent) was second to that from state appropriations (24 percent). Tuition and fees constituted the largest revenue category for private not-for-profit and private for-profit 2- and 4-year institutions, the second largest category for public 4-year institutions, and the third largest category for public 2-year institutions. Across all sectors, the shares for tuition and fees were generally larger for 4-year institutions than they were for 2-year institutions (see table A-50-2).

Historically, investment return has generally been among the largest revenue sources for private not-for-profit institutions. In contrast, private for-profit institutions typically receive little revenue from this source, while public institutions receive a moderate amount. Changes in the value of endowment funds from investments affect total revenue and can fluctuate from year to year. For example, in 2008–09, private not-for-profit institutions saw a loss in investment return of $64 billion, which decreased total revenue and caused other revenue sources to account for larger shares of the total (see table A-50-1). Investment

income at public institutions was affected to a lesser degree (a loss of $9 billion).

In 2008–09, total expenses were $273 billion at public institutions, $141 billion at private not-for-profit institutions, and $16 billion at private for-profit institutions (see table A-50-3). At public and private not-for-profit institutions, instruction was the largest expense category (27 and 33 percent, respectively). At private for-profit institutions, instruction constituted 24 percent of total expenses but student services and academic and institutional support (a category which covers a wide range of administrative costs) was the largest category at 67 percent. Other relatively large categories at public institutions (those accounting for 8–10 percent of expenses) were research, institutional support, auxiliary enterprises, and hospitals. At private not-for-profit institutions, some of the other larger categories (those accounting for 10–14 percent of expenses) were research, institutional support, and auxiliary enterprises.

Public and private not-for-profit institutions spent the most per student on instruction in 2008–09 ($7,534 and 15,215, respectively); private for-profit institutions spent $3,069 per student.

Variations were found when comparing expenses at 2- and 4-year institutions in 2008–09. For example, public 2-year and private for-profit 2-year institutions spent a greater share of their budgets on instruction than their 4-year counterparts did (37 vs. 25 percent at public institutions and 33 vs. 21 percent at private for-profit institutions) (see table A-50-4). Private not-for-profit 2- and 4-year institutions each spent 33 percent of their budgets on instruction.

For more information: *Tables A-50-1 through A-50-4*
Glossary: *Consumer Price Index (CPI), Full-time Equivalent (FTE) enrollment, Private institution, Public institution, Revenues, Tuition*

Technical Notes

Auxiliary enterprises are essentially self-supporting operations, such as residence halls, that exist to provide a service to students, faculty, or staff, and that charge a fee that is directly related to, although not necessarily equal to, the cost of the service. Academic support includes services that directly support an institution's primary missions of instruction, research, or public service. Institutional support includes general administrative services, executive direction and planning, legal and fiscal operations, and community relations. Student services includes expenses associated with

admissions, registrar activities, and activities whose primary purpose is to contribute to students' emotional and physical well-being and to their intellectual, cultural, and social development outside the context of the formal instructional program. Data are adjusted by the Consumer Price Index (CPI) to constant 2009–10 dollars. For more information on the CPI, see *supplemental note 10*. For more information on the Integrated Postsecondary Education Data System (IPEDS) and IPEDS classification of institutions, see *supplemental notes 3 and 8*.

Figure 50-1. Revenue per student from tuition and fees for degree-granting postsecondary institutions, by institutional control and level: Academic year 2008–09

[In constant 2009–10 dollars]

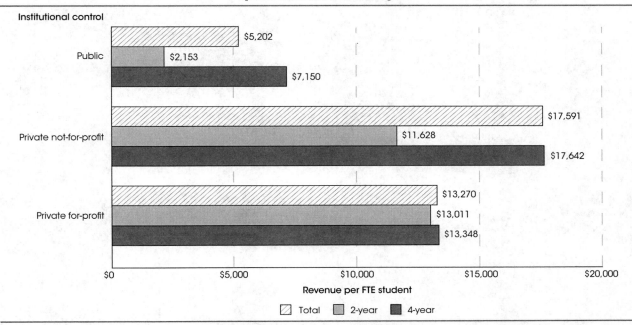

Institutional control

NOTE: Full-time-equivalent (FTE) enrollment includes full-time students plus the full-time equivalent of part-time students. Data are adjusted by the Consumer Price Index (CPI) to constant 2009–10 dollars. For more information on the CPI, see *supplemental note 10*. For more information on the Integrated Postsecondary Education Data System (IPEDS) and IPEDS classification of institutions, see *supplemental notes 3 and 8*.
SOURCE: U.S. Department of Education, National Center for Education Statistics, 2008–09 Integrated Postsecondary Education Data System, Spring 2010.

Figure 50-2. Expenses per student at 4-year degree-granting postsecondary institutions, by institutional control and purpose: Academic year 2008–09

[In constant 2009–10 dollars]

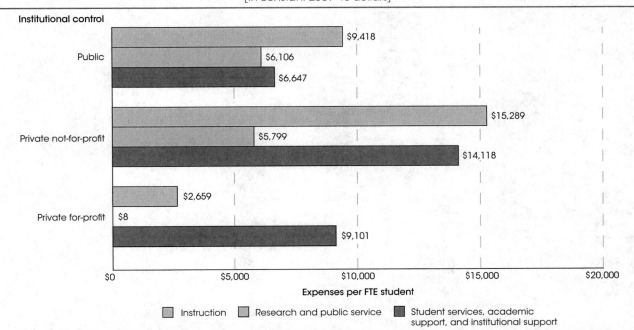

Institutional control

NOTE: Full-time-equivalent (FTE) enrollment includes full-time students plus the full-time equivalent of part-time students. Data are adjusted by the Consumer Price Index (CPI) to constant 2009–10 dollars. For more information on the CPI, see *supplemental note 10*. For more information on the Integrated Postsecondary Education Data System (IPEDS) and IPEDS classification of institutions, see *supplemental notes 3 and 8*.
SOURCE: U.S. Department of Education, National Center for Education Statistics, 2008–09 Integrated Postsecondary Education Data System, Spring 2010.

Appendix A
Supplemental Tables

Appendix A contains all of the supplemental tables for the indicators in this volume.

The indicator tables are numbered sequentially according to indicator with a numbered suffix added to reflect the order of the supplemental table in each indicator. For example, indicator 13 has two supplemental tables, so the tables are numbered Table A-13-1 and A-13-2.

The standard errors for the supplemental tables in appendix A are not included here, but can be found on the NCES website at http://nces.ed.gov/programs/coe.

Enrollment Trends by Age

Table A-1-1. Percentage of the population ages 3–34 enrolled in school, by age group: October 1970–2009

October of year	Total, ages 3–34	Ages 3–4[1]	Ages 5–6	Ages 7–13	Ages 14–15	Ages 16–17	Ages 18–19 Total	In secondary[2]	In college	Ages 20–24 Total	Ages 20–21	Ages 22–24	Ages 25–29	Ages 30–34
1970	56.4	20.5	89.5	99.2	98.1	90.0	47.7	10.5	37.3	21.5	31.9	14.9	7.5	4.2
1971	56.2	21.2	91.6	99.1	98.6	90.2	49.2	11.5	37.7	21.9	32.2	15.4	8.0	4.9
1972	54.9	24.4	91.9	99.2	97.6	88.9	46.3	10.4	35.9	21.6	31.4	14.8	8.6	4.6
1973	53.5	24.2	92.5	99.2	97.5	88.3	42.9	10.0	32.9	20.8	30.1	14.5	8.5	4.5
1974	53.6	28.8	94.2	99.3	97.9	87.9	43.1	9.9	33.2	21.4	30.2	15.1	9.6	5.7
1975	53.7	31.5	94.7	99.3	98.2	89.0	46.9	10.2	36.7	22.4	31.2	16.2	10.1	6.6
1976	53.1	31.3	95.5	99.2	98.2	89.1	46.2	10.2	36.0	23.3	32.0	17.1	10.0	6.0
1977	52.5	32.0	95.8	99.4	98.5	88.9	46.2	10.4	35.7	22.9	31.8	16.5	10.8	6.9
1978	51.2	34.2	95.3	99.1	98.4	89.1	45.4	9.8	35.6	21.8	29.5	16.3	9.4	6.4
1979	50.3	35.1	95.8	99.2	98.1	89.2	45.0	10.3	34.6	21.7	30.2	15.8	9.6	6.4
1980	49.7	36.7	95.7	99.3	98.2	89.0	46.4	10.5	35.9	22.3	31.0	16.3	9.3	6.4
1981	48.9	36.0	94.0	99.2	98.0	90.6	49.0	11.5	37.5	22.5	31.6	16.5	9.0	6.9
1982	48.6	36.4	95.0	99.2	98.5	90.6	47.8	11.3	36.5	23.5	34.0	16.8	9.6	6.3
1983	48.4	37.5	95.4	99.2	98.3	91.7	50.4	12.8	37.6	22.7	32.5	16.6	9.6	6.4
1984	47.9	36.3	94.5	99.2	97.8	91.5	50.1	11.5	38.6	23.7	33.9	17.3	9.1	6.3
1985	48.3	38.9	96.1	99.2	98.1	91.7	51.6	11.2	40.4	24.0	35.3	16.9	9.2	6.1
1986	48.2	38.9	95.3	99.2	97.6	92.3	54.6	13.1	41.5	23.6	33.0	17.9	8.8	6.0
1987	48.6	38.3	95.1	99.5	98.6	91.7	55.6	13.1	42.5	25.5	38.7	17.5	9.0	5.8
1988	48.7	38.2	96.0	99.7	98.9	91.6	55.6	13.9	41.8	26.1	39.1	18.2	8.3	5.9
1989	49.0	39.1	95.2	99.3	98.8	92.7	56.0	14.4	41.6	27.0	38.5	19.9	9.3	5.7
1990	50.2	44.4	96.5	99.6	99.0	92.5	57.2	14.5	42.7	28.6	39.7	21.0	9.7	5.8
1991	50.7	40.5	95.4	99.6	98.8	93.3	59.6	15.6	44.0	30.2	42.0	22.2	10.2	6.2
1992	51.4	39.7	95.5	99.4	99.1	94.1	61.4	17.1	44.3	31.6	44.0	23.7	9.8	6.1
1993	51.8	40.4	95.4	99.5	98.9	94.0	61.6	17.2	44.4	30.8	42.7	23.6	10.2	5.9
1994	53.3	47.3	96.7	99.4	98.8	94.4	60.2	16.2	43.9	32.0	44.9	24.0	10.8	6.7
1995	53.7	48.7	96.0	98.9	98.9	93.6	59.4	16.3	43.1	31.5	44.9	23.2	11.6	5.9
1996	54.1	48.3	94.0	97.7	98.0	92.8	61.5	16.7	44.9	32.5	44.4	24.8	11.9	6.1
1997	55.6	52.6	96.5	99.1	98.9	94.3	61.5	16.7	44.7	34.3	45.9	26.4	11.8	5.7
1998	55.8	52.1	95.6	98.9	98.4	93.9	62.2	15.7	46.4	33.0	44.8	24.9	11.9	6.6
1999	56.0	54.2	96.0	98.7	98.2	93.6	60.6	16.5	44.1	32.8	45.3	24.5	11.1	6.2
2000	55.9	52.1	95.6	98.2	98.7	92.8	61.2	16.5	44.7	32.5	44.1	24.6	11.4	6.7
2001	56.4	52.4	95.3	98.3	98.1	93.4	61.1	17.1	44.0	34.1	46.1	25.5	11.8	6.9
2002	57.1	56.4	95.5	98.3	98.5	94.4	63.2	17.6	45.7	35.0	48.5	26.0	12.3	6.7
2003	56.2	55.1	94.5	98.3	97.5	94.9	64.5	17.9	46.6	35.6	48.3	27.8	11.8	6.8
2004	56.2	54.0	95.4	98.4	98.5	94.5	64.4	16.6	47.8	35.2	48.9	26.3	13.0	6.6
2005	56.5	53.6	95.4	98.6	98.0	95.1	67.6	18.3	49.3	36.1	48.7	27.3	11.9	6.9
2006	56.0	55.7	94.6	98.3	98.3	94.6	65.5	19.3	46.2	35.0	47.5	26.7	11.7	7.2
2007	56.1	54.5	94.7	98.4	98.7	94.3	66.8	17.9	48.9	35.7	48.4	27.3	12.4	7.2
2008	56.2	52.8	93.8	98.7	98.6	95.2	66.0	17.4	48.6	36.9	50.1	28.2	13.2	7.3
2009	56.5	52.4	94.1	98.2	98.0	94.6	68.9	19.1	49.8	38.7	51.7	30.4	13.5	8.1

[1] Beginning in 1994, new procedures were used to collect enrollment data on children ages 3–4. As a result, pre-1994 data may not be comparable to data from 1994 or later.

[2] Includes the few 18- to 19-year-old students (between 0 and 0.17 percent of students) who were enrolled in elementary school.

NOTE: Detail may not sum to totals because of rounding. Includes enrollment in any type of graded public, parochial, or other private schools. Includes nursery or preschools, kindergartens, elementary schools, high schools, colleges, universities, and professional schools. Attendance may be on a full- or part-time basis and during the day or night. Excludes enrollments in schools that do not advance students toward a regular school degree (e.g., trade schools, business colleges, and correspondence courses). This table uses a different data source than table A-1-2; therefore, estimates for 2009 are not directly comparable to the total enrollment estimates in table A-1-2. For more information on the Current Population Survey (CPS), see *supplemental note 2*.
SOURCE: U.S. Department of Commerce, Census Bureau, Current Population Survey (CPS), October Supplement, 1970–2009.

This indicator continues on page 140.

Enrollment Trends by Age

Table A-1-2. Age range for compulsory school attendance, policies on kindergarten education, and percentage of the population ages 3–34 enrolled in school, by age group and state or jurisdiction: 2009

State or jurisdiction	Compulsory age of attendance[1]	Kindergarten education[1]		School districts required to offer		Percentage of the population ages 3–34 enrolled in school									
		Attendance required	Program	Full-day program	Ages 3–4	Ages 5–17				Ages 18–19			Ages 20–24	Ages 25–34
						Total	Ages 5–6	Ages 7–13	Ages 14–17	Total	In secondary[2]	In college		
United States	†	†	†	†	**48.3**	**96.9**	**92.2**	**98.3**	**96.7**	**73.4**	**26.9**	**46.4**	**41.3**	**13.2**
Alabama	7 to 17		X	X	43.3	96.7	89.9	98.6	96.5	71.9	29.4	42.5	41.7	11.6
Alaska	7 to 16				33.6	96.9	88.8	99.0	96.6	60.6	39.7	20.9	33.3	14.6
Arizona	6 to 16[3]		X		32.5	96.1	88.4	98.5	96.2	65.1	29.3	35.8	36.6	13.6
Arkansas	5 to 17[3,4]	X	X	X	50.8	96.2	91.9	97.5	95.8	69.7	27.5	42.2	33.5	12.5
California	6 to 18		X		49.4	97.5	93.8	98.6	97.5	74.3	24.6	49.7	43.3	14.6
Colorado	6 to 17		X		50.3	96.7	93.1	98.4	95.6	71.5	31.0	40.5	41.2	12.6
Connecticut	5 to 18[4]	X	X		60.9	97.7	94.5	98.5	97.6	77.3	20.9	56.4	44.9	14.1
Delaware	5 to 16	X	X		50.6	97.3	92.3	98.7	97.2	78.9	23.6	55.4	42.1	13.8
District of Columbia	5 to 18	X	X		55.6	96.8	98.2	97.5	95.2	84.2	14.4	69.8	40.5	16.0
Florida	6 to 16[5]		X		49.3	96.4	91.8	97.9	96.0	70.6	29.5	41.1	42.1	13.4
Georgia	6 to 16		X	X	51.6	97.2	94.2	98.5	96.5	69.7	27.9	41.8	38.7	12.9
Hawaii	6 to 18		X		57.6	96.2	92.7	98.6	94.4	63.4	21.2	42.1	34.6	15.3
Idaho	7 to 16				30.5	95.9	86.1	98.7	96.5	69.4	23.6	45.7	31.6	12.7
Illinois	7 to 17		X[6]		55.9	97.3	93.3	98.5	97.0	75.5	26.9	48.6	43.9	13.8
Indiana	7 to 18[3]		X		40.5	96.6	88.1	98.6	97.1	74.0	32.9	41.1	43.3	12.2
Iowa	6 to 16		X		47.9	97.4	94.1	98.5	97.2	78.5	25.3	53.2	44.3	13.4
Kansas	7 to 18[3]		X		44.8	97.0	92.6	98.2	97.3	73.2	27.6	45.6	42.6	14.6
Kentucky	6 to 16		X		44.3	96.5	89.9	98.4	96.5	67.3	22.5	44.8	35.6	11.3
Louisiana	7 to 18[3]	X	X	X	55.9	97.6	95.6	98.7	96.7	68.3	28.5	39.9	39.0	10.4
Maine	7 to 17[3]		X		42.8	96.5	90.5	98.3	96.1	70.1	24.9	45.2	44.5	9.9
Maryland	5 to 16[4]	X	X	X	51.0	97.1	93.5	97.9	97.2	74.5	21.9	52.7	39.5	16.0
Massachusetts	6 to 16[3]		X		61.7	97.2	94.0	98.2	97.2	82.4	23.0	59.4	49.5	14.2
Michigan	6 to 18				48.3	96.8	94.2	98.1	96.0	74.6	25.7	49.0	46.0	15.3
Minnesota	7 to 16[3]		X		47.5	96.5	90.2	97.8	97.3	80.1	32.5	47.6	43.3	12.5
Mississippi	6 to 17		X	X	51.7	96.1	92.4	97.5	95.3	73.0	28.5	44.5	39.7	11.6
Missouri	7 to 17		X		43.2	96.3	91.7	98.1	95.2	74.0	32.6	41.4	39.3	14.1
Montana	7 to 16[3]		X		43.7	96.3	88.9	98.4	96.3	71.7	28.0	43.6	39.4	12.5
Nebraska	6 to 18		X		48.8	97.2	92.7	98.6	97.3	71.9	25.8	46.1	37.8	13.1
Nevada	7 to 18[3]	X	X		30.6	95.5	86.1	98.7	94.3	57.2	25.3	31.9	30.5	10.8
New Hampshire	6 to 18				51.5	97.7	92.5	98.9	97.9	81.6	31.3	50.4	39.6	10.6

See notes at end of table.

Table A-1-2. Age range for compulsory school attendance, policies on kindergarten education, and percentage of the population ages 3–34 enrolled in school, by age group and state or jurisdiction: 2009—Continued

| | Kindergarten education[1] | | | | Percentage of the population ages 3–34 enrolled in school | | | | | | | | | |
| | | | School districts required to offer | | | Ages 5–17 | | | | Ages 18–19 | | | | |
State or jurisdiction	Compulsory age of attendance[1]	Attendance required	Program	Full-day program	Ages 3–4	Total	Ages 5–6	Ages 7–13	Ages 14–17	Total	In secondary[2]	In college	Ages 20–24	Ages 25–34
United States	†	†	†	†	**48.3**	**96.9**	**92.2**	**98.3**	**96.7**	**73.4**	**26.9**	**46.4**	**41.3**	**13.2**
New Jersey	6 to 16				66.2	97.4	93.9	98.5	97.1	78.1	29.3	48.8	43.9	11.2
New Mexico	5 to 18[3]	X	X		42.1	95.7	87.3	98.5	94.7	68.0	31.6	36.4	36.8	15.4
New York	6 to 16[7]				57.2	96.9	94.8	97.7	96.5	79.2	23.0	56.2	46.6	12.3
North Carolina	7 to 16		X	X	45.9	96.6	91.0	98.2	96.7	71.1	24.7	46.3	39.0	13.4
North Dakota	7 to 16				31.8	95.0	90.0	96.2	95.3	78.5	17.9	60.7	42.2	13.5
Ohio	6 to 18	X	X[6]		46.9	96.6	90.8	97.8	97.3	74.8	30.9	43.9	44.4	14.5
Oklahoma	5 to 18	X	X	(8)	40.6	97.5	95.2	98.5	96.8	69.9	30.7	39.1	37.7	11.3
Oregon	7 to 18		X		44.2	95.6	86.7	97.8	95.8	70.1	27.9	42.3	40.1	13.6
Pennsylvania	8 to 17[3]				49.3	96.5	90.0	98.1	96.7	77.8	24.3	53.4	42.9	12.3
Rhode Island	6 to 16	X	X		50.1	96.7	90.4	99.2	95.5	80.1	16.5	63.7	52.5	13.1
South Carolina	5 to 17[4]	X	X	X[6]	51.8	97.4	93.2	98.7	97.0	70.9	26.3	44.6	36.2	12.6
South Dakota	6 to 18[3,9]		X		36.2	96.5	90.6	98.5	95.6	73.4	32.5	40.9	37.5	11.0
Tennessee	6 to 17[4]	X	X		41.2	96.7	91.2	98.2	96.7	68.8	29.1	39.6	34.7	12.2
Texas	6 to 18		X		43.6	96.8	92.1	98.4	96.5	68.3	29.7	38.5	36.6	11.9
Utah	6 to 18		X		40.2	96.8	88.8	98.6	97.9	66.9	23.7	43.2	48.0	16.3
Vermont	6 to 16[3]		X		53.9	98.1	93.0	99.2	98.5	74.4	15.7	58.8	46.6	13.6
Virginia	5 to 18[3,4]	X	X		49.6	96.9	90.7	98.5	97.2	77.2	24.2	53.0	39.9	13.8
Washington	8 to 18		X		42.6	96.6	90.1	98.4	96.7	69.9	31.1	38.8	36.0	12.5
West Virginia	6 to 17	X	X	X	35.3	95.1	89.3	97.8	93.5	71.7	27.8	43.9	41.5	9.5
Wisconsin	6 to 18		X		47.6	97.5	94.2	98.5	97.4	79.3	26.8	52.5	42.6	12.6
Wyoming	7 to 16[3]		X		46.6	96.1	88.9	98.4	96.4	70.4	25.2	45.2	36.4	11.9

† Not applicable.
X State has policy.
[1] Requirements are for 2010.
[2] Includes the few 18- to 19-year-old students (between 0 and 0.92 percent of students in each state) who were enrolled in elementary school in 2009.
[3] Child may be exempted from compulsory attendance if he/she meets state requirements for early withdrawal without meeting conditions for a diploma or equivalency.
[4] Parent/guardian may delay child's entry until a later age per state law/regulation.
[5] Attendance is compulsory until age 18 for Manatee County students, unless they earn a high school diploma prior to reaching their 18th birthday.
[6] State requires districts with full-day programs to offer half-day programs.
[7] New York City and Buffalo require school attendance until age 17 unless employed; Syracuse requires kindergarten attendance at age 5.
[8] Beginning in 2011–12, it will be mandatory for all districts in Oklahoma to offer full-day kindergarten.
[9] Compulsory attendance beginning at age 5 effective July 1, 2010.
NOTE: Includes enrollment in public, private, and home school. This includes nursery school, kindergarten, elementary and high school, college, and graduate or professional school. Excludes enrollments in schools that do not advance students toward a regular school degree, such as trade schools, business colleges, and correspondence courses. This table uses a different data source than table A-1-1; therefore, total enrollment estimates are not directly comparable to the 2009 estimates in table A-1-2. For more information on the American Community Survey, see *supplemental note 3*.
SOURCE: Education Commission of the States (ECS), ECS StateNotes, *Compulsory School Age Requirements*, retrieved August 9, 2010, from http://www.ecs.org/clearinghouse/86/62/8662.pdf; *State Kindergarten Statutes: State Comparisons*, retrieved September 22, 2010, from http://mb2.ecs.org/reports/Report.aspx?id=14; and supplemental information retrieved from various state websites. U.S. Department of Commerce, Census Bureau, American Community Survey (ACS), 2009.

Table A-2-1. Actual and projected public school enrollment in grades prekindergarten (preK) through 12, by grade level and region: Selected school years, 1970–71 through 2020–21

[Totals in thousands]

School year	Total enrollment			Total and percent enrollment for grades preK–12, by region							
				Northeast		Midwest		South		West	
	Grades preK–12	Grades preK–8	Grades 9–12	Total	Percent	Total	Percent	Total	Percent	Total	Percent
1970–71	45,894	32,558	13,336	9,860	21.5	12,936	28.2	14,759	32.2	8,339	18.2
1975–76	44,819	30,515	14,304	9,679	21.6	12,295	27.4	14,654	32.7	8,191	18.3
1980–81	40,877	27,647	13,231	8,215	20.1	10,698	26.2	14,134	34.6	7,831	19.2
1985–86	39,422	27,034	12,388	7,318	18.6	9,862	25.0	14,117	35.8	8,124	20.6
1990–91	41,217	29,878	11,338	7,282	17.7	9,944	24.1	14,807	35.9	9,184	22.3
1991–92	42,047	30,506	11,541	7,407	17.6	10,080	24.0	15,081	35.9	9,479	22.5
1992–93	42,823	31,088	11,735	7,526	17.6	10,198	23.8	15,357	35.9	9,742	22.7
1993–94	43,465	31,504	11,961	7,654	17.6	10,289	23.7	15,591	35.9	9,931	22.8
1994–95	44,111	31,896	12,215	7,760	17.6	10,386	23.5	15,851	35.9	10,114	22.9
1995–96	44,840	32,338	12,502	7,894	17.6	10,512	23.4	16,118	35.9	10,316	23.0
1996–97	45,611	32,762	12,849	8,006	17.6	10,638	23.3	16,373	35.9	10,594	23.2
1997–98	46,127	33,071	13,056	8,085	17.5	10,704	23.2	16,563	35.9	10,775	23.4
1998–99	46,539	33,344	13,195	8,145	17.5	10,722	23.0	16,713	35.9	10,959	23.5
1999–2000	46,857	33,486	13,371	8,196	17.5	10,726	22.9	16,842	35.9	11,093	23.7
2000–01	47,204	33,686	13,517	8,222	17.4	10,730	22.7	17,007	36.0	11,244	23.8
2001–02	47,672	33,936	13,736	8,250	17.3	10,745	22.5	17,237	36.2	11,440	24.0
2002–03	48,183	34,114	14,069	8,297	17.2	10,819	22.5	17,471	36.3	11,596	24.1
2003–04	48,540	34,201	14,339	8,292	17.1	10,809	22.3	17,673	36.4	11,766	24.2
2004–05	48,795	34,178	14,618	8,271	17.0	10,775	22.1	17,892	36.7	11,857	24.3
2005–06	49,113	34,204	14,909	8,240	16.8	10,819	22.0	18,103	36.9	11,951	24.3
2006–07	49,316	34,235	15,081	8,258	16.7	10,819	21.9	18,294	37.1	11,945	24.2
2007–08	49,293	34,205	15,087	8,122	16.5	10,770	21.8	18,425	37.4	11,976	24.3
2008–09	49,266	34,285	14,980	8,053	16.3	10,743	21.8	18,491	37.5	11,979	24.3
Projected											
2009–10	49,282	34,440	14,842	7,960	16.2	10,700	21.7	18,600	37.7	12,022	24.4
2010–11	49,306	34,637	14,668	7,887	16.0	10,654	21.6	18,691	37.9	12,073	24.5
2011–12	49,422	34,892	14,530	7,831	15.8	10,622	21.5	18,814	38.1	12,155	24.6
2012–13	49,642	35,129	14,512	7,790	15.7	10,619	21.4	18,977	38.2	12,256	24.7
2013–14	49,914	35,368	14,545	7,762	15.6	10,631	21.3	19,146	38.4	12,374	24.8
2014–15	50,268	35,579	14,689	7,752	15.4	10,662	21.2	19,339	38.5	12,515	24.9
2015–16	50,659	35,829	14,830	7,753	15.3	10,699	21.1	19,531	38.6	12,676	25.0
2016–17	51,038	36,161	14,877	7,758	15.2	10,730	21.0	19,709	38.6	12,842	25.2
2017–18	51,430	36,491	14,939	7,770	15.1	10,760	20.9	19,883	38.7	13,017	25.3
2018–19	51,803	36,803	15,000	7,784	15.0	10,783	20.8	20,043	38.7	13,194	25.5
2019–20	52,204	37,121	15,083	7,805	15.0	10,805	20.7	20,211	38.7	13,383	25.6
2020–21	52,666	37,444	15,222	7,836	14.9	10,846	20.6	20,399	38.7	13,585	25.8

NOTE: The most recent year of actual data is 2008–09, and 2020–21 is the last year for which projected data are available. For more information on projections, see NCES 2011-026. Some data have been revised from previously published figures. For a list of states in each region, see *supplemental note 1*. Detail may not sum to totals because of rounding.
SOURCE: U.S. Department of Education, National Center for Education Statistics, Statistics of Public Elementary and Secondary Day Schools, 1955–56 through 1984–85; Common Core of Data (CCD), "State Nonfiscal Survey of Public Elementary/Secondary Education," 1985–86 through 2008–09, and National Elementary and Secondary Enrollment Model, 1972–2008.

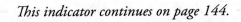

This indicator continues on page 144.

Table A-2-2. Projected percent change in public school enrollment in grades prekindergarten (preK) through 12, by grade level, region, and state or jurisdiction: School years 2008–09 and 2020–21

[Numbers in thousands]

Region and state or jurisdiction	Grades preK–12			Grades preK–8			Grade 9–12		
	Actual enrollment 2008–09	Projected enrollment 2020–21	Projected percent change	Actual enrollment 2008–09	Projected enrollment 2020–21	Projected percent change	Actual enrollment 2008–09	Projected enrollment 2020–21	Projected percent change
United States	**49,265**	**52,666**	**6.9**	**34,285**	**37,444**	**9.2**	**14,980**	**15,221**	**1.6**
Northeast	8,052	7,836	-2.7	5,476	5,505	0.5	2,576	2,331	-9.5
Connecticut	567	552	-2.6	392	395	0.6	175	158	-9.9
Maine	193	195	0.8	129	136	5.3	64	58	-8.4
Massachusetts	959	919	-4.2	667	650	-2.5	292	269	-8.1
New Hampshire	198	193	-2.7	133	138	3.4	65	55	-15.1
New Jersey	1,381	1,396	1.0	957	975	1.9	425	421	-0.9
New York	2,741	2,602	-5.1	1,843	1,814	-1.6	898	788	-12.2
Pennsylvania	1,775	1,739	-2.1	1,194	1,223	2.4	581	515	-11.3
Rhode Island	145	144	-0.8	98	104	6.2	47	40	-15.4
Vermont	92	98	5.6	62	71	13.9	30	27	-11.7
Midwest	10,743	10,846	1.0	7,374	7,622	3.4	3,370	3,224	-4.3
Illinois	2,120	2,143	1.1	1,479	1,515	2.5	641	628	-2.0
Indiana	1,046	1,059	1.2	730	747	2.3	316	312	-1.2
Iowa	488	499	2.4	336	346	3.1	152	154	1.0
Kansas	471	500	6.2	331	351	6.1	140	149	6.2
Michigan	1,660	1,552	-6.5	1,119	1,105	-1.2	541	448	-17.3
Minnesota	836	950	13.6	560	662	18.2	276	287	4.2
Missouri	918	932	1.5	635	658	3.6	282	274	-3.1
Nebraska	293	316	7.9	203	219	7.9	90	97	8.0
North Dakota	95	94	-0.5	64	66	2.6	31	29	-6.9
Ohio	1,817	1,752	-3.6	1,239	1,221	-1.5	578	531	-8.1
South Dakota	127	139	9.4	88	95	8.5	39	44	11.3
Wisconsin	874	910	4.1	590	636	7.9	284	274	-3.8
South	18,491	20,399	10.3	13,167	14,672	11.4	5,324	5,726	7.6
Alabama	746	728	-2.4	528	517	-2.2	218	211	-3.0
Arkansas	479	495	3.3	342	351	2.8	137	144	4.5
Delaware	125	142	12.9	87	99	13.9	39	43	10.8
District of Columbia	69	76	10.3	51	59	15.5	18	17	-4.2
Florida	2,631	2,788	5.9	1,849	2,051	10.9	782	736	-5.8
Georgia	1,656	1,826	10.3	1,186	1,321	11.4	470	504	7.2
Kentucky	670	669	-0.2	472	469	-0.7	198	200	0.9
Louisiana	685	668	-2.4	504	488	-3.2	181	180	-0.2
Maryland	844	921	9.2	576	662	14.8	267	259	-3.0
Mississippi	492	468	-4.9	352	333	-5.4	140	135	-3.8
North Carolina	1,489	1,713	15.1	1,059	1,224	15.5	430	489	13.9
Oklahoma	645	672	4.2	468	484	3.4	177	188	6.2
South Carolina	718	754	5.0	508	536	5.7	211	218	3.5
Tennessee	972	1,031	6.1	685	733	7.0	287	299	3.9
Texas	4,752	5,830	22.7	3,447	4,202	21.9	1,306	1,629	24.7
Virginia	1,236	1,352	9.4	855	960	12.3	381	392	3.0
West Virginia	283	267	-5.5	199	185	-7.4	83	83	-0.9

See notes at end of table.

Table A-2-2. **Projected percent change in public school enrollment in grades prekindergarten (preK) through 12, by grade level, region, and state or jurisdiction: School years 2008–09 and 2020–21—Continued**

[Numbers in thousands]

Region and state or jurisdiction	Grades preK–12			Grades preK–8			Grade 9–12		
	Actual enrollment 2008–09	Projected enrollment 2020–21	Projected percent change	Actual enrollment 2008–09	Projected enrollment 2020–21	Projected percent change	Actual enrollment 2008–09	Projected enrollment 2020–21	Projected percent change
United States	**49,265**	**52,666**	**6.9**	**34,285**	**37,444**	**9.2**	**14,980**	**15,221**	**1.6**
West	11,979	13,585	13.4	8,269	9,645	16.6	3,710	3,941	6.2
Alaska	131	163	24.8	89	119	32.8	41	45	7.5
Arizona	1,088	1,373	26.2	772	996	29.0	316	378	19.5
California	6,323	6,908	9.3	4,306	4,875	13.2	2,016	2,034	0.9
Colorado	818	966	18.0	580	677	16.7	238	288	21.0
Hawaii	179	188	5.0	126	135	7.0	54	54	0.2
Idaho	275	327	18.7	194	231	19.4	82	96	17.1
Montana	142	149	4.7	97	104	7.8	45	44	-1.9
Nevada	433	556	28.4	308	402	30.3	125	155	23.6
New Mexico	330	367	11.2	231	261	12.8	99	106	7.6
Oregon	575	650	13.0	395	462	16.8	180	188	4.6
Utah	560	625	11.7	404	463	14.5	155	162	4.3
Washington	1,037	1,213	17.0	705	854	21.1	332	360	8.3
Wyoming	87	99	13.8	61	67	10.4	27	32	21.5

NOTE: The most recent year of actual data is 2008–09, and 2020–21 is the last year for which projected data are available. Detail may not sum to totals because of rounding. For more information on projections, see NCES 2011-026.
SOURCE: U.S. Department of Education, National Center for Education Statistics, Common Core of Data (CCD), "State Nonfiscal Survey of Public Elementary/Secondary Education," 2008–09; and Public State Elementary and Secondary Enrollment Model, 1980–2008.

Table A-3-1. Number and percentage distribution of public charter schools and students, by selected student and school characteristics: Selected school years, 1999–2000 through 2008–09

Characteristic	1999–2000[1]	2001–02	2003–04	2005–06	2007–08	2008–09
Student characteristics						
Total, number	**339,678**	**571,029**	**789,479**	**1,012,906**	**1,276,731**	**1,433,116**
Sex						
Male	51.1	50.8	50.4	49.9	49.5	49.6
Female	48.9	49.2	49.6	50.1	50.5	50.4
Race/ethnicity						
White	42.5	42.6	41.8	40.5	38.8	37.9
Black	33.5	32.5	31.9	32.1	31.8	31.0
Hispanic	19.6	20.1	21.5	22.4	24.5	25.1
Asian/Pacific Islander	2.8	3.1	3.2	3.6	3.8	3.8
American Indian/Alaska Native	1.5	1.7	1.5	1.4	1.2	1.1
School characteristics						
Total, number	**1,524**	**2,348**	**2,977**	**3,780**	**4,388**	**4,694**
Total, number reporting membership	**1,456**	**2,261**	**2,921**	**3,690**	**4,289**	**4,601**
School level						
Elementary	55.7	51.7	52.1	52.9	54.1	54.4
Secondary	24.9	24.6	26.4	28.1	27.5	26.8
Combined	18.9	23.0	21.4	18.8	18.4	18.8
Enrollment size						
Under 300	77.0	73.5	70.9	69.5	65.5	63.7
300–499	12.0	13.7	15.6	16.6	19.4	20.4
500–999	8.7	10.0	10.3	10.9	12.0	12.6
1,000 or more	2.4	2.8	3.2	3.0	3.1	3.2
Racial/ethnic concentration						
More than 50 percent White	50.9	50.7	48.2	46.0	42.7	40.3
More than 50 percent Black	26.6	23.7	24.4	26.0	26.1	26.2
More than 50 percent Hispanic	11.4	12.4	13.4	14.8	17.7	18.7
Percentage of students in school eligible for free or reduced-price lunch						
0–25 percent	37.4	30.0	29.2	33.5	20.7	24.0
26–50 percent	11.6	12.2	16.3	15.6	15.9	16.1
51–75 percent	10.6	12.5	16.3	17.3	19.3	20.3
76–100 percent	13.0	14.1	20.3	23.2	22.9	30.1
Missing/school did not participate	27.3	31.3	17.9	10.4	21.3	9.5
Locale						
City	†	†	52.5	53.1	54.6	55.1
Suburban	†	†	22.2	22.5	21.8	21.0
Town	†	†	9.6	8.9	8.5	7.8
Rural	†	†	15.8	15.5	15.2	16.1

† Not applicable.

[1] Data for New Jersey were not available and therefore not included in the estimates.

NOTE: A *public charter school* is a school that provides free public elementary and/or secondary education to eligible students under a specific charter granted by the state legislature or other appropriate authority. Charter schools can be administered by regular school districts, state education agencies (SEAs), or chartering organizations. Data are for schools reporting student membership. *Student membership* is defined as an annual headcount of students enrolled in school on October 1 or the school day closest to that date. The Common Core of Data (CCD) allows a student to be reported for only a single school or agency. For example, a vocational school (identified as a "shared time" school) may provide classes to students from other schools and report no membership of its own. Race categories exclude persons of Hispanic ethnicity. For more information on race/ethnicity, poverty status, and locale, see *supplemental note 1*. For more information on the CCD, see *supplemental note 3*.

SOURCE: U.S. Department of Education, National Center for Education Statistics, Common Core of Data (CCD), "Public Elementary/Secondary School Universe Survey," 1999–2000 (version 1b), 2001–02 (version 1a), 2003–04 (version 1a), 2005–06 (version 1a), 2007–08 (version 1b), and 2008–09 (version 1b).

Table A-3-2. Number and percentage distribution of students and schools, by school type, level, and selected student and school characteristics: School year 2008–09

Characteristic	Public charter schools				Traditional public schools			
	Total[1]	Elementary	Secondary	Combined	Total[1]	Elementary	Secondary	Combined
Student characteristics								
Total, number	1,433,116	746,933	291,033	395,122	47,620,670	30,683,274	15,779,923	1,125,124
Sex								
Male	49.6	50.0	49.5	48.9	51.3	51.4	51.0	53.4
Female	50.4	50.0	50.5	51.1	48.7	48.6	49.0	46.6
Race/ethnicity								
White	37.9	33.6	32.4	50.0	55.4	54.0	58.0	58.6
Black	31.0	36.2	29.0	22.7	16.5	16.6	16.3	18.2
Hispanic	25.1	24.6	32.1	20.7	21.4	22.7	19.0	17.6
Asian/Pacific Islander	3.8	4.1	3.4	3.8	4.9	4.9	5.1	2.8
American Indian/Alaska Native	1.1	0.9	1.7	1.0	1.2	1.2	1.2	2.5
School characteristics								
Total, number	4,694	2,512	1,256	865	94,012	64,570	23,019	4,758
Total, number of schools, percentage distribution	100.0	54.4	26.8	18.8	100.0	71.3	24.0	4.5
Total, number of reporting membership	4,601	2,504	1,233	863	90,219	64,337	21,625	4,075
Enrollment size								
Under 300	63.7	61.4	76.0	52.7	29.8	25.2	35.7	68.6
300–499	20.4	22.7	15.9	20.3	28.0	33.5	14.4	13.3
500–999	12.6	14.3	5.6	17.7	32.8	37.4	22.9	13.9
1,000 or more	3.2	1.5	2.5	9.3	9.4	3.9	27.0	4.3
Racial/ethnic concentration								
More than 50 percent White	40.3	37.1	38.2	52.6	63.3	62.3	67.4	57.4
More than 50 percent Black	26.2	31.8	20.6	17.7	10.5	10.4	9.8	15.7
More than 50 percent Hispanic	18.7	17.1	24.7	14.5	13.0	13.9	11.1	9.3
Percentage of students in school eligible for free or reduced-price lunch								
0–25 percent	24.0	21.6	26.2	27.8	24.8	23.6	28.8	20.6
26–50 percent	16.1	15.7	17.8	15.1	29.5	27.6	36.2	25.4
51–75 percent	20.3	19.3	22.4	19.9	24.9	25.8	21.7	27.4
76–100 percent	30.1	34.5	25.2	24.4	18.5	21.2	10.4	19.5
Missing/school did not participate	9.5	8.9	8.4	12.7	2.3	1.8	3.0	7.0
Locale								
City	55.1	57.5	56.4	46.1	24.6	26.0	20.2	25.5
Suburban	21.0	21.8	20.1	19.9	28.1	30.2	23.8	18.7
Town	7.8	6.0	9.2	11.4	14.4	13.8	16.4	12.9
Rural	16.1	14.8	14.2	22.6	32.9	30.0	39.6	42.8

[1] Total number of schools does not always equal the sum of schools by level because the total may include ungraded schools and schools that did not report grade spans.

NOTE: A *public charter school* is a school that provides free public elementary and/or secondary education to eligible students under a specific charter granted by the state legislature or other appropriate authority. Charter schools can be administered by regular school districts, state education agencies (SEAs), or chartering organizations. Data are for schools reporting student membership. *Student membership* is defined as an annual headcount of students enrolled in school on October 1 or the school day closest to that date. The Common Core of Data (CCD) allows a student to be reported for only a single school or agency. For example, a vocational school (identified as a "shared time" school) may provide classes to students from other schools and report no membership of its own. Race categories exclude persons of Hispanic ethnicity. For more information on race/ethnicity, poverty status, and locale, see *supplemental note 1*. For more information on the CCD, see *supplemental note 3*.

SOURCE: U.S. Department of Education, National Center for Education Statistics, Common Core of Data (CCD), "Public Elementary/Secondary School Universe Survey," 2008–09 (version 1b).

Table A-3-3. Number and percentage of public charter schools and students, by state or jurisdiction: School years 1999–2000 and 2008–09

Region and state or jurisdiction	1999–2000					2008–09				
	Schools			Students		Schools			Students	
	Number	As a percent of all public schools	Percent-age distribu-tion	Number	As a percent of all public school students	Number	As a percent of all public schools	Percent-age distribu-tion	Number	As a percent of all public school students
United States	**1,456**	**1.6**	**100.0**	**339,678**	**0.7**	**4,601**	**4.9**	**100.0**	**1,433,116**	**2.9**
Northeast	105	0.7	7.2	26,525	0.3	394	2.6	8.6	161,638	2.0
Connecticut	16	1.5	1.1	2,148	0.4	17	1.5	0.4	4,536	0.8
Maine[1]	†	†	†	†	†	†	†	†	†	†
Massachusetts	40	2.1	2.7	12,518	1.3	61	3.3	1.3	26,384	2.8
New Hampshire	0	0.0	0.0	0	0.0	12	2.5	0.3	585	0.3
New Jersey[2]	†	†	†	†	†	61	2.4	1.3	19,271	1.4
New York	0	0.0	0.0	0	0.0	105	2.3	2.3	34,683	1.3
Pennsylvania	47	1.5	3.2	11,413	0.6	127	4.0	2.8	73,051	4.1
Rhode Island	2	0.6	0.1	446	0.3	11	3.5	0.2	3,128	2.2
Vermont[1]	†	†	†	†	†	†	†	†	†	†
Midwest	354	1.4	24.3	77,697	0.7	1,150	4.6	25.0	324,950	3.0
Illinois	17	0.4	1.2	6,152	0.3	39	1.0	0.8	30,789	1.5
Indiana[3]	†	†	†	†	†	51	2.7	1.1	16,442	1.6
Iowa[3]	†	†	†	†	†	4	0.3	0.1	655	0.1
Kansas	0	0.0	0.0	0	0.0	35	2.5	0.8	4,344	0.9
Michigan	172	4.8	11.8	46,078	2.8	272	7.2	5.9	103,606	6.4
Minnesota	57	2.8	3.9	7,794	0.9	172	8.1	3.7	29,501	3.6
Missouri	15	0.7	1.0	4,303	0.5	41	1.8	0.9	17,165	1.9
Nebraska[1]	†	†	†	†	†	†	†	†	†	†
North Dakota[1]	†	†	†	†	†	†	†	†	†	†
Ohio	48	1.3	3.3	9,809	0.5	324	8.6	7.0	86,824	4.8
South Dakota[1]	†	†	†	†	†	†	†	†	†	†
Wisconsin	45	2.1	3.1	3,561	0.4	212	9.4	4.6	35,624	4.1
South	431	1.5	29.6	76,304	0.5	1,352	4.2	29.4	408,363	2.2
Alabama[1]	†	†	†	†	†	†	†	†	†	†
Arkansas	0	0.0	0.0	0	0.0	30	2.7	0.7	6,989	1.5
Delaware	1	0.5	0.1	115	0.1	18	8.5	0.4	8,626	7.0
District of Columbia	27	14.3	1.9	6,432	8.3	86	39.8	1.9	24,279	35.4
Florida	112	3.6	7.7	17,251	0.7	394	10.6	8.6	117,640	4.5
Georgia	18	1.0	1.2	11,005	0.8	62	2.8	1.3	33,894	2.0
Kentucky[1]	†	†	†	†	†	†	†	†	†	†
Louisiana	15	1.0	1.0	2,449	0.3	65	4.5	1.4	26,012	3.8
Maryland[3]	†	†	†	†	†	34	2.4	0.7	9,829	1.2
Mississippi[4]	1	0.1	0.1	347	0.1	1	0.1	†	371	0.1
North Carolina	77	3.6	5.3	12,691	1.0	95	3.8	2.1	35,677	2.4
Oklahoma	0	†	†	0	†	16	0.9	0.3	5,418	0.8
South Carolina	4	0.4	0.3	327	†	36	3.1	0.8	8,638	1.2
Tennessee[3]	†	†	†	†	†	13	0.8	0.3	3,103	0.3
Texas	176	2.4	12.1	25,687	0.6	498	6.0	10.8	127,637	2.7
Virginia	0	0.0	0.0	0	0.0	4	0.2	0.1	250	0.0
West Virginia[1]	†	†	†	†	†	†	†	†	†	†

See notes at end of table.

Table A-3-3. Number and percentage of public charter schools and students, by state or jurisdiction: School years 1999–2000 and 2008–09—Continued

| Region and state or jurisdiction | 1999–2000 | | | | | 2008–09 | | | | |
| | Schools | | | Students | | Schools | | | Students | |
	Number	As a percent of all public schools	Percent-age distribu-tion	Number	As a percent of all public school students	Number	As a percent of all public schools	Percent-age distribu-tion	Number	As a percent of all public school students
United States	**1,456**	**1.6**	**100.0**	**339,678**	**0.7**	**4,601**	**4.9**	**100.0**	**1,433,116**	**2.9**
West	566	2.9	38.9	159,152	1.4	1,705	7.6	37.1	538,165	4.5
Alaska	18	3.6	1.2	2,300	1.7	24	4.7	0.5	4,847	3.7
Arizona	220	14.2	15.1	31,176	3.7	475	23.3	10.3	105,209	9.7
California	236	2.8	16.2	104,730	1.8	744	7.5	16.2	284,986	4.6
Colorado	69	4.4	4.7	17,822	2.5	148	8.4	3.2	61,460	7.5
Hawaii	2	0.8	0.1	790	0.4	31	10.8	0.7	7,328	4.1
Idaho	8	1.2	0.5	915	0.4	31	4.4	0.7	11,898	4.3
Montana[1]	†	†	†	†	†	†	†	†	†	†
Nevada	5	1.0	0.3	898	0.3	29	4.7	0.6	8,915	2.1
New Mexico	1	0.1	0.1	22	†	67	8.0	1.5	11,735	3.6
Oregon	1	0.1	0.1	109	†	87	6.7	1.9	14,366	2.6
Utah	6	0.8	0.4	390	0.1	66	6.8	1.4	27,117	4.8
Washington[1]	†	†	†	†	†	†	†	†	†	†
Wyoming	0	0.0	0.0	0	0.0	3	0.8	0.1	304	0.3

† Not applicable.
[1] State has not passed a charter school law.
[2] Data for New Jersey were not available in 1990–2000 and therefore not included in the estimates.
[3] State did not have a charter school law in 1990–2000.
[4] Mississippi first passed a charter school law in 1997 which expired in 2009; a new charter school law was passed in 2010.
NOTE: A *public charter school* is a school that provides free public elementary and/or secondary education to eligible students under a specific charter granted by the state legislature or other appropriate authority. Charter schools can be administered by regular school districts, state education agencies (SEAs), or chartering organizations. Data are for schools reporting student membership. *Student membership* is defined as an annual headcount of students enrolled in school on October 1 or the school day closest to that date. The Common Core of Data (CCD) allows a student to be reported for only a single school or agency. For example, a vocational school (identified as a "shared time" school) may provide classes to students from other schools and report no membership of its own. Detail may not sum to totals due to rounding. For more information on geographic region, see *supplemental note 1*. For more information on the CCD, see *supplemental note 3*.
SOURCE: U.S. Department of Education, National Center for Education Statistics, Common Core of Data (CCD), "Public Elementary/ Secondary School Universe Survey," 1999–2000 (version 1b) and 2008–09 (version 1b).

Table A-4-1. Total enrollment and percentage distribution of students enrolled in private elementary and secondary schools, by school type and grade level: Various school years, 1995–96 through 2009–10

Grade level and school year	Total	Catholic				Other religious				Non-sectarian
		Total	Parochial	Diocesan	Private	Total	Conservative Christian	Affiliated	Unaffiliated	
					Enrollment, in thousands					
Grades preK–12										
1995–96	5,918	2,660	1,459	851	351	2,095	787	697	611	1,163
1997–98	5,944	2,666	1,439	874	353	2,097	824	647	627	1,182
1999–2000	6,018	2,660	1,398	881	382	2,193	871	646	676	1,164
2001–02	6,320	2,673	1,310	979	384	2,328	937	663	728	1,319
2003–04	6,099	2,520	1,183	963	374	2,228	890	651	688	1,351
2005–06	6,073	2,403	1,063	957	383	2,303	957	697	649	1,367
2007–08	5,910	2,308	946	970	392	2,283	883	527	873	1,319
2009–10	5,488	2,160	856	909	395	2,076	737	516	823	1,252
Grades preK–8										
1995–96	4,756	2,042	1,368	575	98	1,753	651	575	527	961
1997–98	4,759	2,047	1,353	598	96	1,744	679	529	537	968
1999–2000	4,789	2,034	1,317	608	109	1,818	713	529	576	937
2001–02	5,023	2,032	1,227	688	118	1,927	765	536	626	1,064
2003–04	4,788	1,887	1,108	671	107	1,836	722	519	594	1,066
2005–06	4,724	1,780	993	673	113	1,865	765	561	539	1,079
2007–08	4,546	1,685	879	688	118	1,834	699	418	717	1,027
2009–10	4,179	1,542	782	643	117	1,666	579	401	685	972
Grades 9–12										
1995–96	1,163	618	91	275	252	342	136	122	84	202
1997–98	1,185	619	86	275	257	353	145	117	90	214
1999–2000	1,229	627	80	273	273	375	158	117	100	228
2001–02	1,296	641	83	292	266	401	172	127	102	255
2003–04	1,311	634	75	292	266	392	167	131	94	285
2005–06	1,349	623	70	284	270	438	192	136	110	288
2007–08	1,364	623	67	282	274	450	184	109	156	292
2009–10	1,309	618	74	266	278	411	158	115	138	280

See notes at end of table.

Table A-4-1. Total enrollment and percentage distribution of students enrolled in private elementary and secondary schools, by school type and grade level: Various school years, 1995–96 through 2009–10—Continued

Grade level and school year	Total	Catholic				Other religious				Non-sectarian
		Total	Parochial	Diocesan	Private	Total	Conservative Christian	Affiliated	Unaffiliated	
					Percentage distribution					
Grades preK-12										
1995–96	100.0	45.0	24.7	14.4	5.9	35.4	13.3	11.8	10.3	19.7
1997–98	100.0	44.8	24.2	14.7	5.9	35.3	13.9	10.9	10.5	19.9
1999–2000	100.0	44.2	23.2	14.6	6.4	36.4	14.5	10.7	11.2	19.3
2001–02	100.0	42.3	20.7	15.5	6.1	36.8	14.8	10.5	11.5	20.9
2003–04	100.0	41.3	19.4	15.8	6.1	36.5	14.6	10.7	11.3	22.1
2005–06	100.0	39.6	17.5	15.8	6.3	37.9	15.8	11.5	10.7	22.5
2007–08	100.0	39.1	16.0	16.4	6.6	38.6	14.9	8.9	14.8	22.3
2009–10	100.0	39.4	15.6	16.6	7.2	37.8	13.4	9.4	15.0	22.8
Grades preK-8										
1995–96	100.0	42.9	28.8	12.1	2.1	36.9	13.7	12.1	11.1	20.2
1997–98	100.0	43.0	28.4	12.6	2.0	36.7	14.3	11.1	11.3	20.3
1999–2000	100.0	42.5	27.5	12.7	2.3	38.0	14.9	11.1	12.0	19.6
2001–02	100.0	40.5	24.4	13.7	2.3	38.4	15.2	10.7	12.5	21.2
2003–04	100.0	39.4	23.1	14.0	2.2	38.3	15.1	10.8	12.4	22.3
2005–06	100.0	37.7	21.0	14.2	2.4	39.5	16.2	11.9	11.4	22.8
2007–08	100.0	37.1	19.3	15.1	2.6	40.3	15.4	9.2	15.8	22.6
2009–10	100.0	36.9	18.7	15.4	2.8	39.9	13.9	9.6	16.4	23.2
Grades 9-12										
1995–96	100.0	53.2	7.8	23.7	21.7	29.4	11.7	10.5	7.2	17.4
1997–98	100.0	52.2	7.3	23.2	21.7	29.8	12.2	9.9	7.6	18.0
1999–2000	100.0	51.0	6.5	22.2	22.2	30.5	12.9	9.5	8.1	18.5
2001–02	100.0	49.4	6.4	22.5	20.5	31.0	13.3	9.8	7.8	19.6
2003–04	100.0	48.3	5.7	22.3	20.3	29.9	12.8	10.0	7.2	21.8
2005–06	100.0	46.2	5.2	21.0	20.0	32.5	14.3	10.1	8.1	21.4
2007–08	100.0	45.7	4.9	20.6	20.1	33.0	13.5	8.0	11.4	21.4
2009–10	100.0	47.2	5.7	20.3	21.2	31.4	12.1	8.8	10.5	21.4

NOTE: Prekindergarten students who are enrolled in private schools that do not offer at least one grade of kindergarten or higher are not part of this universe. Catholic schools include parochial, diocesan, and private Catholic schools. Affiliated religious schools have a specific religious orientation or purpose but are not Catholic. Unaffiliated schools have a more general religious orientation or purpose but are not classified as Conservative Christian or affiliated with a specific religion. Nonsectarian schools do not have a religious orientation or purpose. Ungraded students are prorated into preK–8 and 9–12 enrollment totals. Detail may not sum to totals because of rounding. For more information on the Private School Universe Survey (PSS), please see *supplemental note 3*.
SOURCE: U.S. Department of Education, National Center for Education Statistics, Private School Universe Survey (PSS), various years, 1995–96 through 2009–10.

Table A-4-2. Private elementary and secondary school enrollment and private enrollment as a percentage of total enrollment in public and private schools, by region and grade level: Various school years, 1995–96 through 2009–10

[Totals in thousands]

Grade level and school year	Total enrollment		Northeast		Midwest		South		West	
	Total	Percent of total enrollment	Total	Percent of total Northeast enrollment	Total	Percent of total Midwest enrollment	Total	Percent of total South enrollment	Total	Percent of total West enrollment
Grades preK–12										
1995–96	5,918	11.7	1,509	16.0	1,525	12.7	1,744	9.8	1,141	10.0
1997–98	5,944	11.4	1,496	15.6	1,528	12.5	1,804	9.8	1,116	9.4
1999–2000	6,018	11.4	1,507	15.5	1,520	12.4	1,863	10.0	1,127	9.2
2001–02	6,320	11.7	1,581	16.1	1,556	12.6	1,975	10.3	1,208	9.6
2003–04	6,099	11.2	1,513	15.4	1,460	11.9	1,944	9.9	1,182	9.1
2005–06	6,073	11.0	1,430	14.8	1,434	11.7	1,976	9.8	1,234	9.4
2007–08	5,910	10.7	1,426	14.9	1,352	11.2	1,965	9.6	1,167	8.9
2009–10	5,488	10.0	1,310	14.0	1,296	10.8	1,842	9.1	1,041	8.0
Grades preK–8										
1995–96	4,756	12.8	1,174	17.2	1,238	14.3	1,413	10.7	931	11.1
1997–98	4,759	12.6	1,165	16.8	1,235	14.1	1,449	10.8	909	10.5
1999–2000	4,789	12.5	1,168	16.7	1,222	13.9	1,487	10.9	913	10.4
2001–02	5,023	12.9	1,216	17.3	1,253	14.3	1,584	11.3	969	10.6
2003–04	4,788	12.3	1,131	16.4	1,167	13.5	1,547	10.9	944	10.2
2005–06	4,724	12.1	1,063	15.9	1,142	13.3	1,551	10.7	969	10.5
2007–08	4,546	11.7	1,047	16.0	1,065	12.6	1,525	10.4	909	9.9
2009–10	4,179	10.8	938	14.6	1,016	12.1	1,424	9.8	802	8.8
Grades 9–12										
1995–96	1,163	8.5	335	13.0	287	8.6	331	7.1	209	6.8
1997–98	1,185	8.3	331	12.5	293	8.5	354	7.2	207	6.4
1999–2000	1,229	8.4	340	12.6	299	8.6	376	7.5	215	6.3
2001–02	1,296	8.6	365	13.1	302	8.6	390	7.5	239	6.8
2003–04	1,311	8.4	382	13.1	294	8.2	397	7.4	238	6.4
2005–06	1,349	8.3	367	12.3	292	7.9	425	7.5	265	6.7
2007–08	1,364	8.3	379	12.7	287	7.8	440	7.6	257	6.5
2009–10	1,309	8.0	372	12.6	280	7.7	418	7.3	239	6.1

NOTE: Prekindergarten students who are enrolled in private schools that do not offer at least one grade of kindergarten or higher are not part of this universe. Ungraded students are prorated into preK–8 and 9–12 enrollment totals. Detail may not sum to totals because of rounding. For more information on geographic region, see *supplemental note 1*. For more information on the Private School Universe Survey (PSS), see *supplemental note 3*.
SOURCE: U.S. Department of Education, National Center for Education Statistics, Private School Universe Survey (PSS), various years, 1995–96 through 2009–10; and Common Core of Data (CCD), "State Nonfiscal Survey of Public Elementary/Secondary Education," various years, 1995–96 through 2009–10.

Table A-4-3. Percentage distribution of students in private schools, by race/ethnicity and selected school characteristics: School year 2009–10

School characteristic	Percentage distribution, by school characteristics	Percentage distribution, by race/ethnicity						
		Total	White	Black	Hispanic	Asian/ Pacific Islander	American Indian/ Alaska Native	Two or more races
Total	**100.0**	**100.0**	**72.6**	**9.2**	**9.4**	**5.7**	**0.4**	**2.7**
Private school typology								
Catholic	39.4	100.0	70.8	7.5	13.3	5.1	0.4	2.8
Parochial	15.6	100.0	70.4	7.2	14.2	5.2	0.3	2.7
Diocesan	16.6	100.0	72.3	7.0	12.3	4.9	0.5	3.0
Private	7.2	100.0	68.4	9.3	13.6	5.1	0.7	2.9
Other religious	37.8	100.0	76.3	10.3	6.2	4.9	0.4	2.0
Conservative Christian	13.4	100.0	73.2	12.2	7.2	4.9	0.6	2.0
Affiliated	9.4	100.0	77.1	8.7	6.2	5.5	0.3	2.3
Unaffiliated	15.0	100.0	78.8	9.5	5.1	4.4	0.4	1.8
Nonsectarian	22.8	100.0	69.2	10.6	7.3	8.5	0.6	3.8
School level								
Elementary	53.5	100.0	71.0	9.0	10.9	5.8	0.4	3.0
Secondary	14.3	100.0	71.7	9.0	11.0	5.4	0.4	2.6
Combined	32.2	100.0	75.2	9.5	6.7	5.7	0.5	2.4
Program emphasis								
Regular	84.7	100.0	73.4	8.7	9.4	5.5	0.4	2.6
Montessori	3.9	100.0	62.7	8.6	9.9	13.1	0.8	5.0
Special program emphasis	2.4	100.0	72.9	6.9	5.7	9.8	0.4	4.2
Special education	2.2	100.0	59.4	22.0	12.5	3.0	0.6	2.5
Alternative	1.7	100.0	65.8	17.0	8.8	4.1	1.0	3.2
Early childhood	5.2	100.0	65.9	11.5	10.9	8.1	0.6	3.0
Enrollment								
Less than 50	5.4	100.0	74.7	12.3	7.3	2.7	0.9	2.1
50–149	17.3	100.0	67.5	14.1	9.8	5.3	0.8	2.6
150–299	25.9	100.0	67.3	11.2	12.1	6.1	0.4	3.0
300–499	21.0	100.0	75.2	7.4	8.5	5.9	0.3	2.7
500–749	14.0	100.0	75.8	6.4	9.2	5.5	0.4	2.7
750 or more	16.3	100.0	77.3	6.2	7.4	6.2	0.3	2.6
Region								
Northeast	23.9	100.0	74.3	10.5	7.7	5.1	0.2	2.1
Midwest	23.6	100.0	80.9	7.9	5.6	3.1	0.5	2.0
South	33.6	100.0	73.1	11.2	9.4	3.9	0.3	2.1
West	19.0	100.0	58.5	5.4	16.6	13.0	1.0	5.5
Locale								
City	41.0	100.0	65.4	11.9	12.3	6.9	0.4	3.2
Suburban	39.0	100.0	73.7	8.8	8.9	5.6	0.3	2.7
Town	7.1	100.0	85.9	3.5	5.4	3.0	0.6	1.6
Rural	12.9	100.0	84.5	4.8	4.1	3.6	1.2	1.7

NOTE: Prekindergarten students who are enrolled in private schools that do not offer at least one grade of kindergarten or higher are not part of this universe. Race categories exclude persons of Hispanic ethnicity. The distribution of prekindergarten private school students are excluded due to racial/ethnic information not being available for an estimated 837,719 students. Catholic schools include parochial, diocesan, and private Catholic schools. Affiliated religious schools have a specific religious orientation or purpose but are not Catholic. Unaffiliated schools have a more general religious orientation or purpose but are not classified as Conservative Christian or affiliated with a specific religion. Nonsectarian schools do not have a religious orientation or purpose. Vocational schools are included with special program emphasis schools. Detail may not sum to totals because of rounding. For more information on race/ethnicity, geographic region, and locale, see *supplemental note 1*. For more information on private schools, private school program emphases, private school typology, and the Private School Universe Survey (PSS), see *supplemental note 3*.
SOURCE: U.S. Department of Education, National Center for Education Statistics, Private School Universe Survey (PSS), 2009–10.

Racial/Ethnic Enrollment in Public Schools

Table A-5-1. Number and percentage distribution of public school students enrolled in prekindergarten through 12th grade by race/ethnicity: October 1989–October 2009

[Numbers in thousands]

October of year	Total	White	Black	Hispanic	Asian	Pacific Islander	American Indian/ Alaska Native	Two or more races
				Enrollment				
1989	42,248	28,689	7,061	4,792	1,243[1]	([1])	402	—
1990	43,086	28,991	7,202	5,054	1,304[1]	([1])	407	—
1991	43,463	29,103	7,373	5,159	1,374[1]	([1])	367	—
1992	44,041	29,304	7,524	5,310	1,455[1]	([1])	351	—
1993	45,079	30,094	7,576	5,457	1,480[1]	([1])	360	—
1994	46,887	30,656	8,039	6,423	1,141[1]	([1])	390	—
1995	47,320	30,788	8,132	6,751	1,065[1]	([1])	309	—
1996	47,487	29,960	8,002	7,025	1,936[1]	([1])	563	—
1997	49,467	30,896	8,560	7,487	1,920[1]	([1])	604	—
1998	48,817	30,164	8,505	7,647	1,946[1]	([1])	555	—
1999	49,338	30,259	8,304	8,080	2,193[1]	([1])	501	—
2000	49,198	29,963	8,337	8,214	2,044[1]	([1])	641	—
2001	50,005	30,427	8,391	8,400	2,125[1]	([1])	662	—
2002	50,443	30,426	8,434	8,981	1,980[1]	([1])	622	—
2003	50,653	29,395	8,232	9,513	1,829	163	314	1,208
2004	50,568	28,738	8,289	9,870	1,967	102	403	1,200
2005	50,835	29,047	8,056	10,141	1,883	89	351	1,269
2006	50,663	28,486	7,977	10,470	1,900	117	336	1,376
2007	51,082	28,357	7,903	10,865	2,080	134	398	1,345
2008	50,768	27,923	8,002	11,093	1,903	86	440	1,322
2009	51,144	28,030	7,839	11,418	1,903	154	444	1,356
				Percentage distribution				
1989	100.0	67.9	16.7	11.3	2.9[1]	([1])	1.0	—
1990	100.0	67.3	16.7	11.7	3.0[1]	([1])	0.9	—
1991	100.0	67.0	17.0	11.9	3.2[1]	([1])	0.8	—
1992	100.0	66.5	17.1	12.1	3.3[1]	([1])	0.8	—
1993	100.0	66.8	16.8	12.1	3.3[1]	([1])	0.8	—
1994	100.0	65.4	17.1	13.7	2.4[1]	([1])	0.8	—
1995	100.0	65.1	17.2	14.3	2.3[1]	([1])	0.7	—
1996	100.0	63.1	16.9	14.8	4.1[1]	([1])	1.2	—
1997	100.0	62.5	17.3	15.1	3.9[1]	([1])	1.2	—
1998	100.0	61.8	17.4	15.7	4.0[1]	([1])	1.1	—
1999	100.0	61.3	16.8	16.4	4.4[1]	([1])	1.0	—
2000	100.0	60.9	16.9	16.7	4.2[1]	([1])	1.3	—
2001	100.0	60.8	16.8	16.8	4.2[1]	([1])	1.3	—
2002	100.0	60.3	16.7	17.8	3.9[1]	([1])	1.2	—
2003	100.0	58.0	16.3	18.8	3.6	0.3	0.6	2.4
2004	100.0	56.8	16.4	19.5	3.9	0.2	0.8	2.4
2005	100.0	57.1	15.8	19.9	3.7	0.2	0.7	2.5
2006	100.0	56.2	15.7	20.7	3.8	0.2	0.7	2.7
2007	100.0	55.5	15.5	21.3	4.1	0.3	0.8	2.6
2008	100.0	55.0	15.8	21.9	3.7	0.2	0.9	2.6
2009	100.0	54.8	15.3	22.3	3.7	0.3	0.9	2.7

— Not available.

[1] From 1989 through 2002, data on Asian and Pacific Islander students were not reported separately; therefore, Pacific Islander students are included with Asian students during this period.

NOTE: Estimates include all public school students enrolled in prekindergarten through 12th grade. Over time, the Current Population Survey (CPS) has had different response options for race/ethnicity. For more information on the Current Population Survey (CPS), see *supplemental note 2*. Race categories exclude persons of Hispanic ethnicity. For more information on race/ethnicity and region, see *supplemental note 1*. Totals include other race/ethnicity categories not separately shown. Detail may not sum to totals because of rounding.

SOURCE: U.S. Department of Commerce, Census Bureau, Current Population Survey (CPS), October Supplement, 1989–2009.

This indicator continues on page 156.

Racial/Ethnic Enrollment in Public Schools

Table A-5-2. **Number of public school students enrolled in prekindergarten through 12th grade, by race/ethnicity and region: Selected years, October 1989–October 2009**

[Numbers in thousands]

Region and October of year	Total	White	Black	Hispanic	Asian	Pacific Islander	American Indian/ Alaska Native	Two or more races
Northeast								
1989	7,433	5,491	1,050	666	197	(¹)	11!	—
1994	8,417	6,048	1,179	929	200	(¹)	11!	—
1999	9,071	6,148	1,286	1,200	405	(¹)	32	—
2000	8,753	5,930	1,361	1,024	399	(¹)	40	—
2001	8,741	5,850	1,375	1,078	377	(¹)	61	—
2002	8,978	6,022	1,372	1,217	341	(¹)	26	—
2003	8,895	5,746	1,429	1,237	321	‡	17!	142
2004	8,742	5,534	1,385	1,223	442	7!	18!	133
2005	8,876	5,600	1,361	1,319	449	7!	11!	128
2006	8,648	5,464	1,305	1,348	379	‡	24!	128
2007	8,535	5,463	1,135	1,305	484	‡	24!	121
2008	8,334	5,003	1,236	1,416	494	—	9!	176
2009	8,471	5,132	1,222	1,523	416	‡	6!	171
Midwest								
1989	10,532	8,458	1,484	355	130	(¹)	105	—
1994	10,992	8,554	1,676	503	120	(¹)	76	—
1999	11,508	8,677	1,683	677	363	(¹)	107	—
2000	11,412	8,671	1,774	628	236	(¹)	103	—
2001	11,685	8,967	1,755	574	246	(¹)	142	—
2002	11,516	8,660	1,699	737	311	(¹)	109	—
2003	11,143	8,271	1,584	738	231	22!	51	246
2004	11,152	8,244	1,551	766	250	3!	61	277
2005	11,057	8,142	1,558	818	200	2!	65	272
2006	11,091	8,055	1,479	894	305	7!	62	288
2007	11,146	7,984	1,480	974	291	14!	72	331
2008	11,266	7,991	1,518	1,098	287	—	54	319
2009	11,147	7,940	1,466	1,058	288	‡	86	307
South								
1989	15,149	9,323	3,963	1,495	190	(¹)	153	—
1994	17,050	9,991	4,569	2,118	217	(¹)	103	—
1999	17,010	9,297	4,674	2,545	361	(¹)	132	—
2000	17,091	9,314	4,493	2,735	368	(¹)	181	—
2001	17,336	9,507	4,521	2,745	429	(¹)	134	—
2002	17,557	9,458	4,643	2,956	325	(¹)	176	—
2003	18,309	9,757	4,578	3,119	374	‡	95	378
2004	18,498	9,767	4,616	3,152	432	15!	119	397
2005	18,432	9,644	4,480	3,414	340	8!	111	434
2006	18,467	9,398	4,558	3,555	344	‡	127	482
2007	18,898	9,530	4,656	3,637	442	17!	163	453
2008	18,860	9,715	4,540	3,657	396	12!	162	378
2009	19,177	9,591	4,488	3,919	551	55	169	405

See notes at end of table.

Table A-5-2. **Number of public school students enrolled in prekindergarten through 12th grade, by race/ethnicity and region: Selected years, October 1989–October 2009—Continued**

[Numbers in thousands]

Region and October of year	Total	White	Black	Hispanic	Asian	Pacific Islander	American Indian/ Alaska Native	Two or more races
West								
1989	9,134	5,418	564	2,276	727	(¹)	133	—
1994	10,428	6,063	615	2,873	605	(¹)	200	—
1999	11,750	6,137	661	3,658	1,064	(¹)	230	—
2000	11,942	6,048	708	3,827	1,041	(¹)	318	—
2001	12,243	6,102	739	4,003	1,073	(¹)	326	—
2002	12,391	6,286	721	4,070	1,004	(¹)	310	—
2003	12,306	5,621	641	4,420	903	128	150	443
2004	12,176	5,193	736	4,729	842	78	205	393
2005	12,470	5,661	657	4,590	893	71	163	434
2006	12,457	5,569	634	4,673	873	107	123	478
2007	12,503	5,380	632	4,949	863	100	140	440
2008	12,308	5,214	707	4,922	727	74	214	449
2009	12,350	5,367	664	4,919	649	95	183	474

— Not available.
! Interpret with caution. The standard error of the estimate is equal to 30 percent or more of the estimate's value.
‡ Reporting standards not met.
¹ From 1989 through 2002, Asian and Pacific Islander students were not reported separately; therefore, Pacific Islander students are included with Asian students during this period.
NOTE: Estimates include all public school students enrolled in prekindergarten through 12th grade. Over time, the Current Population Survey (CPS) has had different response options for race/ethnicity. Race categories exclude persons of Hispanic ethnicity. For more information on the Current Population Survey (CPS), see *supplemental note 2*. For more information on race/ethnicity and region, see *supplemental note 1*. Totals include other race/ethnicity categories not separately shown. Detail may not sum to totals because of rounding.
SOURCE: U.S. Department of Commerce, Census Bureau, Current Population Survey (CPS), October Supplement, selected years, 1989–2009.

Racial/Ethnic Enrollment in Public Schools

Table A-5-3. Percentage distribution of public school students enrolled in prekindergarten through 12th grade, by race/ethnicity and region: Selected years, October 1989–October 2009

[Numbers in thousands]

Region and October of year	Total	White	Black	Hispanic	Asian	Pacific Islander	American Indian/ Alaska Native	Two or more races
Northeast								
1989	100.0	73.9	14.1	9.0!	2.6!¹	(¹)	0.1!	—
1994	100.0	71.9	14.0	11.0	2.4!¹	(¹)	0.1!	—
1999	100.0	67.8	14.2	13.2	4.5!¹	(¹)	0.4!	—
2000	100.0	67.7	15.6	11.7	4.6!¹	(¹)	0.5!	—
2001	100.0	66.9	15.7	12.3	4.3!¹	(¹)	0.7!	—
2002	100.0	67.1	15.3	13.6	3.8!¹	(¹)	0.3!	—
2003	100.0	64.6	16.1	13.9	3.6!	‡	0.2!	1.6!
2004	100.0	63.3	15.8	14.0	5.1!	‡	0.2!	1.5!
2005	100.0	63.1	15.3	14.9	5.1!	‡	0.1!	1.4!
2006	100.0	63.2	15.1	15.6	4.4!	‡	0.3!	1.5!
2007	100.0	64.0	13.3	15.3	5.7!	‡	0.3!	1.4!
2008	100.0	60.0	14.8	17.0	5.9!	—	0.1!	2.1!
2009	100.0	60.6	14.4	18.0	4.9!	‡	0.1!	2.0!
Midwest								
1989	100.0	80.3	14.1	3.4	1.2¹	(¹)	1.0	—
1994	100.0	77.8	15.2	4.6	1.1¹	(¹)	0.7	—
1999	100.0	75.4	14.6	5.9	3.2¹	(¹)	0.9	—
2000	100.0	76.0	15.5	5.5	2.1¹	(¹)	0.9	—
2001	100.0	76.7	15.0	4.9	2.1¹	(¹)	1.2	—
2002	100.0	75.2	14.8	6.4	2.7¹	(¹)	0.9	—
2003	100.0	74.2	14.2	6.6	2.1	0.2!	0.5	2.2
2004	100.0	73.9	13.9	6.9	2.2	‡	0.5	2.5
2005	100.0	73.6	14.1	7.4	1.8	‡	0.6	2.5
2006	100.0	72.6	13.3	8.1	2.7	0.1!	0.6	2.6
2007	100.0	71.6	13.3	8.7	2.6	0.1!	0.6	3.0
2008	100.0	70.9	13.5	9.7	2.5	—	0.5	2.8
2009	100.0	71.2	13.1	9.5	2.6	‡	0.8	2.8
South								
1989	100.0	61.5	26.2	9.9	1.3¹	(¹)	1.0	—
1994	100.0	58.6	26.8	12.4	1.3¹	(¹)	0.6	—
1999	100.0	54.7	27.5	15.0	2.1¹	(¹)	0.8	—
2000	100.0	54.5	26.3	16.0	2.2¹	(¹)	1.1	—
2001	100.0	54.8	26.1	15.8	2.5¹	(¹)	0.8	—
2002	100.0	53.9	26.4	16.8	1.8¹	(¹)	1.0	—
2003	100.0	53.3	25.0	17.0	2.0	‡	0.5	2.1
2004	100.0	52.8	25.0	17.0	2.3	0.1!	0.6	2.1
2005	100.0	52.3	24.3	18.5	1.8	‡	0.6	2.4
2006	100.0	50.9	24.7	19.3	1.9	‡	0.7	2.6
2007	100.0	50.4	24.6	19.2	2.3	0.1!	0.9	2.4
2008	100.0	51.5	24.1	19.4	2.1	0.1!	0.9	2.0
2009	100.0	50.0	23.4	20.4	2.9	0.3	0.9	2.1

See notes at end of table.

Table A-5-3. Percentage distribution of public school students enrolled in prekindergarten through 12th grade, by race/ethnicity and region: Selected years, October 1989–October 2009—Continued

[Numbers in thousands]

Region and October of year	Total	White	Black	Hispanic	Asian	Pacific Islander	American Indian/ Alaska Native	Two or more races
West								
1989	100.0	59.3	6.2	24.9	8.0[1]	(¹)	1.5	—
1994	100.0	58.1	5.9	27.5	5.8[1]	(¹)	1.9	—
1999	100.0	52.2	5.6	31.1	9.1[1]	(¹)	2.0	—
2000	100.0	50.6	5.9	32.0	8.7[1]	(¹)	2.7	—
2001	100.0	49.8	6.0	32.7	8.8[1]	(¹)	2.7	—
2002	100.0	50.7	5.8	32.8	8.1[1]	(¹)	2.5	—
2003	100.0	45.7	5.2	35.9	7.3	1.0	1.2	3.6
2004	100.0	42.6	6.0	38.8	6.9	0.6	1.7	3.2
2005	100.0	45.4	5.3	36.8	7.2	0.6	1.3	3.5
2006	100.0	44.7	5.1	37.5	7.0	0.9	1.0	3.8
2007	100.0	43.0	5.1	39.6	6.9	0.8	1.1	3.5
2008	100.0	42.4	5.7	40.0	5.9	0.6	1.7	3.6
2009	100.0	43.5	5.4	39.8	5.3	0.8	1.5	3.8

— Not available.
! Interpret with caution. The standard error of the estimate is equal to 30 percent or more of the estimate's value.
‡ Reporting standards not met.
[1] From 1989 through 2002, Asian and Pacific Islander students were not reported separately; therefore, Pacific Islander students are included with Asian students during this period.
NOTE: Estimates include all public school students enrolled in prekindergarten through 12th grade. Over time, the Current Population Survey (CPS) has had different response options for race/ethnicity. For more information on the Current Population Survey (CPS), see *supplemental note 2*. Race categories exclude persons of Hispanic ethnicity. For more information on race/ethnicity and region, see *supplemental note 1*. Totals include other race/ethnicity categories not separately shown. Detail may not sum to totals because of rounding.
SOURCE: U.S. Department of Commerce, Census Bureau, Current Population Survey (CPS), October Supplement, selected years, 1989–2009.

Table A-5-4. Percentage distribution of public school students enrolled in prekindergarten through 12th grade, by race/ethnicity and state or jurisdiction: 2009

State or jurisdiction	Total	White	Black	Hispanic	Asian	Pacific Islander	American Indian/ Alaska Native	Two or more races
United States	**100.0**	**53.5**	**15.3**	**22.7**	**4.0**	**0.2**	**0.8**	**3.2**
Alabama	100.0	57.8	34.4	4.1	1.0	‡	0.5	2.2
Alaska	100.0	53.0	6.1	7.2	4.0	0.9	17.1	11.6
Arizona	100.0	41.0	4.5	43.6	2.0	0.2!	5.1	3.4
Arkansas	100.0	64.2	21.4	9.6	1.0	0.1!	0.7	2.8
California	100.0	27.4	6.2	52.1	9.8	0.4	0.4	3.5
Colorado	100.0	57.8	4.3	30.3	2.2	0.1!	0.5	4.2
Connecticut	100.0	62.4	11.6	18.5	3.4	‡	0.2!	3.3
Delaware	100.0	52.9	26.5	12.8	3.2	—	0.2!	3.9
District of Columbia	100.0	8.4	76.4	12.5	0.8!	—	—	1.3!
Florida	100.0	46.7	22.1	25.7	2.3	0.1!	0.2	2.5
Georgia	100.0	47.0	35.7	11.7	2.8	0.1!	0.1	2.4
Hawaii	100.0	14.6	2.2!	16.1	23.5	11.5	‡	31.6
Idaho	100.0	76.5	0.9	16.8	0.9	0.2!	1.5	3.1
Illinois	100.0	52.7	17.8	22.6	3.9	—	0.1!	2.6
Indiana	100.0	75.7	11.7	8.1	1.3	‡	0.1	3.0
Iowa	100.0	82.9	3.2	7.9	1.7	—	0.4!	3.7
Kansas	100.0	71.9	6.1	14.4	2.0	‡	0.9	4.4
Kentucky	100.0	80.9	10.1	4.3	1.2	‡	0.3	3.0
Louisiana	100.0	48.1	43.0	4.2	1.4	—	0.5	2.5
Maine	100.0	89.1	3.1	2.2	1.2!	—	0.6!	3.9
Maryland	100.0	46.4	35.6	9.7	4.5	‡	0.1!	3.2
Massachusetts	100.0	69.6	7.9	14.1	5.0	—	0.1!	2.8
Michigan	100.0	69.5	17.7	6.5	2.7	‡	0.5	3.0
Minnesota	100.0	75.9	6.6	7.1	5.2	—	1.1	3.9
Mississippi	100.0	44.2	50.7	2.4	0.4	‡	0.3!	1.8
Missouri	100.0	74.6	14.9	5.2	1.2	0.1!	0.3	3.5
Montana	100.0	78.1	0.4!	5.2	0.4!	0.1!	9.7	6.0
Nebraska	100.0	73.8	6.9	13.5	2.4	—	1.0	2.0
Nevada	100.0	41.5	8.9	38.6	5.2	0.6	1.5	3.5
New Hampshire	100.0	88.4	2.0	4.6	2.2	‡	0.2!	2.0

See notes at end of table.

Table A-5-4. Percentage distribution of public school students enrolled in prekindergarten through 12th grade, by race/ethnicity and state or jurisdiction: 2009—Continued

State or jurisdiction	Total	White	Black	Hispanic	Asian	Pacific Islander	American Indian/ Alaska Native	Two or more races
United States	**100.0**	**53.5**	**15.3**	**22.7**	**4.0**	**0.2**	**0.8**	**3.2**
New Jersey	100.0	51.9	15.6	21.7	7.5	‡	#	2.6
New Mexico	100.0	27.6	2.3	55.9	1.1	—	10.6	2.3
New York	100.0	49.2	18.5	22.5	6.7	#	0.2	2.2
North Carolina	100.0	55.1	26.4	11.4	2.2	#	1.2	3.4
North Dakota	100.0	84.1	1.0	2.1	‡	‡	8.5	3.0!
Ohio	100.0	75.2	15.2	4.2	1.5	‡	0.1	3.7
Oklahoma	100.0	59.2	9.4	12.6	1.3	0.1!	7.2	9.7
Oregon	100.0	67.2	2.2	19.4	3.8	0.6	1.3	5.4
Pennsylvania	100.0	71.9	14.4	8.2	2.5	‡	0.1	2.8
Rhode Island	100.0	65.4	7.2	19.9	4.0	—	0.7	2.3
South Carolina	100.0	53.5	36.7	5.8	1.2	‡	0.2!	2.4
South Dakota	100.0	75.4	2.6!	4.4	0.7	—	12.8	3.9
Tennessee	100.0	67.1	22.7	6.0	1.2	0.1!	0.1	2.6
Texas	100.0	34.5	12.4	47.8	3.1	0.1	0.3	1.7
Utah	100.0	75.4	1.8	15.7	1.7	0.8	1.5	2.9
Vermont	100.0	90.8	2.4!	1.9	1.4!	—	‡	2.5
Virginia	100.0	57.3	23.3	9.8	4.9	#	0.3	4.1
Washington	100.0	63.2	4.6	17.5	5.6	0.6	1.5	6.6
West Virginia	100.0	91.6	3.8	1.6	0.6	—	0.1!	2.2
Wisconsin	100.0	75.1	8.8	8.6	3.3	‡	1.2	2.9
Wyoming	100.0	79.7	0.8!	11.2	0.3!	—	2.9	5.0

— Not available.
Rounds to zero.
! Interpret with caution. The standard error of the estimate is equal to 30 percent or more of the estimate's value.
‡ Reporting standards not met.
NOTE: The 2009 American Community Survey (ACS) includes noninstitutionalized and institutionalized group quarters. Therefore, due to this and other methodological differences between the Current Population Survey (CPS) and ACS, enrollment estimates from the two surveys are not directly comparable. For more information on the ACS, see *supplemental note 3*. Totals include other race/ethnicity categories not separately shown. Race categories exclude persons of Hispanic ethnicity. Detail may not sum to totals because of rounding. For more information on race/ethnicity and region, see *supplemental note 1*.
SOURCE: U.S. Department of Commerce, Census Bureau, American Community Survey (ACS), 2009.

Table A-6-1. Number and percentage of children ages 5–17 who spoke only English at home, who spoke a language other than English at home and who spoke English with difficulty, and percent enrolled in school: Selected years, 1980–2009

[Numbers in thousands]

Characteristic	1980	1990	2000	2006	2007	2008	2009
Total, number	**47,917**	**45,217**	**53,076**	**53,406**	**53,217**	**53,012**	**53,300**
Total, percent enrolled in school	**95.1**	**92.5**	**96.8**	**96.2**	**96.4**	**96.8**	**96.9**
Spoke only English at home							
Number	43,226	38,926	43,297	42,562	42,367	42,125	42,096
Percent of total population	90.2	86.1	81.6	79.7	79.6	79.5	79.0
Percent enrolled in school	95.4	92.7	97.1	96.3	96.6	96.9	97.0
Spoke a language other than English at home							
Number	4,691	6,291	9,779	10,845	10,850	10,887	11,204
Percent of total population	9.8	13.9	18.4	20.3	20.4	20.5	21.0
Percent enrolled in school	92.9	91.2	95.6	95.8	95.9	96.2	96.3
Spoke English with difficulty							
Number	1,941	2,373	3,503	2,758	2,739	2,673	2,654
Percent of total population	4.1	5.2	6.6	5.2	5.1	5.0	5.0
Percent enrolled in school	89.8	87.9	92.3	92.1	92.0	92.8	93.3
Percent of those who spoke a language other than English at home	41.4	37.7	35.8	25.4	25.2	24.6	23.7

NOTE: Respondents were asked whether each child in the household spoke a language other than English at home. Those who answered "yes" were asked how well each child could speak English using the following categories: "very well," "well," "not well," and "not at all." All children who were reported to speak English less than "very well" were considered to have difficulty speaking English. Spanish-language versions of the questionnaires were available to respondents. Detail may not sum to totals because of rounding. For more information on the Long Form Decennial Census and the American Community Survey, see *supplemental note 3*.
SOURCE: U.S. Department of Commerce, Census Bureau, Long Form Decennial Census, 1980, 1990, and 2000, and American Community Survey (ACS), 2006–2009.

Table A-6-2. Number and percentage of children ages 5–17 who spoke a language other than English at home and who spoke English with difficulty, by age and selected characteristics: 2009

[Numbers in thousands]

		Spoke a language other than English at home									
				Spoke English with difficulty							
	Total, ages 5–17	Number	Percent	Total, ages 5–17		Ages 5–9		Ages 10–13		Ages 14–17	
Characteristic				Number	Percent	Number	Percent	Number	Percent	Number	Percent
Total	**53,300**	**11,204**	**21.0**	**2,654**	**5.0**	**1,373**	**6.8**	**632**	**3.9**	**649**	**3.9**
Language spoken at home											
Spanish	8,043	8,043	100.0	1,950	24.2	1,031	32.9	455	19.0	464	18.4
Other Indo-European[1]	1,484	1,484	100.0	279	18.8	134	23.8	66	15.7	79	15.7
Asian/Pacific Islander[2]	1,244	1,244	100.0	333	26.8	167	33.9	83	22.2	83	22.1
Other	433	433	100.0	92	21.3	42	24.6	27	20.1	23	18.1
Race/ethnicity[3]											
White	30,090	1,724	5.7	339	1.1	141	1.3	74	0.8	124	1.3
Black	7,448	425	5.7	98	1.3	33	1.2	27	1.2	38	1.5
Hispanic	11,258	7,403	65.8	1,819	16.2	998	21.8	432	12.5	389	12.0
Mexican	7,942	5,398	68.0	1,422	17.9	815	24.9	331	13.6	276	12.3
Puerto Rican	1,029	458	44.5	68	6.6	29	7.1	17	5.6	22	7.0
Cuban	254	164	64.5	31	12.4	14	15.1	8	8.9	10	12.8
Dominican	286	245	85.5	56	19.5	20	18.8	16	18.6	20	21.0
Central American	756	607	80.3	147	19.4	75	24.5	37	15.8	35	16.2
South American	478	351	73.4	59	12.3	26	14.7	15	9.9	18	11.8
Other Hispanic	512	179	35.0	36	7.0	19	9.1	8	5.4	9	5.7
Asian	2,163	1,384	64.0	350	16.2	179	20.5	86	13.1	85	13.5
Asian Indian	415	272	65.5	39	9.5	24	12.3	9	7.3	7	6.9
Chinese	483	340	70.4	89	18.4	45	23.5	22	14.6	22	15.5
Filipino	341	128	37.6	26	7.5	12	9.2	7	6.4	7	6.6
Japanese	57	30	53.4	13	22.8	8	35.2	4	20.3	2	8.9
Korean	197	139	70.5	40	20.0	17	24.7	9	15.4	13	19.4
Vietnamese	271	216	79.5	69	25.4	37	33.0	16	19.3	16	21.1
Other Asian	399	259	65.0	75	18.7	36	23.6	20	16.2	18	15.2
Pacific Islander	77	23	29.3	5	6.0	2	6.1	1 !	5.8	1 !	5.9 !
American Indian/Alaska Native	392	59	15.1	10	2.6	3	2.4	3	2.5	4	2.9
Two or more races	1,708	129	7.5	24	1.4	12	1.7	5	1.1	6	1.3
Citizenship											
U.S.-born citizen	50,801	9,144	18.0	1,892	3.7	1,136	5.8	399	2.6	357	2.3
Naturalized U.S. citizen	514	286	55.7	58	11.2	15	11.3	16	9.8	27	12.2
Non-U.S. citizen	1,985	1,773	89.3	704	35.5	223	44.7	217	31.8	265	32.9
Poverty status[4]											
Poor	9,780	3,112	31.8	956	9.8	517	12.8	232	7.9	207	7.4
Near-poor	11,237	3,341	29.7	827	7.4	439	9.9	195	5.7	194	5.7
Nonpoor	31,451	4,619	14.7	824	2.6	394	3.5	192	2.0	238	2.3

! Interpret with caution. The standard error of the estimate is equal to 30 percent or more of the estimate's value.
[1] An Indo-European language other than Spanish (e.g., French, German, Portuguese, etc.).
[2] Any native spoken language that linguists classify variously as a Sino-Tibetan, Austroasiatic, or Austronesian language.
[3] Race categories exclude persons of Hispanic ethnicity. Totals may include some racial/ethnic categories not shown separately.
[4] Children in families whose incomes are below the poverty threshold are classified as *poor,* those in families with incomes at 100–199 percent of the poverty threshold are classified as *near-poor,* and those in families with incomes at 200 percent or more of the poverty threshold are classified as *nonpoor.* Detail may not sum to totals because of missing values for poverty.
NOTE: Respondents were asked whether each child in the household spoke a language other than English at home. Those who answered "yes" were asked how well each child could speak English using the following categories: "very well," "well," "not well," and "not at all." All children who were reported to speak English less than "very well" were considered to have difficulty speaking English. A Spanish-language version of the American Community Survey (ACS) was available to respondents. Detail may not sum to totals because of rounding. For more information on race/ethnicity and poverty status, see *supplemental note 1.* For more information on the ACS, see *supplemental note 3.*
SOURCE: U.S. Department of Commerce, Census Bureau, American Community Survey (ACS), 2009.

Table A-6-3. Number and percentage of children ages 5–17 who spoke a language other than English at home and who spoke English with difficulty, by language spoken, region, and state or jurisdiction: 2009

[Numbers in thousands]

Region and state or jurisdction	Total, ages 5–17	Spoke a language other than English at home							
		Total, ages 5–17		Spoke English with difficulty					
				Total, ages 5–17		Percent distribution by language spoken			
		Number	Percent	Number	Percent	Spanish	Other Indo-European[1]	Asian/ Pacific Islander[2]	Other
United States	**53,300**	**11,204**	**21.0**	**2,654**	**5.0**	**73.5**	**10.5**	**12.6**	**3.5**
Northeast	9,054	1,879	20.8	410	4.5	53.4	25.6	15.1	5.8
Connecticut	599	111	18.6	20	3.3	57.8	19.2	21.8	‡
Maine	202	12	6.0	5!	2.5!	19.6!	28.1!	‡	51.4
Massachusetts	1,048	208	19.8	43	4.1	51.4	28.3	15.5	4.8
New Hampshire	214	18	8.5	5	2.4	52.9	23.1!	‡	‡
New Jersey	1,493	399	26.8	73	4.9	65.4	17.2	13.5	3.9
New York	3,205	877	27.4	204	6.4	50.7	26.2	16.6	6.5
Pennsylvania	2,031	214	10.5	51	2.5	45.3	39.0	12.2	3.5!
Rhode Island	167	36	21.4	8	4.6	88.1	‡	‡	‡
Vermont	94	4	4.5	‡	‡	‡	#	‡	#
Midwest	11,563	1,349	11.7	331	2.9	62.1	16.3	14.6	7.0
Illinois	2,284	523	22.9	125	5.5	78.5	10.2	7.9	3.4
Indiana	1,143	93	8.1	27	2.3	63.6	23.3	12.8	‡
Iowa	511	41	8.0	8	1.6	71.7	14.9!	10.4!	‡
Kansas	495	59	11.9	13	2.7	79.6	7.6!	10.2!	‡
Michigan	1,733	169	9.7	34	1.9	42.9	23.6	14.1	19.3
Minnesota	892	111	12.4	30	3.4	32.8	13.1	43.0	11.2
Missouri	1,024	69	6.8	19	1.8	48.7	26.2	12.7	12.3!
Nebraska	314	36	11.6	11	3.6	72.9	‡	16.4	10.5!
North Dakota	100	5	5.2	2	1.9	51.3!	‡	#	27.6!
Ohio	1,978	133	6.7	32	1.6	45.1	34.1	10.1	10.8
South Dakota	140	9	6.1	2	1.5	40.1!	‡	‡	‡
Wisconsin	949	101	10.7	28	2.9	57.2	16.2	26.0	0.6
South	19,847	3,658	18.4	878	4.4	81.9	7.8	8.4	2.0
Alabama	813	43	5.3	10	1.2	70.2	‡	16.7!	‡
Arkansas	505	50	9.9	11	2.3	82.5	7.7!	8.9!	‡
Delaware	148	16	11.1	3	1.8	74.1	9.2!	16.7!	#
District of Columbia	75	9	11.5	3	3.5	72.6	20.1!	#	‡
Florida	2,895	756	26.1	145	5.0	74.7	18.7	5.6	1.0!
Georgia	1,839	250	13.6	53	2.9	74.9	7.4	15.7	2.1!
Kentucky	729	38	5.1	11	1.5	54.0	21.4	20.6	‡
Louisiana	806	44	5.5	8	1.0	67.7	8.1!	24.3	#
Maryland	970	149	15.3	34	3.5	54.9	20.3	19.8	5.1
Mississippi	544	19	3.5	5	1.0	78.9	‡	‡	‡
North Carolina	1,619	200	12.4	51	3.1	78.9	6.7	11.1	3.3!
Oklahoma	649	62	9.6	13	2.1	88.3	5.5!	5.8!	‡
South Carolina	767	57	7.4	16	2.0	74.7	10.6	9.6!	‡
Tennessee	1,068	75	7.1	17	1.6	75.9	11.0	9.6!	‡
Texas	4,823	1,706	35.4	458	9.5	90.9	2.7	4.9	1.5
Virginia	1,322	177	13.4	39	2.9	58.5	12.4	25.7	3.4!
West Virginia	277	7	2.5	3	1.0	68.6	‡	‡	‡

See notes at end of table.

Table A-6-3. Number and percentage of children ages 5–17 who spoke a language other than English at home and who spoke English with difficulty, by language spoken, region, and state or jurisdiction: 2009—Continued

[Numbers in thousands]

| Region and state or jurisdiction | Total, ages 5–17 | Spoke a language other than English at home | | Spoke English with difficulty | | | | | |
| | | | | Total, ages 5–17 | | Percent distribution by language spoken | | | |
		Number	Percent	Number	Percent	Spanish	Other Indo-European[1]	Asian/Pacific Islander[2]	Other
United States	**53,300**	**11,204**	**21.0**	**2,654**	**5.0**	**73.5**	**10.5**	**12.6**	**3.5**
West	12,836	4,318	33.6	1,035	8.1	77.9	4.9	14.5	2.7
Alaska	130	21	16.4	4	3.2	‡	‡	36.6	54.2
Arizona	1,214	373	30.7	76	6.3	83.4	3.8	4.2	8.6
California	6,686	2,995	44.8	717	10.7	80.2	3.7	14.9	1.2
Colorado	864	164	19.0	41	4.7	81.3	5.1	10.7	2.8!
Hawaii	200	30	15.2	9	4.7	‡	‡	91.2	‡
Idaho	296	32	11.0	9	2.9	65.6	‡	19.8!	12.4!
Montana	159	6	3.6	1!	0.8!	‡	60.4!	‡	‡
Nevada	483	153	31.7	43	8.9	84.3	4.2!	‡	3.1!
New Mexico	362	110	30.5	21	5.8	91.4	2.2!	‡	‡
Oregon	631	126	20.0	30	4.7	74.1	8.1	12.3	‡
Utah	598	73	12.2	17	2.8	74.2	7.1!	15.0!	‡
Washington	1,122	227	20.3	65	5.8	57.3	18.4	19.0	5.3!
Wyoming	90	5	5.7	1!	1.5!	‡	‡	‡	#

Rounds to zero.
! Interpret with caution. The standard error of the estimate is equal to 30 percent or more of the estimate's value.
‡ Reporting standards not met.
[1] An Indo-European language other than Spanish (e.g., French, German, Portuguese, etc.).
[2] Any native spoken language that linguists classify variously as a Sino-Tibetan, Austroasiatic, or Austronesian language.
NOTE: Respondents were asked whether each child in the household spoke a language other than English at home. Those who answered "yes" were asked how well each child could speak English using the following categories: "very well," "well," "not well," and "not at all." All children who were reported to speak English less than "very well" were considered to have difficulty speaking English. A Spanish-language version of the American Community Survey (ACS) was available to respondents. Detail may not sum to totals because of rounding. For more information on geographic region, see *supplemental note 1*. For more information on the ACS, see *supplemental note 3*.
SOURCE: U.S. Department of Commerce, Census Bureau, American Community Survey (ACS), 2009.

Table A-7-1. Number and percentage distribution of 3- to 21-year-olds served under the Individuals with Disabilities Education Act (IDEA), Part B, and number served as a percentage of total public school enrollment, by type of disability: Selected school years, 1980–81 through 2008–09

Type of disability	1980–81	1990–91	1995–96	2000–01	2004–05	2005–06	2006–07	2007–08	2008–09
	Number served (in thousands)								
All disabilities	**4,144**	**4,710**	**5,572**	**6,296**	**6,719**	**6,713**	**6,686**	**6,606**	**6,483**
Specific learning disabilities	1,462	2,129	2,578	2,868	2,798	2,735	2,665	2,573	2,476
Speech or language impairments	1,168	985	1,022	1,409	1,463	1,468	1,475	1,456	1,426
Intellectual disability	830	534	571	624	578	556	534	500	478
Emotional disturbance	347	389	437	481	489	477	464	442	420
Hearing impairments	79	58	67	78	79	79	80	79	78
Orthopedic impairments	58	49	63	83	73	71	69	67	70
Other health impairments	98	55	133	303	521	570	611	641	659
Visual impairments	31	23	25	29	29	29	29	29	29
Multiple disabilities	68	96	93	133	140	141	142	138	130
Deaf-blindness	3	1	1	1	2	2	2	2	2
Autism	—	—	28	94	191	223	258	296	336
Traumatic brain injury	—	—	9	16	24	24	25	25	26
Developmental delay	—	—	—	178	332	339	333	358	354
Preschool disabled[1]	†	390	544	†	†	†	†	†	†
	Percentage distribution of children served								
All disabilities	**100.0**	**100.0**	**100.0**	**100.0**	**100.0**	**100.0**	**100.0**	**100.0**	**100.0**
Specific learning disabilities	35.3	45.2	46.3	45.5	41.6	40.7	39.9	39.0	38.2
Speech or language impairments	28.2	20.9	18.3	22.4	21.8	21.9	22.1	22.0	22.0
Intellectual disability	20.0	11.3	10.2	9.9	8.6	8.3	8.0	7.6	7.4
Emotional disturbance	8.4	8.3	7.8	7.6	7.3	7.1	6.9	6.7	6.5
Hearing impairments	1.9	1.2	1.2	1.2	1.2	1.2	1.2	1.2	1.2
Orthopedic impairments	1.4	1.0	1.1	1.3	1.1	1.1	1.0	1.0	1.1
Other health impairments	2.4	1.2	2.4	4.8	7.7	8.5	9.1	9.7	10.2
Visual impairments	0.7	0.5	0.4	0.5	0.4	0.4	0.4	0.4	0.4
Multiple disabilities	1.6	2.0	1.7	2.1	2.1	2.1	2.1	2.1	2.0
Deaf-blindness	0.1	#	#	#	#	#	#	#	#
Autism	—	—	0.5	1.5	2.8	3.3	3.9	4.5	5.2
Traumatic brain injury	—	—	0.2	0.2	0.4	0.4	0.4	0.4	0.4
Developmental delay	—	—	—	2.8	4.9	5.1	5.0	5.4	5.5
Preschool disabled[1]	†	8.3	9.8	†	†	†	†	†	†

See notes at end of table.

Table A-7-1. **Number and percentage distribution of 3- to 21-year-olds served under the Individuals with Disabilities Education Act (IDEA), Part B, and number served as a percentage of total public school enrollment, by type of disability: Selected school years, 1980–81 through 2008–09—Continued**

Type of disability	1980–81	1990–91	1995–96	2000–01	2004–05	2005–06	2006–07	2007–08	2008–09
	Number served as a percentage of total public school enrollment[2]								
All disabilities	**10.1**	**11.4**	**12.4**	**13.3**	**13.8**	**13.7**	**13.6**	**13.4**	**13.2**
Specific learning disabilities	3.6	5.2	5.8	6.1	5.7	5.6	5.4	5.2	5.0
Speech or language impairments	2.9	2.4	2.3	3.0	3.0	3.0	3.0	3.0	2.9
Intellectual disability	2.0	1.3	1.3	1.3	1.2	1.1	1.1	1.0	1.0
Emotional disturbance	0.8	0.9	1.0	1.0	1.0	1.0	0.9	0.9	0.9
Hearing impairments	0.2	0.1	0.1	0.2	0.2	0.2	0.2	0.2	0.2
Orthopedic impairments	0.1	0.1	0.1	0.2	0.2	0.1	0.1	0.1	0.1
Other health impairments	0.2	0.1	0.3	0.6	1.1	1.2	1.2	1.3	1.3
Visual impairments	0.1	0.1	0.1	0.1	0.1	0.1	0.1	0.1	0.1
Multiple disabilities	0.2	0.2	0.2	0.3	0.3	0.3	0.3	0.3	0.3
Deaf-blindness	#	#	#	#	#	#	#	#	#
Autism	—	—	0.1	0.2	0.4	0.5	0.5	0.6	0.7
Traumatic brain injury	—	—	#	#	#	#	0.1	0.1	0.1
Developmental delay	—	—	—	0.4	0.7	0.7	0.7	0.7	0.7
Preschool disabled[1]	†	0.9	1.2	†	†	†	†	†	†

— Not available.
† Not applicable.
# Rounds to zero.
[1] In 1980–81, data were collected for preschool-age children ages 3–5 by disability type; those data are combined above with data for children and youth ages 6–21. However, the 1986 Amendments to the Education of the Handicapped Act (now known as the Individuals with Disabilities Education Act (IDEA)) mandated that data not be collected by disability for students ages 3–5. For this reason, data from the 1990s on preschoolers with disabilities are reported in a separate row. Beginning in 2000–01, states were again required to report data on preschool children by disability.
[2] Based on the total prekindergarten through 12th-grade enrollment in public schools.
NOTE: Prior to October 1994, children and youth with disabilities were served under Title I of the Elementary and Secondary Education Act as well as under IDEA, Part B. Data reported in this table for years prior to 1995–96 include children and youth ages 0–21 served under Title I. Includes children and youth in the 50 states, the District of Columbia, and the Bureau of Indian Education schools. Data for 2007–08 and 2008–09 do not include Vermont. In 2006–07, the total number of 3- to 21-year-olds served under IDEA in Vermont was 14,010. Detail may not sum to totals because of rounding. For more information on student disabilities, see *supplemental note 7*. For more information on the Common Core of Data (CCD), see *supplemental note 3*.
SOURCE: U.S. Department of Education, Office of Special Education Programs, Annual Report to Congress on the Implementation of the Individuals with Disabilities Education Act, selected years, 1980 through 2008; and Individuals with Disabilities Education Act (IDEA) database, retrieved October 18, 2010, from http://www.ideadata.org/PartBdata.asp. National Center for Education Statistics, Statistics of Public Elementary and Secondary School Systems,1980–81; and Common Core of Data (CCD), "State Nonfiscal Survey of Public Elementary/Secondary Education," selected years, 1990–91 through 2008–09.

Table A-7-2. Percentage distribution of students ages 6–21 served under the Individuals with Disabilities Education Act (IDEA), Part B, by educational environment and type of disability: Selected school years, 1990–91 through 2008–09

| Year and type of disability | All environments | Regular school, time in general classes | | | Separate school for students with disabilities | | Separate residential facility | | Parentally placed in regular private schools | Home-bound/hospital placement | Correctional facility |
		80 percent or more	79–40 percent	Less than 40 percent	Public	Private	Public	Private			
All students with disabilities											
1990–91	100.0	33.1	36.4	25.0	2.9	1.3	0.6	0.3	—	0.5	—
1994–95	100.0	44.8	28.5	22.4	2.0	1.0	0.5	0.3	—	0.6	—
1995–96	100.0	45.7	28.5	21.5	2.1	1.0	0.4	0.3	—	0.5	—
1996–97	100.0	46.1	28.3	21.4	2.0	1.0	0.4	0.3	—	0.5	—
1997–98	100.0	46.8	28.8	20.4	1.8	1.0	0.4	0.3	—	0.5	—
1998–99	100.0	46.0	29.9	20.0	1.8	1.1	0.4	0.3	—	0.5	—
1999–2000	100.0	45.9	29.8	20.3	1.9	1.0	0.4	0.3	—	0.5	—
2000–01	100.0	46.5	29.8	19.5	1.9	1.1	0.4	0.3	—	0.5	—
2001–02	100.0	48.2	28.5	19.2	1.7	1.2	0.4	0.4	—	0.4	—
2002–03	100.0	48.2	28.7	19.0	1.7	1.2	0.3	0.4	—	0.5	—
2003–04	100.0	49.9	27.7	18.5	1.7	1.1	0.3	0.4	—	0.5	—
2004–05	100.0	51.9	26.5	17.6	1.8	1.2	0.3	0.3	—	0.4	—
2005–06	100.0	54.2	25.1	16.7	1.8	1.2	0.3	0.3	—	0.5	—
2006–07	100.0	53.7	23.7	17.6	2.9[1]	([1])	0.4[1]	([1])	1.0[2]	0.4	0.4
2007–08	100.0	56.8	22.4	15.4	3.0[1]	([1])	0.4[1]	([1])	1.1[2]	0.4	0.4
2008–09											
All students with disabilities	**100.0**	**58.0**	**21.7**	**15.1**	**3.0**[1]	**(**[1]**)**	**0.4**[1]	**(**[1]**)**	**1.1**[2]	**0.4**	**0.4**
Specific learning disabilities	100.0	60.9	28.4	8.6	0.6[1]	([1])	0.1[1]	([1])	0.9[2]	0.2	0.4
Speech or language impairments	100.0	86.4	5.7	4.7	0.3[1]	([1])	#[1]	([1])	2.8[2]	#	#
Intellectual disability	100.0	16.2	27.4	48.9	6.0[1]	([1])	0.4[1]	([1])	0.2[2]	0.5	0.3
Emotional disturbance	100.0	39.2	19.4	23.2	13.1[1]	([1])	2.0[1]	([1])	0.2[2]	1.1	1.9
Hearing impairments	100.0	53.3	17.2	15.8	8.3[1]	([1])	3.9[1]	([1])	1.2[2]	0.2	0.1
Orthopedic impairments	100.0	51.3	16.6	24.8	4.9[1]	([1])	0.2[1]	([1])	0.8[2]	1.4	0.1
Other health impairments	100.0	60.1	24.6	24.8	1.6[1]	([1])	0.2[1]	([1])	1.0[2]	1.0	0.3
Visual impairments	100.0	61.6	13.9	12.0	6.6[1]	([1])	4.1[1]	([1])	1.2[2]	0.6	0.1
Multiple disabilities	100.0	13.2	16.5	46.2	19.1[1]	([1])	1.9[1]	([1])	0.3[2]	2.6	0.2
Deaf-blindness	100.0	30.0	16.7	29.1	15.5[1]	([1])	7.0[1]	([1])	0.6[2]	1.3	0.1
Autism	100.0	36.1	18.3	35.8	8.3[1]	([1])	0.6[1]	([1])	0.6[2]	0.3	#
Traumatic brain injury	100.0	45.0	23.2	23.0	6.0[1]	([1])	0.6[1]	([1])	0.6[2]	1.5	0.2
Developmental delay	100.0	61.8	20.6	16.2	0.7[1]	([1])	0.1[1]	([1])	0.5[2]	0.2	#

— Not available.

\# Rounds to zero.

[1] Data for 2006, 2007, and 2008 combine public and private schools as well as public and private residential facilities.

[2] Students who are enrolled by their parents or guardians in regular private schools and have their basic education paid through private resources, but receive special education services at public expense. These students are not included under "Regular school, time in general classes."

NOTE: Includes children and youth in the 50 states, the District of Columbia, and the Bureau of Indian Education schools. Data for 2007–08 and 2008–09 do not include Vermont. Detail may not sum to totals because of rounding. For more information about student disabilities, see *supplemental note 7*.

SOURCE: U.S. Department of Education, Office of Special Education Programs, Individuals with Disabilities Education Act (IDEA) database, retrieved October 18, 2010, from https://www.ideadata.org/arc_toc9.asp#partbLRE.

This page intentionally left blank.

Undergraduate Enrollment

Table A-8-1. Number and percentage of actual and projected undergraduate enrollment in degree-granting postsecondary institutions, by sex, attendance status, and control of institution: Selected years, fall 1970–2020

[Numbers in thousands]

Fall of year	Total	Sex				Attendance status			
		Male		Female		Full-time		Part-time	
		Number	Percent	Number	Percent	Number	Percent	Number	Percent
1970	7,369	4,250	57.7	3,119	42.3	5,280	71.7	2,089	28.3
1975	9,679	5,257	54.3	4,422	45.7	6,168	63.7	3,511	36.3
1980	10,475	5,000	47.7	5,475	52.3	6,362	60.7	4,113	39.3
1985	10,597	4,962	46.8	5,635	53.2	6,320	59.6	4,277	40.4
1990	11,959	5,380	45.0	6,579	55.0	6,976	58.3	4,983	41.7
1991	12,439	5,571	44.8	6,868	55.2	7,221	58.1	5,218	41.9
1992	12,538	5,583	44.5	6,955	55.5	7,244	57.8	5,293	42.2
1993	12,324	5,484	44.5	6,840	55.5	7,179	58.3	5,144	41.7
1994	12,263	5,422	44.2	6,840	55.8	7,169	58.5	5,094	41.5
1995	12,232	5,401	44.2	6,831	55.8	7,145	58.4	5,086	41.6
1996	12,327	5,421	44.0	6,906	56.0	7,299	59.2	5,028	40.8
1997	12,451	5,469	43.9	6,982	56.1	7,419	59.6	5,032	40.4
1998	12,437	5,446	43.8	6,991	56.2	7,539	60.6	4,898	39.4
1999	12,681	5,559	43.8	7,122	56.2	7,735	61.0	4,946	39.0
2000	13,155	5,778	43.9	7,377	56.1	7,923	60.2	5,232	39.8
2001	13,716	6,004	43.8	7,711	56.2	8,328	60.7	5,388	39.3
2002	14,257	6,192	43.4	8,065	56.6	8,734	61.3	5,523	38.7
2003	14,480	6,227	43.0	8,253	57.0	9,045	62.5	5,435	37.5
2004	14,781	6,340	42.9	8,441	57.1	9,284	62.8	5,496	37.2
2005	14,964	6,409	42.8	8,555	57.2	9,446	63.1	5,518	36.9
2006	15,184	6,514	42.9	8,671	57.1	9,571	63.0	5,613	37.0
2007	15,604	6,728	43.1	8,876	56.9	9,841	63.1	5,763	36.9
2008	16,366	7,067	43.2	9,299	56.8	10,255	62.7	6,111	37.3
2009	17,565	7,595	43.2	9,970	56.8	11,143	63.4	6,422	36.6
Projected									
2010	17,645	7,643	43.3	10,001	56.7	11,176	63.3	6,469	36.7
2011	17,731	7,670	43.3	10,061	56.7	11,231	63.3	6,500	36.7
2012	17,746	7,661	43.2	10,084	56.8	11,217	63.2	6,529	36.8
2013	17,908	7,691	42.9	10,217	57.1	11,289	63.0	6,620	37.0
2014	18,197	7,756	42.6	10,440	57.4	11,439	62.9	6,757	37.1
2015	18,451	7,808	42.3	10,643	57.7	11,569	62.7	6,882	37.3
2016	18,697	7,861	42.0	10,836	58.0	11,696	62.6	7,001	37.4
2017	18,921	7,912	41.8	11,009	58.2	11,815	62.4	7,106	37.6
2018	19,161	7,972	41.6	11,188	58.4	11,950	62.4	7,211	37.6
2019	19,402	8,043	41.5	11,360	58.5	12,104	62.4	7,299	37.6
2020	19,582	8,100	41.4	11,482	58.6	12,224	62.4	7,358	37.6

See notes at end of table.

Table A-8-1. Number and percentage of actual and projected undergraduate enrollment in degree-granting postsecondary institutions, by sex, attendance status, and control of institution: Selected years, fall 1970–2020—Continued

[Numbers in thousands]

		Control of institution							
		Public		Private					
				Total		Not-for-profit		For-profit	
Fall of year	Total	Number	Percent	Number	Percent	Number	Percent	Number	Percent
1970	7,369	5,620	76.3	1,748	23.7	1,730	23.5	18	0.2
1975	9,679	7,826	80.9	1,853	19.1	1,815	18.7	39	0.4
1980	10,475	8,442	80.6	2,033	19.4	1,927	18.4	106	1.0
1985	10,597	8,477	80.0	2,120	20.0	1,929	18.2	191	1.8
1990	11,959	9,710	81.2	2,250	18.8	2,043	17.1	206	1.7
1991	12,439	10,148	81.6	2,291	18.4	2,072	16.7	219	1.8
1992	12,538	10,216	81.5	2,321	18.5	2,102	16.8	220	1.8
1993	12,324	10,012	81.2	2,312	18.8	2,099	17.0	213	1.7
1994	12,263	9,945	81.1	2,317	18.9	2,100	17.1	217	1.8
1995	12,232	9,904	81.0	2,328	19.0	2,105	17.2	223	1.8
1996	12,327	9,935	80.6	2,392	19.4	2,112	17.1	279	2.3
1997	12,451	10,007	80.4	2,443	19.6	2,140	17.2	303	2.4
1998	12,437	9,950	80.0	2,487	20.0	2,153	17.3	334	2.7
1999	12,681	10,110	79.7	2,571	20.3	2,183	17.2	388	3.1
2000	13,155	10,539	80.1	2,616	19.9	2,213	16.8	403	3.1
2001	13,716	10,986	80.1	2,730	19.9	2,258	16.5	472	3.4
2002	14,257	11,433	80.2	2,824	19.8	2,306	16.2	518	3.6
2003	14,480	11,523	79.6	2,957	20.4	2,347	16.2	611	4.2
2004	14,781	11,651	78.8	3,130	21.2	2,389	16.2	741	5.0
2005	14,964	11,698	78.2	3,266	21.8	2,418	16.2	848	5.7
2006	15,184	11,847	78.0	3,337	22.0	2,448	16.1	889	5.9
2007	15,604	12,138	77.8	3,466	22.2	2,470	15.8	996	6.4
2008	16,366	12,591	76.9	3,775	23.1	2,537	15.5	1,238	7.6
2009	17,565	13,387	76.2	4,179	23.8	2,593	14.8	1,585	9.0
Projected									
2010	17,645	13,599	77.1	4,046	22.9	—	—	—	—
2011	17,731	13,662	77.1	4,069	22.9	—	—	—	—
2012	17,746	13,676	77.1	4,070	22.9	—	—	—	—
2013	17,908	13,805	77.1	4,103	22.9	—	—	—	—
2014	18,197	14,032	77.1	4,165	22.9	—	—	—	—
2015	18,451	14,233	77.1	4,218	22.9	—	—	—	—
2016	18,697	14,427	77.2	4,270	22.8	—	—	—	—
2017	18,921	14,605	77.2	4,316	22.8	—	—	—	—
2018	19,161	14,794	77.2	4,367	22.8	—	—	—	—
2019	19,402	14,981	77.2	4,421	22.8	—	—	—	—
2020	19,582	15,119	77.2	4,462	22.8	—	—	—	—

— Not available.

[1] Projections are based on reported data through 2009. The most recent year of actual data is 2009, and 2020 is the last year for which projected data are available. For more information on projections, see NCES 2011-026.

NOTE: Data through 1995 are for institutions of higher education, while later data are for degree-granting institutions. Data for 1999 were imputed using alternative procedures. For more information, see NCES 2001-083, appendix E. Detail may not sum to totals because of rounding. Some data have been revised from previously published figures. For more information on the Integrated Postsecondary Education Data System (IPEDS), see *supplemental note 3*. For more information on the Classification of Postsecondary Education Institutions, see *supplemental note 8*. See the glossary for definitions of full-time and part-time enrollment.

SOURCE: U.S. Department of Education, National Center for Education Statistics, Higher Education General Information Survey (HEGIS), "Fall Enrollment in Colleges and Universities" surveys, 1970 through 1985; 1990 through 2009 Integrated Postsecondary Education Data System, "Fall Enrollment Survey" (IPEDS-EF:90–99), Spring 2001 through Spring 2010; and Enrollment in Degree-Granting Institutions Model, 1980–2009.

Undergraduate Enrollment

Table A-8-2. Actual and projected undergraduate enrollment in degree-granting 4- and 2-year postsecondary institutions, by sex, attendance status, and control of institution: Selected years, fall 1970–2020

[In thousands]

Fall of year	Total	Sex		Attendance status		Control of institution			
							Private		
		Male	Female	Full-time	Part-time	Public	Total	Not-for-profit	For-profit
4-year institutions									
1970	5,049	2,875	2,174	4,051	998	3,425	1,624	1,617	8
1975	5,709	3,092	2,618	4,407	1,302	3,990	1,720	1,702	18
1980	5,949	2,953	2,996	4,608	1,341	4,113	1,836	1,813	23
1985	6,066	2,960	3,106	4,629	1,437	4,207	1,858	1,820	38
1990	6,719	3,147	3,572	5,092	1,627	4,713	2,006	1,954	52
1995	6,739	3,073	3,667	5,168	1,571	4,626	2,113	2,030	84
2000	7,207	3,220	3,987	5,706	1,501	4,842	2,365	2,154	211
2005	8,476	3,729	4,747	6,800	1,676	5,514	2,962	2,375	588
2006	8,666	3,809	4,857	6,928	1,738	5,622	3,043	2,409	634
2007	8,986	3,957	5,029	7,148	1,837	5,813	3,172	2,437	736
2008	9,394	4,131	5,264	7,423	1,972	5,951	3,443	2,501	942
2009	10,044	4,399	5,645	7,895	2,149	6,285	3,759	2,559	1,200
Projected[1]									
2010	10,105	4,447	5,658	8,017	2,089	6,437	3,669	—	—
2015	10,531	4,547	5,984	8,296	2,235	6,707	3,825	—	—
2016	10,657	4,578	6,079	8,381	2,275	6,786	3,871	—	—
2017	10,768	4,606	6,162	8,458	2,310	6,856	3,912	—	—
2018	10,890	4,639	6,251	8,546	2,344	6,934	3,957	—	—
2019	11,022	4,681	6,341	8,650	2,371	7,017	4,005	—	—
2020	11,122	4,716	6,406	8,733	2,389	7,080	4,042	—	—
2-year institutions									
1970	2,319	1,375	945	1,229	1,090	2,195	124	113	11
1975	3,970	2,165	1,805	1,761	2,209	3,836	134	113	21
1980	4,526	2,047	2,479	1,754	2,772	4,329	198	114	83
1985	4,531	2,002	2,529	1,691	2,840	4,270	261	109	153
1990	5,240	2,233	3,007	1,884	3,356	4,996	244	89	154
1995	5,493	2,329	3,164	1,977	3,515	5,278	215	75	140
2000	5,948	2,559	3,390	2,217	3,731	5,697	251	59	192
2005	6,488	2,680	3,808	2,647	3,841	6,184	304	44	260
2006	6,519	2,705	3,814	2,643	3,875	6,225	293	39	254
2007	6,618	2,771	3,847	2,693	3,925	6,324	294	33	260
2008	6,971	2,936	4,035	2,832	4,139	6,640	331	35	296
2009	7,521	3,197	4,325	3,249	4,273	7,101	420	35	385
Projected[1]									
2010	7,539	3,196	4,343	3,159	4,380	7,162	377	—	—
2015	7,920	3,261	4,659	3,273	4,647	7,527	393	—	—
2016	8,040	3,283	4,757	3,314	4,726	7,641	399	—	—
2017	8,153	3,306	4,846	3,356	4,796	7,748	404	—	—
2018	8,271	3,333	4,937	3,403	4,867	7,860	410	—	—
2019	8,381	3,362	5,019	3,453	4,928	7,965	416	—	—
2020	8,459	3,384	5,076	3,490	4,969	8,039	421	—	—

— Not available.

[1] Projections are based on reported data through 2009. The most recent year of actual data is 2009, and 2020 is the last year for which projected data are available. For more information on projections, see NCES 2011-026.
NOTE: Beginning in 1980, 2-year institutions include schools accredited by the Accrediting Commission of Career Schools and Colleges of Technology. Data through 1995 are for institutions of higher education, while later data are for degree-granting institutions. Detail may not sum to totals because of rounding. Some data have been revised from previously published figures. For more information on the Integrated Postsecondary Education Data System (IPEDS), see supplemental note 3. For more information on the Classification of Postsecondary Education Institutions, see supplemental note 8. See the glossary for definitions of full-time and part-time enrollment.
SOURCE: U.S. Department of Education, National Center for Education Statistics, Higher Education General Information Survey (HEGIS), "Fall Enrollment in Colleges and Universities" surveys, 1970 through 1985; 1990 through 2009 Integrated Postsecondary Education Data System, "Fall Enrollment Survey" (IPEDS-EF:90–99), Spring 2001 through Spring 2010; and Enrollment in Degree-Granting Institutions Model, 1980–2009.

Table A-8-3. Total undergraduate enrollment and percentage distribution of students in degree-granting institutions, by race/ethnicity and sex: Selected years, fall 1976–2009

Race/ethnicity and sex	Enrollment (in thousands)					Percentage distribution of students				
	1976	1980	1990	2000	2009	1976	1980	1990	2000	2009
Total	**9,419**	**10,469**	**11,959**	**13,155**	**17,565**	**100.0**	**100.0**	**100.0**	**100.0**	**100.0**
White	7,740	8,481	9,273	8,983	10,915	82.2	81.0	77.5	68.3	62.1
Black	943	1,019	1,147	1,549	2,577	10.0	9.7	9.6	11.8	14.7
Hispanic	353	433	725	1,351	2,362	3.7	4.1	6.1	10.3	13.4
Asian/Pacific Islander	169	249	500	846	1,142	1.8	2.4	4.2	6.4	6.5
American Indian/Alaska Native	70	78	95	139	189	0.7	0.7	0.8	1.1	1.1
Nonresident alien	143	210	219	288	378	1.5	2.0	1.8	2.2	2.2
Male	4,897	4,997	5,380	5,778	7,595	100.0	100.0	100.0	100.0	100.0
White	4,052	4,055	4,184	4,010	4,860	82.8	81.1	77.8	69.4	64.0
Black	431	428	448	577	938	8.8	8.6	8.3	10.0	12.4
Hispanic	192	211	327	583	997	3.9	4.2	6.1	10.1	13.1
Asian/Pacific Islander	91	129	254	402	534	1.9	2.6	4.7	7.0	7.0
American Indian/Alaska Native	35	35	40	56	77	0.7	0.7	0.7	1.0	1.0
Nonresident alien	96	140	126	150	189	2.0	2.8	2.3	2.6	2.5
Female	4,522	5,472	6,579	7,377	9,970	100.0	100.0	100.0	100.0	100.0
White	3,688	4,426	5,088	4,973	6,055	81.6	80.9	77.3	67.4	60.7
Black	513	591	699	972	1,639	11.3	10.8	10.6	13.2	16.4
Hispanic	161	222	398	768	1,365	3.6	4.1	6.0	10.4	13.7
Asian/Pacific Islander	78	120	246	444	608	1.7	2.2	3.7	6.0	6.1
American Indian/Alaska Native	35	43	56	82	113	0.8	0.8	0.8	1.1	1.1
Nonresident alien	47	70	93	138	189	1.0	1.3	1.4	1.9	1.9

NOTE: Race categories exclude persons of Hispanic ethnicity. Because of underreporting and nonreporting of racial/ethnic data, some estimates are slightly lower than corresponding data in other published tables. Nonresident aliens are shown separately because information about their race/ethnicity is not available. See the glossary for the definition of nonresident alien. For more information on race/ethnicity, see *supplemental note 1*. Data through 1995 are for institutions of higher education, while later data are for degree-granting institutions. For more information on the Classification of Postsecondary Education Institutions, see *supplemental note 8*. For more information on the Integrated Postsecondary Education Data System (IPEDS), see *supplemental note 3*. Detail may not sum to totals because of rounding.
SOURCE: U.S. Department of Education, National Center for Education Statistics, Higher Education General Information Survey (HEGIS), "Fall Enrollment in Colleges and Universities" surveys, 1976 through 1980; 1990 through 2009 Integrated Postsecondary Education Data System, "Fall Enrollment Survey" (IPEDS-EF:90–99), Spring 2001 through Spring 2010; and Enrollment in Degree-Granting Institutions Model, 1980–2009.

Table A-9-1. Number and percentage distribution of actual and projected postbaccalaureate enrollment in degree-granting institutions, by sex, attendance status, and control of institution: Fall 1976–2020

[Numbers in thousands]

| Fall of year | Total | Sex | | | | Attendance status | | | |
| | | Male | | Female | | Full-time | | Part-time | |
		Number	Percent	Number	Percent	Number	Percent	Number	Percent
1976	1,578	905	57.3	673	42.7	684	43.3	894	56.7
1977	1,569	892	56.8	677	43.2	699	44.5	870	55.5
1978	1,576	880	55.8	696	44.2	705	44.7	871	55.3
1979	1,572	863	54.9	709	45.1	715	45.5	857	54.5
1980	1,622	874	53.9	748	46.1	736	45.4	886	54.6
1981	1,617	867	53.6	750	46.4	732	45.3	885	54.7
1982	1,601	861	53.8	740	46.2	737	46.0	864	54.0
1983	1,619	865	53.5	753	46.5	747	46.2	872	53.8
1984	1,624	857	52.8	767	47.2	751	46.2	873	53.8
1985	1,650	856	51.9	794	48.1	756	45.8	895	54.2
1986	1,706	867	50.8	839	49.2	767	45.0	938	55.0
1987	1,720	864	50.2	857	49.8	769	44.7	952	55.3
1988	1,739	864	49.7	875	50.3	794	45.7	944	54.3
1989	1,796	879	48.9	917	51.1	820	45.7	976	54.3
1990	1,860	904	48.6	955	51.4	845	45.4	1,015	54.6
1991	1,920	931	48.5	989	51.5	894	46.6	1,026	53.4
1992	1,950	941	48.3	1,009	51.7	918	47.1	1,032	52.9
1993	1,981	944	47.6	1,037	52.4	948	47.9	1,033	52.1
1994	2,016	950	47.1	1,066	52.9	969	48.1	1,047	51.9
1995	2,030	941	46.4	1,089	53.6	984	48.4	1,047	51.6
1996	2,041	932	45.7	1,108	54.3	1,004	49.2	1,036	50.8
1997	2,052	927	45.2	1,124	54.8	1,019	49.7	1,032	50.3
1998	2,070	923	44.6	1,147	55.4	1,025	49.5	1,045	50.5
1999	2,110	931	44.1	1,179	55.9	1,051	49.8	1,059	50.2
2000	2,157	944	43.7	1,213	56.3	1,087	50.4	1,070	49.6
2001	2,212	956	43.2	1,256	56.8	1,120	50.6	1,093	49.4
2002	2,355	1,010	42.9	1,345	57.1	1,212	51.5	1,143	48.5
2003	2,431	1,033	42.5	1,398	57.5	1,281	52.7	1,150	47.3
2004	2,491	1,047	42.0	1,444	58.0	1,326	53.2	1,166	46.8
2005	2,524	1,047	41.5	1,476	58.5	1,351	53.5	1,173	46.5
2006	2,575	1,061	41.2	1,514	58.8	1,386	53.8	1,188	46.2
2007	2,644	1,088	41.2	1,556	58.8	1,429	54.0	1,215	46.0
2008	2,737	1,122	41.0	1,615	59.0	1,493	54.5	1,244	45.5
2009	2,862	1,174	41.0	1,688	59.0	1,579	55.2	1,283	44.8
Projected[1]									
2010	2,932	1,214	41.4	1,718	58.6	1,603	54.7	1,329	45.3
2011	2,952	1,221	41.3	1,732	58.7	1,618	54.8	1,335	45.2
2012	2,976	1,228	41.3	1,748	58.7	1,633	54.9	1,343	45.1
2013	3,035	1,245	41.0	1,790	59.0	1,667	54.9	1,368	45.1
2014	3,118	1,267	40.6	1,851	59.4	1,713	54.9	1,405	45.1
2015	3,195	1,287	40.3	1,908	59.7	1,755	54.9	1,440	45.1
2016	3,266	1,306	40.0	1,960	60.0	1,792	54.9	1,474	45.1
2017	3,325	1,322	39.7	2,004	60.3	1,821	54.8	1,504	45.2
2018	3,380	1,335	39.5	2,044	60.5	1,846	54.6	1,533	45.4
2019	3,413	1,342	39.3	2,071	60.7	1,858	54.4	1,555	45.6
2020	3,429	1,345	39.2	2,084	60.8	1,860	54.2	1,569	45.7

See notes at end of table.

Table A-9-1. Number and percentage distribution of actual and projected postbaccalaureate enrollment in degree-granting institutions, by sex, attendance status, and control of institution: Fall 1976–2020—Continued

[Numbers in thousands]

| Fall of year | Total | Public | | Private | | | | | |
| | | | | Total | | Not-for-profit | | For-profit | |
		Number	Percent	Number	Percent	Number	Percent	Number	Percent
1976	1,578	1,033	65.5	544	34.5	541	34.3	3	0.2
1977	1,569	1,004	64.0	565	36.0	561	35.8	4	0.2
1978	1,576	999	63.4	577	36.6	574	36.4	4	0.2
1979	1,572	990	63.0	582	37.0	578	36.8	4	0.2
1980	1,622	1,015	62.6	606	37.4	601	37.1	5	0.3
1981	1,617	999	61.8	618	38.2	614	37.9	5	0.3
1982	1,601	983	61.4	618	38.6	613	38.3	4	0.3
1983	1,619	986	60.9	633	39.1	628	38.8	5	0.3
1984	1,624	984	60.6	640	39.4	634	39.0	6	0.4
1985	1,650	1,002	60.7	648	39.3	643	38.9	5	0.3
1986	1,706	1,053	61.8	652	38.2	644	37.8	8	0.5
1987	1,720	1,055	61.3	666	38.7	662	38.5	3	0.2
1988	1,739	1,058	60.9	681	39.1	—	—	—	—
1989	1,796	1,090	60.7	706	39.3	—	—	—	—
1990	1,860	1,135	61.0	724	39.0	717	38.5	8	0.4
1991	1,920	1,162	60.5	758	39.5	747	38.9	11	0.6
1992	1,950	1,168	59.9	781	40.1	771	39.5	11	0.5
1993	1,981	1,177	59.4	804	40.6	790	39.9	14	0.7
1994	2,016	1,189	59.0	828	41.0	810	40.2	18	0.9
1995	2,030	1,189	58.6	841	41.4	824	40.6	17	0.8
1996	2,041	1,185	58.1	855	41.9	830	40.7	25	1.2
1997	2,052	1,189	57.9	863	42.1	838	40.8	25	1.2
1998	2,070	1,188	57.4	882	42.6	852	41.2	30	1.5
1999	2,110	1,199	56.8	911	43.2	869	41.2	42	2.0
2000	2,157	1,213	56.3	943	43.7	896	41.6	47	2.2
2001	2,212	1,247	56.4	965	43.6	910	41.1	55	2.5
2002	2,355	1,319	56.0	1,035	44.0	959	40.7	76	3.2
2003	2,431	1,336	54.9	1,096	45.1	994	40.9	101	4.2
2004	2,491	1,330	53.4	1,162	46.6	1,022	41.0	140	5.6
2005	2,524	1,324	52.5	1,199	47.5	1,036	41.1	163	6.5
2006	2,575	1,333	51.8	1,242	48.2	1,065	41.4	177	6.9
2007	2,644	1,353	51.2	1,291	48.8	1,101	41.6	190	7.2
2008	2,737	1,381	50.5	1,356	49.5	1,125	41.1	231	8.4
2009	2,862	1,424	49.8	1,438	50.2	1,172	40.9	267	9.3
Projected[1]									
2010	2,932	1,460	49.8	1,474	50.3	—	—	—	—
2011	2,952	1,469	49.8	1,485	50.3	—	—	—	—
2012	2,976	1,481	49.8	1,500	50.4	—	—	—	—
2013	3,035	1,510	49.8	1,531	50.5	—	—	—	—
2014	3,118	1,551	49.8	1,572	50.4	—	—	—	—
2015	3,195	1,590	49.8	1,611	50.4	—	—	—	—
2016	3,266	1,625	49.8	1,645	50.4	—	—	—	—
2017	3,325	1,655	49.8	1,674	50.4	—	—	—	—
2018	3,380	1,682	49.8	1,700	50.3	—	—	—	—
2019	3,413	1,699	49.8	1,715	50.2	—	—	—	—
2020	3,429	1,707	49.8	1,722	50.2	—	—	—	—

— Not available.

[1] Projections are based on reported data through 2009. The most recent year of actual data is 2009, and 2020 is the last year for which projected data are available. For more information on projections, see NCES 2011-026. Data for 1999 were imputed using alternative procedures. For more information, see NCES 2001-083, appendix E.

NOTE: Postbaccalaureate enrollment is the number of students with a bachelor's degree who are enrolled in graduate-level or first-professional programs. Detail may not sum to totals because of rounding. For more information on the Integrated Postsecondary Education Data System (IPEDS), see *supplemental note 3*. For more information on the Classification of Postsecondary Education Institutions, see *supplemental note 8*. See the glossary for definitions of full-time and part-time enrollment.

SOURCE: U.S. Department of Education, National Center for Education Statistics, Higher Education General Information Survey (HEGIS), "Fall Enrollment in Colleges and Universities" surveys, 1967 through 1985; 1986 through 2009 Integrated Postsecondary Education Data System, "Fall Enrollment Survey" (IPEDS-EF:86–99), and Spring 2001 through Spring 2010; and Enrollment in Degree-Granting Institutions Model, 1980–2009.

Table A-9-2. Total postbaccalaureate enrollment and percentage distribution of students in degree-granting institutions, by race/ethnicity and sex: Selected years, Fall 1976–2009

Race/ethnicity and sex	Enrollment (in thousands)					Percentage distribution of students				
	1976[1]	1980[1]	1990	2000	2009	1976	1980	1990	2000	2009
Total	**1,578**	**1,622**	**1,860**	**2,157**	**2,862**	**99.3**	**99.7**	**100.0**	**100.0**	**100.0**
Race/ethnicity										
White	1,336	1,352	1,450	1,479	1,816	84.7	83.4	78.0	68.6	63.4
Black	90	88	100	181	342	5.7	5.4	5.4	8.4	12.0
Hispanic	31	39	58	111	184	2.0	2.4	3.1	5.1	6.4
Asian/Pacific Islander	29	38	72	133	195	1.8	2.3	3.9	6.2	6.8
American Indian/Alaska Native	6	6	7	13	18	0.4	0.4	0.4	0.6	0.6
Nonresident alien	75	95	173	241	306	4.8	5.9	9.3	11.2	10.7
Sex and race/ethnicity										
Male	898	871	904	944	1,174	56.9	53.7	48.6	43.7	41.0
White	762	718	677	625	734	48.3	44.3	36.4	29.0	25.6
Black	39	36	37	58	99	2.5	2.2	2.0	2.7	3.5
Hispanic	18	20	27	45	69	1.1	1.3	1.5	2.1	2.4
Asian/Pacific Islander	17	23	40	64	87	1.1	1.4	2.2	3.0	3.1
American Indian/Alaska Native	4	3	3	5	7	0.2	0.2	0.2	0.2	0.2
Nonresident alien	58	71	120	147	178	3.7	4.4	6.5	6.8	6.2
Female	669	747	955	1,213	1,688	42.4	46.1	51.4	56.3	59.0
White	574	634	773	854	1,081	36.4	39.1	41.6	39.6	37.8
Black	50	52	63	123	244	3.2	3.2	3.4	5.7	8.5
Hispanic	13	18	31	66	115	0.8	1.1	1.7	3.1	4.0
Asian/Pacific Islander	11	15	32	69	108	0.7	0.9	1.7	3.2	3.8
American Indian/Alaska Native	3	3	4	8	12	0.2	0.2	0.2	0.4	0.4
Nonresident alien	18	24	53	94	129	1.1	1.5	2.8	4.3	4.5

[1] Race/ethnicity estimates may not sum to totals due to underreporting and nonreporting of racial/ethnic data.
NOTE: Postbaccalaureate enrollment is the number of students with a bachelor's degree who are enrolled in graduate-level or first-professional programs. Race categories exclude persons of Hispanic ethnicity. Nonresident aliens are shown separately because information about their race/ethnicity is not available. See the glossary for the definition of nonresident alien. For more information on race/ethnicity, see *supplemental note 1*. For more information on the Integrated Postsecondary Education Data System (IPEDS), see *supplemental note 3*. Detail may not sum to totals because of rounding.
SOURCE: U.S. Department of Education, National Center for Education Statistics, Higher Education General Information Survey (HEGIS), "Fall Enrollment in Colleges and Universities" surveys, 1976 and 1980; and 1990, 2000, and 2009 Integrated Postsecondary Education Data System (IPEDS), Spring 2001 and 2010.

This page intentionally left blank.

Appendix A—Supplemental Tables 177

Reading Performance

Table A-10-1. Average reading scale scores, selected percentile scores, and percentage of students at each achievement level, by grade: Selected years, 1992–2009

Grade, scale score, percentile, and achievement level	1992[1]	1994[1]	1998[1]	1998	2002	2003[2]	2005	2007[2]	2009
Grade 4									
Average scale score	217*	214*	217*	215*	219*	218*	219*	221	221
Percentile									
10th	170*	159*	167*	163*	170*	169*	171*	174	175
25th	194*	189*	193*	191*	196*	195*	196*	199	199
50th	219*	219*	220*	217*	221*	221*	221*	224	223
75th	242*	243	244	242*	244*	244*	244*	246	245
90th	261*	263	263	262	263*	264	263	264	264
Percentage at each achievement level									
Below *Basic*	38*	40*	38*	40*	36*	37*	36*	33	33
At or above *Basic*	62*	60*	62*	60*	64*	63*	64*	67	67
At or above *Proficient*	29*	30*	31*	29*	31*	31*	31*	33	33
At *Advanced*	6*	7	7	7	7*	8	8	8	8
Grade 8									
Average scale score	260*	260*	264	263	264	263	262*	263*	264
Percentile									
10th	213*	211*	217	216	220	217*	216*	217*	219
25th	237*	236*	242	241*	244	242*	240*	242*	243
50th	262*	262*	267	266	267	266	265*	265*	267
75th	285*	286	288	288	288	288	286*	287*	288
90th	305	305	305	306	305	306	305	305	305
Percentage at each achievement level									
Below *Basic*	31*	30*	26	27*	25	26*	27*	26*	25
At or above *Basic*	69*	70*	74	73*	75	74*	73*	74*	75
At or above *Proficient*	29*	30*	33	32	33	32	31*	31*	32
At *Advanced*	3	3	3	3	3	3*	3	3	3
Grade 12									
Average scale score	292*	287	291*	290*	287	—	286*	—	288
Percentile									
10th	249*	239	242*	240*	237	—	235*	—	238
25th	271*	264	268*	267*	263	—	262	—	264
50th	294*	290	293*	293*	289	—	288*	—	291
75th	315	313	317	317	312*	—	313	—	315
90th	333*	332*	337	336	332*	—	333	—	335
Percentage at each achievement level									
Below *Basic*	20*	25	23*	24*	26	—	27	—	26
At or above *Basic*	80*	75	77*	76*	74	—	73	—	74
At or above *Proficient*	40	36	40	40	36	—	35*	—	38
At *Advanced*	4*	4	6	6	5*	—	5	—	5

— Not available.

*Score is significantly different ($p < .05$) from 2009.

[1] Testing accommodations (e.g., extended time, small group testing) for children with disabilities and English language learners were not permitted in 1992 and 1994; students were tested with and without accommodations in 1998. The footnoted column represents the sample without accommodations.

[2] The 12th-grade National Assessment of Educational Progress (NAEP) reading assessment was not administered in 2003 or 2007.

NOTE: The NAEP reading scale ranges from 0 to 500. Achievement levels define what students should know and be able to do: *Basic* indicates partial mastery of fundamental skills, *Proficient* indicates demonstrated competency over challenging subject matter, and *Advanced* indicates superior performance. The percentage of students at or above *Proficient* includes students at the *Proficient* and the *Advanced* achievement levels. Similarly, the percentage of students at or above *Basic* includes students at the *Basic*, *Proficient*, and *Advanced* achievement levels. For more information on NAEP, see *supplemental note 4*.

SOURCE: U.S. Department of Education, National Center for Education Statistics, National Assessment of Educational Progress (NAEP), selected years, 1992–2009 Reading Assessments, NAEP Data Explorer.

Table A-10-2. Average reading scale scores, by grade and selected student and school characteristics: Selected years, 1992–2009

Student or school characteristic	Grade 4			Grade 8			Grade 12		
	1992[1]	2007	2009	1992[1]	2007	2009	1992[1]	2005	2009
Total	**217***	**221**	**221**	**260***	**263***	**264**	**292***	**286***	**288**
Sex									
Male	213*	218	218	254*	258*	259	287*	279*	282
Female	221*	224	224	267*	268	269	297*	292	294
Race/ethnicity									
White	224*	231	230	267*	272*	273	297	293*	296
Black	192*	203	205	237*	245*	246	273*	267	269
Hispanic	197*	205	205	241*	247*	249	279	272	274
Asian/Pacific Islander	216*	232*	235	268	271*	274	290	287*	298
American Indian/Alaska Native	‡	203	204	‡	247*	251	‡	279	283
School type									
Traditional public	—	221	221	—	263*	264	—	285*	289
Public charter	—	214	212	—	260	257	—	—	276
Private	232	234	235	278	280	282	308	—	‡
Percentage of students in school eligible for free or reduced-price lunch									
0–25 percent	—	235	237	—	275*	277	—	292*	299
26–50 percent	—	223	223	—	263*	265	—	282*	286
51–75 percent	—	212*	215	—	253*	256	—	273	276
76–100 percent	—	200	202	—	241	243	—	266	266
Locale									
City	—	215	216	—	257*	259	—	—	286
Suburban	—	226	225	—	267	268	—	—	292
Town	—	219	218	—	262	261	—	—	287
Rural	—	222	222	—	264	265	—	—	286
Student disability and English language learner status[2]									
Students with disabilities (SD)	‡	194	193	‡	229*	233	‡	245*	254
English language learner (ELL)	‡	191	191	‡	226	223	‡	251*	243

— Not available.

‡ Reporting standards not met.

*Score is significantly different ($p < .05$) from 2009.

[1] Testing accommodations (e.g., extended time, small group testing) for children with disabilities and English language learners were not permitted in 1992.

[2] In 1992, the exclusion rates for SD students were 4 percent for grade 4 and 5 percent for grade 8, and the exclusion rates for ELL students were 2 percent for grade 4 and 2 percent for grade 8. In 2007, the exclusion rates for SD students were 4 percent for grade 4 and 4 percent for grade 8, and the exclusion rates for ELL students were 2 percent for grade 4 and 1 percent for grade 8. In 2009, the exclusion rate for SD students was 4 percent for grade 4, 3 percent for grade 8, and 3 percent for grade 12, and the exclusion rates for ELL students were 2 percent for grade 4, 1 percent for grade 8 and 1 percent for grade 12.

NOTE: The National Assessment of Educational Progress (NAEP) reading scale ranges from 0 to 500. The 12th-grade NAEP Reading Assessment was not administered in 2007. For more information on NAEP, see *supplemental note 4*. Race categories exclude persons of Hispanic ethnicity. For more information on free or reduced-priced lunch or race/ethnicity, see *supplemental note 1*.

SOURCE: U.S. Department of Education, National Center for Education Statistics, National Assessment of Educational Progress (NAEP), selected years, 1992–2009 Reading Assessments, NAEP Data Explorer.

Table A-10-3. Average reading scale scores and achievement-level results for public school students, by grade and state or jurisdiction: 2007 and 2009

State or jurisdiction	Grade 4						Grade 8						Grade 12		
	Average score		At or above Basic		At or above Proficient		Average score		At or above Basic		At or above Proficient		Average score	At or above Basic	At or above Proficient
	2007	2009	2007	2009	2007	2009	2007	2009	2007	2009	2007	2009	2009	2009	2009
United States	**220**	**220**	**66**	**66**	**32**	**32**	**261**	**262***	**73**	**74***	**29**	**30***	**287**	**73**	**37**
Alabama	216	216	62	62	29	28	252	255*	62	66	21	24	—	—	—
Alaska	214	211*	62	59	29	27	259	259	71	72	27	27	—	—	—
Arizona	210	210	56	56	24	25	255	258	65	68	24	27	—	—	—
Arkansas	217	216	64	63	29	29	258	258	70	69	25	27	280	68	29
California	209	210	53	54	23	24	251	253	62	64	21	22	—	—	—
Colorado	224	226	70	72	36	40	266	266	79	78	35	32	—	—	—
Connecticut	227	229	73	76	41	42	267	272*	77	81*	37	43*	292	78	43
Delaware	225	226	73	73	34	35	265	265	77	78	31	31	—	—	—
District of Columbia	197	202*	39	44*	14	17*	241	242	48	51	12	14	—	—	—
Florida	224	226	70	73	34	36	260	264*	71	76*	28	32	283	70	32
Georgia	219	218	66	63	28	29	259	260	70	72	26	27	—	—	—
Hawaii	213	211	59	57	26	26	251	255*	62	67*	20	22	—	—	—
Idaho	223	221	70	69	35	32	265	265	78	77	32	33	290	78	39
Illinois	219	219	65	65	32	32	263	265	75	77	30	33	292	78	40
Indiana	222	223	68	70	33	34	264	266	76	79	31	32	—	—	—
Iowa	225	221*	74	69*	36	34	267	265	80	77	36	32	291	79	39
Kansas	225	224	72	72	36	35	267	267	81	80	35	33	—	—	—
Kentucky	222	226*	68	72	33	36	262	267*	73	79*	28	33*	—	—	—
Louisiana	207	207	52	51	20	18	253	253	64	64	19	20	—	—	—
Maine	226	224	73	70	36	35	270	268	83	80*	37	35	—	—	—
Maryland	225	226	69	70	36	37	265	267	76	77	33	36	—	—	—
Massachusetts	236	234	81	80	49	47	273	274	84	83	43	43	295	80	46
Michigan	220	218	66	64	32	30	260	262	72	72	28	31	—	—	—
Minnesota	225	223	73	70	37	37	268	270	80	82	37	38	—	—	—
Mississippi	208	211	51	55	19	22	250	251	60	62	17	19	—	—	—
Missouri	221	224	67	70	32	36*	263	267*	75	79*	31	34	—	—	—
Montana	227	225	75	73	39	35	271	270	85	84	39	38	—	—	—
Nebraska	223	223	71	70	35	35	267	267	79	80	35	35	—	—	—
Nevada	211	211	57	57	24	24	252	254	63	65	22	22	—	—	—
New Hampshire	229	229	76	77	41	41	270	271	82	81	37	39	293	79	44

See notes at end of table.

Table A-10-3. Average reading scale scores and achievement-level results for public school students, by grade and state or jurisdiction: 2007 and 2009—Continued

State or jurisdiction	Grade 4 Average score 2007	2009	Percentage of students At or above Basic 2007	2009	At or above Proficient 2007	2009	Grade 8 Average score 2007	2009	Percentage of students At or above Basic 2007	2009	At or above Proficient 2007	2009	Grade 12 Average score 2009	Percentage of students At or above Basic 2009	At or above Proficient 2009
United States	**220**	**220**	**66**	**66**	**32**	**32**	**261**	**262***	**73**	**74***	**29**	**30***	**287**	**73**	**37**
New Jersey	231	229	77	76	43	40	270	273	81	83	39	42	288	74	39
New Mexico	212	208*	58	52*	24	20*	251	254*	62	66	17	22*	—	—	—
New York	224	224	69	71	36	36	264	264	75	75	32	33	—	—	—
North Carolina	218	219	64	65	29	32	259	260	71	70	28	29	—	—	—
North Dakota	226	226	75	76	35	35	268	269	84	86	32	34	—	—	—
Ohio	226	225	73	71	36	36	268	269	79	80	36	37	—	—	—
Oklahoma	217	217	65	65	27	28	260	259	72	73	26	26	—	—	—
Oregon	215	218	62	65	28	31	266	265	77	76	34	33	—	—	—
Pennsylvania	226	224	73	70	40	37	268	271*	79	81	36	40	—	—	—
Rhode Island	219	223*	65	69*	31	36*	258	260	69	72	27	28	—	—	—
South Carolina	214	216	59	62	26	28	257	257	69	68	25	24	—	—	—
South Dakota	223	222	71	70	34	33	270	270	83	84	37	37	292	82	40
Tennessee	216	217	61	63	27	28	259	261	71	73	26	28	—	—	—
Texas	220	219	66	65	30	28	261	260	73	73	28	27	—	—	—
Utah	221	219	69	67	34	31	262	266*	75	78*	30	33	—	—	—
Vermont	228	229	74	75	41	41	273	272	84	84	42	41	—	—	—
Virginia	227	227	74	74	38	38	267	266	79	78	34	32	—	—	—
Washington	224	221	70	68	36	33	265	267	77	78	34	36	—	—	—
West Virginia	215	215	63	62	28	26	255	255	68	67	23	22	279	68	29
Wisconsin	223	220	70	67	36	33	264	266	76	78	33	34	—	—	—
Wyoming	225	223*	73	72	36	33*	266	268	80	82	33	34	—	—	—

— Not available.

* Change in score or percentage is statistically significant from 2007 ($p < .05$).

NOTE: At the state level, the National Assessment of Educational Progress (NAEP) includes only students in public schools, while other reported national results in this indicator include both public and private school students. In 2009, 11 states participated in the pilot state NAEP reading assessment at grade 12. The 12th-grade NAEP Reading Assessment was not administered in 2007. The NAEP reading scale ranges from 0 to 500. For more information on NAEP, see *supplemental note 4.*

SOURCE: U.S. Department of Education, National Center for Education Statistics, National Assessment of Educational Progress (NAEP), 2007 and 2009 Reading Assessments, NAEP Data Explorer.

Reading Achievement Gaps

Table A-11-1. Average reading scale scores and selected achievement gaps of 4th-, 8th-, and 12th-grade students, by sex and race/ethnicity: Selected years, 1992–2009

Sex and race/ethnicity	1992[1]	1994[1]	1998[1]	1998	2000[1]	2000	2002	2003	2005	2007	2009
Grade 4											
Total	**217**	**214**	**217**	**215**	**217**	**213**	**219**	**218**	**219**	**221**	**221**
Sex											
Male	213	209	214	212	212	208	215	215	216	218	218
Female	221	220	220	217	222	219	222	222	222	224	224
Male-female achievement gap	-8	-10*	-6	-5	-10*	-11*	-6	-7	-6	-7	-7
Race/ethnicity											
White	224	224	226	225	225	224	229	229	229	231	230
Black	192	185	193	193	191	190	199	198	200	203	205
Hispanic	197	188	195	193	197	190	201	200	203	205	205
Asian/Pacific Islander	216	220	221	215	229	225	224	226	229	232	235
American Indian/Alaska Native	‡	211	‡	‡	204	214	207	202	204	203	204
Black-White achievement gap	-32*	-38*	-33*	-32*	-34*	-34*	-30*	-31*	-29*	-27	-26
Hispanic-White achievement gap	-27	-35*	-31*	-32*	-29	-35*	-28	-28*	-26	-26	-25
Grade 8											
Total	**260**	**260**	**264**	**263**	—	—	**264**	**263**	**262**	**263**	**264**
Sex											
Male	254	252	257	256	—	—	260	258	257	258	259
Female	267	267	270	270	—	—	269	269	267	268	269
Male-female achievement gap	-13*	-15*	-13*	-14*	—	—	-9	-11*	-10*	-10	-9
Race/ethnicity											
White	267	267	271	270	—	—	272	272	271	272	273
Black	237	236	243	244	—	—	245	244	243	245	246
Hispanic	241	243	245	243	—	—	247	245	246	247	249
Asian/Pacific Islander	268	265	267	264	—	—	267	270	271	271	274
American Indian/Alaska Native	‡	248	‡	‡	—	—	250	246	249	247	251
Black-White achievement gap	-30	-30	-28	-26	—	—	-27	-28	-28	-27	-26
Hispanic-White achievement gap	-26	-24	-26	-27	—	—	-26	-27*	-25	-25	-24
Grade 12											
Total	**292**	**287**	**291**	**290**	—	—	**287**	—	**286**	—	**288**
Sex											
Male	287	280	283	282	—	—	279	—	279	—	282
Female	297	294	298	298	—	—	295	—	292	—	294
Male-female achievement gap	-10	-14	-16*	-16*	—	—	-16*	—	-13	—	-12
Race/ethnicity											
White	297	293	297	297	—	—	292	—	293	—	296
Black	273	265	271	269	—	—	267	—	267	—	269
Hispanic	279	270	276	275	—	—	273	—	272	—	274
Asian/Pacific Islander	290	278	288	287	—	—	286	—	287	—	298
American Indian/Alaska Native	‡	274	‡	‡	—	—	‡	—	279	—	283
Black-White achievement gap	-24	-29	-26	-27	—	—	-25	—	-26	—	-27
Hispanic-White achievement gap	-19	-23	-21	-22	—	—	-20	—	-21	—	-22

— Not available.
‡ Reporting standards not met.
*Change in gap is statistically significant from 2009 (*p* < .05).
[1] Testing accommodations (e.g., extended time, small group testing) for children with disabilities and English language learners were not permitted in 1992 and 1994; students were tested with and without accommodations in 1998 and 2000. The footnoted column represents the sample without accommodations.
NOTE: Detail may not sum to totals because of rounding. The National Assessment of Educational Progress (NAEP) reading scale ranges from 0 to 500. The 12th-grade NAEP reading assessment was not administered in 2000, 2003, or 2007. For more information on NAEP, see *supplemental note 4*. Race categories exclude persons of Hispanic ethnicity. For more information on race/ethnicity, see *supplemental note 1*.
SOURCE: U.S. Department of Education, National Center for Education Statistics, National Assessment of Educational Progress (NAEP), selected years, 1992–2009 Reading Assessments, NAEP Data Explorer.

Table A-11-2. Average reading scale scores and selected achievement gaps of 4th-, 8th-, and 12th-grade students, by selected student and school characteristics: Selected years, 1992–2009

Student or school characteristic	1992[1]	1994[1]	1998[1]	1998	2000[1]	2000	2002	2003	2005	2007	2009
Grade 4											
Total	217	214	217	215	217	213	219	218	219	221	221
Percentage of students in school eligible for free or reduced-price lunch											
0–25 percent (low poverty)	—	—	233	231	233	231	233	233	234	235	237
26–50 percent	—	—	219	218	218	218	221	221	221	223	223
51–75 percent	—	—	207	205	205	205	210	211	211	212	215
76–100 percent (high poverty)	—	—	190	187	191	184	196	194	197	200	202
Gap between high-poverty and low-poverty schools	—	—	-43 *	-44 *	-42 *	-48 *	-37 *	-39 *	-37 *	-35	-35
English language learner (ELL) status											
ELL	‡	‡	‡	174	‡	167	183	186	187	188	188
Non-ELL	‡	‡	‡	217	‡	216	221	221	222	224	224
Gap between ELL and non-ELL students	—	—	—	-43	—	-49	-38	-35	-35	-36	-36
Grade 8											
Total	260	260	264	263	—	—	264	263	262	263	264
Percentage of students in school eligible for free or reduced-price lunch											
0–25 percent (low poverty)	—	—	275	273	—	—	276	275	274	275	277
26–50 percent	—	—	261	262	—	—	264	263	262	263	265
51–75 percent	—	—	251	252	—	—	254	253	252	253	256
76–100 percent (high poverty)	—	—	243	240	—	—	240	239	240	241	243
Gap between high-poverty and low-poverty schools	—	—	-32	-33	—	—	-36	-36	-34	-34	-34
English language learner (ELL) status											
ELL	‡	‡	‡	218	—	—	224	222	224	223	219
Non-ELL	‡	‡	‡	264	—	—	266	265	264	265	266
Gap between ELL and non-ELL students	—	—	—	-46	—	—	-42	-43	-40	-42	-47
Grade 12											
Total	292	287	291	290	—	—	287	—	286	—	288
Percentage of students in school eligible for free or reduced-price lunch											
0–25 percent (low poverty)	—	—	296	296	—	—	293	—	292	—	299
26–50 percent	—	—	286	284	—	—	282	—	282	—	286
51–75 percent	—	—	274	275	—	—	275	—	273	—	276
76–100 percent (high poverty)	—	—	274	272	—	—	268	—	266	—	266
Gap between high-poverty and low-poverty schools	—	—	-22	-23	—	—	-25	—	-26	—	-33
English language learner (ELL) status											
ELL	‡	‡	‡	244	—	—	245	—	247	—	240
Non-ELL	‡	‡	‡	291	—	—	288	—	288	—	290
Gap between ELL and non-ELL students	—	—	—	-46 *	—	—	-43 *	—	-40 *	—	-50

— Not available.
‡ Reporting standards not met.
*Change in gap is statistically significant from 2009 ($p < .05$).
[1] Testing accommodations (e.g., extended time, small group testing) for children with disabilities and English language learners were not permitted in 1992 and 1994; students were tested with and without accommodations in 1998 and 2000. The footnoted column represents the sample without accommodations.
NOTE: The National Assessment of Educational Progress (NAEP) reading scale ranges from 0 to 500. The 12th-grade NAEP reading assessment was not administered in 2000, 2003, or 2007. For more information on NAEP, see *supplemental note 4*. For more information on free or reduced-price lunch, see *supplemental note 1*.
SOURCE: U.S. Department of Education, National Center for Education Statistics, National Assessment of Educational Progress (NAEP), selected years, 1992–2009 Reading Assessments, NAEP Data Explorer.

Mathematics Performance

Table A-12-1. Average mathematics scale scores, selected percentile scores, and percentage of students at each achievement level, by grade: Selected years, 1990–2009

Grade, scale score, and achievement level	1990[1]	1992[1]	1996[1]	1996	2000	2003	2005	2007	2009
Grade 4									
Average scale score	213*	220*	224*	224*	226*	235*	238*	240	240
Percentile									
10th	171*	177*	182*	182*	184*	197*	200*	202	202
25th	193*	199*	204*	203*	205*	216*	220*	222	221
50th	214*	221*	226*	225*	227*	236*	239*	242	241
75th	235*	242*	246*	245*	248*	255*	258*	260	260
90th	253*	259*	262*	262*	265*	270*	273*	275	275
Percentage at each achievement level									
Below *Basic*	50*	41*	36*	37*	35*	23*	20*	18	18
At or above *Basic*	50*	59*	64*	63*	65*	77*	80*	82	82
At or above *Proficient*	13*	18*	21*	21*	24*	32*	36*	39	39
At *Advanced*	1	2*	2*	2*	3*	4*	5*	6	6
Grade 8									
Average scale score	263*	268*	272*	270*	273*	278*	279*	281*	283
Percentile									
10th	215*	221*	224*	221*	223*	230*	231*	235	236
25th	239*	243*	248*	245*	249*	254*	255*	258*	259
50th	264*	269*	273*	273*	275*	279*	280*	283*	284
75th	288*	294*	298*	297*	300*	303*	304*	306*	308
90th	307*	315*	317*	316*	320*	323*	324*	327*	329
Percentage at each achievement level									
Below *Basic*	48*	42*	38*	39*	37*	32*	31*	29*	27
At or above *Basic*	52*	58*	62*	61*	63*	68*	69*	71*	73
At or above *Proficient*	15*	21*	24*	23*	26*	29*	30*	32*	34
At *Advanced*	2*	3*	4*	4*	5*	5*	6*	7*	8
Grade 12									
Average scale score	—	—	—	—	—	—	150*	—	153
Percentile									
10th	—	—	—	—	—	—	105*	—	110
25th	—	—	—	—	—	—	127*	—	130
50th	—	—	—	—	—	—	151*	—	154
75th	—	—	—	—	—	—	174*	—	177
90th	—	—	—	—	—	—	194	—	197
Percentage at each achievement level									
Below *Basic*	—	—	—	—	—	—	39*	—	36
At or above *Basic*	—	—	—	—	—	—	61*	—	64
At or above *Proficient*	—	—	—	—	—	—	23*	—	26
At *Advanced*	—	—	—	—	—	—	2	—	3

— Not available.

*Score is significantly different (*p* < .05) from 2009.

[1] Testing accommodations (e.g., extended time, small group testing) for children with disabilities and English language learners were not permitted in 1990 and 1992. Students in grades 4 and 8 were tested with and without accommodations in 1996. The footnoted column represents the sample without accommodations.

NOTE: Average mathematics scale scores include public and private school students. At grades 4 and 8, the National Assessment of Educational Progress (NAEP) mathematics scale ranges from 0 to 500. The framework for the 12th-grade mathematics assessment was revised in 2005; as a result, the 2005 and 2009 results cannot be compared with those from previous years. At grade 12, mathematics scores on the revised assessment range from 0 to 300. The 12th-grade mathematics assessment was not administered in 2007. Achievement levels define what students should know and be able to do: *Basic* indicates partial mastery of fundamental skills, *Proficient* indicates demonstrated competency over challenging subject matter, and *Advanced* indicates superior performance. The percentage of students at or above *Proficient* includes students at the *Proficient* and the *Advanced* achievement levels. Similarly, the percentage of students at or above *Basic* includes students at the *Basic*, *Proficient*, and *Advanced* achievement levels. Detail may not sum to totals because of rounding. For more information on NAEP, see *supplemental note 4*.

SOURCE: U.S. Department of Education, National Center for Education Statistics, National Assessment of Educational Progress (NAEP), selected years, 1990–2009 Mathematics Assessments, NAEP Data Explorer.

Table A-12-2. Average mathematics scale scores, by grade and selected student and school characteristics: Selected years, 1990–2009

Student or school characteristic	Grade 4			Grade 8			Grade 12	
	1990[1]	2007	2009	1990[1]	2007	2009	2005	2009
Total	**213***	**240**	**240**	**263***	**281***	**283**	**150***	**153**
Sex								
Male	214*	241	241	263*	282*	284	151*	155
Female	213*	239	239	262*	280*	282	149*	152
Race/ethnicity								
White	220*	248	248	270*	291*	293	157*	161
Black	188*	222	222	237*	260*	261	127*	131
Hispanic	200*	227	227	246*	265*	266	133*	138
Asian/Pacific Islander	225*	253	255	275*	297*	301	163*	175
American Indian/Alaska Native	‡	228	225	‡	264	266	134*	144
School type								
Traditional public	—	240	240	—	281*	283	—	154
Public charter	—	234	231	—	273	275	—	138
Private	224*	246	246	‡	293	296	‡	‡
Percentage of students in school eligible for free or reduced-price lunch								
0–25 percent	—	252*	254	—	296*	298	158*	166
26–50 percent	—	242	242	—	282*	284	147*	150
51–75 percent	—	234	234	—	271*	274	136*	140
76–100 percent	—	222	223	—	259	260	122*	130
Locale								
City	—	235	235	—	275*	279	—	152
Suburban	—	244	243	—	286	287	—	157
Town	—	238	238	—	280	279	—	151
Rural	—	240	241	—	282*	284	—	151
English language learner status[2]								
Non-English language learner	‡	242	242	‡	283*	285	151*	154
English language learner (ELL)	‡	217	218	‡	246*	243	120	117

— Not available.
‡ Reporting standards not met.
*Score is significantly different ($p < .05$) from 2009.
[1] Testing accommodations (e.g., extended time, small group testing) for children with disabilities and English language learners were not permitted in 1990. The footnoted column represents the sample without accommodations.
[2] The percentages of English language learners (ELL) excluded from the National Assessment of Educational Progress (NAEP) may vary across years. In 2005, the exclusion rate was 1 percent at grade 12 for ELL students. In 2007, the exclusion rate was 1 percent at both grade 4 and grade 8 for ELL students. In 2009 the exclusion rate was 1 percent for grade 4 and the percentage of ELL students excluded from the assessment rounded to zero for grade 8 and grade 12.
NOTE: Average mathematics scale scores include public and private school students. At grades 4 and 8, the NAEP mathematics scale ranges from 0 to 500. The framework for the 12th-grade mathematics assessment was revised in 2005; as a result, the 2005 and 2009 results cannot be compared with those from previous years. At grade 12, mathematics scores on the revised assessment range from 0 to 300. For more information on NAEP, see *supplemental note 4*. Race categories exclude persons of Hispanic ethnicity. For more information on race/ethnicity or free or reduced-priced lunch, see *supplemental note 1*.
SOURCE: U.S. Department of Education, National Center for Education Statistics, National Assessment of Educational Progress (NAEP), selected years, 1990–2009 Mathematics Assessments, NAEP Data Explorer.

Mathematics Performance

Table A-12-3. Average mathematics scale scores and achievement-level results for public school students, by grade and state or jurisdiction: 2007 and 2009

State or jurisdiction	Grade 4							Grade 8							Grade 12		
	Average score		At or above *Basic*		At or above *Proficient*			Average score		At or above *Basic*		At or above *Proficient*			Average score	At or above *Basic*	At or above *Proficient*
	2007	2009	2007	2009	2007	2009		2007	2009	2007	2009	2007	2009		2009	2009	2009
United States	**239**	**239**	**81**	**81**	**39**	**38**		**280**	**282***	**70**	**71***	**31**	**33***		**152**	**63**	**25**
Alabama	229	228	70	70	26	24		266	269	55	58	18	20		—	—	—
Alaska	237	237	79	78	38	38		283	283	73	75	32	33		—	—	—
Arizona	232	230	74	71	31	28		276	277	66	67	26	29		—	—	—
Arkansas	238	238	81	80	37	36		274	276	65	67	24	27		146	59	16
California	230	232	70	72	30	30		270	270	59	59	24	23		—	—	—
Colorado	240	243*	82	84	41	45		286	287	75	76	37	40		—	—	—
Connecticut	243	245	84	86	45	46		282	289*	73	78*	35	40*		156	69	29
Delaware	242	239*	87	84*	40	36*		283	284	74	75	31	32		—	—	—
District of Columbia	214	219*	49	56*	14	17*		248	254*	34	40*	8	11*		—	—	—
Florida	242	242	86	86	40	40		277	279	68	70	27	29		148	59	19
Georgia	235	236	79	78	32	34		275	278*	64	67	25	27		—	—	—
Hawaii	234	236	77	77	33	37		269	274*	59	65*	21	25*		—	—	—
Idaho	241	241	85	85	40	41		284	287*	75	78*	34	38*		153	66	23
Illinois	237	238	79	80	36	38		280	282	70	73	31	33		154	67	26
Indiana	245	243*	89	87	46	42*		285	287	76	78	35	36		—	—	—
Iowa	243	243	87	87	43	41		285	284	77	76	35	34		156	71	25
Kansas	248	245	89	89	51	46		290	289	81	79	40	39		—	—	—
Kentucky	235	239*	79	81	31	37*		279	279	69	70	27	27		—	—	—
Louisiana	230	229	73	72	24	23		272	272	64	62	19	20		—	—	—
Maine	242	244	85	87	42	45		286	286	78	78	34	35		—	—	—
Maryland	240	244*	80	85*	40	44		286	288	74	75	37	40		—	—	—
Massachusetts	252	252	93	92	58	57		298	299	85	85	51	52		163	75	36
Michigan	238	236	80	78	37	35		277	278	66	68	29	31		—	—	—
Minnesota	247	249	87	89	51	54		292	294	81	83	43	47		—	—	—
Mississippi	228	227	70	69	21	22		265	265	54	54	14	15		—	—	—
Missouri	239	241	82	83	38	41		281	286*	72	77*	30	35*		—	—	—
Montana	244	244	88	88	44	45		287	292*	79	82*	38	44*		—	—	—
Nebraska	238	239	80	82	38	38		284	284	74	75	35	35		—	—	—
Nevada	232	235*	74	79*	30	32		271	274*	60	63	23	25		—	—	—
New Hampshire	249	251*	91	92	52	56		288	292*	78	82*	38	43*		160	74	32

See notes at end of table.

Table A-12-3. Average mathematics scale scores and achievement-level results for public school students, by grade and state or jurisdiction: 2007 and 2009—Continued

	Grade 4						Grade 8						Grade 12		
	Average score		At or above Basic		At or above Proficient		Average score		At or above Basic		At or above Proficient		Average score	At or above Basic	At or above Proficient
			Percentage of students						Percentage of students					Percentage of students	
State or jurisdiction	2007	2009	2007	2009	2007	2009	2007	2009	2007	2009	2007	2009	2009	2009	2009
United States	**239**	**239**	**81**	**81**	**39**	**38**	**280**	**282***	**70**	**71***	**31**	**33***	**152**	**63**	**25**
New Jersey	249	247	90	88	52	49	289	293*	77	80	40	44	156	67	31
New Mexico	228	230	70	72	24	26	268	270	57	59	17	20	—	—	—
New York	243	241	85	83	43	40	280	283	70	73	30	34	—	—	—
North Carolina	242	244	85	87	41	43	284	284	73	74	34	36	—	—	—
North Dakota	245	245	91	91	46	45	292	293	86	86	41	43	—	—	—
Ohio	245	244	87	85	46	45	285	286	76	76	35	36	—	—	—
Oklahoma	237	237	82	82	33	33	275	276	66	68	21	24	—	—	—
Oregon	236	238	79	80	35	37	284	285	73	75	35	37	—	—	—
Pennsylvania	244	244	85	84	47	46	286	288	77	78	38	40	—	—	—
Rhode Island	236	239*	80	81	34	39*	275	278*	65	68	28	28	—	—	—
South Carolina	237	236	80	78	36	34	282	280	71	69	32	30	—	—	—
South Dakota	241	242	86	86	41	42	288	291*	81	83	39	42	160	77	29
Tennessee	233	232	76	74	29	28	274	275	64	65	23	25	—	—	—
Texas	242	240	87	85	40	38	286	287	78	78	35	36	—	—	—
Utah	239	240	83	81	39	41	281	284*	72	75	32	35	—	—	—
Vermont	246	248*	89	89	49	51	291	293*	81	81	41	43	—	—	—
Virginia	244	243	87	85	42	43	288	286	77	76	37	36	—	—	—
Washington	243	242	84	84	44	43	285	289*	75	78	36	39*	—	—	—
West Virginia	236	233*	81	77*	33	28*	270	270	61	61	19	19	141	52	13
Wisconsin	244	244	85	85	47	45	286	288	76	79	37	39	—	—	—
Wyoming	244	242*	88	87	44	40*	287	286	80	78	36	35	—	—	—

— Not available.

*Score or percentage is statistically significant from 2007 (p < .05).

NOTE: At the state level, the National Assessment of Educational Progress (NAEP) includes only students in public schools, while other reported national results in this indicator include both public and private school students. At grades 4 and 8, the NAEP mathematics scale ranges from 0 to 500. The framework for the 12th-grade mathematics assessment was revised in 2005; scores on the revised assessment range from 0 to 300. Twelfth-graders were assessed in mathematics using the revised assessment in 2005 and 2009 but state-level data are not available for 2005. In 2009, 11 states participated in the pilot state NAEP mathematics assessment. For more information on NAEP, see *supplemental note 4.*

SOURCE: U.S. Department of Education, National Center for Education Statistics, National Assessment of Educational Progress (NAEP), 2007 and 2009 Mathematics Assessments, NAEP Data Explorer.

Table A-13-1. Average mathematics scale scores and selected achievement gaps of 4th-, 8th-, and 12th-grade students, by sex and race/ethnicity: Selected years, 1990–2009

Sex and race/ethnicity	1990[1]	1992[1]	1996[1]	1996	2000	2003	2005	2007	2009
Grade 4									
Total	**213**	**220**	**224**	**224**	**226**	**235**	**238**	**240**	**240**
Sex									
Male	214	221	226	224	227	236	239	241	241
Female	213	219	222	223	224	233	237	239	239
Male-female achievement gap	1	2	3	#	3	3*	3	2	2
Race/ethnicity									
White	220	227	231	232	234	243	246	248	248
Black	188	193	199	198	203	216	220	222	222
Hispanic	200	202	205	207	208	222	226	227	227
Asian/Pacific Islander	225	231	226	229	‡	246	251	253	255
American Indian/Alaska Native	‡	‡	‡	217	208	237	226	228	225
Black-White achievement gap	-32*	-35*	-32*	-34*	-31*	-27*	-26	-26	-26
Hispanic-White achievement gap	-20	-25*	-27	-25	-27*	-22	-20	-21	-21
Grade 8									
Total	**263**	**268**	**272**	**270**	**273**	**278**	**279**	**281**	**283**
Sex									
Male	263	268	272	271	274	278	280	282	284
Female	262	269	272	269	272	277	278	280	282
Male-female achievement gap	1	-1	-1	2	2	2	2	2	2
Race/ethnicity									
White	270	277	281	281	284	288	289	291	293
Black	237	237	242	240	244	252	255	260	261
Hispanic	246	249	251	251	253	259	262	265	266
Asian/Pacific Islander	275	290	‡	‡	288	291	295	297	301
American Indian/Alaska Native	‡	‡	‡	‡	259	263	264	264	266
Black-White achievement gap	-33	-40*	-39*	-41*	-40*	-35*	-34*	-32	-32
Hispanic-White achievement gap	-24	-28	-30	-30	-31*	-29*	-27	-26	-26
Grade 12									
Total	—	—	—	—	—	—	**150**	—	**153**
Sex									
Male	—	—	—	—	—	—	151	—	155
Female	—	—	—	—	—	—	149	—	152
Male-female achievement gap	—	—	—	—	—	—	3	—	3
Race/ethnicity									
White	—	—	—	—	—	—	157	—	161
Black	—	—	—	—	—	—	127	—	131
Hispanic	—	—	—	—	—	—	133	—	138
Asian/Pacific Islander	—	—	—	—	—	—	163	—	175
American Indian/Alaska Native	—	—	—	—	—	—	134	—	144
Black-White achievement gap	—	—	—	—	—	—	-31	—	-30
Hispanic-White achievement gap	—	—	—	—	—	—	-24	—	-23

— Not available.
Rounds to zero.
‡ Reporting standards not met.
* Change in gap is statistically significant from 2009 ($p < .05$).
[1] Testing accommodations (e.g., extended time, small group testing) for children with disabilities and English language learners were not permitted in 1990 and 1992. Students in 4th and 8th grade were tested with and without accommodations in 1996. The footnoted column represents the sample without accommodations.
NOTE: The National Assessment of Educational Progress (NAEP) mathematics scores range from 0 to 500 for grades 4 and 8. The framework for the 12th-grade mathematics assessment was revised in 2005; as a result, the 2005 and 2009 results cannot be compared with those from previous years. At grade 12, mathematics scores on the revised assessment range from 0 to 300. Assessments were not conducted in grade 12 in 2007. For more information on NAEP, see *supplemental note 4*. Race categories exclude persons of Hispanic ethnicity. For more information on race/ethnicity, see *supplemental note 1*.
SOURCE: U.S. Department of Education, National Center for Education Statistics, National Assessment of Educational Progress (NAEP), selected years, 1990–2009 Mathematics Assessments, NAEP Data Explorer.

Table A-13-2. Average mathematics scale scores and selected achievement gaps of 4th-, 8th-, and 12th-grade students, by selected student and school characteristics: Selected years, 2000–09

Student or school characteristic	2000	2003	2005	2007	2009
Grade 4					
Total	226	235	238	240	240
Percentage of students in school eligible for free or reduced-price lunch					
0–25 percent (low poverty)	239	247	250	252	254
26–50 percent	227	237	240	242	242
51–75 percent	216	229	232	234	234
76–100 percent (high poverty)	205	216	220	222	223
Gap between high poverty and low poverty schools	-34	-31	-30	-30	-31
English language learner (ELL) students					
ELL students	199	214	216	217	218
Non-ELL students	227	237	240	242	242
Gap between ELL and non-ELL students	-28	-23	-24	-25	-24
Grade 8					
Total	273	278	279	281	283
Percentage of students in school eligible for free or reduced-price lunch					
0–25 percent (low poverty)	287	291	293	296	298
26–50 percent	270	278	280	282	284
51–75 percent	260	266	268	271	274
76–100 percent (high poverty)	246	251	254	259	260
Gap between high poverty and low poverty schools	-41	-40	-38	-37	-38
English language learner (ELL) students					
ELL students	234	242	244	246	243
Non-ELL students	274	279	281	283	285
Gap between ELL and non-ELL students	-40	-38*	-37*	-38*	-42
Grade 12					
Total	—	—	150	—	153
Percentage of students in school eligible for free or reduced-price lunch					
0–25 percent (low poverty)	—	—	158	—	166
26–50 percent	—	—	147	—	150
51–75 percent	—	—	136	—	140
76–100 percent (high poverty)	—	—	122	—	130
Gap between high poverty and low poverty schools	—	—	-36	—	-36
English language learner (ELL) students					
ELL students	—	—	120	—	117
Non-ELL students	—	—	151	—	154
Gap between ELL and non-ELL students	—	—	-31*	—	-38

— Not available.

* Change in gap is statistically significant from 2009 (*p* < .05).

NOTE: The National Assessment of Educational Progress (NAEP) mathematics scores range from 0 to 500 for grades 4 and 8. The framework for the 12th-grade mathematics assessment was revised in 2005; as a result, the 2005 and 2009 results cannot be compared with those from previous years. At grade 12, mathematics scores on the revised assessment range from 0 to 300. Assessments were not conducted in grade 12 in 2007. The percentages of English language learners (ELL) excluded from NAEP may vary across years. In 2007, the exclusion rate was 1 percent at both grade 4 and grade 8 for ELL students. In 2009 the exclusion rate was 1 percent for grade 4 and the percentage of ELL students excluded from the assessment rounded to zero for grade 8 and grade 12. For more information on NAEP, see *supplemental note 4.* For more information on free or reduced-price lunch, see *supplemental note 1.*
SOURCE: U.S. Department of Education, National Center for Education Statistics, National Assessment of Educational Progress (NAEP), selected years, 2000–2009 Mathematics Assessments, NAEP Data Explorer.

Table A-14-1. **Average science scale scores, selected percentile scores, and percentage of students at each achievement level, by grade: 2009**

Percentile and achievement level	Grade 4	Grade 8	Grade 12
Average scale score	150	150	150
Percentile			
10th	104	103	104
25th	128	128	126
50th	153	153	151
75th	175	175	174
90th	192	192	194
Percentage at each achievement level			
Below *Basic*	28	37	40
At or above *Basic*	72	63	60
At or above *Proficient*	34	30	21
At *Advanced*	1	2	1

NOTE: The National Assessment of Educational Progress (NAEP) science scale ranges from 0 to 300. Achievement levels define what students should know and be able to do: *Basic* indicates partial mastery of fundamental skills, *Proficient* indicates demonstrated competency over challenging subject matter, and *Advanced* indicates superior performance. The percentage of students at or above *Proficient* includes students at the *Proficient* and the *Advanced* achievement levels. Similarly, the percentage of students at or above *Basic* includes students at the *Basic, Proficient,* and *Advanced* achievement levels. Detail may not sum to totals because of rounding. For more information on NAEP, see *supplemental note 4.*
SOURCE: U.S. Department of Education, National Center for Education Statistics, National Assessment of Educational Progress (NAEP), 2009 Science Assessment, NAEP Data Explorer.

Table A-14-2. Average science scale scores and achievement-level results, by grade and selected student and school characteristics: 2009

Student or school characteristic	Grade 4			Grade 8			Grade 12		
	Average scale score	At or above *Basic*	At or above *Proficient*	Average scale score	At or above *Basic*	At or above *Proficient*	Average scale score	At or above *Basic*	At or above *Proficient*
Total	**150**	**72**	**34**	**150**	**63**	**30**	**150**	**60**	**21**
Sex									
Male	151	73	35	152	65	34	153	63	24
Female	149	72	32	148	62	27	147	58	18
Race/ethnicity									
White	163	87	47	162	78	42	159	72	27
Black	127	47	11	126	33	8	125	29	4
Hispanic	131	53	14	132	43	12	134	42	‡
Asian/Pacific Islander	160	81	45	160	73	41	164	73	36
American Indian/Alaska Native	135	57	17	137	48	17	144	53	13
School type									
Public	149	71	32	149	62	29	—	—	—
Private	163	85	48	164	80	44	—	—	—
Percentage of students in school eligible for free or reduced-price lunch									
0–25 percent	167	89	54	165	81	46	163	74	32
26–50 percent	155	79	37	154	68	32	148	59	17
51–75 percent	144	68	25	141	52	20	136	44	9
76–100 percent	126	46	11	124	33	8	124	29	4
Locale									
City	142	63	27	142	54	24	146	55	19
Suburban	154	76	38	154	67	34	154	64	25
Town	150	74	33	149	63	28	150	61	19
Rural	155	79	37	154	69	33	150	61	19
Student disability and English language learner status[1]									
Student with disability (SD)	132	54	18	126	36	12	123	30	6
English language learner (ELL)	117	35	5	107	16	3	107	12	1

— Not available.

‡ Reporting standards not met.

[1] The percentages of students excluded from National Assessment of Educational Progress (NAEP) may vary across years. The exclusion rates for the 2009 science assessment for SD students were 2 percent at grades 4, 8, and 12 and for ELL students were 1 percent at grade 4 and less than 1 percent at grades 8 and 12.

NOTE: Race categories exclude persons of Hispanic ethnicity. For more information on race/ethnicity or free or reduced-priced lunch, see *supplemental note 1*. Data by school type for grade 12 are not available, as the private school participation rate did not meet reporting standards. The NAEP science scale ranges from 0 to 300. Achievement levels define what students should know and be able to do: *Basic* indicates partial mastery of fundamental skills, *Proficient* indicates demonstrated competency over challenging subject matter, and *Advanced* indicates superior performance. The percentage of students at or above *Proficient* includes students at the *Proficient* and the *Advanced* achievement levels. Similarly, the percentage of students at or above *Basic* includes students at the *Basic, Proficient,* and *Advanced* achievement levels. For more information on NAEP, see *supplemental note 4*.

SOURCE: U.S. Department of Education, National Center for Education Statistics, National Assessment of Educational Progress (NAEP), 2009 Science Assessment, NAEP Data Explorer.

Science Performance

Table A-14-3. Average science scale scores and achievement-level results for public school 4th- and 8th-grade students, by state or jurisdiction: 2009

State or jurisdiction	Grade 4					Grade 8				
	Average scale score	Below *Basic*	At or above *Basic*	At or above *Proficient*	At *Advanced*	Average scale score	Below *Basic*	At or above *Basic*	At or above *Proficient*	At *Advanced*
United States	**149**	**29**	**71**	**32**	**1**	**149**	**38**	**62**	**29**	**1**
Alabama	143	35	65	27	#	139	49	51	19	1
Alaska	—	—	—	—	—	—	—	—	—	—
Arizona	138	39	61	22	#	141	46	54	22	1
Arkansas	146	31	69	29	#	144	42	58	24	1
California	136	42	58	22	1	137	52	48	20	1
Colorado	155	23	77	39	1	156	30	70	36	2
Connecticut	156	22	78	40	1	155	31	69	35	2
Delaware	153	23	77	34	#	148	38	62	25	1
District of Columbia	—	—	—	—	—	—	—	—	—	—
Florida	151	25	75	32	#	146	43	57	25	1
Georgia	144	34	66	27	#	147	42	58	27	2
Hawaii	140	37	63	25	#	139	50	50	17	#
Idaho	154	21	79	35	#	158	28	72	37	2
Illinois	148	31	69	32	1	148	39	61	28	1
Indiana	153	22	78	35	#	152	33	67	32	1
Iowa	157	20	80	41	1	156	28	72	35	1
Kansas	—	—	—	—	—	—	—	—	—	—
Kentucky	161	17	83	45	1	156	29	71	34	1
Louisiana	141	37	63	25	#	139	49	51	20	#
Maine	160	15	85	42	1	158	27	73	35	1
Maryland	150	28	72	33	1	148	40	60	28	2
Massachusetts	160	17	83	45	1	160	26	74	41	4
Michigan	150	28	72	34	#	153	34	66	35	2
Minnesota	158	19	81	43	1	159	26	74	40	2
Mississippi	133	46	54	17	#	132	59	41	15	#
Missouri	156	21	79	40	1	156	29	71	36	2
Montana	160	15	85	43	#	162	21	79	43	2
Nebraska	—	—	—	—	—	—	—	—	—	—
Nevada	141	36	64	23	#	141	46	54	20	1
New Hampshire	163	12	88	47	1	160	23	77	39	2

See notes at end of table.

Table A-14-3. Average science scale scores and achievement-level results for public school 4th- and 8th-grade students, by state or jurisdiction: 2009—Continued

	Grade 4					Grade 8				
State or jurisdiction	Average scale score	Below *Basic*	At or above *Basic*	At or above *Proficient*	At *Advanced*	Average scale score	Below *Basic*	At or above *Basic*	At or above *Proficient*	At *Advanced*
United States	**149**	**29**	**71**	**32**	**1**	**149**	**38**	**62**	**29**	**1**
New Jersey	155	22	78	39	1	155	30	70	34	1
New Mexico	142	37	63	24	#	143	45	55	21	1
New York	148	30	70	30	#	149	39	61	31	2
North Carolina	148	31	69	30	1	144	44	56	24	1
North Dakota	162	14	86	45	#	162	20	80	42	1
Ohio	157	21	79	41	1	158	27	73	37	2
Oklahoma	148	27	73	28	#	146	40	60	25	1
Oregon	151	27	73	34	1	154	32	68	35	1
Pennsylvania	154	24	76	38	1	154	32	68	35	2
Rhode Island	150	26	74	34	#	146	41	59	26	1
South Carolina	149	28	72	33	1	143	45	55	23	1
South Dakota	157	19	81	40	#	161	23	77	40	2
Tennessee	148	30	70	33	#	148	39	61	28	2
Texas	148	30	70	29	1	150	36	64	29	2
Utah	154	23	77	38	1	158	28	72	39	2
Vermont	—	—	—	—	—	—	—	—	—	—
Virginia	162	16	84	46	1	156	30	70	36	2
Washington	151	26	74	35	1	155	31	69	34	2
West Virginia	148	27	73	28	#	145	42	58	22	1
Wisconsin	157	21	79	41	1	157	27	73	38	1
Wyoming	156	20	80	37	#	158	26	74	36	1

— Not available.
Rounds to zero.
NOTE: The National Assessment of Educational Progress (NAEP) science scale ranges from 0 to 300. Data for grade 12 by state are not available. For grades 4 and 8, Alaska, the District of Columbia, Kansas, Nebraska, and Vermont did not participate in the 2009 science assessment at the state level. Achievement levels define what students should know and be able to do: *Basic* indicates partial mastery of fundamental skills, *Proficient* indicates demonstrated competency over challenging subject matter, and *Advanced* indicates superior performance. The percentage of students at or above *Proficient* includes students at the *Proficient* and the *Advanced* achievement levels. Similarly, the percentage of students at or above *Basic* includes students at the *Basic, Proficient,* and *Advanced* achievement levels. Detail may not sum to totals because of rounding. For more information on NAEP, see *supplemental note 4.*
SOURCE: U.S. Department of Education, National Center for Education Statistics, National Assessment of Educational Progress (NAEP), 2009 Science Assessment, NAEP Data Explorer.

Table A-15-1. Average scores of 15-year-old students on combined reading literacy scale and reading literacy subscales, by country: 2009

Country	Combined reading literacy score	Reading literacy subscale		
		Access and retrieve	Integrate and interpret	Reflect and evaluate
OECD average	**493**	**495**	**493**	**494** *
OECD countries				
Australia	515 *	513 *	513 *	523 *
Austria	470 *	477 *	471 *	463 *
Belgium	506	513 *	504	505
Canada	524 *	517 *	522 *	535 *
Chile	449 *	444 *	452 *	452 *
Czech Republic	478 *	479 *	488	462 *
Denmark	495	502 *	492	493 *
Estonia	501	503 *	500	503 *
Finland	536 *	532 *	538 *	536 *
France	496	492	497	495 *
Germany	497	501	501	491 *
Greece	483 *	468 *	484 *	489 *
Hungary	494	501	496	489 *
Iceland	500	507 *	503	496 *
Ireland	496	498	494	502
Israel	474 *	463 *	473 *	483 *
Italy	486 *	482 *	490	482 *
Japan	520 *	530 *	520 *	521
Korea, Republic of	539 *	542 *	541 *	542 *
Luxembourg	472 *	471 *	475 *	471 *
Mexico	425 *	433 *	418 *	432 *
Netherlands	508	519 *	504	510
New Zealand	521 *	521 *	517 *	531 *
Norway	503	512 *	502	505
Poland	500	500	503	498 *
Portugal	489 *	488	487	496 *
Slovak Republic	477 *	491	481 *	466 *
Slovenia	483 *	489	489	470 *
Spain	481 *	480 *	481 *	483 *
Sweden	497	505 *	494	502 *
Switzerland	501	505 *	502	497 *
Turkey	464 *	467 *	459 *	473 *
United Kingdom	494	491	491	503 *
United States	**500**	**492**	**495**	**512**

See notes at end of table.

Table A-15-1. Average scores of 15-year-old students on combined reading literacy scale and reading literacy subscales, by country: 2009—Continued

Country	Combined reading literacy score	Reading literacy subscale		
		Access and retrieve	Integrate and interpret	Reflect and evaluate
Non-OECD countries				
Albania	385 *	380 *	393 *	376 *
Argentina	398 *	394 *	398 *	402 *
Azerbaijan	362 *	361 *	373 *	335 *
Brazil	412 *	407 *	406 *	424 *
Bulgaria	429 *	430 *	436 *	417 *
Chinese Taipei	495	496	499	493 *
Colombia	413 *	404 *	411 *	422 *
Croatia	476 *	492	472 *	471 *
Dubai-UAE	459 *	458 *	457 *	466 *
Hong Kong-China	533 *	530 *	530 *	540 *
Indonesia	402 *	399 *	397 *	409 *
Jordan	405 *	394 *	410 *	407 *
Kazakhstan	390 *	397 *	397 *	373 *
Kyrgyz Republic	314 *	299 *	327 *	300 *
Latvia	484 *	476 *	484 *	492 *
Liechtenstein	499	508 *	498	498 *
Lithuania	468 *	476 *	469 *	463 *
Macao-China	487 *	493	488	481 *
Montenegro, Republic of	408 *	408 *	420 *	383 *
Panama	371 *	363 *	372 *	377 *
Peru	370 *	364 *	371 *	368 *
Qatar	372 *	354 *	379 *	376 *
Romania	424 *	423 *	425 *	426 *
Russian Federation	459 *	469 *	467 *	441 *
Serbia, Republic of	442 *	449 *	445 *	430 *
Shanghai-China	556 *	549 *	558 *	557 *
Singapore	526 *	526 *	525 *	529 *
Thailand	421 *	431 *	416 *	420 *
Trinidad and Tobago	416 *	413 *	419 *	413 *
Tunisia	404 *	393 *	393 *	427 *
Uruguay	426 *	424 *	423 *	436 *

* Significantly different from U.S. average ($p < .05$).
NOTE: The Organization for Economic Co-operation and Development (OECD) average is the average of the national averages of the OECD member countries, with each country weighted equally. Because the Program for International Student Assessment (PISA) is principally an OECD study, the results for non-OECD countries are displayed separately from those of the OECD member countries and are not included in the OECD average. Scores are reported on a scale of 0 to 1,000. Italics indicate education systems in non-national entities. UAE is the United Arab Emirates. For more information on PISA, see *supplemental note 5*.
SOURCE: Fleischman, H.L., Hopstock, P.J., Pelczar, M.P., and Shelley, B.E. (2010). *Highlights From PISA 2009: Performance of U.S. 15-Year-Old Students in Reading, Mathematics, and Science Literacy in an International Context* (NCES 2011-004), table 3; data from the Organization for Economic Co-operation and Development (OECD), Program for International Student Assessment (PISA), 2009.

Table A-15-2. **Average scores of 15-year-old students on combined reading literacy scale, by sex and country: 2009**

Country	Combined reading literacy score		Female-male score difference*
	Female	Male	
OECD average	**513**	**474**	**39**
OECD countries			
Australia	533	496	37
Austria	490	449	41
Belgium	520	493	27
Canada	542	507	34
Chile	461	439	22
Czech Republic	504	456	48
Denmark	509	480	29
Estonia	524	480	44
Finland	563	508	55
France	515	475	40
Germany	518	478	40
Greece	506	459	47
Hungary	513	475	38
Iceland	522	478	44
Ireland	515	476	39
Israel	495	452	42
Italy	510	464	46
Japan	540	501	39
Korea, Republic of	558	523	35
Luxembourg	492	453	39
Mexico	438	413	25
Netherlands	521	496	24
New Zealand	544	499	46
Norway	527	480	47
Poland	525	476	50
Portugal	508	470	38
Slovak Republic	503	452	51
Slovenia	511	456	55
Spain	496	467	29
Sweden	521	475	46
Switzerland	520	481	39
Turkey	486	443	43
United Kingdom	507	481	25
United States	**513**	**488**	**25**

See notes at end of table.

Table A-15-2. **Average scores of 15-year-old students on combined reading literacy scale, by sex and country: 2009—Continued**

Country	Combined reading literacy score		
	Female	Male	Female-male score difference*
Non-OECD countries			
Albania	417	355	62
Argentina	415	379	37
Azerbaijan	374	350	24
Brazil	425	397	29
Bulgaria	461	400	61
Chinese Taipei	514	477	37
Colombia	418	408	9
Croatia	503	452	51
Dubai-UAE	485	435	51
Hong Kong-China	550	518	33
Indonesia	420	383	37
Jordan	434	377	57
Kazakhstan	412	369	43
Kyrgyz Republic	340	287	53
Latvia	507	460	47
Liechtenstein	516	484	32
Lithuania	498	439	59
Macao-China	504	470	34
Montenegro, Republic of	434	382	53
Panama	387	354	33
Peru	381	359	22
Qatar	397	347	50
Romania	445	403	43
Russian Federation	482	437	45
Serbia, Republic of	462	422	39
Shanghai-China	576	536	40
Singapore	542	511	31
Thailand	438	400	38
Trinidad and Tobago	445	387	58
Tunisia	418	387	31
Uruguay	445	404	42

* *p* < .05. All differences between females and males are significantly different at the .05 level of statistical significance. Differences were computed using unrounded numbers.
NOTE: The Organization for Economic Co-operation and Development (OECD) average is the average of the national averages of the OECD member countries, with each country weighted equally. Because the Program for International Student Assessment (PISA) is principally an OECD study, the results for non-OECD countries are displayed separately from those of the OECD countries and are not included in the OECD average. Scores are reported on a scale of 0 to 1,000. Italics indicate education systems in non-national entities. UAE is the United Arab Emirates. Detail may not sum to totals due to rounding. For more information on PISA, see *supplemental note 5*.
SOURCE: Fleischman, H.L., Hopstock, P.J., Pelczar, M.P., and Shelley, B.E. (2010). *Highlights From PISA 2009: Performance of U.S. 15-Year-Old Students in Reading, Mathematics, and Science Literacy in an International Context* (NCES 2011-004), table 4; data from the Organization for Economic Co-operation and Development (OECD), Program for International Student Assessment (PISA), 2009.

Table A-15-3. Average scores of U.S. 15-year-old students on combined reading literacy scale, by race and ethnicity: 2009

Race and ethnicity	Combined reading literacy score
U.S. average	**500**
White	525 *
Black	441 *
Hispanic	466 *
Asian	541 *
Native Hawaiian/Other Pacific Islander	‡
American Indian/Alaska Native	‡
Two or more races	502
OECD average	**493**

‡ Reporting standards not met.
* $p < .05$. Significantly different from the U.S. and OECD averages at the .05 level of statistical significance.
NOTE: Race categories exclude people of Hispanic ethnicity. For more information on race/ethnicity, see *supplemental note 1*. The Organization for Economic Co-operation and Development (OECD) average is the average of the national averages of the OECD member countries, with each country weighted equally. Scores are reported on a scale of 0 to 1,000. For more information on PISA, see *supplemental note 5*.
SOURCE: Fleischman, H.L., Hopstock, P.J., Pelczar, M.P., and Shelley, B.E. (2010). *Highlights From PISA 2009: Performance of U.S. 15-Year-Old Students in Reading, Mathematics, and Science Literacy in an International Context* (NCES 2011-004), table 5; data from the Organization for Economic Co-operation and Development (OECD), Program for International Student Assessment (PISA), 2009.

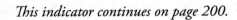

This indicator continues on page 200.

Table A-15-4. Average scores of 15-year-old students on reading literacy scale, by country: 2000, 2003, 2006, and 2009

Country	Reading literacy score			
	2000	2003	2006	2009
OECD average[1]	**496**	—	—	**495**
OECD countries				
Australia	528	525	513	515
Austria[2]	492	491	490	470
Belgium	507	507	501	506
Canada	534	528	527	524
Chile	410	—	442	449
Czech Republic	492	489	483	478
Denmark	497	492	494	495
Estonia	—	—	501	501
Finland	546	543	547	536
France	505	496	488	496
Germany	484	491	495	497
Greece	474	472	460	483
Hungary	480	482	482	494
Iceland	507	492	484	500
Ireland	527	515	517	496
Israel	452	—	439	474
Italy	487	476	469	486
Japan	522	498	498	520
Korea, Republic of	525	534	556	539
Luxembourg	441	479	479	472
Mexico	422	400	410	425
Netherlands[3]	—	513	507	508
New Zealand	529	522	521	521
Norway	505	500	484	503
Poland	479	497	508	500
Portugal	470	478	472	489
Slovak Republic	—	469	466	477
Slovenia	—	—	494	483
Spain	493	481	461	481
Sweden	516	514	507	497
Switzerland	494	499	499	501
Turkey	—	441	447	464
United Kingdom[4]	—	—	495	494
United States[5]	**504**	**495**	—	**500**

See notes at end of table.

Table A-15-4. Average scores of 15-year-old students on reading literacy scale, by country: 2000, 2003, 2006, and 2009—Continued

Country	Reading literacy score			
	2000	2003	2006	2009
Non-OECD countries				
Albania	349	—	—	385
Argentina	418	—	374	398
Azerbaijan	—	—	353	362
Brazil	396	403	393	412
Bulgaria	430	—	402	429
Chinese Taipei	—	—	496	495
Colombia	—	—	385	413
Croatia	—	—	477	476
Dubai-UAE	—	—	—	459
Hong Kong-China	525	510	536	533
Indonesia	371	382	393	402
Jordan	—	—	401	405
Kazakhstan	—	—	—	390
Kyrgyz Republic	—	—	285	314
Latvia	458	491	479	484
Liechtenstein	483	525	510	499
Lithuania	—	—	470	468
Macao-China	—	498	492	487
Montenegro, Republic of[6]	—	412	392	408
Panama	—	—	—	371
Peru	327	—	—	370
Qatar	—	—	312	372
Romania[7]	—	—	396	424
Russian Federation	462	442	440	459
Serbia, Republic of[6]	—	412	401	442
Shanghai-China	—	—	—	556
Singapore	—	—	—	526
Thailand	431	420	417	421
Trinidad and Tobago	—	—	—	416
Tunisia	—	375	380	404
Uruguay	—	434	413	426

— Not available.

[1] The Organization for Economic Co-operation and Development (OECD) average used to report on trends in reading literacy is based on 27 OECD member countries with comparable data for 2000 and 2009. The seven current OECD members not included in the OECD average used to report on trends in reading literacy include the Slovak Republic and Turkey, which joined PISA in 2003; Estonia and Slovenia, which joined PISA in 2006; Luxembourg, which experienced substantial changes in its assessment conditions between 2000 and 2003; and the Netherlands and the United Kingdom, which did not meet the PISA response rate standards in 2000.

[2] The OECD excluded the data for Austria from the trend analysis in its report (*PISA 2009 Results: Learning Trends—Changes in Student Performance Since 2000 [Volume V]*, available at http://www.pisa.oecd.org) because of a concern over a data collection issue in 2009; however, after consultation with Austrian officials, the National Center for Education Statistics kept the Austrian data in the U.S. trend reporting.

[3] Although the Netherlands participated in PISA 2000, technical problems with its sample prevent its results from being included.

[4] Because of low response rates, 2000 and 2003 data for the United Kingdom are not presented.

[5] PISA 2006 reading literacy results are not reported for the United States because of an error in printing the test booklets. For more details, see Baldi et al. 2007 (available at http://nces.ed.gov/pubsearch/pubsinfo.asp?pubid=2008016).

[6] The Republics of Montenegro and Serbia were a united country under the PISA 2003 assessment.

[7] The 2000 results for Romania were not reported by OECD due to delayed submission of data.

NOTE: Because the Program for International Student Assessment (PISA) is principally an OECD study, the results for non-OECD countries are displayed separately from those of the OECD countries and are not included in the OECD average. Scores are reported on a scale of 0 to 1,000. Italics indicate education systems in non-national entities. UAE is the United Arab Emirates. For more information on PISA, see *supplemental note 5*.

SOURCE: Fleischman, H.L., Hopstock, P.J., Pelczar, M.P., and Shelley, B.E. (2010). *Highlights From PISA 2009: Performance of U.S. 15-Year-Old Students in Reading, Mathematics, and Science Literacy in an International Context* (NCES 2011-004), supplemental table R5; data from the Organization for Economic Co-operation and Development (OECD), Program for International Student Assessment (PISA), 2000, 2003, 2006, and 2009.

Table A-16-1. Average scores of 15-year-old students on mathematics literacy scale, by country: 2003 and 2009

Country	Mathematics literacy score		Change in score, 2003 to 2009
	2003	2009	
OECD average[1]	500**	499**	#
OECD countries			
Australia	524	514	-10*
Austria[2]	506	496	-10*
Belgium	529	515	-14*
Canada	532	527	-6
Chile	—	421	—
Czech Republic	516	493	-24*
Denmark	514	503	-11*
Estonia	—	512	—
Finland	544	541	-4
France	511	497	-14*
Germany	503	513	10*
Greece	445	466	21*
Hungary	490	490	#
Iceland	515	507	-8*
Ireland	503	487	-16*
Israel	—	447	—
Italy	466	483	17*
Japan	534	529	-5
Korea, Republic of	542	546	4
Luxembourg	493	489	-4
Mexico	385	419	33*
Netherlands	538	526	-12*
New Zealand	523	519	-4
Norway	495	498	3
Poland	490	495	5
Portugal	466	487	21*
Slovak Republic	498	497	-2
Slovenia	—	501	—
Spain	485	483	-2
Sweden	509	494	-15*
Switzerland	527	534	7
Turkey	423	445	22*
United Kingdom[3]	‡	492	‡
United States	**483**	**487**	**5**

See notes at end of table.

Table A-16-1. **Average scores of 15-year-old students on mathematics literacy scale, by country: 2003 and 2009—Continued**

Country	Mathematics literacy score		Change in score, 2003 to 2009
	2003	2009	
OECD average[1]	**500****	**499****	#
Non-OECD countries			
Albania	—	377	—
Argentina	—	388	—
Azerbaijan	—	431	—
Brazil	356	386	30*
Bulgaria	—	428	—
Chinese Taipei	—	543	—
Colombia	—	381	—
Croatia	—	460	—
Dubai-UAE	—	453	—
Hong Kong-China	550	555	4
Indonesia	360	371	11
Jordan	—	387	—
Kazakhstan	—	405	—
Kyrgyz Republic	—	331	—
Latvia	483	482	-1
Liechtenstein	536	536	#
Lithuania	—	477	—
Macao-China	527	525	-2
Montenegro, Republic of[4]	437	403	—
Panama	—	360	—
Peru	—	365	—
Qatar	—	368	—
Romania	—	427	—
Russian Federation	468	468	-1
Serbia, Republic of[4]	437	442	6
Shanghai-China	—	600	—
Singapore	—	562	—
Thailand	417	419	2
Trinidad and Tobago	—	414	—
Tunisia	359	371	13*
Uruguay	422	427	5

— Not available.
Rounds to zero.
‡ Reporting standards not met.
* *p* < .05. Country average in 2003 is significantly different from the country average in 2009 at the .05 level of statistical significance.
** *p* < .05. U.S. average is significantly different from the Organization for Economic Co-operation and Development (OECD) average at the .05 level of statistical significance.
[1] The OECD average used to report on trends in mathematics literacy is based on 29 countries that participated in both the 2003 and 2009 assessments, met all technical standards, and that are currently members of the OECD. The five current members not included in this OECD average are Chile, Estonia, Israel, and Slovenia, which did not participate in 2003, as well as the United Kingdom, which did not meet PISA standards for the 2003 assessment.
[2] The OECD excluded the data for Austria from the trend analysis in its report (*PISA 2009 Results: Learning Trends—Changes in Student Performance Since 2000 [Volume V]*, available at http://www.pisa.oecd.org) because of a concern over a data collection issue in 2009; however, after consultation with Austrian officials, the National Center for Education Statistics kept the Austrian data in the U.S. trend reporting.
[3] Because of low response rates, 2003 data for the United Kingdom are not presented.
[4] The Republics of Montenegro and Serbia were a united country under the PISA 2003 assessment. Therefore, these countries have the same average score in 2003.
NOTE: The Program for International Student Assessment (PISA) mathematics framework was revised in 2003. Because of changes in the framework, it is not possible to compare mathematics learning outcomes from PISA 2000 with those from PISA 2003, 2006, and 2009. For more details, see the PISA 2009 international report (OECD 2010). Because PISA is principally an OECD study, the results for non-OECD countries are displayed separately from those of the OECD countries and are not included in the OECD average. Italics indicate education systems in non-national entities. UAE is the United Arab Emirates. Scores are reported on a scale from 0 to 1,000. For more information on PISA, see *supplemental note 5*.
SOURCE: Fleischman, H. L., Hopstock, P. J., Pelczar, M. P., and Shelley, B. E. (2010). *Highlights From PISA 2009: Performance of U.S. 15-Year-Old Students in Reading, Mathematics, and Science Literacy in an International Context* (NCES 2011-004), supplemental table M2; data from the Organization for Economic Co-operation and Development (OECD), Program for International Student Assessment (PISA), 2003 and 2009. Organization for Economic Co-operation and Development. (2010). *Learning Trends: Changes in Student Performance Since 2000 (Volume V)*, Annex B1, Table V.3.1.

International Mathematics and Science Literacy

Table A-16-2. Average scores of 15-year-old students on mathematics literacy scale, by sex and country: 2003 and 2009

Country	2003			2009		
	Male	Female	Male-female score difference	Male	Female	Male-female score difference
OECD average	**506**	**494**	**11***	**501**	**490**	**12***
OECD countries						
Australia	527	522	5	519	509	10*
Austria	509	502	8	506	486	19*
Belgium	533	525	8	526	504	22*
Canada	541	530	11*	533	521	12*
Chile	—	—	—	431	410	21*
Czech Republic	524	509	15*	495	490	5
Denmark	523	506	17*	511	495	16*
Estonia	—	—	—	516	508	9*
Finland	548	541	7*	542	539	3
France	515	507	9*	505	489	16*
Germany	508	499	9*	520	505	16*
Greece	455	436	19*	473	459	14*
Hungary	494	486	8*	496	484	12*
Iceland	508	523	-15*	508	505	3
Ireland	510	495	15*	491	483	8
Israel	—	—	—	451	443	8
Italy	475	457	18*	490	475	15*
Japan	539	530	8	534	524	9
Korea, Republic of	552	528	23*	548	544	3
Luxembourg	502	485	17*	499	479	19*
Mexico	391	380	11*	425	412	14*
Netherlands	540	535	5	534	517	17*
New Zealand	531	516	14*	523	515	8
Norway	498	492	6	500	495	5
Poland	493	487	6	497	493	3
Portugal	472	460	12*	493	481	12*
Slovak Republic	507	489	19*	498	495	3
Slovenia	—	—	—	502	501	1
Spain	490	481	9*	493	474	19*
Sweden	512	506	7*	493	495	-2
Switzerland	535	518	17*	544	524	20*
Turkey	430	415	15*	451	440	11*
United Kingdom[1]	‡	‡	‡	503	482	20*
United States	**486**	**480**	**6***	**497**	**477**	**20***

See notes at end of table.

Table A-16-2. Average scores of 15-year-old students on mathematics literacy scale, by sex and country: 2003 and 2009—Continued

Country	2003			2009		
	Male	Female	Male-female score difference	Male	Female	Male-female score difference
OECD average	**506**	**494**	**11***	**501**	**490**	**12***
Non-OECD countries						
Albania	—	—	—	372	383	-11*
Argentina	—	—	—	394	383	10*
Azerbaijan	—	—	—	435	427	8*
Brazil	365	348	16*	394	379	16*
Bulgaria	—	—	—	426	430	-4
Chinese Taipei	—	—	—	546	541	5
Colombia	—	—	—	398	366	32*
Croatia	—	—	—	465	454	11*
Dubai-UAE	—	—	—	454	451	2
Hong Kong-China	552	548	4	561	547	14*
Indonesia	362	358	3	371	372	-1
Jordan	—	—	—	386	387	#
Kazakhstan	—	—	—	405	405	-1
Kyrgyz Republic	—	—	—	328	334	-6*
Latvia	485	482	3	483	481	2
Liechtenstein	550	521	29*	547	523	24*
Lithuania	—	—	—	474	480	-6*
Macao-China	538	517	21*	531	520	11*
Montenegro, Republic of [2]	—	—	—	408	396	12*
Panama	—	—	—	362	357	5
Peru	—	—	—	374	356	18*
Qatar	—	—	—	366	371	-5*
Romania	—	—	—	429	425	3
Russian Federation	473	463	10*	469	467	2
Serbia, Republic of [2]	437	436	1	448	437	12*
Shanghai-China	—	—	—	599	601	-1
Singapore	—	—	—	565	559	5*
Thailand	415	419	-4	421	417	4
Trinidad and Tobago	—	—	—	410	418	-8*
Tunisia	365	353	12*	378	366	12*
Uruguay	428	416	12*	433	421	12*

— Not available.

Rounds to zero.

‡ Reporting standards not met.

* $p < .05$. Male average is significantly different from the female average at the .05 level of statistical significance.

[1] Because of low response rates, 2003 data for the United Kingdom are not presented.

[2] The Republics of Montenegro and Serbia were a united country under the PISA 2003 assessment.

NOTE: The Program for International Student Assessment (PISA) mathematics framework was revised in 2003. Because of changes in the framework, it is not possible to compare mathematics learning outcomes from PISA 2000 with those from PISA 2003, 2006, and 2009. Because PISA is principally an Organization for Economic Co-operation and Development (OECD) study, the results for non-OECD countries are displayed separately from those of the OECD countries and are not included in the OECD average. Italics indicate education systems in non-national entities. UAE is the United Arab Emirates. Scores are reported on a scale from 0 to 1,000. For more information on PISA, see supplemental note 5.

SOURCE: Organization for Economic Co-operation and Development. (2004). *Learning for Tomorrow's World—First Results from PISA 2003, Table 2.5c.* Organization for Economic Co-operation and Development. (2010). *PISA 2009 Results: What Students Know and Can Do: Student Performance in Reading, Mathematics and Science (Volume I),* Table I.3.3.

Table A-16-3.   Average scores of 15-year-old students on science literacy scale, by country: 2006 and 2009

Country	Science literacy score		Change in score, 2006 to 2009
	2006	2009	
OECD average	**498****	**501**	**3**
OECD countries			
Australia	527	527	#
Austria[1]	511	494	-17*
Belgium	510	507	-4
Canada	534	529	-6
Chile	438	447	9
Czech Republic	513	500	-12*
Denmark	496	499	3
Estonia	531	528	-4
Finland	563	554	-9*
France	495	498	3
Germany	516	520	5
Greece	473	470	-3
Hungary	504	503	-1
Iceland	491	496	5
Ireland	508	508	#
Israel	454	455	1
Italy	475	489	13*
Japan	531	539	8
Korea, Republic of	522	538	16*
Luxembourg	486	484	-2
Mexico	410	416	6
Netherlands	525	522	-3
New Zealand	530	532	2
Norway	487	500	13*
Poland	498	508	10*
Portugal	474	493	19*
Slovak Republic	488	490	2
Slovenia	519	512	-7*
Spain	488	488	#
Sweden	503	495	-8
Switzerland	512	517	5
Turkey	424	454	30*
United Kingdom	515	514	-1
United States	**489**	**502**	**13***

See notes at end of table.

Table A-16-3. Average scores of 15-year-old students on science literacy scale, by country: 2006 and 2009—Continued

Country	Science literacy score		Change in score, 2006 to 2009
	2006	2009	
OECD average	498**	501	3
Non-OECD countries			
Albania	—	391	—
Argentina	391	401	10
Azerbaijan	382	373	-9
Brazil	390	405	15*
Bulgaria	434	439	5
Chinese Taipei	532	520	-12*
Colombia	388	402	14*
Croatia	493	486	-7
Dubai-UAE	—	466	—
Hong Kong-China	542	549	7
Indonesia	393	383	-11
Jordan	422	415	-7
Kazakhstan	—	400	—
Kyrgyz Republic	322	330	8
Latvia	490	494	4
Liechtenstein	522	520	-2
Lithuania	488	491	3
Macao-China	511	511	#
Montenegro, Republic of	412	401	-11*
Panama	—	376	—
Peru	—	369	—
Qatar	349	379	30*
Romania	418	428	10
Russian Federation	479	478	-1
Serbia, Republic of	436	443	7
Shanghai-China	—	575	—
Singapore	—	542	—
Thailand	421	425	4
Trinidad and Tobago	—	410	—
Tunisia	386	401	15*
Uruguay	428	427	-1

— Not available.
Rounds to zero.
* p < .05. Country average in 2006 is significantly different from the country average in 2009 at the .05 level of statistical significance.
** p < .05. U.S. average is significantly different from the Organization for Economic Co-operation and Development (OECD) average at the .05 level of statistical significance.
[1] The OECD excluded the data for Austria from the trend analysis in its report (PISA 2009 Results: Learning Trends—Changes in Student Performance Since 2000 [Volume V], available at http://www.pisa.oecd.org) because of a concern over a data collection issue in 2009; however, after consultation with Austrian officials, the National Center for Education Statistics kept the Austrian data in the U.S. trend reporting.
NOTE: The Program for International Student Assessment (PISA) science framework was revised in 2006. Because of changes in the framework, it is not possible to compare science learning outcomes from PISA 2000 and 2003 with those from PISA 2006 and 2009. For more details, see the PISA 2009 international report (OECD 2010). Because PISA is principally an OECD study, the results for non-OECD countries are displayed separately from those of the OECD countries and are not included in the OECD average. Italics indicate education systems in non-national entities. UAE is the United Arab Emirates. Scores are reported on a scale from 0 to 1,000. For more information on PISA, see supplemental note 5.
SOURCE: Fleischman, H. L., Hopstock, P. J., Pelczar, M. P., and Shelley, B. E. (2010). Highlights From PISA 2009: Performance of U.S. 15-Year-Old Students in Reading, Mathematics, and Science Literacy in an International Context (NCES 2011-004), supplemental table S2; data from the Organization for Economic Co-operation and Development (OECD), Program for International Student Assessment (PISA), 2006 and 2009. Organization for Economic Co-operation and Development. (2010). Learning Trends: Changes in Student Performance Since 2000 (Volume V), Annex B1, Table V.3.4.

International Mathematics and Science Literacy

Table A-16-4. Average scores of 15-year-old students on science literacy scale, by sex and country: 2006 and 2009

Country	2006			2009		
	Male	Female	Male-female score difference	Male	Female	Male-female score difference
OECD average	**501**	**499**	**2**	**501**	**501**	**#**
OECD countries						
Australia	527	527	#	527	528	-1
Austria	515	507	8	498	490	8
Belgium	511	510	1	510	503	6
Canada	536	532	4	531	526	5*
Chile	448	426	22*	452	443	9*
Czech Republic	515	510	5	498	503	-5
Denmark	500	491	9*	505	494	12*
Estonia	530	533	-4	527	528	-1
Finland	562	565	-3	546	562	-15*
France	497	494	3	500	497	3
Germany	519	512	7	523	518	6
Greece	468	479	-11*	465	475	-10*
Hungary	507	501	6	503	503	#
Iceland	488	494	-6	496	495	2
Ireland	508	509	#	507	509	-3
Israel	456	452	3	453	456	-3
Italy	477	474	3	488	490	-2
Japan	533	530	3	534	545	-12
Korea, Republic of	521	523	-2	537	539	-2
Luxembourg	491	482	9*	487	480	7*
Mexico	413	406	7*	419	413	6*
Netherlands	528	521	7*	524	520	4
New Zealand	528	532	-4	529	535	-6
Norway	484	489	-4	498	502	-4
Poland	500	496	3	505	511	-6*
Portugal	477	472	5	491	495	-3
Slovak Republic	491	485	6	490	491	-1
Slovenia	515	523	-8*	505	519	-14*
Spain	491	486	4	492	485	7*
Sweden	504	503	1	493	497	-4
Switzerland	514	509	6*	520	512	8*
Turkey	418	430	-12*	448	460	-12*
United Kingdom	520	510	10*	519	509	9*
United States	**489**	**489**	**1**	**509**	**495**	**14***

See notes at end of table.

Table A-16-4. Average scores of 15-year-old students on science literacy scale, by sex and country: 2006 and 2009—Continued

Country	2006			2009		
	Male	Female	Male-female score difference	Male	Female	Male-female score difference
OECD average	**501**	**499**	**2**	**501**	**501**	**#**
Non-OECD countries						
Albania	—	—	—	377	406	-29*
Argentina	384	397	-13*	397	404	-8*
Azerbaijan	379	386	-8*	370	377	-7*
Brazil	395	386	9*	407	404	3
Bulgaria	426	443	-17*	430	450	-20*
Chinese Taipei	536	529	7	520	521	-1
Colombia	393	384	9	413	392	21*
Croatia	492	494	-2	482	491	-9
Dubai-UAE	—	—	—	453	480	-27*
Hong Kong-China	546	539	7	550	548	3
Indonesia	399	387	12	378	387	-9*
Jordan	408	436	-29*	398	433	-35*
Kazakhstan	—	—	—	396	405	-9*
Kyrgyz Republic	319	325	-6*	318	340	-22*
Latvia	486	493	-7*	490	497	-7*
Liechtenstein	516	527	-11	527	511	16*
Lithuania	483	493	-9*	483	500	-17*
Macao-China	513	509	4	510	512	-2
Montenegro, Republic of	411	413	-2	395	408	-13*
Panama	—	—	—	375	377	-2
Peru	—	—	—	372	367	5
Qatar	334	365	-32*	366	393	-26*
Romania	417	419	-2	423	433	-10*
Russian Federation	481	478	3	477	480	-3
Serbia, Republic of	433	438	-5	442	443	-1
Shanghai-China	—	—	—	574	575	-1
Singapore	—	—	—	541	542	-1
Thailand	411	428	-17*	418	431	-13*
Trinidad and Tobago	—	—	—	401	419	-18*
Tunisia	383	388	-5	401	400	1
Uruguay	427	430	-3	427	428	-1

— Not available.
Rounds to zero.
* *p* < .05. Male average is significantly different from the female average at the .05 level of statistical significance.
NOTE: The Program for International Student Assessment (PISA) science framework was revised in 2006. Because of changes in the framework, it is not possible to compare science learning outcomes from PISA 2000 and 2003 with those from PISA 2006 and 2009. For more details, see the PISA 2009 international report (OECD 2010). Because PISA is principally an Organization for Economic Co-operation and Development (OECD) study, the results for non-OECD countries are displayed separately from those of the OECD countries and are not included in the OECD average. Italics indicate education systems in non-national entities. UAE is the United Arab Emirates. Scores are reported on a scale from 0 to 1,000. For more information on PISA, see *supplemental note 5*.
SOURCE: Organization for Economic Co-operation and Development. (2007). *PISA 2006: Science Competencies for Tomorrow's World* (Volume II), Table 2.1c. Organization for Economic Co-operation and Development. (2010). *PISA 2009 Results: What Students Know and Can Do: Student Performance in Reading, Mathematics and Science (Volume I)*, Table I.3.6.

Annual Earnings of Young Adults

Table A-17-1. Median annual earnings and percentage of full-time, full-year wage and salary workers ages 25–34, by educational attainment, sex, and race/ethnicity: Selected years, 1980–2009

Educational attainment, sex, and race/ethnicity	Median earnings [In constant 2009 dollars]							Percentage of wage and salary workers who worked full-time for a full-year in 2009[1]
	1980	1985	1990	1995	2000	2005	2009	
Total[2]	**$39,000**	**$38,900**	**$36,100**	**$35,200**	**$37,400**	**$36,200**	**$38,000**	**61.0**
Less than high school completion[3]	28,600	25,900	24,600	22,300	23,700	22,800	21,000	47.0
High school diploma or equivalent	36,400	33,900	31,600	29,300	31,100	30,600	30,000	55.3
Some college[4]	39,000	39,900	36,900	32,800	34,900	34,600	33,500	58.7
Associate's degree	—	—	—	35,200	37,400	37,300	36,000	65.1
Bachelor's degree or higher	46,900	49,800	48,100	46,500	49,800	48,300	50,000	69.4
Bachelor's degree	—	—	—	43,600	48,600	44,800	45,000	69.1
Master's degree or higher	—	—	—	56,300	56,100	54,900	60,000	70.0
Male	45,000	43,900	41,000	38,000	41,100	38,400	40,000	62.8
Less than high school completion[3]	31,200	28,600	26,300	25,300	24,900	24,200	23,000	49.2
High school diploma or equivalent	44,000	39,900	36,100	33,800	36,100	33,000	32,900	57.4
Some college[4]	46,900	45,900	41,000	36,600	41,000	38,400	39,000	62.7
Associate's degree	—	—	—	36,600	46,100	42,800	42,000	70.1
Bachelor's degree or higher	52,100	54,600	52,100	52,500	57,300	54,900	55,000	71.8
Bachelor's degree	—	—	—	49,300	56,100	49,400	51,000	70.6
Master's degree or higher	—	—	—	62,400	66,000	60,400	70,000	75.6
Female	31,200	31,900	32,000	31,000	33,600	33,000	35,000	58.9
Less than high school completion[3]	21,300	19,900	19,700	18,300	19,400	18,700	19,000	42.7
High school diploma or equivalent	28,600	27,900	26,300	24,800	26,200	26,400	25,000	51.8
Some college[4]	31,200	31,900	32,800	28,200	29,900	30,800	29,300	54.1
Associate's degree	—	—	—	33,800	32,400	33,000	31,000	60.8
Bachelor's degree or higher	38,700	41,600	42,700	42,200	44,200	43,900	45,000	67.2
Bachelor's degree	—	—	—	39,400	43,600	41,700	40,100	67.9
Master's degree or higher	—	—	—	49,300	49,800	51,600	54,000	65.7
White	40,300	39,900	39,100	36,600	39,900	38,400	40,000	62.5
Less than high school completion[3]	31,200	29,900	26,900	24,900	24,900	25,300	25,000	41.0
High school diploma or equivalent	37,400	35,900	32,800	31,000	34,300	33,000	32,000	55.9
Some college[4]	41,300	39,900	39,100	33,800	37,400	35,100	35,000	59.0
Associate's degree	—	—	—	36,600	39,900	38,400	39,900	65.4
Bachelor's degree or higher	46,900	49,900	49,300	47,900	49,800	49,400	50,000	69.5
Bachelor's degree	—	—	—	45,000	49,800	45,000	45,000	69.4
Master's degree or higher	—	—	—	56,300	56,100	54,900	58,000	69.5
Black	31,200	29,900	29,600	29,600	31,300	31,400	30,000	57.4
Less than high school completion[3]	23,000	20,100	19,700	19,700	23,700	22,800	23,200	38.1
High school diploma or equivalent	31,200	27,900	26,100	25,300	26,200	25,300	25,000	48.9
Some college[4]	33,800	29,900	32,000	31,000	32,400	32,000	29,500	57.7
Associate's degree	—	—	—	31,000	31,100	30,800	28,000	63.2
Bachelor's degree or higher	39,000	39,900	41,000	38,700	43,600	42,800	45,000	73.5
Bachelor's degree	—	—	—	36,600	41,100	39,500	40,000	73.1
Master's degree or higher	—	—	—	47,900	‡	48,300	55,000	74.7

See notes at end of table.

Table A-17-1. Median annual earnings and percentage of full-time, full-year wage and salary workers ages 25–34, by educational attainment, sex, and race/ethnicity: Selected years, 1980–2009—Continued

Educational attainment, sex, and race/ethnicity	Median earnings [In constant 2009 dollars]							Percentage of wage and salary workers who worked full-time for a full-year in 2009[1]
	1980	1985	1990	1995	2000	2005	2009	
Hispanic	$32,000	$30,100	$27,900	$26,500	$28,600	$27,500	$29,000	58.2
Less than high school completion[3]	26,000	22,800	21,100	21,100	22,400	22,000	20,000	51.8
High school diploma or equivalent	31,200	29,900	27,900	26,700	28,600	26,400	26,000	58.2
Some college[4]	39,000	37,900	32,800	28,200	33,600	35,100	32,400	61.1
Associate's degree	—	—	—	33,800	37,400	37,300	31,000	66.2
Bachelor's degree or higher	42,500	47,900	44,300	42,200	47,300	45,000	46,000	64.4
Bachelor's degree	—	—	—	40,500	44,800	43,900	45,000	64.2
Master's degree or higher	—	—	—	‡	‡	55,600	53,000	65.3
Asian	—	—	38,100[5]	35,600[5]	44,800[5]	43,900	50,000	66.7
Less than high school completion[3]	—	—	‡[5]	‡[5]	‡[5]	‡	‡	‡
High school diploma or equivalent	—	—	27,100[5]	28,200[5]	31,100[5]	29,700	26,000	59.3
Some college[4]	—	—	32,800[5]	26,200[5]	34,900[5]	33,000	38,000	57.4
Associate's degree	—	—	—[5]	28,200[5]	37,400[5]	38,400	36,500	70.3
Bachelor's degree or higher	—	—	49,300[5]	46,500[5]	62,300[5]	54,900	60,000	70.5
Bachelor's degree	—	—	—[5]	42,900[5]	61,000[5]	54,900	50,000	69.7
Master's degree or higher	—	—	—[5]	53,500[5]	66,000[5]	60,400	70,000	71.6
Pacific Islander	—	—	([5])	([5])	([5])	‡	‡	46.9
American Indian/Alaska Native	—	—	32,800	28,200	29,900	33,000	30,000	59.8
Two or more races	—	—	—	—	—	37,300	34,000	50.2

— Not available.
‡ Reporting standards not met.
[1] Full-time, full-year wage workers as a percentage of the population ages 25–34 who reported working or looking for work in 2009.
[2] Totals for 1980 and 1985 include other racial/ethnic groups not shown.
[3] Young adults in this category did not earn a high school diploma or receive alternative credentials, such as a General Educational Development (GED) certificate.
[4] Due to changes in categories across time, the category "some college" prior to 1992 is not comparable with "some college" from 1992 onward. Prior to 1992, "some college" may have included students who earned an associate's degree.
[5] From 1989 through 2002, data for Asians and Pacific Islanders were not reported separately; therefore, Pacific Islanders are included with Asians during this period.
NOTE: Earnings are presented in constant dollars by means of the Consumer Price Index (CPI) to eliminate inflationary factors and to allow for direct comparison across years. For more information on the CPI, see *supplemental note 10*. *Full-year worker* refers to those who were employed 50 or more weeks during the previous year; *full-time worker* refers to those who were usually employed 35 or more hours per week. For more information on the Current Population Survey, see *supplemental note 2*. Race categories exclude persons of Hispanic ethnicity. Estimates for educational attainment categories for Pacific Islander, American Indian/Alaska Native, and Two or more races subgroups did not meet reporting standards. For more information on race/ethnicity, see *supplemental note 1*.
SOURCE: U.S. Department of Commerce, Census Bureau, Current Population Survey (CPS), Annual Social and Economic Supplement, selected years, 1981–2010.

Employment Outcomes of Young Adults

Table A-18-1. Percentage distribution of adults ages 25–34, by employment status and educational attainment: Selected years, 1990–2010

Employment status and educational attainment	1990	2000	2005	2006	2007	2008	2009	2010
Total	**100.0**	**100.0**	**100.0**	**100.0**	**100.0**	**100.0**	**100.0**	**100.0**
Employed full time	67.6	71.7	66.6	67.9	68.3	67.8	61.8	60.8
Employed part time	11.0	9.8	10.2	10.0	10.5	10.3	12.4	12.4
Unemployed	4.8	3.4	4.8	4.5	4.1	4.9	8.4	8.9
Not in the labor force	16.6	15.0	18.5	17.6	17.1	16.9	17.4	17.9
Educational attainment and employment status								
Less than high school	100.0	100.0	100.0	100.0	100.0	100.0	100.0	100.0
Employed full time	49.5	55.1	52.1	54.1	52.8	49.1	39.6	40.6
Employed part time	10.8	8.9	9.8	9.2	10.9	11.3	15.0	14.5
Unemployed	9.6	7.3	8.2	7.8	7.3	10.0	13.6	14.0
Not in the labor force	30.0	28.6	29.9	29.0	29.1	29.6	31.8	30.9
High school diploma or equivalent	100.0	100.0	100.0	100.0	100.0	100.0	100.0	100.0
Employed full time	66.0	70.4	63.8	66.3	66.3	64.1	55.9	55.0
Employed part time	11.7	9.8	9.2	9.2	10.1	9.9	13.1	13.1
Unemployed	5.3	4.1	6.1	5.2	5.0	6.9	11.3	12.9
Not in the labor force	17.0	15.7	20.8	19.2	18.6	19.1	19.7	19.0
Some college	—	100.0	100.0	100.0	100.0	100.0	100.0	100.0
Employed full time	—	70.0	64.7	65.6	64.5	65.1	59.6	55.9
Employed part time	—	12.0	13.0	11.4	13.0	12.6	13.7	14.0
Unemployed	—	3.2	4.8	5.1	4.3	4.6	9.1	9.5
Not in the labor force	—	14.8	17.5	17.9	18.2	17.7	17.6	20.6
Associate's degree	—	100.0	100.0	100.0	100.0	100.0	100.0	100.0
Employed full time	—	73.3	71.6	71.3	72.9	73.7	67.4	65.4
Employed part time	—	11.1	11.4	11.3	12.0	10.7	13.9	13.5
Unemployed	—	3.1	3.9	3.1	3.2	3.5	6.5	7.0
Not in the labor force	—	12.5	13.1	14.3	11.9	12.1	12.2	14.1
Bachelor's degree or higher	100.0	100.0	100.0	100.0	100.0	100.0	100.0	100.0
Employed full time	78.7	80.6	75.2	75.8	77.6	77.8	74.9	74.1
Employed part time	9.4	8.4	9.2	9.8	8.9	9.0	9.7	9.9
Unemployed	2.0	1.5	2.3	2.4	2.0	2.0	4.0	4.0
Not in the labor force	9.9	9.6	13.3	12.0	11.6	11.3	11.4	12.0
Bachelor's degree	—	100.0	100.0	100.0	100.0	100.0	100.0	100.0
Employed full time	—	80.3	74.7	74.9	76.6	76.4	73.5	73.1
Employed part time	—	8.2	9.0	9.8	9.0	9.7	10.0	10.0
Unemployed	—	1.4	2.4	2.7	2.2	2.2	4.4	4.3
Not in the labor force	—	10.0	13.9	12.6	12.1	11.7	12.0	12.5
Master's degree or higher	—	100.0	100.0	100.0	100.0	100.0	100.0	100.0
Employed full time	—	81.3	76.6	78.2	80.3	81.4	78.1	76.9
Employed part time	—	9.1	9.9	9.7	8.4	7.1	8.8	9.5
Unemployed	—	1.6!	1.8	1.6	1.3	1.3	3.1	3.1
Not in the labor force	—	8.1	11.6	10.4	10.1	10.2	9.9	10.6

— Not available.
! Interpret with caution. The standard error of the estimate is equal to 30 percent or more of the estimate's value.
NOTE: Persons who were employed 35 or more hours during the previous week were classified as working full time; those who worked fewer hours were classified as working part time. Detail may not sum to totals because of rounding. Race categories exclude persons of Hispanic ethnicity. Over time, the Current Population Survey (CPS) has had different response options for race/ethnicity. For more information on race/ethnicity, see *supplemental note 1*. For more information on the CPS, see *supplemental note 2*.
SOURCE: U.S. Department of Commerce, Census Bureau, Current Population Survey (CPS), Annual Social and Economic Supplement (ASEC), selected years, 1991–2011.

Table A-18-2. Percentage distribution of adults ages 25–34, by race/ethnicity, employment status, and educational attainment: 2010

Race/ethnicity, employment status, and educational attainment	Total	White	Black	Hispanic	Asian	Pacific Islander	American Indian/ Alaska Native	Two or more races
Total	**100.0**	**100.0**	**100.0**	**100.0**	**100.0**	**100.0**	**100.0**	**100.0**
Employed full time	60.8	64.2	53.9	55.6	60.6	59.5	50.0	55.6
Employed part time	12.4	12.3	10.4	14.6	10.6	11.0!	13.1	13.6
Unemployed	8.9	7.8	14.5	9.4	5.3	11.4!	9.7	11.2
Not in the labor force	17.9	15.7	21.2	20.5	23.5	18.0	27.2	19.6
Educational attainment and employment status								
Less than high school	100.0	100.0	100.0	100.0	100.0	‡	100.0	100.0
Employed full time	40.6	38.2	28.1	44.9	38.3	‡	51.0	27.1!
Employed part time	14.5	11.9	9.1	17.1	17.3	‡	‡	18.9!
Unemployed	14.0	16.2	22.8	11.0	8.9!	‡	‡	17.3!
Not in the labor force	30.9	33.7	40.0	27.0	35.4	‡	39.2	36.7
High school diploma or equivalent	100.0	100.0	100.0	100.0	100.0	100.0	100.0	100.0
Employed full time	55.0	56.2	47.0	57.4	63.0	60.7	44.7	48.3
Employed part time	13.1	13.2	10.9	14.3	13.7	‡	15.2!	12.0
Unemployed	12.9	12.4	18.3	10.6	7.1	11.3!	13.6	18.8
Not in the labor force	19.0	18.2	23.8	17.8	16.2	22.3!	26.5!	20.9
Some college	100.0	100.0	100.0	100.0	100.0	‡	100.0	100.0
Employed full time	55.9	56.6	53.3	57.5	49.8	‡	41.2	58.5
Employed part time	14.0	14.5	13.0	12.6	15.4	‡	15.0!	14.5
Unemployed	9.5	9.0	13.8	8.4	3.5!	‡	11.4!	8.8!
Not in the labor force	20.6	19.9	19.9	21.5	31.3	‡	32.5	18.2
Associate's degree	100.0	100.0	100.0	100.0	100.0	‡	100.0	100.0
Employed full time	65.4	67.4	60.5	62.5	68.4	‡	42.2	50.8
Employed part time	13.5	13.1	11.7	14.9	14.0	‡	23.5!	23.7
Unemployed	7.0	6.6	10.3	7.8	‡	‡	‡	‡
Not in the labor force	14.1	12.9	17.4	14.8	15.8	‡	34.3!	19.3!
Bachelor's degree or higher	100.0	100.0	100.0	100.0	100.0	‡	100.0	100.0
Employed full time	74.1	76.0	76.5	70.5	62.8	‡	73.6	71.7
Employed part time	9.9	10.4	6.7	11.4	8.0	‡	12.3!	9.0
Unemployed	4.0	3.3	6.7	5.0	5.4	‡	‡	5.7!
Not in the labor force	12.0	10.3	10.0	13.1	23.9	‡	‡	13.6
Bachelor's degree	100.0	100.0	100.0	100.0	100.0	‡	100.0	100.0
Employed full time	73.1	74.9	75.9	69.6	60.0	‡	75.6	66.5
Employed part time	10.0	10.3	6.9	11.7	9.3	‡	‡	10.4!
Unemployed	4.3	3.7	7.4	5.0	5.7	‡	‡	6.5!
Not in the labor force	12.5	11.1	9.8	13.6	25.0	‡	‡	16.7
Master's degree or higher	100.0	100.0	100.0	100.0	100.0	‡	‡	‡
Employed full time	76.9	79.0	78.1	73.8	67.2	‡	‡	‡
Employed part time	9.5	10.6	6.4!	10.4	5.9	‡	‡	‡
Unemployed	3.1	2.3	4.9!	4.7!	4.9	‡	‡	‡
Not in the labor force	10.6	8.1	10.6	11.1	22.1	‡	‡	‡

! Interpret with caution. The standard error of the estimate is equal to 30 percent or more of the estimate's value.
‡ Reporting standards not met.
NOTE: Persons who were employed 35 or more hours during the previous week were classified as working full time; those who worked fewer hours were classified as working part time. Detail may not sum to totals because of rounding. Race categories exclude persons of Hispanic ethnicity. Over time, the Current Population Survey (CPS) has had different response options for race/ethnicity. For more information on race/ethnicity, see *supplemental note 1*. For more information on the CPS, see *supplemental note 2*.
SOURCE: U.S. Department of Commerce, Census Bureau, Current Population Survey (CPS), Annual Social and Economic Supplement (ASEC), 2011.

Public High School Graduation Rates

Table A-19-1. Averaged freshman graduation rate for public high school students and number of graduates, by state or jurisdiction: School years 2001–02 through 2007–08

State or jurisdiction	Averaged freshman graduation rate						
	2001–02	2002–03	2003–04	2004–05	2005–06	2006–07	2007–08
United States	**72.6**	**73.9**	**74.3**[1]	**74.7**	**73.4**[1]	**73.9**	**74.7**[1]
Alabama	62.1	64.7	65.0	65.9	66.2	67.1	69.0
Alaska	65.9	68.0	67.2	64.1	66.5	69.0	69.1
Arizona	74.7	75.9	66.8	84.7	70.5	69.6	70.7
Arkansas	74.8	76.6	76.8	75.7	80.4	74.4	76.4
California	72.7	74.1	73.9	74.6	69.2	70.7	71.2
Colorado	74.7	76.4	78.7	76.7	75.5	76.6	75.4
Connecticut	79.7	80.9	80.7	80.9	80.9	81.8	82.2
Delaware	69.5	73.0	72.9	73.0	76.3	71.9	72.1
District of Columbia	68.4	59.6	68.2	66.3	65.4	54.8	56.0
Florida	63.4	66.7	66.4	64.6	63.6	65.0	66.9
Georgia	61.1	60.8	61.2	61.7	62.4	64.1	65.4
Hawaii	72.1	71.3	72.6	75.1	75.5	75.4	76.0
Idaho	79.3	81.4	81.5	81.0	80.5	80.4	80.1
Illinois	77.1	75.9	80.3	79.4	79.7	79.5	80.4
Indiana	73.1	75.5	73.5	73.2	73.3	73.9	74.1
Iowa	84.1	85.3	85.8	86.6	86.9	86.5	86.4
Kansas	77.1	76.9	77.9	79.2	77.5	78.8	79.0
Kentucky	69.8	71.7	73.0	75.9	77.2	76.4	74.4
Louisiana	64.4	64.1	69.4	63.9	59.5	61.3	63.5
Maine	75.6	76.3	77.6	78.6	76.3	78.5	79.1
Maryland	79.7	79.2	79.5	79.3	79.9	80.0	80.4
Massachusetts	77.6	75.7	79.3	78.7	79.5	80.8	81.5
Michigan	72.9	74.0	72.5	73.0	72.2	77.0	76.3
Minnesota	83.9	84.8	84.7	85.9	86.2	86.5	86.4
Mississippi	61.2	62.7	62.7	63.3	63.5	63.5	63.9
Missouri	76.8	78.3	80.4	80.6	81.0	81.9	82.4
Montana	79.8	81.0	80.4	81.5	81.9	81.5	82.0
Nebraska	83.9	85.2	87.6	87.8	87.0	86.3	83.8
Nevada	71.9	72.3	57.4	55.8	55.8	54.2	56.3
New Hampshire	77.8	78.2	78.7	80.1	81.1	81.7	83.3

See notes at end of table.

Table A-19-1. Averaged freshman graduation rate for public high school students and number of graduates, by state or jurisdiction: School years 2001–02 through 2007–08—Continued

State or jurisdiction	Number of graduates						
	2001–02	2002–03	2003–04	2004–05	2005–06	2006–07	2007–08
United States	**2,621,534**	**2,719,947**	**2,753,438**[1]	**2,799,250**	**2,815,544**[1]	**2,892,351**	**2,999,508**[1]
Alabama	35,887	36,741	36,464	37,453	37,918	38,912	41,346
Alaska	6,945	7,297	7,236	6,909	7,361	7,666	7,855
Arizona	47,175	49,986	45,508	59,498	54,091	55,954	61,667
Arkansas	26,984	27,555	27,181	26,621	28,790	27,166	28,725
California	325,895	341,097	343,480	355,217	343,515	356,641	374,561
Colorado	40,760	42,379	44,777	44,532	44,424	45,628	46,082
Connecticut	32,327	33,667	34,573	35,515	36,222	37,541	38,419
Delaware	6,482	6,817	6,951	6,934	7,275	7,205	7,388
District of Columbia	3,090	2,725	3,031	2,781	3,150	2,944	3,352
Florida	119,537	127,484	131,418	133,318	134,686	142,284	149,046
Georgia	65,983	66,890	68,550	70,834	73,498	77,829	83,505
Hawaii	10,452	10,013	10,324	10,813	10,922	11,063	11,613
Idaho	15,874	15,858	15,547	15,768	16,096	16,242	16,567
Illinois	116,657	117,507	124,763	123,615	126,817	130,220	135,143
Indiana	56,722	57,897	56,008	55,444	57,920	59,887	61,901
Iowa	33,789	34,860	34,339	33,547	33,693	34,127	34,573
Kansas	29,541	29,963	30,155	30,355	29,818	30,139	30,737
Kentucky	36,337	37,654	37,787	38,399	38,449	39,099	39,339
Louisiana	37,905	37,610	37,019	36,009	33,275	34,274	34,401
Maine	12,593	12,947	13,278	13,077	12,950	13,151	14,350
Maryland	50,881	51,864	52,870	54,170	55,536	57,564	59,171
Massachusetts	55,272	55,987	58,326	59,665	61,272	63,903	65,197
Michigan	95,001	100,301	98,823	101,582	102,582	111,838	115,183
Minnesota	57,440	59,432	59,096	58,391	58,898	59,497	60,409
Mississippi	23,740	23,810	23,735	23,523	23,848	24,186	24,795
Missouri	54,487	56,925	57,983	57,841	58,417	60,275	61,717
Montana	10,554	10,657	10,500	10,335	10,283	10,122	10,396
Nebraska	19,910	20,161	20,309	19,940	19,764	19,873	20,035
Nevada	16,270	16,378	15,201	15,740	16,455	17,149	18,815
New Hampshire	12,452	13,210	13,309	13,775	13,988	14,452	14,982

See notes at end of table.

Table A-19-1. Averaged freshman graduation rate for public high school students and number of graduates, by state or jurisdiction: School years 2001–02 through 2007–08—Continued

State or jurisdiction	Averaged freshman graduation rate						
	2001–02	2002–03	2003–04	2004–05	2005–06	2006–07	2007–08
United States	**72.6**	**73.9**	**74.3**[1]	**74.7**	**73.4**[1]	**73.9**	**74.7**[1]
New Jersey	85.8	87.0	86.3	85.1	84.8	84.4	84.6
New Mexico	67.4	63.1	67.0	65.4	67.3	59.1	66.8
New York	60.5	60.9	60.9	65.3	67.4	68.9	70.9
North Carolina	68.2	70.1	71.4	72.6	71.8	68.6	72.8
North Dakota	85.0	86.4	86.1	86.3	82.2	83.1	83.8
Ohio	77.5	79.0	81.3	80.2	79.2	78.7	79.0
Oklahoma	76.0	76.0	77.0	76.9	77.8	77.8	78.0
Oregon	71.0	73.7	74.2	74.2	73.0	73.8	76.7
Pennsylvania	80.2	81.7	82.2	82.5	83.5	83.0	82.7
Rhode Island	75.7	77.7	75.9	78.4	77.8	78.4	76.4
South Carolina	57.9	59.7	60.6	60.1	61.0	58.9	62.2
South Dakota	79.0	83.0	83.7	82.3	84.5	82.5	84.4
Tennessee	59.6	63.4	66.1	68.5	70.7	72.6	74.9
Texas	73.5	75.5	76.7	74.0	72.5	71.9	73.1
Utah	80.5	80.2	83.0	84.4	78.6	76.6	74.3
Vermont	82.0	83.6	85.4	86.5	82.3	88.5	89.3
Virginia	76.7	80.6	79.3	79.6	74.5	75.5	77.0
Washington	72.2	74.2	74.6	75.0	72.9	74.8	71.9
West Virginia	74.2	75.7	76.9	77.3	76.9	78.2	77.3
Wisconsin	84.8	85.8	85.8	86.7	87.5	88.5	89.6
Wyoming	74.4	73.9	76.0	76.7	76.1	75.8	76.0

See notes at end of table.

Table A-19-1. Averaged freshman graduation rate for public high school students and number of graduates, by state or jurisdiction: School years 2001–02 through 2007–08—Continued

State or jurisdiction	Number of graduates						
	2001–02	2002–03	2003–04	2004–05	2005–06	2006–07	2007–08
United States	**2,621,534**	**2,719,947**	**2,753,438**[1]	**2,799,250**	**2,815,544**[1]	**2,892,351**	**2,999,508**[1]
New Jersey	77,664	81,391	83,826	86,502	90,049	93,013	94,994
New Mexico	18,094	16,923	17,892	17,353	17,822	16,131	18,264
New York	140,139	143,818	142,526	153,203	161,817	168,333	176,310
North Carolina	65,955	69,696	72,126	75,010	76,710	76,031	83,307
North Dakota	8,114	8,169	7,888	7,555	7,192	7,159	6,999
Ohio	110,608	115,762	119,029	116,702	117,356	117,658	120,758
Oklahoma	36,852	36,694	36,799	36,227	36,497	37,100	37,630
Oregon	31,153	32,587	32,958	32,602	32,394	33,446	34,949
Pennsylvania	114,943	119,933	123,474	124,758	127,830	128,603	130,298
Rhode Island	9,006	9,318	9,258	9,881	10,108	10,384	10,347
South Carolina	31,302	32,482	33,235	33,439	34,970	35,108	35,303
South Dakota	8,796	8,999	9,001	8,585	8,589	8,346	8,582
Tennessee	40,894	44,113	46,096	47,967	50,880	54,502	57,486
Texas	225,167	238,111	244,165	239,717	240,485	241,193	252,121
Utah	30,183	29,527	30,252	30,253	29,050	28,276	28,167
Vermont	7,083	6,970	7,100	7,152	6,779	7,317	7,392
Virginia	66,519	72,943	72,042	73,667	69,597	73,997	77,369
Washington	58,311	60,435	61,274	61,094	60,213	62,801	61,625
West Virginia	17,128	17,287	17,339	17,137	16,763	17,407	17,489
Wisconsin	60,575	63,272	62,784	63,229	63,003	63,968	65,183
Wyoming	6,106	5,845	5,833	5,616	5,527	5,441	5,494

[1] The 2003–04 national estimates include imputed data for New York and Wisconsin. The 2005–06 national estimates include imputed data for the District of Columbia, Pennsylvania, and South Carolina. The 2007–08 estimate for Maine includes graduates of semi-private schools.
NOTE: The averaged freshman graduation rate is the number of graduates divided by the estimated freshman enrollment count 4 years earlier. This count is the sum of the number of 8th-graders 5 years earlier, the number of 9th-graders 4 years earlier, and the number of 10th-graders 3 years earlier, divided by 3. Ungraded students were allocated to individual grades proportional to each state's enrollment in those grades. Graduates include only those who earned regular diplomas or diplomas for advanced academic achievement (e.g., honors diploma) as defined by the state or jurisdiction. For more information on the Common Core of Data (CCD), see *supplemental note 3.* For more information on measures of student progress and persistence, see *supplemental note 6.*
SOURCE: U.S. Department of Education, National Center for Education Statistics, Common Core of Data (CCD), "NCES Common Core of Data State Dropout and Completion Data File," school year 2007–08, version 1a; and "State Nonfiscal Survey of Public Elementary/Secondary Education," 2002–03, Version 1b; 2003–04, Version 1b; 2004–05, Version 1b; 2005–06, Version 1b, and 2006–07, Version 1b.

Table A-20-1. Status dropout rates of 16- through 24-year-olds in the civilian, noninstitutionalized population, by race/ethnicity: October Current Population Survey (CPS) 1980–2009

| Year | Total[1] | Race/ethnicity | | | | |
		White	Black	Hispanic	Asian/ Pacific Islander	American Indian/ Alaska Native
1980	14.1	11.4	19.1	35.2	—	—
1981	13.9	11.4	18.4	33.2	—	—
1982	13.9	11.4	18.4	31.7	—	—
1983	13.7	11.2	18.0	31.6	—	—
1984	13.1	11.0	15.5	29.8	—	—
1985	12.6	10.4	15.2	27.6	—	—
1986	12.2	9.7	14.2	30.1	—	—
1987	12.7	10.4	14.1	28.6	—	—
1988	12.9	9.6	14.5	35.8	—	—
1989	12.6	9.4	13.9	33.0	7.5	21.6
1990	12.1	9.0	13.2	32.4	4.9!	16.4!
1991	12.5	8.9	13.6	35.3	3.5!	18.7!
1992	11.0	7.7	13.7	29.4	5.7	17.5!
1993	11.0	7.9	13.6	27.5	5.8	14.6!
1994	11.5	7.7	12.6	30.0	5.8	10.2!
1995	12.0	8.6	12.1	30.0	3.9	13.4!
1996	11.1	7.3	13.0	29.4	5.3	13.0
1997	11.0	7.6	13.4	25.3	6.9	14.5
1998	11.8	7.7	13.8	29.5	4.1	11.8
1999	11.2	7.3	12.6	28.6	4.3	‡
2000	10.9	6.9	13.1	27.8	3.8	14.0
2001	10.7	7.3	10.9	27.0	3.6	13.1
2002	10.5	6.5	11.3	25.7	3.9	16.8
2003	9.9	6.3	10.9	23.5	3.9	15.0
2004	10.3	6.8	11.8	23.8	3.6	17.0
2005	9.4	6.0	10.4	22.4	2.9	14.0
2006	9.3	5.8	10.7	22.1	3.6	14.7
2007	8.7	5.3	8.4	21.4	6.1	19.3
2008	8.0	4.8	9.9	18.3	4.4	14.6
2009	8.1	5.2	9.3	17.6	3.4	13.2

— Not available.
! Interpret with caution. The standard error of the estimate is equal to 30 percent or more of the estimate's value.
‡ Reporting standards not met.
[1] Total includes other race/ethnicity categories not separately shown.
NOTE: The *status dropout rate* is the percentage of 16- through 24-year-olds who are not enrolled in high school and have not earned a high school credential (either a diploma or an equivalency credential such as a General Educational Development [GED] certificate). The status dropout rate includes all dropouts regardless of when they last attended school. Estimates from 1987 and onward reflect new editing procedures for cases with missing data on school enrollment items. This table uses a different data source than tables A-20-2 and A-20-3; therefore, estimates for 2009 are not directly comparable to the estimates in tables A-20-2 and A-20-3. Race categories exclude persons of Hispanic ethnicity. One should use caution when making comparisons between data from 1995 and earlier and data from 1996 and later because of differing response options for race/ethnicity over time. For more information on race/ethnicity and the CPS, see *supplemental notes 1* and *2*. For more information on measures of student persistence and progress, see *supplemental note 6*.
SOURCE: U.S. Department of Commerce, Census Bureau, Current Population Survey (CPS), October Supplement, 1980–2009.

Table A-20-2. Number of status dropouts and status dropout rates of 16- through 24-year-olds in the household and noninstitutionalized group quarters population, by nativity and school or student characteristics: American Community Survey (ACS) 2009

School or student characteristic	Number of status dropouts (in thousands)	Status dropout rate (percent)	Percent of all status dropouts	Dropout rate for those born in the United States[1] (percent)	Dropout rate for those born outside of the United States[1] (percent)
Total[2]	**3,167**	**8.2**	**100.0**	**6.8**	**19.6**
Sex					
Male	1,850	9.4	58.4	7.6	22.9
Female	1,317	7.0	41.6	5.9	15.8
Race/ethnicity					
White	1,261	5.5	39.8	5.5	5.0
Black	518	9.5	16.4	9.7	6.6
Hispanic	1,226	17.5	38.7	10.2	32.5
Asian	50	3.2	1.6	2.2	4.2
Native Hawaiian/Pacific Islander	5	8.7	0.2	8.0	10.3
American Indian/Alaska Native	47	15.3	1.5	15.3	‡
Two or more races	52	6.1	1.7	6.2	4.2
Race/ethnicity by sex					
Male					
White	717	6.1	38.8	6.1	5.4
Black	295	10.9	15.9	11.3	6.3
Hispanic	749	20.5	40.5	11.4	37.1
Asian	28	3.5	1.5	2.8	4.3
Native Hawaiian/Pacific Islander	3	8.4	0.1	8.1!	8.9!
American Indian/Alaska Native	25	16.6	1.4	16.7	‡
Two or more races	28	6.6	1.5	6.8	3.8!
Female					
White	544	4.8	41.3	4.8	4.6
Black	223	8.0	16.9	8.1	7.0
Hispanic	477	14.2	36.2	9.0	26.5
Asian	22	2.9	1.7	1.6	4.2
Native Hawaiian/Pacific Islander	3	9.0	0.2	7.9	12.3!
American Indian/Alaska Native	22	14.0	1.7	13.9	‡
Two or more races	24	5.6	1.9	5.6	4.6!
Age					
16	114	2.7	3.6	2.4	6.2
17	176	4.2	5.6	3.8	8.0
18	329	7.1	10.4	6.4	14.9
19	375	8.7	11.8	7.7	17.3
20–24	2,173	10.3	68.6	8.2	23.6
Region					
Northeast	432	6.4	13.6	5.2	14.9
Midwest	603	7.1	19.0	6.4	16.9
South	1,301	9.2	41.1	7.8	21.3
West	831	9.1	26.2	6.8	21.9

! Interpret with caution. The standard error of the estimate is equal to 30 percent or more of the estimate's value.
‡ Reporting standards not met.
[1] United States refers to the 50 states and the District of Columbia.
[2] Total includes other race/ethnicity categories not separately shown.
NOTE: The *status dropout rate* is the percentage of 16- through 24-year-olds who are not enrolled in high school and have not earned a high school credential (either a diploma or an equivalency credential such as a General Educational Development [GED] certificate). The status dropout rate includes all dropouts regardless of when they last attended school. This table uses a different data source than table A-20-1; therefore, estimates are not directly comparable to the 2009 estimates in table A-20-1. Noninstitutionalized group quarters include college and university housing, military quarters, facilities for workers and religious groups, and temporary shelters for the homeless. Among those counted in noninstitutionalized group quarters in the ACS, only the residents of military barracks are not included in the civilian noninstitutionalized population in the Current Population Survey. Detail may not sum to totals because of rounding. Race categories exclude persons of Hispanic ethnicity. For more information on race/ethnicity and region, see *supplemental note 1*. For more information on the ACS, see *supplemental note 3*. For more information on measures of student persistence and progress, see *supplemental note 6*.
SOURCE: U.S. Department of Commerce, Census Bureau, American Community Survey (ACS), 2009.

Status Dropout Rates

Table A-20-3. Status dropout rates of 16- through 24-year-olds and number of status dropouts in the household and group quarters population, by housing type and school or student characteristics: American Community Survey (ACS) 2009

School or student characteristic	Total status dropout rate (percent)	Institutionalized group quarters[1]		Noninstitutionalized group quarters and households[2]	
		Number of status dropouts	Status dropout rate (percent)	Number of status dropouts	Status dropout rate (percent)
Total[3]	8.6	205,000	40.1	3,167,400	8.2
Sex					
Male	10.1	185,100	41.4	1,850,000	9.4
Female	7.1	19,900	31.1	1,317,400	7.0
Race/ethnicity					
White	5.6	51,200	31.2	1,260,700	5.5
Black	10.7	90,200	44.3	517,800	9.5
Hispanic	17.9	53,200	46.7	1,225,500	17.5
Asian	3.3	1,900	45.2	50,200	3.2
Native Hawaiian/Pacific Islander	9.5	‡	‡	5,300	8.7
American Indian/Alaska Native	15.9	3,100	40.6	46,800	15.3
Two or more races	6.5	4,700	30.2	52,400	6.1
Race/ethnicity by sex					
Male					
White	6.3	41,900	31.7	717,100	6.1
Black	13.2	85,300	45.5	294,700	10.9
Hispanic	21.2	48,900	47.8	748,600	20.5
Asian	3.7	1,800	47.0	28,200	3.5
Native Hawaiian/Pacific Islander	9.4	‡	‡	2,600	8.4
American Indian/Alaska Native	17.6	2,500	42.5	25,100	16.6
Two or more races	7.4	4,200	31.3	28,100	6.6
Female					
White	4.9	9,300	29.3	543,500	4.8
Black	8.2	5,000	30.6	223,000	8.0
Hispanic	14.3	4,200	36.9	476,900	14.2
Asian	2.9	‡	‡	22,000	2.9
Native Hawaiian/Pacific Islander	9.7	‡	‡	2,700	9.0
American Indian/Alaska Native	14.2	‡	‡	21,800	14.0
Two or more races	5.7	450!	22.7!	24,400	5.6
Age					
16	2.8	4,800	14.4	113,700	2.7
17	4.4	10,900	24.5	175,800	4.2
18	7.5	18,400	45.3	329,400	7.1
19	9.1	23,900	45.5	375,100	8.7
20–24	10.8	147,100	43.3	2,173,300	10.3
Region					
Northeast	6.8	33,400	39.5	432,100	6.4
Midwest	7.4	34,000	33.0	603,200	7.1
South	9.7	95,800	45.2	1,301,200	9.2
West	9.5	41,800	37.7	830,900	9.1

! Interpret with caution. The standard error of the estimate is equal to 30 percent or more of the estimate's value.
‡ Reporting standards not met.
[1] Institutionalized group quarters include adult and juvenile correctional facilities, nursing facilities, and other health care facilities.
[2] Noninstitutionalized group quarters, such as college and university housing, military quarters, facilities for workers and religious groups, and temporary shelters for the homeless, are included in the noninstitutionalized category. Among those counted in noninstitutionalized group quarters in the ACS, only the residents of military barracks are not included in the civilian noninstitutionalized population in the Current Population Survey.
[3] Total includes other race/ethnicity categories not separately shown.
NOTE: The *status dropout rate* is the percentage of 16- through 24-year-olds who are not enrolled in high school and have not earned a high school credential (either a diploma or an equivalency credential such as a General Educational Development [GED] certificate). The status dropout rate includes all dropouts regardless of when they last attended school. This table uses a different data source than table A-20-1; therefore, total status dropout rate estimates are not directly comparable to the 2009 estimates in table A-20-1. However, estimates for noninstitutionalized group quarters and households include similar populations as those included in the 2009 estimates in table A-20-1. Race categories exclude persons of Hispanic ethnicity. For more information on race/ethnicity, see *supplemental note 1*. For more information on the ACS, see *supplemental note 3*. For more information on measures of student persistence and progress, see *supplemental note 6*.
SOURCE: U.S. Department of Commerce, Census Bureau, American Community Survey (ACS), 2009.

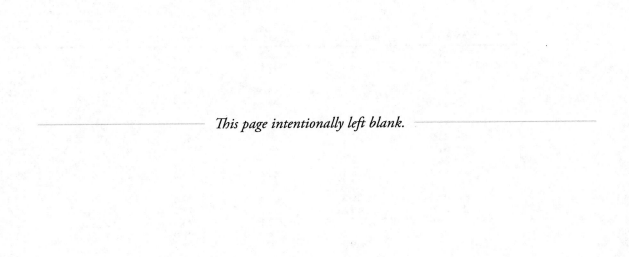

This page intentionally left blank.

Table A-21-1. Percentage of high school completers who were enrolled in 2- or 4-year colleges the October immediately following high school completion, by family income: 1975–2009

Year	Total	Low income Annual	Low income Moving average[1]	Middle income	High income	Gap between High income and Low income[2]	Gap between High income and Middle income
1975	50.7	31.2	34.8	46.2	64.5	29.7	18.3
1976	48.8	39.3	32.3	40.5	63.0	30.6	22.5
1977	50.6	27.7	32.4	44.2	66.3	33.8	22.0
1978	50.1	31.4	29.8	44.3	64.0	34.2	19.6
1979	49.3	30.5	31.5	43.2	63.2	31.6	19.9
1980	49.3	32.4	32.3	42.5	65.2	32.9	22.8
1981	53.9	33.9	33.0	49.2	67.6	34.6	18.4
1982	50.6	32.8	33.7	41.7	70.9	37.1	29.2
1983	52.7	34.6	34.1	45.2	70.3	36.3	25.1
1984	55.2	34.7	36.4	48.4	74.0	37.6	25.6
1985	57.7	40.2	36.0	50.6	74.6	38.5	24.0
1986	53.8	33.9	36.7	48.5	71.0	34.3	22.6
1987	56.8	36.8	37.5	50.1	73.8	36.3	23.8
1988	58.9	42.5	42.4	54.7	72.8	30.4	18.1
1989	59.6	48.5	45.9	55.3	70.7	24.8	15.3
1990	60.1	46.9	45.0	54.4	76.6	31.6	22.2
1991	62.5	39.5	42.2	58.4	78.2	36.0	19.8
1992	61.9	40.8	43.5	57.1	79.0	35.5	22.0
1993	62.6	50.4	44.7	56.9	79.3	34.6	22.4
1994	61.9	43.3	42.0	57.8	77.9	35.9	20.1
1995	61.9	34.2	42.0	56.0	83.5	41.4	27.4
1996	65.0	48.3	47.0	62.8	78.0	31.0	15.2
1997	67.0	57.0	50.5	60.7	82.2	31.7	21.5
1998	65.6	46.4	50.4	64.7	77.5	27.0	12.8
1999	62.9	48.0	48.0	60.1	75.4	27.4	15.3
2000	63.3	49.7	47.1	59.5	76.9	29.8	17.4
2001	61.7	43.5	49.8	56.6	80.0	30.2	23.5
2002	65.2	56.4	50.6	60.7	78.2	27.6	17.5
2003	63.9	52.0	52.5	59.1	77.9	25.5	18.9
2004	66.7	48.5	51.4	63.2	80.1	28.8	17.0
2005	68.6	53.5	51.0	65.1	81.2	30.2	16.1
2006	66.0	50.9	54.5	61.4	80.7	26.2	19.3
2007	67.2	58.4	55.2	63.3	78.2	23.0	14.8
2008	68.6	55.5	56.0	65.3	81.9	25.9	16.6
2009	70.1	54.1	54.8	66.8	84.2	29.4	17.4

[1] Due to the small sample size for the low-income category, data are subject to relatively large sampling errors. Therefore, moving averages are used to produce more stable estimates. The 3-year moving average is an arithmetic average of the year indicated, the year immediately preceding, and the year immediately following. For 1975 and 2009, a 2-year moving average is used: data for 1975 reflect an average of 1975 and 1976, and data for 2009 reflect an average of 2008 and 2009.
[2] Refers to the moving average rates for the low-income category.
NOTE: Includes high school completers ages 16–24, who account for about 98 percent of all high school completers in a given year. Before 1992, *high school completer* referred to those who had completed 12 years of schooling. As of 1992, *high school completer* refers to those who have received a high school diploma or equivalency certificate. *Low income* refers to the bottom 20 percent of all family incomes, *high income* refers to the top 20 percent of all family incomes, and *middle income* refers to the 60 percent in between. For more information on the Current Population Survey (CPS), educational attainment, and family income, see *supplemental note 2*.
SOURCE: U.S. Department of Commerce, Census Bureau, Current Population Survey (CPS), October Supplement, 1975–2009.

Table A-21-2. Percentage of high school completers who were enrolled in 2- or 4-year colleges the October immediately following high school completion, by race/ethnicity: 1975–2009

Year	White	Black		Hispanic		Asian		Gap between White and		
		Annual	Moving average[1]	Annual	Moving average[1]	Annual	Moving average[1]	Black[2]	Hispanic[2]	Asian[2]
1975	51.1	41.7	43.0	58.0	55.2	—	—	8.1 !	‡	—
1976	48.8	44.4	45.3	52.7	53.6	—	—	3.5 !	‡	—
1977	50.8	49.5	46.8	50.8	48.8	—	—	4.0 !	‡	—
1978	50.5	46.4	47.5	42.0	46.1	—	—	‡	‡	—
1979	49.9	46.7	45.2	45.0	46.3	—	—	4.7 !	‡	—
1980	49.8	42.7	44.0	52.3	49.6	—	—	5.9 !	‡	—
1981	54.9	42.7	40.3	52.1	48.7	—	—	14.6	6.2 !	—
1982	52.7	35.8	38.8	43.2	49.4	—	—	13.9	‡	—
1983	55.0	38.2	38.0	54.2	46.7	—	—	17.1	8.4 !	—
1984	59.0	39.8	39.9	44.3	49.3	—	—	19.1	9.7 !	—
1985	60.1	42.2	39.5	51.0	46.1	—	—	20.5	13.9 !	—
1986	56.8	36.9	43.5	44.0	42.3	—	—	13.3	14.5 !	—
1987	58.6	52.2	44.2	33.5	45.0	—	—	14.4	13.6 !	—
1988	61.1	44.4	49.7	57.1	48.5	—	—	11.4 !	12.6 !	—
1989	60.7	53.4	48.0	55.1	52.7	—	—	12.7	8.0 !	—
1990	63.0	46.8	48.9	42.7	52.5	—	—	14.1	10.6 !	—
1991	65.4	46.4	47.2	57.2	52.6	—	—	18.2	12.8 !	—
1992	64.3	48.2	50.0	55.0	58.2	—	—	14.3	6.1 !	—
1993	62.9	55.6	51.3	62.2	55.7	—	—	11.6 !	7.3 !	—
1994	64.5	50.8	52.4	49.1	55.0	—	—	12.1	9.5 !	—
1995	64.3	51.2	52.9	53.7	51.6	—	—	11.4	12.7	—
1996	67.4	56.0	55.4	50.8	57.6	—	—	12.1	9.8 !	—
1997	68.2	58.5	58.8	65.6	55.3	—	—	9.4 !	12.9	—
1998	68.5	61.9	59.8	47.4	51.9	—	—	8.8 !	16.6	—
1999	66.3	58.9	58.6	42.3	47.4	—	—	7.7 !	18.9	—
2000	65.7	54.9	56.3	52.9	48.6	—	—	9.4 !	17.1	—
2001	64.2	54.6	56.3	51.7	52.7	—	—	7.8 !	11.4	—
2002	68.9	59.4	57.2	53.3	54.7	—	—	11.7	14.1	—
2003	66.2	57.5	60.0	58.6	57.7	84.1	80.0	6.2 !	8.5 !	-13.8 !
2004	68.8	62.5	58.8	61.8	57.7	75.6	81.6	10.0	11.1	-12.8
2005	73.2	55.7	58.2	54.0	57.5	86.7	80.9	15.0	15.7	-7.7 !
2006	68.5	55.5	55.6	57.9	58.5	82.3	85.1	12.9	10.0	-16.6
2007	69.5	55.7	55.7	64.0	62.0	88.8	85.8	13.9	7.5 !	-16.3
2008	71.7	55.7	60.3	63.9	62.3	88.4	90.1	11.4	9.4	-18.4
2009	71.3	69.5	62.6	59.3	61.6	92.1	90.4	8.7 !	9.7 !	-19.1

— Not available.

! Interpret with caution. The standard error of the estimate is equal to 30 percent or more of the estimate's value.

‡ Reporting standards not met.

[1] Due to the small sample sizes for the Black, Hispanic, and Asian categories, data are subject to relatively large sampling errors. Therefore, moving averages are used to produce more stable estimates. The 3-year moving average is an arithmetic average of the year indicated, the year immediately preceding, and the year immediately following. For 1975 and 2009, a 2-year moving average is used: data for 1975 reflect an average of 1975 and 1976, and data for 2009 reflect an average of 2008 and 2009.

[2] Refers to the moving average rates for the Black, Hispanic and Asian categories.

NOTE: Includes high school completers ages 16–24, who account for about 98 percent of all high school completers in a given year. Before 1992, *high school completer* referred to those who had completed 12 years of schooling. As of 1992, *high school completer* refers to those who have received a high school diploma or equivalency certificate. Race categories exclude persons of Hispanic ethnicity. From 2003 onward, data for Asians and Pacific Islanders are collected separately. Data for the Asian category are not available prior to 2003. For more information on the Current Population Survey (CPS), educational attainment, and race/ethnicity, see *supplemental note 2*.

SOURCE: U.S. Department of Commerce, Census Bureau, Current Population Survey (CPS), October Supplement, 1975–2009.

Immediate Transition to College

Table A-21-3. Percentage of high school completers who were enrolled in 2- or 4-year colleges the October immediately following high school completion, by sex and level of institution: 1975–2009

Year	Total 2-year[1]	Total 4-year[1]	Male Total	Male 2-year[1]	Male 4-year[1]	Female Total	Female 2-year[1]	Female 4-year[1]
1975	18.2	32.6	52.6	19.0	33.6	49.0	17.4	31.6
1976	15.6	33.3	47.2	14.5	32.7	50.3	16.6	33.8
1977	17.5	33.1	52.1	17.2	35.0	49.3	17.8	31.5
1978	17.0	33.1	51.1	15.6	35.5	49.3	18.3	31.0
1979	17.5	31.8	50.4	16.9	33.5	48.4	18.1	30.3
1980	19.4	29.9	46.7	17.1	29.7	51.8	21.6	30.2
1981	20.5	33.5	54.8	20.9	33.9	53.1	20.1	33.0
1982	19.1	31.5	49.1	17.5	31.6	52.0	20.6	31.4
1983	19.2	33.5	51.9	20.2	31.7	53.4	18.4	35.1
1984	19.4	35.8	56.0	17.7	38.4	54.5	21.0	33.5
1985	19.6	38.1	58.6	19.9	38.8	56.8	19.3	37.5
1986	19.3	34.5	55.8	21.3	34.5	51.9	17.3	34.6
1987	18.9	37.9	58.3	17.3	41.0	55.3	20.3	35.0
1988	21.9	37.1	57.1	21.3	35.8	60.7	22.4	38.3
1989	20.7	38.9	57.6	18.3	39.3	61.6	23.1	38.5
1990	20.1	40.0	58.0	19.6	38.4	62.2	20.6	41.6
1991	24.9	37.7	57.9	22.9	35.0	67.1	26.8	40.3
1992	23.0	38.9	60.0	22.1	37.8	63.8	23.9	40.0
1993	22.8	39.8	59.9	22.9	37.0	65.2	22.8	42.4
1994	21.0	40.9	60.6	23.0	37.5	63.2	19.1	44.1
1995	21.5	40.4	62.6	25.3	37.4	61.3	18.1	43.2
1996	23.1	41.9	60.1	21.5	38.5	69.7	24.6	45.1
1997	22.8	44.3	63.6	21.4	42.2	70.3	24.1	46.2
1998	24.4	41.3	62.4	24.4	38.0	69.1	24.3	44.8
1999	21.0	41.9	61.4	21.0	40.5	64.4	21.1	43.3
2000	21.4	41.9	59.9	23.1	36.8	66.2	20.0	46.2
2001	19.7	42.0	59.7	18.6	41.1	63.6	20.7	42.9
2002	21.7	43.5	62.1	20.5	41.7	68.3	23.0	45.3
2003	21.5	42.5	61.2	21.9	39.3	66.5	21.0	45.5
2004	22.4	44.2	61.4	21.8	39.6	71.5	23.1	48.5
2005	24.0	44.6	66.5	24.7	41.8	70.4	23.4	47.0
2006	24.7	41.3	65.8	24.9	40.9	66.1	24.5	41.7
2007	24.1	43.1	66.1	22.7	43.4	68.3	25.5	42.8
2008	27.7	40.9	65.9	24.9	41.0	71.6	30.6	40.9
2009	27.7	42.4	66.0	25.1	40.9	73.8	30.1	43.8

[1] From 1975 through 1986, due to a skip pattern in the Current Population Survey (CPS), about 3–9 percent of high school completers ages 16–24 who immediately enrolled in college were not asked the question about the level of institution attended. Such respondents were assumed to have had the same probability of enrolling in a 2- or 4-year institution as those who were asked the question.

NOTE: Includes high school completers ages 16–24, who account for about 98 percent of all high school completers in each year. Before 1992, *high school completer* referred to those who had completed 12 years of schooling. As of 1992, *high school completer* refers to those who have received a high school diploma or equivalency certificate. For more information on the CPS and educational attainment, see *supplemental note 2*. Detail may not sum to totals because of rounding.

SOURCE: U.S. Department of Commerce, Census Bureau, Current Population Survey (CPS), October Supplement, 1975–2009.

Remedial Coursetaking

Table A-22-1. Percentage of first-year undergraduate students who took remedial education courses, by number of courses and selected characteristics: 2007–08

	First-year undergraduates						
			Number who took a remedial course in 2007–08, in thousands	Percent who took remedial courses in 2007–08			
Selected characteristic	Number of students, in thousands	Percent who ever took a remedial course[1]		Any courses	1 course	2 courses	3 or more courses
Total	**8,517**	**36.2**	**1,724**	**20.2**	**9.3**	**6.5**	**4.4**
Sex							
Male	3,714	32.8	719	19.4	8.9	6.5	3.9
Female	4,802	38.8	1,005	20.9	9.7	6.5	4.8
Race/ethnicity of student							
White	4,897	31.3	881	18.0	8.8	5.4	3.9
Black	1,397	45.1	344	24.7	11.3	7.7	5.6
Hispanic	1,386	43.3	323	23.3	9.5	8.8	5.0
Asian	455	38.0	90	19.8	7.2	7.3	5.2
Pacific Islander	69	40.0	13	19.3	7.9!	9.2	‡
American Indian/Alaska Native	82	46.8	24	29.0	12.0	9.0	8.0
Two or more races	205	32.8	43	20.9	12.2	5.2	3.5
Other	26	35.6	6	23.2	7.7!	9.9!	‡
Age							
15 to 23	5,260	34.6	1,168	22.2	10.1	7.4	4.7
24 to 29	1,347	39.5	261	19.4	8.9	6.1	4.4
30 or older	1,910	38.1	295	15.5	7.5	4.3	3.6
Attendance status							
Exclusively full-time	4,010	31.4	786	19.6	8.8	6.2	4.6
Exclusively part-time	3,426	39.8	650	19.0	9.2	5.9	3.9
Mixed full- and part-time	1,081	42.5	288	26.7	11.8	9.6	5.3
Student housing status							
On-campus	1,081	23.1	185	17.1	8.8	5.1	3.2
Off-campus, not with relatives	4,327	37.3	777	18.0	8.4	5.4	4.1
With parents or relatives	2,538	39.8	646	25.4	11.0	8.9	5.6
Control and level of institution							
Public less-than-2-year	80	31.5	7	9.1	4.7	0.7!	3.7
Public 2-year	4,855	41.9	1,160	23.9	10.7	8.0	5.2
Public 4-year nondoctorate	690	38.6	175	25.3	12.0	8.8	4.5
Public 4-year doctorate	823	24.2	142	17.2	10.0	4.5	2.7
Private not-for-profit less than 4-year	53	33.0	6	10.7	4.6	1.8!	4.3
Private not-for-profit 4-year nondoctorate	415	25.8	68	16.5	6.9	5.4	4.1
Private not-for-profit 4-year doctorate	319	22.3	43	13.3	6.9	3.7	2.7
Private for-profit less-than-2-year	380	26.7	22	5.7	2.2	1.4	2.0
Private for-profit, 2 years or more	904	28.8	103	11.4	4.9	2.9	3.6

! Interpret with caution. Estimates are unstable.
‡ Reporting standards not met.
[1] Although these data are for first-year undergraduates, student status was determined by accumulation of credits. Students attending postsecondary education part time, or not completing the credit accumulation requirements for second-year status, could be considered first-year students for more than 1 year. Therefore, there is a distinction between having "ever" taken a remedial course and having taken one in 2007–08.
NOTE: Data are based on a sample survey of students who enrolled at any time during the school year. Data include the 50 states, the District of Columbia, and Puerto Rico. Detail may not sum to totals because of survey item nonresponse and rounding. Race categories exclude persons of Hispanic ethnicity.
SOURCE: U.S. Department of Education, National Center for Education Statistics, 2007–08 National Postsecondary Student Aid Study (NPSAS:08).

Postsecondary Graduation Rates

Table A-23-1. Percentage of students seeking a bachelor's degree at 4-year institutions who completed a bachelor's degree, by control of institution, time to degree attainment, and sex: Cohort years 1996 and 2002

Time to degree attainment and sex	1996 starting cohort				2002 starting cohort			
	Total	Public	Private not-for-profit	Private for-profit	Total	Public	Private not-for-profit	Private for-profit
All students								
4 years	33.7	26.0	48.6	21.8	36.4	29.9	51.0	14.2
5 years	50.2	45.9	59.2	25.4	52.3	49.2	61.3	17.2
6 years	55.4	51.7	63.1	28.0	57.2	54.9	64.6	22.0
Male								
4 years	28.5	20.8	43.6	22.3	31.3	24.5	46.3	17.0
5 years	46.2	41.6	55.8	25.6	48.7	45.3	58.5	19.9
6 years	52.0	48.1	60.4	28.0	54.1	51.7	61.9	23.6
Female								
4 years	38.0	30.3	52.6	21.1	40.5	34.3	54.7	11.6
5 years	53.6	49.5	61.8	25.1	55.2	52.5	63.5	14.7
6 years	58.2	54.7	65.4	27.9	59.7	57.5	66.7	20.5

NOTE: The rate was calculated in the manner required for disclosure and reporting purposes under the Student Right-To-Know Act; this calculation is the total number of students who completed a degree within the specified time to degree attainment divided by the revised cohort minus any allowable exclusions. The revised cohort is the spring 2009 estimate of the number of students who entered the institution in 1996 or 2002 as first-time, full-time undergraduates seeking a bachelor's or equivalent degree. Students who transferred to another institution and graduated from the other institution are not counted as completers at their initial institution. The number of completers used in the calculation of the graduation rate for each time-to-degree designation is cumulative; for example, the 6-year graduation rate includes all students who graduated in 4 years and 5 years, as well as those who graduated in 6 years. For more information on the Integrated Postsecondary Education Data System (IPEDS), see *supplemental note 3.*
SOURCE: U.S. Department of Education, National Center for Education Statistics, Integrated Postsecondary Education Data System (IPEDS), Spring 2003 and Spring 2009, Graduation Rates component.

Table A-23-2. Percentage of students seeking a bachelor's degree at 4-year institutions who completed a bachelor's degree within 6 years, by race/ethnicity, control of institution, sex, and admissions acceptance rate: Cohort years 1996 and 2002

Characteristic	Total	White	Black	Hispanic	Asian/ Pacific Islander	American Indian/ Alaska Native
			1996 starting cohort			
Total	**55.4**	**58.1**	**38.9**	**45.7**	**63.4**	**38.0**
Public	51.7	54.3	36.8	42.1	59.5	35.3
Male	48.1	50.8	30.3	37.5	55.2	33.1
Female	54.7	57.4	41.0	45.7	63.5	37.0
Private not-for-profit	63.1	65.7	44.6	55.7	73.5	48.1
Male	60.4	63.0	38.9	52.1	71.5	46.7
Female	65.4	67.9	48.4	58.3	75.0	49.2
Private for-profit	28.0	33.2	19.2	24.6	28.9	23.1
Male	28.0	32.3	19.4	26.7	31.7	30.8
Female	27.9	34.5	19.0	21.9	24.9	17.3
			2002 starting cohort			
Total	**57.2**	**60.2**	**40.1**	**48.9**	**67.1**	**38.3**
Public	54.9	57.4	39.4	46.3	64.7	35.7
Male	51.7	54.4	32.9	41.4	61.3	32.2
Open admissions	27.2	31.7	16.0	23.1	31.3	9.1
90 percent or more accepted	40.8	42.9	26.3	27.4	49.3	32.3
75.0 to 89.9 percent accepted	49.1	51.5	34.1	39.8	50.5	27.6
50.0 to 74.9 percent accepted	55.6	58.4	36.0	46.4	61.7	40.3
25.0 to 49.9 percent accepted	64.1	71.8	34.6	48.2	75.5	59.0
Less than 25.0 percent accepted	73.1	75.5	44.0	69.5	85.3	66.7
Female	57.5	59.9	43.7	50.0	67.7	38.3
Open admissions	33.7	37.8	23.2	32.1	40.5	13.0
90 percent or more accepted	46.0	48.0	33.6	37.0	53.9	36.3
75.0 to 89.9 percent accepted	54.8	56.9	43.7	47.5	56.0	35.1
50.0 to 74.9 percent accepted	61.7	64.1	48.1	55.2	68.3	46.5
25.0 to 49.9 percent accepted	69.8	77.8	46.5	56.4	81.3	70.9
Less than 25.0 percent accepted	71.8	71.1	46.6	77.5	92.2	71.1
Private not-for-profit	64.6	67.2	44.9	59.5	75.3	49.8
Male	61.9	64.8	38.6	55.4	73.8	46.6
Open admissions	32.9	42.2	17.5	23.0	44.9	20.6
90 percent or more accepted	48.9	51.4	22.9	40.5	58.6	45.2
75.0 to 89.9 percent accepted	56.2	58.9	37.5	47.7	58.1	40.8
50.0 to 74.9 percent accepted	60.0	63.6	40.1	49.1	65.3	48.3
25.0 to 49.9 percent accepted	78.4	81.8	49.8	72.9	85.3	65.8
Less than 25.0 percent accepted	88.8	91.6	59.5	87.9	95.8	77.6
Female	66.7	69.1	49.4	62.2	76.3	52.1
Open admissions	37.7	45.7	27.8	31.4	36.0	21.2
90 percent or more accepted	57.8	60.3	33.0	43.6	58.8	43.7
75.0 to 89.9 percent accepted	62.3	64.8	46.1	57.3	62.4	48.6
50.0 to 74.9 percent accepted	65.9	69.2	50.2	58.8	68.5	54.1
25.0 to 49.9 percent accepted	79.9	82.7	60.4	76.7	88.6	74.9
Less than 25.0 percent accepted	89.5	91.1	70.4	92.7	96.5	84.1
Private for-profit	22.0	25.5	16.3	27.5	35.5	17.1
Male	23.6	27.8	16.6	26.7	38.4	23.5
Female	20.5	23.1	16.1	28.3	31.3	12.0

NOTE: The rate was calculated in the manner required for disclosure and reporting purposes under the Student Right-To-Know Act; this calculation is the total number of students who completed a degree within the specified time to degree attainment divided by the revised cohort minus any allowable exclusions. The revised cohort is the spring 2009 estimate of the number of students who entered the institution in 1996 or 2002 as first-time, full-time undergraduates seeking a bachelor's or equivalent degree. Students who transferred to another institution and graduated from the other institution are not counted as completers at their initial institution. Data are not shown by acceptance rate for private for-profit institutions due to the relatively small number of institutions that did not have open admissions. For more information on the Integrated Postsecondary Education Data System (IPEDS), see *supplemental note 3*. Race categories exclude persons of Hispanic ethnicity. Persons with unknown race/ethnicity and nonresident aliens are not shown. For more information on race/ethnicity, see *supplemental note 1*.
SOURCE: U.S. Department of Education, National Center for Education Statistics, Integrated Postsecondary Education Data System (IPEDS), Spring 2003 and Spring 2009, Graduation Rates component.

Table A-23-3. Percentage of students seeking a certificate or associate's degree at 2-year institutions who completed a certificate program or associate's degree within 150 percent of the normal time required to do so, by race/ethnicity, control of institution, and sex: Cohort years 1999 and 2005

Control of institution and sex	Total	White	Black	Hispanic	Asian/Pacific Islander	American Indian/ Alaska Native
			1999 starting cohort			
Total	**29.3**	**30.7**	**23.3**	**27.0**	**30.8**	**25.1**
Public	22.9	25.3	15.3	16.6	24.2	18.1
Male	21.6	23.7	14.1	15.0	21.8	17.3
Female	24.2	26.8	16.2	17.9	26.7	18.8
Private not-for-profit	44.7	45.6	42.4	36.9	56.6	51.3
Male	43.6	43.7	34.5	43.7	59.5	48.1
Female	45.7	47.3	47.1	33.3	54.0	53.1
Private for-profit	61.0	64.6	51.3	63.2	64.4	54.2
Male	63.2	67.5	49.0	62.9	67.5	56.2
Female	59.1	61.8	52.7	63.4	61.6	52.6
			2005 starting cohort			
Total	**27.5**	**28.5**	**22.6**	**25.7**	**31.5**	**24.9**
Public	20.6	22.9	12.1	15.6	25.8	18.2
Male	19.9	22.1	12.0	14.6	23.5	18.7
Female	21.2	23.8	12.1	16.4	28.2	17.8
Private not-for-profit	48.2	52.3	41.6	47.3	41.6	14.8
Male	44.5	49.1	38.7	42.9	43.7	10.4
Female	51.3	54.9	44.9	49.6	40.1	18.0
Private for-profit	57.7	62.9	47.8	61.4	65.8	55.8
Male	57.7	64.8	43.1	57.5	65.7	56.3
Female	57.7	61.6	49.4	63.3	65.8	55.7

NOTE: The rate was calculated in the manner required for disclosure and reporting purposes under the Student Right-To-Know Act; this calculation is the total number of students who completed a degree within the specified time to degree attainment divided by the revised cohort minus any allowable exclusions. The revised cohort is the spring 2009 estimate of the number of students who entered the institution in 1999 or 2005 as first-time, full-time undergraduates seeking a certificate or associate's degree. Students who transferred to another institution and graduated from the other institution are not counted as completers at their initial institution. For more information on the Integrated Postsecondary Education Data System (IPEDS), see *supplemental note 3*. Race categories exclude persons of Hispanic ethnicity. Persons with unknown race/ethnicity and nonresident aliens are not shown. For more information on race/ethnicity, see *supplemental note 1*.
SOURCE: U.S. Department of Education, National Center for Education Statistics, Integrated Postsecondary Education Data System (IPEDS), Spring 2003 and Spring 2009, Graduation Rates component.

This page intentionally left blank.

Table A-24-1. Percentage of 25- to 29-year-olds who attained selected levels of education, by race/ethnicity and sex: Selected years, March 1975–2010

Educational attainment and year	Total[1]			White			Black		
	Total	Male	Female	Total	Male	Female	Total	Male	Female
High school diploma or equivalent[2]									
1975	83.1	84.5	81.8	86.6	88.0	85.2	71.1	72.3	70.1
1980	85.4	85.4	85.5	89.2	89.1	89.2	76.7	74.7	78.3
1985	86.1	85.9	86.4	89.5	89.2	89.9	80.5	80.6	80.5
1990	85.7	84.4	87.0	90.1	88.6	91.7	81.7	81.4	82.0
1995	86.8	86.3	87.4	92.5	92.0	93.0	86.7	88.4	85.3
2000	88.1	86.7	89.4	94.0	92.9	95.2	86.8	87.6	86.2
2005	86.1	84.9	87.3	92.8	91.8	93.8	86.9	86.6	87.3
2006	86.4	84.4	88.5	93.4	92.3	94.6	86.3	84.2	88.0
2007	87.0	84.9	89.1	93.5	92.7	94.2	87.7	87.4	87.9
2008	87.8	85.8	89.9	93.7	92.6	94.7	87.5	85.7	89.2
2009	88.6	87.5	89.8	94.6	94.4	94.8	88.9	88.8	89.0
2010	88.8	87.4	90.2	94.5	94.6	94.4	89.6	87.9	91.1
Some college[3]									
1975	41.6	47.4	36.0	44.3	50.4	38.3	27.5	29.7	25.8
1980	44.7	47.6	41.9	48.0	51.1	44.9	32.4	32.6	32.3
1985	43.7	44.2	43.3	46.4	46.8	46.0	34.4	34.2	34.5
1990	44.5	43.7	45.3	48.3	47.3	49.3	36.1	35.0	36.9
1995	54.1	52.3	55.8	59.8	57.5	62.1	45.1	45.3	44.8
2000	58.3	55.1	61.5	64.1	60.5	67.7	52.7	50.4	54.6
2005	56.7	52.1	61.4	64.3	59.7	68.9	49.0	41.9	55.1
2006	57.8	53.3	62.4	66.3	62.1	70.4	49.9	44.8	54.3
2007	57.7	52.5	63.0	65.6	61.1	70.0	50.0	45.9	53.6
2008	59.2	53.9	64.8	67.1	62.4	71.9	51.0	44.5	56.7
2009	59.9	54.7	65.3	68.1	63.5	72.9	53.4	45.2	60.6
2010	61.2	55.9	66.8	69.3	64.9	73.9	54.7	48.8	60.0
Bachelor's degree[4]									
1975	21.9	25.2	18.7	23.8	27.3	20.2	10.5	11.1	10.0
1980	22.5	24.0	21.0	25.0	26.8	23.2	11.6	10.5	12.4
1985	22.2	23.1	21.3	24.4	25.5	23.3	11.6	10.3	12.6
1990	23.2	23.7	22.8	26.4	26.6	26.2	13.4	15.1	11.9
1995	24.7	24.5	24.9	28.8	28.4	29.2	15.4	17.4	13.7
2000	29.1	27.9	30.1	34.0	32.3	35.8	17.8	18.4	17.4
2005	28.6	25.3	32.0	34.1	30.4	37.8	17.5	14.3	20.3
2006	28.4	25.3	31.6	34.3	31.4	37.2	18.7	15.2	21.7
2007	29.6	26.3	33.0	35.5	31.9	39.2	19.5	18.9	20.0
2008	30.8	26.8	34.9	37.1	32.6	41.7	20.4	19.0	21.6
2009	30.6	26.6	34.8	37.2	32.6	42.0	18.9	14.8	22.6
2010	31.7	27.8	35.7	38.6	34.8	42.4	19.4	15.0	23.3
Master's degree[5]									
1995	4.5	4.9	4.1	5.3	5.6	5.0	1.8	2.2!	1.4!
2000	5.4	4.7	6.2	5.8	4.9	6.7	3.7	2.1!	4.9
2005	6.2	5.1	7.3	7.4	6.0	8.7	2.6	1.1!	4.0
2006	6.4	5.1	7.8	7.5	5.8	9.2	3.2	1.7	4.5
2007	6.3	5.0	7.6	7.6	5.7	9.4	3.5	3.3	3.7
2008	7.0	5.3	8.7	8.2	5.9	10.4	4.4	3.4	5.2
2009	7.4	6.1	8.8	8.9	7.4	10.4	4.2	3.2	5.1
2010	6.8	5.2	8.5	7.7	6.3	9.2	4.7	2.9	6.2

See notes at end of table.

Table A-24-1. Percentage of 25- to 29-year-olds who attained selected levels of education, by race/ethnicity and sex: Selected years, March 1975–2010—Continued

Educational attainment and year	Hispanic			Asian/Pacific Islander		
	Total	Male	Female	Total	Male	Female
High school diploma or equivalent[2]						
1975	53.1	52.2	53.9	—	—	—
1980	58.0	57.0	58.9	—	—	—
1985	60.9	58.6	63.1	—	—	—
1990	58.2	56.6	59.9	89.9	95.3	85.1
1995	57.1	55.7	58.7	90.8	90.5	91.2
2000	62.8	59.2	66.4	93.7	92.1	95.2
2005	63.3	63.2	63.3	95.6	96.8	94.5
2006	63.2	60.5	66.6	96.4	97.2	95.6
2007	65.0	60.5	70.7	96.8	95.9	97.7
2008	68.3	65.6	71.9	95.9	95.6	96.1
2009	68.9	66.2	72.5	95.4	96.4	94.5
2010	69.4	65.7	74.1	93.7	93.8	93.6
Some college[3]						
1975	21.8	26.3	17.6	—	—	—
1980	23.2	25.9	20.5	—	—	—
1985	26.9	26.9	27.0	—	—	—
1990	23.4	22.9	23.9	62.8	69.3	57.0
1995	28.7	26.7	30.9	76.4	75.4	77.6
2000	32.8	29.0	36.6	78.2	79.3	77.3
2005	32.8	31.8	34.0	80.3	78.2	82.2
2006	31.7	28.3	35.9	80.9	80.0	81.8
2007	33.9	28.2	41.1	80.4	78.6	82.1
2008	35.9	30.8	42.5	80.2	78.9	81.5
2009	34.5	30.7	39.5	78.6	80.2	77.1
2010	36.8	30.2	45.1	76.3	75.9	76.7
Bachelor's degree[4]						
1975	8.8	10.4	7.3	—	—	—
1980	7.7	8.4	6.9	—	—	—
1985	11.1	10.9	11.2	—	—	—
1990	8.1	7.3	9.1	42.2	47.6	37.4
1995	8.9	7.8	10.1	43.1	42.0	44.5
2000	9.7	8.3	11.0	54.3	55.5	53.1
2005	11.2	10.2	12.4	59.9	58.4	61.3
2006	9.5	6.9	12.8	59.6	58.7	60.4
2007	11.6	8.6	15.4	59.5	58.5	60.3
2008	12.4	10.0	15.5	57.9	54.1	61.6
2009	12.2	11.0	13.8	56.4	55.2	57.6
2010	13.5	10.8	16.8	52.5	49.0	55.8
Master's degree[5]						
1995	1.6	2.0!	1.2!	10.9	12.6	8.9
2000	2.1	1.5	2.7	15.5	17.2	13.9
2005	2.1	1.7	2.5	16.9	19.7	14.4
2006	1.5	1.1	2.0	20.1	20.5	19.7
2007	1.5	0.6	2.6	17.5	18.4	16.5
2008	2.0	1.2	2.9	19.9	20.9	18.9
2009	1.9	1.2	2.7	21.1	20.4	21.7
2010	2.5	1.5	3.8	17.9	15.0	20.6

— Not available.
! Interpret data with caution (estimates are unstable).
[1] Included in the totals but not shown separately are estimates for persons from other racial/ethnic groups.
[2] Prior to 1992, *high school completers* referred to those who completed 12 years of schooling; from 1992 to 2010, the term refers to those who have received a high school diploma or equivalency certificate.
[3] Prior to 1992, *some college* meant completing 1 or more years of college; from 1992 to 2010, the term means completing any college at all.
[4] Data prior to 1992 were for completing 4 years of college; from 1992 to 2010, data are for earning a bachelor's degree.
[5] Estimates for attainment of a master's degree prior to 1992 are not available.
NOTE: Detail may not sum to totals as estimates of educational attainment represent the percentage who achieved at least the cited credential. For more information on educational attainment of 25- to 29-year-olds, see *supplemental note 6*. For more information on the Current Population Survey (CPS), see *supplemental note 2*. Race categories exclude persons of Hispanic ethnicity. For more information on race/ethnicity, see *supplemental note 1*.
SOURCE: U.S. Department of Commerce, Census Bureau, Current Population Survey (CPS), Annual Social and Economic Supplement, selected years, 1975–2010.

Table A-25-1. Percentage of the population 25 to 64 years old who attained selected levels of education, by country: 2001, 2005, and 2008

Country	High school			Bachelor's degree or higher		
	2001	2005	2008	2001	2005	2008
OECD countries						
OECD average	**64.6**	**68.5**	**72.4**	**14.8**	**18.6**	**20.8**
Australia	58.9	65.0	69.9	19.2	22.7	25.9
Austria[1]	75.7	80.6	81.0	6.6	9.1	10.7
Belgium[1]	58.5	66.1	69.6	12.1	13.8	16.4
Canada	81.9	85.2	87.1	20.4	23.3	25.2
Chile	—	50.0	68.0	—	10.3	15.7
Czech Republic	86.2	89.9	90.9	11.1	13.1	14.5
Denmark	80.2	81.0	77.6	7.5	26.0	27.5
Estonia	—	89.1	88.5	—	22.2	22.3
Finland	73.8	78.8	81.1	14.8	18.1	21.5
France	63.9	66.3	70.0	11.9	14.8	16.4
Germany	82.6	83.1	85.3	13.5	14.8	16.4
Greece	51.4	57.1	61.1	12.4	14.5	16.8
Hungary	70.2	76.4	79.7	14.1	16.9	18.7
Iceland	56.9	62.9	64.1	18.8	25.9	27.9
Ireland	57.6	64.5	69.5	14.0	18.4	22.2
Israel	—	79.2	81.2	—	29.8	28.8
Italy	43.3	50.1	53.3	10	11.7	14.0
Japan	83.1	—	—	19.2	22.3	24.3
Korea	68.0	75.5	79.1	17.5	22.7	25.6
Luxembourg	‡	‡	‡	‡	‡	‡
Mexico	21.6	21.3	33.6	13.3	13.8	14.9
Netherlands[1]	65.0	71.8	73.3	21.0	28.3	29.8
New Zealand	75.7	78.7	72.1	13.9	19.7	25.1
Norway[1]	85.2	77.2	80.7	25.6	30.3	33.6
Poland	45.9	51.4	87.1	11.9	16.9	19.6
Portugal	19.9	26.5	28.2	6.6	12.8	14.3
Slovak Republic	85.1	85.7	89.9	10.3	12.8	14.0
Slovenia	—	80.3	82.0	—	10.6	11.8
Spain	40.0	48.8	51.2	16.9	19.9	20.0
Sweden	80.6	83.6	85.0	16.9	20.6	23.4
Switzerland	87.4	83.0	86.8	15.8	19.0	23.3
Turkey	24.3	27.2	30.3	8.9	9.7	12.0
United Kingdom	63.0	66.7	69.6	18.0	20.8	23.6
United States	**87.7**	**87.8**	**88.7**	**28.3**	**29.6**	**31.5**
Reporting partner countries						
Brazil	—	29.5	38.8	—	7.8	10.8
Russian Federation[2]	88.0	88.9	—	20.8	20.8	—

— Not available.

‡ Reporting standards not met.

[1] Data from 2000 reported for 2001 for high school and bachelor's degree or higher data.

[2] Data from 2002 shown for 2001, and data from 2003 reported for 2005 for high school and bachelor's degree or higher data.

NOTE: OECD average refers to the mean of the data values for all reporting Organization for Economic Co-operation and Development (OECD) countries, to which each country reporting data contributes equally. High school attainment data in this table refer to degrees classified by the Organization for Economic Co-operation and Development (OECD) as International Standard Classification of Education (ISCED) level 3. ISCED level 3 corresponds to high school completion in the United States. ISCED level 3C short programs do not correspond to high school completion; these short programs are excluded from this table. Bachelor's degree or higher attainment data in this table refer to degrees classified by the OECD as ISCED level 5A or 6. ISCED level 5A, first award, corresponds to the bachelor's degree in the United States; ISCED level 5A, second award, corresponds to master's and first-professional degrees in the United States; and ISCED level 6 corresponds to doctoral degrees in the United States. For more information on ISCED levels, please see *supplemental note 11.*

SOURCE: Organization for Economic Co-operation and Development (OECD), *Education at a Glance,* 2002, 2007, and 2010, Tables A1.2a and A1.3a.

Table A-25-2. Percentage of the population 25 to 64 years old who attained selected levels of education, by age group and country: 2008

Country	High school					Bachelor's degree or higher				
	Total, 25 to 64 years old	25 to 34 years old	35 to 44 years old	45 to 54 years old	55 to 64 years old	Total, 25 to 64 years old	25 to 34 years old	35 to 44 years old	45 to 54 years old	55 to 64 years old
OECD countries										
OECD average	**72.4**	**80.8**	**76.1**	**69.3**	**59.9**	**20.8**	**26.6**	**21.9**	**18.2**	**15.5**
Australia	69.9	82.5	72.6	66.0	55.5	25.9	32.2	27.4	23.4	18.9
Austria	81.0	87.7	84.8	79.0	70.5	10.7	13.5	11.7	9.2	7.9
Belgium	69.6	83.1	77.2	64.4	52.1	16.4	22.8	18.2	13.8	10.5
Canada	87.1	91.9	90.2	85.6	79.6	25.2	29.8	28.5	21.1	21.1
Chile	68.0	84.5	74.2	65.5	39.3	15.7	22.3	13.6	13.1	13.9
Czech Republic	90.9	94.2	93.9	89.7	85.1	14.5	17.7	14.4	14.8	10.6
Denmark	77.6	86.1	81.9	73.6	69.1	27.5	34.9	29.3	24.9	21.0
Estonia	88.5	85.1	93.2	91.9	82.8	22.3	23.5	22.5	22.3	20.6
Finland	81.1	90.1	87.8	82.3	65.9	21.5	32.9	24.0	17.3	13.6
France	70.0	82.9	76.7	64.3	55.0	16.4	23.7	18.2	11.6	11.8
Germany	85.3	85.8	86.9	85.8	82.2	16.4	17.5	17.3	15.9	15.0
Greece	61.1	74.8	68.8	56.4	39.2	16.8	18.6	18.6	16.3	12.7
Hungary	79.7	85.6	82.8	78.4	70.5	18.7	22.9	18.6	16.6	16.0
Iceland	64.1	69.0	68.3	60.9	55.8	27.9	30.6	32.1	26.0	21.0
Ireland	69.5	84.7	74.5	61.9	44.7	22.2	30.6	23.4	17.2	12.1
Israel	81.2	87.5	83.6	77.0	72.3	28.8	28.9	30.1	28.2	27.6
Italy	53.3	68.9	57.1	49.4	35.2	14.0	19.6	14.6	11.5	9.5
Japan	—	—	—	—	—	24.3	30.9	25.8	25.3	16.0
Korea	79.1	97.6	93.3	68.1	40.4	25.6	34.5	31.7	18.9	10.5
Luxembourg	‡	‡	‡	‡	‡	‡	‡	‡	‡	‡
Mexico	33.6	39.8	36.3	30.2	19.1	14.9	18.5	14.6	14.0	8.9
Netherlands	73.3	82.4	77.3	71.3	62.2	29.8	37.5	29.7	28.1	24.4
New Zealand	72.1	79.5	74.3	70.5	62.1	25.1	33.6	25.9	21.9	18.2
Norway	80.7	84.0	81.9	78.4	78.3	33.6	43.8	36.3	28.7	25.3
Poland	87.1	92.8	90.9	87.0	76.0	19.6	32.1	18.8	13.0	12.0
Portugal	28.2	46.7	28.7	20.0	13.5	14.3	23.2	14.5	9.9	7.7
Slovak Republic	89.9	94.5	93.3	88.4	80.9	14.0	17.8	13.1	13.4	9.9
Slovenia	82.0	92.4	84.8	77.9	71.5	11.8	18.4	12.3	9.0	6.9
Spain	51.2	65.0	56.7	45.0	29.1	20.0	25.7	21.9	17.2	11.9
Sweden	85.0	91.2	90.4	83.6	75.0	23.4	32.4	24.3	19.3	17.8
Switzerland	86.8	90.3	88.2	85.5	82.7	23.3	28.8	25.0	20.8	18.0
Turkey	30.3	40.3	27.0	24.4	18.7	12.0	15.5	10.6	9.6	9.5
United Kingdom	69.6	76.6	69.7	67.0	63.4	23.6	30.7	23.3	20.3	18.5
United States	**88.7**	**88.1**	**88.6**	**89.2**	**88.8**	**31.5**	**32.3**	**33.1**	**29.6**	**31.1**
Reporting partner countries										
Brazil	38.8	49.8	40.0	32.7	23.2	10.8	11.0	11.6	10.6	9.1
Russian Federation	—	—	—	—	—	—	—	—	—	—

— Not available.
‡ Reporting standards not met.
NOTE: OECD average refers to the mean of the data values for all reporting Organization for Economic Co-operation and Development (OECD) countries, to which each country reporting data contributes equally. High school attainment data in this table refer to degrees classified by the Organization for Economic Co-operation and Development (OECD) as International Standard Classification of Education (ISCED) level 3. ISCED level 3 corresponds to high school completion in the United States. ISCED level 3C short programs do not correspond to high school completion; these short programs are excluded from this table. Bachelor's degree or higher attainment data in this table refer to degrees classified by the OECD as ISCED level 5A or 6. ISCED level 5A, first award, corresponds to the bachelor's degree in the United States; ISCED level 5A, second award, corresponds to master's and first-professional degrees in the United States; and ISCED level 6 corresponds to doctoral degrees in the United States. For more information on ISCED levels, please see *supplemental note 11*.
SOURCE: Organization for Economic Co-operation and Development (OECD), *Education at a Glance 2010*, Tables A1.2a and A1.3a.

Degrees Earned

Table A-26-1. Number of degrees conferred by degree-granting institutions and percentage of degrees conferred to females, by level of degree: Academic years 1994–95 through 2008–09

Academic year	Associate's		Bachelor's		Master's	
	Number	Percent conferred to females	Number	Percent conferred to females	Number	Percent conferred to females
1994–95	539,691	59.5	1,160,134	54.6	397,629	55.1
1995–96	555,216	60.5	1,164,792	55.1	406,301	55.9
1996–97	571,226	60.8	1,172,879	55.6	419,401	56.9
1997–98	558,555	61.0	1,184,406	56.1	430,164	57.1
1998–99	559,954	61.0	1,200,303	56.8	439,986	57.7
1999–2000	564,933	60.2	1,237,875	57.2	457,056	58.0
2000–01	578,865	60.0	1,244,171	57.3	468,476	58.5
2001–02	595,133	60.0	1,291,900	57.4	482,118	58.7
2002–03	634,016	60.0	1,348,811	57.5	513,339	58.8
2003–04	665,301	60.9	1,399,542	57.5	558,940	58.9
2004–05	696,660	61.6	1,439,264	57.4	574,618	59.3
2005–06	713,066	62.1	1,485,242	57.5	594,065	60.0
2006–07	728,114	62.2	1,524,092	57.4	604,607	60.6
2007–08	750,164	62.3	1,563,069	57.3	625,023	60.6
2008–09	787,325	62.1	1,601,368	57.2	656,784	60.4
	Increase in the number of degrees conferred					
1998–99 to 2008–09	227,371	†	401,065	†	216,798	†
	Percentage change in the number of degrees conferred					
1998–99 to 2008–09	40.6	†	33.4	†	49.3	†

See notes at end of table.

Table A-26-1. Number of degrees conferred by degree-granting institutions and percentage of degrees conferred to females, by level of degree: Academic years 1994–95 through 2008–09—Continued

Academic year	First-professional[1]		Doctoral[2]	
	Number	Percent conferred to females	Number	Percent conferred to females
1994–95	75,800	40.8	44,446	39.4
1995–96	76,734	41.7	44,652	39.9
1996–97	78,730	42.1	45,876	40.8
1997–98	78,598	42.9	46,010	42.0
1998–99	78,439	43.5	44,077	42.9
1999–2000	80,057	44.7	44,808	44.1
2000–01	79,707	46.2	44,904	44.9
2001–02	80,698	47.3	44,160	46.3
2002–03	80,897	48.2	46,042	47.1
2003–04	83,041	49.2	48,378	47.7
2004–05	87,289	49.8	52,631	48.8
2005–06	87,655	49.8	56,067	48.9
2006–07	90,064	50.0	60,616	50.1
2007–08	91,309	49.7	63,712	51.0
2008–09	92,004	49.0	67,716	52.3
	Increase in the number of degrees conferred			
1998–99 to 2008–09	13,565	†	23,639	†
	Percentage change in the number of degrees conferred			
1998–99 to 2008–09	17.3	†	53.6	†

† Not applicable.
[1] Includes first-professional degrees such as M.D., D.D.S., and law degrees. See glossary for a definition of first-professional degree.
[2] Includes Ph.D., Ed.D., and comparable degrees at the doctoral level. See glossary for a definition of doctoral degree.
NOTE: For more information on the Integrated Postsecondary Education Data System (IPEDS), see *supplemental note 3*. For more information on the classification of postsecondary education institutions, see *supplemental note 8*.
SOURCE: U.S. Department of Education, National Center for Education Statistics, 1994–95 through 2008–09 Integrated Postsecondary Education Data System (IPEDS), "Completions Survey" (IPEDS-C:94–99) and Fall 2000 through Fall 2009.

Table A-26-2. Number and percentage change in degrees conferred by degree-granting institutions, percentage distribution of degrees conferred, and percentage of degrees conferred to females, by level of degree and race/ethnicity: Academic years 1998–99, 2003–04, and 2008–09

Level of degree and race/ethnicity	Number			Percent change, 1998–99 to 2008–09	Percentage distribution			Percent conferred to females		
	1998–99	2003–04	2008–09	2008–09	1998–99	2003–04	2008–09	1998–99	2003–04	2008–09
Associate's	559,954	665,301	787,325	40.6	100.0	100.0	100.0	61.0	60.9	62.1
White	409,086	456,047	522,985	27.8	73.1	68.5	66.4	60.7	59.7	61.2
Black	57,439	81,183	101,487	76.7	10.3	12.2	12.9	66.2	68.0	68.5
Hispanic	48,670	72,270	97,921	101.2	8.7	10.9	12.4	60.2	61.5	62.5
Asian/Pacific Islander	27,586	33,149	40,914	48.3	4.9	5.0	5.2	57.7	58.0	58.1
American Indian/ Alaska Native	6,424	8,119	8,834	37.5	1.1	1.2	1.1	65.1	66.3	65.2
Nonresident alien	10,749	14,533	15,184	41.3	1.9	2.2	1.9	54.1	60.2	59.9
Bachelor's	1,200,303	1,399,542	1,601,368	33.4	100.0	100.0	100.0	56.8	57.5	57.2
White	907,245	1,026,114	1,144,612	26.2	75.6	73.3	71.5	56.2	56.6	56.0
Black	102,214	131,241	156,615	53.2	8.5	9.4	9.8	65.9	66.6	65.9
Hispanic	70,085	94,644	129,526	84.8	5.8	6.8	8.1	59.1	60.6	60.9
Asian/Pacific Islander	74,197	92,073	112,510	51.6	6.2	6.6	7.0	53.9	55.1	54.9
American Indian/ Alaska Native	8,423	10,638	12,222	45.1	0.7	0.8	0.8	60.5	60.1	60.3
Nonresident alien	38,139	44,832	45,883	20.3	3.2	3.2	2.9	45.8	48.3	51.3
Master's	439,986	558,940	656,784	49.3	100.0	100.0	100.0	57.7	58.9	60.4
White	313,487	369,582	424,188	35.3	71.2	66.1	64.6	59.6	61.1	62.2
Black	32,541	50,657	70,010	115.1	7.4	9.1	10.7	69.1	71.1	71.8
Hispanic	17,838	29,666	39,439	121.1	4.1	5.3	6.0	60.6	63.6	64.0
Asian/Pacific Islander	22,072	30,952	39,944	81.0	5.0	5.5	6.1	52.5	53.6	53.7
American Indian/ Alaska Native	2,016	3,192	3,759	86.5	0.5	0.6	0.6	61.8	64.7	64.4
Nonresident alien	52,032	74,891	79,444	52.7	11.8	13.4	12.1	40.2	40.2	42.4
First-professional[1]	78,439	83,041	92,004	17.3	100.0	100.0	100.0	43.5	49.2	49.0
White	58,720	60,379	65,439	11.4	74.9	72.7	71.1	41.6	47.0	46.1
Black	5,333	5,930	6,571	23.2	6.8	7.1	7.1	58.8	62.1	62.0
Hispanic	3,864	4,273	5,089	31.7	4.9	5.1	5.5	46.6	51.3	52.8
Asian/Pacific Islander	8,152	9,964	12,182	49.4	10.4	12.0	13.2	46.8	54.6	56.1
American Indian/ Alaska Native	612	565	659	7.7	0.8	0.7	0.7	45.6	51.3	50.1
Nonresident alien	1,758	1,930	2,064	17.4	2.2	2.3	2.2	35.1	45.9	50.0
Doctoral[2]	44,077	48,378	67,716	53.6	100.0	100.0	100.0	42.9	47.7	52.3
White	27,838	28,214	39,648	42.4	63.2	58.3	58.6	47.1	51.9	56.9
Black	2,136	2,900	4,434	107.6	4.8	6.0	6.5	59.1	65.0	66.5
Hispanic	1,302	1,662	2,540	95.1	3.0	3.4	3.8	52.0	53.9	57.0
Asian/Pacific Islander	2,299	2,632	3,875	68.6	5.2	5.4	5.7	41.8	50.9	54.3
American Indian/ Alaska Native	194	217	332	71.1	0.4	0.4	0.5	52.6	58.5	58.4
Nonresident alien	10,308	12,753	16,887	63.8	23.4	26.4	24.9	27.3	32.6	36.6

[1] Includes first-professional degrees such as M.D., D.D.S., and law degrees. See glossary for a definition of first-professional degree.
[2] Includes Ph.D., Ed.D, and comparable degrees at the doctoral level. See glossary for a definition of doctoral degree.
NOTE: Reported racial/ethnic distributions of students by level of degree, field of degree, and sex were used to estimate race/ethnicity for students whose race/ethnicity was not reported. Race categories exclude persons of Hispanic ethnicity. Nonresident aliens are shown separately because information about their race/ethnicity is not available. Detail may not sum to totals because of rounding. For more information on race/ethnicity, see *supplemental note 1*. For more information on the Integrated Postsecondary Education Data System (IPEDS), see *supplemental note 3*. For more information on the classification of postsecondary education institutions, see *supplemental note 8*.
SOURCE: U.S. Department of Education, National Center for Education Statistics, 1998–99, 2003–04, and 2008–09 Integrated Postsecondary Education Data System (IPEDS), "Completions Survey" (IPEDS-C:99) and Fall 2004 and 2009.

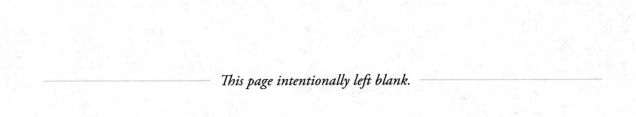
This page intentionally left blank.

Table A-27-1. Number and percentage of public schools, by school level and selected school characteristics: School years 1998–99 and 2008–09

School characteristic	1998–99				2008–09			
	Total[1]	Elementary	Secondary	Combined	Total[1]	Elementary	Secondary	Combined
	Number							
Total, all schools[2]	**90,874**	**63,382**	**21,790**	**5,067**	**98,706**	**67,082**	**24,275**	**5,623**
School type								
Regular	83,642	62,412	18,601	2,495	88,801	65,949	19,399	2,793
Special education	1,974	515	259	870	2,289	535	328	938
Vocational	1,077	8	640	367	1,409	1	1,187	82
Alternative	4,181	447	2,290	1,335	6,207	597	3,361	1,810
Charter schools	507	310	110	84	4,694	2,512	1,256	865
Title I school	—	—	—	—	62,305	48,741	10,889	2,657
Schools with a magnet program	1,165	865	274	26	3,021	2,191	729	92
	Percentage							
Total, all schools[2]	**100.0**	**69.7**	**24.0**	**5.6**	**100.0**	**68.0**	**24.6**	**5.7**
School type								
Regular	92.0	98.5	85.4	49.2	90.0	98.3	79.9	49.7
Special education	2.2	0.8	1.2	17.2	2.3	0.8	1.4	16.7
Vocational	1.2	#	2.9	7.2	1.4	#	4.9	1.5
Alternative	4.6	0.7	10.5	26.3	6.3	0.9	13.8	32.2
Charter schools	0.6	0.5	0.5	1.7	4.8	3.7	5.2	15.4
Title I schools	—	—	—	—	63.1	72.7	44.9	47.3
Schools with a magnet program	1.3	1.4	1.3	0.5	3.1	3.3	3.0	1.6
Enrollment size[3]	100.0	100.0	100.0	100.0	100.0	100.0	100.0	100.0
Less than 300	30.8	27.1	34.3	68.1	31.5	26.6	37.9	65.8
300–499	26.3	31.2	14.5	12.1	27.6	33.1	14.5	14.5
500–999	33.3	37.1	26.0	15.0	31.8	36.5	22.0	14.5
1,000 or more	9.6	4.7	25.3	4.8	9.1	3.8	25.7	5.1
Racial/ethnic concentration[3]								
More than 50 percent White	72.0	71.2	76.4	62.8	62.7	62.0	66.1	57.1
More than 50 percent Black	10.9	11.4	8.8	13.8	11.5	11.4	10.5	16.4
More than 50 percent Hispanic	8.2	8.7	6.8	6.8	13.4	14.1	11.8	10.3
Percentage of students in school eligible for free or reduced-price lunch	100.0	100.0	100.0	100.0	100.0	100.0	100.0	100.0
0–25 percent	22.1	18.8	31.4	25.6	24.7	23.6	28.6	21.9
26–50 percent	20.9	20.6	23.0	16.2	28.9	27.1	35.2	23.6
51–75 percent	14.5	16.3	9.1	17.2	24.7	25.6	21.7	26.1
76–100 percent	9.7	11.8	3.7	9.4	19.1	21.7	11.2	20.4
Missing/school did not participate	32.8	32.4	32.8	31.5	2.7	2.0	3.3	8.0

See notes at end of table.

Table A-27-1. **Number and percentage of public schools, by school level and selected school characteristics: School years 1998–99 and 2008–09—Continued**

School characteristic	1998–99				2008–09			
	Total[1]	Elementary	Secondary	Combined	Total[1]	Elementary	Secondary	Combined
Region	100.0	100.0	100.0	100.0	100.0	100.0	100.0	100.0
Northeast	16.2	17.4	13.7	8.6	15.5	16.6	14.0	9.1
Midwest	29.2	28.5	31.5	28.5	26.9	26.3	29.8	23.7
South	33.0	32.8	32.3	40.2	34.4	34.5	31.5	38.4
West	21.6	21.3	22.5	22.7	23.1	22.5	24.7	28.8
School locale	†	†	†	†	100.0	100.0	100.0	100.0
City	†	†	†	†	26.0	27.2	22.1	28.3
Suburban	†	†	†	†	27.5	29.8	23.4	19.3
Town	†	†	†	†	14.4	13.5	16.4	14.5
Rural	†	†	†	†	32.0	29.4	38.2	37.9

— Not available.
† Not applicable.
# Rounds to zero.
[1] Total number of schools does not always equal the sum of schools by level because the total may include ungraded schools and schools that did not report grade spans.
[2] Includes charter, Title I, and magnet schools.
[3] Schools that did not report enrollment were excluded from the percentage distribution.
NOTE: A charter school is a school that provides free public elementary and/or secondary education to eligible students under a specific charter granted by the state legislature or other appropriate authority and that is designated by such authority to be a charter school. A Title I school is designated under appropriate state and federal regulations as a high-poverty school that is eligible for participation in programs authorized by Title I of P.L. 107-110. A magnet program is a special program designed to attract students of different racial/ethnic backgrounds in an effort to reduce, prevent, or eliminate racial isolation and/or provide an academic or social focus on a particular theme. A large number of schools did not report whether they were Title I or not in 1998–99. Race categories exclude persons of Hispanic ethnicity. For more information on race/ethnicity, the free or reduced-price lunch program, region, and locale, see *supplemental note 1*. Detail may not sum to totals because of rounding. For more information on the Common Core of Data (CCD), see *supplemental note 3*.
SOURCE: U.S. Department of Education, National Center for Education Statistics, Common Core of Data (CCD), "Public Elementary/ Secondary School Universe Survey," 1998–99 (version 1c) and 2008–09 (version 1b).

Table A-28-1. Number and percentage of public school students across schools, by percentage of students in school eligible for free or reduced-price lunch, school level, and race/ethnicity: School year 2008–09

| Race/ethnicity | Number of students[1] | Total | Percentage of students in school eligible for free or reduced-price lunch | | | | |
			0–25	26–50	51–75	76–100	Missing/ school does not participate
			Total[2]				
Total[3]	**49,053,786**	**100.0**	**28.5**	**29.2**	**23.3**	**17.3**	**1.8**
White	26,655,206	100.0	39.0	35.7	18.9	4.5	1.9
Black	8,225,299	100.0	10.5	21.1	30.5	35.2	2.7
Hispanic	10,439,072	100.0	13.3	19.6	29.5	36.6	1.0
Asian/Pacific Islander	2,419,695	100.0	41.2	26.1	18.5	12.9	1.3
American Indian/Alaska Native	583,384	100.0	13.5	26.7	30.4	26.5	2.8
			Elementary				
Total[3]	**31,430,207**	**100.0**	**25.3**	**26.3**	**24.8**	**22.1**	**1.5**
White	16,615,628	100.0	35.6	34.1	22.8	6.0	1.6
Black	5,288,220	100.0	8.3	16.9	28.5	44.0	2.3
Hispanic	7,077,394	100.0	11.5	15.6	27.5	44.7	0.7
Asian/Pacific Islander	1,551,549	100.0	39.8	23.9	18.7	16.5	1.1
American Indian/Alaska Native	361,356	100.0	10.2	23.5	32.6	30.8	2.9
			Secondary				
Total[3]	**16,070,956**	**100.0**	**35.0**	**34.9**	**20.3**	**7.9**	**1.8**
White	9,181,992	100.0	46.3	38.7	11.6	1.6	1.8
Black	2,632,013	100.0	14.8	30.1	34.6	17.7	2.8
Hispanic	3,075,913	100.0	17.2	28.6	34.5	18.5	1.2
Asian/Pacific Islander	820,013	100.0	43.9	30.2	18.2	6.2	1.4
American Indian/Alaska Native	190,366	100.0	19.4	34.6	27.1	16.3	2.7

[1] Includes students enrolled in schools that did not report free or reduced-price lunch eligibility.
[2] Includes students who attended combined elementary and secondary schools not shown separately.
[3] Includes students whose racial/ethnic group was not reported.
NOTE: The National School Lunch Program is a federally assisted meal program. To be eligible, a student must be from a household with an income at or below 130 percent of the poverty threshold for free lunch, or between 130 percent and 185 percent of the poverty threshold for reduced-price lunch. Race categories exclude persons of Hispanic ethnicity. Persons with unknown race/ethnicity are not shown. For more information on race/ethnicity and poverty, see *supplemental note 1*. For more information on the Common Core of Data (CCD), see *supplemental note 3*. Percent detail may not sum to percent totals because of rounding.
SOURCE: U.S. Department of Education, National Center for Education Statistics, Common Core of Data (CCD), "Public Elementary/ Secondary School Universe Survey," 2008–09.

Table A-28-2. Number and percentage of public school students within schools, by percentage of students in school eligible for free or reduced-price lunch, locale, and race/ethnicity: School year 2008–09

| Locale and race/ethnicity | Number of students[1] | Total | Percentage of students in school eligible for free or reduced-price lunch | | | |
			0–25	26–50	51–75	76–100
Total	**49,053,786**	**100.0**	**100.0**	**100.0**	**100.0**	**100.0**
White	26,655,206	54.3	74.5	66.5	44.1	14.1
Black	8,225,299	16.8	6.2	12.1	21.9	34.2
Hispanic	10,439,072	21.3	10.0	14.3	26.9	45.1
Asian/Pacific Islander	2,419,695	4.9	7.1	4.4	3.9	3.7
American Indian/Alaska Native	583,384	1.2	0.6	1.1	1.6	1.8
Race/ethnicity unknown	731,130	1.5	1.6	1.6	1.5	1.1
Total	**49,053,786**	**100.0**	**100.0**	**100.0**	**100.0**	**100.0**
City	14,323,420	29.2	17.3	20.9	32.7	58.1
Suburban	17,047,823	34.8	52.1	31.9	26.4	22.8
Town	5,998,669	12.2	6.7	16.8	16.1	8.5
Rural	11,683,874	23.8	23.8	30.3	24.7	10.7
City	14,323,420	100.0	100.0	100.0	100.0	100.0
White	4,513,958	31.5	57.6	51.0	27.4	9.9
Black	3,830,395	26.7	9.4	18.3	29.5	37.5
Hispanic	4,644,213	32.4	17.7	20.0	34.5	46.4
Asian/Pacific Islander	1,002,691	7.0	12.7	7.7	6.1	4.6
American Indian/Alaska Native	117,453	0.8	0.7	1.0	0.9	0.7
Race/ethnicity unknown	214,710	1.5	1.9	1.9	1.6	1.0
Suburban	17,047,823	100.0	100.0	100.0	100.0	100.0
White	9,512,154	55.8	75.6	57.5	32.5	11.9
Black	2,499,270	14.7	6.1	15.6	25.4	28.0
Hispanic	3,572,687	21.0	8.7	18.1	34.1	54.6
Asian/Pacific Islander	1,040,628	6.1	7.4	5.9	5.2	3.5
American Indian/Alaska Native	91,145	0.5	0.4	0.7	0.7	0.5
Race/ethnicity unknown	331,939	1.9	1.8	2.3	2.2	1.5
Town	5,998,669	100.0	100.0	100.0	100.0	100.0
White	4,104,322	68.4	86.0	80.1	61.1	25.9
Black	664,085	11.1	2.8	5.4	13.9	32.4
Hispanic	929,312	15.5	7.3	9.7	19.5	36.0
Asian/Pacific Islander	113,280	1.9	2.1	2.2	1.7	1.1
American Indian/Alaska Native	124,042	2.1	1.0	1.6	2.5	3.5
Race/ethnicity unknown	63,628	1.1	0.8	1.0	1.3	1.0
Rural	11,683,874	100.0	100.0	100.0	100.0	100.0
White	8,524,772	73.0	81.1	79.2	67.6	32.4
Black	1,231,549	10.5	5.1	7.9	13.5	30.8
Hispanic	1,292,860	11.1	7.8	8.8	14.0	25.4
Asian/Pacific Islander	263,096	2.3	4.0	1.9	1.2	1.1
American Indian/Alaska Native	250,744	2.1	0.7	1.2	2.7	9.6
Race/ethnicity unknown	120,853	1.0	1.3	1.0	0.9	0.8

[1] Includes students enrolled in schools that did not report free or reduced-price lunch eligibility.
NOTE: The National School Lunch Program is a federally assisted meal program. To be eligible, a student must be from a household with an income at or below 130 percent of the poverty threshold for free lunch, or between 130 percent and 185 percent of the poverty threshold for reduced-price lunch. Race categories exclude persons of Hispanic ethnicity. For more information on race/ethnicity, locale, and poverty, see *supplemental note 1*. For more information on the Common Core of Data (CCD), see *supplemental note 3*. Percent detail may not sum to percent totals because of rounding.
SOURCE: U.S. Department of Education, National Center for Education Statistics, Common Core of Data (CCD), "Public Elementary/Secondary School Universe Survey," 2008–09.

School-Age Children Living in Poverty

Table A-29-1. Percentage of 5- to 17-year-olds in families living in poverty, by region and state or jurisdiction: Selected years, 1990 through 2009

Region and state or jurisdiction	1990[1]	2000[2]	2008	2009	From 1990 to 2009	From 1990 to 2000	From 2000 to 2009	From 2008 to 2009
					Percentage point difference			
United States	**17.0**	**15.4**	**17.1**	**18.6**	**1.6**	**-1.6**	**3.2**	**1.6**
Northeast	14.3	14.3	15.0	15.7	1.4!	‡	1.4!	0.7!
Connecticut	9.8	9.6	11.5	11.5	1.7!	‡	1.9!	‡
Maine	12.3	12.0	16.7	16.0	3.7!	‡	4.0!	‡
Massachusetts	12.2	11.4	11.1	12.8	‡	-0.8	1.4!	1.7!
New Hampshire	6.4	6.7	8.4	9.5	3.2!	‡	2.8!	‡
New Jersey	10.8	10.5	11.7	12.6	1.9	‡	2.1	‡
New York	18.1	19.1	18.6	18.9	0.8!	1.0	‡	‡
Pennsylvania	14.5	13.6	15.6	16.5	2.0	-0.9	2.9	‡
Rhode Island	12.3	15.6	13.9	16.7	4.4!	3.3	‡	‡
Vermont	10.7	9.9	12.3	10.6	‡	-0.8!	‡	‡
Midwest	14.9	12.0	15.6	17.8	2.8	-2.9	5.8	2.2
Illinois	15.9	13.4	15.9	18.0	2.1	-2.5	4.6	2.1!
Indiana	12.8	10.6	16.2	17.4	4.6	-2.2	6.8	‡
Iowa	12.6	9.5	13.8	14.3	‡	-3.2	4.8	‡
Kansas	12.8	10.4	13.1	15.9	3.1!	-2.4	5.5	‡
Michigan	16.7	12.7	18.2	20.5	3.8	-4.0	7.8	2.3!
Minnesota	11.4	8.7	10.3	13.0	1.6!	-2.7	4.3	2.6!
Missouri	16.2	14.4	17.3	18.7	2.5!	-1.9	4.3	‡
Nebraska	12.0	11.1	13.2	13.8	‡	-0.9	2.7!	‡
North Dakota	15.9	12.2	12.7	12.1	‡	-3.6	‡	‡
Ohio	16.2	12.9	17.0	20.0	3.8	-3.3	7.1	3.1
South Dakota	18.7	15.5	18.1	16.6	‡	-3.3	‡	‡
Wisconsin	13.3	10.0	12.4	16.4	3.1	-3.3	6.4	4.0
South	20.5	17.6	19.1	20.8	‡	-2.9!	3.2	1.6
Alabama	23.2	20.3	20.2	22.3	‡	-2.9	2.0!	‡
Arkansas	23.8	20.1	23.1	24.9	‡	-3.7	4.8	‡
Delaware	11.0	10.9	16.2	14.8	3.8!	‡	3.8!	‡
District of Columbia	24.1	30.4	25.4	32.5	8.4!	6.3	‡	‡
Florida	17.5	16.6	16.9	19.9	2.4	-0.9	3.4	3.0
Georgia	18.9	16.1	18.4	20.4	1.5!	-2.7	4.3	2.0!
Kentucky	23.2	19.4	22.0	23.6	‡	-3.9	4.2	‡
Louisiana	30.4	25.3	22.1	22.7	-7.7	-5.1	-2.6!	‡
Maryland	10.5	9.8	10.2	10.1	‡	-0.7	‡	‡
Mississippi	32.6	26.0	29.1	29.3	-3.3!	-6.6	3.2!	‡
North Carolina	16.0	14.9	18.9	20.6	4.6	-1.1	5.7	1.7!
Oklahoma	19.9	17.7	21.4	21.8	1.9!	-2.2	4.1	‡
South Carolina	20.0	17.9	19.8	22.6	2.6!	-2.1	4.7	2.7!
Tennessee	19.5	16.6	19.7	21.0	1.5!	-2.9	4.5	‡
Texas	23.4	19.3	21.0	22.8	‡	-4.0	3.5	1.8
Virginia	12.4	11.4	13.3	13.1	‡	-1.0	1.6!	‡
West Virginia	24.0	22.9	19.5	21.4	-2.6!	-1.1	‡	‡

See notes at end of table.

Table A-29-1. **Percentage of 5- to 17-year-olds in families living in poverty, by region and state or jurisdiction: Selected years, 1990 through 2009—Continued**

Region and state or jurisdiction	1990[1]	2000[2]	2008	2009	Percentage point difference			
					From 1990 to 2009	From 1990 to 2000	From 2000 to 2009	From 2008 to 2009
United States	**17.0**	**15.4**	**17.1**	**18.6**	**1.6**	**-1.6**	**3.2**	**1.6**
West	16.2	16.2	16.6	18.2	2.0!	‡	2.0	1.6
Alaska	9.6	10.3	9.8	11.9	‡	0.7!	‡	‡
Arizona	20.3	17.8	19.8	21.7	1.4!	-2.5	3.9	1.9!
California	17.2	18.5	17.8	18.9	1.7	1.3	‡	1.2!
Colorado	13.7	10.0	14.0	16.1	2.4	-3.7	6.1	2.1!
Hawaii	10.5	12.9	8.2	12.9	2.4!	2.4	‡	4.7!
Idaho	14.4	12.6	16.2	17.3	2.9!	-1.8	4.7	‡
Montana	18.4	17.1	18.0	17.2	‡	-1.3	‡	‡
Nevada	11.7	12.3	14.0	16.5	4.8	0.6!	4.2	‡
New Mexico	26.3	23.6	23.0	25.6	‡	-2.7	‡	‡
Oregon	13.4	12.8	16.4	18.7	5.3	-0.6!	5.9	‡
Utah	10.9	8.9	9.7	11.8	‡	-2.0	2.9!	‡
Washington	12.8	12.2	13.7	15.6	2.8	-0.6	3.4	1.9!
Wyoming	12.6	12.5	11.8	10.8	‡	‡	‡	‡

! Interpret with caution. The standard error of the estimate is equal to 30 percent or more of the estimate's value.
‡ Reporting standards not met. The standard error of the estimate is equal to 50 percent or more of the estimate's value.
[1] Based on 1989 incomes collected in the 1990 decennial census.
[2] Based on 1999 incomes collected in the 2000 decennial census.
NOTE: Children in families include own children and all other children in the household who are related to the householder by birth, marriage, or adoption. For more information on poverty and region, see *supplemental note 1*. For more information on the American Community Survey, see *supplemental note 3*.
SOURCE: U.S. Department of Commerce, Census Bureau, 1990 Summary Tape File 3 (STF 3), "Median Household Income in 1989" and "Poverty Status in 1989 by Family Type and Age," retrieved May 12, 2005, from http://factfinder.census.gov/servlet/ DTGeoSearchByListServlet?ds_name=DEC_1990_STF3_&_lang=en&_ts=134048804959; Decennial Census, 1990, Minority Economic Profiles, unpublished data; Decennial Census, 2000, Summary Social, Economic, and Housing Characteristics; Census 2000 Summary File 4 (SF 4), "Poverty Status in 1999 of Related Children Under 18 Years by Family Type and Age," retrieved March 28, 2005, from http://factfinder.census. gov/servlet/DTGeoSearchByListServlet?ds_name=DEC_2000_SF4_U&_lang=en&_ts=134049420077; and American Community Survey (ACS), 2008 and 2009.

Rates of School Crime

Table A-30-1.   Rate of nonfatal incidents of crime against students ages 12–18 at school and away from school, by type of crime: Selected years, 1992–2008

[Per 1,000 students]

Location and year	At school				Away from school			
	Total	Theft	Violent	Serious violent[1]	Total	Theft	Violent	Serious violent[1]
1992	144	95	48	10	138	68	71	32
1993	155	96	59	12	139	69	70	35
1994	150	94	56	13	129	60	69	33
1995	135	85	50	9	119	61	58	23
1996	121	78	43	9	117	62	55	26
1997	102	63	40	8	117	58	59	24
1998	101	58	43	9	95	46	48	21
1999	92	59	33	7	78	39	39	18
2000	72	46	26	5	74	40	34	14
2001	73	45	28	6	61	33	28	11
2002	64	40	24	3	55	29	26	11
2003	73	45	28	6	60	28	32	12
2004	55	33	22	4	48	27	21	9
2005	56	32	24	5	46	23	24	10
2007	57	31	26	4	41	21	20	6
2008	47	24	24	4	38	19	19	8

[1] Serious violent crime is also included in violent crime.
NOTE: Total nonfatal crime includes violent crime and theft. Violent crime includes serious violent crime and simple assault. Serious violent crime includes rape, sexual assault, robbery, and aggravated assault. Theft includes purse snatching, pickpocketing, all burglaries, attempted forcible entry, and all attempted and completed thefts except motor vehicle thefts. Theft does not include robbery in which threat or use of force is involved. "At school" includes inside the school building, on school property, or on the way to or from school. Detail may not sum to totals because of rounding. There were changes in the sample design and survey methodology in the 2006 National Crime Victimization Survey (NCVS) that affected survey estimates. Due to this redesign, 2006 data are not presented. Data from 2007 onward are comparable to earlier years. For more information on NCVS, see *supplemental note 3*.
SOURCE: U.S. Department of Justice, Bureau of Justice Statistics, National Crime Victimization Survey (NCVS), selected years, 1992–2008.

Table A-30-2. Rate of nonfatal incidents of crime against students ages 12–18 at school and away from school, by type of crime and selected student characteristics: 2008

[Per 1,000 students]

Student characteristic	At school				Away from school			
	Total	Theft	Violent	Serious violent[1]	Total	Theft	Violent	Serious violent[1]
Total	**47**	**24**	**24**	**4**	**38**	**19**	**19**	**8**
Sex								
Male	55	26	29	6	45	20	25	10
Female	40	21	19	3!	31	18	12	5
Age								
12–14	49	22	27	5	25	14	12	4
15–18	46	25	21	4	49	24	25	11
Race/ethnicity[2]								
White	44	21	23	2!	40	21	19	6
Black	68	31	37	7!	40	16	25	15
Hispanic	47	27	20	9!	31	17	14	9!
Other	32	21!	11!	‡	38	24	15!	‡
Household income								
Less than $15,000	72	19!	54	‡	77	20!	57	14!
$15,000–29,999	41	25	16!	‡	62	29	33	10!
$30,000–49,999	49	26	23	6!	35	17	18	9!
$50,000–74,999	56	24	31	6!	31	18	12!	5!
$75,000 or more	41	25	16	1!	35	21	14	7!

! Interpret data with caution. The standard error of the estimate is equal to 30 percent or more of the estimate's value.
‡ Reporting standards not met.
[1] Serious violent crime is also included in violent crime.
[2] Other includes Asian, Pacific Islander, and American Indian/Alaska Native. Race categories exclude persons of Hispanic ethnicity.
NOTE: Total crime includes violent crime and theft. Violent crime includes serious violent crime and simple assault. Serious violent crime includes rape, sexual assault, robbery, and aggravated assault. Theft includes purse snatching, pickpocketing, all burglaries, attempted forcible entry, and all attempted and completed thefts except motor vehicle thefts. Theft does not include robbery in which threat or use of force is involved. "At school" includes inside the school building, on school property, or on the way to or from school. Detail may not sum to totals because of rounding and missing data on student characteristics. For more information on the National Crime Victimization Survey, see *supplemental note 3*.
SOURCE: U.S. Department of Justice, Bureau of Justice Statistics, National Crime Victimization Survey (NCVS), 2008.

Characteristics of Full-Time Teachers

Table A-31-1. Number and percentage distribution of full-time teachers, by school level, sector, and selected teacher characteristics: School years 1999–2000 and 2007–08

| Teacher characteristic | All teachers[1] | | Elementary | | | | | |
| | | | 1999–2000 | | | 2007–08 | | |
	1999–2000	2007–08	All	Public	Private	All	Public	Private
Total, number[1]	**3,107,900**	**3,501,400**	**1,931,800**	**1,755,500**	**176,300**	**2,103,400**	**1,936,400**	**166,900**
Total, percentage	**†**	**†**	**100.0**	**90.9**	**9.1**	**100.0**	**92.1**	**7.9**
Sex	100.0	100.0	100.0	100.0	100.0	100.0	100.0	100.0
Male	25.3	24.9	14.9	15.2	12.5	15.4	15.6	12.8
Female	74.7	75.1	85.1	84.8	87.5	84.6	84.4	87.2
Age	100.0	100.0	100.0	100.0	100.0	100.0	100.0	100.0
Under 30	17.7	18.2	18.2	17.9	20.8	18.7	18.7	18.6
30–39	21.9	26.1	21.9	21.9	21.8	26.3	26.8	20.9
40–49	31.1	23.6	31.4	31.7	27.9	23.8	23.9	22.2
50–59	26.0	25.7	25.2	25.3	24.0	25.6	25.4	28.2
60 and over	3.3	6.4	3.3	3.1	5.5	5.6	5.2	10.2
Race/ethnicity[2]	100.0	100.0	100.0	100.0	100.0	100.0	100.0	100.0
White	84.6	82.9	83.4	82.9	87.8	82.3	82.0	85.7
Black	7.3	6.9	8.0	8.4	4.7	7.2	7.4	5.2
Hispanic	5.6	7.2	6.0	6.1	4.7	7.7	7.9	6.0
Asian	1.6	1.3	1.8	1.8	2.1	1.3	1.3	2.0
Native Hawaiian/ Pacific Islander	—	0.2	—	—	—	0.2!	0.2!	0.2!
American Indian/ Alaska Native	0.8	0.5	0.8	0.8	0.8	0.4	0.4	0.4!
Two or more races	—	0.9	—	—	—	0.8	0.9	0.5!
Highest degree earned[3]	100.0	100.0	100.0	100.0	100.0	100.0	100.0	100.0
Less than bachelor's	1.3	1.5	0.7	0.2	5.6	0.8	0.2	7.1
Bachelor's	53.5	49.1	55.9	54.7	68.1	50.7	49.6	63.3
Postbaccalaureate	45.2	49.5	43.4	45.1	26.3	48.5	50.1	29.7
Master's	40.0	42.8	38.5	40.0	23.3	42.3	43.6	27.3
Education specialist or professional diploma	4.5	5.7	4.5	4.7	2.5	5.7	6.0	1.9
Doctoral or first-professional	0.8	1.0	0.5	0.5	0.5	0.5	0.5	0.5!
Average base salary, in constant 2009–10 dollars[4]	$49,800	$50,100	$49,100	$50,700	$32,500	$49,300	$50,500	$34,900
Base salary, in constant 2009–10 dollars, percentage[4]	100.0	100.0	100.0	100.0	100.0	100.0	100.0	100.0
Less than $30,000	6.0	3.9	6.8	2.9	45.1	4.7	2.1	34.4
$30,000–$44,000	40.3	39.2	41.3	40.9	44.8	40.5	39.7	49.3
$45,000–$59,000	29.3	34.1	28.9	31.0	8.4	33.5	35.3	13.2
$60,000–$74,000	17.1	15.8	16.3	17.8	1.5	14.8	15.8	2.8
$75,000 or more	7.4	7.1	6.7	7.3	0.3!	6.5	7.0	0.3!

See notes at end of table.

Table A-31-1. Number and percentage distribution of full-time teachers, by school level, sector, and selected teacher characteristics: School years 1999–2000 and 2007–08—Continued

	Secondary					
	1999–2000			2007–08		
Teacher characteristic	All	Public	Private	All	Public	Private
Total, number[1]	**983,100**	**919,800**	**63,300**	**1,093,400**	**1,032,800**	**60,600**
Total, percentage	**100.0**	**93.6**	**6.4**	**100.0**	**94.5**	**5.5**
Sex	100.0	100.0	100.0	100.0	100.0	100.0
Male	45.0	44.8	46.9	41.7	41.3	47.1
Female	55.0	55.2	53.1	58.3	58.7	52.9
Age	100.0	100.0	100.0	100.0	100.0	100.0
Under 30	16.5	16.2	20.2	17.6	17.5	18.6
30–39	21.6	21.7	20.0	25.6	26.0	17.9
40–49	30.7	30.9	28.1	23.2	23.3	20.6
50–59	28.1	28.3	26.1	26.2	26.1	27.3
60 and over	3.2	3.0	5.5	7.5	7.0	15.6
Race/ethnicity[2]	100.0	100.0	100.0	100.0	100.0	100.0
White	86.2	85.9	91.0	83.5	83.1	89.6
Black	6.4	6.7	1.8	6.7	7.0	1.9!
Hispanic	5.2	5.1	5.7	6.9	7.0	5.7
Asian	1.3	1.3	1.2	1.3	1.3	1.7!
Native Hawaiian/ Pacific Islander	—	—	—	0.2!	0.2!	‡
American Indian/ Alaska Native	0.9	0.9	0.4!	0.5	0.5	0.5!
Two or more races	—	—	—	0.9	0.9	0.6!
Highest degree earned[3]	100.0	100.0	100.0	100.0	100.0	100.0
Less than bachelor's	1.5	1.5	2.0	1.8	1.8	1.4!
Bachelor's	48.8	48.9	47.5	44.6	44.5	46.3
Postbaccalaureate	49.7	49.7	50.5	53.6	53.7	52.3
Master's	43.9	43.8	45.6	45.9	45.9	45.0
Education specialist or professional diploma	4.7	4.8	3.1	6.2	6.3	4.4
Doctoral or first-professional	1.2	1.1	1.8	1.6	1.5	2.9!
Average base salary, in constant 2009–10 dollars[4]	$51,200	$51,900	$40,600	$51,600	$52,100	$43,800
Base salary, in constant 2009–10 dollars, percentage[4]	100.0	100.0	100.0	100.0	100.0	100.0
Less than $30,000	4.4	3.3	19.9	2.3	1.8	11.2
$30,000–$44,000	38.4	37.7	48.7	36.8	36.2	48.0
$45,000–$59,000	30.0	30.4	23.2	35.1	35.5	28.1
$60,000–$74,000	18.6	19.4	6.3	17.6	18.1	9.6
$75,000 or more	8.7	9.1	1.8	8.2	8.5	3.1

— Not available.

† Not applicable.

! Interpret with caution. The standard error of the estimate is equal to 30 percent or more of the estimate's value.

‡ Reporting standards not met.

[1] Included in the total but not shown separately are full-time teachers in combined schools. There were 3.1 million full-time teachers in 1999–2000 and 3.5 million full-time teachers in 2007–08. This analysis focuses on full-time teachers who taught in elementary and secondary schools. These teachers made up 84 percent of all teachers in public and private schools in 1999–2000 and 82 percent in 2007–08.

[2] Race categories exclude persons of Hispanic ethnicity. In 1999–2000, "Asian" and "Native Hawaiian/Pacific Islander" were not reported separately; therefore, "Native Hawaiian/Pacific Islander" is included in "Asian." Respondents were not able to report more than one race in the 1999–2000 questionnaire. For more information on race/ethnicity, see *supplemental note 1*.

[3] "Less than bachelor's" includes teachers with an associate's degree and those without a postsecondary degree; in 2007–08, it also includes those with vocational certificates. "Education specialist/professional diploma" includes teachers with a certificate of advanced graduate studies in 1999–2000 and 2007–08. See glossary for the definition of first-professional degrees and a list of these degrees.

[4] Average base salary was calculated in 2009–10 school year constant dollars and adjusted using the Consumer Price Index (CPI). For more information on the CPI, see *supplemental note 10*.

NOTE: Detail may not sum to totals because of rounding. For more information on the Schools and Staffing Survey (SASS), see *supplemental note 3*.

SOURCE: U.S. Department of Education, National Center for Education Statistics, Schools and Staffing Survey (SASS), "Public School Teacher and Private School Teacher Data Files," 1999–2000 and 2007–08 and "Charter School Teacher Data File," 1999–2000.

Characteristics of Full-Time Teachers

Table A-31-2. Number and percentage distribution of full-time teachers, by school level, sector, and selected teaching characteristics: School years 1999–2000 and 2007–08

Teaching characteristic	Elementary					
	1999–2000			2007–08		
	All	Public	Private	All	Public	Private
Total, number[1]	**1,931,800**	**1,755,500**	**176,300**	**2,103,400**	**1,936,400**	**166,900**
Total, percentage	**100.0**	**90.9**	**9.1**	**100.0**	**92.1**	**7.9**
Years of teaching experience	100.0	100.0	100.0	100.0	100.0	100.0
3 or fewer	16.7	16.2	22.5	17.3	17.0	20.2
4–9	23.3	23.2	23.8	27.9	28.0	25.9
10–19	26.6	26.2	29.9	27.8	27.9	25.5
20 or more	33.4	34.4	23.8	27.1	27.0	28.5
Average years of teaching experience	14.4	14.6	12.6	13.5	13.5	13.7
Main teaching assignment						
Elementary						
General	57.5	56.7	65.8	53.8	53.1	61.9
English	3.0	2.9	3.7	4.0	4.0	4.0
English as a second language	1.3	1.4	‡	0.8	0.9	0.1 !
Mathematics	0.9	0.7	2.2	1.2	1.1	2.3
Special education	8.7	9.4	1.9	8.7	9.3	1.4
Other	8.7	8.3	12.1	8.6	8.0	15.8
Secondary						
English	4.7	4.8	3.5	5.2	5.2	4.7
English as a second language	0.2	0.2	‡	0.3	0.4	#
Foreign language	0.6	0.6	0.3 !	0.4	0.4	0.6
Mathematics	3.3	3.3	2.9	4.2	4.3	2.6
Science	2.7	2.7	2.4	2.8	2.8	3.0
Social sciences	2.7	2.7	3.2	3.4	3.5	2.2
Special education	0.8	0.8	0.4 !	2.0	2.2	0.1 !
Vocational/technical	0.8	0.9	‡	0.8	0.9	#
Other	4.2	4.5	1.4	3.8	4.0	1.3
Certification type[2]	100.0	100.0	100.0	100.0	100.0	100.0
Regular	86.5	89.8	54.5	86.1	88.5	57.3
Probationary	3.1	2.2	11.8	3.8	3.9	2.6
Provisional	2.7	2.7	2.9	—	—	—
Temporary	0.9	0.8	1.9	4.7	4.8	3.4
Waiver or emergency	0.5	0.5	0.5	2.0	2.0	1.7
No certification	6.3	4.0	28.4	3.4	0.7	35.0

See notes at end of table.

Table A-31-2. Number and percentage distribution of full-time teachers, by school level, sector, and selected teaching characteristics: School years 1999–2000 and 2007–08—Continued

| | Secondary | | | | | |
| Teaching characteristic | 1999–2000 | | | 2007–08 | | |
	All	Public	Private	All	Public	Private
Total, number[1]	**983,100**	**919,800**	**63,300**	**1,093,400**	**1,032,800**	**60,600**
Total, percentage	**100.0**	**93.6**	**6.4**	**100.0**	**94.5**	**5.5**
Years of teaching experience	100.0	100.0	100.0	100.0	100.0	100.0
3 or fewer	15.8	15.5	20.2	16.8	16.8	16.4
4–9	22.9	22.9	23.7	28.0	28.0	26.9
10–19	24.5	24.5	25.1	27.3	27.4	25.3
20 or more	36.7	37.1	31.0	28.0	27.8	31.4
Average years of teaching experience	15.1	15.2	14.0	13.7	13.6	15.2
Main teaching assignment						
Elementary						
General	0.3	0.3	‡	0.2!	0.2!	‡
English	#	#	‡	0.1!	0.1!	#
English as a second language	‡	‡	‡	#	#	#
Mathematics	#	#	‡	0.1!	0.1!	#
Special education	1.4	1.5	0.1!	0.6	0.6	0.6
Other	0.2	0.2	‡	0.2	0.2	‡
Secondary						
English	15.8	15.6	18.0	16.8	16.8	15.3
English as a second language	0.8	0.8	0.5!	0.9	0.9	#
Foreign language	5.8	5.6	9.1	5.6	5.4	9.6
Mathematics	13.2	13.1	14.9	14.3	14.3	13.7
Science	12.0	12.0	12.3	12.1	11.9	14.8
Social sciences	11.6	11.4	13.5	12.2	12.2	13.4
Special education	8.3	8.7	3.4	9.3	9.7	2.3!
Vocational/technical	10.6	11.0	3.5	11.5	12.1	2.8
Other	20.0	19.7	24.5	16.1	15.5	26.1
Certification type[2]	100.0	100.0	100.0	100.0	100.0	100.0
Regular	87.5	89.6	56.5	85.0	86.8	54.7
Probationary	2.9	2.6	7.8	4.3	4.5	1.7
Provisional	2.5	2.6	1.9	—	—	—
Temporary	1.0	1.0	1.8	4.1	4.3	1.4!
Waiver or emergency	0.6	0.6	0.3!	3.0	3.2	0.9!
No certification	5.5	3.7	31.8	3.5	1.3	41.4

— Not available.
Rounds to zero.
! Interpret with caution. The standard error of the estimate is equal to 30 percent or more of the estimate's value.
‡ Reporting standards not met.
[1] There were 3.1 million full-time teachers in 1999–2000 and 3.5 million full-time teachers in 2007–08. This analysis focuses on full-time teachers who taught in elementary and secondary schools. These teachers made up 84 percent of all teachers in public and private schools in 1999–2000 and 82 percent in 2007–08.
[2] The regular certification category includes regular or standard state certificates and advanced professional certificates (for both public and private school teachers) and full certificates granted by an accrediting or certifying body other than the state (for private school teachers only). Probationary certificates are for those who have satisfied all requirements except the completion of a probationary period. Provisional certificates are for those who are still participating in an "alternative certification program." Temporary certificates are for those who require additional college coursework and/or student teaching. Waivers or emergency certificates are for those with insufficient teacher preparation who must complete a regular certification program in order to continue teaching. No certification indicates that the teacher did not hold any certification in the state where the teacher had taught. The SASS questionnaire was redesigned in 2007–08 and the teacher certification question no longer included provisional certification as an option.
NOTE: Detail may not sum to totals because of rounding. For more information on the Schools and Staffing Survey (SASS), see *supplemental note 3.*
SOURCE: U.S. Department of Education, National Center for Education Statistics, Schools and Staffing Survey (SASS), "Public School Teacher and Private School Teacher Data Files," 1999–2000 and 2007–08 and "Charter School Teacher Data File," 1999–2000.

Teacher Turnover: Stayers, Leavers, and Movers

Table A-32-1. Number and percentage of public and private school teacher stayers, movers, and leavers: Various school years 1988–89 through 2008–09

Sector and year	Number				Percent		
	Total base year teachers[1]	Stayers	Movers	Leavers	Stayers	Movers	Leavers
Public							
1988–89	2,386,500	2,065,800	188,400	132,300	86.5	7.9	5.6
1991–92	2,553,500	2,237,300	185,700	130,500	87.6	7.3	5.1
1994–95	2,555,800	2,205,300	182,900	167,600	86.3	7.2	6.6
2000–01	2,994,700	2,542,200	231,000	221,400	84.9	7.7	7.4
2004–05	3,214,900	2,684,200	261,100	269,600	83.5	8.1	8.4
2008–09	3,380,300	2,854,900	255,700	269,800	84.5	7.6	8.0
Private							
1988–89	311,900	242,500	29,700	39,700	77.8	9.5	12.7
1991–92	353,800	287,100	23,200	43,500	81.1	6.6	12.3
1994–95	376,900	310,100	21,700	45,000	82.3	5.8	11.9
2000–01	448,600	354,800	37,600	56,200	79.1	8.4	12.5
2004–05	465,300	374,600	27,600	63,100	80.5	5.9	13.6
2008–09	487,300	386,000	24,000	77,300	79.2	4.9	15.9

[1] Base year refers to the year in which the Schools and Staffing Survey (SASS) was administered. The SASS is administered a year prior to the Teacher Follow-up Survey (TFS). The total number of base year teachers for any year is slightly lower than in previously published counts, as all teachers who responded to SASS but were ineligible for the TFS (e.g., because they died or moved out of the country) were removed from the weighted count of base year teachers.

NOTE: *Stayers* are those teachers who remained at the same school. *Movers* are those teachers who moved to a different school. *Leavers* are those teachers who left the profession. For more information on the Schools and Staffing Survey (SASS), see *supplemental note 3*. Detail may not sum to totals because of rounding.

SOURCE: Keigher, A. (2010). *Teacher Attrition and Mobility: Results From the 2008–09 Teacher Follow-up Survey* (NCES 2010-353), data from U.S. Department of Education, National Center for Education Statistics, Teacher Follow-up Survey (TFS), "Current Teacher Data File" and "Former Teacher Data File," 1988–89, 1991–92, 1994–95, 2000–2001, 2004–05, and 2008–09.

Table A-32-2. Percentage distribution of teacher stayers, movers, and leavers, by school sector and selected school characteristics in the base year: School year 2008–09

School characteristic in base year[1]	All school teachers			Public school teachers			Private school teachers		
	Stayers	Movers	Leavers	Stayers	Movers	Leavers	Stayers	Movers	Leavers
Total, number	**3,240,900**	**279,700**	**347,100**	**2,854,900**	**255,700**	**269,800**	**386,000**	**24,000**	**77,300**
Total, percentage	**83.8**	**7.2**	**9.0**	**84.5**	**7.6**	**8.0**	**79.2**	**4.9**	**15.9**
School classification									
Traditional public	84.6	7.5	7.9	84.6	7.5	7.9	†	†	†
Public charter	76.2	11.4	12.5	76.2	11.4	12.5	†	†	†
School level									
Elementary	84.3	7.6	8.1	84.8	7.7	7.5	78.9	6.4	14.6
Secondary	84.0	7.0	9.0	84.1	7.1	8.8	82.3	5.4!	12.2
Combined	79.6	5.6	14.8	81.4	9.3	9.3!	78.4	3.1	18.6
Enrollment size									
Less than 300	79.2	8.7	12.0	81.7	10.4	7.9	75.2	6.0	18.8
300–499	83.2	7.5	9.4	83.0	7.9	9.1	84.9	3.4!	11.7
500–999	85.7	7.0	7.2	85.7	7.2	7.1	86.1	4.4	9.4!
1,000 or more	85.1	6.1	8.8	85.4	6.3	8.3	77.2	‡	20.9
Racial/ethnic concentration									
More than 50 percent White	84.4	6.4	9.2	85.2	6.8	8.0	80.5	4.5	15.1
More than 50 percent Black	81.0	11.1	7.9	82.0	11.1	7.0	60.0	12.4!	27.6!
More than 50 percent Hispanic	86.3	8.2	5.5	86.4	8.2	5.4	84.7	‡	6.5!
Other	81.3	7.7	11.0	82.0	8.1	9.9	75.1	4.8!	20.1
Percentage of students in school eligible for free or reduced-price lunch									
0–25 percent	85.8	5.6	8.7	86.3	5.6	8.1	78.5	4.9	16.6
26–50 percent	82.9	7.6	9.5	83.0	7.8	9.2	81.1	‡	15.9
51–75 percent	83.6	7.8	8.6	83.8	7.7	8.6	74.6	‡	11.8!
76–100 percent	83.8	10.7	5.6	83.9	10.8	5.3	80.4	‡	‡
School did not participate in free or reduced-price lunch	80.5	5.2	14.3	87.4	6.8!	‡	79.3	4.9	15.8
Region									
Northeast	85.3	5.0	9.8	86.2	4.9	8.9	80.3	5.0	14.7
Midwest	86.2	6.1	7.7	87.3	6.4	6.4	78.8	3.8	17.3
South	81.4	8.7	9.9	82.0	9.1	8.9	77.5	5.4	17.2
West	84.0	8.1	7.9	84.3	8.4	7.3	81.9	5.3	12.9
Locale									
City	83.4	7.4	9.1	84.5	8.0	7.5	78.6	5.2	16.2
Suburban	83.6	7.1	9.3	84.3	7.5	8.3	79.1	4.8	16.2
Town	84.7	7.6	7.6!	84.9	7.6	7.5!	82.1	7.5!	10.3
Rural	84.1	6.9	9.0	84.4	7.2	8.4	80.4	3.4!	16.3

† Not applicable.
! Interpret with caution. The standard error of the estimate is equal to 30 percent or more of the estimate's value.
‡ Reporting standards not met.
[1] Base year refers to the year in which the Schools and Staffing Survey (SASS) was administered. SASS is administered a year prior to the Teacher Follow-up Survey (TFS). The total number of base year teachers for any year is slightly lower than in previously published counts, as all teachers who responded to SASS but were ineligible for the TFS (e.g., because they died or moved out of the country) were removed from the weighted count of base year teachers.
NOTE: *Stayers* are those teachers who remained at the same school. *Movers* are those teachers who moved to a different school. *Leavers* are those teachers who left the profession. Race categories exclude persons of Hispanic ethnicity. For more information on race/ethnicity, poverty, region, and locale, see *supplemental note 1*. For more information on the Schools and Staffing Survey (SASS), see *supplemental note 3*. Detail may not sum to totals because of rounding.
SOURCE: U.S. Department of Education, National Center for Education Statistics, Teacher Follow-up Survey (TFS), "Current Teacher Data File" and "Former Teacher Data File," 2008–09.

Table A-32-3. Number and percentage distribution of teacher stayers, movers, and leavers, by school sector and selected teacher characteristics in the base year: School year 2008–09

Teacher characteristic in base year[1]	All school teachers			Public school teachers			Private school teachers		
	Stayers	Movers	Leavers	Stayers	Movers	Leavers	Stayers	Movers	Leavers
Total, number	**3,240,900**	**279,700**	**347,100**	**2,854,900**	**255,700**	**269,800**	**386,000**	**24,000**	**77,300**
Total, percentage	**83.8**	**7.2**	**9.0**	**84.5**	**7.6**	**8.0**	**79.2**	**4.9**	**15.9**
Sex									
Male	83.7	7.5	8.8	84.4	7.8	7.9	80.0	5.7	14.3
Female	83.8	7.2	9.0	84.5	7.5	8.0	78.9	4.7	16.4
Age									
Under 30	75.2	14.1	10.7	76.1	14.7	9.2	68.9	10.0	21.1
30–39	83.4	7.0	9.6	84.4	7.3	8.4	76.9	4.9	18.2
40–49	88.9	6.4	4.6	89.6	6.6	3.9	83.7	5.4	10.9
50–59	85.8	5.3	8.9	85.9	5.7	8.4	85.2	2.4	12.4
60 and over	81.5	2.1	16.4	82.4	2.0!	15.6	77.7	2.7!	19.6
Race/ethnicity									
White	84.4	6.7	8.9	85.0	7.0	8.0	80.7	4.6	14.7
Black	79.8	10.3	9.9	80.5	10.4	9.0	67.2	8.6!	24.2!
Hispanic	82.0	10.3	7.7	83.8	10.7	5.6!	69.2	‡	23.7!
Asian, Native Hawaiian, or Other Pacific Islander	76.3	‡	12.9!	80.1	‡	8.0!	58.7!	‡	‡
American Indian/Alaska Native	79.1!	‡	‡	82.5!	‡	‡	‡	‡	‡
Two or more races	85.5	‡	‡	82.5	‡	‡	100.0	#	#
Highest degree earned[2]									
Less than bachelor's	77.9	‡	‡	80.8	‡	‡	72.9	‡	25.9
Bachelor's	83.2	8.1	8.7	83.9	8.7	7.4	79.2	5.0	15.8
Postbaccalaureate									
Master's	85.1	6.3	8.6	85.8	6.4	7.8	78.5	5.2	16.3
Education specialist or professional diploma	80.5	9.4	10.1!	79.8	9.7	10.5!	88.9	‡	‡
Doctoral or first-professional	84.4	‡	10.4!	82.5	‡	‡	89.3	‡	‡
Years as a teacher									
3 or fewer	75.2	12.8	11.9	76.2	14.1	9.7	70.5	6.5	22.9
4–9	82.4	8.5	9.1	83.4	8.6	7.9	74.8	7.8	17.4
10–19	89.7	4.9	5.3	90.4	5.2	4.4	84.3	2.8	12.9
20 or more	84.3	4.9	10.8	84.0	5.2	10.8	85.8	2.7	11.4

See notes at end of table.

Table A-32-3. Number and percentage distribution of teacher stayers, movers, and leavers, by school sector and selected teacher characteristics in the base year: School year 2008–09—Continued

Teacher characteristic in base year[1]	All school teachers			Public school teachers			Private school teachers		
	Stayers	Movers	Leavers	Stayers	Movers	Leavers	Stayers	Movers	Leavers
Total, number	**3,240,900**	**279,700**	**347,100**	**2,854,900**	**255,700**	**269,800**	**386,000**	**24,000**	**77,300**
Total, percentage	**83.8**	**7.2**	**9.0**	**84.5**	**7.6**	**8.0**	**79.2**	**4.9**	**15.9**
Teaching status									
Full-time	84.8	7.3	7.9	85.2	7.5	7.3	82.0	5.2	12.8
Part-time	74.8	6.8	18.4	77.0	7.8	15.2	67.5	3.6!	28.9
Certification type[3]									
Regular	85.1	6.7	8.2	85.2	6.9	7.9	84.3	4.0	11.7
Probationary	79.6	14.1!	6.3!	79.7	14.3!	‡	77.8	‡	‡
Temporary	82.9	8.7	8.4!	83.7	8.5	7.7!	67.8	‡	‡
Waiver or emergency	79.3	14.5	6.2!	78.2	15.7	6.0!	89.5	‡	‡
No certification	73.1	6.0	20.9	67.5	‡	‡	74.2	5.5	20.3
Main teaching assignment									
Early childhood/general elementary	86.1	7.2	6.7	87.0	7.4	5.6	79.7	6.5	13.8
Special education	77.4	9.8	12.8	78.0	9.8	12.3	62.9	‡	27.5!
Arts/music	88.3	6.8	4.9	88.4	7.5	4.1	87.9	‡	9.0
English/language arts	81.7	7.1	11.2	81.8	7.7	10.5	80.5	2.9!	16.5
Mathematics	85.6	6.1	8.3	85.6	6.7	7.7	85.3	‡	12.7!
Natural sciences	83.4	6.7	9.9	83.9	7.1	9.0!	80.6	4.8!	14.6!
Social sciences	84.0	7.6!	8.3	84.2	8.2!	7.6	83.3	4.3!	12.4!
Other	82.4	6.4	11.1	84.2	6.7	9.1	72.3	4.9	22.8
Median base salary, in constant 2009–10 dollars[4]	$46,000	$43,500	$44,700	$47,000	$44,000	$48,100	$34,400	$31,700	$30,200
Base salary, in constant 2009–10 dollars[4]									
Less than $30,000	80.3	6.0	13.7	86.0	7.3	6.7	74.9	4.9	20.2
$30,000–$44,999	82.6	8.8	8.5	83.0	9.2	7.8	79.7	6.2	14.1
$45,000–$59,999	84.2	6.6	9.2	84.1	6.9	9.1	86.0	3.4!	10.7!
$60,000–$74,999	85.4	6.8	7.8	85.6	7.1	7.2	81.9	‡	17.3!
$75,000 or more	89.8	‡	6.3!	89.8	‡	6.4!	90.9	‡	‡

\# Rounds to zero.
! Interpret with caution. The standard error of the estimate is equal to 30 percent or more of the estimate's value.
‡ Reporting standards not met.
[1] Base year refers to the year in which the Schools and Staffing Survey (SASS) was administered. SASS is administered a year prior to the Teacher Follow-up Survey (TFS). The total number of base year teachers for any year is slightly lower than in previously published counts, as all teachers who responded to SASS but were ineligible for the TFS (e.g., because they died or moved out of the country) were removed from the weighted count of base year teachers.
[2] "Less than bachelor's" includes teachers with an associate's degree, those with vocational certificates, and those without a degree. "Education specialist/professional diploma" includes teachers with a certificate of advanced graduate studies. See glossary for the definition and a list of first-professional degrees.
[3] The regular certification category includes regular or standard state certificates and advanced professional certificates (for both public and private school teachers) and full certificates granted by an accrediting or certifying body other than the state (for private school teachers only). Probationary certificates are for those who have satisfied all requirements except the completion of a probationary period. Temporary certificates are for those who require additional college coursework and/or student teaching. Waivers or emergency certificates are for those with insufficient teacher preparation who must complete a regular certification program in order to continue teaching. No certification indicates that the teacher did not hold any certification in the state where they had taught.
[4] Average base salary was calculated in 2009–10 school year constant dollars and adjusted using the Consumer Price Index (CPI). For more information on the CPI, see supplemental note 10.
NOTE: Stayers are those teachers who remained at the same school. Movers are those teachers who moved to a different school. Leavers are those teachers who left the profession. Race categories exclude persons of Hispanic ethnicity. For more information on race/ethnicity, see supplemental note 1. Detail may not sum to totals because of rounding. For more information on the Schools and Staffing Survey (SASS), see supplemental note 3.
SOURCE: U.S. Department of Education, National Center for Education Statistics, Teacher Follow-up Survey (TFS), "Current Teacher Data File" and "Former Teacher Data File," 2008–09.

Table A-33-1. Number and percentage distribution of school principals, by school level, school type, and selected principal characteristics: School years 1999–2000 and 2007–08

| Principal characteristic | All principals[1] | | Elementary | | | | | |
| | | | 1999–2000 | | | 2007–08 | | |
	1999–2000	2007–08	All	Public	Private	All	Public	Private
Total, number	**110,000**	**118,400**	**75,900**	**60,100**	**15,800**	**78,500**	**62,300**	**16,100**
Total, percentage	**100.0**	**100.0**	**100.0**	**79.2**	**20.8**	**100.0**	**79.5**	**20.5**
Sex	100.0	100.0	100.0	100.0	100.0	100.0	100.0	100.0
Male	53.7	49.0	44.9	48.2	32.4	40.1	41.1	36.3
Female	46.3	51.0	55.1	51.8	67.6	59.9	58.9	63.7
Age	100.0	100.0	100.0	100.0	100.0	100.0	100.0	100.0
Under 40	11.1	18.6	10.5	9.9	12.9	18.5	19.2	15.9
40–44	12.7	14.0	12.5	12.6	12.5	13.9	14.8	10.5
45–49	22.6	14.4	22.6	23.7	18.6	14.4	14.8	13.2
50–54	30.0	18.5	30.0	32.0	22.4	17.7	18.6	14.3
55 and over	23.7	34.4	24.3	21.8	33.6	35.4	32.6	46.1
Race/ethnicity[2]	100.0	100.0	100.0	100.0	100.0	100.0	100.0	100.0
White	83.9	82.4	82.2	81.2	86.2	80.7	79.5	85.4
Black	9.8	9.7	11.1	11.8	8.1	10.1	10.9	6.9
Hispanic	4.7	5.9	5.1	5.6	3.2	7.0	7.6	5.1
Asian	0.9	0.8	1.0	0.7	1.9	0.9	0.7!	1.6
Native Hawaiian/ Pacific Islander	—	0.1!	—	—	—	0.1!	‡	‡
American Indian/ Alaska Native	0.7	0.6	0.6	0.7	0.6!	0.6!	0.7!	‡
Two or more races	—	0.6	—	—	—	0.5	0.5!	0.8!
Highest degree earned	100.0	100.0	100.0	100.0	100.0	100.0	100.0	100.0
Bachelor's or less	8.7	8.8	7.6	1.8	29.3	7.6	1.2	32.2
Master's	53.4	58.5	54.1	53.9	54.7	59.4	61.3	52.0
Education specialist or professional diploma[3]	28.1	24.5	29.5	34.6	9.9	25.3	29.1	10.5
Doctoral or first-professional	9.8	8.1	8.9	9.7	6.1	7.7	8.3	5.2

See notes at end of table.

Table A-33-1. Number and percentage distribution of school principals, by school level, school type, and selected principal characteristics: School years 1999–2000 and 2007–08—Continued

Principal characteristic	Secondary					
	1999–2000			2007–08		
	All	Public	Private	All	Public	Private
Total, number	**23,100**	**20,500**	**2,600**	**24,500**	**21,600**	**2,900**
Total, percentage	**100.0**	**88.6**	**11.4**	**100.0**	**88.0**	**12.0**
Sex	100.0	100.0	100.0	100.0	100.0	100.0
Male	76.9	78.2	66.3	70.6	71.5	64.4
Female	23.1	21.8	33.7	29.4	28.5	35.6
Age	100.0	100.0	100.0	100.0	100.0	100.0
Under 40	9.9	10.0	9.6	18.7	19.0	16.2
40–44	13.1	12.9	14.6	14.4	14.6	12.9
45–49	22.8	23.1	20.4	15.1	15.4	12.8
50–54	32.8	33.5	28.0	21.0	21.5	17.3
55 and over	21.4	20.6	27.3	30.8	29.5	40.8
Race/ethnicity[2]	100.0	100.0	100.0	100.0	100.0	100.0
White	86.6	85.6	94.5	85.0	84.1	91.2
Black	7.6	8.4	‡	9.2	9.8	4.9!
Hispanic	4.0	4.1	3.1!	4.1	4.5	‡
Asian	0.7!	0.8!	‡	‡	‡	‡
Native Hawaiian/ Pacific Islander	—	—	—	0.1!	0.1!	‡
American Indian/ Alaska Native	1.1	1.1	‡	0.6!	0.4!	‡
Two or more races	—	—	—	‡	‡	‡
Highest degree earned	100.0	100.0	100.0	100.0	100.0	100.0
Bachelor's degree or less	2.9	1.4	14.5	3.3	1.3!	18.0
Master's	56.1	55.7	58.6	60.8	61.0	59.5
Education specialist or professional diploma[3]	29.5	31.3	16.0	26.6	28.6	11.8
Doctoral or first-professional	11.5	11.6	10.9	9.3	9.1	10.7

See notes at end of table.

Characteristics of School Principals

Table A-33-1. Number and percentage distribution of school principals, by school level, school type, and selected principal characteristics: School years 1999–2000 and 2007–08—Continued

| Principal characteristic | All principals[1] | | Elementary | | | | | |
| | | | 1999–2000 | | | 2007–08 | | |
	1999–2000	2007–08	All	Public	Private	All	Public	Private
Total, number	**110,000**	**118,400**	**75,900**	**60,100**	**15,800**	**78,500**	**62,300**	**16,100**
Total, percentage	**100.0**	**100.0**	**100.0**	**79.2**	**20.8**	**100.0**	**79.5**	**20.5**
Number of years as a principal	100.0	100.0	100.0	100.0	100.0	100.0	100.0	100.0
3 or fewer	29.6	34.4	29.6	29.5	29.9	34.0	34.1	33.5
4–9	29.9	33.2	28.9	30.0	24.8	33.2	35.3	25.0
10–19	27.8	22.7	28.5	28.5	28.5	22.9	23.0	22.7
20 or more	12.7	9.7	13.0	12.0	16.8	9.9	7.6	18.7
Number of years of teaching experience prior to becoming a principal	100.0	100.0	100.0	100.0	100.0	100.0	100.0	100.0
3 or fewer	9.9	10.1	7.8	4.9	18.8	7.9	3.2	25.9
4–9	29.7	31.5	29.1	29.5	27.4	31.0	33.0	23.1
10–19	43.1	41.1	44.8	47.1	36.0	43.5	46.2	33.0
20 or more	17.3	17.2	18.4	18.5	17.8	17.6	17.5	17.9
Median annual salary, in constant 2009–10 dollars[4]	$78,100	$81,900	$78,100	$83,200	$46,100	$81,900	$86,000	$51,200
Annual salary, in constant 2009–10 dollars, percentage[4]	100.0	100.0	100.0	100.0	100.0	100.0	100.0	100.0
Less than $30,000	3.6	3.4	3.1	0.2	14.3	2.4	‡	11.5
$30,000–44,999	7.1	5.4	7.3	0.9	32.2	5.1	0.6!	23.6
$45,000–59,999	10.9	10.5	10.7	6.3	27.9	10.1	4.8	31.7
$60,000–74,999	21.4	21.0	22.0	23.8	14.7	21.4	22.4	17.0
$75,000–99,999	39.5	37.4	41.0	49.9	6.6	39.8	47.4	8.9
$100,000 or more	17.4	22.3	15.8	18.8	4.3	21.2	24.7	7.2

See notes at end of table.

Table A-33-1. Number and percentage distribution of school principals, by school level, school type, and selected principal characteristics: School years 1999–2000 and 2007–08—Continued

	Secondary					
	1999–2000			2007–08		
Principal characteristic	All	Public	Private	All	Public	Private
Total, number	**23,100**	**20,500**	**2,600**	**24,500**	**21,600**	**2,900**
Total, percentage	**100.0**	**88.6**	**11.4**	**100.0**	**88.0**	**12.0**
Number of years as a principal	100.0	100.0	100.0	100.0	100.0	100.0
3 or fewer	29.6	30.3	23.4	35.0	35.5	31.0
4–9	33.5	33.7	32.0	35.6	36.6	28.8
10–19	26.2	25.9	28.8	22.7	22.5	24.3
20 or more	10.8	10.1	15.8	6.6	5.4	15.9
Number of years of teaching experience prior to becoming a principal	100.0	100.0	100.0	100.0	100.0	100.0
3 or fewer	7.4	6.4	15.5	8.4	6.8	20.4
4–9	31.1	31.6	27.3	34.5	34.9	31.5
10–19	44.0	44.8	37.7	39.7	41.5	26.7
20 or more	17.5	17.2	19.6	17.4	16.8	21.4
Median annual salary, in constant 2009–10 dollars[4]	$84,800	$86,900	$66,500	$88,000	$90,100	$67,600
Annual salary, in constant 2009–10 dollars, percentage[4]	100.0	100.0	100.0	100.0	100.0	100.0
Less than $30,000	1.2	0.1	10.7	0.7!	‡	5.7!
$30,000–44,999	1.5	0.6	9.1	1.8	0.8!	8.8
$45,000–59,999	7.9	6.3	21.5	5.8	3.6	22.2
$60,000–74,999	21.1	21.3	20.1	19.6	19.4	21.2
$75,000–99,999	42.4	44.8	23.1	39.5	41.8	22.2
$100,000 or more	25.8	27.0	15.6	32.6	34.3	19.8

— Not available.
! Interpret with caution. The standard error of the estimate is equal to 30 percent or more of the estimate's value.
‡ Reporting standards not met.
[1] Included in the total but not shown separately are principals in combined schools. This analysis focuses on principals in elementary and secondary schools. These principals made up 90 percent of all principals in 1999–2000 and 87 percent in 2007–08.
[2] Race categories exclude persons of Hispanic ethnicity. In 1999–2000, "Asian" and "Native Hawaiian/Pacific Islander" were not reported separately; therefore, "Native Hawaiian/Pacific Islander" is included in "Asian." Respondents were not able to report two or more races in the 1999–2000 questionnaire. For more information on race/ethnicity, see *supplemental note 1.*
[3] "Education specialist or professional diploma" is a certificate of advanced graduate studies. See glossary for the definition of this type of degree and for a list of first-professional degrees.
[4] Median annual salary was calculated in 2009–10 school year constant dollars and adjusted using the Consumer Price Index (CPI). For more information on the CPI, see *supplemental note 10.*
NOTE: Principals from Bureau of Indian Education schools were excluded from the analysis. Detail may not sum to totals because of rounding. For more information on the Schools and Staffing Survey (SASS), see *supplemental note 3.*
SOURCE: U.S. Department of Education, National Center for Education Statistics, Schools and Staffing Survey (SASS), "Public School Principal and Private School Principal Data Files," 1999–2000 and 2007–08, and "Charter School Principal Data File," 1999–2000.

Principal Turnover: Stayers, Leavers, and Movers

Table A-34-1. Number and percentage distribution of principal stayers, movers, and leavers, by sector and selected school characteristics in the base year: School year 2008–09

School characteristic	All school principals				Public school principals				Private school principals			
	Stayers	Movers	Leavers	Other	Stayers	Movers	Leavers	Other	Stayers	Movers	Leavers	Other
Total, number	**93,150**	**7,060**	**13,640**	**3,290**	**71,440**	**6,210**	**10,690**	**1,570**	**21,580**	**830**	**2,930**	**1,710**
Total, percentage	**79.5**	**6.0**	**11.6**	**2.8**	**79.5**	**6.9**	**11.9**	**1.8**	**79.8**	**3.1**	**10.8**	**6.3**
School classification												
Traditional public	79.8	6.9	11.9	1.5	79.8	6.9	11.9	1.5	†	†	†	†
Public charter	72.0	7.7!	12.8	7.4!	72.0	7.7!	12.8	7.4!	†	†	†	†
School level												
Elementary	80.2	6.3	11.0	2.5	80.4	7.0	11.0	1.5	79.7	3.6	10.6	6.1
Secondary	78.2	5.9	13.1	2.8	78.6	6.3	13.1	1.9	74.8	3.0!	12.9	9.4!
Combined	78.1	4.5	12.8	4.6	73.4	7.5	15.9	‡	81.6	2.2!	10.5	5.6
Enrollment size												
Less than 300	78.2	5.4	11.8	4.6	78.3	7.4	12.0	2.3!	78.2	3.1	11.5	7.3
300–499	78.9	7.2	12.0	2.0	77.8	7.7	12.5	2.0	88.1	2.7!	7.5	1.7!
500–999	81.7	5.6	11.4	1.3	81.6	5.7	11.5	1.3!	83.1	4.6	9.7	2.6!
1,000 or more	81.2	7.0	10.9	0.9!	80.7	7.3	11.1	0.9!	92.5	#	‡	‡
Racial/ethnic concentration												
More than 50 percent White	81.0	5.3	11.3	2.4	81.5	6.1	11.4	1.1	79.8	2.8	11.2	6.2
More than 50 percent Black	72.6	8.0	12.7	6.7	71.5	9.5	12.8	6.3	77.2	‡	12.4	8.2!
More than 50 percent Hispanic	75.7	8.1	13.7	2.4!	74.9	8.4	14.4	2.4!	83.2	5.4!	8.0!	‡
Other concentration	79.5	6.6	11.6	2.3	79.4	7.2	12.1	‡	79.8	4.1!	9.7	6.4!
Percentage of students in school eligible for free or reduced-price lunch												
0–25 percent	82.1	5.6	11.4	1.0!	81.9	6.0	11.2	0.9!	83.4	2.9	12.5	‡
26–50 percent	81.7	6.6	10.4	1.4	81.9	6.7	10.3	1.2!	78.0	‡	12.4!	5.2!
51–75 percent	79.8	6.2	12.0	2.0	79.8	6.4	12.2	1.6!	79.6	‡	6.9!	12.4!
76–100 percent	74.1	8.7	13.7	3.5	74.2	9.1	13.4	3.3!	72.8	‡	17.7	‡
Missing/school did not participate	77.8	3.7	11.6	6.9	69.3	‡	19.0	‡	79.6	3.1	10.0	7.3
Region												
Northeast	79.9	5.1	10.8	4.3	81.2	6.1	11.1	1.6!	76.7	2.5	10.2	10.6
Midwest	78.9	6.9	11.9	2.4	77.9	7.7	12.3	2.1	82.5	3.9	10.5	3.1!
South	79.3	6.3	11.9	2.5	79.0	7.2	12.4	1.5!	80.3	3.3	10.1	6.3
West	80.4	5.3	11.7	2.6	80.8	6.1	11.3	1.8!	79.0	2.3!	13.2	5.5
Locale												
City	79.6	6.3	11.2	2.9	78.3	7.6	11.4	2.7	82.4	3.3	10.9	3.4
Suburban	82.2	4.8	10.2	2.8	82.0	5.5	10.8	1.8!	82.7	3.2	8.7	5.4
Town	77.6	5.8	14.3	2.2!	77.9	6.5	14.0	‡	76.5	2.1!	16.1	5.4!
Rural	77.7	7.1	12.2	3.0	78.8	7.9	12.3	1.0!	72.2	3.0!	11.7	13.2

\# Rounds to zero.
† Not applicable.
! Interpret with caution. The standard error of the estimate is equal to 30 percent or more of the estimate's value.
‡ Reporting standards not met.
NOTE: Estimates and percentages for all school principals include BIE school principal rates and therefore public and private school estimates may not add to totals for all schools. *Stayers* are 2007–08 principals who were principals in the same schools in 2008–09. *Movers* are 2007–08 principals who were principals in different schools in 2008–09. *Leavers* are 2007–08 principals who were no longer principals in 2008–09. "Other" includes principals who had left their 2007–08 school, but for whom it was not possible to determine a mover or leaver status in 2008–09. For more information on the Schools and Staffing Survey (SASS), see *supplemental note 3*. Race categories exclude persons of Hispanic ethnicity. Schools with "Other" racial/ethnic concentration are those with more than 50 percent enrollment of a racial/ethnic group other than White, Black, or Hispanic, and schools where no racial ethnic group makes up more than 50 percent of total enrollment. Due to school nonresponse, student racial/ethnic concentration data are missing on 4,890 principals. For more information on race/ethnicity, poverty, region, and locale, see *supplemental note 1*. Detail may not sum to totals because of rounding.
SOURCE: U.S. Department of Education, National Center for Education Statistics, Schools and Staffing Survey (SASS), "Public School and Private School Data Files," 2007–08; "Public School Principal Status and Private School Principal Status Data Files," 2008–09.

Table A-34-2. Number and percentage distribution of principal stayers, movers, and leavers, by sector and selected principal characteristics in the base year: School year 2008–09

Principal characteristic	All school principals				Public school principals				Private school principals			
	Stayers	Movers	Leavers	Other	Stayers	Movers	Leavers	Other	Stayers	Movers	Leavers	Other
Total, number	**93,150**	**7,060**	**13,640**	**3,290**	**71,440**	**6,210**	**10,690**	**1,570**	**21,580**	**830**	**2,930**	**1,710**
Total, percentage	**79.5**	**6.0**	**11.6**	**2.8**	**79.5**	**6.9**	**11.9**	**1.8**	**79.8**	**3.1**	**10.8**	**6.3**
Sex												
Male	77.6	6.5	12.6	3.2	77.6	7.5	13.0	1.9	77.7	3.2	11.1	8.0
Female	81.3	5.5	10.7	2.4	81.3	6.4	10.8	1.6	81.6	3.0	10.6	4.8
Age												
Under 30	74.4	‡	13.6!	‡	88.2	‡	‡	‡	61.1	‡	23.6!	‡
30–39	79.7	8.5	8.6	3.2	81.3	9.6	7.3	1.8!	72.2	3.5!	14.5	9.8!
40–49	83.1	6.3	7.6	3.0	83.4	7.1	7.6	1.9!	82.1	2.7	7.6	7.6
50–59	79.1	5.6	13.0	2.2	78.8	6.2	13.5	1.5	80.4	3.6	11.2	4.8
60 and over	73.4	3.4	20.0	3.3	66.9	4.1!	26.7	‡	83.0	2.2	9.9	4.9
Race/ethnicity												
White	80.1	5.9	11.6	2.4	80.1	6.8	11.9	1.3	80.4	3.0	10.9	5.7
Black	77.0	6.7	11.4	4.9!	77.4	7.2	11.3	4.1!	74.9	4.3!	11.8!	9.0!
Hispanic	79.4	6.1!	10.8	3.7!	79.1	6.6!	11.7	‡	80.9	‡	6.2!	9.7!
Asian, Native Hawaiian, or Other Pacific Islander	70.1	‡	10.2!	‡	61.7	‡	‡	‡	85.9	‡	‡	#
American Indian/ Alaska Native	70.3	‡	16.0!	‡	74.3	‡	18.0!	‡	‡	#	#	‡
Two or more races	60.1	‡	26.5!	‡	66.1	‡	‡	#	45.9!	#	‡	‡
Highest degree earned[1]												
Less than bachelor's	69.6	‡	10.8!	19.2!	100.0	#	#	#	69.0	‡	11.0!	19.6!
Bachelor's	81.8	4.3!	8.3	5.6	76.8	‡	‡	6.3!	82.9	3.7!	8.0	5.4
Postbaccalaureate Master's	80.3	6.4	11.1	2.2	80.1	7.1	11.2	1.5	80.9	3.2	10.8	5.0
Education specialist or professional diploma	79.6	6.0	12.5	1.9	79.6	6.3	12.2	1.9	79.4	3.3!	15.5	‡
Doctoral or first-professional	74.8	6.5	15.7	3.0	74.2	7.2	16.5	2.1!	77.1	3.5!	12.9	6.5!
Years of experience as principal at any school												
Less than 3	78.8	8.0	9.7	3.5	80.5	9.5	8.0	2.0	72.9	2.7	15.6	8.8
3–5	81.1	6.4	9.3	3.2	82.2	6.8	9.1	1.8	76.2	4.6	10.1	9.1
6–9	82.0	5.2	10.8	2.0	82.1	5.7	10.8	1.4!	81.2	3.4	10.5	5.0
10 or more	77.6	4.7	15.3	2.5	74.5	5.6!	18.2	1.7!	84.7	2.6	8.5	4.2
Median base salary, in constant 2009–10 dollars[2]	$81,900	$81,600	$81,900	$65,700	$86,000	$81,900	$88,800	$85,800	$51,600	$53,600	$50,300	$38,200

\# Rounds to zero.
! Interpret with caution. The standard error of the estimate is equal to 30 percent or more of the estimate's value.
‡ Reporting standards not met.
[1] "Less than bachelor's" includes teachers with an associate's degree, those with vocational certificates, and those without a degree. "Education specialist/professional diploma" includes teachers with a certificate of advanced graduate studies. See glossary for the definition and a list of first-professional degrees.
[2] Median base salary and base salary percentages were calculated in 2009–10 school year constant dollars and adjusted using the Consumer Price Index (CPI). For more information on the CPI, see *supplemental note 10*.
NOTE: Estimates and percentages for all school principals include BIE school principal rates and therefore public and private school estimates may not add to totals for all schools. *Stayers* are 2007–08 principals who were principals in the same schools in 2008–09. *Movers* are 2007–08 principals who were principals in different schools in 2008–09. *Leavers* are 2007–08 principals who were no longer principals in 2008–09. "Other" includes principals who had left their 2007–08 school, but for whom it was not possible to determine a mover or leaver status in 2008–09. Race categories exclude persons of Hispanic ethnicity. For more information on race/ethnicity, see *supplemental note 1*. Detail may not sum to totals because of rounding. For more information on the Schools and Staffing Survey (SASS), see *supplemental note 3*.
SOURCE: U.S. Department of Education, National Center for Education Statistics, Schools and Staffing Survey (SASS), "Public School Principal and Private School Principal Data Files," 2007–08; "Public School Principal Status and Private School Principal Status Data Files," 2008–09.

Table A-34-3. Percentage distribution of school principal leavers, by total years of experience as a principal in any school in 2007–08 and 2008–09 status: School year 2008–09

2008–09 status of all leavers	Total	Total years of experience as a principal in any school in 2007–08			
		Less than 3 years	3–5 years	6–9 years	10 or more years
Public school principals					
Retired—not working outside of home	45.4	18.8	20.2	38.6	68.2
Not retired	54.6	81.2	79.8	61.4	31.8
Private school principals					
Retired—not working outside of home	22.1	‡	16.0!	13.4!	40.3
Not retired	77.9	88.0	84.0	86.6	59.7

! Interpret with caution. The standard error of the estimate is equal to 30 percent or more of the estimate's value.
‡ Reporting standards not met.
NOTE: *Leavers* are 2007–08 principals who were no longer principals in 2008–09. For more information on the Schools and Staffing Survey (SASS), see *supplemental note 3.* Detail may not sum to totals because of rounding.
SOURCE: U.S. Department of Education, National Center for Education Statistics, Schools and Staffing Survey (SASS), "Public School and Private School Data Files," 2007–08; "Public School Principal Status and Private School Principal Status Data Files," 2008–09.

This page intentionally left blank.

Table A-35-1.   Total revenues and percentage distribution for public elementary and secondary schools, by revenue source: School years 1989–90 through 2007–08

| | Revenues, in billions of constant 2009–10 dollars | | | | | | Percentage distribution | | | | | |
| | | | | Local | | | | | | Local | | |
Year	Total	Federal	State	Total	From property taxes	From other sources	Total	Federal	State	Total	From property taxes	From other sources
1989–90	$356.0	$21.7	$167.7	$166.6	$127.8	$38.8	100.0	6.1	47.1	46.8	35.9	10.9
1990–91	361.5	22.3	170.5	168.7	130.1	38.6	100.0	6.2	47.2	46.7	36.0	10.7
1991–92	367.9	24.3	170.6	173.0	134.7	38.3	100.0	6.6	46.4	47.0	36.6	10.4
1992–93	376.6	26.2	172.5	177.9	132.5	45.3	100.0	7.0	45.8	47.2	35.2	12.0
1993–94	385.6	27.2	174.1	184.3	144.9	39.4	100.0	7.1	45.2	47.8	37.6	10.2
1994–95	393.6	26.8	184.1	182.8	141.2	41.6	100.0	6.8	46.8	46.4	35.9	10.6
1995–96	403.6	26.8	191.7	185.1	142.8	42.3	100.0	6.6	47.5	45.9	35.4	10.5
1996–97	416.1	27.4	199.7	189.0	145.3	43.6	100.0	6.6	48.0	45.4	34.9	10.5
1997–98	436.7	29.8	211.2	195.7	149.0	46.8	100.0	6.8	48.4	44.8	34.1	10.7
1998–99	457.6	32.3	223.0	202.3	157.4	44.9	100.0	7.1	48.7	44.2	34.4	9.8
1999–2000	477.5	34.7	236.4	206.4	159.7	46.7	100.0	7.3	49.5	43.2	33.4	9.8
2000–01	496.8	36.0	247.1	213.7	164.1	49.6	100.0	7.3	49.7	43.0	33.0	10.0
2001–02	510.2	40.3	251.2	218.7	171.6	47.1	100.0	7.9	49.2	42.9	33.6	9.2
2002–03	523.8	44.6	255.0	224.1	176.8	47.4	100.0	8.5	48.7	42.8	33.7	9.0
2003–04	538.1	48.8	253.2	236.1	187.0	49.1	100.0	9.1	47.1	43.9	34.8	9.1
2004–05	551.5	50.7	258.4	242.4	189.8	52.6	100.0	9.2	46.9	44.0	34.4	9.5
2005–06	567.0	51.8	263.7	251.5	194.2	57.3	100.0	9.1	46.5	44.4	34.2	10.1
2006–07	590.0	50.1	279.9	260.1	199.9	60.2	100.0	8.5	47.4	44.1	33.9	10.2
2007–08	598.6	48.8	289.4	260.4	201.2	59.2	100.0	8.2	48.3	43.5	33.6	9.9

NOTE: Detail may not sum to totals because of rounding. Estimates are revised from previous publications. Revenues are in constant 2009–10 dollars, adjusted using the Consumer Price Index (CPI). For more information about the CPI and revenues for public elementary and secondary schools, see *supplemental note 10*. For more information about the Common Core of Data, see *supplemental note 3*.
SOURCE: U.S. Department of Education, National Center for Education Statistics, Common Core of Data (CCD), "National Public Education Financial Survey," 1989–90 through 2007–08.

This indicator continues on page 264.

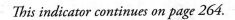

Public School Revenue Sources

Table A-35-2. Total revenues and percentage distribution for public elementary and secondary schools, by revenue source and state: School year 2007–08

| State | Revenues, in billions of constant 2009–10 dollars | | | | | | Percentage distribution | | | | | |
| | | | | Local | | | | | | Local | | |
	Total	Federal	State	Total	From property taxes	From other sources	Total	Federal	State	Total	From property taxes	From other sources
United States	**$598.6**	**$48.8**	**$289.4**	**$260.4**	**$201.2**	**$59.2**	**100.0**	**8.2**	**48.3**	**43.5**	**33.6**	**9.9**
Alabama	7.9	0.8	4.8	2.3	1.0	1.3	100.0	9.7	60.6	29.8	13.1	16.7
Alaska	2.3	0.3	1.6	0.5	0.2	0.3	100.0	13.4	66.3	20.4	8.9	11.4
Arizona	10.5	1.1	5.4	4.0	3.1	0.8	100.0	10.6	51.7	37.7	29.6	8.1
Arkansas	4.8	0.5	2.7	1.6	1.3	0.3	100.0	10.8	56.7	32.5	26.5	6.0
California	72.9	6.8	44.7	21.4	15.9	5.5	100.0	9.4	61.3	29.3	21.8	7.6
Colorado	8.3	0.6	3.5	4.2	3.3	1.0	100.0	6.9	42.2	50.9	39.4	11.6
Connecticut	9.7	0.4	3.8	5.4	5.3	0.2	100.0	4.4	39.6	56.0	54.2	1.8
Delaware	1.7	0.1	1.1	0.5	0.4	0.1	100.0	7.9	62.0	30.1	25.0	5.1
District of Columbia	1.4	0.2	†	1.2	0.4	0.9	100.0	11.4	†	88.6	25.3	63.3
Florida	30.0	2.6	11.7	15.8	12.9	2.9	100.0	8.6	38.8	52.5	43.0	9.6
Georgia	19.1	1.5	8.7	8.9	6.0	2.9	100.0	8.0	45.4	46.6	31.4	15.2
Hawaii	2.6	0.3	2.2	0.1	0.0	0.1	100.0	12.2	84.8	3.0	†	3.0
Idaho	2.2	0.2	1.5	0.5	0.4	0.1	100.0	9.9	67.1	23.1	17.5	5.6
Illinois	26.0	2.0	8.1	15.9	13.3	2.5	100.0	7.9	31.2	60.9	51.2	9.7
Indiana	12.6	0.9	6.7	5.0	3.3	1.6	100.0	7.1	53.5	39.4	26.4	13.0
Iowa	5.4	0.4	2.5	2.5	1.6	0.9	100.0	7.6	46.5	45.9	30.1	15.8
Kansas	5.7	0.4	3.3	2.0	1.5	0.5	100.0	7.9	57.5	34.7	25.9	8.7
Kentucky	6.7	0.7	3.8	2.1	1.4	0.7	100.0	10.8	57.3	31.9	21.3	10.6
Louisiana	8.0	1.3	3.6	3.1	1.1	2.0	100.0	16.8	44.8	38.4	13.8	24.7
Maine	2.7	0.2	1.2	1.2	1.1	0.1	100.0	9.0	44.9	46.1	43.1	3.0
Maryland	13.4	0.7	5.6	7.0	3.3	3.7	100.0	5.5	42.1	52.4	24.5	28.0
Massachusetts	15.0	0.8	6.3	7.9	7.4	0.6	100.0	5.1	41.9	53.0	49.1	3.9
Michigan	20.1	1.6	11.6	7.0	5.8	1.2	100.0	7.8	57.5	34.7	28.9	5.7
Minnesota	10.5	0.6	6.9	3.0	1.7	1.3	100.0	5.9	65.9	28.2	16.2	12.0
Mississippi	4.5	0.7	2.4	1.3	1.0	0.3	100.0	16.1	54.5	29.4	22.4	7.0
Missouri	10.1	0.8	3.4	5.9	4.5	1.5	100.0	8.1	33.3	58.6	44.2	14.4
Montana	1.6	0.2	0.8	0.6	0.4	0.2	100.0	12.1	49.7	38.2	22.9	15.2
Nebraska	3.4	0.3	1.1	1.9	1.7	0.3	100.0	9.1	33.1	57.8	49.6	8.2
Nevada	4.5	0.3	1.4	2.8	1.3	1.5	100.0	6.6	30.8	62.6	29.4	33.2
New Hampshire	2.7	0.1	1.0	1.5	1.4	0.1	100.0	5.2	38.6	56.2	52.7	3.5

See notes at end of table.

Table A-35-2. Total revenues and percentage distribution for public elementary and secondary schools, by revenue source and state: School year 2007–08—Continued

| | Revenues, in billions of constant 2008–09 dollars | | | | | | Percentage distribution | | | | | |
| | | | | Local | | | | | | Local | | |
State	Total	Federal	State	Total	From property taxes	From other sources	Total	Federal	State	Total	From property taxes	From other sources
United States	**$598.6**	**$48.8**	**$289.4**	**$260.4**	**$201.2**	**$59.2**	**100.0**	**8.2**	**48.3**	**43.5**	**33.6**	**9.9**
New Jersey	25.5	1.0	10.7	13.7	12.8	0.9	100.0	4.0	42.1	54.0	50.3	3.7
New Mexico	3.7	0.5	2.6	0.6	0.4	0.2	100.0	13.6	70.8	15.6	11.1	4.5
New York	54.0	3.2	24.2	26.6	23.8	2.8	100.0	6.0	44.8	49.2	44.0	5.2
North Carolina	12.7	1.3	8.4	3.1	2.4	0.7	100.0	10.0	65.7	24.3	18.6	5.8
North Dakota	1.1	0.1	0.4	0.5	0.4	0.1	100.0	13.8	36.3	49.9	39.1	10.8
Ohio	23.3	1.7	10.6	11.0	8.8	2.2	100.0	7.3	45.6	47.1	37.7	9.5
Oklahoma	5.6	0.7	3.0	1.9	1.3	0.6	100.0	11.8	54.2	34.0	23.8	10.2
Oregon	6.3	0.6	3.3	2.4	1.8	0.6	100.0	9.1	52.3	38.6	28.9	9.7
Pennsylvania	25.6	1.8	9.3	14.4	10.7	3.7	100.0	7.2	36.5	56.3	41.9	14.3
Rhode Island	2.3	0.2	0.9	1.2	1.2	#	100.0	7.8	39.9	52.3	50.6	1.7
South Carolina	8.0	0.7	4.0	3.2	2.4	0.8	100.0	9.2	50.8	40.0	29.6	10.4
South Dakota	1.2	0.2	0.4	0.6	0.5	0.1	100.0	15.3	33.9	50.8	41.6	9.2
Tennessee	8.4	0.9	3.8	3.7	1.7	2.0	100.0	10.5	45.6	43.9	20.5	23.5
Texas	46.7	4.7	20.9	21.1	18.1	3.0	100.0	10.0	44.8	45.2	38.7	6.5
Utah	4.5	0.4	2.6	1.6	1.1	0.5	100.0	7.8	56.7	35.6	24.7	10.8
Vermont	1.5	0.1	1.3	0.1	#	0.1	100.0	6.3	85.9	7.9	0.1	7.7
Virginia	14.9	0.9	6.1	7.9	3.8	4.1	100.0	6.2	41.0	52.9	25.6	27.3
Washington	11.4	0.9	7.1	3.3	2.6	0.7	100.0	8.1	62.5	29.4	23.2	6.3
West Virginia	3.2	0.4	1.9	1.0	0.8	0.1	100.0	10.9	59.1	29.9	25.9	4.0
Wisconsin	10.7	0.7	5.4	4.7	4.2	0.5	100.0	6.4	50.0	43.6	39.0	4.6
Wyoming	1.6	0.1	0.9	0.7	0.4	0.2	100.0	6.4	52.8	40.8	27.2	13.6

† Not applicable.
# Rounds to zero.
NOTE: Detail may not sum to totals because of rounding. Both the District of Columbia and Hawaii have only one school district each; therefore, neither is comparable to the other states. Revenues are in constant 2009–10 dollars, adjusted using the Consumer Price Index (CPI). For more information about the CPI and revenues for public elementary and secondary schools, see *supplemental note 10*. For more information about the Common Core of Data, see *supplemental note 3*.
SOURCE: U.S. Department of Education, National Center for Education Statistics, Common Core of Data (CCD), "National Public Education Financial Survey," 2007–08.

Table A-36-1. Total expenditures per student in fall enrollment in public elementary and secondary schools, percentage distribution of current expenditures, and percent change of total expenditures by type and object: Selected school years 1989–90 through 2007–08

Type and object	Expenditures			Percentage distribution of current expenditures			Percent change of total expenditures		
	1989–90	1998–99	2007–08	1989–90	1998–99	2007–08	1989–90 to 1998–99	1998–99 to 2007–08	1989–90 to 2007–08
	[In current dollars]								
Total expenditures[1]	**$5,174**	**$7,533**	**$11,952**	†	†	†	**46**	**59**	**131**
Current expenditures[2]	4,643	6,508	10,297	100	100	100	40	58	122
Salaries	3,045	4,225	6,175	66	65	60	39	46	103
Employee benefits	775	1,078	2,093	17	17	20	39	94	170
Purchased services	383	583	1,001	8	9	10	52	72	161
Supplies	347	507	840	7	8	8	46	66	142
Tuition and other	93	115	189	2	2	2	24	64	104
Capital outlay	439	849	1,336	†	†	†	94	57	205
Interest on school debt	93	176	319	†	†	†	89	81	242
	[In constant 2009–10 dollars[3]]								
Total expenditures[1]	**$8,832**	**$9,923**	**$12,236**	†	†	†	**12**	**23**	**39**
Current expenditures[2]	7,925	8,572	10,542	100	100	100	8	23	33
Salaries	5,198	5,565	6,321	66	65	60	7	14	22
Employee benefits	1,323	1,420	2,142	17	17	20	7	51	62
Purchased services	654	768	1,025	8	9	10	17	33	57
Supplies	592	668	860	7	8	8	13	29	45
Tuition and other	158	151	193	2	2	2	-4	28	22
Capital outlay	749	1,119	1,368	†	†	†	49	22	83
Interest on school debt	159	232	326	†	†	†	46	41	105

† Not applicable.
[1] Excludes "Other current expenditures" such as community services, private school programs, adult education, and other programs not allocable to expenditures per student at public schools.
[2] Includes estimated data for 1989–90 for food services and enterprise operations by object because those data were not collected for that year.
[3] Expenditures are in constant 2009–10 dollars, adjusted using the Consumer Price Index (CPI). For more information about the CPI, see *supplemental note 10*.
NOTE: Detail may not sum to totals because of rounding. Estimates are revised from previous editions. The category of total expenditures is broken down by type (current expenditures, capital outlay, and interest on debt). Current expenditures, which is one component of total expenditures, can be broken down by both the service or commodity bought (object) as well as the activity that is supported by the service or commodity bought (function). For more information about classifications of expenditures, see *supplemental note 10*. For more information about the Common Core of Data (CCD), see *supplemental note 3*.
SOURCE: U.S. Department of Education, National Center for Education Statistics, Common Core of Data (CCD), "National Public Education Financial Survey," 1989–90, 1998–99, and 2007–08.

Table A-36-2. Current expenditures per student in fall enrollment in public elementary and secondary schools, percentage distribution of current expenditures, and percent change of current expenditures, by function and object: Selected school years 1989–90 through 2007–08

[In constant 2009–10 dollars]

Function and object	Expenditures			Percentage distribution of current expenditures			Percent change of current expenditures		
	1989–90	1998–99	2007–08	1989–90	1998–99	2007–08	1989–90 to 1998–99	1998–99 to 2007–08	1989–90 to 2007–08
Current expenditures	**$7,925**	**$8,572**	**$10,542**	**100**	**100**	**100**	**8**	**23**	**33**
Instruction	4,781	5,286	6,411	60	62	61	11	21	34
Salaries	3,551	3,838	4,299	45	45	41	8	12	21
Employee benefits	872	963	1,441	11	11	14	11	50	65
Purchased services	108	156	255	1	2	2	45	64	136
Supplies	180	243	294	2	3	3	35	21	63
Tuition and other	70	87	122	1	1	1	24	41	75
Administration	688	662	796	9	8	8	-4	20	16
Salaries	455	452	509	6	5	5	-1	13	12
Employee benefits	120	116	171	2	1	2	-3	47	42
Purchased services	69	65	83	1	1	1	-6	28	21
Supplies	15	14	15	#	#	#	-3	4	1
Tuition and other	29	14	17	#	#	#	-51	18	-42
Student and staff support[1]	887	1,074	1,436	11	13	14	21	34	62
Salaries	578	672	852	7	8	8	16	27	47
Employee benefits	154	171	282	2	2	3	11	65	83
Purchased services	74	135	197	1	2	2	81	46	164
Supplies	52	61	73	1	1	1	19	18	41
Tuition and other	28	34	33	#	#	#	20	#	16
Operation and maintenance	853	832	1,027	11	10	10	-2	23	20
Transportation	338	346	448	4	4	4	2	29	32
Food services	342	347	399	4	4	4	2	15	17
Enterprise operations[2]	36	25	25	#	#	#	-32	0	-32

Rounds to zero.
[1] Includes expenditures for student support, other instructional staff, and other support services.
[2] Includes expenditures for operations funded by sales of products or services, along with amounts for direct program support made available by state education agencies for local school districts.
NOTE: Detail may not sum to totals because of rounding. Estimates are revised from previous editions. Expenditures are in constant 2009–10 dollars, adjusted using the Consumer Price Index (CPI). For more information about the CPI, see *supplemental note 10*. The category of total expenditures is broken down by type (current expenditures, capital outlay, and interest on debt). Current expenditures, which is one component of total expenditures, can be broken down by both the service or commodity bought (object) as well as the activity that is supported by the service or commodity bought (function). Breakouts of operation and maintenance, transportation, food services and enterprise operations by object are also available, but are not shown. For more information about classifications of expenditures, see *supplemental note 10*. For more information about the Common Core of Data (CCD), see *supplemental note 3*.
SOURCE: U.S. Department of Education, National Center for Education Statistics, Common Core of Data (CCD), "National Public Education Financial Survey," 1989–90, 1998–99, and 2007–08.

Variations in Instruction Expenditures

Table A-37-1. Variation and percentage distribution of variation in instruction expenditures per student in unified public elementary and secondary school districts, by source of variation: School years 1989–90 through 2007–08

School year	Theil coefficient[1]			Percentage distribution		
	Total	Between-state component	Within-state component	Total	Between-state component	Within-state component
1989–90	0.0448	0.0322	0.0125	100.0	72.0	28.0
1990–91	0.0469	0.0346	0.0123	100.0	73.8	26.2
1991–92	0.0434	0.0320	0.0115	100.0	73.6	26.4
1992–93	0.0437	0.0324	0.0113	100.0	74.2	25.8
1993–94	0.0405	0.0301	0.0104	100.0	74.3	25.7
1994–95	0.0389	0.0288	0.0100	100.0	74.2	25.8
1995–96	0.0373	0.0279	0.0094	100.0	74.8	25.2
1996–97	0.0349	0.0257	0.0092	100.0	73.7	26.3
1997–98	0.0332	0.0246	0.0086	100.0	74.0	26.0
1998–99	0.0335	0.0249	0.0087	100.0	74.2	25.8
1999–2000	0.0337	0.0253	0.0085	100.0	74.9	25.1
2000–01	0.0370	0.0280	0.0090	100.0	75.7	24.3
2001–02	0.0373	0.0283	0.0089	100.0	76.1	23.9
2002–03	0.0391	0.0303	0.0088	100.0	77.6	22.4
2003–04	0.0420	0.0327	0.0093	100.0	77.9	22.1
2004–05	0.0456	0.0359	0.0097	100.0	78.7	21.3
2005–06	0.0487	0.0380	0.0107	100.0	78.1	21.9
2006–07	0.0505	0.0397	0.0108	100.0	78.6	21.4
2007–08	0.0522	0.0410	0.0113	100.0	78.4	21.6

[1] The *Theil coefficient* measures variation for groups within a set (i.e., states within the country) and indicates relative variation and any differences that may exist among them. It can be decomposed into components measuring between-state and within-state variation in expenditures per student. It has a minimum value of zero, and increasing values indicate increases in the variation, with a maximum possible value of 1.0. The value of the *Theil coefficient* remains unchanged if expenditures in all districts are increased by the same percentage; therefore it was not necessary to adjust instruction expenditures for inflation at the national level. For more information on the variation in expenditures per student and the *Theil coefficient,* see *supplemental note 10.*
NOTE: Detail may not sum to totals because of rounding. Some data have been revised from previously published data. Public elementary and secondary unified districts are those districts that serve both elementary and secondary grades. In 2007–08, approximately 92 percent of all public elementary and secondary school students were enrolled in unified school districts. For more information on the classifications of expenditures for elementary and secondary education, see *supplemental note 10.* For more information on the Common Core of Data (CCD), see *supplemental note 3.*
SOURCE: U.S. Department of Education, National Center for Education Statistics (NCES), Common Core of Data (CCD), "NCES Longitudinal School District Fiscal-Nonfiscal (FNF) File, Fiscal Years 1990 through 2002" and "School District Finance Survey (Form F-33)," 2002–03 through 2007–08.

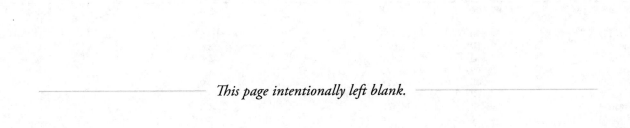

This page intentionally left blank.

Education Expenditures by Country

Table A-38-1. Annual educational expenditures per student on public and private institutions, and expenditures as a percentage of gross domestic product (GDP) in OECD countries, by level of education: 2007

Country	Expenditures per student		Expenditures as a percentage of GDP			GDP per capita
	Elementary and secondary	Postsecondary	Total[1]	Elementary and secondary	Postsecondary	
OECD average	**$7,401**	**$12,471**	**5.7**	**3.6**	**1.5**	**$32,219**
Australia	7,590	14,726	5.2	3.5	1.5	37,615
Austria	9,959	15,039	5.4	3.6	1.3	36,839
Belgium	8,333	13,482	6.1	4.1	1.3	34,662
Canada[2]	8,045	20,278	6.1	3.5	2.6	36,397
Chile[3]	2,245	6,626	6.4	3.9	2.0	14,106
Czech Republic	4,712	8,209	4.6	2.8	1.2	23,995
Denmark	9,448	16,466	7.1	4.3	1.7	36,326
Estonia	4,637	5,214	5.0	3.3	1.3	20,620
Finland	7,216	13,566	5.6	3.6	1.6	35,322
France	8,070	12,773	6.0	3.9	1.4	32,495
Germany	7,243	13,823	4.7	3.0	1.1	34,683
Greece	—	—	—	—	—	27,793
Hungary[4,5]	4,371	6,721	4.9	3.2	0.9	18,763
Iceland	8,949	9,309	7.8	5.1	1.2	36,325
Ireland	7,791	12,631	4.7	3.5	1.2	44,381
Israel	5,345	11,435	7.4	4.1	1.8	26,444
Italy[6]	7,771	8,673	4.5	3.1	0.9	31,016
Japan	8,012	14,201	4.9	2.8	1.5	33,635
Korea, Republic of	6,663	8,920	7.0	4.0	2.4	26,574
Luxembourg[7]	15,579	—	—	—	—	82,456
Mexico	2,165	6,971	5.7	3.8	1.2	14,128
Netherlands	8,571	15,969	5.6	3.7	1.5	39,594
New Zealand	5,454	9,905	5.9	4.0	1.5	27,020
Norway[5]	10,855	17,140	5.5	3.7	1.3	53,672
Poland[4]	3,804	5,576	5.3	3.4	1.3	16,312
Portugal[4]	5,898	10,398	5.6	3.5	1.6	22,638
Slovak Republic[8]	3,296	5,736	4.0	2.5	0.9	20,270
Slovenia	7,267	8,559	5.6	3.6	1.3	26,557
Spain	7,671	12,548	4.8	2.9	1.1	31,469
Sweden	8,773	18,361	6.3	4.1	1.6	36,785
Switzerland[9]	11,702	20,883	5.5	4.0	1.2	41,800
Turkey	—	—	—	—	—	13,362
United Kingdom	8,622	15,463	5.8	4.2	1.3	34,957
United States	10,768	27,010	7.6	4.0	3.1	46,434

— Not available.
[1] Includes expenditures for preprimary, elementary/secondary, postsecondary nontertiary, and postsecondary education, and education not classified by level.
[2] Data are for 2006. Postsecondary includes public academic institutions only.
[3] Data are for 2008.
[4] Expenditures per student include public institutions only.
[5] Expenditures as a percentage of GDP include public institutions only.
[6] Elementary and secondary expenditures per student include public institutions only.
[7] Luxembourg data are excluded from percentages because of anomalies with respect to their GDP per capita data. (Large revenues from international finance institutions distort the wealth of the population.) Expenditures include public institutions only.
[8] Expenditures on tertiary vocational programs (International Standard Classification of Education [ISCED] level 5B) are included under elementary and secondary.
[9] Expenditures per student and postsecondary expenditures as a percentage of GDP include public institutions only.
NOTE: Education expenditures are from public revenue sources (governments) and private revenue sources. Private sources include payments from households for school-based expenses such as tuition, transportation fees, book rentals, or food services, as well as funds raised by institutions through endowments or returns on investments. Per student expenditures are calculated based on public and private full-time-equivalent (FTE) enrollment figures and on current expenditures and capital outlays from both public and private sources, where data are available. Elementary/secondary expenditures generally include postsecondary nontertiary (ISCED level 4) education. Postsecondary nontertiary expenditures are included under postsecondary for Canada and are not available for France, Greece, Italy, Luxembourg, Portugal, and the United States. Postsecondary includes all tertiary-level data (ISCED levels 5A, 5B, and 6). For more information on the International Standard Classification of Education (ISCED), see *supplemental note 11*. For more information on classification of expenditures for international comparisons, see *supplemental note 10*. Purchasing power parity (PPP) indices are used to convert other currencies to U.S. dollars. Within-country consumer price indices are used to adjust the PPP indices to account for inflation because the fiscal year has a different starting date in different countries. OECD average reflects the unweighted average of countries reporting data.
SOURCE: Organization for Economic Co-operation and Development (OECD), Center for Educational Research and Innovation. (2010). *Education at a Glance, 2010: OECD Indicators*, tables B1.1a, B1.2, B2.1, and X2.1.

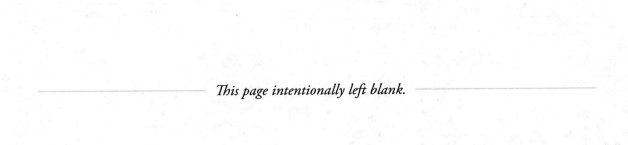

This page intentionally left blank.

Table A-39-1. Number and percentage distribution of fall undergraduate enrollment in degree-granting institutions, by control and level of institution and selected student characteristics: Fall 2009

Student characteristic	Total, all institutions	Public		Private, not-for-profit		Private, for profit	
		4-year	2-year	4-year	2-year	4-year	2-year
Total	**17,565,320**	**6,285,149**	**7,101,444**	**2,558,594**	**34,767**	**1,200,172**	**385,194**
Sex							
Male	7,595,481	2,867,053	3,050,243	1,090,833	12,299	441,035	134,018
Female	9,969,839	3,418,096	4,051,201	1,467,761	22,468	759,137	251,176
Race/ethnicity							
White	10,915,263	4,135,164	4,176,793	1,769,073	19,770	637,614	176,849
Black	2,577,417	764,423	1,040,434	329,763	7,631	330,442	104,724
Hispanic	2,362,481	702,490	1,223,620	194,205	3,322	156,771	82,073
Asian/Pacific Islander	1,142,301	451,061	478,391	152,224	1,744	43,319	15,562
American Indian/Alaska Native	189,428	66,276	85,142	18,838	1,373	14,062	3,737
Nonresident alien	378,430	165,735	97,064	94,491	927	17,964	2,249
Attendance status and age							
Full time	11,143,499	4,904,272	2,880,631	2,119,871	23,483	870,633	344,609
Under 25	8,775,443	4,333,533	2,136,470	1,846,921	15,201	276,118	167,200
25 to 34	1,485,537	427,580	453,005	160,629	4,779	333,114	106,430
35 and over	861,638	140,357	287,062	105,078	3,439	258,160	67,542
Age unknown	20,881	2,802	4,094	7,243	64	3,241	3,437
Part time	6,421,821	1,380,877	4,220,813	438,723	11,284	329,539	40,585
Under 25	2,977,409	654,948	2,094,673	130,727	4,127	78,248	14,686
25 to 34	1,736,154	406,737	1,050,717	130,536	3,693	130,467	14,004
35 and over	1,675,394	315,287	1,060,931	165,660	3,404	118,669	11,443
Age unknown	32,864	3,905	14,492	11,800	60	2,155	452

See notes at end of table.

Table A-39-1. **Number and percentage distribution of fall undergraduate enrollment in degree-granting institutions, by control and level of institution and selected student characteristics: Fall 2009—Continued**

Student characteristic	Total, all institutions	Public		Private, not-for-profit		Private, for profit	
		4-year	2-year	4-year	2-year	4-year	2-year
Total	**100.0**	**35.8**	**40.4**	**14.6**	**0.2**	**6.8**	**2.2**
Sex							
Male	100.0	37.7	40.2	14.4	0.2	5.8	1.8
Female	100.0	34.3	40.6	14.7	0.2	7.6	2.5
Race/ethnicity							
White	100.0	37.9	38.3	16.2	0.2	5.8	1.6
Black	100.0	29.7	40.4	12.8	0.3	12.8	4.1
Hispanic	100.0	29.7	51.8	8.2	0.1	6.6	3.5
Asian/Pacific Islander	100.0	39.5	41.9	13.3	0.2	3.8	1.4
American Indian/Alaska Native	100.0	35.0	44.9	9.9	0.7	7.4	2.0
Nonresident alien	100.0	43.8	25.6	25.0	0.2	4.7	0.6
Attendance status and age							
Full time	100.0	44.0	25.9	19.0	0.2	7.8	3.1
Under 25	100.0	49.4	24.3	21.0	0.2	3.1	1.9
25 to 34	100.0	28.8	30.5	10.8	0.3	22.4	7.2
35 and over	100.0	16.3	33.3	12.2	0.4	30.0	7.8
Age unknown	100.0	13.4	19.6	34.7	0.3	15.5	16.5
Part time	100.0	21.5	65.7	6.8	0.2	5.1	0.6
Under 25	100.0	22.0	70.4	4.4	0.1	2.6	0.5
25 to 34	100.0	23.4	60.5	7.5	0.2	7.5	0.8
35 and over	100.0	18.8	63.3	9.9	0.2	7.1	0.7
Age unknown	100.0	11.9	44.1	35.9	0.2	6.6	1.4

NOTE: Degree-granting institutions grant associate's or higher degrees and participate in Title IV federal financial aid programs. Race categories exclude persons of Hispanic ethnicity. For more information on race/ethnicity, see *supplemental note 1*. For more information on IPEDS, see *supplemental note 3*. Institutions in this indicator are classified based on the highest degree offered. For more information on the classification of postsecondary institutions, see *supplemental note 8*. Detail may not sum to totals due to rounding.
SOURCE: U.S. Department of Education, National Center for Education Statistics, 2009 Integrated Postsecondary Education Data System (IPEDS), Spring 2010, Fall Enrollment.

Table A-39-2. Number and percentage distribution of degree-granting undergraduate institutions, retention rates, and overall graduation rates, by level, control, and acceptance rate of institution: Fall 2008

Level and control of institution and acceptance rate	Total number of institutions	Percentage distribution	Retention rate[1]		Overall graduation rate by fall 2008 (2002 cohort for 4-year institutions and 2005 cohort for 2-year institutions)[2]
			Full-time	Part-time	
4-year institutions					
All institutions	**2,401**	**100.0**	**76.6**	**45.5**	**57.2**
Open admissions (no application criteria)	526	21.9	57.1	45.8	27.1
75 percent or more accepted	618	25.7	74.2	44.0	53.1
50.0 to 74.9 percent accepted	873	36.4	79.3	45.9	59.9
25.0 to 49.9 percent accepted	331	13.8	82.1	46.2	73.1
Less than 25 percent accepted	53	2.2	95.3	60.1	82.8
Public institutions	629	100.0	78.2	47.7	54.9
Open admissions (no application criteria)	108	17.2	63.7	44.2	30.7
75 percent or more accepted	185	29.4	74.7	47.3	50.6
50.0 to 74.9 percent accepted	251	39.9	81.2	51.0	58.9
25.0 to 49.9 percent accepted	75	11.9	83.6	61.7	67.3
Less than 25 percent accepted	10	1.6	92.7	77.3	72.6
Private not-for-profit institutions	1,245	100.0	79.1	43.6	64.6
Open admissions (no application criteria)	165	13.3	57.3	43.3	35.4
75 percent or more accepted	350	28.1	75.3	39.0	58.9
50.0 to 74.9 percent accepted	516	41.4	78.0	45.1	63.4
25.0 to 49.9 percent accepted	174	14.0	86.7	52.1	79.2
Less than 25 percent accepted	40	3.2	96.5	89.4	89.1
Private for-profit institutions	527	100.0	49.7	43.2	22.0
Open admissions (no application criteria)	253	48.0	48.6	48.0	13.0
75 percent or more accepted	83	15.7	51.2	39.2	34.9
50.0 to 74.9 percent accepted	106	20.1	52.0	32.1	39.5
25.0 to 49.9 percent accepted	82	15.6	47.9	29.9	31.9
Less than 25 percent accepted	3	0.6	76.1	39.4	72.0
2-year institutions					
All institutions	**1,708**	**100.0**	**61.0**	**40.3**	**27.5**
Public institutions	999	58.5	60.0	40.1	20.6
Private not-for-profit institutions	83	4.9	59.2	59.5	48.2
Private for-profit institutions	626	36.7	69.0	47.3	57.7

[1] For 4-year institutions, the retention rate is the percentage of first-time, bachelor's degree-seeking students who return to the institution to continue their studies the following fall, in this case fall 2009. For 2-year institutions, the retention rate is the percentage of first-time degree/certificate-seeking students enrolled in the fall who either returned to the institution or successfully completed their program by the following fall.
[2] The overall graduation rate is the percentage of full-time, first-time students who graduated within 150 percent of normal program completion time. For a bachelor's degree, this represents 6 years.
NOTE: Degree-granting institutions grant associate's or higher degrees and participate in Title IV federal financial aid programs. For more information on IPEDS, see *supplemental note 3*. Institutions in this indicator are classified based on the highest degree offered. For more information on the classification of postsecondary institutions, see *supplemental note 8*. Detail may not sum to totals because of rounding.
SOURCE: U.S. Department of Education, National Center for Education Statistics, 2009 Integrated Postsecondary Education Data System (IPEDS), Spring 2010, Graduation Rates.

This page intentionally left blank.

Table A-40-1. Number of associate's and bachelor's degrees awarded by degree-granting institutions, percentage of total, number and percentage awarded to females, and percent change, by selected fields of study: Academic years 1998–99 and 2008–09

Field of study	1998–99				2008–09				1998–99 to 2008–09		
	Number	Percent of total	Number to females	Percent to females	Number	Percent of total	Number to females	Percent to females	Change in number of degrees	Percent change	Percent change for females
Associate's degrees											
Total[1]	**559,954**	**100.0**	**341,537**	**61.0**	**787,325**	**100.0**	**489,184**	**62.1**	**227,371**	**40.6**	**43.2**
Liberal arts and sciences, general studies, and humanities	181,977	32.5	113,768	62.5	263,853	33.5	161,635	61.3	81,876	45.0	42.1
Health professions and related clinical sciences	93,218	16.6	79,707	85.5	165,163	21.0	140,893	85.3	71,945	77.2	76.8
Business	95,897	17.1	66,361	69.2	127,848	16.2	82,113	64.2	31,951	33.3	23.7
Engineering and engineering technologies	57,292	10.2	7,504	13.1	52,933	6.7	5,709	10.8	-4,359	-7.6	-23.9
Security and protective services	17,430	3.1	5,981	34.3	33,033	4.2	15,803	47.8	15,603	89.5	164.2
Computer and information sciences	22,445	4.0	10,200	45.4	30,006	3.8	7,453	24.8	7,561	33.7	-26.9
Visual and performing arts	17,640	3.2	9,698	55.0	18,629	2.4	11,836	63.5	989	5.6	22.0
Multi/interdisciplinary studies	8,661	1.5	4,663	53.8	15,459	2.0	9,504	61.5	6,798	78.5	103.8
Education	10,165	1.8	7,683	75.6	14,123	1.8	12,083	85.6	3,958	38.9	57.3
Social sciences and history	4,550	0.8	2,957	65.0	9,142	1.2	5,889	64.4	4,592	100.9	99.2
Legal professions and studies	9,133	1.6	8,198	89.8	9,062	1.2	8,125	89.7	-71	-0.8	-0.9
Family and consumer sciences	8,063	1.4	7,410	91.9	9,020	1.1	8,664	96.1	957	11.9	16.9
Communications and communications technologies	5,167	0.9	2,421	46.9	7,525	1.0	2,901	38.6	2,358	45.6	19.8
Agriculture and natural resources	6,632	1.2	2,313	34.9	5,724	0.7	1,969	34.4	-908	-13.7	-14.9
Public administration and social service professions	3,881	0.7	3,268	84.2	4,178	0.5	3,595	86.0	297	7.7	10.0
Psychology	1,625	0.3	1,230	75.7	3,949	0.5	3,205	81.2	2,324	143.0	160.6
Physical sciences and science technologies	2,399	0.4	1,201	50.1	3,617	0.5	1,497	41.4	1,218	50.8	24.6
Biological and biomedical sciences	2,213	0.4	1,447	65.4	2,364	0.3	1,608	68.0	151	6.8	11.1
Precision production	2,201	0.4	296	13.4	2,126	0.3	138	6.5	-75	-3.4	-53.4
Foreign languages, literatures, and linguistics	1,705	0.3	1,220	71.6	1,627	0.2	1,366	84.0	-78	-4.6	12.0

See notes at end of table.

Table A-40-1. Number of associate's and bachelor's degrees awarded by degree-granting institutions, percentage of total, number and percentage awarded to females, and percent change, by selected fields of study: Academic years 1998–99 and 2008–09—Continued

Field of study	1998–99				2008–09				1998–99 to 2008–09		
	Number	Percent of total	Number to females	Percent to females	Number	Percent of total	Number to females	Percent to females	Change in number of degrees	Percent change	Percent change for females
Bachelor's degrees											
Total[1]	1,200,303	100.0	681,557	56.8	1,601,368	100.0	915,986	57.2	401,065	33.4	34.4
Business	240,947	20.1	118,697	49.3	347,985	21.7	170,123	48.9	107,038	44.4	43.3
Social sciences and history	124,658	10.4	62,922	50.5	168,500	10.5	83,303	49.4	43,842	35.2	32.4
Health professions and related clinical sciences	85,214	7.1	70,027	82.2	120,488	7.5	102,696	85.2	35,274	41.4	46.7
Education	107,086	8.9	80,862	75.5	101,708	6.4	80,549	79.2	-5,378	-5.0	-0.4
Psychology	73,636	6.1	55,332	75.1	94,271	5.9	72,783	77.2	20,635	28.0	31.5
Visual and performing arts	54,404	4.5	32,123	59.0	89,140	5.6	54,089	60.7	34,736	63.8	68.4
Engineering and engineering technologies	72,445	6.0	12,952	17.9	84,636	5.3	13,961	16.5	12,191	16.8	7.8
Communication and communications technologies	52,460	4.4	31,510	60.1	83,109	5.2	51,891	62.4	30,649	58.4	64.7
Biological and biomedical sciences	64,608	5.4	36,433	56.4	80,756	5.0	47,831	59.2	16,148	25.0	31.3
English language and literature/letters	49,800	4.1	33,515	67.3	55,462	3.5	37,489	67.6	5,662	11.4	11.9
Liberal arts and sciences, general studies, and humanities	34,772	2.9	22,601	65.0	47,096	2.9	30,480	64.7	12,324	35.4	34.9
Security and protective services	24,601	2.0	10,516	42.7	41,800	2.6	20,727	49.6	17,199	69.9	97.1
Computer and information sciences and support services	30,574	2.5	8,276	27.1	37,994	2.4	6,779	17.8	7,420	24.3	-18.1
Multi/interdisciplinary studies	27,545	2.3	18,532	67.3	37,444	2.3	25,587	68.3	9,899	35.9	38.1
Parks, recreation, leisure, and fitness studies	16,532	1.4	8,356	50.5	31,667	2.0	15,001	47.4	15,135	91.5	79.5
Agriculture and natural resources	23,916	2.0	10,052	42.0	24,988	1.6	11,887	47.6	1,072	4.5	18.3
Public administration and social service professions	20,287	1.7	16,496	81.3	23,851	1.5	19,477	81.7	3,564	17.6	18.1
Physical sciences and science technologies	18,285	1.5	7,282	39.8	22,466	1.4	9,167	40.8	4,181	22.9	25.9
Family and consumer sciences	16,059	1.3	14,127	88.0	21,905	1.4	19,151	87.4	5,846	36.4	35.6
Foreign languages, literatures, and linguistics	15,821	1.3	11,078	70.0	21,158	1.3	14,856	70.2	5,337	33.7	34.1

[1] Includes other fields not shown separately.

NOTE: For more information on fields of study for postsecondary degrees, see *supplemental note 9*. The 2000 *Classification of Instructional Programs* was initiated in 2002–03. Estimates for 1998–99 have been reclassified when necessary to conform to the new taxonomy. For more information on the Classification of Postsecondary Education Institutions, see *supplemental note 8*. For more information on the Integrated Postsecondary Education Data System (IPEDS), see *supplemental note 3*.
SOURCE: U.S. Department of Education, National Center for Education Statistics, 1998–99 and 2008–09 Integrated Postsecondary Education Data System, "Completions Survey" (IPEDS-C:99) and Fall 2009.

Graduate and First-Professional Fields of Study

Table A-41-1. Number of master's, doctoral, and first-professional degrees awarded by degree-granting institutions, percentage of total, number and percentage awarded to females, and percent change, by selected fields of study: Academic years 1998–99 and 2008–09

| Field of study | 1998–99 | | | | 2008–08 | | | | 1998–99 to 2008–09 | | |
	Number	Percent of total	Number of females	Percent female	Number	Percent of total	Number of females	Percent female	Change in number of degrees	Percent change	Percent change for females
Master's degrees											
Total[1]	**439,986**	**100.0**	**253,838**	**57.7**	**656,784**	**100.0**	**396,786**	**60.4**	**216,798**	**49.3**	**56.3**
Education	118,048	26.8	90,051	76.3	178,564	27.2	138,240	77.4	60,516	51.3	53.5
Business	107,477	24.4	42,777	39.8	168,375	25.6	76,394	45.4	60,898	56.7	78.6
Health professions and related clinical sciences	40,707	9.3	31,505	77.4	62,620	9.5	50,751	81.0	21,913	53.8	61.1
Engineering and engineering technologies	26,739	6.1	5,341	20.0	38,205	5.8	8,610	22.5	11,466	42.9	61.2
Public administration and social service professions	24,925	5.7	18,369	73.7	33,933	5.2	25,587	75.4	9,008	36.1	39.3
Psychology	15,688	3.6	11,698	74.6	23,415	3.6	18,626	79.5	7,727	49.3	59.2
Social sciences and history	14,431	3.3	6,975	48.3	19,240	2.9	9,635	50.1	4,809	33.3	38.1
Computer and information sciences and support services	12,858	2.9	3,987	31.0	17,907	2.7	4,844	27.1	5,049	39.3	21.5
Visual and performing arts	10,753	2.4	6,210	57.8	14,918	2.3	8,593	57.6	4,165	38.7	38.4
Biological and biomedical sciences	6,913	1.6	3,666	53.0	9,898	1.5	5,698	57.6	2,985	43.2	55.4
English language and literature/letters	7,288	1.7	4,846	66.5	9,261	1.4	6,260	67.6	1,973	27.1	29.2
Communication and communications technologies	5,556	1.3	3,555	64.0	7,567	1.2	5,108	67.5	2,011	36.2	43.7
Theology and religious vocations	4,679	1.1	1,851	39.6	7,541	1.1	2,702	35.8	2,862	61.2	46.0
Library science	4,752	1.1	3,761	79.1	7,091	1.1	5,747	81.0	2,339	49.2	52.8
Architecture and related services	4,172	0.9	1,778	42.6	6,587	1.0	2,930	44.5	2,415	57.9	64.8
Security and protective services	2,249	0.5	937	41.7	6,128	0.9	3,299	53.8	3,879	172.5	252.1
Physical sciences and science technologies	5,124	1.2	1,758	34.3	5,658	0.9	2,225	39.3	534	10.4	26.6
Multi/interdisciplinary studies	3,073	0.7	1,935	63.0	5,344	0.8	3,398	63.6	2,271	73.9	75.6
Mathematics and statistics	3,286	0.7	1,385	42.1	5,211	0.8	2,147	41.2	1,925	58.6	55.0
Legal professions and studies	3,308	0.8	1,341	40.5	5,150	0.8	2,467	47.9	1,842	55.7	84.0
Doctoral degrees[2]											
Total[1]	**44,077**	**100.0**	**18,931**	**42.9**	**67,716**	**100.0**	**35,437**	**52.3**	**23,639**	**53.6**	**87.2**
Health professions and related clinical sciences	1,920	4.4	1,199	62.4	12,112	17.9	8,921	73.7	10,192	530.8	644.0
Education	6,394	14.5	4,096	64.1	9,028	13.3	6,072	67.3	2,634	41.2	48.2
Engineering and engineering technologies	5,461	12.4	785	14.4	7,990	11.8	1,731	21.7	2,529	46.3	120.5
Biological and biomedical sciences	5,024	11.4	2,149	42.8	6,957	10.3	3,665	52.7	1,933	38.5	70.5
Psychology	4,695	10.7	3,185	67.8	5,477	8.1	3,999	73.0	782	16.7	25.6
Physical sciences and science technologies	4,142	9.4	998	24.1	5,048	7.5	1,632	32.3	906	21.9	63.5
Social sciences and history	3,855	8.7	1,585	41.1	4,234	6.3	1,881	44.4	379	9.8	18.7

See notes at end of table

Table A-41-1. Number of master's, doctoral, and first-professional degrees awarded by degree-granting institutions, percentage of total, number and percentage awarded to females, and percent change, by selected fields of study: Academic years 1998–99 and 2008–09—Continued

Field of study	1998–99				2008–09				1998–99 to 2008–09		
	Number	Percent of total	Number of females	Percent female	Number	Percent of total	Number of females	Percent female	Change in number of degrees	Percent change	Percent change for females
Doctoral degrees[2]											
Total[1]	**44,077**	**100.0**	**18,931**	**42.9**	**67,716**	**100.0**	**35,437**	**52.3**	**23,639**	**53.6**	**87.2**
Business	1,201	2.7	358	29.8	2,123	3.1	821	38.7	922	76.8	129.3
Computer and information sciences and support services	801	1.8	151	18.9	1,580	2.3	354	22.4	779	97.3	134.4
Visual and performing arts	1,130	2.6	556	49.2	1,569	2.3	843	53.7	439	38.8	51.6
Mathematics and statistics	1,090	2.5	287	26.3	1,535	2.3	476	31.0	445	40.8	65.9
Theology and religious vocations	1,440	3.3	235	16.3	1,520	2.2	354	23.3	80	5.6	50.6
Agriculture and natural resources	1,231	2.8	376	30.5	1,328	2.0	587	44.2	97	7.9	56.1
Multi/interdisciplinary studies	754	1.7	363	48.1	1,273	1.9	701	55.1	519	68.8	93.1
English language and literature/letters	1,407	3.2	847	60.2	1,271	1.9	807	63.5	-136	-9.7	-4.7
Foreign languages, literatures, and linguistics	1,049	2.4	605	57.7	1,111	1.6	685	61.7	62	5.9	13.2
Public administration and social service professions	532	1.2	293	55.1	812	1.2	506	62.3	280	52.6	72.7
Philosophy and religious studies	584	1.3	149	25.5	686	1.0	214	31.2	102	17.5	43.6
Communication and communications technologies	352	0.8	169	48.0	535	0.8	310	57.9	183	52.0	83.4
Family and consumer sciences/human sciences	323	0.7	239	74.0	333	0.5	267	80.2	10	3.1	11.7
First-professional degrees[3]											
Total[1]	**78,439**	**100.0**	**34,100**	**43.5**	**92,004**	**100.0**	**45,104**	**49.0**	**13,565**	**17.3**	**32.3**
Law	39,167	49.9	17,539	44.8	44,045	47.9	20,185	45.8	4,878	12.5	15.1
Medicine	15,562	19.8	6,608	42.5	15,987	17.4	7,823	48.9	425	2.7	18.4
Pharmacy	3,992	5.1	2,673	67.0	11,291	12.3	7,280	64.5	7,299	182.8	172.4
Theology	5,558	7.1	1,572	28.3	5,362	5.8	1,776	33.1	-196	-3.5	13.0
Dentistry	4,144	5.3	1,470	35.5	4,918	5.3	2,281	46.4	774	18.7	55.2
Osteopathic	2,135	2.7	797	37.3	3,665	4.0	1,867	50.9	1,530	71.7	134.3
Chiropractic	3,639	4.6	1,045	28.7	2,512	2.7	928	36.9	-1,127	-31.0	-11.2
Veterinary medicine	2,226	2.8	1,501	67.4	2,377	2.6	1,851	77.9	151	6.8	23.3
Optometry	1,285	1.6	648	50.4	1,338	1.5	872	65.2	53	4.1	34.6
Podiatry	578	0.7	161	27.9	431	0.5	181	42.0	-147	-25.4	12.4

[1] Includes other fields not shown separately.
[2] Includes Ph.D., Ed.D., and comparable degrees at the doctoral level.
[3] An award that requires completion of a degree program that meets all of the following criteria: (1) completion of the academic requirements to begin practice in the profession; (2) at least 2 years of college work before entering the degree program; and (3) a total of at least 6 academic years of college work to complete the degree program, including previously required college work plus the work required in the professional program itself. See glossary for a complete list of first-professional degrees.
NOTE: For more information on fields of study for postsecondary degrees, see *supplemental note 9*. The 2000 edition of *Classification of Instructional Programs* was initiated in 2002–03. Estimates for 1998–99 have been reclassified when necessary to conform to the new taxonomy. For more information on the classification of postsecondary education institutions, see *supplemental note 8*. For more information on the Integrated Postsecondary Education Data System (IPEDS), see *supplemental note 3*.
SOURCE: U.S. Department of Education, National Center for Education Statistics, 1998–99 and 2008–09 Integrated Postsecondary Education Data System, "Completions Survey" (IPEDS-C:99) and Fall 2009.

Table A-42-1. Number and percentage distribution of degrees conferred by degree-granting institutions, by control of institution and level of degree: Academic years 1998–99 through 2008–09

Level of degree and academic year	Number of degrees conferred					Percentage distribution of degrees conferred				
			Total	Private					Private	
	Total	Public	Total	Not-for-profit	For-profit	Total	Public	Total	Not-for-profit	For-profit
Associate's										
1998–99	559,954	448,334	111,620	47,611	64,009	100.0	80.1	19.9	8.5	11.4
1999–2000	564,933	448,446	116,487	46,337	70,150	100.0	79.4	20.6	8.2	12.4
2000–01	578,865	456,487	122,378	45,711	76,667	100.0	78.9	21.1	7.9	13.2
2001–02	595,133	471,660	123,473	45,761	77,712	100.0	79.3	20.7	7.7	13.1
2002–03	634,016	498,279	135,737	46,183	89,554	100.0	78.6	21.4	7.3	14.1
2003–04	665,301	524,875	140,426	45,759	94,667	100.0	78.9	21.1	6.9	14.2
2004–05	696,660	547,519	149,141	45,344	103,797	100.0	78.6	21.4	6.5	14.9
2005–06	713,066	557,134	155,932	46,442	109,490	100.0	78.1	21.9	6.5	15.4
2006–07	728,114	566,535	161,579	43,829	117,750	100.0	77.8	22.2	6.0	16.2
2007–08	750,164	578,520	171,644	44,788	126,856	100.0	77.1	22.9	6.0	16.9
2008–09	787,325	596,098	191,227	46,929	144,298	100.0	75.7	24.3	6.0	18.3
Bachelor's										
1998–99	1,200,303	790,287	410,016	393,680	16,336	100.0	65.8	34.2	32.8	1.4
1999–2000	1,237,875	810,855	427,020	406,958	20,062	100.0	65.5	34.5	32.9	1.6
2000–01	1,244,171	812,438	431,733	408,701	23,032	100.0	65.3	34.7	32.8	1.9
2001–02	1,291,900	841,180	450,720	424,322	26,398	100.0	65.1	34.9	32.8	2.0
2002–03	1,348,811	875,596	473,215	442,060	31,155	100.0	64.9	35.1	32.8	2.3
2003–04	1,399,542	905,718	493,824	451,518	42,306	100.0	64.7	35.3	32.3	3.0
2004–05	1,439,264	932,443	506,821	457,963	48,858	100.0	64.8	35.2	31.8	3.4
2005–06	1,485,242	955,369	529,873	467,836	62,037	100.0	64.3	35.7	31.5	4.2
2006–07	1,524,092	975,513	548,579	477,805	70,774	100.0	64.0	36.0	31.4	4.6
2007–08	1,563,069	996,435	566,634	490,685	75,949	100.0	63.7	36.3	31.4	4.9
2008–09	1,601,368	1,020,435	580,933	496,260	84,673	100.0	63.7	36.3	31.0	5.3
Master's										
1998–99	439,986	238,501	201,485	192,152	9,333	100.0	54.2	45.8	43.7	2.1
1999–2000	457,056	243,157	213,899	203,591	10,308	100.0	53.2	46.8	44.5	2.3
2000–01	468,476	246,054	222,422	210,789	11,633	100.0	52.5	47.5	45.0	2.5
2001–02	482,118	249,820	232,298	218,034	14,264	100.0	51.8	48.2	45.2	3.0
2002–03	513,339	265,643	247,696	232,709	14,987	100.0	51.7	48.3	45.3	2.9
2003–04	558,940	285,138	273,802	245,562	28,240	100.0	51.0	49.0	43.9	5.1
2004–05	574,618	291,505	283,113	248,031	35,082	100.0	50.7	49.3	43.2	6.1
2005–06	594,065	293,517	300,548	255,424	45,124	100.0	49.4	50.6	43.0	7.6
2006–07	604,607	291,971	312,636	261,700	50,936	100.0	48.3	51.7	43.3	8.4
2007–08	625,023	299,923	325,100	270,246	54,854	100.0	48.0	52.0	43.2	8.8
2008–09	656,784	308,206	348,578	285,098	63,480	100.0	46.9	53.1	43.4	9.7
First-professional										
1998–99	78,439	31,693	46,746	46,315	431	100.0	40.4	59.6	59.0	0.5
1999–2000	80,057	32,247	47,810	47,301	509	100.0	40.3	59.7	59.1	0.6
2000–01	79,707	32,633	47,074	46,828	246	100.0	40.9	59.1	58.8	0.3
2001–02	80,698	33,439	47,259	47,020	239	100.0	41.4	58.6	58.3	0.3
2002–03	80,897	33,549	47,348	47,116	232	100.0	41.5	58.5	58.2	0.3
2003–04	83,041	34,499	48,542	48,278	264	100.0	41.5	58.5	58.1	0.3
2004–05	87,289	35,768	51,521	51,259	262	100.0	41.0	59.0	58.7	0.3
2005–06	87,655	36,269	51,386	50,902	484	100.0	41.4	58.6	58.1	0.6
2006–07	90,064	36,855	53,209	52,746	463	100.0	40.9	59.1	58.6	0.5
2007–08	91,309	37,278	54,031	53,225	806	100.0	40.8	59.2	58.3	0.9
2008–09	92,004	37,357	54,647	53,572	1,075	100.0	40.6	59.4	58.2	1.2

See notes at end of table.

Table A-42-1.   Number and percentage distribution of degrees conferred by degree-granting institutions, by control of institution and level of degree: Academic years 1998–99 through 2008–09—Continued

Level of degree and academic year	Number of degrees conferred					Percentage distribution of degrees conferred				
			Private					Private		
	Total	Public	Total	Not-for-profit	For-profit	Total	Public	Total	Not-for-profit	For-profit
Doctoral										
1998–99	44,077	28,134	15,943	15,501	442	100.0	63.8	36.2	35.2	1.0
1999–2000	44,808	28,408	16,400	15,800	600	100.0	63.4	36.6	35.3	1.3
2000–01	44,904	28,187	16,717	15,920	797	100.0	62.8	37.2	35.5	1.8
2001–02	44,160	27,622	16,538	15,882	656	100.0	62.5	37.5	36.0	1.5
2002–03	46,042	28,062	17,980	17,138	842	100.0	60.9	39.1	37.2	1.8
2003–04	48,378	29,706	18,672	17,501	1,171	100.0	61.4	38.6	36.2	2.4
2004–05	52,631	31,743	20,888	19,552	1,336	100.0	60.3	39.7	37.1	2.5
2005–06	56,067	33,767	22,300	20,830	1,470	100.0	60.2	39.8	37.2	2.6
2006–07	60,616	36,230	24,386	22,483	1,903	100.0	59.8	40.2	37.1	3.1
2007–08	63,712	38,315	25,397	23,037	2,360	100.0	60.1	39.9	36.2	3.7
2008–09	67,716	39,911	27,805	25,169	2,636	100.0	58.9	41.1	37.2	3.9

NOTE: Includes only institutions that participated in Title IV federal financial aid programs. For more information on the Integrated Postsecondary Education Data System (IPEDS) and IPEDS classification of institutions, see *supplemental notes 3* and *8*. See the glossary for the definitions of first-professional degree and doctoral degree. Detail may not sum to totals because of rounding.
SOURCE: U.S. Department of Education, National Center for Education Statistics, 1998–99 through 2008–09 Integrated Postsecondary Education Data System (IPEDS), "Completions Survey" (IPEDS-C:99), and Fall 2000 through Fall 2009.

Table A-42-2.   Number of degree-granting institutions, by control and level of institution: Academic years 1998–99 through 2008–09

Academic year	All institutions			Public			Private								
										Not-for-profit			For-profit		
	Total	2-year	4-year	Total	2-year	4-year	Total	2-year	4-year	Total	2-year	4-year	Total	2-year	4-year
1998–99	4,048	1,713	2,335	1,681	1,069	612	2,367	644	1,723	1,695	164	1,531	672	480	192
1999–2000	4,084	1,721	2,363	1,682	1,068	614	2,402	653	1,749	1,681	150	1,531	721	503	218
2000–01	4,182	1,732	2,450	1,698	1,076	622	2,484	656	1,828	1,695	144	1,551	789	512	277
2001–02	4,197	1,710	2,487	1,713	1,085	628	2,484	625	1,859	1,676	135	1,541	808	490	318
2002–03	4,168	1,702	2,466	1,712	1,081	631	2,456	621	1,835	1,665	127	1,538	791	494	297
2003–04	4,236	1,706	2,530	1,720	1,086	634	2,516	620	1,896	1,664	118	1,546	852	502	350
2004–05	4,216	1,683	2,533	1,700	1,061	639	2,516	622	1,894	1,637	112	1,525	879	510	369
2005–06	4,276	1,694	2,582	1,693	1,053	640	2,583	641	1,942	1,647	113	1,534	936	528	408
2006–07	4,314	1,685	2,629	1,688	1,045	643	2,626	640	1,986	1,640	107	1,533	986	533	453
2007–08	4,352	1,677	2,675	1,685	1,032	653	2,667	645	2,022	1,624	92	1,532	1,043	553	490
2008–09	4,409	1,690	2,719	1,676	1,024	652	2,733	666	2,067	1,629	92	1,537	1,104	574	530

NOTE: Includes only institutions that participate in Title IV federal financial aid programs. Changes in counts of institutions over time are partly affected by increases or decreases in the number of institutions submitting separate data for branch campuses. For more information on the Integrated Postsecondary Education Data System (IPEDS) and IPEDS classification of institutions, see *supplemental notes 3* and *8*.
SOURCE: U.S. Department of Education, National Center for Education Statistics, 1998–99 through 2008–09 Integrated Postsecondary Education Data System (IPEDS), "Institutional Characteristics Survey" (IPEDS-IC:98–99), and Fall 2000 through Fall 2008.

Table A-43-1. Number and percentage of undergraduate students in postsecondary institutions taking distance education courses, by selected characteristics: 2003–04 and 2007–08

Selected characteristic	2003–04			
	Taking any distance education courses		Taking their entire program through distance education	
	Number of students (in thousands)	Percent of all students	Number of students (in thousands)	Percent of all students
Total	**2,961**	**15.5**	**973**	**5.1**
Sex				
Male	1,099	13.6	365	4.5
Female	1,862	17.0	609	5.5
Race/ethnicity				
White	1,944	16.2	630	5.3
Black	400	14.9	131	4.9
Hispanic	329	13.4	109	4.5
Asian	145	14.0	55	5.4
Native Hawaiian/Pacific Islander	19	19.1	‡	7.2
American Indian/Alaska Native	27	15.5	11	6.1
Two or more races	64	16.5	21	5.3
Other and unknown	33	13.4	9	3.5
Age				
15 through 23	1,283	11.7	353	3.2
24 through 29	592	18.4	213	6.6
30 or older	1,086	22.4	408	8.4
Attendance status				
Exclusively full-time	1,179	12.7	360	3.9
Exclusively part-time	1,251	18.7	470	7.0
Mixed full-time and part-time	531	17.3	143	4.7
Type of job student had				
No job	533	12.4	158	3.7
Regular job only	2,282	17.2	768	5.8
Work-study/assistantship job only	60	8.8	18	2.6
Both regular job and work-study/ assistantship job	86	11.1	29	3.7
Student housing status				
On-campus	194	7.2	48	1.8
Off-campus	1,851	17.7	634	6.1
With parents or relatives	604	13.2	171	3.7
Attended more than one institution	312	23.4	120	9.1
Dependency status				
Dependent	1,064	11.1	291	3.0
Independent, no dependents, not married[1]	454	15.6	152	5.2
Independent, no dependents, married	269	19.6	101	7.4
Independent, with dependents, not married[1]	522	20.5	180	7.1
Independent, with dependents, married	653	25.1	251	9.6

See notes at end of table.

Table A-43-1. Number and percentage of undergraduate students in postsecondary institutions taking distance education courses, by selected characteristics: 2003–04 and 2007–08—Continued

| | 2007–08 | | | |
| | Taking any distance education courses | | Taking their entire program through distance education | |
Selected characteristic	Number of students (in thousands)	Percent of all students	Number of students (in thousands)	Percent of all students
Total	**4,277**	**20.4**	**769**	**3.7**
Sex				
Male	1,679	18.6	297	3.3
Female	2,598	21.8	472	4.0
Race/ethnicity				
White	2,803	21.7	489	3.8
Black	592	20.2	145	5.0
Hispanic	484	16.4	74	2.5
Asian	225	18.2	37	3.0
Native Hawaiian/Pacific Islander	27	17.7	‡	1.3!
American Indian/Alaska Native	39	22.1	‡	2.0!
Two or more races	99	20.1	15	3.0
Other and unknown	8	13.4	‡	4.7!
Age				
15 through 23	1,891	15.1	169	1.4
24 through 29	938	25.9	192	5.3
30 or older	1,448	30.1	408	8.5
Attendance status				
Exclusively full-time	1,648	16.5	299	3.0
Exclusively part-time	1,839	24.8	373	5.0
Mixed full-time and part-time	791	22.3	97	2.7
Type of job student had				
No job	708	16.1	121	2.8
Regular job only	3,259	22.3	607	4.2
Work-study/assistantship job only	112	12.9	13	1.5
Both regular job and work-study/ assistantship job	198	18.7	27	2.5
Student housing status				
On-campus	263	8.9	13	0.5
Off-campus	2,709	24.0	606	5.4
With parents or relatives	854	17.1	83	1.7
Attended more than one institution	452	27.1	66	4.0
Dependency status				
Dependent	1,589	14.3	108	1.0
Independent, no dependents, not married[1]	788	24.0	155	4.7
Independent, no dependents, married	356	28.7	83	6.6
Independent, with dependents, not married[1]	712	25.5	197	7.0
Independent, with dependents, married	833	33.0	227	9.0

See notes at end of table.

Table A-43-1. Number and percentage of undergraduate students in postsecondary institutions taking distance education courses, by selected characteristics: 2003–04 and 2007–08—Continued

Selected characteristic	2003–04			
	Taking any distance education courses		Taking their entire program through distance education	
	Number of students (in thousands)	Percent of all students	Number of students (in thousands)	Percent of all students
Total	**2,961**	**15.5**	**973**	**5.1**
Veteran status				
Veteran	140	22.5	48	7.6
Not veteran	2,821	15.3	926	5.0
Field of study				
Business/management	550	18.7	206	7.0
Computer science	177	19.4	65	7.2
Education	218	17.1	58	4.6
Engineering	96	12.1	26	3.3
Health	427	17.4	138	5.6
Humanities	276	14.0	76	3.9
Life sciences	81	11.0	20	2.8
Mathematics	12	12.7	‡	3.8!
Physical sciences	12	10.1	‡	1.1!
Social/behavioral sciences	165	12.4	46	3.5
Vocational/technical	62	13.1	20	4.3
Undeclared/no major	622	15.0	233	5.6
Other	265	14.4	79	4.3
Control and level of institution				
Public	2,373	16.2	723	4.9
4-year	823	13.5	245	4.0
2-year	1,540	18.2	475	5.6
Less-than-2-year	11	11.8	3	3.0
Private not-for-profit	353	12.4	122	4.3
4-year	340	12.4	118	4.3
2-year	10	11.3	3	3.3
Less-than-2-year	4	17.3	1	6.8
Private for-profit	235	15.3	128	8.4
4-year	155	26.2	91	15.4
2-year	52	12.1	26	6.1
Less-than-2-year	27	5.4	11	2.1

See notes at end of table.

Table A-43-1. Number and percentage of undergraduate students in postsecondary institutions taking distance education courses, by selected characteristics: 2003–04 and 2007–08—Continued

| Selected characteristic | 2007–08 | | | |
| | Taking any distance education courses | | Taking their entire program through distance education | |
	Number of students (in thousands)	Percent of all students	Number of students (in thousands)	Percent of all students
Total	**4,277**	**20.4**	**769**	**3.7**
Veteran status				
Veteran	191	29.0	58	8.9
Not veteran	4,087	20.2	710	3.5
Field of study				
Business/management	811	23.9	203	6.0
Computer science	190	27.1	56	8.0
Education	272	22.3	38	3.1
Engineering	166	15.8	24	2.3
Health	667	22.2	122	4.1
Humanities	620	19.5	77	2.4
Life sciences	174	15.5	20	1.8
Mathematics	16	15.0	‡	‡
Physical sciences	22	12.5	‡	0.3!
Social/behavioral sciences	226	16.9	30	2.2
Vocational/technical	94	18.5	18	3.4
Undeclared/no major	605	20.6	101	3.4
Other	414	18.9	81	3.7
Control and level of institution				
Public	3,423	21.5	436	2.7
4-year	1,210	18.1	146	2.2
2-year	2,206	24.2	288	3.2
Less-than-2-year	8	8.2	‡	2.2!
Private not-for-profit	429	14.1	88	2.9
4-year	412	14.0	84	2.8
2-year	12	20.2	4	6.1
Less-than-2-year	5	16.3	‡	2.5
Private for-profit	425	21.3	245	12.3
4-year	301	29.7	193	19.0
2-year	97	18.0	44	8.3
Less-than-2-year	28	6.2	7	1.6

! Interpret data with caution. Estimate is unstable because the standard error represents more than 30 percent of the estimate.
‡ Reporting standards not met.
[1] Includes separated.
NOTE: Estimates pertain to all postsecondary students who enrolled at any time during the school year at an institution participating in Title IV programs. Distance education participation includes participation at any institution for students attending more than one institution during the school year. Data include Puerto Rico. Detail may not sum to totals because of survey item nonresponse and rounding. Race categories exclude persons of Hispanic ethnicity. For more information on race/ethnicity, please see *supplemental note 1*. For more information on the classification of postsecondary education institutions, see *supplemental note 8*.
SOURCE: U.S. Department of Education, National Center for Education Statistics, 2003–04 and 2007–08 National Postsecondary Student Aid Study (NPSAS:04 and NPSAS:08).

Table A-43-2. Number and percentage of postbaccalaureate students in postsecondary institutions taking distance education courses, by selected characteristics: 2007–08

Selected characteristic	Taking any distance education courses		Taking their entire program through distance education	
	Number of students (in thousands)	Percent of total enrollment	Number of students (in thousands)	Percent of total enrollment
Total	**763**	**22.1**	**302**	**8.7**
Sex				
Male	268	19.3	104	7.5
Female	495	23.9	199	9.6
Race/ethnicity				
White	532	23.1	211	9.2
Black	102	25.1	42	10.4
Hispanic	60	21.8	20	7.4
Asian	47	12.7	16	4.3
Native Hawaiian/Pacific Islander	‡	31.5!	‡	13.9!
American Indian/Alaska Native	‡	17.0!	‡	3.4!
Two or more races	17	24.1	‡	15.3
Age				
15 through 23	59	14.9	‡	1.6
24 through 29	220	16.0	75	5.4
30 or older	484	28.8	221	13.1
Attendance status				
Exclusively full-time	213	15.2	74	5.3
Exclusively part-time	441	28.4	192	12.3
Mixed full-time and part-time	110	21.7	36	7.2
Type of job student had				
No job	55	12.3	21	4.8!
Regular job only	613	28.1	260	11.9
Work-study/assistantship job only	38	8.0	‡	1.2
Both regular job and work-study/ assistantship job	58	16.0	16	4.3
Dependency status				
Dependent	†	†	†	†
Independent, no dependents, not married[1]	275	15.8	82	4.7
Independent, no dependents, married	125	22.0	54	9.4
Independent, with dependents, not married[1]	92	29.0	34	10.7
Independent, with dependents, married	271	32.8	133	16.0

See notes at end of table.

Table A-43-2. Number and percentage of postbaccalaureate students in postsecondary institutions taking distance education courses, by selected characteristics: 2007–08—Continued

Selected characteristic	Taking any distance education courses		Taking their entire program through distance education	
	Number of students (in thousands)	Percent of total enrollment	Number of students (in thousands)	Percent of total enrollment
Total	**763**	**22.1**	**302**	**8.7**
Veteran status				
Veteran	39	36.3	20	18.8
Not veteran	724	21.6	282	8.4
Field of study				
Business/management	156	26.1	76	12.8
Education	229	27.7	80	9.7
Computer science, mathematics and engineering	60	19.5	28	9.3
Health	90	22.3	37	9.1
Humanities	36	15.5	7	3.1
Law	10	6.0	‡	1.7
Life sciences	23	13.7	‡	4.2
Social/behavioral sciences	44	18.7	21	9.1
Other[2]	116	22.3	43	8.2
Control of institution				
Public	401	22.9	150	8.6
Private not-for-profit	267	18.3	88	6.0
Private for-profit	95	37.7	64	25.4

† Not applicable.
! Interpret data with caution. Estimate is unstable because the standard error represents more than 30 percent of the estimate.
‡ Reporting standards not met.
[1] Includes separated.
[2] Includes physical sciences, other programs, and students with no major.
NOTE: Estimates pertain to all postsecondary students who enrolled at any time during the school year at an institution participating in Title IV programs. Distance education participation includes participation at any institution for students attending more than one institution during the school year. Data include Puerto Rico. Detail may not sum to totals because of survey item nonresponse and rounding. Race categories exclude persons of Hispanic ethnicity. For more information on race/ethnicity, please see *supplemental note 1.* For more information on the classification of postsecondary education institutions, see *supplemental note 8.*
SOURCE: U.S. Department of Education, National Center for Education Statistics, 2007–08 National Postsecondary Student Aid Study (NPSAS:08).

Faculty Salary, Benefits, and Total Compensation

Table A-44-1. Percentage distribution of full-time faculty, and average total compensation, salary, and fringe benefits in current year dollars for faculty at degree-granting postsecondary institutions, by faculty type and level and control of institution: Selected academic years, 1979–80 through 2009–10

[In current year dollars]

Academic rank and level and control of institution	1979–80 Percent distribution of faculty	1979–80 Average	1989–90 Percent distribution of faculty	1989–90 Average	1999–2000 Percent distribution of faculty	1999–2000 Average	2009–10 Percent distribution of faculty	2009–10 Average	Percent change in average 1979–80 to 2009–10	Percent change in average 1999–2000 to 2009–10
Total compensation	**100.0**	**$25,600**	**100.0**	**$48,300**	**100.0**	**$69,100**	**100.0**	**$95,600**	**273.9**	**38.3**
Salary										
All faculty	100.0	21,400	100.0	40,100	100.0	55,900	100.0	74,600	247.9	33.5
Professor	25.5	28,500	30.7	52,900	30.7	74,400	26.9	103,700	264.0	39.3
Associate professor	25.5	21,500	24.6	39,500	24.2	54,500	23.1	74,100	244.9	36.0
Assistant professor	26.2	17,500	24.1	32,700	23.0	45,000	24.1	62,200	256.1	38.4
Faculty with no academic rank	22.8	17,000	20.7	29,000	22.1	40,200	25.9	55,600	227.5	38.4
All institutions	100.0	21,400	100.0	40,100	100.0	55,900	100.0	74,600	247.9	33.5
Public doctoral universities	25.8	23,400	28.3	44,600	27.2	62,700	30.2	82,200	251.6	31.1
Private doctoral universities	8.2	25,000	10.7	50,000	10.2	74,300	13.0	97,700	291.0	31.5
Public master's colleges/ universities	24.5	21,700	20.3	40,200	19.6	52,600	16.3	68,200	214.7	29.6
Private master's colleges/ universities	8.0	19,700	9.8	35,900	11.1	51,000	10.4	67,800	243.9	33.1
Public other 4-year colleges	2.5	19,400	2.4	35,600	2.6	48,100	3.7	61,500	217.6	28.0
Private other 4-year colleges	9.1	17,200	8.5	32,700	7.6	47,600	6.2	66,200	284.7	39.0
Public 2-year colleges	21.1	20,500	19.4	34,400	21.4	48,200	20.1	62,300	204.3	29.1
Private 2-year colleges	0.7	13,300	0.6	24,500	0.4	35,900	0.2	44,700	235.4	24.6
Fringe benefits										
All institutions	100.0	4,100	100.0	8,200	100.0	13,200	100.0	21,000	409.1	58.6
Public doctoral universities	25.8	4,400	28.3	9,700	27.2	14,500	30.2	22,100	405.4	52.6
Private doctoral universities	8.2	4,800	10.7	10,000	10.2	18,300	13.0	26,400	456.6	44.6
Public master's colleges/ universities	24.5	4,400	20.3	8,900	19.6	12,400	16.3	20,400	360.3	64.5
Private master's colleges/ universities	8.0	3,700	9.8	7,400	11.1	12,500	10.4	19,100	417.9	52.2
Public other 4-year colleges	2.5	3,600	2.4	7,000	2.6	11,000	3.7	18,800	423.0	70.2
Private other 4-year colleges	9.1	3,300	8.5	6,300	7.6	12,000	6.2	19,100	484.5	58.6
Public 2-year colleges	21.1	3,900	19.4	6,100	21.4	11,100	20.1	18,300	373.3	64.6
Private 2-year colleges	0.7	2,300	0.6	3,900	0.4	9,000	0.2	11,300	389.9	25.0

Rounds to zero.
NOTE: Average total compensation is the sum of salary (which excludes outside income) and fringe benefits (which may include benefits such as retirement plans, medical/dental plans, group life insurance, or other benefits). Private institutions include private not-for-profit and private for-profit institutions. Institutions are classified based on the number of highest degrees awarded. For more information on the classification of postsecondary institutions, see supplemental note 8. Data are reported for the 50 states and D.C. and exclude Puerto Rico and the territories. Salaries reflect an average of all faculty on 9- and 10-month contracts rather than a weighted average based on contract length that appears in some other reports of the National Center for Education Statistics. Faculty categories are defined by the institution; the "Other" category includes instructors, lecturers, and faculty with no academic rank. Data on faculty benefits have not been collected since the early 1980s. Salaries, benefits, and compensation adjusted by the Consumer Price Index (CPI) to constant 2009–10 dollars. Detail may not sum to totals because of rounding. For more information on the CPI, see supplemental note 10. For more information on the Integrated Postsecondary Education Data System (IPEDS), see supplemental note 3.
SOURCE: U.S. Department of Education, National Center for Education Statistics, 1979–80 Higher Education General Information Survey (HEGIS), "Faculty Salaries, Tenure, and Fringe Benefits Survey"; and 1989–90, 1999–2000, and 2009–10 Integrated Postsecondary Education Data System (IPEDS), "Salaries, Tenure, and Fringe Benefits of Full-Time Instructional Faculty Survey" (IPEDS-SA:89–99), "Completions Survey" (IPEDS-C:89–99), Fall 2009 and Winter 2009–10.

Table A-44-2. Percentage distribution of full-time faculty, and average total compensation, salary, and fringe benefits in constant 2009–10 dollars for faculty at degree-granting postsecondary institutions, by faculty type and level and control of institution: Selected academic years, 1979–80 through 2009–10

[In constant 2009–10 dollars]

Academic rank and level and control of institution	1979–80 Percent distribution of faculty	1979–80 Average	1989–90 Percent distribution of faculty	1989–90 Average	1999–2000 Percent distribution of faculty	1999–2000 Average	2009–10 Percent distribution of faculty	2009–10 Average	Percent change in average 1979–80 to 2009–10	Percent change in average 1999–2000 to 2009–10
Total compensation	**100.0**	**$71,400**	**100.0**	**$82,500**	**100.0**	**$88,500**	**100.0**	**$95,600**	**33.9**	**8.0**
Salary										
All faculty	100.0	59,900	100.0	68,400	100.0	71,600	100.0	74,600	24.6	4.3
Professor	25.5	79,500	30.7	90,400	30.7	95,300	26.9	103,700	30.4	8.8
Associate professor	25.5	60,000	24.6	67,300	24.2	69,800	23.1	74,100	23.6	6.2
Assistant professor	26.2	48,800	24.1	55,900	23.0	57,600	24.1	62,200	27.5	8.1
Faculty with no academic rank	22.8	47,400	20.7	49,500	22.1	51,400	25.9	55,600	17.3	8.1
All institutions	100.0	59,900	100.0	68,400	100.0	71,600	100.0	74,600	24.6	4.3
Public doctoral universities	25.8	65,300	28.3	76,100	27.2	80,300	30.2	82,200	26.0	2.4
Private doctoral universities	8.2	69,800	10.7	85,300	10.2	95,100	13.0	97,700	40.1	2.7
Public master's colleges/universities	24.5	60,500	20.3	68,600	19.6	67,400	16.3	68,200	12.7	1.2
Private master's colleges/universities	8.0	55,000	9.8	61,200	11.1	65,200	10.4	67,800	23.2	3.9
Public other 4-year colleges	2.5	54,100	2.4	60,700	2.6	61,500	3.7	61,500	13.8	#
Private other 4-year colleges	9.1	48,000	8.5	55,900	7.6	60,900	6.2	66,200	37.8	8.6
Public 2-year colleges	21.1	57,100	19.4	58,800	21.4	61,800	20.1	62,300	9.0	0.8
Private 2-year colleges	0.7	37,200	0.6	41,800	0.4	46,000	0.2	44,700	20.1	-2.7
Fringe benefits										
All institutions	100.0	11,500	100.0	14,100	100.0	16,900	100.0	21,000	82.4	23.9
Public doctoral universities	25.8	12,200	28.3	16,500	27.2	18,500	30.2	22,100	81.0	19.2
Private doctoral universities	8.2	13,300	10.7	17,000	10.2	23,400	13.0	26,400	99.4	13.0
Public master's colleges/universities	24.5	12,400	20.3	15,100	19.6	15,900	16.3	20,400	64.9	28.5
Private master's colleges/universities	8.0	10,300	9.8	12,700	11.1	16,100	10.4	19,100	85.5	18.9
Public other 4-year colleges	2.5	10,000	2.4	12,000	2.6	14,100	3.7	18,800	87.3	32.9
Private other 4-year colleges	9.1	9,100	8.5	10,800	7.6	15,400	6.2	19,100	109.3	23.9
Public 2-year colleges	21.1	10,800	19.4	10,400	21.4	14,200	20.1	18,300	69.5	28.5
Private 2-year colleges	0.7	6,400	0.6	6,700	0.4	11,500	0.2	11,300	75.5	-2.3

NOTE: Average total compensation is the sum of salary (which excludes outside income) and fringe benefits (which may include benefits such as retirement plans, medical/dental plans, group life insurance, or other benefits). Private institutions include private not-for-profit and private for-profit institutions. Institutions are classified based on the number of highest degrees awarded. For more information on the classification of postsecondary institutions, see *supplemental note 8*. Data are reported for the 50 states and D.C. and exclude Puerto Rico and the territories. Salaries reflect an average of all faculty on 9- and 10-month contracts rather than a weighted average based on contract length that appears in some other reports of the National Center for Education Statistics. Faculty categories are defined by the institution; the "Other" category includes instructors, lecturers, and faculty with no academic rank. Data on faculty benefits have not been collected since the early 1980s. Salaries, benefits, and compensation adjusted by the Consumer Price Index (CPI) to constant 2009–10 dollars. Detail may not sum to totals because of rounding. For more information on the CPI, see *supplemental note 10*. For more information on the Integrated Postsecondary Education Data System (IPEDS), see *supplemental note 3*.
SOURCE: U.S. Department of Education, National Center for Education Statistics, 1979–80 Higher Education General Information Survey (HEGIS), "Faculty Salaries, Tenure, and Fringe Benefits Survey"; and 1989–90, 1999–2000, and 2009–10 Integrated Postsecondary Education Data System (IPEDS), "Salaries, Tenure, and Fringe Benefits of Full-Time Instructional Faculty Survey" (IPEDS-SA:89–99), "Completions Survey" (IPEDS-C:89–99), Fall 2009 and Winter 2009–10.

Table A-45-1. Percentage of 16- to 24-year-old college students who were employed, by attendance status, hours worked per week, and institution level and control: Selected years, October 1970 through October 2009

| | Full-time students | | | | Part-time students | | | |
| | | Hours worked per week[1] | | | | Hours worked per week[1] | | |
Year	Percent employed[2]	Less than 20 hours	20–34 hours	35 or more hours	Percent employed[2]	Less than 20 hours	20–34 hours	35 or more hours
Total								
1970	33.8	19.3	10.4	3.8	82.2	5.0	15.8	60.3
1975	35.3	18.2	12.0	4.7	80.9	6.0	19.5	52.6
1980	40.0	21.5	14.0	3.9	84.5	7.9	22.5	52.6
1985	44.2	21.8	17.3	4.3	86.1	6.0	26.8	52.5
1990	45.7	20.6	19.3	4.8	83.7	4.0	26.0	52.7
1995	47.2	19.1	20.3	6.5	82.9	8.6	30.4	42.3
2000	52.0	20.1	21.7	8.9	84.9	8.6	27.8	47.5
2001	47.0	17.4	20.6	7.9	84.5	8.1	25.8	48.9
2002	47.8	17.3	20.9	8.5	78.9	8.7	25.3	43.4
2003	47.7	17.1	20.7	8.8	79.0	7.8	27.2	42.8
2004	49.0	17.7	21.6	8.6	81.5	8.5	27.4	44.1
2005	49.1	17.8	21.1	9.0	85.0	10.2	27.1	47.1
2006	46.5	15.1	22.0	8.1	81.0	7.3	27.6	45.5
2007	45.5	15.4	20.7	8.7	81.2	6.8	27.2	45.9
2008	45.3	15.6	20.1	8.7	79.4	9.3	24.7	44.4
2009	40.6	15.6	17.6	6.2	76.2	10.1	27.5	36.9
Enrolled in public 4-year institutions								
1990	43.0	19.8	18.6	3.7	87.4	4.2!	27.9	54.7
1995	48.8	19.4	22.6	5.6	86.7	9.6	30.8	45.0
2000	50.5	19.1	21.5	9.0	87.3	8.5	26.4	50.9
2001	45.9	16.6	20.9	7.5	86.7	7.5	27.9	49.5
2002	47.7	17.2	21.0	8.0	78.5	7.5	22.8	47.4
2003	47.5	17.3	20.7	8.2	81.7	9.3	27.3	43.7
2004	49.7	17.4	22.0	8.8	83.0	9.0	27.4	44.3
2005	49.6	17.8	22.7	8.0	86.3	9.0	26.8	49.7
2006	46.6	13.9	22.9	8.6	80.5	7.1	26.4	46.0
2007	44.7	14.9	20.1	8.9	78.3	6.4	23.1	48.5
2008	44.1	15.1	19.2	8.8	83.9	9.3	24.7	49.5
2009	40.6	14.7	18.7	5.8	78.7	11.1	25.7	39.8
Enrolled in private 4-year institutions								
1990	38.1	24.0	9.9	3.5	89.9	‡	31.9	53.1
1995	38.6	21.6	10.7	4.6	80.1	14.9	26.8	36.5
2000	45.8	23.6	14.9	5.4	78.0	‡	18.5	52.6
2001	38.7	19.7	11.6	6.3	83.6	7.9!	23.3	51.6
2002	39.8	17.4	15.1	6.0	77.6	16.6	17.4	42.1
2003	41.1	19.0	12.8	8.4	69.2	9.3!	17.5	40.7
2004	40.6	19.6	15.0	5.3	73.0	‡	21.2	49.2
2005	42.3	20.1	13.8	7.0	88.5	10.6!	34.5	43.2
2006	36.9	18.1	12.4	5.1	83.0	6.1!	21.0	55.9
2007	38.7	18.0	13.0	6.7	83.9	‡	14.3!	61.2
2008	38.0	18.5	12.4	5.6	84.4	‡	21.4	55.3
2009	35.2	18.6	10.7	5.1	93.9	7.5!	22.1	62.4

See notes at end of table.

Table A-45-1. **Percentage of 16- to 24-year-old college students who were employed, by attendance status, hours worked per week, and institution level and control: Selected years, October 1970 through October 2009—Continued**

Year	Full-time students				Part-time students			
		Hours worked per week[1]				Hours worked per week[1]		
	Percent employed[2]	Less than 20 hours	20–34 hours	35 or more hours	Percent employed[2]	Less than 20 hours	20–34 hours	35 or more hours
Enrolled in public 2-year institutions								
1990	61.2	19.1	31.2	9.2	81.5	4.1	24.9	51.1
1995	52.9	15.6	25.3	10.9	81.1	6.1	32.5	40.5
2000	63.9	20.6	29.9	11.9	85.5	9.9	30.0	44.9
2001	58.1	18.0	28.0	10.6	83.2	8.9	25.2	47.4
2002	55.1	17.4	26.3	11.0	79.2	8.6	29.8	39.6
2003	54.7	15.4	28.1	10.3	80.6	6.6	29.6	43.4
2004	55.1	17.0	27.1	10.3	81.9	9.0	28.7	43.1
2005	54.2	15.6	24.2	13.4	82.0	10.8	25.8	44.8
2006	55.3	15.8	28.8	9.2	80.7	8.2	30.0	42.2
2007	54.0	15.2	28.7	9.6	83.4	7.1	33.7	40.9
2008	52.9	14.6	26.9	10.7	74.8	9.7	25.9	37.8
2009	45.4	16.0	20.5	7.8	71.8	10.3	30.6	29.4

! Interpret with caution. The standard error of the estimate is equal to 30 percent or more of the estimate's value.
‡ Reporting standards not met.
[1] Excludes those who were employed but not at work during the survey week; therefore, detail may not sum to total percentage employed. *Hours worked per week* refers to the number of hours the respondent worked at all jobs during the survey week.
[2] Includes those who were employed but not at work during the survey week.
NOTE: College includes both 2- and 4-year institutions. College students were classified as full time if they were taking at least 12 hours of classes (or at least 9 hours of graduate classes) during an average school week and as part time if they were taking fewer hours. For more information on the Current Population Survey (CPS), see *supplemental note 2*.
SOURCE: U.S. Department of Commerce, Census Bureau, Current Population Survey (CPS), October Supplement, selected years, 1970–2009.

College Student Employment

Table A-45-2. Percentage of 16- to 24-year-old college students who were employed, by attendance status, hours worked per week, and selected characteristics: October 2009

Characteristic	Full-time students				Part-time students			
		Hours worked per week[1]				Hours worked per week[1]		
	Percent employed[2]	Less than 20 hours	20–34 hours	35 or more hours	Percent employed[2]	Less than 20 hours	20–34 hours	35 or more hours
Total	**40.6**	**15.6**	**17.6**	**6.2**	**76.2**	**10.1**	**27.5**	**36.9**
Sex								
Male	35.6	12.5	16.2	5.8	72.5	8.8	24.2	37.4
Female	45.0	18.3	18.9	6.6	79.2	11.1	30.2	36.4
Race/ethnicity								
White	44.5	18.6	18.6	5.9	79.0	11.0	24.6	41.7
Black	28.9	8.1	13.5	7.1	73.3	‡	42.4	23.0
Hispanic	38.8	10.8	18.7	8.7	73.7	11.8	28.5	32.6
Asian	25.6	9.2	12.0	3.5!	63.1	‡	16.2!	36.7
Pacific Islander	‡	‡	‡	‡	‡	‡	‡	‡
American Indian/ Alaska Native	‡	‡	‡	‡	‡	‡	‡	‡
Two or more races	44.5	15.3	25.4	‡	‡	‡	‡	‡
Level and control of institution								
2-year	44.1	15.6	19.7	7.7	71.2	9.8	29.9	30.1
Public	45.4	16.0	20.5	7.8	71.8	10.3	30.6	29.4
Private	28.5	9.7!	9.5!	7.5!	‡	‡	‡	‡
4-year	39.4	15.6	16.9	5.7	81.7	10.4	25.0	44.2
Public	40.6	14.7	18.7	5.8	78.7	11.1	25.7	39.8
Private	35.2	18.6	10.7	5.1	93.9	7.5!	22.1	62.4
Student enrollment level								
Undergraduate	40.2	15.8	17.5	5.7	74.2	11.2	29.7	31.9
Sex								
Male	34.9	12.8	15.8	5.2	70.7	10.4	25.5	33.2
Female	44.9	18.5	19.0	6.2	77.0	11.8	32.9	31.0
Race/ethnicity								
White	44.4	18.9	18.6	5.4	77.1	12.6	26.7	36.2
Black	28.4	8.5	13.2	6.5	71.0	‡	47.5	16.8
Hispanic	37.8	10.5	18.5	8.5	72.9	12.1	27.2	32.7
Asian	21.7	8.7	9.5	2.5!	‡	‡	‡	‡
Pacific Islander	‡	‡	‡	‡	‡	‡	‡	‡
American Indian/ Alaska Native	‡	‡	‡	‡	‡	‡	‡	‡
Two or more races	45.9	15.8	26.2	‡	‡	‡	‡	‡
Level and control of institution								
2-year	43.5	15.1	19.8	7.5	70.2	10.3	30.8	28.1
Public	44.9	15.9	20.5	7.4	70.9	10.9	31.5	27.5
Private	23.1	4.1	10.5	8.5	‡	‡	‡	‡
4-year	39.0	16.0	16.6	5.1	79.7	12.4	28.2	37.1
Public	40.2	14.9	18.5	5.5	77.6	12.8	27.0	36.1
Private	34.6	20.4	9.8	3.6	93.7	‡	36.2	43.7
Graduate	45.4	13.0	19.3	12.3	88.0	‡	14.8	66.4

! Interpret with caution. The standard error of the estimate is equal to 30 percent or more of the estimate's value.
‡ Reporting standards not met.
[1] Excludes those who were employed but not at work during the survey week; therefore, detail may not sum to total percentage employed. *Hours worked per week* refers to the number of hours the respondent worked at all jobs during the survey week.
[2] Includes those who were employed but not at work during the survey week.
NOTE: College includes both 2- and 4-year institutions. College students were classified as full time if they were taking at least 12 hours of classes (or at least 9 hours of graduate classes) during an average school week and as part time if they were taking fewer hours. Race categories exclude persons of Hispanic ethnicity. For more information on race/ethnicity, see *supplemental note 1*. For more information on the Current Population Survey (CPS), see *supplemental note 2*.
SOURCE: U.S. Department of Commerce, Census Bureau, Current Population Survey (CPS), October Supplement, 2009.

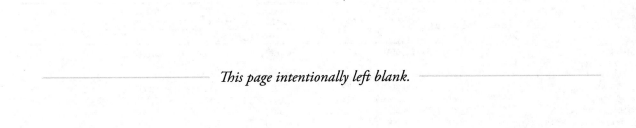

This page intentionally left blank.

Federal Grants and Loans to Undergraduates

Table A-46-1. Percentage of full-time, full-year undergraduates who received loans and grants, and average annual amounts received by recipients, by source of aid, dependency status, income, and institution control and level: Academic year 1999–2000, 2003–04, and 2007–08

[In constant 2009–10 dollars]

Characteristic	Total				Federal			
	Loans		Grants		Loans		Grants	
	Percent	Average dollars	Percent	Average dollars	Percent	Average dollars	Percent	Average dollars
	1999–2000							
Total	**44.5**	**$6,500**	**59.2**	**$6,500**	**43.4**	**$5,700**	**30.6**	**$3,300**
Dependency status and income								
Dependent undergraduates	44.4	6,000	56.9	7,100	43.2	5,100	23.4	3,100
Low-income	47.8	5,800	83.6	7,100	46.9	5,200	73.2	3,600
Middle-income	49.0	6,000	54.4	7,100	47.8	5,100	13.1	2,100
High-income	33.0	6,400	39.0	6,900	31.5	5,100	0.7	2,100
Independent undergraduates	44.8	7,900	66.2	4,900	43.9	7,300	51.7	3,500
Control and level of institution								
Public less-than-2-year	4.6	6,600	48.3	3,800	4.6	6,500	39.8	3,100
Public 2-year	12.8	4,900	49.3	3,400	11.9	4,200	32.4	3,200
Public 4-year	48.6	5,900	54.8	4,900	47.6	5,500	28.9	3,200
Private not-for-profit less-than-2-year	7.4	‡	84.3	3,900	‡	‡	84.3	3,300
Private not-for-profit 2-year	26.6	6,200	72.6	6,600	26.6	5,400	35.4	3,400
Private not-for-profit 4-year	61.3	7,500	75.9	10,900	59.7	6,000	27.5	3,500
Private for-profit less-than-2-year	74.0	6,000	74.1	3,200	73.3	5,300	72.1	3,100
Private for-profit 2-year	86.7	6,800	68.9	4,700	85.7	6,000	58.1	3,300
Private for-profit 4-year	73.4	8,200	51.7	4,700	73.0	7,700	35.5	3,200
	2003–04							
Total	**48.0**	**6,700**	**63.5**	**6,600**	**46.5**	**5,600**	**33.9**	**3,800**
Dependency status and income								
Dependent undergraduates	46.8	6,300	61.0	7,200	45.1	4,900	25.9	3,600
Low-income	49.3	5,900	85.9	8,200	47.9	5,100	73.1	4,300
Middle-income	49.9	6,300	58.5	6,600	48.2	4,900	17.1	2,300
High-income	38.5	6,600	43.8	6,900	36.6	4,700	1.0	1,900
Independent undergraduates	51.6	7,800	70.6	5,400	50.4	7,200	56.4	4,000
Control and level of institution								
Public less-than-2-year	17.5	6,200	52.5	3,700	16.9	5,500	37.4	3,300
Public 2-year	17.5	4,300	52.1	3,900	16.2	4,000	35.0	3,700
Public 4-year	51.9	6,300	59.9	5,500	50.2	5,500	30.6	3,700
Private not-for-profit less-than-2-year	25.0	4,100	78.8	5,100	21.4	4,400	76.7	4,100
Private not-for-profit 2-year	46.3	5,900	75.8	6,800	43.6	5,100	46.8	4,200
Private not-for-profit 4-year	64.9	7,900	81.7	11,100	63.1	5,800	31.7	4,000
Private for-profit less-than-2-year	69.9	6,000	69.9	3,800	68.0	5,200	59.9	3,400
Private for-profit 2-year	88.5	7,100	80.4	5,600	88.0	5,900	72.7	3,800
Private for-profit 4-year	82.1	9,100	69.0	5,400	80.8	7,600	48.5	4,100

See notes at end of table.

Table A-46-1. Percentage of full-time, full-year undergraduates who received loans and grants, and average annual amounts received by recipients, by source of aid, dependency status, income, and institution control and level: Academic year 1999–2000, 2003–04, and 2007–08—Continued

[In constant 2009–10 dollars]

Characteristic	Total				Federal			
	Loans		Grants		Loans		Grants	
	Percent	Average dollars	Percent	Average dollars	Percent	Average dollars	Percent	Average dollars
	2007–08							
Total	**53.1**	**$8,200**	**65.3**	**$7,400**	**49.3**	**$5,600**	**33.4**	**$3,800**
Dependency status and income								
Dependent undergraduates	49.5	7,900	63.1	8,100	45.6	4,900	25.4	3,800
Low-income	54.0	6,900	88.5	9,000	51.2	5,200	79.9	4,400
Middle-income	53.6	8,000	61.4	7,700	49.4	4,900	15.0	2,500
High-income	39.2	8,600	46.2	7,800	34.9	4,700	0.8	3,200
Independent undergraduates	64.2	9,200	72.4	5,400	60.8	7,100	58.6	3,700
Control and level of institution								
Public less-than-2-year	26.3	6,700	55.1	3,700	23.2	5,400	48.5	3,400
Public 2-year	22.5	5,000	55.7	3,800	19.6	4,200	36.7	3,600
Public 4-year	52.7	7,200	60.4	6,300	48.7	5,400	28.8	3,900
Private not-for-profit less-than-2-year	‡	‡	81.2!	4,100	‡	‡	77.2!	3,900
Private not-for-profit 2-year	50.7	9,300	67.0	7,200	47.6	5,600	52.4	5,100
Private not-for-profit 4-year	65.0	10,000	81.2	12,600	60.6	5,700	28.0	4,200
Private for-profit less-than-2-year	77.9	7,200	75.5	3,800	67.5	5,500	72.8	3,500
Private for-profit 2-year	95.3	10,300	79.0	4,500	94.2	6,700	73.6	3,700
Private for-profit 4-year	94.2	10,300	68.8	4,000	91.9	6,700	55.5	3,200

! Interpret data with caution. Estimate is unstable because the standard error represents more than 30 percent of the estimate.
‡ Reporting standards not met.
NOTE: Total loans include federal, state, institutional, and private loans. Total grants include federal, state, institutional, and private grants, including employer reimbursements. Federal loans include Perkins loans, subsidized and unsubsidized Stafford loans, and Supplemental Loans to Students (SLS). Federal grants are primarily Pell Grants and Supplemental Educational Opportunity Grants (SEOG), but also include Byrd scholarships. Parent Loans for Undergraduate Students (PLUS), veterans' benefits, and tax credits are not included in this table. Average aid amounts are calculated for recipients only. Income for dependent students is based on parents' annual income in the prior year. The cutoff points for low, middle, and high income were obtained by identifying the incomes below the 25th percentile (low-income), between the 25th and 75th percentiles (middle-income), and at the 75th percentile and above (high-income). Data adjusted to 2009–10 dollars using the Consumer Price Index for All Urban Consumers (CPI-U). For more information about the CPI-U, see *supplemental note 10*. For more information on the National Postsecondary Student Aid Study (NPSAS), see *supplemental note 3*.
SOURCE: U.S. Department of Education, National Center for Education Statistics, 1999–2000, 2003–04, and 2007–08 National Postsecondary Student Aid Studies (NPSAS:2000, NPSAS:04, and NPSAS:08).

Price of Attending an Undergraduate Institution

Table A-47-1. Average total price of attendance, grants, net price, and loans for all full-time, full-year, dependent undergraduates attending only one institution, by institution control and level: Academic years 1999–2000, 2003–04, and 2007–08

[In constant 2009–10 dollars]

Control and level of institution	1999–2000	2003–04	2007–08
Public less than 2-year			
Total price of attendance	$10,700	$13,100	$16,200
Grants	700	1,700	1,100
Net price	10,000	11,500	15,100
Loans	‡	700!	1,300!
Public 2-year			
Total price of attendance	10,900	11,400	12,100
Grants	1,400	1,700	1,800
Net price	9,500	9,700	10,300
Loans	400	600	900
Public 4-year			
Total price of attendance	15,800	17,500	19,300
Grants	2,500	3,100	3,700
Net price	13,300	14,400	15,600
Loans	3,100	3,800	4,600
Private not-for-profit less than 2-year			
Total price of attendance	15,800	‡	18,500!
Grants	2,400!	‡	2,900!
Net price	13,300	‡	‡
Loans	‡	‡	‡
Private not-for-profit 2-year			
Total price of attendance	19,100	21,000	23,800
Grants	5,100	5,300	4,100!
Net price	14,000	15,700	19,800
Loans	2,100	4,100	7,800
Private not-for-profit 4-year			
Total price of attendance	31,200	34,200	37,400
Grants	8,900	9,700	10,900
Net price	22,300	24,500	26,600
Loans	6,100	7,000	8,500
Private for-profit less than 2-year			
Total price of attendance	19,400	21,000	21,000
Grants	2,100	2,300	2,400
Net price	17,300	18,700	18,600
Loans	5,400	5,400	6,600
Private for-profit 2-year			
Total price of attendance	24,000	25,000	27,900
Grants	2,500	4,900	3,100
Net price	21,500	20,100	24,700
Loans	8,400	9,600	11,800
Private for-profit 4-year			
Total price of attendance	26,000	27,300	33,500
Grants	3,200	4,700	2,600
Net price	22,800	22,500	30,900
Loans	9,700	11,200	15,800

! Interpret with caution. The standard error of the estimate is equal to 30 percent or more of the estimate's value.
‡ Reporting standards not met.
NOTE: *Full time* refers to students who attended full time (as defined by the institution) for the full year (at least 9 months). Grants include the total amount of all grants and scholarships received during the academic year, including federal grants, state grants, institutional grants, and outside grants. Outside grants include employer tuition reimbursements and grants from private sources. *Net price* is an estimate of the cash outlay that students and their families need to make in a given year to cover educational expenses. It is calculated here as the total price of attendance including loans and minus grants. Information on the use of tax credits by individual families is not available and therefore could not be taken into account in calculating net price. Loans includes the total amount of all loans received during the 2007–08 academic year, including federal Parent Loans to Undergraduate Students (PLUS), all federal loans to students, state loans, institutional loans, and other private commercial or alternative loans. Averages were computed for all students, including those who did not receive financial aid. Data were adjusted by the Consumer Price Index for All Urban Consumers (CPI-U) to constant 2009–10 dollars. For more information on the CPI-U, see *supplemental note 10*. Estimates exclude students who were not U.S. citizens or permanent residents and therefore ineligible for federal student aid and students who attended more than one institution in a year, due to the difficulty of matching information on price and aid. Details may not sum to totals due to rounding.
SOURCE: U.S. Department of Education, National Center for Education Statistics, 1999–2000, 2003–04, and 2007–08 National Postsecondary Student Aid Studies (NPSAS:2000, NPSAS:04, and NPSAS:08).

Table A-47-2. Average net price for all full-time, full-year, dependent undergraduates after grants, by sex, family income, and race/ethnicity: Academic years 1999–2000, 2003–04, and 2007–08

[In constant 2009–10 dollars]

Sex, race/ethnicity, and family income	1999–2000	2003–04	2007–08
Average net price	**$15,100**	**$16,000**	**$17,700**
Sex			
Male	15,400	16,300	18,000
Female	14,900	15,800	17,400
Family income			
Low income	10,600	11,500	12,000
Middle income	15,100	15,900	17,300
High income	19,100	20,200	22,700
Race/ethnicity			
White	16,000	16,800	18,700
Black	12,300	13,200	14,900
Hispanic	11,600	13,200	14,300
Asian	14,600	16,200	17,700
American Indian/Alaskan Native	13,600	12,900	13,400
Pacific Islander/Hawaiian	13,900	15,100	18,900
Two or more races	13,700	16,700	16,700

NOTE: *Full time* refers to students who attended full time (as defined by the institution) for the full year (at least 9 months). *Net price* is an estimate of the cash outlay that students and their families need to make in a given year to cover educational expenses. It is calculated here as the total price of attendance including loans and minus grants. Information on the use of tax credits by individual families is not available and therefore could not be taken into account in calculating net price. Averages were computed for all students, including those who did not receive financial aid. Data were adjusted by the Consumer Price Index for All Urban Consumers (CPI-U) to constant 2009–10 dollars. For more information on the CPI-U, see *supplemental note 10*. Estimates exclude students who were not U.S. citizens or permanent residents and therefore ineligible for federal student aid and students who attended more than one institution in a year, due to the difficulty of matching information on price and aid. The cutoff points for low, middle, and high income were obtained by identifying the incomes below the 25th percentile (low income), between the 25th and 75th percentile (middle income), and at the 75th percentile and above (high income). Race categories exclude persons of Hispanic ethnicity. For more information on race/ethnicity, see *supplemental note 1*.
SOURCE: U.S. Department of Education, National Center for Education Statistics, 1999–2000, 2003–04, and 2007–08 National Postsecondary Student Aid Studies (NPSAS:2000, NPSAS:04, and NPSAS:08).

Price of Graduate and First-Professional Attendance

Table A-48-1. Average annual tuition and fees, total price, amount of aid, and net price for all full-time graduate and first-professional students, and percentage of all students attending full time, by level, degree program, and institution control: Academic years 2003–04 and 2007–08

[In constant 2009–10 dollars]

Characteristic	Percent attending full time	Average for full-time students						Net price (total price minus grants)
		Tuition and fees	Total price[1]	Total aid	Grants	Loans	Assistant-ships and other aid	
				2003–04				
Master's degree students								
Total	**21.3**	**$13,500**	**$32,000**	**$16,300**	**$3,300**	**$10,400**	**$2,500**	**$28,700**
Degree program								
Business administration (M.B.A.)	19.9	17,700	38,200	16,700	3,000	12,500	1,300	35,200
Education (any master's)	11.5	9,600	26,400	12,600	1,900	9,600	1,000	24,500
Any other master's degree	27.8	13,300	31,700	17,000	3,800	10,100	3,200	28,000
Institution control								
Public	20.4	8,700	25,700	13,900	3,300	6,800	3,800	22,400
Private not-for-profit	20.8	20,100	39,400	20,000	3,800	14,800	1,400	35,600
Doctoral degree students								
Total	**47.7**	**16,800**	**38,500**	**26,500**	**10,100**	**7,200**	**9,300**	**28,400**
Degree program								
Ph.D. (except in education)	53.1	17,400	39,100	28,100	12,600	3,200	12,300	26,500
Education (any doctorate)[2]	20.2	12,500	32,400	16,300	5,900	5,100	5,300	26,500
Any other doctoral degree[3]	52.4	16,300	38,500	25,100	4,800	17,500	2,800	33,700
Institution control								
Public	45.3	11,800	32,900	24,700	9,700	5,400	9,700	23,200
Private not-for-profit	51.8	23,900	46,700	29,500	10,800	9,700	8,900	35,800
First-professional degree students								
Total	**76.5**	**18,900**	**41,200**	**28,300**	**3,500**	**23,700**	**1,100**	**37,600**
Degree program								
Medicine (M.D.)	90.9	19,200	45,200	32,300	4,000	26,400	1,900	41,200
Other health science degree	89.4	18,200	40,400	28,100	2,300	24,800	1,100	38,100
Law (L.L.B. or J.D.)	76.5	19,700	40,300	27,200	3,800	22,600	700	36,500
Theology (M.Div., M.H.L., B.D.)	22.4	11,000	27,600	13,400	5,900	6,900	700	21,700
Institution control								
Public	87.8	11,100	33,700	24,600	2,800	20,800	1,100	30,900
Private not-for-profit	68.9	25,600	47,600	31,500	4,200	26,200	1,100	43,400

See notes at end of table.

Table A-48-1. Average annual tuition and fees, total price, amount of aid, and net price for all full-time graduate and first-professional students, and percentage of all students attending full time, by level, degree program, and institution control: Academic years 2003–04 and 2007–08—Continued

[In constant 2009–10 dollars]

Characteristic	Percent attending full time	Average for full-time students						
		Tuition and fees	Total price[1]	Total aid	Grants	Loans	Assistant-ships and other aid	Net price (total price minus grants)
				2007–08				
Master's degree students								
Total	26.0	$14,700	$34,600	$19,300	$4,500	$12,600	$2,200	$30,100
Degree program								
Business administration (M.B.A.)	30.6	15,200	37,100	18,300	4,200	13,300	800	32,900
Education (any master's)	16.5	10,900	29,400	16,000	2,900	11,600	1,500	26,500
Any other master's degree	30.2	15,800	35,500	20,900	5,200	12,700	3,000	30,300
Institution control								
Public	21.8	10,600	29,000	18,600	5,200	9,200	4,200	23,900
Private not-for-profit	25.6	20,600	39,600	20,900	4,600	15,000	1,300	35,000
Doctoral degree students								
Total	52.9	16,800	39,700	26,900	9,200	8,300	9,400	30,500
Degree program								
Ph.D. (except in education)	57.7	17,300	40,000	27,100	12,000	3,100	12,000	27,900
Education (any doctorate)[2]	22.8	12,300	34,500	21,900	4,400	11,300	6,100	30,100
Any other doctoral degree[3]	59.2	16,900	40,200	27,400	3,700	19,600	4,100	36,400
Institution control								
Public	47.8	11,900	33,700	24,900	9,100	4,700	11,200	24,700
Private not-for-profit	61.8	24,200	47,100	29,100	10,800	9,800	8,500	36,300
First-professional degree students								
Total	78.4	24,200	46,500	32,000	3,600	27,400	900	42,900
Degree program								
Medicine (M.D.)	87.2	21,100	46,100	31,900	2,700	28,100	1,100	43,400
Other health science degree	81.7	20,000	42,700	31,300	3,000	27,200	1,000	39,700
Law (L.L.B. or J.D.)	76.6	28,100	49,200	33,200	4,200	28,200	900	45,000
Theology (M.Div., M.H.L., B.D.)	44.3	16,200	33,900	17,600	7,000	10,300	300	26,900
Institution control								
Public	82.2	13,500	37,300	27,700	3,000	23,400	1,300	34,400
Private not-for-profit	75.6	32,600	53,700	35,300	4,100	30,500	700	49,600

[1] Total price (also known as the student budget) includes tuition and fees, books and materials, and living expenses.
[2] Ph.D. in education, Ed.D., or any other doctoral degree in which education is the field of study.
[3] Examples include D.B.A. (Doctor of Business Administration), D.F.A. (Doctor of Fine Arts), and D.P.A. (Doctor of Public Administration).
NOTE: Data presented are limited to full-time students who attended for the full year at only one institution to keep financial aid and price data comparable. *Full-time* students includes unaided students. "Other aid" includes aid that could not be characterized as federal, state, or institutional, such as employer aid, outside grants, and veteran's benefits. "Total" includes data for private for-profit institutions, which are not shown separately. Detail may not sum to totals because of rounding. Some data are revised from previously published figures. Data were adjusted to constant 2009–10 dollars using the Consumer Price Index For All Urban Consumers (CPI-U). for more information on the CPI-U, see *supplemental note 10*. For more information on the National Postsecondary Student Aid Study (NPSAS), see *supplemental note 3*.
SOURCE: U.S. Department of Education, National Center for Education Statistics, 2003–04 and 2007–08 National Postsecondary Student Aid Study (NPSAS:04 and NPSAS:08).

Price of Graduate and First-Professional Attendance

Table A-48-2. Percentage of full-time graduate and first-professional students with aid and the average annual amount of aid for students receiving each type of aid, by type of aid, level, degree program, and institution control: Academic years 2003–04 and 2007–08

Characteristic	Percent				Average (for full-time students with each type of aid, in constant 2009–10 dollars)			
	Any aid	Grants	Loans	Assistant-ships and other aid	Total aid	Grants	Loans	Assistant-ships and other aid
					2003–04			
Master's degree students								
Total	**80.5**	**40.3**	**56.9**	**25.9**	**$20,200**	**$8,200**	**$18,300**	**$9,700**
Degree program								
Business administration (M.B.A.)	76.4	39.9	57.6	16.2	21,900	7,500	21,700	‡
Education (any master's)	70.7	25.7	59.1	12.6	17,800	7,500	16,300	‡
Any other master's degree	84.1	44.1	56.2	31.8	20,300	8,500	17,900	10,100
Institution control								
Public	78.2	43.0	45.8	37.2	17,700	7,600	14,900	10,200
Private not-for-profit	82.8	39.0	67.2	16.9	24,200	9,800	22,000	8,400
Doctoral degree students								
Total	**92.4**	**65.9**	**34.2**	**55.5**	**28,700**	**15,300**	**20,900**	**16,700**
Degree program								
Ph.D. (except in education)	95.4	74.4	21.1	68.3	29,400	17,000	15,100	18,000
Education (any doctorate)[1]	79.7	51.0	34.8	41.8	20,400	11,500	14,700	12,600
Any other doctoral degree[2]	88.3	48.8	66.4	27.7	28,400	9,800	26,300	10,300
Institution control								
Public	93.6	70.6	30.6	60.6	26,400	13,700	17,500	15,900
Private not-for-profit	90.6	60.3	38.3	49.7	32,600	18,000	25,400	18,000
First-professional degree students								
Total	**90.3**	**40.6**	**81.3**	**15.4**	**31,400**	**8,700**	**29,100**	**7,100**
Degree program								
Medicine (M.D.)	89.0	41.2	78.0	16.9	36,300	9,800	33,900	11,000
Other health science degree	92.3	40.8	84.0	17.2	30,500	5,600	29,500	6,100
Law (L.L.B. or J.D.)	91.1	39.1	84.3	13.7	29,800	9,900	26,900	5,200
Theology (M.Div., M.H.L., B.D.)	74.2	53.5	45.6	12.7	‡	‡	‡	‡
Institution control								
Public	90.6	42.5	80.9	14.4	27,200	6,500	25,700	7,600
Private not-for-profit	90.1	38.9	81.6	16.3	34,900	10,800	32,100	6,800

See notes at end of table.

Table A-48-2. Percentage of full-time graduate and first-professional students with aid and the average annual amount of aid for students receiving each type of aid, by type of aid, level, degree program, and institution control: Academic years 2003–04 and 2007–08—Continued

	Percent				Average (for full-time students with each type of aid, in constant 2009–10 dollars)			
Characteristic	Any aid	Grants	Loans	Assistant-ships and other aid	Total aid	Grants	Loans	Assistant-ships and other aid
				2007–08				
Master's degree students								
Total	**84.8**	**42.5**	**60.0**	**22.2**	**$22,800**	**$10,600**	**$21,000**	**$10,100**
Degree program								
Business administration (M.B.A.)	83.5	42.0	58.9	10.5	22,000	10,000	22,600	7,400
Education (any master's)	83.1	35.2	66.2	15.7	19,200	8,200	17,500	9,500
Any other master's degree	85.9	45.2	58.3	28.8	24,300	11,400	21,700	10,500
Institution control								
Public	86.5	49.5	52.2	38.0	21,500	10,500	17,700	10,900
Private not-for-profit	81.9	42.1	60.8	16.3	25,500	10,900	24,600	8,200
Doctoral degree students								
Total	**93.0**	**59.7**	**35.3**	**57.1**	**28,900**	**15,400**	**23,600**	**16,400**
Degree program								
Ph.D. (except in education)	94.5	70.1	19.5	67.5	28,700	17,200	15,900	17,800
Education (any doctorate)[1]	89.3	45.4	52.7	50.5	24,500	9,800	21,400	12,100
Any other doctoral degree[2]	90.4	39.3	67.4	34.7	30,300	9,600	29,000	11,800
Institution control								
Public	92.0	64.5	28.0	67.4	27,100	14,100	16,600	16,600
Private not-for-profit	94.5	61.8	35.2	51.7	30,800	17,500	27,800	16,500
First-professional degree students								
Total	**88.1**	**40.3**	**81.2**	**14.8**	**36,300**	**9,000**	**33,700**	**6,400**
Degree program								
Medicine (M.D.)	83.7	33.2	77.2	14.8	38,100	8,100	36,400	7,400
Other health science degree	91.7	42.8	86.9	12.4	34,100	7,000	31,300	8,500
Law (L.L.B. or J.D.)	89.0	41.3	81.8	16.1	37,300	10,100	34,400	5,300
Theology (M.Div., M.H.L., B.D.)	87.3	68.3	67.6	10.0	20,100	10,200	‡	‡
Institution control								
Public	88.1	42.1	81.1	14.4	31,400	7,100	28,900	8,800
Private not-for-profit	88.1	39.0	81.3	15.0	40,100	10,600	37,500	4,600

‡ Reporting standards not met.
[1] Ph.D. in education, Ed.D., or any other doctoral degree in which education is the field of study.
[2] Examples include D.B.A. (Doctor of Business Administration), D.F.A. (Doctor of Fine Arts), and D.P.A. (Doctor of Public Administration).
NOTE: Data presented are limited to full-time students who attended for the full year at only one institution to keep financial aid and price data comparable. "Other aid" includes aid that could not be characterized as federal, state, or institutional, such as employer aid, outside grants, and veteran's benefits. "Total" includes data for private for-profit institutions, which are not shown separately. Some data are revised from previously published figures. Data were adjusted to constant 2009–10 dollars using the Consumer Price Index For All Urban Consumers (CPI-U). for more information on the CPI-U, see *supplemental note 10.*
SOURCE: U.S. Department of Education, National Center for Education Statistics, 2003–04 and 2007–08 National Postsecondary Student Aid Study (NPSAS:04 and NPSAS:08).

Price of Graduate and First-Professional Attendance

Table A-48-3. Average annual tuition and fees, aid, and net tuition after grants for part-time graduate students, by level, degree program, and institution control: Academic years 2003–04 and 2007–08

[In constant 2009–10 dollars]

Characteristic	Average tuition and fees	Percent with grants	Percent with employer aid[1]	Average grants	Average employer aid[1]	Net tuition after grants[2] (all part-time students)	Percent attending part time
			2003–04				
Master's degree students							
Total	**$6,200**	**41.2**	**25.8**	**$2,000**	**$1,000**	**$4,700**	**43.4**
Degree program							
Business administration (M.B.A.)	7,400	59.1	48.6	3,300	2,700	4,900	35.7
Education (any master's)	5,400	34.9	22.1	1,300	600	4,400	49.1
Any other master's degree	6,300	40.1	21.2	2,000	800	4,800	42.9
Institution control							
Public	4,300	38.9	23.5	1,600	700	3,200	48.4
Private not-for-profit	9,000	44.4	28.2	2,500	1,400	6,900	40.6
Doctoral degree students							
Total	**6,600**	**48.2**	**20.6**	**3,800**	**600**	**4,400**	**33.2**
Degree program							
Ph.D. (except in education)	6,300	52.0	14.9	4,900	500	3,600	29.3
Education (any doctorate)[3]	5,500	41.4	26.3	1,900	800	4,100	57.0
Any other doctoral degree[4]	8,900	47.2	27.7	3,200	900	6,800	27.5
Institution control							
Public	5,500	48.4	17.5	3,700	500	3,500	36.0
Private not-for-profit	8,200	44.8	22.6	3,900	1,000	5,500	28.0
			2007–08				
Master's degree students							
Total	**7,000**	**42.1**	**30.4**	**2,300**	**1,500**	**5,200**	**32.4**
Degree program							
Business administration (M.B.A.)	9,100	53.3	47.6	4,200	3,400	5,800	27.6
Education (any master's)	5,800	32.9	23.3	1,300	700	4,900	35.4
Any other master's degree	7,200	44.9	29.8	2,500	1,400	5,300	32.3
Institution control							
Public	4,900	41.2	29.2	1,900	1,100	3,600	35.1
Private not-for-profit	9,600	44.9	32.8	3,000	2,000	7,100	32.0
Doctoral degree students							
Total	**7,800**	**51.1**	**19.1**	**3,900**	**900**	**5,200**	**22.5**
Degree program							
Ph.D. (except in education)	7,700	56.5	16.2	4,800	800	4,600	19.7
Education (any doctorate)[3]	7,200	45.6	25.7	2,700	1,100	5,400	43.7
Any other doctoral degree[4]	8,800	44.5	16.7	3,100	800	6,700	16.7
Institution control							
Public	6,500	55.9	18.2	4,400	900	3,800	26.3
Private not-for-profit	9,800	42.1	21.7	3,100	1,000	7,400	17.1

[1] Employer aid is considered a type of grant aid and therefore is included in the estimates for grants.
[2] If grants were greater than tuition, net tuition was set to zero. Consequently, average net tuition may be larger than average tuition and fees minus average grants.
[3] Ph.D. in education, Ed.D., or any other doctoral degree in which education is the field of study.
[4] Examples include D.B.A. (Doctor of Business Administration), D.F.A. (Doctor of Fine Arts), and D.P.A. (Doctor of Public Administration).
NOTE: Data presented are limited to part-time students who attended for the full year at only one institution to keep financial aid and price comparable. "Total" includes data for private for-profit institutions, which are not shown separately. Too few first-professional students enrolled part time to present the data. Part-time students includes unaided students. Detail may not sum to totals because of rounding. Some data are revised from previously published figures. Data were adjusted to constant 2009–10 dollars using the Consumer Price Index For All Urban Consumers (CPI-U). for more information on the CPI-U, see *supplemental note 10*.
SOURCE: U.S. Department of Education, National Center for Education Statistics, 2003–04 and 2007–08 National Postsecondary Student Aid Study (NPSAS:04 and NPSAS:08).

This page intentionally left blank.

Table A-49-1. Average tuition and fees, percentage of students with loans, and average loan amounts at degree-granting institutions, by level and control of institution: 2007–08 and 2008–09

Level and control of institution	2007–08			2008–09		
	Average tuition and fees	Percentage of first-time, full-time students with student loans	Average loan amount	Average tuition and fees	Percentage of first-time, full-time students with student loans	Average loan amount
	[In current dollars]					
All institutions	**$8,412**	**45.6**	**$6,009**	**$8,813**	**48.6**	**$6,974**
2-year institutions	2,519	32.0	5,407	2,618	34.9	6,082
Public	2,061	19.4	3,488	2,136	21.1	4,152
Private not-for-profit	11,789	54.1	5,323	12,603	58.1	6,089
Private for-profit	13,363	77.9	7,195	13,725	77.5	7,736
4-year institutions	11,414	52.6	6,198	12,021	55.8	7,268
Public	5,943	45.2	5,190	6,312	46.9	5,972
Private not-for-profit	23,328	60.3	6,435	24,636	60.6	7,638
Private for-profit	15,226	68.7	8,799	15,168	81.4	9,661
	[In constant 2009–10 dollars]					
All institutions	**$8,612**	**45.6**	**$6,152**	**$8,898**	**48.6**	**$7,042**
2-year institutions	2,579	32.0	5,536	2,644	34.9	6,141
Public	2,110	19.4	3,571	2,156	21.1	4,193
Private not-for-profit	12,069	54.1	5,449	12,725	58.1	6,148
Private for-profit	13,680	77.9	7,366	13,858	77.5	7,811
4-year institutions	11,685	52.6	6,345	12,137	55.8	7,338
Public	6,084	45.2	5,314	6,373	46.9	6,029
Private not-for-profit	23,883	60.3	6,588	24,875	60.6	7,712
Private for-profit	15,588	68.7	9,009	15,315	81.4	9,754

NOTE: Degree-granting institutions grant associate's or higher degrees and participate in Title IV federal financial aid programs. Tuition and fees amounts for public institutions are the averages for in-state students. Tuition and fee data are collected in the fall and loan data are collected in the spring. For more information on the Integrated Postsecondary Data System (IPEDS) and IPEDS classification of institutions, see *supplemental notes 3* and *8.* Data were adjusted to constant 2009–10 dollars using the Consumer Price Index For All Urban Consumers (CPI-U). For more information on the CPI-U, see *supplemental note 10.*
SOURCE: U.S. Department of Education, National Center for Education Statistics, 2007–08 and 2008–09 Integrated Postsecondary Education Data System (IPEDS), Spring 2008 and Spring 2009.

Table A-49-2. Number of students at degree-granting institutions who have entered the repayment phase of student loans, number of students in default, and 2-year student loan cohort default rates, by level and control of institution: Fiscal years 2006–08

Level and control of institution	Number of students who have entered repayment phase	Number of students who have entered repayment and are in default	2-year cohort default rate[1]
	Fiscal year 2006		
All institutions	**3,715,745**	**181,492**	**4.9**
2-year institutions	805,741	71,175	8.8
Public	562,215	45,881	8.2
Private not-for-profit	12,138	827	6.8
Private for-profit	231,388	24,467	10.6
4-year institutions	2,910,004	110,317	3.8
Public	1,451,795	49,632	3.4
Private not-for-profit	1,003,880	23,051	2.3
Private for-profit	454,329	37,634	8.3
	Fiscal year 2007		
All institutions	**3,158,499**	**202,247**	**6.4**
2-year institutions	759,050	79,954	10.5
Public	508,950	49,257	9.7
Private not-for-profit	11,194	1,048	9.4
Private for-profit	238,906	29,649	12.4
4-year institutions	2,399,449	122,293	5.1
Public	1,225,091	53,512	4.4
Private not-for-profit	737,206	25,496	3.5
Private for-profit	437,152	43,285	9.9
	Fiscal year 2008		
All institutions	**3,179,704**	**213,339**	**6.7**
2-year institutions	764,620	81,007	10.6
Public	514,091	50,428	9.8
Private not-for-profit	11,966	996	8.3
Private for-profit	238,563	29,583	12.4
4-year institutions	2,415,084	132,332	5.5
Public	1,218,257	53,644	4.4
Private not-for-profit	718,215	26,361	3.7
Private for-profit	478,612	52,327	10.9

[1] The 2-year cohort default rate is the percentage of borrowers who enter repayment on certain Federal Family Education Loan (FFEL) Program or William D. Ford Federal Direct Loan (Direct Loan) Program loans during a particular federal fiscal year (a fiscal year runs from October 1 to September 30) and default or meet other specified conditions within the cohort default period. The cohort default period is the two-year period that begins on October 1 of the fiscal year when the borrower enters repayment and ends on September 30 of the following fiscal year.
NOTE: Degree-granting institutions grant associate's or higher degrees and participate in Title IV federal financial aid programs. For more information on the Integrated Postsecondary Data System (IPEDS), see *supplemental note 3*. Default rates were calculated using student counts by institution from the Federal Student Aid Cohort Default Rate Database and the IPEDS classification of institutions. For more information on the IPEDS classification of institutions, see *supplemental note 8*. The repayment phase is the period when student loans must be repaid and generally begins 6 months after a student leaves an institution.
SOURCE: U.S. Department of Education, Federal Student Aid, Direct Loan and Federal Family Education Loan Programs, Cohort Default Rate Database, retrieved November 5, 2010, from http://www2.ed.gov/offices/OSFAP/defaultmanagement/cdr.html.

Postsecondary Revenues and Expenses

Table A-50-1. Total and per-student revenue of public, private not-for-profit, and private for-profit degree-granting postsecondary institutions, by source of funds: Selected academic years, 2004–05 through 2008–09

[Numbers in 2009–10 constant dollars]

Control of institution and source of funds	Total 2004–05 revenue (in millions)	Total 2008–09 revenue (in millions)	Percentage distribution of total revenue			Revenue per FTE student[1]		
			2004–05	2007–08	2008–09	2004–05	2007–08	2008–09
Public institutions								
Total	$234,842	$267,385	100.0	100.0	100.0	$28,404	$28,823	$26,831
Operating revenues	136,767	158,799	58.2	55.5	59.4	16,542	15,996	15,935
Tuition and fees[2]	38,526	51,840	16.4	17.5	19.4	4,660	5,053	5,202
Grants and contracts	44,376	43,096	18.9	15.3	16.1	5,367	4,420	4,325
Federal (excludes FDSL[3])	30,071	26,092	12.8	9.3	9.8	3,637	2,683	2,618
State	6,818	7,403	2.9	2.9	2.8	825	823	743
Local	7,487	9,600	3.2	3.2	3.6	906	914	963
Auxiliary enterprises	17,673	21,358	7.5	7.5	8.0	2,138	2,154	2,143
Hospitals	21,772	27,302	9.3	9.2	10.2	2,633	2,647	2,740
Other operating revenues	14,420	15,202	6.1	6.0	5.7	1,744	1,723	1,526
Nonoperating revenues	85,517	92,448	36.4	38.4	34.6	10,343	11,064	9,277
Federal appropriations	1,784	2,011	0.8	0.7	0.8	216	194	202
State appropriations	55,325	65,486	23.6	24.9	24.5	6,692	7,187	6,571
Local appropriations	7,687	9,787	3.3	3.4	3.7	930	980	982
Government grants	3,919	15,747	1.7	4.4	5.9	474	1,273	1,580
Gifts	4,606	5,894	2.0	2.2	2.2	557	638	591
Investment income[4]	9,523	-9,488	4.1	1.9	-3.5	1,152	555	-952
Other nonoperating revenues	2,674	3,011	1.1	0.8	1.1	323	237	302
Other revenues	12,557	16,138	5.3	6.1	6.0	1,519	1,763	1,619
Private not-for-profit institutions								
Total	140,151	69,064	100.0	100.0	100.0	55,223	46,961	22,621
Tuition and fees	41,394	53,708	29.5	36.4	77.8	16,310	17,110	17,591
Federal government[5]	19,699	21,024	14.1	14.5	30.4	7,762	6,814	6,886
State governments	1,470	1,816	1.0	1.3	2.6	579	626	595
Local governments	488	575	0.3	0.4	0.8	192	178	188
Private gifts, grants, and contracts[6]	16,739	17,672	11.9	15.1	25.6	6,596	7,079	5,788
Investment return[4]	30,432	-64,205	21.7	4.6	-93.0	11,991	2,174	-21,029
Educational activities	3,596	4,791	2.6	3.5	6.9	1,417	1,636	1,569
Auxiliary enterprises	10,824	13,559	7.7	9.3	19.6	4,265	4,360	4,441
Hospitals	10,378	14,803	7.4	9.6	21.4	4,089	4,485	4,848
Other	5,131	5,321	3.7	5.3	7.7	2,022	2,498	1,743
Private for-profit institutions								
Total	10,979	19,374	100.0	100.0	100.0	15,751	15,978	15,358
Tuition and fees	9,567	16,740	87.1	87.2	86.4	13,725	13,937	13,270
Federal government	674	1,408	6.1	6.0	7.3	967	953	1,116
State and local governments	63	130	0.6	0.4	0.7	91	67	103
Private gifts, grants, and contracts	7	80	0.1	#	0.4	10	5	64
Investment return[4]	25	39	0.2	0.4	0.2	35	64	31
Educational activities	232	368	2.1	1.8	1.9	333	288	292
Auxiliary enterprises	252	396	2.3	2.2	2.0	362	350	314
Other	159	213	1.5	2.0	1.1	229	313	169

Rounds to zero.
[1] Full-time-equivalent (FTE) enrollment includes full-time students plus the full-time equivalent of part-time students.
[2] Net of allowances and discounts.
[3] Federal Direct Student Loans.
[4] Revenue from endowments, as reported in investment income or return, can fluctuate from year to year.
[5] Includes independent operations.
[6] Includes contracts and contributions from affiliated entities.
NOTE: Data are adjusted by the Consumer Price Index (CPI) to constant 2009–10 dollars. For more information on the CPI, see *supplemental note 10*. Detail may not sum to totals because of rounding. For more information on the Integrated Postsecondary Education Data System (IPEDS), see *supplemental note 3*.
SOURCE: U.S. Department of Education, National Center for Education Statistics, 2004–05 through 2008–09 Integrated Postsecondary Education Data System, Spring 2006 through Spring 2010.

This indicator continues on page 308.

Postsecondary Revenues and Expenses

Table A-50-2. Total and per-student revenue of public, private not-for-profit, and private for-profit 2- and 4-year degree-granting postsecondary institutions, by source of funds: 2004–05 and 2008–09

[Numbers in 2009–10 constant dollars]

Control of institution and source of funds	Total revenue (in millions)			
	2-year institutions		4-year institutions	
	2004–05	2008–09	2004–05	2008–09
Public institutions				
Total	**$41,045**	**$50,953**	**$193,797**	**$216,432**
Operating revenues	16,396	15,563	120,371	143,236
Tuition and fees[2]	6,857	8,362	31,669	43,478
Grants and contracts	7,057	4,359	37,319	38,736
Federal (excludes FDSL[3])	4,740	1,914	25,331	24,178
State	1,720	1,877	5,098	5,527
Local	597	569	6,890	9,032
Auxiliary enterprises	1,788	1,967	15,884	19,391
Hospitals	#	#	21,772	27,302
Other operating revenues	694	874	13,727	14,328
Nonoperating revenues	22,646	32,599	62,872	59,849
Federal appropriations	148	76	1,636	1,935
State appropriations	12,160	14,623	43,165	50,863
Local appropriations	7,388	9,302	299	485
Government grants	1,904	7,460	2,015	8,287
Gifts	277	259	4,329	5,635
Investment income[4]	417	470	9,106	-9,958
Other nonoperating revenues	351	409	2,322	2,602
Other revenues	2,003	2,791	10,554	13,347
Private not-for-profit institutions				
Total	**622**	**447**	**139,529**	**68,618**
Tuition and fees	349	299	41,046	53,409
Federal government[5]	77	59	19,622	20,965
State governments	23	20	1,447	1,796
Local governments	4	1	484	574
Private gifts, grants, and contracts[6]	68	46	16,671	17,625
Investment return[4]	23	-32	30,409	-64,173
Educational activities	14	6	3,582	4,786
Auxiliary enterprises	40	37	10,784	13,522
Hospitals	#	#	10,378	14,803
Other	25	11	5,107	5,310
Private for-profit institutions				
Total	**3,287**	**4,608**	**7,692**	**14,766**
Tuition and fees	2,703	3,785	6,864	12,955
Federal government	328	510	346	898
State and local governments	42	50	21	80
Private gifts, grants, and contracts	3	9	4	72
Investment return[4]	7	3	17	35
Educational activities	58	41	174	327
Auxiliary enterprises	51	98	202	298
Other	95	111	65	102

See notes at end of table.

Table A-50-2. Total and per-student revenue of public, private not-for-profit, and private for-profit 2- and 4-year degree-granting postsecondary institutions, by source of funds: 2004–05 and 2008–09—Continued

[Numbers in 2009–10 constant dollars]

Control of institution and source of funds	Percentage distribution of total revenue				Revenue per FTE student[1]			
	2-year institutions		4-year institutions		2-year institutions		4-year institutions	
	2004–05	2008–09	2004–05	2008–09	2004–05	2008–09	2004–05	2008–09
Public institutions								
Total	**100.0**	**100.0**	**100.0**	**100.0**	**$13,425**	**$13,911**	**$38,846**	**$35,593**
Operating revenues	39.9	30.5	62.1	66.2	5,000	4,006	24,128	23,556
Tuition and fees[2]	16.7	16.4	16.3	20.1	2,091	2,153	6,348	7,150
Grants and contracts	17.2	8.6	19.3	17.9	2,152	1,122	7,480	6,370
Federal (excludes FDSL[3])	11.5	3.8	13.1	11.2	1,446	493	5,077	3,976
State	4.2	3.7	2.6	2.6	524	483	1,022	909
Local	1.5	1.1	3.6	4.2	182	146	1,381	1,485
Auxiliary enterprises	4.4	3.9	8.2	9.0	545	506	3,184	3,189
Hospitals	#	#	11.2	12.6	#	#	4,364	4,490
Other operating revenues	1.7	1.7	7.1	6.6	212	225	2,751	2,356
Nonoperating revenues	55.2	64.0	32.4	27.7	6,906	8,392	12,602	9,842
Federal appropriations	0.4	0.1	0.8	0.9	45	20	328	318
State appropriations	29.6	28.7	22.3	23.5	3,708	3,764	8,652	8,365
Local appropriations	18.0	18.3	0.2	0.2	2,253	2,395	60	80
Government grants	4.6	14.6	1.0	3.8	581	1,920	404	1,363
Gifts	0.7	0.5	2.2	2.6	84	67	868	927
Investment income[4]	1.0	0.9	4.7	-4.6	127	121	1,825	-1,638
Other nonoperating revenues	0.9	0.8	1.2	1.2	107	105	465	428
Other revenues	4.9	5.5	5.4	6.2	1,519	1,513	2,116	2,195
Private not-for-profit institutions								
Total	**100.0**	**100.0**	**100.0**	**100.0**	**20,422**	**17,370**	**55,646**	**22,665**
Tuition and fees	56.1	66.9	29.4	77.8	11,453	11,628	16,369	17,642
Federal government[5]	12.4	13.2	14.1	30.6	2,535	2,292	7,825	6,925
State governments	3.7	4.6	1.0	2.6	764	795	577	593
Local governments	0.6	0.1	0.3	0.8	119	24	193	190
Private gifts, grants, and contracts[6]	10.9	10.4	11.9	25.7	2,229	1,802	6,649	5,822
Investment return[4]	3.7	-7.2	21.8	-93.5	754	-1,252	12,127	-21,197
Educational activities	2.2	1.2	2.6	7.0	450	214	1,428	1,581
Auxiliary enterprises	6.4	8.2	7.7	19.7	1,307	1,432	4,301	4,467
Hospitals	#	#	7.4	21.6	#	#	4,139	4,890
Other	4.0	2.5	3.7	7.7	810	435	2,037	1,754
Private for-profit institutions								
Total	**100.0**	**100.0**	**100.0**	**100.0**	**15,853**	**15,837**	**15,708**	**15,215**
Tuition and fees	82.2	82.2	89.2	87.7	13,036	13,011	14,016	13,348
Federal government	10.0	11.1	4.5	6.1	1,583	1,753	706	925
State and local governments	1.3	1.1	0.3	0.5	203	173	43	82
Private gifts, grants, and contracts	0.1	0.2	0.1	0.5	15	30	8	74
Investment return[4]	0.2	0.1	0.2	0.2	35	11	35	37
Educational activities	1.8	0.9	2.3	2.2	280	139	355	337
Auxiliary enterprises	1.5	2.1	2.6	2.0	244	337	411	307
Other	2.9	2.4	0.8	0.7	457	383	132	105

Rounds to zero.
[1] Full-time-equivalent (FTE) enrollment includes full-time students plus the full-time equivalent of part-time students.
[2] Net of allowances and discounts.
[3] Federal Direct Student Loans.
[4] Revenue from endowments, as reported in investment income or return, can fluctuate from year to year.
[5] Includes independent operations.
[6] Includes contracts and contributions from affiliated entities.
NOTE: Data are adjusted by the Consumer Price Index (CPI) to constant 2009–10 dollars. For more information on the CPI, see *supplemental note 10.* Detail may not sum to totals because of rounding. For more information on the Integrated Postsecondary Education Data System (IPEDS) and IPEDS classification of institutions, see *supplemental notes 3* and *8.*.
SOURCE: U.S. Department of Education, National Center for Education Statistics, 2004–05 and 2008–09 Integrated Postsecondary Education Data System, Spring 2006 and Spring 2010.

Postsecondary Revenues and Expenses

Table A-50-3. Total and per-student expenses of public, private not-for-profit, and private for-profit degree-granting postsecondary institutions, by purpose: Selected academic years, 2004–05 through 2008–09

[Numbers in 2009–10 constant dollars]

Control of institution and purpose	Total 2004–05 expenses (in millions)	Total 2008–09 expenses (in millions)	Percentage distribution of total expenses			Expenses per FTE student[1]		
			2004–05	2007–08	2008–09	2004–05	2007–08	2008–09
Public institutions[2]								
Total	$215,794	$273,030	100.0	100.0	100.0	$26,100	$27,439	$27,398
Instruction	59,657	75,079	27.6	27.5	27.5	7,215	7,548	7,534
Research	22,551	26,651	10.5	9.7	9.8	2,728	2,663	2,674
Public service	9,481	11,245	4.4	4.1	4.1	1,147	1,135	1,128
Academic support	14,259	18,805	6.6	6.8	6.9	1,725	1,879	1,887
Student services	10,042	12,939	4.7	4.7	4.7	1,215	1,283	1,298
Institutional support	17,455	23,079	8.1	8.5	8.5	2,111	2,328	2,316
Operation and maintenance of plant	13,578	17,840	6.3	6.5	6.5	1,642	1,790	1,790
Depreciation	9,593	13,719	4.4	4.9	5.0	1,160	1,347	1,377
Scholarships/fellowships[3]	8,403	11,105	3.9	3.7	4.1	1,016	1,016	1,114
Auxiliary enterprises	16,664	20,588	7.7	7.5	7.5	2,016	2,053	2,066
Hospitals	20,105	25,945	9.3	9.2	9.5	2,432	2,520	2,604
Other operating expenditures and deductions	6,701	5,777	3.1	1.8	2.1	810	491	580
Nonoperating expenses	7,306	10,259	3.4	5.1	3.8	884	1,387	1,029
Private not-for-profit institutions								
Total	110,394	141,349	100.0	100.0	100.0	43,498	45,023	46,296
Instruction	36,258	46,453	32.8	33.1	32.9	14,287	14,915	15,215
Research	12,813	15,263	11.6	10.8	10.8	5,049	4,881	4,999
Public service	2,000	2,299	1.8	1.6	1.6	788	736	753
Academic support	9,342	12,580	8.5	8.9	8.9	3,681	4,008	4,120
Student services	8,192	11,012	7.4	7.8	7.8	3,228	3,495	3,607
Institutional support	14,690	19,401	13.3	13.8	13.7	5,788	6,193	6,354
Auxiliary enterprises	10,944	13,708	9.9	10.0	9.7	4,312	4,492	4,490
Hospitals	9,181	11,931	8.3	8.1	8.4	3,617	3,627	3,908
Independent operations	4,224	5,158	3.8	3.7	3.6	1,664	1,648	1,690
Other	2,749	3,545	2.5	2.3	2.5	1,083	1,027	1,161
Private for-profit institutions								
Total	8,831	16,364	100.0	100.0	100.0	12,669	13,849	12,973
Instruction	2,314	3,871	26.2	23.2	23.7	3,320	3,217	3,069
Research and public service	8	10	0.1	0.1	0.1	11	9	8
Student services, academic and institutional support	5,693	11,005	64.5	66.9	67.2	8,168	9,261	8,724
Auxiliary enterprises	270	397	3.1	3.0	2.4	387	419	314
Other	546	1,082	6.2	6.8	6.6	784	942	858

[1] Full-time-equivalent (FTE) enrollment includes full-time students plus the full-time equivalent of part-time students.
[2] For 2007–08 and 2008–09 data, all expenses reported by institutions for operations and maintenance and depreciation have been aggregated into the general categories of operations and maintenance and depreciation, even in cases where a particular expense was originally disaggregated into a purpose category.
[3] Excludes discounts and allowances. In 2008–09, about 59 percent of the total scholarships were reported under discounts and allowances
NOTE: Data are adjusted by the Consumer Price Index (CPI) to constant 2009–10 dollars. For more information on the CPI, see *supplemental note 10.* Detail may not sum to totals because of rounding. For more information on the Integrated Postsecondary Education Data System (IPEDS), see *supplemental note 3.*
SOURCE: U.S. Department of Education, National Center for Education Statistics, 2004–05 through 2008–09 Integrated Postsecondary Education Data System, Spring 2006 through Spring 2010.

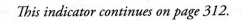

This indicator continues on page 312.

Postsecondary Revenues and Expenses

Table A-50-4. Total and per-student expenses of public, private not-for-profit, and private for-profit 2- and 4-year degree-granting postsecondary institutions, by purpose: 2004–05 and 2008–09

[Numbers in 2009–10 constant dollars]

Control of institution and purpose	Total expenses (in millions)			
	2-year institutions		4-year institutions	
	2004–05	2008–09	2004–05	2008–09
Public institutions[2]				
Total	$38,602	$47,667	$177,192	$225,363
Instruction	14,957	17,813	44,700	57,266
Research	22	22	22,529	26,629
Public service	662	745	8,819	10,499
Academic support	2,842	3,505	11,417	15,300
Student services	3,567	4,327	6,476	8,613
Institutional support	5,303	6,573	12,152	16,506
Operation and maintenance of plant	3,291	4,034	10,287	13,805
Depreciation	1,456	2,000	8,137	11,720
Scholarships/fellowships[3]	2,949	3,949	5,453	7,156
Auxiliary enterprises	2,071	2,295	14,593	18,293
Hospitals	#	#	20,105	25,945
Other operating expenditures and deductions	789	1,480	5,912	4,297
Nonoperating expenses	694	925	6,612	9,334
Private not-for-profit institutions				
Total	604	496	109,790	140,853
Instruction	207	166	36,051	46,287
Research	1	#	12,812	15,262
Public service	7	4	1,994	2,295
Academic support	34	42	9,308	12,538
Student services	91	68	8,101	10,944
Institutional support	174	142	14,516	19,259
Auxiliary enterprises	45	37	10,899	13,671
Hospitals	#	#	9,181	11,931
Independent operations	#	#	4,224	5,158
Other	46	37	2,704	3,508
Private for-profit institutions				
Total	2,841	3,965	5,990	12,399
Instruction	884	1,291	1,430	2,580
Research and public service	4	2	4	8
Student services, academic and institutional support	1,583	2,172	4,111	8,832
Auxiliary enterprises	90	121	180	276
Other	281	379	266	703

See notes at end of table.

Table A-50-4. Total and per-student expenses of public, private not-for-profit, and private for-profit 2- and 4-year degree-granting postsecondary institutions, by purpose: 2004–05 and 2008–09—Continued

[Numbers in 2009–10 constant dollars]

Control of institution and purpose	Percentage distribution of total expenses				Expenses per FTE student[1]			
	2-year institutions		4-year institutions		2-year institutions		4-year institutions	
	2004–05	2008–09	2004–05	2008–09	2004–05	2008–09	2004–05	2008–09
Public institutions[2]								
Total	100.0	100.0	100.0	100.0	$11,772	$12,271	$35,517	$37,062
Instruction	38.7	37.4	25.2	25.4	4,561	4,585	8,960	9,418
Research	0.1	#	12.7	11.8	7	6	4,516	4,379
Public service	1.7	1.6	5.0	4.7	202	192	1,768	1,727
Academic support	7.4	7.4	6.4	6.8	867	902	2,289	2,516
Student services	9.2	9.1	3.7	3.8	1,088	1,114	1,298	1,416
Institutional support	13.7	13.8	6.9	7.3	1,617	1,692	2,436	2,714
Operation and maintenance of plant	8.5	8.5	5.8	6.1	1,004	1,039	2,062	2,270
Depreciation	3.8	4.2	4.6	5.2	444	515	1,631	1,927
Scholarships/fellowships[3]	7.6	8.3	3.1	3.2	899	1,016	1,093	1,177
Auxiliary enterprises	5.4	4.8	8.2	8.1	632	591	2,925	3,008
Hospitals	#	#	11.3	11.5	#	#	4,030	4,267
Other operating expenditures and deductions	2.0	3.1	3.3	1.9	241	381	1,185	707
Nonoperating expenses	1.8	1.9	3.7	4.1	212	238	1,325	1,535
Private not-for-profit institutions								
Total	100.0	100.0	100.0	100.0	19,845	19,314	43,785	46,525
Instruction	34.3	33.5	32.8	32.9	6,810	6,467	14,378	15,289
Research	0.1	0.1	11.7	10.8	17	13	5,110	5,041
Public service	1.1	0.7	1.8	1.6	219	140	795	758
Academic support	5.7	8.4	8.5	8.9	1,132	1,614	3,712	4,142
Student services	15.0	13.8	7.4	7.8	2,972	2,662	3,231	3,615
Institutional support	28.8	28.7	13.2	13.7	5,718	5,535	5,789	6,361
Auxiliary enterprises	7.4	7.5	9.9	9.7	1,474	1,453	4,347	4,516
Hospitals	#	#	8.4	8.5	#	#	3,661	3,941
Independent operations	#	#	3.8	3.7	#	#	1,684	1,704
Other	7.6	7.4	2.5	2.5	1,504	1,428	1,078	1,159
Private for-profit institutions								
Total	100.0	100.0	100.0	100.0	13,704	13,628	12,231	12,776
Instruction	31.1	32.6	23.9	20.8	4,263	4,437	2,920	2,659
Research and public service	0.1	0.1	0.1	0.1	20	8	7	8
Student services, academic and institutional support	55.7	54.8	68.6	71.2	7,634	7,467	8,394	9,101
Auxiliary enterprises	3.2	3.0	3.0	2.2	433	414	368	285
Other	9.9	9.6	4.4	5.7	1,354	1,303	542	724

\# Rounds to zero.

[1] Full-time-equivalent (FTE) enrollment includes full-time students plus the full-time equivalent of part-time students.

[2] For 2008–09 data, all expenses reported by institutions for operations and maintenance and depreciation have been aggregated into the general categories of operations and maintenance and depreciation, even in cases where a particular expense was originally disaggregated into a purpose category.

[3] Excludes discounts and allowances. In 2008–09, about 59 percent of the total scholarships were reported under discounts and allowances.

NOTE: Data are adjusted by the Consumer Price Index (CPI) to constant 2009–10 dollars. For more information on the CPI, see *supplemental note 10*. Detail may not sum to totals because of rounding. For more information on the Integrated Postsecondary Education Data System (IPEDS) and IPEDS classification of institutions, see *supplemental notes 3 and 8*.

SOURCE: U.S. Department of Education, National Center for Education Statistics, 2004–05 and 2008–09 Integrated Postsecondary Education Data System, Spring 2006 and Spring 2010.

Appendix B
Supplemental Notes

Appendix B

Supplemental Notes

Contents

NOTE 1: Commonly Used Variables

Certain common variables, such as parents' education, race/ethnicity, community type, poverty, and region are used in the various surveys cited in *The Condition of Education 2011.* The definitions for these variables can vary across surveys and sometimes between different time periods of a single survey. This supplemental note describes how several common variables used in various indicators in this volume are defined in each of the surveys. In addition, this note describes how certain terms are used in these indicators.

Race/Ethnicity

The categories denoting race and ethnicity in *The Condition of Education* are in accordance with the 1997 Office of Management and Budget (OMB) standard classification scheme. The 1997 standards emphasize self-reporting or self-identification as the preferred method for collecting data on race and ethnicity. However, while the federal categories provide a standardized format for purposes of collecting and presenting data on race and ethnicity, the standard was not designed to capture the full complexity of race and ethnicity in the United States.

The 1997 standards do not establish criteria or qualifications (such as blood quantum levels) that are to be used in determining a particular individual's racial or ethnic classification. They do not specify how an individual should classify himself or herself. In situations where self-reporting is not practicable or feasible, observer identification may be used. For *indicator 4,* which uses data from the Private School Universe Survey, racial/ethnic classifications are based on school reports of race/ethnicity for aggregate K–12 enrollment. The 1997 standards reflect a change in data collection policy, making it possible for federal agencies to collect information that reflects the increasing diversity of the United States population.

Under the OMB standards, "Hispanic or Latino" is an ethnicity category, not a racial category. Agencies that collect data on race and ethnicity separately must collect data on ethnicity first. Ethnicity is categorized as follows:

- *Hispanic or Latino:* A person of Cuban, Mexican, Puerto Rican, South or Central American, or other Spanish culture or origin, regardless of race.

Race categories presented in *The Condition of Education 2011* exclude persons of Hispanic ethnicity; thus, the race/ethnicity categories are mutually exclusive.

Racial groupings are as follows:

- *American Indian or Alaska Native:* A person having origins in any of the original peoples of North and South America (including Central America)

who maintains tribal affiliation or community attachment.

- *Asian:* A person having origins in any of the original peoples of the Far East, Southeast Asia, and the Indian subcontinent; this includes, for example, people from Cambodia, China, India, Japan, Korea, Malaysia, Pakistan, the Philippines, Thailand, and Vietnam.

- *Black or African American:* A person having origins in any of the Black racial groups of Africa.

- *Native Hawaiian or Other Pacific Islander:* A person having origins in any of the original peoples of Hawaii, Guam, Samoa, or other Pacific Islands.

- *White:* A person having origins in any of the original peoples of Europe, North Africa, or the Middle East.

- *Two or more races:* A person who reported any combination of two or more races and not Hispanic/Latino ethnicity.

In *The Condition of Education,* the following terms are typically used to represent the above categories: White, Black, Hispanic, Asian, Pacific Islander, American Indian/Alaska Native, and Two or more races. Not all categories are shown in all indicators. In some cases, categories are omitted because there are insufficient data in some of the smaller categories or because the data collection design did not distinguish between groups (between Asians and Pacific Islanders, for example). For example, in the Common Core of Data (CCD), the categories Asian and Pacific Islander are combined and "Two or more races" is used by some, not all, respondents. In other cases, omissions occur because only comparable data categories are shown. For example, the category "Two or more races," which was introduced in the 2000 Census and became a regular category for data collection in the Current Population Survey (CPS) in 2003, is sometimes excluded from indicators that present a historical series of data with constant categories, and it is sometimes included within the category "Other." For further details on these classifications, see the source documentation of the particular survey and http://www.census.gov/popest/race.html.

In *The Condition of Education 2011,* the above definitions of race/ethnicity apply to *indicators 3, 4, 5, 6, 8, 9, 10, 11, 12, 13, 14, 15, 17, 18, 20, 21, 22, 23, 24, 26, 27, 28, 30, 31, 32, 33, 34, 39, 43, 45,* and *47. Indicators 32* and *34* combine Asians and Native Hawaiian or Other Pacific Islanders due to insufficient data. These definitions may or may not apply to *indicators 23, 26,* and *39,* which use data from the Integrated Postsecondary Education Data System (IPEDS). The above definitions are currently being phased into the IPEDS data collection, and will be

NOTE 1: Commonly Used Variables

fully implemented in the 2011–12 data collection. For more information on IPEDS, see *supplemental note 3*.

Locale

Federal departments and agencies use various classification systems to define community types. Indicators in *The Condition of Education* use the National Center for Education Statistics (NCES) system of *locale codes*.

The CCD uses the "locale code" system to classify the type of geographic area where a school is physically located. Locale assignments are based on latitude and longitude values developed from reported address information. The assignments include four primary categories—(1) city, (2) suburban, (3) town, and (4) rural—and each primary category includes three subcategories. City and suburban areas are subdivided into small, midsize, and large, while town and rural areas are subdivided into fringe, distant, and remote according to their proximity to urban areas (see exhibit B-1). These 12 categories are based on four geographic concepts defined by the Census Bureau: *urbanized areas, urban clusters, core based statistical areas,* and *principal cities.* Urbanized Areas and Urban Clusters are densely settled areas defined by collections of Census blocks and block groups, the smallest geographic units for which the Census Bureau determines population. Urban cores with populations of 50,000 or more are classified as Urbanized

Areas, while those with populations of less than 50,000 but greater than 2,500 are classified as Urban Clusters. All nonurban territory is classified as Rural. A Core Based Statistical Area (CBSA) includes at least one urban core population of 10,000 or more and adjacent territory that has a high degree of social and economic integration with the core as measured by commuting ties. CBSAs are composed of one or more contiguous counties, and are classified as Metropolitan Statistical Areas if they contain a population core of 50,000 or more. A principal city is an incorporated place or Census-designated place that serves as a primary population and economic center in a CBSA. NCES city locale assignments are based on principal cities of Metropolitan Statistical Areas. For more information about urban areas, see http://www.census.gov/geo/www/ua/ua_2k.html. For more information about Core Based Statistical Areas, see http://www.census.gov/population/www/metroareas/metroarea.html.

Assignments of locale codes to local education agencies (LEAs) are based on enrolled-weighted locale assignments of the schools operated by the LEA. If a majority of students in the LEA attend schools located in a single locale, the LEA is assigned to that locale. Most LEAs in the CCD are assigned based on a majority locale. If a majority of students in an LEA do not attend schools within a single locale, the LEA is reevaluated to see if a majority of its students are located in one of the four primary categories (city, suburban, town, and rural). If so, then the LEA is assigned to the largest subcategory

Exhibit B-1.   NCES urban-centric locale categories

Locale	Definition
City	
Large	Territory inside an urbanized area and inside a principal city with population of 250,000 or more
Midsize	Territory inside an urbanized area and inside a principal city with population less than 250,000 and greater than or equal to 100,000
Small	Territory inside an urbanized area and inside a principal city with population less than 100,000
Suburban	
Large	Territory outside a principal city and inside an urbanized area with population of 250,000 or more
Midsize	Territory outside a principal city and inside an urbanized area with population less than 250,000 and greater than or equal to 100,000
Small	Territory outside a principal city and inside an urbanized area with population less than 100,000
Town	
Fringe	Territory inside an urban cluster that is less than or equal to 10 miles from an urbanized area
Distant	Territory inside an urban cluster that is more than 10 miles and less than or equal to 35 miles from an urbanized area
Remote	Territory inside an urban cluster that is more than 35 miles from an urbanized area
Rural	
Fringe	Census-defined rural territory that is less than or equal to 5 miles from an urbanized area, as well as rural territory that is less than or equal to 2.5 miles from an urban cluster.
Distant	Census-defined rural territory that is more than 5 miles but less than or equal to 25 miles from an urbanized area, as well as rural territory that is more than 2.5 miles but less than or equal to 10 miles from an urban cluster.
Remote	Census-defined rural territory that is more than 25 miles from an urbanized area and is also more than 10 miles from an urban cluster

SOURCE: U.S. Department of Education, National Center for Education Statistics. Common Core of Data (CCD). Identification of Locale Codes, retrieved April 10, 2009 from http://nces.ed.gov/ccd/rural_locales.asp.

within that primary category. If the LEA does not have a majority of its students in a specific locale or within a primary category, then the LEA is assigned the locale that accounts for a plurality of its students. In cases where an LEA does not enroll students or does not report student enrollment to the CCD, the LEA is assigned a locale based on its reported address location.

Although geographic locale assignments are included in the CCD and other NCES surveys, data products and publications often consolidate the full set of locales and present data only for the four primary categories. The CCD adopted the 12-category locale framework in 2006. Prior to that, the CCD relied on an eight-category framework that classified areas primarily on the basis of metropolitan area boundaries.

In *The Condition of Education 2011,* urban-centric locale codes are used in *indicators 3, 4, 27, 28, 32,* and *34.*

Poverty

Data on household income and the number of people living in the household are combined with estimates of the poverty threshold, published by the Census Bureau, to determine the poverty status of children (or adults). The thresholds used to determine poverty status for an individual differ for each survey year. The weighted average poverty thresholds for various household sizes for 1990, 1995, and 2000 through 2009 are shown in exhibit B-2. (For thresholds for other years, see http://www.census.gov/hhes/www/poverty/data/threshld/index.html.)

In *indicator 6,* children in families whose incomes are below the poverty threshold are classified as *poor,* those in families with incomes at 100–199 percent of the poverty threshold are classified as *near-poor,* and those in families with incomes at 200 percent or more of the poverty threshold are classified as *nonpoor.*

In *indicator 29,* poverty status is based on Census Bureau guidelines for the year that corresponds with the year of the estimate. Poverty status for the 9-month estimates reflects poverty status at the time of the 9-month data collection, poverty status for the 2-year estimates reflects poverty status at the time of the 2-year collection, and poverty status for the preschool estimates reflects poverty status at the time of the preschool year collection. Census Bureau guidelines identify a dollar amount that would allow a household to meet its needs, given its size and composition. For example, in 2002, a family of four was considered to live below the poverty threshold if its income was less than or equal to $18,392. Children in families whose incomes were below the poverty threshold were classified as being in poverty.

Eligibility or approval for the National School Lunch Program also serves as a measure of poverty status. The National School Lunch Program is a federally assisted meal program operated in public and private nonprofit schools and residential child care centers. Unlike the poverty thresholds discussed above, which rely on dollar amounts determined by the Census Bureau, eligibility for the National School Lunch Program relies on the federal income poverty guidelines of the Department of Health and Human Services. To be eligible for free lunch, a student must be from a household with an income at or below 130 percent of the federal poverty guideline; to be eligible for reduced-price lunch, a student must be from a household with an income between 130 percent and 185 percent of the federal poverty guideline. Title I basic program funding relies on free lunch eligibility numbers as one (of four) possible poverty measures for levels of Title I federal funding.

In *The Condition of Education 2011,* eligibility for the National School Lunch Program applies to *indicators 3, 10, 11, 12, 13, 14, 27,* and *28;* approval for the National School Lunch Program applies to *indicators 32* and *34.*

Exhibit B-2. **Weighted average poverty thresholds, by household size: Selected years, 1990–2009**

[In current dollars]

| Year | Household size | | | | | | | |
	2	3	4	5	6	7	8	9 or more
1990	$8,509	$10,419	$13,359	$15,792	$17,839	$20,241	$22,582	$26,848
1995	9,933	12,158	15,569	18,408	20,804	23,552	26,237	31,280
2000	11,239	13,738	17,603	20,819	23,528	26,754	29,701	35,060
2001	11,569	14,128	18,104	21,405	24,195	27,517	30,627	36,286
2002	11,756	14,348	18,392	21,744	24,576	28,001	30,907	37,062
2003	12,015	14,680	18,810	22,245	25,122	28,544	31,589	37,656
2004	12.334	15,067	19,307	22,831	25,788	29,236	32,641	39,048
2005	12,755	15,577	19,971	23,613	26,683	30,249	33,610	40,288
2006	13,167	16,079	20,614	24,382	27,560	31,205	34,774	41,499
2007	13,542	16,537	21,201	21,201	28,345	32,094	35,764	42,681
2008	14,051	17,163	22,025	26,049	29,456	33,529	37,220	44,346
2009	13,991	17,098	21,954	25,991	29,405	33,372	37,252	44,366

SOURCE: U.S. Census Bureau, Current Population Survey (CPS). Retrieved March 9, 2011 from http://www.census.gov/hhes/www/poverty/data/threshld/index.html.

NOTE 1: Commonly Used Variables

Geographic Region

The regional classification systems in exhibit B-3 represent the four geographical regions of the United States as defined by the Census Bureau of the U.S. Department of Commerce. In *The Condition of Education 2011*, indicators *2, 3, 4, 5, 6, 20, 27, 29, 32*, and *34* use this system.

Exhibit B-3. **U.S. Census Bureau, Regional Classification**

Northeast	South	Midwest	West
Connecticut (CT)	Alabama (AL)	Illinois (IL)	Alaska (AK)
Maine (ME)	Arkansas (AR)	Indiana (IN)	Arizona (AZ)
Massachusetts (MA)	Delaware (DE)	Iowa (IA)	California (CA)
New Hampshire (NH)	District of Columbia (DC)	Kansas (KS)	Colorado (CO)
New Jersey (NJ)	Florida (FL)	Michigan (MI)	Hawaii (HI)
New York (NY)	Georgia (GA)	Minnesota (MN)	Idaho (ID)
Pennsylvania (PA)	Kentucky (KY)	Missouri (MO)	Montana (MT)
Rhode Island (RI)	Louisiana (LA)	Nebraska (NE)	Nevada (NV)
Vermont (VT)	Maryland (MD)	North Dakota (ND)	New Mexico (NM)
	Mississippi (MS)	Ohio (OH)	Oregon (OR)
	North Carolina (NC)	South Dakota (SD)	Utah (UT)
	Oklahoma (OK)	Wisconsin (WI)	Washington (WA)
	South Carolina (SC)		Wyoming (WY)
	Tennessee (TN)		
	Texas (TX)		
	Virginia (VA)		
	West Virginia (WV)		

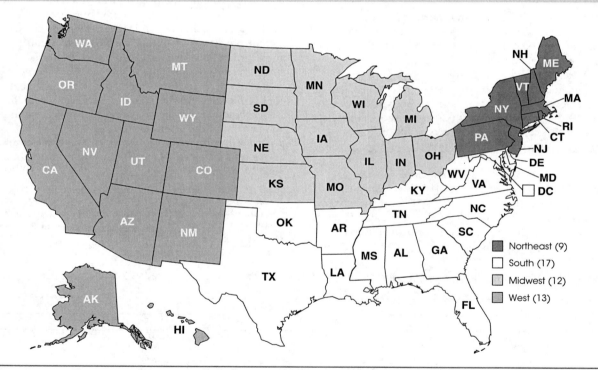

SOURCE: U.S. Census Bureau. Census Regions and Divisions of the United States, retrieved April 10, 2009 from http://www.census.gov/geo/www/us_regdiv.pdf.

NOTE 2: The Current Population Survey (CPS)

The Current Population Survey (CPS) is a monthly survey of about 60,000 households from the 50 states and the District of Columbia. It is conducted by the Census Bureau, which is part of the U.S. Department of Commerce, for the Bureau of Labor Statistics. The survey has been conducted for more than 50 years.

The CPS sample is scientifically selected to represent the civilian, noninstitutional U.S. population. This includes the household population, people living in noninstitutional group quarters, and members of the military living off post or with their families on post. Thus, inmates in correctional institutions and patients in long-term medical or custodial facilities are not included in the sample, nor are military personnel living in barracks. Interviewers ask a knowledgeable adult household member (known as the "household respondent") to answer all of the month's questionnaires for all members of the household. Respondents are interviewed to obtain information about the employment status of each member of the household age 15 or older. However, published data focus on those age 16 and over. The sample provides estimates for the nation as a whole, as well as for individual states and other geographic areas.

Estimates obtained from the CPS include employment, unemployment, earnings, hours of work, and other measures. They are available by a variety of demographic characteristics, including age, sex, race/ethnicity, marital status, and education attainment. They are also available by occupation, industry, and class of worker (e.g., government, private, self-employed). Supplemental questions to produce estimates on topics such as school enrollment, income, previous work experience, health, employee benefits, and work schedules are often added to the regular CPS questionnaire.

Each year, the Annual Social and Economic (ASEC) Supplement and October supplemental questionnaires contain questions of relevance to education policy. The ASEC Supplement, formerly known as the March CPS Supplement, is a primary source of detailed information on income and work experience in the United States. The October Supplement routinely gathers data on school enrollment, school characteristics, and educational attainment for elementary, secondary, and postsecondary education. Related data are also collected about preschooling and the general adult population. In addition, NCES funds additional items on education-related topics such as language proficiency, disabilities, computer use and access, student mobility, and private school tuition. Responses are collected for all household members age 3 and over.

CPS interviewers initially used printed questionnaires. However, since 1994, the Census Bureau has used Computer-Assisted Personal and Telephone Interviewing (CAPI and CATI) to collect data. These technologies allow interviewers to administer a complex questionnaire with increasing consistency and reductions in interviewer error. In 1994, the survey methodology for CPS was changed, and weights were adjusted. For more information on CPS data collections, please visit http://www.census.gov/apsd/techdoc/cps/cps-main.html.

The following section contains definitions of selected variables that are used in *The Condition of Education 2011*. Further information on the CPS can be found at http://www.census.gov/cps.

Definitions of Selected Variables

Employment Status

Indicator 18 examines employment status using data from the ASEC Supplement, which contains questions on the employment of adults in the previous week. Respondents can report that they were employed (either full or part time), unemployed (looking for work or on layoff), or not in the labor force (due to being retired, having unpaid employment, or some other reason).

Indicator 45 looks at employment status using data from the October CPS and its supplement, which also contains questions on employment of adults in the previous week. In this indicator, employed persons are persons age 16 or older who, during the reference week, (1) did any work at all (at least 1 hour) as paid employees or (2) were not working but had jobs or businesses from which they were temporarily absent because of vacation, illness, bad weather, child care problems, maternity or paternity leave, labor-management dispute, job training, or other family or personal reasons, whether or not they were paid for the time off or were seeking other jobs.

Hours Worked per Week

Indicator 45 presents data from the October CPS and its supplement on the number of hours worked per week. This estimate is the number of hours a respondent worked in all jobs in the week prior to the survey interview. The population for this variable includes any employed person who also worked in the week prior to the survey interview. The sum of the categories may not equal the total percentage employed because those who were employed but did not work in the previous week were excluded.

NOTE 2: The Current Population Survey (CPS)

Family Income

Indicator 21 uses data on family income, collected as part of the October CPS, to measure a student's economic standing. The October CPS determines family income from a single question asked of the household respondent. Family income includes all monetary income from all sources (including jobs, businesses, interest, rent, and social security payments) over a 12-month period. The income of nonrelatives living in the household is excluded, but the income of all family members age 15 or older (age 14 or older in years prior to 1989), including those temporarily living outside of the household, is included.

In *indicator 21*, family income of a recent high school graduate is defined as the income of the household where the graduate has membership. A household is defined as the group of individuals whose usual place of residence at the time of the interview is the sample unit. The following considerations guide the determination of household members:

- *Persons staying in the sample housing unit at the time of the interview:* Persons for whom the household is their usual place of residence are included in the household membership. Persons who are living in the household temporarily (such as students) and who have living quarters held elsewhere are not considered part of the household unless they are living with their spouse or children.

- *Persons who usually live in the sample housing unit and are absent at the time of the interview:* Individuals who are temporarily absent and who have no other usual place of residence are classified as household members even if they are not present in the household during the survey week. If such persons are away temporarily attending school, they are considered part of the household unless they are living with their spouse or children.

Families in the bottom 20 percent of all family incomes are classified as low income; families in the top 20 percent of all family incomes are classified as high income; and families in the 60 percent between these two categories are classified as middle income. Exhibit B-4 shows the current dollar amount of the breakpoints between low and middle income and between middle and high income that are used in *indicator 21*. For example, the income for low-income families in 2009 ranged from $0 to $18,000; for middle-income families, from $18,100 to $86,700; and for high-income families, from $86,800 and higher.

Median Earnings

Indicator 17 uses data on earnings that are collected as part of the March CPS. The March CPS collects information on earnings from individuals who were full-year workers (individuals who were employed 50 or more weeks in the previous year) and full-time workers (those who were usually employed 35 or more hours per week). Earnings include all wage and salary income. Unlike mean earnings, median earnings either do not change or change very little in response to extreme observations.

Race/Ethnicity

Over time, the CPS has had different response options for race/ethnicity. From 1972 through 1988, the response options were limited to White, Black, Hispanic, and Other. From 1989 through 1995, the response options were White, Black, American Indian/Aleut Eskimo, Asian/Pacific Islander, Hispanic, and Other. In 1996, Census revised procedures for editing and allocating the race variable to offset an underestimation of data on American Indians and Asians/Pacific Islanders. One should use caution when making comparisons between data from 1995 and earlier and data from 1996 and later. From 1996 through 2002, the response options were White, Black, American Indian/Aleut Eskimo, Asian/Pacific Islander, and Hispanic. Since 2003, the response options have been White, Black, American Indian/Alaska Native, Asian, Hawaiian/Pacific Islander, and Hispanic, and respondents have been allowed to select two or more race categories. In *The Condition of Education 2011*, persons of Hispanic ethnicity are classified as Hispanic regardless of their race response(s). Thus, the race/ethnicity categories are mutually exclusive.

Exhibit B-4. Dollar value (in current dollars rounded to the nearest hundreds) at the breakpoint between low- and middle-income and between middle- and high-income categories of family income: October 1975–2009

Year	Breakpoints between low- and middle-income	Breakpoints between middle- and high-income
1975	4,400	17,000
1976	4,600	18,300
1977	4,900	20,000
1978	5,300	21,600
1979	5,800	23,700
1980	6,100	25,300
1981	6,500	27,100
1982	7,200	31,200
1983	7,300	32,300
1984	7,500	34,200
1985	7,900	36,400
1986	8,400	38,100
1987	8,800	39,600
1988	9,300	42,100
1989	9,500	43,900
1990	9,600	46,200
1991	10,500	48,300
1992	10,700	49,600
1993	10,800	50,600
1994	11,900	55,500
1995	11,700	56,100
1996	12,300	58,100
1997	12,800	60,800
1998	13,900	64,900
1999	14,700	68,200
2000	15,300	71,900
2001	16,300	75,000
2002	16,700	75,000
2003	16,600	75,500
2004	16,000	77,100
2005	16,800	80,700
2006	18,000	84,500
2007	18,400	85,000
2008	19,000	88,100
2009	18,000	86,800

SOURCE: U.S. Department of Commerce, Census Bureau, Current Population Survey (CPS), October Supplement. 1975–2009.

Indicators 17, 18, 20, 21, 24, and *45* present data by race/ethnicity using CPS data. For more information on race/ethnicity, see *supplemental note 1.*

Enrolled in School

Indicators 1, 5, 21, and *45* use data from the October CPS and information from its supplemental questionnaire on enrollment in school.

Status Dropout Rate

Indicator 20 reports *status dropout rates* using data from the October CPS. The status dropout rate is one of a number of rates that are used to report high school dropout and completion behavior in the United States. Status dropout rates measure the percentage of individuals within a given age range who are not enrolled in high school and lack a high school credential, irrespective of when they dropped out. Status dropout rates are distinct from event dropout rates, which measure the proportion of students who drop out of high school in a given year; event dropout rates have been reported in a previous volume of *The Condition of Education* (NCES 2004-077, *indicator 16*) and are featured in the annual report *Trends in High School Dropout and Completion Rates in the United States* (see, for example, NCES 2011-012). For more information on measures of student persistence and progress featured in *The Condition of Education 2011,* see *supplemental note 6.*

The status dropout rate is the percentage of civilian, noninstitutionalized young people ages 16 through 24 who are not in high school and have not earned a high school credential (either a diploma or equivalency credential such as a General Educational Development [GED] certificate). The numerator of the status dropout rate for a given year is the number of individuals ages 16 through 24 who, as of October of that year, had not completed high school and were not currently enrolled in school. The denominator is the total number of individuals ages 16 through 24 who were in the United States in October of that year. Status dropout rates count as dropouts individuals who never attended school and immigrants who did not complete the equivalent of a high school education in their home country. The inclusion of these individuals is appropriate because the status dropout rate is designed to report the percentage of youth and young adults in the United States who lack what is now considered a basic level of education. However, the status dropout rate should not be used as a measure of the performance of U.S. schools because it counts as dropouts individuals who may have never attended a U.S. school.

The CPS October Supplement items used to identify status dropouts include (1) "Is...attending or enrolled in regular school?" and (2) "What is the highest level of school...completed or the highest degree...received?" (See the *Educational Attainment* section below for details on how the second question changed between 1972 and 1992.) Beginning in 1986, the Census Bureau instituted new editing procedures for cases with missing data on school enrollment, (i.e., missing data relating to the first October Supplement item cited above). These changes were made in an effort to improve data quality. The effect of the editing changes was evaluated by applying both the earlier and revised editing procedures to the 1986 data. The changes resulted in an increase in the number of students enrolled in school and a slightly lowered status dropout rate (12.2 percent based on the earlier procedures and 12.1 percent based on the revised ones). The difference in the two rates is not statistically significant. While the change in the procedures occurred in 1986, the revised procedures are reflected in *indicator 20* beginning with 1987 data.

NOTE 2: The Current Population Survey (CPS)

Educational Attainment

Data from CPS questions on educational attainment are used in *indicators 17, 21,* and *24.* From 1972 to 1991, two CPS questions provided data on the number of years of school completed: (1) "What is the highest grade or year of regular school...has ever attended?" and (2) "Did... complete that grade (year)?" An individual's educational attainment was considered to be his or her last fully completed year of school. Individuals who completed 12 years of schooling were deemed to be high school graduates, as were those who began but did not complete the first year of college. Respondents who completed 16 or more years of schooling were counted as college graduates.

Beginning in 1992, the CPS combined the two questions into the following question: "What is the highest level of school... completed or the highest degree...received?" This change means that some data collected before 1992 are not strictly comparable with data collected from 1992 onward, and that care must be taken when making comparisons across years. The revised question changed the response categories from "highest grade completed" to "highest level of schooling or degree completed." In the revised response categories, several of the lower grade levels are combined into a single summary category such as "1st, 2nd, 3rd, or 4th grades." Several categories are added, including "12th grade, no diploma"; "High school graduate, high school diploma, or the equivalent"; and "Some college but no degree." College degrees are now listed by level, allowing for a more precise description of educational attainment. The revised question emphasizes credentials received rather than the last grade level attended or completed. The new categories include the following:

- High school graduate, high school diploma, or the equivalent (e.g., GED)
- Some college but no degree
- Associate's degree in college, occupational/ vocational program
- Associate's degree in college, academic program
- Bachelor's degree (e.g., B.A., A.B., B.S.)
- Master's degree (e.g., M.A., M.S., M.Eng., M.Ed., M.S.W., M.B.A.)
- Professional school degree (e.g., M.D., D.D.S., D.V.M., LL.B., J.D.)
- Doctorate degree (e.g., Ph.D., Ed.D.)

High School Completion

The pre-1988 questions about educational attainment did not specifically consider high school equivalency certificates (i.e., GEDs). Consequently, an individual who attended 10th grade, dropped out without completing that grade, and subsequently received a high school equivalency credential would not have been counted as completing high school. The revised question allows for these individuals to be counted as high school completers. Since 1988, an additional question has also asked respondents if they have a high school diploma or the equivalent, such as a GED. People who respond "yes" are classified as high school completers. Before 1988, the number of individuals who earned a high school equivalency certificate was small compared to the number of high school graduates, so the subsequent increase caused by including equivalency certificate recipients in the total number of people counted as "high school completers" was small in the years immediately after the change was made.

Before 1992, the CPS considered individuals who completed 12th grade to be high school graduates. A revision in 1992 added the response category "12th grade, no diploma." Individuals who select this response are not counted as graduates. Historically, the number of individuals in this category has been small.

Some College

Based on the question used in 1992 and in subsequent surveys, the response for an individual who attended college for less than a full academic year would be "some college but no degree." Before 1992, the appropriate response would have been "attended first year of college and did not complete it," thereby excluding those individuals with 1–3 years of college from the calculation of the percentage of the population. With the revised question, such respondents are placed in the "some college but no degree" category. Thus, the percentage of individuals with some college might be larger than the percentage with 1–3 years of college, because "some college" includes those who have not completed an entire year of college, but "1–3 years of college" does not. Therefore, it is not appropriate to make comparisons between the percentage of those with "some college but no degree" (using the post-1991 question) and the percentage of those who completed "1–3 years of college" (using the two pre-1992 questions).

In *The Condition of Education*, the "some college" category for years preceding 1992 includes only the response "1–3 years of college." After 1991, the "some college" category included those who responded "some college but no degree"; "associate's degree in college, occupational/ vocational program"; and "associate's degree in college, academic program." The effect of this change to the "some college" category is indicated by the fact that in 1992, some 48.9 percent of 25- to 29-year-olds reported completing some college or more, compared with 45.3 percent in 1991 (see *indicator 25,* table 25-2, in NCES 2008-031). The 3.6 percentage point difference is statistically significant. Some of the increase between 1991 and 1992 may be the result of individuals who completed less than 1 year of postsecondary education responding differently to the "some college" category; that is, they included themselves in the category in 1992 but did not include themselves in the category in 1991.

Another potential difference in the "some college" category is how individuals who have completed a certificate or type of award other than a degree respond to the questions, introduced in 1992, about their educational attainment. Some may answer "some college, no degree"; others may indicate only high school completion; and still others may equate their certificate with one of the types of associate's degrees. No information is available on the tendencies of individuals with a postsecondary credential other than a bachelor's or higher degree to respond to the new attainment question introduced in 1992.

College Completion

Some students attend college for 4 or more years without earning a bachelor's degree, so some researchers are concerned that the college completion rate, based on the pre-1992 category "4th year or higher of college completed," overstates the number of respondents with a bachelor's degree (or higher). In fact, however, the completion rates among those ages 25–29 in 1992 and 1993 were similar to the completion rates for 1990 and 1991, before the change in the question's wording. Thus, there appears to be good reason to conclude that the change has not affected the completion rates reported in *The Condition of Education 2011.*

NOTE 3: Other Surveys

American Community Survey (ACS)

The Census Bureau introduced the American Community Survey (ACS) in 1996. Fully implemented in 2005, it provides a large monthly sample of demographic, socioeconomic, and housing data comparable in content to the Long Form of the Decennial Census. Aggregated over time, these data will serve as a replacement for the Long Form of the Decennial Census. The survey includes questions mandated by federal law, federal regulations, and court decisions.

Since 2005, the survey has been mailed to approximately 250,000 addresses in the United States and Puerto Rico each month, or about 2.5 percent of the population annually. A larger proportion of addresses in small governmental units (e.g., American Indian reservations, small counties, and towns) also receive the survey. The monthly sample size is designed to approximate the ratio used in the 2000 Census, which requires more intensive distribution in these areas. The ACS covers the U.S. resident population, which includes the entire civilian, noninstitutionalized population; incarcerated persons; institutionalized persons; and the active duty military who are in the United States. In 2006, the ACS began interviewing residents in group quarter facilities. Institutionalized group quarters include adult and juvenile correctional facilities, nursing facilities, and other health care facilities. Noninstitutionalized group quarters include college and university housing, military barracks, and other noninstitutional facilities such as workers and religious group quarters and temporary shelters for the homeless.

National-level data from the ACS are available from 2000 onward. Annual results were available for areas with populations of 65,000 or more beginning in the summer of 2006; for areas with populations of 20,000 or more in the summer of 2008; and for all areas—down to the census tract level. This schedule is based on the time it will take to collect data from a sample size large enough to produce accurate results for different size geographic units.

Indicators 1, 5, 6, 20, and *29* use data from the ACS. Indicator *20* examines the status dropout rate by looking at an ACS question in which respondents were asked whether they had attended school or college at any time in the last 3 months and what degree or level of school was the highest they had completed. The status dropout rate is the percentage of 16- through 24-year-olds surveyed by the ACS who are not enrolled in high school and have not earned a high school credential (either a diploma or equivalency credential such as a General Educational Development [GED] certificate). For more information on the status dropout rate, see *supplemental*

note 6. For further details on the ACS, see http://www.census.gov/acs/www/.

Common Core of Data (CCD)

The Common Core of Data (CCD), a program of the National Center for Education Statistics (NCES), is the Department of Education's primary statistical database on public elementary and secondary education in the United States. It is a comprehensive, annual, national database of information concerning all public elementary and secondary schools (approximately 101,000) and school districts (approximately 18,000). The database contains data that are designed to be comparable across all states. The CCD consists of five surveys that state education departments complete annually from their administrative records. The database includes a general description of schools and school districts; data on students and staff, including demographics; and fiscal data, including revenues and current expenditures.

Indicators 2, 3, 4, 7, 19, 27, 28, 35, 36, and *37* use data from the CCD. Further information about the database is available at http://www.nces.ed.gov/ccd/.

Integrated Postsecondary Education Data System (IPEDS)

The Integrated Postsecondary Education Data System (IPEDS) is the core program that NCES uses for collecting data on postsecondary education. IPEDS is a single, comprehensive system that encompasses all identified institutions whose primary purpose is to provide postsecondary education. Before IPEDS, some of the same information was collected through the Higher Education General Information Survey (HEGIS). *Indicators 8* and *9* use data from HEGIS.

IPEDS consists of institution-level data that can be used to describe trends in postsecondary education at the institution, state, and/or national levels. For example, researchers can use IPEDS to analyze information on (1) enrollments of undergraduates, first-time freshmen, and graduate and first-professional students by race/ethnicity and sex; (2) institutional revenue and expenditure patterns by source of income and type of expense; (3) completions (awards) by level of program, level of award, race/ethnicity, and sex; (4) characteristics of postsecondary institutions, including tuition, room and board charges, and calendar systems; (5) status of career and technical education programs; and (6) other issues of interest.

Participation in IPEDS was a requirement for more than 6,900 institutions that participated in Title IV federal student financial aid programs, such as Pell Grants or Stafford Loans, during the corresponding academic years.

Title IV institutions include traditional colleges and universities, 2-year institutions, and for-profit degree- and non-degree-granting institutions (such as schools of cosmetology), among others. These categories are further disaggregated by financial control (public, private not-for-profit, and private for-profit), resulting in nine institutional categories or sectors. Institutions that do not participate in Title IV programs may participate in the IPEDS data collection on a voluntary basis.

The structure of the IPEDS collection of data on degrees conferred changed beginning with the 2007–08 academic year. Prior to 2007–08, colleges reported the number of first-professional degrees separate from the number of doctoral degrees. In addition, doctoral degrees were reported as a single category. In the 2008–09 academic year, institutions were required (optional in the 2007–08 academic year) to discontinue reporting first-professional degrees as a separate category and to integrate them into the master's and doctoral degrees categories; additionally, required in the 2008–09 academic year, the doctoral degrees could be reported in three different classifications: "professional practice," "research/scholarship," and "other." In order to present consistent national data over time, the data for the institutions reporting in the new structure were cross-walked to the old structure. The master's and doctoral degrees awarded in fields of study classified in the Classification of Instruction Programs (CIP) as "formerly considered first-professional" were reclassified as first-professional degree awards. Therefore, data presented in *The Condition of Education* on completed degrees from 2007–08 onward may not match reported totals within other publications. The specific fields and CIP programs cross-walked in this manner were the following:

51.0401 Dentistry (D.D.S. or D.M.D.)

51.1201 Medicine (M.D.)

51.1701 Optometry (O.D.)

51.1901 Osteopathic medicine (D.O.)

51.2001 Pharmacy (Pharm.D.)

51.2101 Podiatry (Pod.D. or D.P.) or podiatric medicine (D.P.M.)

51.2401 Veterinary medicine (D.V.M.)

51.0101 Chiropractic (D.C. or D.C.M.)

22.0101 Law (LL.B. or J.D.)

39.0602 Theology (M. Div., M.H.L., B.D., or Ord. and M.H.L./Rav.).

Indicators 8, 9, 22, 23, 26, 39, 40, 41, 42, 44, 49, and *50* use data from IPEDS. The institutional categories used in these indicators are described in *supplemental note 8*. Further information about IPEDS is available at http://nces.ed.gov/ipeds/.

Federal Student Aid Cohort Default Rate Database

The U.S Department of Education releases official cohort default rates once per year. The FY 2008 official cohort default rates, the most recent cohort default rates available, were delivered to both domestic and foreign schools on September 13, 2010.

For schools having 30 or more borrowers entering repayment in a fiscal year, the school's cohort default rate is the percentage of a school's borrowers who enter repayment on certain Federal Family Education Loans (FFELs) and/or William D. Ford Federal Direct Loans (Direct Loans) during that fiscal year and default (or meet the other specified condition) within the cohort default period. For schools with 29 or fewer borrowers entering repayment during a fiscal year, the cohort default rate is an "average rate" based on borrowers entering repayment over a 3-year period.

The phrase "cohort default period" refers to the 2-year period that begins on October 1 of the fiscal year when the borrower enters repayment and ends on September 30 of the following fiscal year. This is the period during which a borrower's default affects the school's cohort default rate.

Cohort default rates are based on federal fiscal years. Federal fiscal years begin October 1 of a calendar year and end on September 30 of the following calendar year. Each federal fiscal year refers to the calendar year in which it ends.

The phrase "cohort fiscal year" refers to the fiscal year for which the cohort default rate is calculated. For example, when calculating the 2008 cohort default rate, the cohort fiscal year is FY 2008 (October 1, 2007, to September 30, 2008).

A Federal Stafford Loan or Direct Stafford/Ford Loan enters repayment under the requirements applicable to the type of loan. In most cases, they enter repayment after a 6-month grace period that begins when the borrower separates (graduates or withdraws) from school or drops below half-time enrollment. The official repayment date is the first day following the end of the 6-month grace period. Use of this date is dependent on the school providing timely notification of any change in a student's enrollment status to the National Student Loan Data System (NSLDS) or the data manager. If the school does not provide timely notification, the data manager will use the best information available to determine the repayment date. This date will be used for purposes of calculating the school's cohort default rate. A Federal Supplemental Loan to Students (SLS) loan enters repayment on the day after the borrower separates from school or drops below half-time enrollment, unless the borrower also has a Federal Stafford Loan that was obtained during the same period of continuous enrollment. In that event, the repayment date of the Federal SLS loan for cohort default rate purposes is the same as the repayment date for the Federal Stafford Loan; generally, this is the first day following the end of the 6-month grace period.

For cohort default rate purposes, a Direct Loan is considered to be in default after 360 days of delinquency (or after 270 days if the borrower's first day of delinquency was before October 7, 1998). If the default date falls within the cohort default period, the borrower will be included in both the denominator and the numerator of the cohort default rate calculation.

Indicator 49 uses data from the Federal Student Aid Cohort Default Rate database.

National Postsecondary Student Aid Study (NPSAS)

The National Postsecondary Student Aid Study (NPSAS) is based on a nationally representative sample of all students in postsecondary education institutions, which comprises undergraduate, graduate, and first-professional students. Each NPSAS survey provides information on the cost of postsecondary education, the distribution of financial aid, and the characteristics of both aided and nonaided students and their families.

For NPSAS:2000, information on approximately 50,000 undergraduate, 11,000 graduate, and 1,000 first-professional students was obtained from more than 900 postsecondary institutions. They represented the nearly 17 million undergraduates, 2.4 million graduate students, and 300,000 first-professional students who were enrolled at some time between July 1, 1999, and June 30, 2000. Weights for NPSAS:2000 were revised to be comparable with financial aid data from NPSAS:2004 and NPSAS:2008. The revised NPSAS:2000 weights produce estimates that differ from the estimates reported in *The Condition of Education 2010*. Using the revised weights has the largest effect on the estimates of average Stafford Loan amounts, and therefore on the averages of all composite financial aid variables that include Stafford loans, such as total loans, total aid, and cumulative loans. The revised weights result in some changes in the estimates for nearly all variables in NPSAS:2000, although there were only minor changes in average grant amounts.

For NPSAS:04, information on approximately 80,000 undergraduates and 11,000 graduate or first-professional students was obtained from about 1,400 postsecondary institutions. These students represented nearly the 19 million undergraduate students, 3 million graduate students, and 300,000 first-professional students who

were enrolled at some time between July 1, 2003, and June 30, 2004.

For NPSAS:08, information on approximately 114,000 undergraduate students and 14,000 graduate or first-professional students was obtained from about 1,600 postsecondary institutions. These students represented the nearly 21 million undergraduate students and 3 million graduate students who were enrolled at some time between July 1, 2007, and June 30, 2008.

NPSAS represents all undergraduate students enrolled in postsecondary institutions in the 50 states, the District of Columbia, and Puerto Rico who were eligible to participate in the federal financial aid programs in Title IV of the Higher Education Act. The survey focuses on how they and their families pay for postsecondary education and includes information on general demographics and other characteristics of these students, types of aid and amounts received, and the cost of attending college. Students attending all controls and levels of institutions are represented, including private (both not-for-profit and for-profit) and public 4-year colleges and universities, 2-year institutions, and less-than-2-year institutions.

To be eligible for inclusion in the institutional sample, an institution must satisfy the following conditions: (1) offer an education program designed for persons who have completed secondary education; (2) offer an academic, occupational, or vocational program of study lasting 3 months or longer; (3) offer access to the general public; (4) offer more than just correspondence courses; (5) be located in the 50 states, the District of Columbia, or the Commonwealth of Puerto Rico; and (6) be other than a U.S. Service Academy.

Part-time and full-time students who are enrolled in academic or vocational courses or programs at these institutions and who are not concurrently enrolled in a high school completion program or who are not enrolled *solely* for the purpose of completing a GED or other high school completion program are eligible for inclusion in NPSAS. The first NPSAS, conducted in 1986–87, sampled students enrolled in fall 1986. Since the 1989–90 NPSAS, students who enrolled at any time during the year have been eligible for inclusion in the survey. This design change provides the opportunity to collect the data necessary for estimating full-year financial aid awards. Unless otherwise specified, all estimates in *The Condition of Education* using data from NPSAS include students in the 50 states, the District of Columbia, and the Commonwealth of Puerto Rico.

Indicator 43 reports data by dependency status. For federal financial aid purposes, all students are considered to be dependent unless they meet one of the following criteria for independence: age 24 or older; enrolled in a graduate or professional program beyond a bachelor's degree; married; orphan or ward of the court; have legal dependents other than a spouse; or on active duty or a veteran of the U.S. armed forces.

Indicators 22, 43, 46, 47, and *48* use data from NPSAS. Further information about the survey is available at http://nces.ed.gov/surveys/npsas/.

National Crime Victimization Survey (NCVS)

The National Crime Victimization Survey (NCVS) is the nation's primary source of information on criminal victimization. Initiated in 1972 and redesigned in 1992, the NCVS annually collects detailed information on the frequency and nature of the crimes of rape, sexual assault, robbery, aggravated and simple assault, theft, household burglary, and motor vehicle theft experienced by Americans and their households each year. The survey measures crimes reported to police as well as those not reported. The NCVS sample consists of about 50,000 households. U.S. Census Bureau personnel interview all household members age 12 or older within each sampled household to determine whether they had been victimized by the measured crimes during the 6 months preceding the interview. Households remain in the sample for 3 years and are interviewed seven times at 6-month intervals. The first of these seven household interviews is used only to bind future interviews by establishing a time frame in order to avoid duplication of crimes reported in the six subsequent interviews. After their seventh interview, households are replaced by a new sample of households. Data are obtained on the frequency, characteristics, and consequences of criminal victimization in the United States. The survey enables the Bureau of Justice Statistics (BJS) to estimate the likelihood of victimization for the population as a whole, as well as for segments of the population such as women, the elderly, members of various racial groups, city dwellers, or other groups. The NCVS provides the largest national forum for victims to describe the impact of crime and the characteristics of violent offenders.

Indicator 30 uses data from NCVS. Further information about the survey is available at http://bjs.ojp.usdoj.gov/index.cfm?ty=dcdetail&iid=245#Methodology.

Private School Universe Survey (PSS)

The Private School Universe Survey (PSS) was established in 1988 to ensure that private school data would be collected on a regular basis. With the help of the Census Bureau, the PSS is conducted biennially to provide the total number of private schools, students, and teachers, and to build a universe of private schools in the 50 states

and the District of Columbia that can serve as a sampling frame of private schools for NCES sample surveys.

The PSS groups elementary and secondary schools according to one of seven program emphases:

- *Regular:* The PSS questionnaire does not provide a definition of this term. Regular schools do not specialize in special, vocational/technical, early childhood, or alternative education and do not have a Montessori or special program emphasis, although they may offer these programs in addition to the regular curriculum.

- *Montessori:* The PSS questionnaire does not provide a definition of this term. Montessori schools provide instruction using Montessori teaching methods.

- *Special program emphasis:* A science/mathematics school, a performing arts high school, a foreign language immersion school, and a talented/gifted school are examples of schools that offer a special program emphasis.

- *Special education:* Special education schools primarily serve students with disabilities.

- *Vocational:* Vocational schools primarily serve students who are being trained for occupations. For *indicator 4,* vocational schools are included with special program emphasis schools.

- *Alternative:* Alternative schools provide nontraditional education. They fall outside the categories of regular, Montessori, special education, early childhood, and vocational education.

- *Early childhood:* Early childhood program schools serve students in prekindergarten, kindergarten, transitional (or readiness) kindergarten, and/or transitional first (or prefirst) grade.

Private schools are assigned to one of three major categories (Catholic, other religious, or nonsectarian) and, within each major category, one of three subcategories based on the school's religious affiliation provided by respondents.

- *Catholic:* Catholic schools are categorized according to governance, provided by Catholic school respondents, into parochial, diocesan, and private schools.

- *Other religious:* Other religious schools have a religious orientation or purpose, but are not Roman Catholic. Other religious schools are categorized according to religious association membership, provided by respondents into conservative Christian, other affiliated, and unaffiliated schools. Conservative Christian schools are those "Other religious" schools with membership in at least

NOTE 3: Other Surveys

one of four associations: Accelerated Christian Education, American Association of Christian Schools, Association of Christian Schools International, or Oral Roberts University Education Fellowship. Affiliated schools are those "Other religious" schools not classified as Conservative Christian with membership in at least 1 of 11 associations—Association of Christian Teachers and Schools, Christian Schools International, Evangelical Lutheran Education Association, Friends Council on Education, General Conference of the Seventh-Day Adventist Church, Islamic School League of America, National Association of Episcopal Schools, National Christian School Association, National Society for Hebrew Day Schools, Solomon Schechter Day Schools, and Southern Baptist Association of Christian Schools—or indicating membership in "other religious school associations." Unaffiliated schools are those "Other religious" schools that have a religious orientation or purpose, but are not classified as Conservative Christian or affiliated.

- *Nonsectarian:* Nonsectarian schools do not have a religious orientation or purpose and are categorized according to program emphasis, provided by respondents, into regular, special emphasis, and special education schools. Regular schools are those that have a regular elementary/secondary or early childhood program emphasis. Special emphasis schools are those that have a Montessori, vocation/technical, alternative, or special program emphasis. Special education schools are those that have a special education program emphasis.

In the most recent PSS data collection, conducted in 2009–10, the survey was sent to 40,302 institutions, with a weighted response rate of 93.6 percent.

Indicator 4 uses data from the PSS. Further information on the survey is available at http://nces.ed.gov/surveys/pss/.

Schools and Staffing Survey (SASS)

The Schools and Staffing Survey (SASS) is a large sample survey of America's elementary and secondary schools. First conducted in 1987–88, SASS periodically surveys and collects data on the following:

- public schools (collecting data on school districts, schools, principals, teachers, and library media centers);

- private schools (collecting data on schools, principals, and teachers [and library media centers for survey years prior to 2003–04]);

- Bureau of Indian Education (BIE) funded schools (collecting data on schools, principals, teachers, and library media centers); and public charter schools (collecting data on schools, principals, teachers, and library media centers).

Responses from each component can be linked together to provide a comprehensive perspective on the context of elementary and secondary education in the United States. To ensure that the samples contain sufficient numbers for estimates, SASS uses a stratified probability sample design. Public and private schools are oversampled into groups based on certain characteristics. After the schools are stratified and sampled, the teachers within the schools are stratified and sampled based on their characteristics. In 1999–2000, public charter schools became a new school sector for SASS, and questionnaires were sent to charter schools, principals, and teachers. Since the 2003–04 SASS, public charter schools have been sampled as part of the public school questionnaire.

Indicators 31 and *33* use data from SASS. The most recent SASS data collection was conducted in 2007–08. Further information about the survey is available at http://nces.ed.gov/surveys/SASS/.

The Teacher Follow-up Survey (TFS)

The Teacher Follow-up Survey (TFS) is a component of SASS that is designed to determine how many teachers remained at the same school, moved to another school, or left the profession in the year following the SASS administration. It has been administered the year following each SASS administration since school year 1988–89. The 2008–09 TFS was administered to a subsample of SASS teachers who completed the SASS in 2007–08. Information was collected by web and paper instruments between February and August 2009.

Within TFS, there are questionnaires for teachers who left teaching since the previous SASS and another for those who are currently teaching either in the same school as the prior year or in a different school. The topics for the Current Teacher questionnaire include teaching status and assignments, ratings of various aspects of teaching, information on decisions to change schools, and ratings of various strategies for retaining more teachers. The topics for the Former Teacher questionnaire include employment status, ratings of various aspects of teaching and their current jobs, and information on decisions to leave teaching.

Indicator 32 uses data from the TFS. Further information about the survey is available at http://nces.ed.gov/surveys/sass/ovrv_whatstfs.asp.

The Principal Follow-up Survey (PFS)

The Principal Follow-up Survey (PFS), first conducted in school year 2008–09, is a component of the 2007–08 SASS. The goal of the PFS was to assess how many principals from school year 2007–08 still worked as a principal in the same school in the 2008–09 school year, how many had moved to become a principal in another school, and how many had left the principalship altogether. Another goal was to measure the percentage of principals who left to retire or seek work in another occupational field. All public, private, and BIE school principals who replied to a 2007–08 SASS principal questionnaire were included in the PFS sample. Information was collected primarily by mail, with telephone follow-up for nonrespondents from March to June 2009.

Indicator 34 uses data from the PFS. Further information about the survey is available at http://nces.ed.gov/surveys/sass/ovrv_pfs.asp.

NOTE 4: National Assessment of Educational Progress

The National Assessment of Educational Progress (NAEP), governed by the National Assessment Governing Board (NAGB), is administered regularly in a number of academic subjects. Since its creation in 1969, NAEP has had two major goals: (1) to assess student performance reflecting current educational and assessment practices, and (2) to measure change in student performance reliably over time. To address these goals, NAEP conducts a main assessment and a long-term trend assessment. The two assessments are administered to separate samples of students at separate times, use separate instruments, and measure different educational content. Thus, results from the two assessments should not be directly compared.

Main NAEP

Indicators 10, 11, 12, 13, and *14* are based on the main NAEP. Begun in 1990, the main NAEP, following the assessment framework developed by NAGB, periodically assesses students' performance in several subjects in grades 4, 8, and 12. NAGB develops the frameworks using standards developed within the field; this is a consensus process involving educators, subject-matter experts, and other interested citizens. Each round of the main NAEP includes a student assessment and background questionnaires (for the student, teacher, and school) to provide information on instructional experiences and the school environment at each grade. While NAEP assessments are not intended to reveal underlying causes for student performance, the results can be viewed in tandem with the changing composition of enrollment and trends in education policy, practice, and expectations for America's youth.

Through 1988, NAEP reported only on the academic achievement of the nation as a whole and subgroups within the population. Because the national samples were not designed to support the reporting of accurate and representative state-level results, Congress passed legislation in 1988 authorizing a voluntary Trial State Assessment (TSA). Separate representative samples of students were selected from each state or jurisdiction that agreed to participate in state NAEP. TSAs were conducted in 1990, 1992, and 1994 and were evaluated thoroughly. Beginning with the 1996 assessment, the authorizing statute no longer considered the state component to be a "trial" assessment.

A significant change to state NAEP occurred in 2001 with the reauthorization of the Elementary and Secondary Education Act, also referred to as the "No Child Left Behind" legislation. This legislation requires states that receive Title I funding to participate every 2 years in state NAEP in reading and mathematics at grades 4 and 8. State participation in other state NAEP subjects, including science and writing, remains voluntary.

The assessments given in the states are exactly the same as those given nationally. The assessments follow the subject area frameworks developed by NAGB and use the latest advances in assessment methodology. State NAEP assessed students at grades 4 and 8 in 2009, and 11 states participated in a pilot-state NAEP reading and mathematics assessment at grade 12. The assessments allow states to monitor their own progress over time in the selected subject areas. They can then compare the knowledge and skills of their students with students in other states and with students across the country.

The ability of the assessments to measure change in student performance over time is sometimes limited by changes in the NAEP framework. While shorter-term trends can be measured in most of the NAEP subjects, data from different assessments are not always comparable. In cases where the framework of a given assessment changes, linking studies are generally conducted to ensure comparability over time. In 2005, NAGB revised the grade 12 mathematics framework to reflect changes in high school mathematics standards and coursework. As a result, even though many questions are repeated from previous assessments, the 2005 and 2009 mathematics results cannot be directly compared with those from previous years.

NAGB called for the development of a new mathematics framework for the 2005 assessment. The revisions made to the mathematics framework for the 2005 assessment were intended to reflect recent curricular emphases and better assess the specific objectives for students in each grade level. The revised mathematics framework focuses on two dimensions: mathematical content and cognitive demand. By considering these two dimensions for each item in the assessment, the framework ensures that NAEP assesses an appropriate balance of content, as well as a variety of ways of knowing and doing mathematics. For grades 4 and 8, comparisons over time can be made among the assessments prior to and after the implementation of the 2005 framework. In grade 12, with the implementation of the 2005 framework, the assessment included more questions on algebra, data analysis, and probability to reflect changes in high school mathematics standards and coursework. Additionally, the measurement and geometry content areas were merged. Grade 12 results could not be placed on the old NAEP scale and could not be directly compared with previous years as the assessment changed. The reporting scale for grade 12 mathematics was changed from 0–500 to 0–300. For more information regarding the 2005 framework revisions, see http://nces.ed.gov/nationsreportcard/mathematics/whatmeasure.asp.

In 2009, a new framework was developed for the 4th-, 8th-, and 12th-grade NAEP reading assessments. The previous framework was first implemented in 1992 and was used for each subsequent assessment from 1994 through 2007. Past NAEP practice has been to start a new trend line when a new framework is introduced.

However, special analyses were conducted in 2009 to determine if the results from the 2009 reading assessment could be compared to results from earlier years despite being based on a new framework. Both a content alignment study and a reading trend or bridge study were conducted to determine if the "new" assessment was comparable to the "old" assessment. Overall, the results of the special analyses suggested that the old and new assessments were similar in terms of their item and scale characteristics and the results they produced for important demographic groups of students. It was determined that the results of the 2009 reading assessment could still be compared to those from earlier assessment years, thereby maintaining the trend lines first established in 1992. For more information regarding the 2009 reading framework revisions, see http://nces.ed.gov/nationsreportcard/reading/whatmeasure.asp.

In 2009, a new framework was developed for the 4th-, 8th-, and 12th-grade NAEP science assessment to keep the content current with key developments in science, curriculum standards, assessments, and research. The 2009 framework, therefore, replaces the framework that was used for earlier NAEP science assessments in 1996, 2000, and 2005. Due to the change in framework, the results from the 2009 science assessment are not comparable to those from previous assessment years. The 2009 science framework organizes science content into three broad content areas, physical science, life science, and Earth and space sciences, reflecting the science curriculum students are generally exposed to in grades K–12. For more information regarding the 2009 science framework and the specific content areas, see http://www.nagb.org/publications/frameworks/science-09.pdf.

The main NAEP results are reported in *The Condition of Education* in terms of average scale scores and achievement levels. The achievement levels define what students who are performing at the *Basic, Proficient,* and *Advanced* levels of achievement should know and be able to do. NAGB establishes new achievement levels whenever a new main NAEP framework is adopted. As provided by law, NCES, upon review of congressionally mandated evaluations of NAEP, has determined that achievement levels are to be used on a trial basis and should be interpreted with caution. NAEP achievement levels have been widely used by national and state officials. The policy definitions of the achievement levels that apply across all grades and subject areas are as follows:

- *Basic:* This level denotes partial mastery of prerequisite knowledge and skills that are fundamental for proficient work at each grade assessed.

- *Proficient:* This level represents solid academic performance for each grade assessed. Students reaching this level have demonstrated competency over challenging subject matter, including subject-matter knowledge, application of such knowledge to real-world situations, and analytical skills appropriate to the subject matter.

- *Advanced:* This level signifies superior performance at each grade assessed.

In *indicators 10, 12,* and *14,* the percentage of students at or above *Proficient* or at or above *Basic* are reported. The percentage of students at or above *Proficient* includes students at the *Proficient* and *Advanced* achievement levels. Similarly, the percentage of students at or above *Basic* includes students at the *Basic, Proficient,* and *Advanced* achievement levels.

NAEP estimates that are potentially unstable (large standard error compared with the estimate) are not flagged as potentially unreliable. This practice for NAEP estimates is consistent with the current output from the NAEP online data analysis tool. The reader should always consult the appropriate standard errors when interpreting these findings. For additional information on NAEP, including technical aspects of scoring and assessment validity and more specific information on achievement levels, see http://nces.ed.gov/nationsreportcard/.

Until 1996, the main NAEP assessments excluded certain subgroups of students identified as "special needs students," that is, students with disabilities and students with limited-English-proficiency. For the 1996 and 2000 mathematics assessments and the 1998 and 2000 reading assessments, the main NAEP included a separate assessment with provisions for accommodating these students (e.g., extended time, small group testing, mathematics questions read aloud, etc.). Thus, for these years, there are results for both the unaccommodated assessment and the accommodated assessment. For the 2002, 2003, and 2005 reading assessments and the 2003 and 2005 mathematics assessments, the main NAEP did not include a separate unaccommodated assessment—only a single accommodated assessment was administered. The switch to a single accommodated assessment instrument was made after it was determined that accommodations in NAEP did not have any significant effect on student scores. *Indicators 10, 11, 12,* and *13* present NAEP results with and without accommodations.

NOTE 5: International Assessments

Program for International Student Assessment (PISA)

Indicators 15 and *16* are based on data collected as part of the Program for International Student Assessment (PISA). PISA is sponsored by the Organization for Economic Co-operation and Development (OECD), an intergovernmental organization of 34 industrialized countries that serves as a forum for member countries to cooperate in research and policy development on social and economic topics of common interest.

PISA seeks to represent the overall yield of learning for 15-year-olds. PISA assumes that by age 15, young people have had a series of learning experiences, both in and out of school, that allow them to perform at particular levels in reading, mathematics, and science. Formal education will have played a major role in student performance, but other factors, such as learning opportunities at home, also play a role. PISA's results provide an indicator of the overall performance of a country's educational system, and they also provide information about other factors that influence performance (e.g., hours of instructional time). By assessing students near the end of compulsory schooling in key knowledge and skills, PISA provides information about how well prepared students will be for their future lives as they approach an important transition point for education and work. PISA thus aims to show how well equipped 15-year-olds are for their futures based on what they have learned up to that point.

PISA was first implemented in 2000 and is based on a 3-year cycle. PISA 2009 was the fourth cycle of the assessment. In each PISA cycle the capabilities of 15-year-olds in reading literacy, mathematics literacy, and science literacy are assessed. However, in each assessment year, PISA provides a detailed examination for one of the three subjects (referred to as a major domain) and a basic examination of the other two subjects (referred to as minor domains). The 2000 assessment focused on reading literacy; the 2003 assessment focused on mathematics literacy; the 2006 assessment focused on science literacy; and the 2009 assessment again focused on reading literacy.

In 2009, 65 countries and other education systems participated in PISA, including the 34 OECD countries, 26 non-OECD countries, and 5 other education systems. Other education systems refer to non-national entities, such as Shanghai-China. To implement PISA, each participating country and education system selected a representative sample of 15-year-olds. The PISA 2009 guidelines specified that a minimum of 4,500 students from a minimum of 150 schools was required in each country and education system in order to meet the minimum sample threshold to participate in the assessment. The guidelines also specified that within

schools, a sample of 35 students was to be selected in an equal probability sample unless fewer than 35 students age 15 were available (in which case all students were selected). PISA 2009 standards required that students in the sample be 15 years and 3 months to 16 years and 2 months old at the beginning of the testing period.

In the United States, the PISA 2009 assessment was administered from September 21, 2009, to November 19, 2009. A total of 5,233 15-year-old students from 165 participating schools in the United States participated in the assessment.

PISA 2009 was developed by international experts and a consortium of test developers with items submitted and reviewed by representatives of each country for possible bias and relevance to PISA's goals. The final assessment consisted of 102 reading items, 36 mathematics items, and 52 science items allocated to 13 test booklets. Each booklet was made up of 4 test clusters, and the average number of items per cluster was 15 items for reading, 12 items for mathematics, and 17 items for science. Each student completed a 2-hour paper-and-pencil assessment. During the assessment, all students answered reading items, but only some students, depending on the test booklet which they received, answered mathematics and/ or science items. In addition to the cognitive assessment, students received a 30-minute questionnaire designed to give information about their backgrounds, attitudes, and experiences in school. Principals in schools where PISA was administered were also given a 30-minute questionnaire to provide information about their schools. For more detailed information on sampling, administration, response rates, and other technical issues related to PISA data, see http://nces.ed.gov/ pubs2011/2011004.pdf.

The OECD developed the *PISA 2009 Assessment Framework: Key Competencies in Reading, Mathematics, and Science* to design the PISA 2009 assessment in a collaborative effort of the PISA Governing Board and an international consortium. The PISA 2009 framework acts as a blueprint for the assessment, outlining what should be assessed.

Reading literacy in PISA 2009 is defined as "understanding, using, reflecting on, and engaging with written texts in order to achieve one's goals, to develop one's knowledge and potential, and to participate in society." Reading literacy is built on three "task characteristics": (1) *situation,* which distinguishes the range of context or purposes for which reading takes place; (2) *text,* the range of materials that are read; and (3) *aspect,* which consists of the mental strategies, approaches or purposes that readers use to negotiate their way into, around, and between texts.

The three reading literacy subscales (*access and retrieve, integrate and interpret,* and *reflect and evaluate*) were derived from three aspect categories: (1) *access and retrieve,* which includes navigating the information space provided to locate and retrieve one or more distinct pieces of information; (2) *integrate and interpret,* which includes developing an understanding of the coherence of the text and make meaning from something that is not stated; and (3) *reflect and evaluate,* which includes drawing upon knowledge, ideas, or attitudes beyond the text in order to relate the information provided within the text to one's own conceptual and experiential frame of reference.

Mathematics literacy in PISA 2009 is defined as "an individual's capacity to identify and understand the role that mathematics plays in the world, to make well-founded judgments and to use and engage with mathematics in ways that meet the needs of that individual's life as a constructive, concerned and reflective citizen."

Science literacy in PISA 2009 is defined as "scientific knowledge and use of that knowledge to identify questions, to acquire new knowledge, to explain scientific phenomena, and to draw evidence based conclusions about science-related issues, understanding of the characteristic features of science as a form of human knowledge and inquiry, awareness of how science and technology shape our material, intellectual, and cultural environments, and willingness to engage in science-related issues, and with the ideas of science, as a reflective citizen." Details on the PISA 2009 framework and the reading, science, and mathematics literacy competencies can be found at http://www.oecd.org/dataoecd/11/40/44455820.pdf.

The PISA 2000 and 2009 OECD averages used in the analysis of trends in reading literacy scores over time are based on the averages of the 27 OECD countries with comparable data for 2000 and 2009. As a result, the reading literacy OECD average score for PISA 2000 differs from previously published reports and the reading literacy OECD average score for PISA 2009 differs from the OECD average score used for analyses other than trend comparisons. The seven current OECD members not included in the OECD average for trend analysis include the Slovak Republic and Turkey, which joined

PISA in 2003; Estonia and Slovenia, which joined PISA in 2006; Luxembourg, which experienced substantial changes in its assessment conditions between 2000 and 2003; and the Netherlands and the United Kingdom, which did not meet the PISA response rate standards in 2000. Though reading literacy scores can be compared for all PISA administrative cycles (2000, 2003, 2006, and 2009), the U.S. averages in 2000 and 2009 are compared with OECD average scores in 2000 and 2009 because reading literacy was the major domain assessed in those years.

The PISA mathematics framework was revised in 2003. Because of changes in the framework, it is not possible to compare mathematics learning outcomes from PISA 2000 with those from PISA 2003, 2006, and 2009. The PISA science framework was revised in 2006. Because of changes in the framework, it is not possible to compare science learning outcomes from PISA 2000 and 2003 with those from PISA 2006 and 2009. Details on the changes to PISA since 2000 can be found at http://www.oecd.org/document/61/0,3746,en_32252351_32235731_46567613_1_1_1_1,00.html.

The PISA 2003 and 2009 OECD averages used in the analysis of trends in mathematics literacy scores over time are based on the 29 OECD countries with comparable data for 2003 and 2009. The five current members not included in the OECD average for trend analysis include Chile, Estonia, Israel, Slovenia, which did not participate in 2003, and the United Kingdom, which did not meet PISA response rate standards for the 2003 assessment.

For science literacy trends, all 34 OECD countries are used.

The OECD excluded the data for Austria from the trend analysis in its report (*PISA 2009 Results: Learning Trend—Changes in Student Performance Since 2000 (Volume V),* available at http://www.pisa.oecd.org) because of a concern over a data collection issue in 2009; however, after consultation with Austrian officials, NCES kept the Austrian data in the U.S. trend reporting.

For more information on PISA, see http://nces.ed.gov/Surveys/PISA.

NOTE 6: Measures of Student Persistence and Progress

Various measures have been developed to provide information about student persistence and progress in formal elementary and secondary education in the United States. Three measures are presented in this report: the public school *averaged freshman graduation rate* (*indicator 19*), the *status dropout rate* (*indicator 20*), and the educational attainment of 25- through 29-year-olds (*indicator 24*). Each of these indicators employs a different analytic method and dataset to document a unique aspect of the complex processes of high school graduation and dropping out of high school. No single data source provides comprehensive information on the graduation and dropout processes on an annual basis, but the three indicators presented here complement one another and draw upon the particular strengths of their respective data. Each indicator has limitations, however, which underscores the importance of having multiple indicators that address the question of student persistence. A brief description of the relevant methodology and data used by each indicator follows.

Public School Averaged Freshman Graduation Rate

The accurate reporting of a high school graduation rate requires student record data on student progression from grade to grade, data on graduation status, and data on students who transfer in and out of a school, district, or state during the high school years, or in other words, cohort data (National Institute of Statistical Sciences (NISS) 2004 Task Force, NCES 2005-105). At the time the on-time graduation rate reporting requirement was enacted in the Elementary and Secondary Education Act of 2001, few states had data collection systems adequate to support the calculation of an accurate on-time graduation rate. Recognizing the need for an interim measure to use while individual states develop student record systems, the leadership in the Department of Education asked NCES to evaluate the array of potential graduation indicators. In response NCES issued a two-volume report that examined the existing measures of high school completion and the newly proposed proxy measures. The analysis provided the technical basis for the Department's selection of an interim graduation rate based on estimating the percentage of an incoming freshman class that graduates 4 years later (NCES 2006-604 and 2006-605). The *averaged freshman graduation rate* (AFGR) appeared in the NCES analysis as the only measure that consistently figured among the best performing indicators.

Indicator 19 examines the percentage of public high school students who graduate on time by using the AFGR. The AFGR is a measure of the percentage of the incoming freshman class that graduates 4 years later. The AFGR is the number of graduates with a regular diploma divided by the estimated count of incoming freshmen 4 years earlier, as reported through the NCES Common Core of Data (CCD), the survey system based on state education departments' annual administrative records. (For more information on the CCD, see *supplemental note 3*.) The estimated count of incoming freshmen is the sum of the number of 8th-graders 5 years earlier, the number of 9th-graders 4 years earlier (when current-year seniors were freshmen), and the number of 10th-graders 3 years earlier, divided by 3. The intent of this averaging is to account for the high rate of grade retention in the freshman year, which adds 9th-grade repeaters from the previous year to the number of students in the incoming freshman class each year. Ungraded students are allocated to individual grades proportional to each state's enrollment in those grades. An advantage of using CCD data to calculate the AFGR is that the data are available on an annual basis by state; however, the demographic details available from the survey are limited.

Status Dropout Rate

Indicator 20 reports *status dropout rates* by race/ethnicity and nativity status. Status dropout rates measure the extent of the dropout problem for a population. As such, these rates can be used to gauge the need for further education and training within that population. *Indicator 20* uses data from the American Community Survey (ACS) and the October Current Population Survey (CPS) to estimate the percentage of the population ages 16 through 24 who are not in high school and have not earned a high school credential (either a diploma or an equivalency credential such as a General Educational Development [GED] certificate), irrespective of when they dropped out. The 2009 ACS allows for more detailed comparisons of status dropout rates by race/ethnicity, nativity, and sex, and, unlike the CPS, includes institutionalized persons, incarcerated persons, and active duty military personnel living in barracks in the United States. The CPS provides several decades of historical trends on status dropouts that are not available from the ACS. The disadvantage of using CPS data to compute status dropout rates for the civilian, noninstitutionalized population is that military personnel and incarcerated or institutionalized persons are excluded. A disadvantage of both the CPS and ACS is that the datasets include as dropouts individuals who never attended U.S. schools, including immigrants who did not complete the equivalent of a high school education in their home country. Estimates of status dropout rates from the ACS and CPS are not directly comparable due to methodological differences, such as differing sampling frames, modes of administration, and question wording. For more information on the CPS, see *supplemental note 2,* and for more information on the ACS, see *supplemental note 3.*

Educational Attainment of 25- to 29-Year-Olds

Indicator 24 examines the educational attainment of adults who are just past the age by which most people are traditionally expected to have completed their postsecondary education. This indicator uses March CPS data to estimate the percentage of civilian, noninstitutionalized people ages 25 through 29 who have achieved the following levels of educational attainment: high school diploma or equivalent (including a credential such as a GED), some college, bachelor's degree, or master's or other advanced degree. Estimates of educational attainment represent the percentage of adults who completed at least the cited credential.

Attainment estimates do not differentiate between those who graduated from public schools, those who graduated from private schools, and those who earned a GED. These estimates also include individuals who never attended high school in the United States but attained a high school diploma or its equivalent in another country. An advantage of using CPS data to compute educational attainment estimates is that estimates can be computed on an annual basis for various demographic subgroups of adults. A disadvantage of using CPS data to compute the educational attainment rate is that these data exclude all military personnel living in barracks and incarcerated or institutionalized persons. For more information on the CPS, see *supplemental note 2*.

NOTE 7: Student Disabilities

Indicator 7 uses data from the U.S. Department of Education's Office of Special Education Programs (OSEP), which collects information on students with disabilities as part of the implementation of the Individuals with Disabilities Education Act (IDEA). OSEP classifies disabilities in 13 categories. (For more detailed definitions of these categories, see the part B and C data dictionaries at http://www.ideadata.org.)

Prior to October 1994, children and youth with disabilities were served under Title I of the Elementary and Secondary Education Act, as well as under the Individuals with Disabilities Education Act (IDEA), Part B. Data reported for years prior to 1994–95 include children ages 0–21 served under Title I. Increases since 1987–88 are due in part to new legislation enacted in fall 1986, which added a mandate for public school special education services for 3- to 5-year-old disabled children.

Disability Categories

Autism

A developmental disability significantly affecting verbal and nonverbal communication and social interaction that adversely affects a child's educational performance, generally evident before age 3. Other characteristics often associated with autism are engagement in repetitive activities and stereotyped movements, resistance to environmental change or change in daily routines, and unusual responses to sensory experiences.

Deaf-Blindness

Concomitant hearing and visual impairments, the combination of which causes such severe communication and other developmental and educational needs that the student cannot be accommodated in special education programs solely for children with deafness or children with blindness.

Developmental Delay

This term may apply to children ages 3 through 9 who are experiencing delays in one or more of the following developmental areas: physical, cognitive, communication, social or emotional, or adaptive, and who, therefore, need special education and related services. It is optional for states to adopt and use this term to describe any child within its jurisdiction. A local education agency (LEA) may use the term if its state has adopted it, but it must conform its use of the term to the state's use of the term.

Emotional Disturbance

A condition exhibiting one or more of the following characteristics over a long period of time and to a marked degree that adversely affects a child's educational performance:

- An inability to learn that cannot be explained by intellectual, sensory, or health factors.

- An inability to build or maintain satisfactory interpersonal relationships with peers and teachers.

- Inappropriate types of behavior or feelings under normal circumstances.

- A general pervasive mood of unhappiness or depression.

- A tendency to develop physical symptoms or fears associated with personal or school problems.

Emotional disturbance includes schizophrenia. However, the term does not apply to children who are socially maladjusted, unless it is determined that they have an emotional disturbance.

Hearing Impairment

An impairment in hearing, whether permanent or fluctuating, that adversely affects a child's educational performance, but that is not included under the traditional definition of deafness.

Although children and youth with deafness are not included in the definition of hearing impairment, they are counted in the hearing impairment category.

Intellectual Disability

Significantly subaverage general intellectual functioning existing concurrently with deficits in adaptive behavior and manifested during the developmental period that adversely affects a child's educational performance.

Multiple Disabilities

Concomitant impairments (such as intellectual disability-blindness, intellectual disability-orthopedic impairment, etc.), the combination of which causes such severe educational needs that the student cannot be accommodated in special education programs solely for one of the impairments. The term does not include deaf-blindness.

Orthopedic Impairment

A severe orthopedic impairment that adversely affects a child's educational performance. The term includes impairments caused by a congenital anomaly (e.g., clubfoot, absence of some member, etc.), impairments caused by disease (e.g., poliomyelitis, bone tuberculosis, etc.), and impairments from other causes (e.g., cerebral palsy, amputations, and fractures or burns that cause contractures).

Other Health Impairment

Having limited strength, vitality, or alertness, including a heightened alertness to environmental stimuli, that results in limited alertness with respect to the educational environment, that

- is due to chronic or acute health problems such as asthma, attention deficit disorder or attention deficit hyperactivity disorder, diabetes, epilepsy, a heart condition, hemophilia, lead poisoning, leukemia, nephritis, rheumatic fever, sickle cell anemia; or Tourette syndrome; and

- adversely affects a child's educational performance.

Specific Learning Disability

A disorder in one or more of the basic psychological processes involved in understanding or in using language, spoken or written, that may manifest itself in an imperfect ability to listen, think, speak, read, write, spell, or do mathematical calculations. This disorder includes conditions such as perceptual disabilities, brain injury, minimal brain dysfunction, dyslexia, and developmental aphasia. The term does not include learning problems that are primarily the result of visual, hearing, or motor disabilities; intellectual disability; emotional disturbance; or environmental, cultural, or economic disadvantage.

Speech or Language Impairment

A communication disorder such as stuttering, impaired articulation, a language impairment, or a voice impairment that adversely affects a child's educational performance.

Traumatic Brain Injury

An acquired injury to the brain caused by an external physical force, resulting in total or partial functional disability, psychosocial impairment, or both, that adversely affects a child's educational performance. The term applies to open or closed head injuries resulting in impairments in one or more areas such as cognition; language; memory; attention; reasoning; abstract thinking; judgment; problem solving; sensory, perceptual, and motor abilities; psychosocial behavior; physical functions; information processing; and speech. The term does not apply to brain injuries that are congenital or degenerative or to brain injuries induced by birth trauma.

Visual Impairments

An impairment in vision that, even with correction, adversely affects a child's educational performance. The term includes both partial sight and blindness.

Preschool Disability

Beginning in 1976, data were collected for preschool age children by disability type; those data are combined with data for children and youth ages 6–21. However, the 1986 Amendments to the Education of the Handicapped Act (now known as IDEA) mandated that data not be collected by disability for students ages 3–5. For this reason, data from the 1990s on preschoolers with disabilities are reported separately. Beginning in 2000–01, states were again required to report preschool children by disability.

NOTE 8: Classification of Postsecondary Education Institutions

The U.S. Department of Education's Integrated Postsecondary Education Data System (IPEDS) employs various categories to classify postsecondary institutions. This supplemental note outlines the different categories used in varying combinations in *indicators 4, 8, 9, 23, 26, 39, 40, 41, 42, 43, 44, 49,* and *50.*

Basic IPEDS Classifications

The term postsecondary institutions is the category used to refer to institutions with formal instructional programs and a curriculum designed primarily for students who have completed the requirements for a high school diploma or its equivalent. This includes programs whose purpose is academic or vocational, as well as continuing professional education programs, and excludes avocational and adult basic education programs. For many analyses, however, comparing all institutions in this broad universe of postsecondary institutions would not be appropriate. Thus, postsecondary institutions are placed in one of three levels, based on the highest award offered at the institution:

- *4-year-and-above institutions:* Institutions or branches that offer programs of at least 4 years' duration or offer programs at or above the baccalaureate level. These institutions award a 4-year degree or higher in one or more programs or award a post-baccalaureate or post-master's. Includes schools that offer post-baccalaureate certificates only or those that offer graduate programs only. Also includes freestanding medical, law, or other first-professional schools.

- *2-year but less-than-4-year institutions:* A postsecondary institution that offers programs of at least 2 but less than 4 years' duration. Includes occupational and vocational schools with programs of at least 1,800 hours and academic institutions with programs of less than 4 years' duration. Does not include bachelor's degree-granting institutions where the baccalaureate-level program can be completed in 3 years.

- *Less-than-2-year institutions:* Institutions or branches that offer programs of less than 2 years' duration below the baccalaureate level. Includes occupational and vocational schools with programs that do not exceed 1,800 contact hours.

Postsecondary institutions are further divided according to these criteria: type of financial control, degree-granting versus non-degree-granting, and Title IV-participating versus non-Title IV-participating.

IPEDS also classifies institutions at each of the three levels of institutions by financial control:

- *Public institutions:* Institutions whose programs and activities are operated by publicly elected or appointed school officials and which are supported primarily by public funds.

- *Private not-for-profit institutions:* Institutions in which the individual(s) or agency in control receives no compensation other than wages, rent, or other expenses for the assumption of risk. These include both independent not-for-profit schools and those affiliated with a religious organization.

- *Private for-profit institutions:* Institutions in which the individual(s) or agency in control receives compensation other than wages, rent, or other expenses for the assumption of risk (e.g., proprietary schools).

Thus, IPEDS divides the universe of postsecondary institutions into nine different "sectors," each comprising a combination of the institution level and the control of the institution. In some sectors (for example, private for-profit 4-year institutions), the number of institutions is small relative to other sectors.

Institutions in any of these nine sectors can be degree- or non-degree-granting, a classification based on whether or not they offer students a formal award such as a degree or certificate:

- *Degree-granting institutions* offer associate's, bachelor's, master's, doctoral, and/or first-professional degrees that a state agency recognizes or authorizes.

- *Non-degree-granting institutions* offer other kinds of credentials and exist at all types of financial control (i.e., public, private not-for-profit, and private for-profit institutions).

The number of 4-year-and-above non-degree-granting institutions is small compared with the total number of non-degree-granting institutions.

Institutions in any of these nine sectors can also be Title IV-participating or not. For an institution to participate in federal Title IV Higher Education Act, Part C, financial aid programs, it must offer a program of study at least 300 clock hours in length; have accreditation recognized by the U.S. Department of Education; have been in business for at least 2 years; and have a Title IV participation agreement with the U.S. Department of Education. All indicators in this volume using IPEDS data present only Title IV-participating institutions. For more information on the Higher Education Act of 2008, see http://www2.ed.gov/policy/highered/leg/hea08/index.html.

In some indicators based on IPEDS data, 4-year-and-above degree-granting institutions are further classified according to the highest degree awarded:

- *Doctoral institutions* award at least 20 doctoral degrees per year.

- *Master's institutions* award at least 20 master's degrees per year.

The remaining institutions are considered to be other 4-year degree-granting institutions. The number of degrees awarded by an institution in a given year is obtained for each institution from data published in the IPEDS "Completions Survey" (IPEDS-C).

Indicators 4, 8, 22, 26, 39, 40, 42, 43, 44, and *49* include 2-year (short for 2-year but less-than-4-year) degree-granting institutions in their analyses.

Indicators 8, 9, 22, 26, 39, 40, 41, 42, 43, 44, and *49* include 4-year-and-above degree-granting institutions in their analyses.

NOTE 9: Fields of Study for Postsecondary Degrees

The general categories for fields of study used in *indicators 40* and *41* were derived from the 2000 edition of the *Classification of Instructional Programs* (CIP-2000), which was initiated in 2002–03. Some category modifications have been made in some instances. These modified aggregations are as follows:

Agriculture and natural resources: agriculture, agriculture operations and related sciences; and natural resources and conservation.

Business: business, management, marketing, and related support services; and personal and culinary services.

Communication and communications technologies: communication, journalism, and related programs; and communications technologies/technicians and support services.

Engineering and engineering technologies: engineering; engineering technologies/construction trades and mechanics and repairers.

Physical sciences and science technologies: physical sciences and science technologies/technicians.

Social science and history: social sciences and history.

Data may differ from previously published figures as data from earlier years have been reclassified when necessary to make them conform to the new taxonomy. Further information about the CIP-2000 is available at http://nces.ed.gov/pubs2002/cip2000/.

NOTE 10: Finance

Using the Consumer Price Index (CPI) to Adjust for Inflation

The Consumer Price Indexes (CPIs) represent changes in the prices of all goods and services purchased for consumption by households. Indexes vary for specific areas or regions, periods of time, major groups of consumer expenditures, and population groups. The CPI reflects spending patterns for two population groups: (1) all urban consumers and urban wage earners and (2) clerical workers. The all urban consumer group represents about 87 percent of the total U.S. population. *Indicators 17, 31, 32, 33, 34, 35, 36, 37, 44, 46, 47, 48, 49,* and *50* in *The Condition of Education 2011* use the U.S. All Items CPI for All Urban Consumers (CPI-U).

CPIs are calculated for both the calendar year and the school year using the CPI-U. The calendar year CPI is the same as the annual CPI-U. The school year CPI is calculated by adding the monthly CPI-U figures, beginning with July of the first year and ending with June of the following year, and then dividing that figure by 12. The school year CPI is rounded to three decimal places. Data for the CPI-U are available on the Bureau of Labor Statistics (BLS) website (http://www.bls.gov/cpi/). Also, figures for both the calendar year CPI and the school year CPI can be obtained from the *Digest of Education Statistics 2010* (NCES 2011-015), an annual publication of the National Center for Education Statistics (NCES).

Although the CPI has many uses, its principal function in *The Condition of Education* is to convert monetary figures (salaries, expenditures, income, etc.) into inflation-adjusted dollars to allow for comparisons over time. For example, due to inflation, the buying power of a salary of a person holding a bachelor's degree or higher in 1995 is not comparable with that of a bachelor's degree-holder in 2010. In order to make such comparisons, the 1995 salary must be converted into constant 2009–10 dollars by multiplying the 1995 salary by a ratio of the 2010 CPI over the 1995 CPI. As a formula, this is expressed as

$$1995 \text{ salary} \times \frac{(2010 \text{ CPI})}{(1995 \text{ CPI})} = \frac{1995 \text{ salary in}}{\text{constant 2010 dollars}}$$

The reader should be aware that there are alternative price indexes to the CPI that could be used to make these adjustments. These alternative adjustments might produce findings that differ from the ones presented here. For more detailed information on how the CPI is calculated or on the other types of price indexes, go to the BLS website (http://www.bls.gov/cpi/).

Classifications of Expenditures

Indicators 36 and *37* examine expenditures for public elementary and secondary education. *Indicator 36* uses total expenditures as a whole, together with the three major functions (categories) of total expenditures: *current expenditures, capital outlay,* and *interest on school debt.* Current expenditures, in turn, is broken into seven subfunctions (subcategories): expenditures for instruction, administration, student and staff support, operation and maintenance, transportation, food services, and enterprise operations. *Indicator 37* uses expenditures for instruction (usually referred to as instruction expenditures) in its analysis.

Total expenditures for elementary and secondary education includes all expenditures allocable to per student costs: these are all current expenditures for regular school programs, capital outlay, and interest on school debt. Expenditures on education by other agencies or equivalent institutions (e.g., the Department of Health and Human Services and the Department of Agriculture) are included. Total expenditures excludes "Other current expenditures" such as community services, private school programs, adult education, and other programs not allocable to expenditures per student at public schools.

Current expenditures includes expenditures for the day-to-day operation of schools and school districts, and includes instruction, administration, student and staff support, operation and maintenance, transportation, food services, and enterprise operations. Thus, current expenditures includes items such as salaries for school personnel, benefits, supplies, purchased services, student transportation, schoolbooks and materials, and energy costs. Current expenditures and each of its seven subfunctions can be further broken down by the object of the expenditure: salaries, employee benefits, purchased services, supplies, and tuition and other.

- *Instruction expenditures* includes expenditures for activities related to the interaction between teachers and students. Includes salaries and benefits for teachers and instructional aides, textbooks, supplies, and purchased services such as instruction via television. Also included are tuition expenditures to other local education agencies.

- *Administration expenditures* includes expenditures for school administration (i.e., the office of the principal, full-time department chairpersons, and graduation expenses), general administration (the superintendent and board of education and their immediate staff), and other support services expenditures.

NOTE 10: Finance

- *Student and staff support expenditures* includes expenditures for student support (attendance and social work, guidance, health, psychological services, speech pathology, audiology, and other student support services), instructional staff services (instructional staff training, educational media [libraries and audiovisual], and other instructional staff support services), and other support services (business support services, central support services, and other support services not reported elsewhere).

- *Operation and maintenance expenditures* includes expenditures for supervision of operations and maintenance; operating buildings (heating, lighting, ventilating, repair, and replacement); care and upkeep of grounds and equipment; vehicle operations and maintenance (other than student transportation); security; and other operations and maintenance services.

- *Transportation includes expenditures* for vehicle operation, monitoring, and vehicle servicing and maintenance.

- *Food services* includes all expenditures associated with providing food to students and staff in a school or school district. The services include preparing and serving regular and incidental meals or snacks in connection with school activities, as well as the delivery of food to schools.

- *Enterprise operations* includes expenditures for activities that are financed, at least in part, by user charges, similar to a private business. These include operations funded by sales of products or services, together with amounts for direct program support made by state education agencies for local school districts.

Capital outlay includes direct expenditures for construction of buildings, roads, and other improvements and for purchases of equipment, land, and existing structures. Includes amounts for additions, replacements, and major alterations to fixed works and structures; the initial installation or extension of service systems and other built-in equipment; and site improvement. The category also encompasses architectural and engineering services, including the development of blueprints.

Interest on debt includes expenditures for long-term debt service interest payments (i.e., those longer than 1 year).

Classifications of Revenue

In *indicator 35,* revenue is classified by source (federal, state, or local). Revenue from federal sources includes direct grants-in-aid to schools or agencies, funds distributed through a state or intermediate agency, and revenue in lieu of taxes to compensate a school district for nontaxable federal institutions within a district's boundary. Revenue from state sources includes both direct funds from state governments and revenue in lieu of taxation. Revenue from local sources includes revenue from such sources as local property and nonproperty taxes, investments, and revenue from student activities, textbook sales, transportation and tuition fees, and food services. Intermediate revenue comes from sources that are not local or state education agencies, but that operate at an intermediate level between local and state education agencies and possess independent fundraising capability—for example, county or municipal agencies. Intermediate revenue is included in local revenue totals. In *indicator 35,* local revenue is classified as either local property tax revenue or other local revenue.

The Variation in Expenditures per Student and the *Theil Coefficient*

Indicator 37 uses the *Theil coefficient* to measure the variation in expenditures per pupil in regular public school elementary and secondary schools in the United States. A comparison of the values of *Theil coefficients* for groups within a set (i.e., districts within the nation) will indicate relative dispersion and any variations that may exist among them. The *Theil coefficient* was subsequently used to measure the trends in variation of a number of items, including expenditures per student (see NCES 2000-020 and Murray, Evans, and Schwab 1998).

The *Theil coefficient* has a convenient property when the individual units of observation (e.g., school districts) can be aggregated into subgroups (e.g., states): the *Theil coefficient* for the aggregation of all the individual units of observation can be decomposed into a measure of the variation within the subgroups and a measure of the variation between the subgroups. Hence, in the examination of the variation in instructional expenditures in the United States, the national variation can be decomposed into measures of between-state and within-state variation.

The between-state *Theil coefficient,* T_B, equals

$$T_B = \sum_{k=1}^{K} (P_k \overline{X}_k / \overline{X}) \ln(\overline{X}_k / \overline{X})$$

where P_k is the enrollment in state k, $\overline{X}_k$ is the student-weighted mean expenditure per student in state k, and $\overline{X}$ is the student-weighted mean expenditure per student for the country.

The within-state *Theil coefficient,* T_w, equals

$$T_W = \sum_{k=1}^{K} (\overline{P}_k \overline{X}_k / X) T_k$$

where T_k is the *Theil coefficient* for state k.

T_k equals

$$T_k = \frac{\sum\limits_{j=1}^{J_k} P_{jk} X_{jk} \ln(X_{jk}/\overline{X}_k)}{\sum\limits_{j=1}^{J_k} P_{jk} X_{jk}}$$

where P_{jk} is the enrollment of district j in state k and X_{jk} is the mean expenditure per student of district j in state k.

The national *Theil coefficient, T,* is

$$T = T_W + T_B$$

Classifications of Expenditures for International Comparisons

Indicator 38 presents international data on public and private expenditures for instructional and noninstructional educational institutions. Instructional educational institutions are educational institutions that directly provide instructional programs (i.e., teaching) to individuals in an organized group setting or through distance education. Business enterprises or other institutions that provide short-term courses of training or instruction to individuals on a "one-to-one" basis are not included. Noninstructional educational institutions are educational institutions that provide administrative, advisory, or professional services to other educational institutions, although they do not enroll students themselves. Examples include national, state, and provincial bodies in the private sector; organizations that provide education-related services such as vocational and psychological counseling; and educational research institutions.

Public expenditures refers to the spending of public authorities at all levels. *Total public expenditures* used for the calculation in *indicator 38* corresponds to the nonrepayable current and capital expenditures of all levels of the government directly related to education. Expenditures that are not directly related to education (e.g., culture, sports, youth activities, etc.) are, in principle, not included. Expenditures on education by other ministries or equivalent institutions (e.g., Health and Agriculture) are included. Public subsidies for students' living expenses are excluded to ensure international comparability of the data.

Private expenditures refers to expenditures funded by private sources (i.e., households and other private entities). "Households" means students and their families. "Other private entities" includes private business firms and nonprofit organizations, including religious organizations, charitable organizations, and business and labor associations. Private expenditures are composed of school fees, the cost of materials such as textbooks and teaching equipment, transportation costs (if organized by the school), the cost of meals (if provided by the school), boarding fees, and expenditures by employers on initial vocational training. Private educational institutions are considered to be service providers and do not include sources of private funding.

Current expenditures includes final consumption expenditures (e.g., compensation of employees, consumption of intermediate goods and services, consumption of fixed capital, and military expenditures); property income paid; subsidies; and other current transfers paid.

Capital expenditures includes spending to acquire and improve fixed capital assets, land, intangible assets, government stocks, and nonmilitary, nonfinancial assets, as well as spending to finance net capital transfers.

NOTE 11: International Education Definitions

Organization for Economic Co-operation and Development (OECD)

The OECD is an intergovernmental organization of 34 industrialized countries that serves as a forum for member countries to cooperate in research and policy development on social and economic topics of common interest. These 34 member countries are included in *indicator 25:* Australia, Austria, Belgium, Canada, Chile, Czech Republic, Denmark, Estonia, Finland, France, Germany, Greece, Hungary, Iceland, Ireland, Israel, Italy, Japan, Korea, Luxembourg, Mexico, Netherlands, New Zealand, Norway, Poland, Portugal, Slovak Republic, Slovenia, Spain, Sweden, Switzerland, Turkey, United Kingdom, and United States. Currently, 25 nonmembers participate as regular observers or full participants in OECD Committees; two of these partner countries, Brazil and the Russian Federation, are included in *indicator 25.*

International Standard Classification of Education (ISCED)

Indicators 25 and *38* uses the 1997 International Standard Classification of Education (ISCED) to compare educational systems in different countries. ISCED is the standard used by many countries to report education statistics to UNESCO and the Organization for Economic Co-operation and Development (OECD). ISCED divides educational systems into the following seven categories, based on six levels of education.

ISCED Level 0: Education preceding the first level (early childhood education) usually begins at age 3, 4, or 5 (sometimes earlier) and lasts from 1 to 3 years, when it is provided. In the United States, this level includes nursery school and kindergarten.

ISCED Level 1: Education at the first level (primary or elementary education) usually begins at age 5, 6, or 7 and continues for about 4 to 6 years. For the United States, the first level starts with 1st grade and ends with 6th grade.

ISCED Level 2: Education at the second level (lower secondary education) typically begins at about age 11 or 12 and continues for about 2 to 6 years. For the United States, the second level starts with 7th grade and typically ends with 9th grade. Education at the lower secondary level continues the basic programs of the first level, although teaching is typically more subject focused, often using more specialized teachers who conduct classes in their field of specialization. The main criterion for distinguishing lower secondary education from primary education is whether programs begin to be organized in

a more subject-oriented pattern, using more specialized teachers conducting classes in their field of specialization. If there is no clear breakpoint for this organizational change, the lower secondary education is considered to begin at the end of 6 years of primary education. In countries with no clear division between lower secondary and upper secondary education, and where lower secondary education lasts for more than 3 years, only the first 3 years following primary education are counted as lower secondary education.

ISCED Level 3: Education at the third level (upper secondary education) typically begins at ages 15 or 16 and lasts for approximately 3 years. In the United States, the third level starts with 10th grade and ends with 12th grade. Upper secondary education is the final stage of secondary education in most OECD countries. Instruction is often organized along subject-matter lines, in contrast to the lower secondary level, and teachers typically must have a higher level, or more subject-specific, qualification. There are substantial differences in the typical duration of programs both across and between countries, ranging from 2 to 5 years of schooling. The main criteria for classifications are (1) national boundaries between lower and upper secondary education and (2) admission into educational programs, which usually requires the completion of lower secondary education or a combination of basic education and life experience that demonstrates the ability to handle the subject matter in upper secondary schools.

ISCED Level 4: Education at the fourth level (postsecondary nontertiary education) straddles the boundary between secondary and postsecondary education. This program of study, which is primarily vocational in nature, is generally taken after the completion of secondary school, typically lasts from 6 months to 2 years. Although the content of these programs may not be significantly more advanced than upper secondary programs, these programs serve to broaden the knowledge of participants who have already gained an upper secondary qualification. This level of education is not included in the analysis for *indicator 25,* but is included for select countries in *indicator 38.*

ISCED Level 5: Education at the fifth level (first stage of tertiary education) includes programs with more advanced content than those offered at the two previous levels. Entry into programs at the fifth level normally requires successful completion of either of the two previous levels. *Indicator 25* makes a distinction between two types of tertiary education.

- *ISCED Level 5A:* Tertiary-type A programs provide an education that is largely theoretical and is intended to provide sufficient qualifications for gaining entry into advanced research programs and professions with high skill requirements. Entry into these programs normally requires the successful completion of an upper secondary education; admission is competitive in most cases. The minimum cumulative theoretical duration at this level is 3 years of full-time enrollment. In the United States, tertiary-type A programs include first university programs that last 4 years and lead to the award of a bachelor's degree and second university programs that lead to a master's degree.

■ *ISCED Level 5B:* Tertiary-type B programs are typically shorter than tertiary-type A programs and focus on practical, technical, or occupational skills for direct entry into the labor market, although they may cover some theoretical foundations in the respective programs. They have a minimum duration of 2 years of full-time enrollment at the tertiary level. In the United States, such programs are often provided at community colleges and lead to an associate's degree. This level of education is not included in the analysis for *indicator 25*.

ISCED Level 6: Education at the sixth level (advanced research qualification) is provided in graduate and professional schools that generally require a university degree or diploma as a minimum condition for admission. Programs at this level lead to the award of an advanced, postgraduate degree, such as a Ph.D. The theoretical duration of these programs is 3 years of full-time enrollment in most countries (for a cumulative total of at least 7 years at levels five and six), although the length of actual enrollment is often longer. Programs at this level are devoted to advanced study and original research.

High school attainment data presented in *indicator 25* refer to ISCED level 3 degrees. ISCED level 3 corresponds to high school completion in the United States. ISCED level 3C short programs do not correspond to high school completion; these short programs are excluded from *indicator 25*. Bachelor's degree or higher data presented in *indicator 25* refer to ISCED level 5A or 6 degrees. ISCED level 5A, first award, corresponds to the bachelor's degree in the United States; ISCED level 5A, second award, corresponds to master's and first-professional degrees in the United States; and ISCED level 6 corresponds to doctoral degrees in the United States.

Appendix C
Glossary

Glossary

A

Achievement levels: National Assessment of Educational Progress (NAEP) achievement levels are set through a National Assessment Governing Board process and define what students should know and be able to do at different levels of performance. The NAEP achievement levels are *Basic, Proficient,* and *Advanced.* The definitions of these levels, which apply across all grades and subject areas, are as follows:

Basic: This level denotes partial mastery of prerequisite knowledge and skills that are fundamental for *proficient* work at each grade.

Proficient: This level represents solid academic performance for each grade assessed. Students reaching this level have demonstrated competency over challenging subject matter, including subject-matter knowledge, application of such knowledge to real-world situations, and analytical skills appropriate to the subject matter.

Advanced: This level signifies superior performance.

The percentage of students at or above *Proficient* includes students at the *Proficient* achievement level and at the *Advanced* achievement level. Similarly, the percentage of students at or above *Basic* includes students at the *Basic,* those at the *Proficient,* and those at the *Advanced* achievement levels. See also *supplemental note 4.*

Alternative school: A public elementary/secondary school that (1) addresses needs of students that typically cannot be met in a regular school, (2) provides nontraditional education, (3) serves as an adjunct to a regular school, or (4) falls outside the categories of regular, special education, or vocational education. Some examples of alternative schools are schools for potential dropouts; residential treatment centers for substance abuse (if they provide elementary or secondary education); schools for chronic truants; and schools for students with behavioral problems.

Associate's degree: An award that normally requires at least 2 but less than 4 years of full-time-equivalent college work.

B

Bachelor's degree: A degree granted for the successful completion of a baccalaureate program of studies, usually requiring at least 4 years (or the equivalent) of full-time college-level study.

C

Charter school: A publicly funded school that, in accordance with an enabling statute, has been granted a charter exempting it from selected state or local rules and regulations. A public charter school may be a newly created school, or it may previously have been a public or private school. In return for funding and autonomy, the charter school must meet accountability standards. A school's charter is typically reviewed every 3 to 5 years and can be revoked if guidelines on curriculum and management are not followed or standards are not met. Charter schools provide free public elementary and/or secondary education and can be administered by regular school districts, state education agencies (SEAs), or chartering organizations. See also Public school.

Classification of Instructional Programs (CIP): A taxonomic coding scheme for secondary and postsecondary instructional programs. It is intended to facilitate the organization, collection, and reporting of program data using classifications that capture the majority of reportable data. The CIP is the accepted federal government statistical standard on instructional program classifications and is used in a variety of education information surveys and databases. See also *supplemental note 10.*

College: A postsecondary educational institution.

Combined school: A school offering both elementary and secondary education. A combined school typically has one or more of grades kindergarten (K) through grade 6 and one or more of grades 9–12. For example, schools with grades K–12, 6–9, or 1–12 are classified as combined schools.

Constant dollars: Dollar amounts that have been adjusted by means of price and cost indexes to eliminate inflationary factors and allow for direct comparison across years.

Consumer Price Index (CPI): This price index measures the average change in the cost of a fixed-market basket of goods and services purchased by consumers.

D

Disabilities, children with: Children who, by reason of having any of the disabilities outlined in *supplemental note 7,* need special education and related services. Types of disabilities include the following:

Specific learning disabilities: Specific learning disabilities are disorders of one or more of the basic psychological processes involved in understanding or in using language, spoken or written, that may manifest themselves in an imperfect ability to listen, think, speak, read, write, spell, or do mathematical calculations. These disorders include conditions such as perceptual disabilities, brain injury, minimal brain dysfunction, dyslexia, and developmental aphasia.

Speech or language impairments: Communication disorders such as stuttering, impaired articulation, a language impairment, or a voice impairment that adversely affects a child's educational performance.

Doctoral degree: An earned degree carrying the title of Doctor. The Doctor of Philosophy degree (Ph.D.) is the highest academic degree and requires mastery within a field of knowledge and demonstrated ability to perform scholarly research. Other doctoral degrees are awarded for fulfilling specialized requirements in professional fields, such as education (Ed.D.), musical arts (D.M.A.), business administration (D.B.A.), and engineering (D. Eng. or D.E.S.). Many doctoral degrees in both academic and professional fields require an earned master's degree as a prerequisite. First-professional degrees, such as M.D. and D.D.S., are not included under this heading. See also First-professional degree.

Dropout: The term is used to describe both the event of leaving school before completing high school and the status of an individual who is not in school and who is not a high school completer. High school completers include both graduates of school programs as well as those completing high school through equivalency programs such as the GED. Transferring from a public school to a private school, for example, is not regarded as a dropout event. A person who drops out of school may later return and graduate but is called a "dropout" at the time he or she leaves school. Measures to describe these often complicated behaviors include the event dropout rate (or the closely related school persistence rate), the status dropout rate, and the high school completion rate. See also Status dropout rate.

E

Education specialist/professional diploma: A certificate of advanced graduate studies that advance educators in their instructional and leadership skills beyond the master's level of competence.

Educational attainment: The highest level of schooling attended and completed. See also High school completion, Associate's degree, Bachelor's degree, Master's degree, Doctoral degree, and First-professional degree.

Elementary school: An elementary/secondary school with one or more grades of K–6 that does not have any grade higher than grade 8. For example, schools with grades K–6, 1–3, or 6–8 are classified as elementary. See also Primary school.

Elementary/secondary school: Elementary/secondary schools include regular schools (i.e., schools that are part of state and local school systems and private elementary/secondary schools, both religiously affiliated and nonsectarian); alternative schools; vocational education schools; and special education schools.

English language learner: A person for whom English is a second language and who has not yet attained proficiency in the English language. See also Limited-English proficient.

Expenditures: Charges incurred, whether paid or unpaid, that are presumed to benefit the current fiscal year. For elementary/secondary schools, these include all charges for current outlays plus capital outlays and interest on school debt. For postsecondary institutions, these include current outlays plus capital outlays. For the government, these include charges net of recoveries and other correcting transactions, other than retirement of debt, investment in securities, extension of credit, or agency transactions. Also, government expenditures include only external transactions, such as the provision of prerequisites or other payments in kind. Aggregates for groups of governments exclude intergovernmental transactions among the governments. See also *supplemental note 10.* Expenditures types include the following:

Current expenditures: Short-term spending that is fully expensed in the fiscal period in which it is incurred. Current expenditures are in contrast to capital expenditures, which refer to spending on long-term assets that are capitalized and amortized over their useful life. Examples of current expenditures include salaries for school personnel, fixed charges, student transportation, book and materials, and energy costs. Expenditures for state administration are excluded. *Instructional expenditures (elementary/secondary):* Current expenditures for activities directly associated with the interaction between teachers and students. These include teacher salaries and benefits, supplies (such as textbooks), and purchased instructional services.

Expenditures per student: Charges incurred for a particular period of time divided by a student unit of measure, such as enrollment, average daily attendance, or average daily membership. See also *supplemental note 10.*

F

Faculty: Persons identified by the institution as such and whose assignments include conducting instruction, research, or public service as a principal activity (or activities). They may hold academic rank titles of professor, associate professor, assistant professor, instructor, lecturer, or the equivalent of any of those academic ranks. Faculty may also include the chancellor/president, provost, vice provosts, deans, directors or the equivalent, as well as associate deans, assistant deans, and executive officers of academic departments (chairpersons, heads or the equivalent) if their principal activity is instruction combined with research and/or public service. Graduate, instruction, and research assistants are not included in this category.

Glossary

Financial aid: Grants, loans, assistantships, scholarships, fellowships, tuition waivers, tuition discounts, veteran's benefits, employer aid (tuition reimbursement), and other monies (other than from relatives/friends) provided to students to help them meet expenses. This includes Title IV subsidized and unsubsidized loans made directly to students.

First-professional degree: An award that requires completion of a degree program that meets all of the following criteria: (1) completion of the academic requirements to begin practice in the profession; (2) at least 2 years of college work before entering the degree program; and (3) a total of at least 6 academic years of college work to complete the degree program, including previously required college work plus the work required in the professional program itself. First-professional degrees may be awarded in the following 10 fields: chiropractic (D.C. or D.C.M.), osteopathic medicine (D.O.), dentistry (D.D.S. or D.M.D.), pharmacy (Pharm.D.), law (L.L.B. or J.D.), podiatry (D.P.M., D.P., or Pod.D.), medicine (M.D.), theology (M.Div., M.H.L., B.D., or Ordination), optometry (O.D.), and veterinary medicine (D.V.M.).

Four-year postsecondary institution: A postsecondary education institution that can award a bachelor's degree or higher. See also Postsecondary education and *supplemental note 8.*

Full-time enrollment: The number of students enrolled in postsecondary education courses with a total credit load equal to at least 75 percent of the normal full-time course load.

Full-time-equivalent (FTE) enrollment: For institutions of higher education, enrollment of full-time students, plus the full-time equivalent of part-time students. The full-time equivalent of the part-time students is estimated using different factors depending on the level and control of institution and level of student.

G

GED certificate: This award is received following successful completion of the General Educational Development (GED) test. The GED program, sponsored by the American Council on Education, enables individuals to demonstrate that they have acquired a level of learning comparable to that of high school graduates. See also High school equivalency certificate.

Graduate: An individual who has received formal recognition for the successful completion of a prescribed program of studies.

Gross domestic product (GDP): Gross national product less net property income from abroad. Both gross national product (GNP) and GDP aggregate only the incomes of residents of a nation, corporate and individual, derived directly from the current production of goods and services by individuals, businesses, and government; gross private domestic investment in infrastructure; and total exports of goods and services. The goods and services included are largely those bought for final use (excluding illegal transactions) in the market economy. A number of inclusions, however, represent imputed values, the most important of which is rental value of owner-occupied housing.

H

High school: A secondary school offering the final years of high school study necessary for graduation, in which the lowest grade is not lower than grade 9. Usually includes grades 10, 11, 12 or grades 9, 10, 11, and 12.

High school completer: An individual has completed high school if he or she has been awarded a high school diploma or an equivalent credential, including a General Educational Development (GED) credential.

High school diploma: A formal document regulated by the state certifying the successful completion of a prescribed secondary school program of studies. In some states or communities, high school diplomas are differentiated by type, such as an academic diploma, a general diploma, or a vocational diploma.

High school equivalency certificate: A formal document certifying that an individual has met the state requirements for high school graduation equivalency by obtaining satisfactory scores on an approved examination and meeting other performance requirements (if any) set by a state education agency or other appropriate body. One particular version of this certificate is the General Educational Development (GED) test. The GED test is a comprehensive test used primarily to appraise the educational development of students who have not completed their formal high school education and who may earn a high school equivalency certificate by achieving satisfactory scores. GEDs are awarded by the states or other agencies, and the test is developed and distributed by the GED Testing Service of the American Council on Education.

I

Individuals with Disabilities Education Act (IDEA): IDEA is a federal law requiring services to children with disabilities throughout the nation. IDEA governs how states and public agencies provide early intervention, special education, and related services to more than 6.8 million eligible infants, toddlers, children, and youth with disabilities. Infants and toddlers with disabilities (birth–age 2) and their families receive early intervention services under IDEA, Part C. Children and youth (ages

3–21) receive special education and related services under IDEA, Part B.

Inflation: A rise in the general level of prices of goods and services in an economy over a period of time, which generally corresponds to a decline in the real value of money or a loss of purchasing power. See also Constant dollars and Purchasing power parity.

L

Limited-English proficient: Refers to an individual who was not born in the United States or whose native language is a language other than English, or who comes from an environment where a language other than English has had a significant impact on the individual's level of English language proficiency. It may also refer to an individual who is migratory, whose native language is a language other than English, and who comes from an environment where a language other than English is dominant; and whose difficulties in speaking, reading, writing, or understanding the English language may be sufficient to deny the individual the ability to meet the state's proficient level of achievement on state assessments as specified under the No Child Left Behind Act, the ability to successfully achieve in classrooms where the language of instruction is English, or the opportunity to participate fully in society. See also English language learner.

M

Magnet school or program: A special school or program designed to reduce, prevent, or eliminate racial isolation and/or to provide an academic or social focus on a particular theme.

Master's degree: A degree awarded for successful completion of a program generally requiring 1 or 2 years of full-time college-level study beyond the bachelor's degree. One type of master's degree, which includes the Master of Arts degree, or M.A., and the Master of Science degree, or M.S., is awarded in the liberal arts and sciences for advanced scholarship in a subject field or discipline and for demonstrated ability to perform scholarly research. A second type of master's degree is awarded for the completion of a professionally oriented program—for example, an M.Ed, in education, an M.B.A. in business administration, an M.F.A. in fine arts, an M.M. in music, an M.S.W. in social work, or an M.P.A. in public administration. A third type of master's degree is awarded in professional fields for study beyond the first-professional degree—for example, the Master of Laws (LL.M.) and Master of Science (M.S.) in various medical specializations.

Measurable difference: Before determining that two estimates in a sample survey are different, a statistical test must be conducted to take into consideration uncertainty due to sampling variability. The statistical test detects the presence of a measurable difference between the two estimates.

N

National School Lunch Program: Established by President Truman in 1946, the program is a federally assisted meal program operated in public and private nonprofit schools and residential child care centers. To be eligible for free lunch, a student must be from a household with an income at or below 130 percent of the federal poverty guideline; to be eligible for reduced-price lunch, a student must be from a household with an income between 130 percent and 185 percent of the federal poverty guideline. See also *supplemental note 1.*

Nonresident alien: A person who is not a citizen of the United States, who is in this country on a temporary basis, and who does not have the right to remain indefinitely.

Nursery school: An instructional program for groups of children during the year or years preceding kindergarten, which provides educational experiences under the direction of teachers. See also Preschool.

O

Organization for Economic Co-operation and Development (OECD): The OECD is an organization of nations whose purpose is to promote trade and economic growth in both member and nonmember nations. OECD's activities inform many aspects of economic and social policy. See also *supplemental note 11.*

P

Part-time enrollment: The number of students enrolled in postsecondary education courses with a total credit load of less than 75 percent of the normal full-time credit load.

Postbaccalaureate enrollment: The number of students with a bachelor's degree who are enrolled in graduate-level or first-professional courses. See also First-professional degree.

Postsecondary education: The provision of a formal instructional program whose curriculum is designed primarily for students who are beyond the compulsory age for high school. This includes programs whose purpose is academic, vocational, and continuing professional education, and excludes avocational and adult basic education programs. See also *supplemental note 8.*

Glossary

Prekindergarten: Preprimary education for children typically ages 3–4 who have not yet entered kindergarten. It may offer a program of general education or special education and may be part of a collaborative effort with Head Start.

Preschool: An instructional program enrolling children generally younger than 5 years of age and organized to provide children with educational experiences under professionally qualified teachers during the year or years immediately preceding kindergarten (or prior to entry into elementary school when there is no kindergarten). See also Nursery school.

Private institution: An institution that is controlled by an individual or agency other than a state, a subdivision of a state, or the federal government; that is usually not supported primarily by public funds; and that is not operated by publicly elected or appointed officials. See also *supplemental note 8*. Types of private institutions include:

Private for-profit institution: A private institution in which the individual(s) or agency in control receives compensation other than wages, rent, or other expenses for the assumption of risk.

Private not-for-profit institution: A private institution in which the individual(s) or agency in control receives no compensation, other than wages, rent, or other expenses for the assumption of risk. These include both independent not-for-profit institutions and those affiliated with a religious organization.

Private school: A school serving students in one or more of grades K–12 that is controlled by an individual or agency other than a state, a subdivision of a state, or the federal government; that is usually not supported primarily by public funds; and that is not operated by publicly elected or appointed officials. Organizations or institutions that provide support for homeschooling but do not offer classroom instruction for students are not included. See also *supplemental note 3*.

Property tax: The sum of money collected from a tax levied against the value of property.

Public institution: A postsecondary educational institution whose programs and activities are operated by publicly elected or appointed school officials and which is supported primarily by public funds. See also supplemental note 8.

Public school: An institution that provides educational services for at least one of grades K–12 (or comparable ungraded levels), has one or more teachers to give instruction, has an assigned administrator, receives public funds as primary support, and is operated by an education or chartering agency. Public schools include regular, special education, vocational/technical, alternative, and charter schools. They also include schools in juvenile detention centers, schools located on military bases and operated by the Department of Defense, and Bureau of Indian Education-funded schools operated by local public school districts. See also Special education school, Vocational school, Alternative school, Charter school, and Traditional public school.

Purchasing Power Parity (PPP) indices: PPP exchange rates, or indices, are the currency exchange rates that equalize the purchasing power of different currencies, meaning that when a given sum of money is converted into different currencies at the PPP exchange rates, it will buy the same basket of goods and services in all countries. PPP indices are the rates of currency conversion that eliminate the difference in price levels among countries. Thus, when expenditures on gross domestic product (GDP) for different countries are converted into a common currency by means of PPP indices, they are expressed at the same set of international prices, so that comparisons among countries reflect only differences in the volume of goods and services purchased.

R

Regular school: A public elementary/secondary school providing instruction and education services that does not focus primarily on special education, vocational/technical education, or alternative education, or on any of the particular themes associated with magnet/special program emphasis schools.

Revenues: Funds that are appropriated to schools and education institutions. Types of revenues include the following:

Revenues from federal sources: Revenues from federal sources include direct grants-in-aid from the federal government; federal grants-in-aid through the state or an intermediate agency; and other revenue, in lieu of taxes that would have accrued had the tax base been subject to taxation.

Revenues from local sources: Revenues from local sources include revenues from a local education agency (LEA), including taxes levied or assessed by an LEA; revenues from a local government to the LEA; tuition received; transportation fees; earnings on investments from LEA holdings; net revenues from food services (gross receipts less gross expenditures); net revenues from student activities (gross receipts less gross expenditures); and other revenues (textbook sales, donations, property rentals).

Revenues from state sources: Revenues from state sources include revenues from an agency of state government including those that can be used without restriction, those for categorical purposes, and revenues in lieu of taxation.

S

Salary: The total amount regularly paid or stipulated to be paid to an individual, before deductions, for personal services rendered while on the payroll of a business or organization.

Secondary school: A school with one or more of grades 7–12 that does not have any grade lower than grade 7. For example, schools with grades 9–12, 7–9, 10–12, or 7–8 are classified as secondary.

Special education school: An elementary/secondary school that (1) focuses primarily on special education, including instruction for any of the following groups of students: hard of hearing, deaf, speech impaired, health impaired, orthopedically impaired, intellectually disabled, seriously emotionally disturbed, multi-handicapped, visually handicapped, deaf and blind, and the learning disabled; and (2) adapts curriculum, materials, or instruction for students served.

Status dropout rate: The status dropout rate is the percentage of young adults who are dropouts, regardless of when they dropped out. The numerator of the status dropout rate for any given year is the number of young adults ages 16–24 who, as of October of that year, had not completed high school and were not currently enrolled. The denominator is the total number of 16- to 24-year-olds in October of that same year.

STEM fields: Science, Technology, Engineering, and Mathematics (STEM) fields of study that are considered to be of particular relevance to advanced societies. For the purposes of *The Condition of Education 2011*, STEM fields include agriculture and natural resources, biological and biomedical sciences, computer and information sciences and support services, engineering and engineering technologies, mathematics and statistics, and physical sciences and science technologies.

Student membership: Student membership is an annual headcount of students enrolled in school on October 1 or the school day closest to that date. The Common Core of Data (CCD) allows a student to be reported for only a single school or agency. For example, a vocational school (identified as a "shared time" school) may provide classes for students from a number of districts and show no membership.

T

Title I school: A school designated under appropriate state and federal regulations as a high-poverty school that is eligible for participation in programs authorized by Title I of the Reauthorization of the Elementary and Secondary Education Act, P.L. 107-110.

Title IV institution: An institution that has a written agreement with the Secretary of Education that allows the institution to participate in any of the Title IV federal student financial assistance programs (other than the State Student Incentive Grant [SSIG] and the National Early Intervention Scholarship and Partnership [NEISP] programs).

Traditional public school: Traditional public schools are publicly funded schools other than public charter schools. See also Public schools and Public charter schools.

Tuition: The amount of money charged to students for instructional services. Tuition may be charged per term, per course, or per credit.

Two-year postsecondary institution: A postsecondary education institution that does not confer bachelor's or higher degrees, but does provide 2-year programs that result in a certificate or an associate's degree, or 2-year programs that fulfill part of the requirements for a bachelor's degree at a 4-year institution. See also Postsecondary education and *supplemental note 8*.

U

Undergraduate student: A student enrolled in a 4- or 5-year bachelor's degree program, an associate's degree program, or a vocational or technical program below the baccalaureate.

V

Vocational school: A secondary school that focuses primarily on vocational, technical, or career education and provides education and training in one or more occupations. They may be part of a regular district (along with academic schools) or in a vocational district (serving more than one academic school district).

Appendix D
Bibliography

Bibliography

NCES Publications

Aud, S., Hussar, W., Planty, M., Snyder, T., Bianco, K., Fox, M., Frohlich, L., Kemp, J., and Drake, L. (2010). *The Condition of Education 2010* (NCES 2010-028). National Center for Education Statistics, Institute of Education Sciences, U.S. Department of Education. Washington, DC: U.S. Government Printing Office.

Battle, D. (2009). *Characteristics of Public, Private, and Bureau of Indian Education Elementary and Secondary School Principals in the United States: Results From the 2007–08 Schools and Staffing Survey* (NCES 2009-323). *National Center for Education* Statistics, Institute of Education Sciences, U.S. Department of Education. Washington, DC. Retrieved March 17, 2011, from http://nces.ed.gov/pubsearch/pubsinfo.asp?pubid=2009323.

Battle, D. (2010). *Principal Attrition and Mobility: Results From the 2008–09 Principal Follow-up Survey* (NCES 2010-337). National Center for Education Statistics, Institute of Education Sciences, U.S. Department of Education. Washington, DC: U.S. Government Printing Office.

Chen, C. (2010). *Numbers and Types of Public Elementary and Secondary Schools From the Common Core of Data: School Year 2008–09* (NCES 2010-345). National Center for Education Statistics, Institute of Education Sciences, U.S. Department of Education. Washington, DC. Retrieved March 17, 2011, from http://nces.ed.gov/pubsearch/pubsinfo.asp?pubid=2010345.

Coopersmith, J. (2009). *Characteristics of Public, Private, and Bureau of Indian Education Elementary and Secondary School Teachers in the United States: Results From the 2007–08 Schools and Staffing Survey* (NCES 2009-324). National Center for Education Statistics, Institute of Education Sciences, U.S. Department of Education. Washington, DC. Retrieved March 17, 2011, from http://nces.ed.gov/pubsearch/pubsinfo.asp?pubid=2009324.

Fleischman, H.L., Hopstock, P.J., Pelczar, M.P., and Shelley, B.E. (2010). *Highlights From PISA 2009: Performance of U.S. 15-Year-Old Students in Reading, Mathematics, and Science Literacy in an International Context* (NCES 2011-004). National Center for Education Statistics, Institute of Education Sciences, U.S. Department of Education. Washington, DC.

Hampden-Thompson, G., Mulligan, G., Kinukawa, A., and Halle, T. (2008). *Issue Brief: Mathematics Achievement of Language-Minority Students During the Elementary Years* (NCES 2009-036). National Center for Education Statistics, Institute of Education Sciences, U.S. Department of Education. Washington, DC.

Hussar, W., and Sonnenberg, W. (2000). *Trends in Disparities in School District Level Expenditures per Pupil* (NCES 2000-020). U.S. Department of Education. Washington, DC: National Center for Education Statistics.

Hussar, W.J., and Bailey, T.M. (2011). *Projections of Education Statistics to 2020* (NCES 2011-026). National Center for Education Statistics, Institute of Education Sciences, U.S. Department of Education. Washington, DC: U.S. Government Printing Office.

Keigher, A. (2010). *Teacher Attrition and Mobility: Results From the 2008–09 Teacher Follow-up Survey. First Look* (NCES 2010-353). National Center for Education Statistics, Institute of Education Sciences, U.S. Department of Education. Washington, DC. Retrieved March 17, 2011, from http://nces.ed.gov/pubsearch/pubsinfo.asp?pubid=2010353.

Snyder, T.D., and Dillow, S.A. (2011). *Digest of Education Statistics 2010* (NCES 2011-015). National Center for Education Statistics, Institute of Education Sciences, U.S. Department of Education. Washington, DC: U.S. Government Printing Office.

U.S. Department of Education, Institute of Education Sciences, National Center for Education Statistics. (2009). *The Nation's Report Card: Mathematics 2009* (NCES 2010-451). Washington, DC: Author.

U.S. Department of Education, Institute of Education Sciences, National Center for Education Statistics. (2009). *The Nation's Report Card: Reading 2009* (NCES 2010-458). Washington, DC: Author.

U.S. Department of Education, Institute of Education Sciences, National Center for Education Statistics. (2010). *The Nation's Report Card: Grade 12 Reading and Mathematics 2009 National and Pilot State Results* (NCES 2011-455). Washington, DC: Author.

U.S. Department of Education, National Center for Education Statistics. (2002). *Classification of Instructional Programs—2000* (NCES 2002-165). Washington, DC: Author.

Other Publications

Education Commission of the States. (2010). *ECS StateNotes: Compulsory School Age Requirements.* Retrieved August 9, 2010, from http://www.ecs.org/clearinghouse/86/62/8662.pdf.

Education Commission of the States. (n.d.). *State Kindergarten Statutes: State Comparisons.* Retrieved September 22, 2010, from http://mb2.ecs.org/reports/Report.aspx?id=14.

Individuals with Disabilities Education Improvement Act of 2004, 20 U.S.C. §1400 et seq. (2004).

Murray, S.E., Evans, W.E., and Schwab, R.M. (1998). Education-Finance Reform and the Distribution of Education Resources. *American Economic Review, 88*(4): 789–812.

Office of Management and Budget Revisions to the Standards for the Classification of Federal Data on Race and Ethnicity, 62 Federal Register 58782–58790 (Oct. 30, 1997).

Nelson, B., Berman, P., Ericson, J., Kamprath, N., Perry, R., Silverman, D., and Solomon, D. (2000). *The State of Charter Schools 2000: Fourth-Year Report.* U.S. Department of Education, Washington, DC: Office of Educational Research and Improvement. Retrieved March 16, 2011, from http://www2.ed.gov/PDFDocs/4yrrpt.pdf.

Organization for Economic Cooperation and Development (2004). *Learning for Tomorrow's World—First Results From PISA 2003.* Paris: OECD Publications. Retrieved March 17, 2011, from http://www.oecd.org/dataoecd/1/60/34002216.pdf.

Organization for Economic Cooperation and Development (2007). *PISA 2006: Science Competencies for Tomorrow's World (Volume II).* OECD Publishing. Retrieved March 17, 2011, from http://www.pisa.oecd.org/cument/2/0,3343,en_32252351_32236191_39718850 1_1_1_1,00.html.

Organization for Economic Cooperation and Development (2010). *PISA 2009 Results: Learning Trends—Changes in Student Performance Since 2000 (Volume V).* OECD Publishing. Retrieved March 17, 2011, from http://www.oecd.org/document/60/0,3343,en_2649_35845621_46609852_1_1_1_1,00.html.

Organization for Economic Cooperation and Development (2010). *PISA 2009 Results: What Students Know and Can Do—Student Performance in Reading, Mathematics and Science (Volume I).* OECD Publishing. Retrieved March 17, 2011, from http://www.pisa.oecd.org/document/53/0,3746,en_32252351_46584327_46584821_1_1_1_1,00.html.

Organization for Economic Cooperation and Development, Center for Educational Research and Innovation (2010). *Education at a Glance, 2010.* Retrieved March 16, 2010, from http://www.oecd.org/edu/eag2010.

Theil, H. (1975). *Theory and Measurement of Consumer Demand: Volume 1.* Amsterdam: North-Holland Publishing Company.

U.S. Department of Education, Office of Special Education and Rehabilitative Services, Office of Special Education Programs. (2010). *29th Annual Report to Congress on the Implementation of the Individuals with Disabilities Education Act, 2007.* Washington, DC: Author.

NCES Surveys

The Common Core of Data (CCD). Available: http://nces.ed.gov/ccd/.

Higher Education General Information Survey (HEGIS). Available: http://www.icpsr.umich.edu/icpsrweb/ICPSR/series/00030.

Integrated Postsecondary Education Data System (IPEDS). Available: http://nces.ed.gov/ipeds/.

National Assessment of Educational Progress (NAEP). Available: http://nces.ed.gov/nationsreportcard/.

National Postsecondary Student Aid Studies (NPSAS), 1999–2008. Available: http://nces.ed.gov/surveys/npsas/about.asp.

Private School Universe Survey (PSS). Available: http://nces.ed.gov/surveys/pss/.

Schools and Staffing Survey (SASS). Available: http://nces.ed.gov/surveys/SASS/.

Teacher Follow-up Survey (TFS). Available: http://nces.ed.gov/surveys/sass/ovrv_whatstfs.asp.

Principal Follow-up Survey (PFS). Available: http://nces.ed.gov/surveys/sass/ovrv_pfs.asp.

Surveys From Other Agencies

Organization for Economic Cooperation and Development (OECD), Program for International Student Assessment (PISA). Available: http://nces.ed.gov/Surveys/PISA.

Bibliography

U.S. Department of Commerce, Census Bureau, American Community Survey (ACS). Available: http://www.census.gov/acs/www/.

U.S. Department of Commerce, Census Bureau, Current Population Survey (CPS). Available: http://www.census.gov/cps/.

- Annual Social and Economic Supplement (ASEC), 1975–2011

- March Supplement, 1996–2010

- October Supplement, 1970–2009

U.S. Department of Commerce, Census Bureau, Long Form Decennial Census, 1980, 1990, and 2000. Available: http://www.census.gov/main/www/cen2000.html.

- Decennial Census, 1990, Minority Economic Profiles, unpublished data

- Decennial Census, 2000, Summary Social, Economic, and Housing Characteristics

- Census 2000 Summary File 4 (SF 4), "Poverty Status in 1999 of Related Children Under 18 Years by Family Type and Age," retrieved March 28, 2005, from http://factfinder.census.gov/servlet/DTGeoSearchByListServlet?ds_name=DEC_2000_SF4_U&_lang=en&_ts=134049420077.

- 1990 Summary Tape File 3 (STF 3), "Median Household Income in 1989" and "Poverty Status in 1989 by Family Type and Age." Retrieved May 12, 2005, from http://factfinder.census.gov/servlet/DTGeoSearchByListServlet?ds_name=DEC_1990_STF3_&_lang=en&_ts=134048804959.

U.S. Department of Education, Federal Student Aid, Direct Loan and Federal Family Education Loan Programs, Cohort Default Rate Database. Available: http://www2.ed.gov/offices/OSFAP/defaultmanagement/cdr.html.

U.S. Department of Justice, Bureau of Justice Statistics, National Crime Victimization Survey (NCVS), 1992–2005 and 2007–2008. Available: http://bjs.ojp.usdoj.gov/index.cfm?ty=dcdetail&iid=245.

Appendix E
Index

Appendix E is the cumulative index for the 2007–2011 print editions of *The Condition of Education.*

The **year** of publication appears in bold type. Arabic numerals (e.g., 2, 3, 4) following the year refer to Indicator numbers. References beginning with "TF" (e.g., TF2, TF3, TF4) refer to page numbers in the Topics in Focus.

Please note that some indicators may no longer appear in the Indicator List on *The Condition of Education* website and can only be found in the Print Editions (PDFs).

Index

A

Academic levels in high school, **2007**:TF16n11

Academic preparation. *See* Coursetaking by high school students

Academic rank, **2007**:44, **2008**:42, **2009**:43, **2010**:44, **2011**:44

Academic standards, New Basics curriculum, **2007**:TF2

Academic support, **2009**:46, **2010**:49, **2011**:50

Accommodations. *See* Testing accommodations

Achievement levels/tests, **2007**:11, **2007**:12

    international comparisons (*See* International comparisons)

    mathematics performance in 4th, 8th, and 12th grade, **2011**:12, **2011**:13

    mathematics performance in 4th and 8th grade, **2008**:13, **2009**:13, **2010**:11, **2010**:12 (*See also* Mathematics)

    reading performance through elementary/secondary level, **2008**:12, **2009**:12, **2010**:9, **2010**:10, **2011**:10, **2011**:11 (*See also* Reading)

    science performance in 4th, 8th, and 12th grade, **2011**:13, **2011**:14

    science performance through elementary/secondary level, **2007**:13 (*See also* Science)

    writing performance in 8th and 12th grade, **2008**:14

Administration, expenditures in public elementary/secondary schools for, **2007**:38, **2008**:35, **2009**:34, **2010**:34, **2011**:36

Adult education, **2007**:10

Adult literacy. *See* Literacy

Advanced degrees. *See* Educational attainment; Graduate degrees

Advanced Placement (AP)

    examinations, **2007**:TF14–TF15

    in foreign languages, **2007**:TF13

    public schools offering, **2007**:TF5–TF7

Affiliated schools, **2007**:4, **2008**:4, **2009**:5, **2010**:3, **2011**:4. *See also* Private elementary/secondary schools

Afterschool activities/care, **2007**:29

Age/Age comparisons. *See also* Grade-level studies

    compulsory school attendance, **2007**:1, **2008**:1, **2009**:1, **2010**:1, **2011**:1

    crime in schools, **2007**:36, **2008**:28

    educational attainment, **2011**:25

    enrollment in postsecondary education by level and control of institution, **2011**:TF8

    home activities and early childhood development, **2009**:2

    mathematics performance, **2007**:15, **2008**:17, **2009**:14, **2010**:13

    preprimary education enrollment by, **2007**:2, **2008**:2

    principals in elementary/secondary schools, **2007**:34, **2010**:29, **2011**:33

    reading performance, **2007**:15, **2008**:17, **2009**:14, **2010**:13

    remedial coursetaking by undergraduates, **2011**:22

Algebra. *See also* Mathematics

    coursetaking by high school students, **2007**:TF9, **2007**:TF11

    international comparisons of skill levels, **2010**:15

Alternative schools, **2009**:31, **2010**:24, **2010**:31, **2011**:4, **2011**:27

American Community Survey (ACS), **2007**:6, **2008**:7, **2009**:8, **2009**:20, **2010**:5, **2010**:19, **2011**:1, **2011**:6, **2011**:20

American students studying abroad, **2010**:40

Art, **2010**:14

Assessment of students. *See* Achievement levels/tests

Assistantships, graduate education, **2007**:48, **2010**:48, **2011**:48

Associate's degrees, **2007**:26, **2008**:26, **2009**:24, **2010**:23, **2011**:26

    awarded by public and private institutions, **2008**:41, **2009**:42, **2010**:43, **2011**:42

    awarded by level and control of institution, **2011**:TF7

    completion rates, **2011**:23, **2011**:TF14

    earnings of young adults affected by, **2008**:20, **2009**:17, **2010**:17, **2011**:17

    by field of study, **2007**:42, **2008**:39, **2009**:40, **2010**:41, **2011**:40

At-risk students, **2010**:24, **2011**:27

Attainment in education. *See* Educational attainment

Attendance status, postsecondary education. *See also* Full-time enrollment at postsecondary institutions; Part-time enrollment at postsecondary institutions

    enrollment, **2007**:1

    by level and control of institution, **2011**:TF8, **2011**:TF9

    undergraduate enrollment, **2007**:8, **2008**:9, **2009**:10, **2010**:7, **2011**:8

Attitudes of students, preparedness for school day, **2007**:22

Index

Index

Elementary schools

    staff in public schools, **2008**:32, **2010**:30

    student/teacher ratios, **2008**:33, **2009**:31, **2010**:31

Elementary/secondary education, **2007**:29–41, **2008**:28–38, **2009**:4–9, **2009**:25–37, **2010**:2–6, **2010**:24–38, **2011**:2–7, **2011**:27–38. *See also* Private elementary/secondary schools; Public elementary/secondary schools

    afterschool activity participation, **2007**:29

    charter schools, **2007**:32

    children who spoke a language other than English at home, **2007**:6, **2008**:7, **2009**:8, **2010**:5, **2011**:6

    crime in schools, **2011**:30

    disabilities, students with, **2010**:6, **2011**:7 (*See also* Disabilities, students with)

    enrollment, **2007**:1, **2007**:3, **2008**:1, **2008**:3, **2009**:1, **2009**:4, **2010**:1, **2011**:1

    enrollment, public schools, **2010**:2, **2011**:2

    grade retention of students, **2009**:18

    graduation rates, **2007**:24, **2008**:21, **2009**:19, **2010**:18, **2011**:19

    high school graduation rates by students with disabilities, **2008**:22

    international comparisons for mathematics, **2009**:15, **2010**:15

    international comparisons of expenditures for, **2008**:38, **2009**:37, **2010**:38, **2011**:38

    mathematics achievement (*See* Mathematics)

    parental educational attainment (*See* Parents, level of education)

    principals, **2007**:34, **2010**:29, **2011**:33

    private schools, **2007**:4, **2008**:4, **2009**:5, **2010**:3, **2011**:4 (*See also* Private elementary/secondary schools)

    race/ethnicity in, **2007**:5, **2008**:5, **2009**:7, **2010**:4, **2011**:5 (*See also* Race/ethnicity)

    reading achievement (*See* Reading)

    school choice, **2007**:32, **2009**:32

    science achievement (*See* Science)

    staff in public schools, **2010**:30

    teachers/teaching (*See* Teachers/Teaching)

    violence at schools, **2008**:28, **2009**:27, **2010**:26

Emotional disturbances, **2008**:22

Employee benefits, **2009**:34, **2010**:34, **2011**:36

Employer financial aid for adult education, **2007**:48, **2010**:48, **2011**:48

Employment status. *See also* Unemployment

    by educational attainment, **2011**:18

    of students while earning postsecondary degree, **2008**:43, **2009**:44, **2010**:45, **2011**:45

    while earning postsecondary degree, **2007**:45 (*See also* Working while attending school (postsecondary education))

    young adults, earnings of, **2009**:17, **2010**:17, **2011**:17

Endowments, **2009**:46, **2010**:49, **2011**:50

Engineering, degrees in, **2007**:42, **2007**:43, **2008**:39, **2008**:40, **2009**:40, **2009**:41, **2010**:41, **2010**:42, **2011**:40, **2011**:41

English, high school

    coursetaking by high school students, **2007**:TF12–TF13

    credits earned and dropout rate, **2007**:TF10

English and literature, degrees in, **2008**:40

English as a Second Language (ESL); English language learner

    language spoken at home, **2007**:6, **2008**:7, **2009**:8, **2010**:5, **2011**:6

    teacher aides for, **2007**:35

English Speakers of Other Languages (ESOL). *See* Limited English proficiency (LEP)

Enrollment, elementary/secondary schools

    by age, **2007**:1, **2008**:1, **2009**:1, **2010**:1, **2011**:1

    charter schools, **2010**:32, **2011**:3

    grade retention of students, **2009**:18

    past and projected, **2007**:3, **2008**:3, **2009**:4, **2010**:2, **2011**:2

    private elementary/secondary schools, **2007**:4, **2008**:4, **2009**:5, **2010**:3, **2011**:4 (*See also* Private elementary/secondary schools)

    public schools, **2008**:30, **2009**:26 (*See also* Public elementary/secondary schools)

    student/teacher ratios, **2007**:30, **2008**:33, **2009**:31, **2010**:31

Enrollment, postsecondary education

    by age, **2007**:1, **2008**:1, **2009**:1, **2010**:1, **2011**:1

    immediately after high school, **2007**:25, **2008**:24, **2009**:21, **2010**:20, **2011**:21

    by institution level and control, **2011**:TF7–TF9

    undergraduate level, **2007**:8, **2008**:9, **2009**:10, **2010**:7, **2011**:8 (*See also* Undergraduate students)

Index

Index

Index

Index

charter schools in central cities, **2007**:32, **2009**:32

crime in schools, **2007**:36, **2008**:28, **2009**:27

expenditures per student by school district, **2007**:40, **2008**:37, **2009**:36, **2010**:36

poverty levels in public schools, **2008**:29, **2009**:25, **2010**:25, **2011**:28

private school enrollments, **2007**:4, **2008**:4

public school characteristics, **2011**:27

public school enrollments, **2008**:30, **2009**:26

students per staff member at public elementary/secondary schools, **2008**:32

student/teacher ratios at public schools, **2009**:31, **2010**:31

teacher pay incentives by, **2010**:37

V

Verbalization in young children, **2009**:3

Violence at schools

declining, **2007**:36

public schools experiencing, **2008**:28, **2009**:27, **2010**:26, **2011**:30

Visual arts

degrees in, **2007**:42, **2007**:43, **2008**:39, **2008**:40, **2009**:40, **2010**:41, **2011**:40

eighth grade performance, **2010**:14

Visual impairments, **2008**:22

Vocational education/schools, **2009**:31, **2010**:31

coursetaking decreasing, **2007**:TF8

percentage of public schools as, **2010**:24, **2011**:27

Volunteerism, parental involvement with children's education, **2009**:30

W

Weapons in schools, **2008**:28, **2009**:27, **2010**:26

Western region schools. *See* Regional distributions

William D. Ford Federal Direct Loan Program, **2011**:49, **2011**:TF13, **2011**:TF15

Women. *See also* Gender

degrees by field of study, **2009**:40, **2010**:41, **2011**:40

earning degrees, **2007**:28, **2008**:27

enrollment rates in college, **2007**:8, **2008**:9

graduate enrollment rates, **2007**:9, **2008**:11

Work experience. *See also* Principals; Teachers/Teaching

turnover rates of principals by, **2011**:34

turnover rates of teachers by, **2011**:32

Working while attending school (postsecondary education), **2007**:45, **2008**:43, **2009**:44, **2010**:45, **2011**:45. *See also* Employment status

Work-related education, **2007**:10

Writing, proficiency levels in 8th and 12th grades, **2008**:14

Y

Young adults

annual earnings of, **2008**:20, **2009**:17, **2010**:17, **2011**:17

not in school or working, **2007**:19

status dropout rates for high school, **2008**:23, **2009**:20, **2010**:19, **2011**:20